To Mom + Dad

with love

Christmas 1990

from Rita

Celebrating Italy

Also by Carol Field

THE HILL TOWNS OF ITALY

THE ITALIAN BAKER

Celebrating Italy

CAROL FIELD

WILLIAM MORROW AND COMPANY, INC. NEW YORK

Illustration on title page: The Triumph of Carneval,
Museo Nazionale delle Arti e Tradizioni Popolari, Rome

Illustrations at the beginning of each chapter, as well as those on pages 48, 154, 190, 191,
193, 295, 303, 319, 339, 342, 361, and 437, are by Donnie Cameron.

Nineteenth-century Bartolomeo Pinelli engravings, pages 14–15, 130–131, 218–219, 275,
294, 301, 328–329, 412, and 438, courtesy of de Bellis Collection, San Francisco State
University Library, San Francisco, California

Other illustrations courtesy of Il Collezionista, Milan

Recognizing the importance of preserving what has been written, it is the policy of William
Morrow and Company, Inc., and its imprints and affiliates to have the books it publishes
printed on acid-free paper, and we exert our best efforts to that end.

Library of Congress Cataloging-in-Publication Data

Field, Carol.
Celebrating Italy / Carol Field.
p.   cm.
Includes bibliographical references and index.
ISBN 0-688-07093-0
1. Festivals—Italy.   2. Cookery, Italian.   3. Italy—Social life and customs.
I. Title.
GT4852.A2F54   1990
394.2′6′0945—dc20   90-35916
CIP

Printed in the United States of America

First Edition

1 2 3 4 5 6 7 8 9 10

BOOK DESIGN BY JOEL AVIROM

FOR JOHN,
who dreamed up this great adventure and was there through it all
and for my father,
JAMES D. HART,
a great celebrant at the feast of life

Spring

*The game of Cuccagna
(the land of plenty),
which no one ever loses
and everyone wins, by
Giuseppe Maria Mitelli,
1691, Raccolta Bertarelli,
Milan*

ACKNOWLEDGMENTS

I could never have written this book without the help and kindness of hundreds of people to whom I turned for assistance during the three years I spent researching and writing it. Some of them are mentioned below, but there were many others as well in various cultural and tourist offices, in restaurants and homes across Italy, and to all of them I want to extend my thanks.

None of it would have been possible without the help of Daniela Falini, a wonderful researcher in Italy who went far beyond the call of duty in being sure that I found the information and people I needed. Without her conscientious help I cannot imagine how this book could have been written.

Invaluable information about festivals and their foods came from Professore Alessandro Falassi in Siena, Avvocato Giovanni Goria in Asti, Professore Salvatore Schifano in Sicily, and Professore Antonio Stanziani in Villa Santa Maria. Bill Pepper convinced me that I could not write this book without a research assistant, and then found Daniela Falini to help me. Carlo and Renato Veggetti were extremely generous in introducing me to bakers all over the country and helping me with the historical research I needed. Carla Schucani at the Pasticceria Sandri in Perugia has been extremely generous and helpful over my many visits. My friends Riccardo and Gianna Bertelli, Shirley and François Caracciolo, Lorenza and Piero Stucchi-Prinetti, and Antonio and Cynthia Piccinardi saw a great deal of me during all my trips and were untiringly hospitable and helpful. I am extremely grateful to all the officials of the Ente Provinciale del Turismo and the Assessorato alla Cultura who answered my letters, gave me important information, and offered assistance. With apologies to anyone I have omitted, I want to list some others who were especially helpful:

Badessa Ildegarde Pitrone at the Convento di Santo Spirito, Agrigento; Cesare Giaccone in Albaretto Torre; Giovanni Battista Minnucci in Aricia; Signor Giovanni Maggiolo in Camogli; Claudio and Mario Bianchi in Cantù; Filippi Beruno in Carru; Roberto Zecca in Caselle Torinese; Lele and Ada Gani in Castel d'Asti; John Meis in Gaiole in Chianti; Giorgio Riva and Federica Albini in Cividale del Friuli; Emilia, Laura, and Artimisia Corbetti and Mario Volpi in Cocullo, and Sofia Carmine and Demetrio Josella in nearby Anversa; Franco Zilliani and his daughter Christina in Cortefranca; Giovanni Galli, Julie Peterson, Faith Heller Willinger and Max Hillinger in Florence, and Gastone and Kathy Manozzi in nearby Troghi; Anna Maria Ciuchini, Pietro Moresini, and Leandro Donati in Gradoli; Giampiero Bedini, Pier Luigi Menichetti, Massimo Monacelli, and Rodolfo Mencarelli in Gubbio; Franco Marco Badia, Walter Bano, Lynn and David Olivetti, Silvana Trebbi, and the Pasticceria Stroppia in Ivrea; Angelo Ferrua, Elvio Cogno, Angelo Gaja, Bruno Ceretto in the Langhe, with Gianni Galli and Gran Maestro Luciano de Giacomi in Alba; Gian Guido d'Amico in Lavagna; Franco Colombani at Il Sole in Maleo; Giacchino Palestro in Mortara, and Josef Egger, Dottore Spora, Peter Seibstock, and Siegfried van Rachelwitz in Merano; Riccardo di Corato, Antonio and Cynthia Piccinardi, Fulco Portinari, Armanda Capeder, Giancarlo Grignani, Dottoressa Roselli and Giancarlo Piccalunga at the Touring Club Italiano, and Amadeo Vergani and Neil Empson in Milan; Daria Luccerini in Montefollonico; Ermendina Lorenzini in Montepulciano; Claudia and Tonino Verro in Neive, Italo Pedroni and Franca Prampolini in Nonantola; Elio Sulla, Alberto and Gennaro Petillo, and their families in Nola, Corrado Costanzo in Noto; Luigi Mazzarella in Ostia; Leo Bertozzi, Arrocato Giorgio Bernardini, and Valerio Ugolotti in Parma; Alberto del Buono in Pienza; Luigi Faffa in nearby Pontevalleceppi; Anna and Gino Perra and family, and Gabriele Pani, his wife and mother-in-law in Quartu Sant'Elena, and Professoressa Enrica Delitala and Anna Mura in Cagliari, Sardinia; Anna Tasca Lanza di Mazzarino, Conte and Contessa Tasca d'Almerita and Mario Lo Menzo at Regaleali, Sicily; Antonio and Malika Nicolai, Mario and Anna Pagano, Luigi Martucci, Vincenzo Mareri, Signora Lantini, Jo Bettoja, Patrizia Barberito, Professor Franco Ferrarotti, Maria Macioti, Maria Grazia Panella, Ugo Farsetti, Daniele Boari, and Paola di Mauro in Rome; Dottore Francesco Bivona and the families Ardagna, Pusillesi, Giammalvo-Carbonello, and Di Stefano-Lombardo in Salemi; Pancrazio Marcomeni and Bianca Caricioli in San Benedetto Po; Vito Teti in Serra San Bruno, Calabria; Signor Federici in Sezze Romano; Antonio Sclavi and his bakers, Paolo Gamberucci, and Giovanni Righi Parenti in Siena; Maria Grammatico in Erice and Mary Taylor Simeti, Giulia Centineo, Dottoressa Giovanna Cangialosi, and the bakeries Spinnelli and Scimone in Palermo; Silvana Belloni and Alvaro Buono in Spello; Professore Italo Merlino in Taranta Peligna; Luigi di Lenardo, Alba Felluga, Isi Benigni, Walter and Patrizia Filiputti, and Ida and Gianni Zamara in Tarcento and Udine; Conte and Contessa Alessandro and Conte Giorgio Cicogna-Mozzone in Terdobbiate; Shirley and Francois Caracciolo, Giuliana and Piero Dorazio, Annetta Mannaioli, Beverly and Bill Pepper, and Anna Maria Petrocchi in Todi; Mario Buri, Federica de Luca, Dottore Bovetti, and Roberto Perino in Torino; Arneo Nizzoli in Villastrada; Antonio de Sanctis, Mayor Salvatore Paolini, and Tommaso Sboro in Villa Santa Maria; Presidente Luigi d'Agostino, Dottore Antonio Giarola, Dottore Tarcisio Caltran, and Cav. Gr. Cr. Rag. Nereo del Bianco in Verona.

I want to offer special thanks to Diane Dexter, whose expertise and enthusiasm made her a wonderful assistant in testing many of these recipes. And to Corby Kummer for his enormously sensitive and helpful reading of the manuscript. Very special thanks to Maggie Waldron for her help with the cover photograph.

Other people whose help I could not have done without include Tim Amlaw, Paola Bagnatori, Lea Bergin, Margaret Cicogna, Susan Cole, Perry Dexter, Marcia Guerrero, Susan Klee, John Mackie, Maria Mendola, Carlo Middione, Elisabetta Nelsen, Doreen Schmidt, and Susan Tompkins.

Special thanks go to my editor, Ann Bramson, ever patient and supportive, and to my two copy editors, Dolores Simon and Sonia Greenbaum, to Joel Avirom for his beautiful book design, to Donnie Cameron for her illustrations, to Linda Kosarin, and to my agent, Fred Hill.

I am extremely fortunate in having an extremely understanding family. Its various members have put up with my long absences in Italy and intense periods of work when I was at home. John, Matthew, and Alison were supportive and encouraging through it all.

This book owes an enormous debt not only to all the people in Italy and America who opened doors for me, literally and metaphorically, but also to the scholars whose books have guided me in my research. I could never have written this book without the books and essays of several particularly important writers whose names appear frequently in the text.

It is likely that Italians will recognize some or all of them, but Americans may well wonder who they are.

Alessandro Falassi is author of several books on the Palio of Siena, as well as the definitive bibliography of Italian folklore and a charming book about Tuscan food, *Pan che canti, vin che salti*. Especially important for the purposes of this book is his *Feste*, a compilation of essays on the festivals of Italy for which he wrote both the introductory chapter on the history of festivals in Italy and the section on Tuscany. Each chapter is written by an expert and focuses on the *feste* of a specific region. In addition Professor Falassi was enormously helpful in helping me formulate the overall outline of this book. Much of the information in the first chapter grew out of our conversations, both in Italy and at UCLA in Los Angeles, for which I am enormously indebted to him. This book would suffer greatly without his contribution, although its mistakes and omissions are purely my own.

Alberto Cattabiani has written several books on religion and popular tradition. His book *Calendario: le feste i miti, leggende e i riti dell'anno* (*The Calendar: Festivals, Myths, Legends, and Rites of the Year*) so intrigued Italians that it was on the best-seller list when it was published in 1988. Franco Cardini, professor of history at the University of Florence, wrote *Il giorno del sacro, il libro delle feste* (*The Sacred Day, a Book of Festivals*), a book that focuses on festivals primarily from a religious, historical, and anthropological view, paying especially close attention to their connection with myth, ritual, and magical rites.

Marina Warner looks at the myth and cult of the Virgin Mary in *Alone of All Her Sex*, a profound and beautifully written book on the protagonist of many of Italy's religious *feste*.

Joseph Campbell's books on myth, especially *The Masks of God* series, guided me along my way as well.

Four magazines were essential to my research: the magazine of the Accademia Italiana della Cucina, *La Gola*, *Lares*, and *Informatore Alimentare*.

xxxxxxxxxxxxxxxxxxxxxxx

Before cooking the foods of the festivals,
please read "Cooking from This Book,"
pages 445–448.

Before planning a trip through Italy,
consult the "Traveler's Calendar" beginning
on page 455.

CONTENTS

A World Hung with Banners

PART THREE
Darkness

PART FOUR
Rebirth

Celebrating Italy

*H*igh in a medieval tower, a lone figure swings back and forth, ringing a gigantic bell with the sheer force of his body. Church bells answer, pealing from every corner of the city, and hundreds of young men fill the streets, singing and shouting at the top of their lungs. Bands beat out the music of celebration on drums and trumpet it through golden horns to announce the beginning of the procession. Beautiful women parade by in Renaissance costumes of brocade and velour, horses stride with polished bridles and red and white plumes, standard bearers follow in brilliant silks, and flag throwers toss banners that ripple in the wind as they pass high in the air. You can see the sun slanting over the cinnamon tiles of the roofs and smell the porchetta fragrant with herbs from the hillside. A great crush of people covers every surface of the sloping piazza. Some even cling to the sides of the Renaissance fountain.

Italians throw themselves into festivities with costumed parades and processions, with competitive games like the jousts of medieval days, and with outrageous displays of sheer physical strength. They feast on epic amounts of food whose colors, fragrances, and flavors tempt the eye and dazzle the taste buds. Festivals can be either sacred or profane, and the Italians have often invented stories to give the celebrations supernatural significance or mythic and legendary beginnings. A feast of polenta? The lord of the land opened his storehouses during a famine in the seventeenth century and out poured coarse grains that were cooked in giant cauldrons to feed thousands of hungry citizens in the village. A celebration of fish? No doubt a local patron saint once caused vast quantities to leap into fishermen's nets. Sometimes it is heroes who rise out of city history and sometimes gods from the great beyond who instigate the celebration, causing eggs and grains to be cooked into gargantuan risotti and tangles of pasta or baked into cookies as tiny as a bean and cakes as high as a house. Festivals are a form of communion, a sharing that reinforces bonds of family and friendship and a sense of identity that stretches across centuries. No wonder they are transfiguring experiences, not only for Italians but for Americans who happen upon them. We, who so often yearn for a sense of meaning and community, respond to the communal joy and feasting and the participating in rites that are profoundly rooted in an ancient country of surpassing beauty.

During festivals "the world is hung with banners," in Joseph Campbell's lovely phrase. Large cities and tiny villages alike are completely changed in magic moments that touch us deeply in an unexpected way. Even people who instinctively dislike crowded spaces can't resist the electrifying enthusiasm of a people in the throes of celebration. Daily events come to a halt as bonfires blaze on hillsides and fireworks explode in ribbons of color against the inky blue sky, beating out a percussive pagan dance of fire. There is nothing Italians like more than exploding fireworks or fires roaring in a country landscape. At festivals, torchlight processions serpentine up a steep mountainside in the silence of night, their tapers lighting up the contours of a hillside. Tiny bulbs outline the towers and arched entrance of a church, and colored lanterns twinkle around the entire piazza in summertime as music fills the air, encouraging everyone to dance until the early morning hours. The city or village is dressed in its finest clothes. Where once medieval streets were empty save for the occasional resident, for one brief morning a year they are carpeted with designs made of flower petals in dazzling nuances of color. Where once a lovely piazza of herringbone brick was dotted with the canvas umbrellas of outdoor restaurants, now a race track made of earth is laid right around its edges. It is suddenly filled with tens of thousands of people, singing songs and clapping hands to the music of horns and the insistent beat of drums ricocheting off the stone buildings that edge the narrow medieval streets. The noise is thrilling. You can hear the echo of centuries of celebration in it. Quantities of food are cooked and served in the city squares; five thousand thrushes or eight thousand spareribs or mountains of polenta feed the assembled celebrants. Barrels of wine are bottomless.

Come back the next day, and it is all gone. Earth still lies in the piazza but the horses have left, the great masses of humanity have decamped, and the emptiness is palpable. The petals have blown away, save for a few blossoms still clinging to the gray stones of the streets. The magic is a memory. The festival is over.

The phenomenon exists all over Italy. The country may be relatively small but many civilizations meet in its concentrated space. This complex and varied terrain encompasses expanses of wild landscape and soft green hills; rocky gorges and dark green forests along with urban piazze; sharp ridges and bare, snow-covered mountains, dramatic beaches, and rich, flat farmland. It is in the countryside, as well as in the famous cities, that history and myth mingle. Over many centuries Arab, Phoenician, Norman, Spanish, and Austrian conquerors have left their cultural and culinary imprints, which is why different foods grow in these soils, different dishes define the festivals of each region, and attitudes and patterns of life change from north to south. The political unification of the peninsula took place in 1860, but it never really took hold of the popular imagination. Family and friends and a close-knit community are what count most to Italians, and it is to them that the Italians pledge allegiance.

Festivals tend to fall into four groups: country festivals called *sagre,* which celebrate the fertility of nature; civic festivals glorifying a city's prosperity, such as the Palio of Siena; religious festivals celebrating divine blessings, such as saints' feast days in every little village and town; and political festivals. All have ritual foods that reflect agriculture and religion and consecrate the event.

People give up days and even weeks of their time to plan and launch a festival. It takes the women of small Sicilian towns the equivalent of two solid weeks to bake the ornamental and sacred breads for San Giuseppe (Saint Joseph's Day). Preparations for the Palio in Siena and the Corsa dei Ceri in Gubbio go on for most of the year. They are so important that the army gives young men leave to go home during the celebration. Citizens far away on the date of the festival have been known to re-create the event wherever they are. Families from Nola who now live in Brooklyn and Greenpoint, near Williamsburg in New York, re-create one of the old baroque-style Gigli, with a six-story-high tower that weighs four thousand pounds. The men lift and dance the structure to the music of a brass band, precisely as the natives of Nola continue to do every June on the feast day of their patron saint, Saint Paulinus. Before the Second World War, natives of Gubbio who were stationed in Somalia re-created the Ceri, which are normally two huge octagonal rocketlike forms joined in

Italian representations of the months

the center, by piling two empty smoked-herring barrels one on top of the other. Men from Siena in prison camps during the war reenacted the Palio as best they could.

The festival is not just a day off, it is time out from ordinary daily life, a moment of truce and a time of communion. In the Middle Ages, to partake of a feast was like being united with one's fellows "as the grains of wheat are united in a loaf of bread." The words are Cyprian's but the attitude is what continues to make festivals so powerful. In preparing for the *festa*, the social distinctions that normally pervade every nuance of relationships in status-conscious Italy are erased. Carpenters work alongside industrialists; bakers and architects and teachers plan and build together. Neighbors try to work out quarrels and grudges.

In Latin the day of the festival, *festum* (plural, *festa*), meant a day of public joy, while *feria* (*ae*) was a day off from work in honor of the gods. *Feria*, which remains the Italian word for holiday, produced *fiera*, an exposition of commercial products. *Sagra* came from the Latin *sacer*, a festival that commemorated the consecration of a church; over time the *sagra* became detached from religious observance and is today a celebration with both exposition and marketplace. These divisions, based on the anthropologist Alessandro Falassi's formulations, define most of Italy's *feste*. But not all.

Some festivals have lost ancient links to religion or pagan myths, and by now have become simply activities to be engaged in during free time, on weekends or vacations. They break up daily routine and are a diversion from normal activities, unlike the fluid time of festivals, when the experience is measured not in minutes and hours but in the flow of the entire event. Examples are found in the political fund-raising events that often occur in competition with a *sagra*. I remember one Festa dell Unità, a Communist party festival during the celebration of the white truffle in Alba. The dishes were delicious, more varied and plentiful than at the city celebration—and they cost less. Falassi calls these meals "the revenge of the proletariat," since most Italians did without meat for so long. The Communists are not the only such sponsors of subsidized feasting, although they have more *feste* than any other party: The Festa dell'Avanti is run by the Socialist party, for example, and the Festa dell'Amicizia, by the Christian Democrats. They all serve an impressive array of local foods, at prices that are extremely reasonable. *Feste* were once really meaningful for the poor, offering them one of their few opportunities to eat meat or sweets during the year.

From medieval times until quite recently, when the system of sharecropping called *mezzadria* was abandoned, those who worked the land brought the first stalks of asparagus, the first handful of cherries, the first wheels of cheese to the *signore*—the *padrone*, the lord of the land. They were perpetuating rituals that began when the ancients gave the first drop of wine to their gods. By tradition the first fruit of the earth is blessed and thus always counts more; but now that people work by the hour the tradition is on the wane. Young girls in Castel Gandolfo still bring the first peaches of the season to the pope in his summer residence in July, although the practice of transporting canteloupes, the melons that get their name from the papal gardens in Cantalupo in the Sabine region where they are cultivated, has died out. Thousands of artichokes are cooked in six entirely different ways in Sezze Romano every April as the first conical, violet-leaved vegetables become ripe. There are *sagre* that celebrate asparagus, cherries, lemons, strawberries, apricots, and every vegetable produced in the Italian soil; festivals in honor of geese, frogs, ducks, and thrushes; others that celebrate tuna and swordfish, oysters, and prosciutto. There are even festivals that honor rosemary and oregano. There are numerous polentatas, but grain festivals celebrating wheat are remarkably few, and they don't always feature loaves of bread. Perhaps the most memorable image of a grain festival comes from Fascist times, when Mussolini created grain fields all over the country. Even the Piazza della Repubblica, in the center of Florence, was planted in grain, and when the time came for the harvest a bare-chested Duce was filmed wielding a scythe and gathering in sheaves to feed the people of Italy.

Italians live in a land with many layers of history. They walk on stones worn smooth by the feet of Etruscans, Romans, and Saracens who came before them. They think nothing of it. They live with centuries of history piled up visibly in the walls and streets and stone cathedrals of every little town. No wonder that their festivals are deeply rooted in the history and mythology of the community. Festivals reenact the primal rhythms of the birth and death of seasons and crops, the rising of the sun and the waning of the moon, the great release of warmth from the sun and of moisture from water that causes crops to be born. If you look beyond the sacred

relics like a saint's tooth or events like horse races, you can find hints of earlier pagan observances that were meant to pacify the gods or to honor the underworld. Festivals are a key to the secrets of the world.

Seasonal festivals are tied to the rhythm of the agricultural year. Spring festivals celebrate the reawakening of nature as seeds respond to the warmth of the sun. Summer celebrates the work of the fields and bringing in the harvest; bundles of wheat fall under the scythe, hay is threshed, fish are pulled out of the sea, and great baskets full of fruits are brought in from orchards and fields. Cows return from Alpine pastures and sheep begin their passage to the lowland valleys where they will pass the next months. The grape harvest comes, and after that olives are picked and pressed into the deep green oil that flavors the food. Once the sun has wheeled across the sky, blazing with the heat that brings fruit to harvest, the year begins to cycle down into autumn, abundance begins to disappear, and funereal events take over. When the grain is sown in October, seeds begin their slumber in the cool earth, lying dormant before the warmth of springtime returns to give them new life. The period between November 1, the Day of the Dead, when ancestors are said to rise out of their graves and return home for a visit, and January 6, Epiphany, is a time when things are unstable and the "doors to the beyond remain open," according to the Italian historian Franco Cardini. It is a time when gifts from the other world arrive via dead ancestors, or from San Nicola (Saint Nicolas), Santa Lucia (Saint Lucy), Jesus or the Befana, the old lady who slides down the chimney with presents for children and also garlic and *carbone*, pieces of "charcoal" that happen to be made out of sugar. Italians don't just wait for food to appear. The *questua*, an ancient ritual of going from house to house asking for gifts and food, brings it forth. Fires blaze as Christmas logs in the fireplace and as great bonfires on the hillsides whose ashes are saved to fertilize the fields.

The *feste* all come to a head at Carnival, when people once disguised themselves in costume and indulged in gluttonous transgressions. License, revelry, and crazed disorder ruled. In ancient Rome a pig was sacrificed at the beginning of Saturnalia, and in later eras a trickster or great buffoon was chosen as the King of Carnival. In his culinary guise, he was portrayed as a pig, reclining on a dais and carried about on a sedan chair. He presided over orgiastic rites full of rich, fatty foods. (Of course he also furnished a great deal of its menu.) Carnival's abundance and excesses still turn the world upside down, if only briefly, but are followed by the penitence and abstinence of Lent and by the rebirth of nature in agriculture at Eastertime. Next comes May, a month of contradictions. The Romans celebrated the goddess Maia and the fertility of spring and wrapped ribbons around maypoles in sexual rites, but the Church took one look at these goings-on and dedicated May to the Virgin Mary, and made it a time of chastity.

During the Roman Empire, the calendar counted no fewer than 182 sacred festival days that were meant to honor or appease the many gods, ask for their divine assistance, and serve food and drink showing gratitude for the abundance of blessings received. The Romans made sacrifices to compensate for their interference in nature as they began to consume the harvest, for they were filled with the dread of destabilizing the mysterious equilibrium between birth, life, death, and the rich earth. So their gifts were meant to propitiate the powerful gods who controlled every aspect of life. There were games and competitions, dramatic processions and rituals to feed or conciliate dead ancestors who returned to earth.

When Christianity became the religion of the state in the fourth century, the Catholic Church simply substituted its own sacred figures for heathen deities, and added the Virgin Mary, who replaced many female divinities, including Cybele, Demeter and Persephone, Athena, Diana, Maia and Ceres, Isis and Aphrodite. Saints, who dispense grace in the name of the Lord, took the place of various local pagan figures who had performed the same function in Roman times. San Giovanni (Saint John the Baptist), who gives people new life with immersion in water, simply took over the summer water festival; and San Giorgio (Saint George), who slew the dragon, took over from the mythical Perseus, who did in the Gorgon Medusa. Christianity added two major new celebrations: Christmas, which replaced the birth of the sun, and Easter, a pastoral feast that replaced the resurrection of Attis and earlier gods of vegetation.

By the time of the Renaissance, the new city-states had created festivals that were extravagant entertainments, full of colorful triumphal carts, jousts, horse races, and violent tournaments, spectacles intended to celebrate the cities' individuality as well as their saints. Lorenzo de' Medici was the consummate deviser of masked entertainments and festivals that, according to Giorgio Vasari, united the "sacred and profane, classicism and innovation, reminiscences of chivalrism and popular discourse. . . ."

By the beginning of the sixteenth century, more than one day in three

in Italy was a festival, which struck the Church as so excessive that it made a serious effort to reduce the number of celebrations. Some *feste* were unquestionably pagan and others only marginally less so, so the Church was more than happy to remove them from observance. A more recent adjustment took place in the 1970s when the Italian government decided that there were too many holidays on the calendar and abolished seven festivals. Five saints, including Saint Valentine, actually lost their national status entirely.

Festival foods and recipes don't exist in a vacuum, but are tied to the calendar and to the countryside in which the events are celebrated. Some foods are served to invoke fertility and to symbolize the beginnings of life. Grains of rice look like little seeds, as do lentils, fava beans, wheat berries, and *farro,* a primitive wheat that is still cooked in a wonderful bean-and-*farro* soup in the area around Lucca. Eggs are like seeds contained in a fragile oval envelope. Pomegranates, the fruit of Persephone, with their slippery seeds, are like little dowries of fertility, as Botticelli's beautiful pregnant Madonna of the Pomegranate in Florence makes clear.

All festival food comes in gigantic amounts because it is meant to convey a message of abundance. Until recently, most people didn't have enough to eat during the year. It is not uncommon to hear stories of a poor childhood when bread on the table was an event and meat a mirage. An old expression says that "when a poor person eats a chicken, it means one of them is sick." Behind the feasting and the meager daily diet lay the rhythm of the seasons, abundance alternating with scarcity, although usually a few days of gastronomic plenty were meant to compensate for the deprivation suffered the rest of the year. Fasting or eating a lean meatless diet (*magro*) could virtually be a lifetime commitment, a case of obeying a holy commandment and making virtue of necessity at the same time. (Nowadays, even in Italy things are changing. The country is much richer, and everyone is concerned with health, cholesterol, grains, cutting calories.)

The other side of the landscape of scarcity is the magical land of milk and honey, where an endless supply of food can be had simply by wishing. Boccaccio forever captured the glories of abundance in his portrait of the land of Cockayne, the land of milk and honey "in a village that they called Bengodi, where they tie up the vineyards with sausages and where you can have a goose for a penny and a gosling thrown in for good measure, and that there was a mountain there made entirely of grated Parmesan cheese upon which there lived people who did nothing but make macaroni and ravioli which they cook in capon broth and later toss off the mountain, and whoever picks up more gets the most; and nearby there flowed a stream of dry white wine, the best you ever drank, without a drop of water in it." Of course the promise of the land of Cockayne was almost entirely a fantasy until a once a year festival like Carnival came along, with its abundance of food for everyone.

Still, food is especially magical on festival days. A piece of Christmas panettone saved to eat on February 3, San Biagio's Day (Saint Blaise), is said to ward off sore throats for the rest of the year; dried chestnuts eaten on January 17, the Feast of Sant'Antonio Abate (Saint Anthony the Abbot), are protection against mosquito bites.

Officially festival eating is divided between eating *magro* (no meat) on the eve of the festival to purify the body and eating *grasso* (meat and rich fatty foods) on the day itself. So widespread was the phenomenon that the struggle between Carnival and Lent was one of the most popular themes in folk wisdom as well as in literature.

Clearly, eating festival foods has more meanings than just tasting ritual soups and sweets from the past. It is actually a way of assimilating wisdom, since these foods communicate the message "I taste, therefore I know." The Italian word for wisdom, *sapienza*, comes from *sapia*, Latin for taste, and eating is a powerful way of consuming God. One meaning of the Christian rite of communion—of eating Christ's body and drinking his blood—is that this food becomes a path to enlightenment. So, the Italians reason, if you can eat the body of Christ, why not the eyes of Santa Lucia during the absence of light in wintertime? Why not the breasts of a saint (*i minni di Sant'Agata*), or the "little pricks" of the angels (*i cazzetti degli angeli*), which may answer the question of the sex of an angel? The eyes of Santa Lucia are fashioned of concentric circles of golden durum bread; the breasts of Sant'Agata (Saint Agatha) are filled with marzipan. "Eating the gods" is a mystical experience, a poetic and playful way of incorporating their virtues. In Giuseppe di Lampedusa's *The Leopard*, Don Fabrizio surveys the enormous table of Sicilian deserts with its "cakes called 'Triumphs of Gluttony,' shameless 'Virgin's cakes' shaped like breasts. Don Fabrizio asked for some of these, and as he held them on his plate [they] looked

like a profane caricature of Saint Agatha claiming her own sliced-off breasts. 'Why ever didn't the Holy Office forbid these puddings when it had the chance? "Triumphs of Gluttony" indeed! (Gluttony, mortal sin!) Saint Agatha's sliced-off teats sold by convents, devoured at dances! Well! Well!' "

In Apulia, Christmas desserts include dita degli apostoli, fingers of the Apostles, fine cylinders of crepes filled with sweetened ricotta; le cartellate, sheets for the baby Jesus; calzoncicchi, the pillow on which he laid his head; and even latte di mandorla, Virgin's milk. The playfulness of the devotion, the casual holy communion is a wonderful indication of the personal level of the relationship between Italians and their saints.

Being part of a festival celebration is like becoming a child again. Cauldrons that stand as high as a man's shoulder bubble over tall pyramids of wood and the food is turned out onto platters the size of a barn door. In Camogli thousands of pounds of fish fry in a pan with a handle eighteen feet long. The Ash Wednesday penitential meal in Gradoli uses 1 ton of pike, 660 pounds of baccalà, and 220 pounds of rice, and those are the merest beginnings. Mountains of potatoes are used to make the gnocchi in Gubbio. The bakers of Lavagna break thousands of eggs for a cake that stands twenty-one feet high.

The sense of fun is just as childlike. In Montefeltro there used to be a festival of the berlingozzo, a liqueur-flavored biscotto, during which people tossed the cookies from a medieval tower that was once used for pouring boiling oil on enemies below. On New Year's Eve in the town of Vita San Secondo, near Asti, people used to be able to go into any trattoria to eat what they wanted and depart without a receiving a bill. They were simply weighed upon entering and weighed upon leaving and asked to pay the difference.

The intensity and color of many Italian festivals have definitely diminished since earlier centuries. In the 1920s Toschi wrote that festivals were losing their grandeur, and by the time World War II was over, there was a definite downhill slide. Once il boom came along, with its economic good times and consumer mentality, folklore was caught between tourism and a mythic past. Regional tourist offices, the equivalent of chambers of commerce and local promotion agencies, took over the revival and organization of many festivals to attract tourists. Local governments poured large infusions of lire into various events, often providing an incentive for creating new festivals or brightening up old ones. Of course some practices are changing. It is hard to have a Christmas log in new apartments built without fireplaces. And there are reports of a community in which Father Christmas delivers presents by parachuting them in. Molto moderno. And what about celebrations of products of the earth that include beauty contests choosing Miss Rice Grain or Miss Truffle? For

Christmas turkeys are gradually replacing capon, and the younger generation shows a definite aversion to Christmas Eve eel. Many young people have never eaten the foods that their grandparents considered irreplaceable, and many families just don't have the time to cook massive feasts as they once did. Machines have entirely changed the grain and grape harvests, and almost no one has major feasts in the fields any more.

So it takes discrimination to find the festivals that have retained their integrity and intensity and that continue to be an expression of Italian culture. The people of Siena and Gubbio live for their Palio and Corsa dei Ceri all year long. In Trapani the Mysteries evoke profound feelings, and it is not unusual to see women standing outside the church as the Madonna is finally brought in, tears sliding down their cheeks. Entire cities and villages are still swept up in excitement of the festival, still feast on great platters of gnocchi and ribbons of pasta, plunge forks into polenta and spoons into cuccia.

Festivals are still part of the dance of life, the great feast at the moment of plenty. They are times when everyone can feel the rhythms of life and the rapture of celebration. They are moments when people can have their culture and eat it too.

PART ONE

Abundance

s May arrives, Italy erupts in bloom. The air is scented with the ripeness that May Day festivals celebrate by tying ribbons and lemons around flowering branches and bringing male and female trees to be "married" on a piazza. It is the month in which Persephone returned to her mother and the month in which grain reappears from its dark winter home. In Teramo, the culinary center of Abruzzo, May 1 is the day to eat le sette virtù, the seven virtues, a minestrone made of the meeting of two seasons. Its ingredients come from cleaning out the pantry at the end of the agricultural year. Out of bins and drawers come seven forms of leftover dried pasta, seven kinds of dried beans, and stock made of seven types of preserved leftovers of the pig, such as the feet. Since it is May, into the minestrone go seven kinds of fresh vegetables, including artichokes, fennel, and fava beans, and seven different fresh herbs. Seven is the number of the cardinal virtues and le sette virtù exalts the frugality of local housewives who waste nothing that is left in the larder. Far to the north in Friuli and Piedmont, May 1 is celebrated by eating a spring-time dish called *frittata primaverile verde alle sette erbe*, a frittata flavored with sage, parsley, thyme, basil, mint, marjoram, and a bitter herb known as *amarella*. It would seem that the magic calendar of ancient ritual still exerts a strong pull, although in truth the frittata is eaten by ever fewer families, and the minestrone, which was cooked in abundance in every country house, can now be found only in a very few restaurants.

The rites of spring—fires, dances, huge banquets, and sexual embraces—once welcomed Walpurgis Night, or Calendimaggio, the eve of May Day, the beginning of what the Celts called "the luminous time." In the Celtic calendar, the first of May was Beltane, the beginning of summer, the day on which the pastoral Celts took their flocks to a pasturage that lasted for six months until their New Year. They celebrated summer by lighting huge fires on hilltops for luck and for protection, and they even brought out a springtime crown, which they stretched on a tree like an early maypole. Maypoles still appear in Italian *feste* as *alberi della cuccagna*, trees from the land of milk and honey, with prosciutto, mortadella, cheeses, and money dangling from a ring at the crown of the pole. The trick is to climb to the top of the tall pole, which is slick with lard, using ashes sprinkled on one's hands to neutralize the grease. As each competitor falls, some of the grease goes with him until someone is finally able to climb to the prize.

Men in Tuscany and young women in Piedmont sing in May with rhyming songs called *maggiolate*. They go from house to house serenading the occupants with accordions and cymbals, wishing them good luck in exchange for gifts of food. Groups of young Piemontese girls, dressed in their best spring outfits, parade through their villages on the first of May, and the one chosen to be the bride of May carries the *maggio*, a green branch garlanded with ribbons, fresh fruits, and lemons.

Assisi celebrates Calendimaggio with an elaborate medieval procession and torchlight parade as silken banners flutter against churches and stone buildings. The upper and lower sections of the city compete with each other in singing love songs, an elegant contest that harks back to medieval times and to earlier Celtic *Campi di Maggio,* battlefields of May, so named because armed warriors assembled in May when there was finally enough food for the horses and wars could begin again.

The Church didn't care for the tournaments or for the freedom they offered men and women in a springtime fragrant with hints of amorous pleasure any more than they liked the celebrations that grew out of the orgiastic Roman rites for various female goddesses. Romans worshiped Flora, the goddess of spring and the harvest, at her festival, the Floralia, from April 23 through May 3. They threw flowers at each other, they watched nude dancing, and they sacrificed a pregnant pig to Maia, the great goddess of the Maytime festivals. Maia gave her name to the month and her spirit to the Queen of the May and her fertility rituals. The pig, *maiale* in Italian, was sacred to Maia, as it was to the goddess Demeter, mother of the harvest. While the Church couldn't get rid of the drinking, the lascivious dancing, or the bawdy songs, it could substitute the Virgin Mary for Maia, and could exchange chastity for sexual license. It has even tried to turn May Day into Labor Day by making San Giuseppe (Saint Joseph) the patron saint of workers and sponsoring processions of workers who march carrying tools of their trades.

When Thomas Ashby traveled from England to Italy in 1929, he attended the Festa of the Madonna del Monte in Marta, in the countryside near Lake Bolsena, where Etruscans once resided. Ashby was struck by rites that seemed to combine all the sacred and pagan elements of May rituals. He saw the picture of the Madonna encircled with loaves of bread and framed by bay leaves, artichokes, apples, cherries, lemons, and oranges. It was carried in and out of the church, where fishermen offered live squid and eels to the Virgin, while other workers proffered the tools and emblems of their agricultural work. Goatherds brought goats with red and yellow ribbons tied around their necks, plowmen held out ox harnesses, and servants from great houses arrived laden with loaves of bread and bottles of wine.

As full as May is of celebrations of the fruits of the earth—of artichokes in Sezze Romano, asparagus in Cilavegna and Fubine, and rice in Villimpenta—it is also a time of religious ceremonies. Lent lasts for forty days, and Easter for fifty, the last day being Pentecost (from the Greek word for fiftieth), which celebrates the descent of the Holy Spirit on the Apostles, and the real beginning of the Church, while Ascension falls on the fortieth day, in recognition of Jesus' flight upward to heaven. For La Festa del Grillo, the outdoor festival of crickets that celebrates Ascension and is held in the Cascine Gardens in Florence, people used to bring food already cooked at home, or bought what *trattorie* had made at impromptu kitchens set up outside: grilled chicken, pollo alla diavola, chicken on a spit, or agnello in umido, great pots of lamb stew. While the food cooked, children went to look for crickets, true symbols of spring, poking a piece of grass into their holes to lure them into a cage already prepared with a leaf of lettuce set on the bottom. It was a lazy feast day, which many people spent stretched out under the shade of trees, eating prosciutto, fennel sausages, and salame, salads of hard-boiled eggs, masses of bread and wine, and for dessert, cantucci di Prato and bocche di dama. The festival continues to be observed, although these days no one hunts for crickets because they are sold in pretty painted cages.

Eggs appear at Easter, birds at Ascension and Pentecost, and fish are celebrated in the height of summer. The warm waters of the straits of Messina are the breeding ground for *pesce spada,* the swordfish, celebrated in Bagnara Calabra (Calabria) in the month of July. They are still hunted on strange fishing boats called *ontri* that have a mast over forty feet tall from which protrudes a platform with just enough room for a lookout. Once he spots one of the giant fish, the boat is steered toward it and a fisherman, positioned on the deck, spears it with a ten-foot-long harpoon. When the Scot Patrick Brydone traveled to Sicily in 1770 as part of his Grand Tour, he was invited to see the capture of the swordfish, which he described as "whale-fishing in miniature" and pronounced "a noble diversion." The fishing is a hunt that remains a primitive rite, and must have had a religious aura centuries ago. It still exerts a powerful hold on those who have seen it. Renato Guttuso, a Sicilian artist, paid the event tribute with a famous painting, and Domenico Modugno, known for his song "*Volare,*" wrote "The Ballad of the Swordfish" ("*La ballata del pesce spada*") elaborating the danger and the drama of the capture. Swordfish usually travel in pairs, and it is said that if the female is caught, the male commits suicide, while if the male is harpooned, the female simply swims away. What implications can be drawn from this behavior, it is not clear, although it is only the fishermen lost to the waters—not the fish of either sex—who are honored in the ceremony.

An even bloodier rite known as the *mattanza,* the killing of the tuna, takes place between the island of Favignana and Trapani in Sicily. At the height of summer the sea runs red with the blood of thousands of the big fish when they are hunted down and driven toward the chambers of death, rooms of diminishing size, where they are finally killed. Tuna have been fished in the waters of Sicily for two thousand years, ever since classical times. The market and the practice of the kill, however, are changing dramatically. The Japanese are becoming the greatest consumers of Sicilian tuna, driving prices so high that a fisherman can now live comfortably for a year on the proceeds of a very few fish.

July ends with harvests. Grain is celebrated in the village of Ielsi in Molise, apricots in Monte Porzio Catone, near Rome, lemons in Amalfi, and lamb in Apulia, where farm contracts expire on July 25, obliging farmers to invite people to a dinner lasting all afternoon, for which quantities of young lamb in a meat sauce are served with barrels of wine.

The Celts had a certain ambivalence about the critical time just before the beginning of May, since they believed the dead were "like seeds buried in mother earth, returned to life in a new form," as philosopher Mircea Eliade explains, overflowing with energy and exuberance. People ate fava beans, the traditional Greek and Roman food of the dead, but they worshiped Belenos, the god of sunlight. This contradiction is a reminder that rites of abundance have a dark side, that death is a shadowy guest at the feast, just as darkness is evoked even at the height of summer, with its heat and flowers and fruits, when the sun is already beginning its descent toward winter.

FESTA DEI SERPARI

SNAKE FESTIVAL IN COCULLO

First Thursday in May

Cocullo, a tiny white stone village perched on a green hillside in Abruzzo, a mountainous region east of Rome, has a mere five hundred inhabitants, but you would never know it on the first Thursday in May. The steep road leading into the town is lined with a mile-long market, making its single appearance of the year, and thousands of people stream by it into the center of the village, two streets with one church, two piazze, and three towers. They are all on their way to an event that ostensibly celebrates the Feast Day of San Domenico (Saint Dominic), but everyone knows that it is really a snake festival. There are dozens of snakes in various sizes and colors and lengths, black and creamy yellow and deep green, mottled and plain. While some are as slender as a garden hose, others are as thick as a man's fist and six or seven feet long. They have been brought to Cocullo by the *serpari,* snake handlers who have gone into the stony fields on March 19 to catch the snakes as they wake from their winter lethargy and slither out into the warmth of the new spring sun. The *serpari* clamp them into terracotta jugs filled with bran or carry them back to Cocullo in sheepskin sacks the size of old-fashioned dinner napkins.

On their big day, the *serpari* arrive in the main piazza of Cocullo, wrapping snakes in bunches around their wrists, knotting them loosely around their necks like neckties, or slinging them casually over their shoulders. The *serpari* move slowly and deliberately, controlling and handling the snakes with a sureness that verges on rite as they stroke and caress them, letting them slide slowly around their shoulders, across their chests, and up their sleeves. They often work in pairs, one holding the reptiles and the other using a Polaroid camera to snap people who line up to be photographed for posterity holding the reptiles. Many boys and young men enthusiastically stretch out their hands to receive the snakes, and a large number of old women dressed in traditional black handle them casually. Almost all the little girls look apprehensive about the entire event but, coaxed by their fearless grandmothers, some manage to wrap the snakes around their arms and smile bravely at the camera. The snakes are generally tranquil, although several times in the course of the morning, one may stiffen around the neck of a young man, hissing, its tongue flicking in and out, its head moving back and forth in a slow, oily rhythm, causing momentary panic until the *serparo*'s nimble fingers grip it at the base of the head and calmly remove it. The *serpari* know that the snakes are not poisonous. They have already made them harmless by waving an old felt hat, and waiting for one of the snakes to get the hat in its jaws, and giving a swift yank, which breaks the fangs.

At first sight, the tiny piazza filled with dark-eyed men holding black and greenish reptiles looks like some terrifying vision out of Dante's Hell, but the men move with such composure and authority that the scene soon ceases to seem strange and the snakes become merely fascinating. As the morning wears on, more and more people are willing to hold the snakes, stroke them, drape them in twos and threes on their shoulders and necks.

The snakes are ancient residents of Cocullo. The cult of San Domenico, who is the ostensible reason for the festival, continues a tradition begun when an ancient people called the Marsi inhabited this territory. They worshiped the goddess Angizia, a snake enchantress who lived in a sacred wood nearby and protected local inhabitants from the venomous serpents that infested the countryside. She was the sister of the sorceress Circe, who had a few powerful charms herself, and she taught the Marsi remedies against snakebite. Now Angizia has been supplanted by San Domenico, who protects against the same menace. Like many saints, he was slipped in by the church to take over pagan rituals that could not be eradicated. San Domenico was originally known for the rather modest feat of speeding up the growth cycle of fava beans, hardly the stuff of which miracles are made, although the humble act takes on meaning since favas are a crucial food eaten at funerals. "They open the door on an unknown world," writes France Cardini, scholar of festivals and myth, and so San Domenico's favas become evidence of the powers of a miracle worker.

San Domenico was a Benedictine monk born in Umbria in 951 who established monasteries and performed miracles, especially saving people

Vipers, wood engraving by Ulysses Aldrovandi

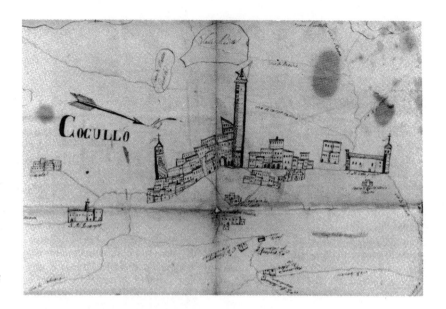

A copy of the design of Cocullo, perhaps from the late seventeenth century

from the bites of venomous snakes and rabid dogs and taming a fierce wolf that was about to spirit a small child away. He came to Cocullo when it was threatened by an invasion of snakes, and like Saint Patrick freed the town by luring the snakes out of their nests and making them harmless. He has been closely connected to the town ever since. Over the years the event has been embellished so that on his festival day the statue of the saint now leaves the church to be festooned with snakes that writhe around its neck.

Of course snakes have had a bad reputation ever since they were assigned the role of fatal tempters and the Church made them agents of Satan and symbols of corruption and evil. Before Christianity, however, snakes were worshiped in many parts of the world for their wisdom, and they were thought to have the gift of prophecy and healing. To this day, the emblem of the medical profession, the staff of Aesculapius, shows two serpents entwined around what was once the god Hermes' magic staff. As guardians of the waters of life, serpents represent knowledge of the secrets of creation. Because they penetrate the earth, they are thought to be intimately connected with the secrets of fertility, and because they shed their skins and renew themselves, like the moon that is reborn each month, they symbolize rebirth and eternal life, as in the Italian expression *aver più anni d'un serpente,* "being older than a serpent." For the people of Abruzzo, who live in a countryside thick with them, snakes represent a connection with the Great Mother Isis, mother of life and the afterlife, who mated with the serpent and made him her phallic consort. Until

The procession of snake charmers with the statue of San Domenico, from La Tribuna Illustrata, *1905*

some time in the last century, the people of Abruzzo believed that the serpent copulated with all women.

For years the people of Cocullo actually partook of the snakes, their totem animals, as a way of incorporating their virtues. But no one talks about roast snake now; instead they make five enormous sweet rings called *ciambellone*, shaped in the form of snakes biting their own tails.

It is a rare festival in which food isn't shared among the people of the town, but in Cocullo the ciambellone are made only for the five men who carry the statue of the saint and the banner of the parish throughout the procession that marks the festivities. To raise funds for the ingredients of the ciambellone, townspeople go from door to door collecting offerings of grain or flour, eggs and money. Then early on Monday, before the festival, four chosen women begin their work in the kitchen of the oldest among them. They make the dough in a huge slant-sided wooden drawer, using their hands to beat seventy eggs into more than thirty pounds of flour and handling the floppy dough with the same ease that the *serpari* hold the snakes. It is an honor to be chosen to make the big sweet cake wreaths, and one by one the women of Cocullo drop by to see how the baking is progressing. Someone brings coffee, another offers to let the old scale hang from her thumb to make sure that the dough for each

wreath really weighs over six pounds. Cocullo's single woodburning oven was destroyed in the earthquake of 1986, so the ciambellone have to be loaded into the back of a three-wheeled Piaggio van, covered with a bedspread, and transported to nearby Anversa, where two young bakers from Cocullo fire up the ovens and make room to cook them.

The festival, which has been held on the first Thursday in May for almost four centuries, is built around an offering of snakes and takes place in both church and piazza. Years ago the entire ceremony was held in the church, where the serpents were waved above the heads of the worshipers during the elevation of the host. Of course some snakes always wriggled free and slithered around the crowded church, which was hot and airless and thick with the smell of incense. The snakes are still very much in the center of things, and are still taken inside the church, where people approach the statue of the saint and offer it money and ex-votos, but the main event now takes place in the piazza and a few small streets of the town.

Church bells ring and a band appears, filling the town with music. Next comes the procession, walking behind the green banner of the parish of Cocullo. The enormous ring-shaped ciambellone used to be slid into place on the wooden brackets and handles by which the statue of the saint was carried. This suggestive arrangement has been replaced by girls from Cocullo, dressed in traditional embroidered red dresses of Abruzzo, holding baskets draped in pink and white linen high above their heads and showing off the five great golden ciambellone. Not to be outdone, the nearby town of Gissi sends an impressive edible pyramid made of rows of colorfully decorated heart-shaped breads alternating with pizzelle, flat waffle-like cookies shaped like shingles, and crowned by an enormous sunburst. This confection rides on a hammered copper jug balanced on a woman's head. Behind the girls come the *serpari,* perhaps twenty of them, proudly holding up knots and clumps of their biggest, longest, and fattest snakes.

The procession moves through the piazza into the church. Mass is celebrated for quite a long time. When the procession reemerges, it contains monks, priests, members of a confraternity, children, and of course the statue of San Domenico. The *serpari* follow the statue closely, holding up the snakes to show their great size and stretching them out, like thick ropes, ready to be tossed and draped on the slippery black wooden statue of the saint. Inevitably one or two refuse to take hold and start to slither away. The *serparo* then dives into the crowd and, swinging the errant snake by the tail, tosses it back onto the statue. As bells chime and trumpets sound, the procession goes through the two main streets of the town with all the snakes tangled on the saint. The virginal young girls of Cocullo, with their great golden wreaths iced and sprinkled with colorful confetti, lead the way. For many years the procession used to end with the snakes being killed in front of the church and then buried outside the city, or being sold at an improvised market to pharmacists for various ointments and cures, to tourists, or to traders interested in their skins. These days ecology triumphs and since snakes no longer threaten the countryside in massive numbers, many are set free and encouraged to return to the fields whence they were taken.

The festival food in Cocullo evokes snakes. One tiny bar and the small stands behind the church sell ciambelle, little twisted wreaths of bread flavored with anise seed, which look like snakes wrapped one around another. With their internal vacancy, they resemble the embracing enclosure of women's sexuality, a perfect counterpoint to the omnipresent serpents. And the ciambelle are not alone. Other towns nearby in Abruzzo make different snake-shaped sweets, including the coffee- and almond-flavored cervone with an interior spine of raspberry jam. All these foods are pagan in origin, and while the festivals cannot be traced to Etruscan times, sweets shaped and coiled to resemble snakes occur only in those regions of Italy where the Etruscans lived. Some are made in Pienza and Chianti in Tuscany and others in Perugia, home of the famous torciglione, a serpent with almonds standing in its scales, a slice of candied orange for a flicking tongue, and coffee beans for eyes.

There are even rubber snakes at the market at the entrance to town, and many who buy them sling them around their necks, looking as brave as the *serpari* in the piazza who caress their snakes and wear them proudly. The market has changed dramatically since earlier days when amulets against the evil eye were the main items for sale. Now there are several trucks, each holding an entire porchetta, the great roast pig stuffed with rosemary and herbs of the countryside that is served at every festival. People wedge slabs of porchetta between panini or big slices of the focaccia-like bread of the area, munch on chickens cooked on whirring spits, and drink cooling sodas as they walk down the hillside away from the saint of the snakes.

Miraculous Liberation of a City Infested with Snakes, engraving of 1488, from a German edition of The Golden Legend *of Jacopo da Varagine*

Biscotti di Cocullo

~~~~~~~~~~~~~~~~~~~~~~~~~~~~

Lemony Cookies from Cocullo

These cookies, really a cross between a graham cracker and lemony short-bread, are perfect for teatime. They were once baked for the band that played for the Festa of San Domenico. Although that tradition has disappeared, there is no reason the cookies should vanish as well. They are extremely easy to make.

Makes 30 cookies

3¾ cups (500 grams) unbleached all-purpose flour
1 cup (200 grams) sugar
½ teaspoon salt
¾ teaspoon baking soda
Grated zest of 1 lemon
¾ teaspoon lemon extract
½ cup plus 2 tablespoons (125 grams) unsalted butter
3 eggs
4 tablespoons rum
About 2 tablespoons milk
1 egg white

In a large bowl, stir the flour, sugar, salt, baking soda, and lemon zest and extract together. Cut in the butter with a pastry blender until the mixture has the granular texture of cornmeal. Beat the whole eggs and rum in a measuring cup until smooth. Add enough milk to measure 1 cup. Add the egg mixture to the dry ingredients and mix until it coheres. Chill well.

On a lightly floured work surface roll the dough out ⅛ inch thick and cut into 5- by 2½-inch rectangles. Brush with egg white and prick the tops generously with the tines of a fork.

Bake on greased or parchment-paper–lined cookie sheets at 400°F until lightly golden, 16 to 18 minutes.

Cervone

~~~~~~~~~~~~~~~~~~~~~~~~~~~~

Spicy Cake Shaped Like a Snake

This spicy cake, in a charming serpentine shape, is one of several such cakes made in Abruzzo. My version is typically fragrant with nutmeg and cloves, orange and honey, but not quite traditional since I have added butter and left out the candied fruits. The cooks of Abruzzo often ice the cake with chocolate fondant and then wash the spine with a cover of powdered sugar and egg white glaze.

(continued)

Makes 2 cakes

¾ cup (150 grams) sugar
½ teaspoon ground cloves
1½ teaspoons ground nutmeg
Grated zest of 1 orange
1 teaspoon baking soda
¾ teaspoon salt
4½ cups plus 2 tablespoons (600 grams) unbleached all-purpose flour
½ cup (112 grams) unsalted butter
¾ cup plus 3 tablespoons (250 grams) honey, boiling
½ cup strong brewed espresso coffee
1 egg
⅓ cup amaretto or rum
⅓ cup jam; amarena or wild cherry is traditional, but raspberry is a fine
  alternative
Coffee beans and candied orange peel for garnish

Mix the sugar, spices, orange zest, baking soda, and salt into the flour.
Cut in the butter with a pastry blender until it is the size of small pebbles.
Pour in the boiling honey, coffee, egg, and liqueur and mix until smooth.
Let cool and then turn out onto a floured surface.

Divide the dough in half. Roll the first half into an 18-inch-long
cylinder. Make a deep trough down the center and carefully spoon half
the jam in it. Pull the edges of the dough out and over the jam and pinch
firmly all along the length to seal it firmly inside. Roll the log over and
carefully place it, seam side down, on a baking sheet lined with parchment
paper. Be sure that the smooth side is up. Bend the dough carefully into
a circle and fashion the snake's head at one end—make it a bit triangular,
tapering to the mouth—and the tail at the other—tapering it as well.
Very firmly set 2 coffee beans for eyes and a thin slice of candied orange
peel for tongue. Repeat with the second piece of dough.

Bake the cakes at 400°F about 30 minutes.

Ciambella

xxxxxxxxxxxxxxxxxxxxxxxxxxxxxx

*Lemon-Flavored
Wreath Cake from
Cocullo*

Four or five women spend the morning grating lemons, beating eggs into
flour, measuring out rum, and shaping this lemon-flavored dough into
giant wreaths. It is one of the few sweets that are not baked in vast
proportions, so the women congregate in a home kitchen and drink coffee
and talk about this year's cakes and last. I like the lemon taste so much
that I have accentuated it a bit by adding a little more extract. Spreading
the icing on the warm cakes with your bare hands is a glorious childlike

experience, which can be followed by sowing handfuls of colored sprinkles over the top.

Makes 1 round cake

3¾ cups (500 grams) unbleached all-purpose flour
1 teaspoon sea salt
¾ cup (150 grams) sugar
1 teaspoon cinnamon
2 tablespoons baking powder
½ teaspoon baking soda
3 tablespoons olive oil
6 tablespoons vegetable oil
3 lemons
3 eggs
4 tablespoons rum
3 tablespoons milk
1½ tablespoons vanilla extract
½ teaspoon lemon extract

I C I N G

2 egg whites
2 tablespoons sugar
Colored sprinkles (optional)

In a large bowl mix the flour, salt, sugar, cinnamon, baking powder, and baking soda. Add the oils and mix with a wooden spoon or with the paddle of an electric mixer until crumbly. Grate the zest of the lemons directly over the mixture. Beat the eggs, rum, milk, and vanilla and lemon extracts together; add to the dry ingredients and stir until completely incorporated.

Shape the dough into a ball. You can bake it free form on a baking sheet lined with parchment paper or set it in a 9½- or 10-inch round baking pan lined with parchment paper. Place the dough in the pan and make a hole in the center of it with your hands. Gradually stretch the dough from the center, increasing the size of the hole to about 6 inches wide. The hole will close up to some extent during the baking.

Bake at 375°F until a tester comes out clean, about 45 minutes.

Icing. Just before the cake finishes baking, beat the egg whites vigorously until they form soft peaks. Add the sugar and beat until glossy.

As soon as the cake tests done, remove it from the oven and with your bare hands spread the icing over the top. Shower with a blizzard of colored sprinkles, if you wish.

Pane al Pizza

Bread Made Like Pizza

Hortus sanitatis,
Giovanni daCuba, 1491,
Ferrara, Biblioteca
Comunale, Ariostea

Wherever we wandered during the festival in Cocullo, we saw great oval breads with rough dimpled tops. They were so big they looked like footprints left by the Yeti; yet there were long lines of people who bought chunks wrapped in waxed paper and ate them as they meandered. One bite was a revelation—an introduction to an extraordinarily fragrant, slightly dark bread made with oil and salt sprinkled directly on top and baked right into the dough. The top is dimpled and even seasoned like focaccia, which undoubtedly explains why it is called *pane al pizza*, bread made just like pizza. It is hard to imagine a bread that could be fuller in taste and richer in flavor. It goes with almost everything—cheese, meats, stews, and salads.

This dough is so wet that it looks impossible to work with; yet sprinkle a couple of tablespoons of flour on your work surface and it will come together very nicely. I have made this bread with no yeast other than what is in the starter and it is delicious, although it does take considerably longer to rise. Should you substitute Biga (see opposite page) for the natural yeast, be prepared for a dough that domes up dramatically in the baking. Although it is not traditional, these breads are wonderful when shaped as round loaves and they keep longer.

Makes 4 medium-sized oval loaves

¼ teaspoon active dry yeast
⅓ cup warm water
3 cups water, room temperature
2 cups (500 grams) Natural Yeast Starter (page 32), measured when cold
1½ cups (200 grams) whole-wheat flour
5¾ cups (800 grams) unbleached all-purpose flour
1 tablespoon sea salt
3 to 4 teaspoons olive oil
Sea salt

By Mixer. Stir the yeast into the warm water in a large mixer bowl; let stand until creamy, about 10 minutes. Add the room temperature water and the starter and mix with the paddle. Add both flours and 1 tablespoon salt and mix until well blended, but do not expect it to come away from the sides of the bowl. Change to the dough hook and knead at medium speed 4 minutes. The dough will be very soft, malleable, and elastic. Finish kneading on a lightly floured surface, adding 1 to 2 extra tablespoons flour if needed, so that it comes together nicely.

First Rise. Place the dough in a lightly oiled container, cover tightly with plastic wrap, and let rise until doubled, about 3 hours.

Shaping and Second Rise. Flour your work surface generously. You can even flour your dough scraper and your hands before pouring the dough out of the bowl. Lightly flour the top of the dough and divide it into 4 equal pieces. Flatten each piece of dough and roll it up lengthwise into a cylinder. Stretch each piece into a rectangle about 9 by 5 inches and dimple it lightly. Cut 4 pieces of parchment paper somewhat larger than the loaves, flour them lightly, and set them on a pizza peel or baking sheet. Place a loaf on each paper. Cover with towels and let rise until doubled, about 2 hours.

Baking. Thirty minutes before baking, heat the oven with baking stones in it to 425°F. Just before baking, dimple each loaf well with your fingertips, spread the tops with a bit of olive oil, and sprinkle with sea salt. Dimple again lightly to be sure the oil stays in the holes. Leave the dough on the pieces of parchment paper and just slide them onto the stones in the oven. You can remove the paper after about 20 minutes. Bake until the loaves ring hollow when tapped on the bottom, about 35 minutes.

Biga
~~~~~~~~~~~~~~~~~~~~~~~~~~~~
Bread Starter

Almost every bread in this book includes a *biga*, a slightly sour starter that enhances the flavor of the wheat. Loaves made with a *biga* last longer and taste richer than those made with commercial yeast. Although it looks complicated, a *biga* is a simple mixture of three ingredients. Dissolve a tiny amount of yeast in warm water, whisk in the flour, cover, and let it sit for up to a day or two, and your starter is made. A *biga* can be refrigerated for several days or frozen for weeks. Take it out of the freezer and it will be bubbling again after three hours at room temperature.

Makes 2⅓ cups

¼ teaspoon active dry yeast or ¹⁄₁₀ small cake (2 grams) fresh yeast
¼ cup warm water
¾ cup plus 1 tablespoon plus 1 teaspoon water, room temperature
2½ cups (330 grams) unbleached all-purpose flour, preferably
    organically grown

Stir the yeast into the warm water and let stand until creamy, about 10 minutes. Stir in the remaining water and then the flour, 1 cup at a time.
   Leave this covered with plastic wrap to rise at room temperature 6 to 24 hours. Refrigerate. You can refresh it by stirring into it:

(continued)

½ cup plus 2 teaspoons water, room temperature
1¼ cups (165 grams) unbleached all-purpose flour, preferably
organically grown

Cover with plastic wrap and let rise at cool room temperature 4 to 6 hours. Refrigerate until ready to use. It will keep several days, becoming sourer and tangier as time passes. To continue refreshing it, use or discard ¾ cup of the *biga* and stir the same amounts of flour and water directly above into the remainder.

Lievito Naturale

Natural Yeast Starter

The search for splendid bread continues. As I traveled through Italy going from festival to festival, I found loaves or great round wheels that I particularly liked, and sought out bakers to learn how they were made. It gradually dawned on me that breads whose doughs bubbled only on the organic wild yeasts made loaves with a fragrance and texture that were even richer and more complex than breads made with a *biga*, a sour sponge using dough left from the previous day's bake.

I knew from artisan bakers that starters could be made from unsulfured and unsprayed wine grapes, but I wondered where most people would find such esoteric produce. I wanted a starter that would be easy for everyone to make and realized that organic raisins could provide the answer. I simply soaked the raisins until they began to bubble and froth, then drained them and used the water to make a starter in the same proportions as for Pugliese bread, a porous full-flavored country loaf. It takes several days to build the full starter, and once it is ready to use the individual rises of the dough take longer, which further develops the flavor of the wheat. The starter must be refreshed at least once a week. It is a straight-forward starter that can replace commercial yeast. Measure what you need by substituting 20 to 35 percent of the weight of the flour in simple breads; use 25 to as much as 40 percent of the flour weight in fruit- and nut-filled doughs. Always use freshly made or recently refreshed yeast in sweet breads so they do not have a sour taste.

There are two ways to measure and use the starter. The first is easy and straightforward, while the second is more finely calibrated and produces a consistent strength. In either case, I advise weighing the sponge since it expands at room temperature, but if you measure it, be sure it is cold when you do.

Makes 2¾ cups (about 660 grams) natural yeast starter, measured cold

2 cups (300 grams) organic raisins
4 cups water, 75° to 80°F temperature
1½ cups plus 2 tablespoons (250 grams) unbleached all-purpose flour,
  preferably organically grown

Set the raisins in a bowl, cover them with water, squeeze them to release
the sugars, and leave at room temperature until the water becomes frothy,
3 to 4 days, although it can take as long as 6 days. Do not worry if bits
of mold begin to form.

Drain the raisins and measure ¾ cup plus 1 tablespoon of the soaking
water. Pour the soaking water into a mixing bowl, add the flour, and stir
well or mix with the paddle attachment of an electric mixer. Cover with
plastic wrap or a tea towel and leave it out at room temperature to bubble
4 to 6 hours. You will see little bubbles have developed on the surface
and the whole mixture has puffed up and expanded. You can proceed
immediately or refrigerate the starter for 24 hours.

Refresh the starter by adding:

¼ cup plus 1 teaspoon water, room temperature
½ cup (75 grams) unbleached all-purpose flour, preferably organically
  grown

Mix well, cover with plastic wrap or a tea towel, and leave out to bubble
again another 4 to 6 hours. You can refrigerate the starter 24 to 72 hours
or you can proceed immediately.

Refresh one final time by adding:

¼ cup plus 1 teaspoon water, room temperature
½ cup plus 1 tablespoon (75 grams) unbleached all-purpose flour,
  preferably organically grown

Stir well, cover with plastic wrap or a tea towel, and leave out to bubble
and triple in volume, 4 to 6 hours. By now it smells sourer than it tastes.
The taste is sweetly sour. Refrigerate the starter. It is now ready to use.

As you use the starter, after taking the amount required by a recipe,
you will need to refresh it every 3 or 4 days, although it keeps for a week,
becoming sourer as it sits. If you neglect it, the starter becomes slick,
develops a slimy skin, and dies. You can freeze the starter, but even if
you only bake every week or two, you can keep the starter alive by
refreshing it. Add ¼ cup plus ½ teaspoon water and ½ cup plus 1 tablespoon flour. If you need more starter, double the amounts since it is the
ratio that matters. Discard the crusty surface and use the softer portion
underneath. If the starter begins to go flat, try soaking more raisins as in
the first step.

(continued)

Same Starter— Larger Amount

These proportions provide enough raisin soaking water to make some natural yeast starter with durum flour too (see below).

Makes 4¼ cups (about 1050 grams) natural yeast starter

3 cups (450 grams) organic raisins
6 cups water, 75° to 80°F temperature
3¾ cups unbleached all-purpose flour, preferably organically grown

In the first step measure 1½ cups plus 2 tablespoons and 1 teaspoon soaking water and mix in the flour. Follow the same procedure and refresh each time by adding:

¼ cup plus 1 teaspoon water
½ cup (75 grams) unbleached all-purpose flour, preferably organically grown

Same Starter— Second Method

Makes 2 cups and 2 tablespoons (about 550 grams) of natural yeast starter

Follow the directions on page 32 for the natural yeast starter, but divide all the measurements in half:

1 cup raisins
2 cup water
¾ cup plus 1 tablespoon unbleached all-purpose flour, preferably organically grown

To refresh the starter, measure ½ cup (120 grams) of the mixture and add to it:

½ cup water
1 cup plus 2 tablespoons (165 grams) unbleached all-purpose flour, preferably organically grown

Follow the directions in the first method. Refresh by measuring ¾ cup (165 grams) of the natural yeast starter and add to it:

¾ cup water
1¾ cup plus 2 tablespoons (250 grams) unbleached all-purpose flour, preferably organically grown

Follow the directions in the first method.

Durum Flour Natural Yeast Starter

Makes 3¼ cups plus 1 tablespoon (800 grams)

1 cup raisin soaking water (see page 33)
1¾ cups (250 grams) durum flour

Mix the soaking water and durum flour vigorously with a wooden spoon or the paddle attachment of an electric mixer for 3 minutes, until the dough is elastic, stretchy, and cohesive. Follow the instructions above.
   Refresh it by adding:

¼ cup plus 1 teaspoon water
½ cup minus 1 tablespoon (60 grams) durum flour

Follow the instructions for the natural yeast starter. The final mixture will be smooth, sticky, and elastic.

SAGRA DEL PESCE

FISH SAGRA IN CAMOGLI

Second Sunday in May

*T*wo tons of fish cooking in a gigantic frying pan, bonfires roaring on the beach, fireworks and food in a Ligurian seaside village: Camogli fries up free fish for anyone who comes on the second Sunday in May. This may not be an ancient festival, but it has its magical moments. It is conceived on such a mammoth scale that attending it is almost like being a child again, dwarfed by the enormous accouterments of life in the grown-up world. The *festa* begins with local fishermen cooking fat anchovy-like fish in a frying pan that is twelve feet in diameter and has a handle eighteen feet long. It's as if Gulliver's frying pan had been hauled up on the beaches near Genoa. The recipe? First bring 700 liters of oil to a boil, lightly dust 1½ tons of fresh little silvery fish with 120 kilos of flour, and slip them in small batches into one of 28 baskets circulating in the bubbling oil. The fishermen are the cooks and instead of wearing white toques they take charge sporting bright red and blue Genovese sailors' berets that look just like Scottish tam-o'-shanters.

Certainly the portions are generous. Everyone gets a container filled with five or six pieces of fish and a chunk of local lemon. Camogli becomes a gigantic picnic as all over town people have lunch sitting on the beach and the beach wall, in empty rowboats and on stone promenades, and on the ubiquitous stone steps. Some even perch on the great open space next to the medieval tower that holds the town aquarium. They pick up the little fish in their fingers, pull out the bones, and eat them, washed down with copious servings of wine. For dessert, perhaps they pick up some camogliese, rum-drenched truffle-like sweets that are made only in Camogli.

Camogli is a seaside village that rises straight out of the water on dramatic stone cliffs, like a miniature Orvieto on the sea. It is framed by a wharf with enormous rocks at one end and little hill towns, such as Santa Margherita, that are strung along the tops of the pine-covered rocky cliffs at the other end. Unlike nearby Portofino this town has not been overrun by tourists. Its narrow alleys, tiny courtyards, and steep steps are still used by fishermen who set off each morning to fish the sea. The six- to eight-story houses are tall and thin, each set directly next to the other on the hill. They were originally painted in different shades of bright pink or lemon yellow or rosy red so the men could distinguish their houses while they were out on the water. To this day the owner of each house must paint it with the specific hue that has been its special color since the Middle Ages or the Renaissance, and must maintain its decoration exactly as it was. Even more remarkable are the many cornices and stone balconies and windows covered with half-opened green shutters that are really trompe l'oeil ornaments painted right onto flat plain façades. Almost every house has its *faux* decoration, even the church, whose flat pink bell tower looks garlanded and is framed and shaded with golden outlines. The entire town is so full of trompe l'oeil that it becomes a game to pick out which are the real balconies and shutters and windows and which have been painted to trick the eye. Even the great banner with the image of the Virgin Mary fluttering in the piazza with the giant frying pan is really only a painted bedsheet. It's as if Magritte had been turned loose on an entire village.

The festival's beginnings are hardly shrouded in mystery—the first one took place in 1952—but there are variations on the theme of its origins. In one version several local men were in danger of drowning, and when they were saved, they vowed to honor San Fortunato, the patron saint of Camogli. In another, San Fortunato took care of a sailor in a terrible storm at sea during World War II. No matter. The *festa* of free fish was born, offering the catch of a single night to San Fortunato. The first year of the festival, six men cooked at three different parts of the wharf; but word got around and the next year it took fifty fishermen and fifteen pans to fry the fish. The following year the event was held in a single location, which compelled the cooks to invent an enormous frying pan, and then to set it on a superstructure in the harbor created especially for the day. In time they made the current frying pan, which weighs 1,500 pounds and sits on top of the 28 gas cylinders used to fire up the jets, which cook 3,500 pounds of fish in a single day.

Once, Camogli's fishermen set off on the Saturday night before the festival to catch the fish for the next day's fry. Bonfires on the shore lit up the night, so the fishermen could look back and see the town, and those fires blazed until the men returned with boats full of fish, which they cooked right on the beach. These days the local fishermen cannot possibly net 3,500 pounds of fish from these Mediterranean waters, so many of the fish come from as far away as the Adriatic and the bonfires blaze spectacularly only for an hour or two before fading, just as the dancing and music start to wind down. Even if its origins are somewhat fanciful, there must always have been a community tradition of frying and sharing, so this festival is probably just a logical and charming extension of something that already existed.

It is worth arriving on Saturday to see the two enormous bonfires being built and then lit on the beach. In the afternoon it is hot and still as construction proceeds, but only a few people lie sunning themselves on the usually crowded beach. Nearby, the form of a wooden dragon is being covered with a green paper skin, while the other soon-to-be bonfire, a windmill forty-five feet high, is being sheathed in bamboo curtaining. The residents of Camogli's two neighborhoods have saved all their old cartons, crates, chairs, boards, baskets, drawers, chests, even rowboats with split hulls, and have packed them into empty cavities in the two bonfire constructions. In the course of construction the dragon receives large red toenails, scales parading down a long sloping back, enormous nostrils (all the better to breathe fire with), a fluttery beard, and a very long tail.

By Saturday night fireworks are popping. The reverberations of the explosions bounce off the stone walls of the town. Young boys light torches of newspaper and enormous sparklers that sizzle hot pink. The tempo intensifies. Bells ring. The clock in the tower bongs eleven times, and

Fishermen, wood etching from Agricoltura vulgare *by Pietro Crescentino, 1511*

when the windmill is finally set on fire, it catches immediately and huge black clouds of smoke billow upward. A few people rush to toss debris into the flames, but most back away instinctively from the great roar as the dragon is torched. The thick crowd, pushed back by the heat, stands silent as the great fires blaze in the air.

Some say Camogli gets its name from *Ca'* (for *Casa*) *Mogli*, house of the wife left behind while her husband went to sea, a reference to all the women who have been widowed by the Mediterranean. Others say it comes from *case a mucchi*, houses all bunched together, and still others from Camuli, the medieval equivalent of an Etruscan name. Sean O'Faolain was particularly taken with its "restless vivacity," brilliant colors, and "the tiny cluttered harbour, . . . crooked houses on every square foot of crooked space, all this way and that, with taverns built over the water, a ruined castle to top the rocks, and a gaudy, glittering, golden church approached by a flight of noble steps."

On the day of the *festa*, the fishermen fire up the twenty-eight enormous gas cylinders to fry the fish in the gigantic frying pan. Inside the pan bubble vats of oil. The cooks flour the fish and fry them—two thousand at a time—in containers that look like giant lettuce baskets, and dish them out to the waiting crowds. The tiny fish—mostly zerro or boga—belong to a family of small deep-sea fish called *pesce azzurro*, blue fish, which includes a number of more familiar species such as anchovies and sardines. On the coasts of Italy, traditional "poor" cooking has always used these fish in such dishes as pasta con le sarde. Being full of protein and mineral salts, they are both cheap and nutritious, but chic they are not.

Even though there are lots of people at the Camogli fish fry, no one shoves or gets impatient, and while standing in line is almost unheard of in Italy, everyone waits peaceably for the free fried fish. The fish fry goes all morning, and after the usual three-hour break at midday, starts up again. On Saturday night and again on Sunday, at the foot of the port, there is a competing fish fry with a larger selection of fish meant to raise funds to buy a new ambulance for the Green Cross. This evening calamari, hake, a fish called *sugharelli*, horse mackerel, and scad are bobbing in the pan. Wine flows freely and kids dance with each other and old people two-step to the little band tucked into a corner of the piazza below the church. People wander slowly through the crowds, buy camogliese to nibble on for dessert, and many take the boat to the tiny cove of San Fruttuoso to see a nearby Romanesque abbey that rises against the perpendicular cliffs before returning home after their feast at the sea.

Gallette

~~~~~~~~~~~~~~~~~~~~~~~~~~~~~

*Small Sourdough
Rolls
from Camogli*

Columbus and his sailors probably survived their long voyages by eating gallette, small dried focacce, the quintessential sailors' bread that was softened by dipping in seawater. Gallette may be basic, but they also are the floor of the most elegant of all Ligurian dishes, cappon magro. The bread goes on the bottom, and on top chefs build a true Renaissance *trionfo di tavola*, triumph of the table, and a magnificent architectural construction with layers of the bounty of Liguria—all manner of elegant fish and poached green vegetables. Eaten fresh, gallette are delicious little sourdough rolls—fine for small sandwiches and snacks.

Makes 14 rolls

2 cups (500 grams) 3-day-old Biga (page 31) or Natural Yeast Starter
   (page 32)
1½ cups plus 2 tablespoons warm water
3¾ cups (500 grams) unbleached all-purpose flour
1 tablespoon plus 1 teaspoon sea salt

By Mixer. Using the paddle attachment mix the *biga* and water slowly until the *biga* breaks up a bit. Add the flour and salt and mix vigorously until the dough is well formed, about 2 minutes. Change to the dough hook and knead 4 minutes at medium speed. Finish by kneading briefly on a floured surface, adding as little flour as possible, until the dough is supple and moist.

By Processor. Mix the starter with the water by squeezing it through your fingers until the starter is fairly well broken up. Refrigerate until cold. Place the flour and salt in the processor bowl fitted with the steel blade. Pulse several times to sift. With the machine running, pour the starter mixture down the feed tube and process until the dough comes together. To knead, process no more than 30 seconds longer. Stop if the motor begins to slow down. Finish kneading on a well-floured surface until the dough is supple and moist. It will remain sticky throughout the kneading, but resist any impulse to add more flour.

First Rise. Set the dough in an oiled bowl, cover with plastic wrap, and let rise until doubled, 3 to 4 hours. If you are using natural yeast, the rise will be slower.

Shaping and Second Rise. Turn the dough out onto a lightly floured surface, knead it briefly, and cut it into 14 pieces. Elongate each piece to a flat oval and dimple it with your fingertips. The rolls look unpromisingly flat, but they will puff and rise. Set on baking sheets lined with parchment paper, cover with a towel, and let rise until puffed but not really doubled, 45 minutes to 1 hour.

Baking. Thirty minutes before baking, heat the oven with baking stones in it to 400°F. Set the baking sheets inside the oven and bake until the rolls puff a bit and look like largish buttons, 35 to 40 minutes. Cool on a rack. If you want real hardtack biscuits, turn off the oven and leave the rolls to harden. Otherwise eat them soon after baking.

Fish, illustration from l'Encyclopédie *by Diderot-D'Alembert*

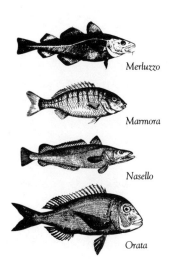

Merluzzo

Marmora

Nasello

Orata

CORSA DEI CERI

RACE OF THE CANDLES
IN GUBBIO

May 15

*C*all it collective madness or mass catharsis, every May 15 a wild race
called the Corsa dei Ceri unleashes a frenzy of excitement in the normally
silent city of Gubbio as three teams of men race up and down narrow
streets of the vertical city carrying three Ceri, gigantic wooden constructions that look like two octagonal rockets joined in the center and tapered
at each end, with a statue of a saint planted on top. They each weigh
about a thousand pounds, stand close to sixteen feet high, and are bolted
to platforms resembling long wooden stretchers with arms at each corner
so the Ceraioli, team members, can hoist and carry them. The people of
Gubbio actually call the event La Corsa dei Matti, The Race of the Crazy,
and cry, "Long live the crazy people of Gubbio." They are so proud of
being considered mad that they give out diplomas of craziness to citizens
during the *festa,* and anyone can become an honorary citizen by racing
three times around the fountain in front of the town hall and being
energetically splashed with its waters.

   The day begins at dawn with drummers banging out a wake-up message
and continues with mass in the tiny whitewashed church of the masons
for the blessing of the small wooden statues of the three saints that ride
on top of the Ceri. In the procession, which traces its way through the
city, are the band, great masses of Ceraioli, the bearers of the Ceri, and
all their followers, one team in red shirts, the next in yellow, the last in
black, each with scarves of a contrasting color. Each of the three Ceri
represents a professional corporation and on top of each sits a saint:

Sant'Ubaldo, patron of the masons and of the city itself; San Giorgio (Saint George), patron of artisans and merchants; and Sant'Antonio (Saint Anthony), who looks after students and farmworkers. Look at them and you can see how society was divided in medieval times: Sant'Ubaldo represents the Church; the warrior San Giorgio, the army; and Sant'Antonio, the peasants and manual workers. Like the Palio in Siena, the race is an event for which the city lives all year long, but unlike the horse race, there is no suspense about the outcome, since everyone knows that the Cero with Sant'Ubaldo on it will win. He is, after all, Gubbio's patron saint, and the celebration happens on the eve of the anniversary of his death. They know that San Giorgio will come in second and Sant'Antonio third, because that is the way they are lined up at the start, and the streets are so narrow that overtaking is out of the question. It is not who wins but how far one Cero can outstrip its adversary or how close on the heels of a competitor it can run that counts. The three groups of Ceraioli, for the moment without their Ceri, parade through the walled city, following a route from gate to gate until they arrive at Gubbio's center, the impressive Piazza Grande. All this time people have been streaming into the city from neighboring Umbrian towns, from Rome, and from other places far away until the piazza is a solid sea of humanity. Every square inch, every window, balcony, and crenellated battlement, is filled with people; even the bell tower—where the bells are rung by a man swinging back and forth with his entire body—is crammed.

Hundreds of Ceraioli jog into the piazza in a ribbon of color, opening a path through the spectators, finding space to stand where minutes before not even a sliver of pavement had been visible. Drummers and trumpeters in medieval dress line the cantilevered stone stairs of the great fourteenth-century Palazzo dei Consoli that look as if they had been poured in liquid layers and frozen. From one direction comes the mayor with a red, white, and green sash across his chest, from another the bishop in his shocking-pink biretta and vestments, and from a third the captain, who is in charge of the event, arrives on horseback to receive the key to the city for the day.

It is time for the Alzata, the raising of the Ceri. A drumroll is the signal for members of all three teams to raise high the great wooden platforms that will hold the Ceri. Seconds later the doors of the Palazzo dei Consoli fly open and out run the members of one group after another. First come the captains with swords raised. Next appear the teams with the gigantic shiny wooden Ceri, which they lay on the wooden platforms. No sooner does each captain leap up on the platform that will hold his Cero than three more men rush out into the piazza, each one carrying a small carved wooden saint. Bells toll and the crowd lets out a tremendous roar as each saint is attached to the top. Next come the men bearing the special sacramental nails that bolt the Ceri to their platforms. And finally, as tension continues to mount, a man from each team dashes down the steps of the palazzo holding high above his head a ceramic amphora full of water. Each man turns his amphora over, letting a great rush of water sluice over where the Cero is inserted into the platform, then he hurls the empty jug right into the dense crowd. People leap up as it crashes, some trying to avoid the shards, others rushing to collect the pieces for good luck.

Bells ring and another huge roar goes up as the captains raise up their platforms in a single fluid movement and race them three times around the square, Sant'Ubaldo first, followed by San Giorgio and then Sant'Antonio. The three teams take off. The enormous weight of the Ceri rests on the shoulders of teams of about twenty men, who continually rotate in and out to share the burden. They keep up a trot, for the saints perched on top must look as if they are really running. They make a circuit of the city, racing along Via Dante, then up Via dei Consoli and Via Gattapone, stopping to drink the water and wine that are offered along the way and to receive flowers that are showered from windows overhead. Finally, they set down their heavy burdens to eat *La Tavola Bona*, a multicourse ceremonial banquet that will fortify them for the great race ahead.

No one can say for sure what the origin of the Ceri is, although they may date back to the twelfth century, when Gubbio was miraculously spared from defeat at the hands of Frederick Barbarossa. The city credited Sant'Ubaldo with its salvation, and while no one knows exactly why the race began, ever since Sant'Ubaldo died, on May 16, 1160, the town has had a solemn procession on the eve of the anniversary of his death. In medieval times the Ceri perhaps were real *ceri*, large votive candles that were carried up to the church of Sant'Ubaldo. It was traditional to offer candles in honor of the patron saint of a city and in his study of Italian festivals Franco Cardini suggests that the saints' figures were veiled with wax, like alternative candles. Today's wooden Ceri are covered with a dark chestnut-colored cloth, and may well be transformations of the earlier wooden figures.

Other explanations speculate that Sant'Ubaldo may actually be the descendant of a pagan sylvan mountain god. Honey bees may have swarmed to make his beard and from them may have come the wax forming the candles. The ceremony may once have been concerned with fertility and the return of life at springtime, for festivals have taken place at just this time of year ever since the Romans celebrated the rebirth of spring and love and fecundity with the Ides of May. The sexual symbolism of the ceremony is quite evident and powerful. Watch the Ceri being inserted horizontally into the long narrow opening of the platform. The whole point of the ceremony is to raise them erect and keep them that way through the entire race. First, however, the water poured over the Cero as it is inserted into the opening makes the wood swell and assures a tight connection between the two. Only then is the amphora thrown into the crowd so that it will break.

Food plays a large part in the celebration of the Ceri, even though honey does not enter into it. Ritual meals begin on the first Sunday of May when the Ceri are brought down from their resting place in the basilica of Sant'Ubaldo to the great hall of the Palazzo dei Consoli. Breakfast is served at 10:30 in the morning to sixty Ceri bearers from each team, and the menu is entirely of lamb, the dish of springtime. It begins with coratella, a highly peppered concoction of the liver, spleen, lungs, and heart of the lamb, which is cooked with onions, parsley, and tomatoes and braised in white wine. Next comes a garlic-scented lamb stew called *fricco alla ceraiola* and roast leg of lamb marbled with rosemary and garlic. Apples and raw fennel are followed by a rum-soaked cake called a *diplomatico,* and local wines flow like rivers. The same menu is served again at lunchtime to a variety of other people.

On the Saturday night before the great race "a taste of baccalà" is served to a relatively small number of officials inside the great Palazzo dei Consoli, and to anyone who wants to buy the same dish outside. For this one night of the year each team opens a tavern that serves wine and snacks—fast food Gubbio style—and the menus vary. The Taverna di Sant'Ubaldo offers tastes of baccalà and is so popular that it is overrun by half the city talking and tasting and drinking wine. Five thousand pieces of baccalà are eaten on this single night! The Taverna dei Capitani sells penne with a creamy sausage and peperoncino sauce, barbecued meat on skewers, local mortadella, and salame on cheese bread, all for four thousand lire (less than three dollars). The wine is free and vast quantities of it are consumed. The Taverna dei Ceraioli serves fava beans and wine, and the wine flows out of the jugs with the same abandon with which it will wash out of the three ceramic amphoras the next day. The citizens of Gubbio fill the piazze of the taverns on Saturday night, singing neighborhood songs and dancing. Dozens of them run three times around the Bargello fountain and are splashed with great handfuls of water. No wonder people say that for anyone from Gubbio to be away on May 15 is the worst possible thing that could happen. The army actually gives official leave to young men to return to be Ceraioli, and many natives of Gubbio come great distances for a ceremony that is woven deep in their sense of self.

The largest celebration is *La Tavola Bona,* the spectacular feast. Seven hundred people—city officials, Ceraioli, guests of the city, and those who

Raising of The Ceri of Gubbio in front of Palazzo dei Consoli by Antonioli, nineteenth century

have returned to Gubbio from far away—are invited to a monumental lunch in the massive barrel-vaulted stone hall of the Palazzo dei Consoli amid Roman sarcophagi, medieval armaments, and banners from the days of the city's glory as an independent commune. In medieval times the rulers of the city who assembled in the great honey-colored hall must have derived satisfaction from the enormous scale and dimensions of the hall, which testified to their powers. Now on this one day a year the hall sees the same sort of energy and celebration that it must have known centuries ago. Sound travels up to the curved vaulting of the fifty-foot ceiling and bounces back, reverberating with the excitement of the crowd. The hall is full of tables of hundreds of Ceraioli who spend half the time on their feet, chanting and singing special songs. There is no real competition between teams yet. All the *capodieci*, the men who steer the teams' awkward and heavy Ceri, are friends, and they move from table to table, hugging each other and singing together. Whole tables of Ceraioli leap up repeatedly, holding their white napkins by a corner and twirling them around in the air and singing. They bang on the tables and clang forks against wineglasses in what sounds like artillery fire. Trumpets blare. Finally, when the band appears, all three teams sing together, jumping up and down on chairs and generally carrying on. After a fanfare, the Triumphal March from *Aïda* announces the arrival of enormous lobsters from the Canary Islands, their shells decorated with baroque designs of whipped butter.

The meal itself changes every year, although traditionally only fish is served, since the race is held on the day before the anniversary of Sant'Ubaldo's death, a time of penitential eating. Only fish! When I attended, ten courses, each more spectacular than the last, poured out of the temporary kitchens set up below the great hall in another vaulted room with thirty-foot ceilings. The cooks are not professionals, but carpenters and plasterers and schoolteachers. A single professional chef directs their efforts. As one hardworking woman said, "If we can't run with the Ceri, this is what we can do." Imagine making gnocchi for twelve hundred. Imagine pans that are four feet long and three feet wide filled with layers of liqueur-soaked cake and pastry cream. Pots are so cavernous that paddles the size of oars are used for stirring. A half-dozen huge tubs are filled to overflowing with prawns and mussels and clams, and oversized baking sheets are spread with polenta perfumed with porcini mushrooms and the white truffles of Umbria.

It is a fair bet that no one here has ever cleaned 200 kilos of clams and 150 of mussels before, or peeled 350 pounds of potatoes for gnocchi, or made mayonnaise with 100 eggs, but the cooks work in relay teams and are amazingly efficient. Everyone glows with pride as dish after dish leaves the confines of the fourteenth-century kitchen downstairs to make its way upstairs to the Ceraioli and guests.

The tables in the great hall are set with five plates stacked one on top of the other. Young waiters in tuxedos bring the courses, beginning with a spicy clam soup. "There are only tastes," the head chef says, arranging a seafood salad in a scallop shell, but after stockfish comes a risotto bursting with mussels, clams, and prawns; then red, white, and green gnocchi with a smoked salmon sauce. Skewers of prawns and calamari are embellished with a side dish of zucchini and tomatoes. The meal ends with a wonderful zuppa alla ceraiola, a local version of zuppa inglese, fragrant with Alkermes, a strawberry-colored liqueur of Tuscany, followed by strawberries in lemon juice.

While seven hundred people eat at *La Tavola Bona*, the thousands who jammed the city in the morning seem to have disappeared. Some have filled up restaurants and *trattorie*, taken picnics onto the broom- and poppy-filled hillsides, or stretched out under the arcade at the foot of the hill, and at the end of the warm afternoon, when the streets still feel deserted, a number of them collect in the great piazza and dance in a big circle as bands play. By five o'clock the crowds have returned. Every window and balcony on the Corso Garibaldi is full, the Piazza Grande hasn't a single open space, and the streets are jammed with people waiting for the great race. Big pieces of confetti float down from windows and shimmer in the late afternoon sun. Excitement and tension are palpable. Horses mounted by medieval warriors clear a path, since the entire Corso is awash with people, leaping up and down like some sort of strange sea life, in anticipation of their first view of the Ceri.

Suddenly a roar breaks loose, like the powerful sound and vibrations from putting an ear to the railroad track as the train, still out of sight, speeds closer and closer. A tidal wave of sound rolls from one end of the

Corso to the other as the three Ceri turn into the main street. They are moving at high speed and the saints appear to be running, Sant'Ubaldo nodding as he passes, Sant'Antonio's cape blowing in the wind. They fly by in a flash. Thick streams of people, anxious to see as much as they can, dash off in hot pursuit, plunging down tiny alleyways, taking short-cuts from one piazza to another. The streets swarm with people, but the huge crowd never collects in a single place, for the city itself is the course. The sound waves of feet send advance warning; next come the horses; then Ceri team members clear the way as they race down the streets, constantly looking over their shoulders to see if the rival Ceri are gaining on them. There are children on their fathers' shoulders, old people, young people, people crowding every balcony and window, and of course hundreds of Ceri team members.

At the Piazza Grande, the Ceraioli rest briefly in anticipation of the final great push up the mountainside. All eyes are on the the palazzo, waiting for the mayor to wave a white handkerchief. When he does, a great bell rings to announce the *birate,* the frenzied circling of the Ceri in the great square. Three times around they go before they dash to the top of Monte Ingino. The Ceri carriers race upward through the streets of Gubbio, which are much too narrow to accommodate more than one at a time; they pause briefly at the ancient gate; and then, with spectators cheering wildly, they fly up the dramatically vertical mountainside in seven or eight minutes, surging through the alleys of the upper part of the city, and onward along the steep and heavily wooded hill. The switch-backs and paths and the summit are densely lined with spectators cheering Sant'Ubaldo on as he arrives first at the top. When the saint makes it to the door of the basilica, his team achieves what it always wants to— it slams the door in the faces of the other saints—and a great cheer goes up from the spectators. San Giorgio is hot on the heels of Sant'Ubaldo, and last comes Sant'Antonio, right on schedule. The doors of the basilica are opened to admit them. All three Ceri are whirled around in the courtyard before being escorted into the church, where they will remain for another year until this crazed *festa* begins all over again.

For all the impassioned feelings loose in the city, this festival is not a competition but a reaffirmation of community. No one really wins or loses, although no team wants its Cero to tip or fall, and the one that stays the closest to the one before it or the farthest from the one behind does best. At the very end, after all the saints go into the church, the women enter to touch and stroke them, say nice things if the saints performed well, and distinctly coarser words if they didn't. A torchlight procession, carrying the statues of the saints, winds down from the basilica to take them back to their resting place at the little whitewashed church of the masons. Singing and dancing go on late into the night. There will

Cero of Sant'Ubaldo

be celebrations the next day, Sant'Ubaldo's actual *festa*, and a miniature race will be run by young boys two Sundays hence, but the big event is over until next year.

After its ecstatic explosion, austere Gubbio subsides into quiet. At the end of the race, the city falls silent again, returning to its somber medieval character. Gubbio is known as the City of Silence, a stony citadel claiming the hillside in a remote Umbrian landscape. The birds continue to wheel overhead, stirring the air over the stone palazzi edging the great piazza with its mammoth arches, over the curved streets and dark winding lanes, over the brief flashes of color in ceramic workshops, and over the great basilica at the top of the hill.

Fricò alla Ceraiola

Lamb Stew

Lamb stew for breakfast? Why not? Lamb is the dish of hope and springtime, the perfect way to begin a festival. It is on the breakfast menu in Gubbio on the first Sunday in May, the great day when the Ceri are brought down the hill into the city. This particular stew is fragrant with garlic and rosemary and the slow cooking makes the lamb tender and succulent. It is easy to make and tastes even better the second day.

Makes 4 to 6 servings

6 tablespoons olive oil
3 pounds (1⅓ kilograms) boneless lamb shoulder, well trimmed and cut
   into small cubes
2 tablespoons fresh rosemary, finely minced
3 large cloves garlic, finely minced
3 tomatoes (about 1 pound, 450 grams), peeled, seeded, and chopped, or
   2 fresh tomatoes and 1 teaspoon tomato paste dissolved in warm
   water
1 cup dry white wine
Salt and pepper

Warm 4 tablespoons of the olive oil in a heavy ovenproof casserole and sauté as many of the lamb pieces as fit comfortably in the pan until browned. Repeat with the remaining lamb, adding a little oil as needed. Pour off the extra fat. In another pan warm the rosemary and garlic briefly in the rest of the oil but do not let the garlic burn. Add the tomatoes and wine and cook over medium heat 4 to 5 minutes. Add the herb and wine mixture and salt and pepper to the lamb, cover, and bake at 325°F until the lamb is tender and the sauce concentrated, about 1½ to 2 hours. If the juices are too thin, remove the meat to a warm platter, raise the heat to high, and reduce the sauce. Pour over the lamb.

Arrosto di Agnello alla Ceraiola

~~~~~~~~~~~~~~~~~~~~~~~~~~~

Roast Lamb from Gubbio

I was amazed enough when I heard that leg of lamb marbled with garlic and rosemary was served for breakfast in Gubbio, but I was even more astonished when I heard how the dish was made. I understood that the roast was tied all around with slices of salame. When I tried it, the lamb had a certain smoky taste and was delicious. When I mentioned it later, I got only blank looks. I finally caught on that what I had been told was to tie up the leg of lamb as if it were a salame. So if you use toothpicks to cover the exterior of the leg with slices of salame, understand that it is not at all traditional in Gubbio and, in fact, the city fathers would probably be horrified. They might also object that I have omitted the pork fatback that is usually chopped with the garlic and rosemary.

Makes 8 servings

1 leg of lamb, about 6½ pounds (3 kilograms)
6 tablespoons finely chopped fresh rosemary
4 to 5 large cloves garlic, finely minced
Salt and pepper
¾ to 1 cup white wine

Have your butcher remove the hip and pelvic bones from the leg of lamb. With a sharp knife, cut numerous slits in the meat. Combine the rosemary and garlic and insert pinches of the mixture into the slits. Tie the roast at 1-inch intervals beginning above the shank as if it were a salame. Salt and pepper the lamb and set it in a lightly oiled roasting pan. Bake at 450°F 15 minutes, then turn the oven down to 350°F and roast another hour. Add the white wine after 25 minutes.

Baccalà Arrosto alla Ceraiola

~~~~~~~~~~~~~~~~~~~~~~~~~~~

Roast Salt Cod

I have to admit I was deeply suspicious. How could anyone cook salt cod for hundreds of people and make it taste good? Could this dish possibly retain the delicate taste of flaky white fish, the crunch of crisp bread crumbs, and the flavor of fresh rosemary? Indeed it could in Gubbio, where it soaked for two days and nights before it was cooked to feed celebrants on the eve of the big race.

Because dried salt cod varies in saltiness, size, and moisture, it is difficult to give precise instructions. I prefer the boneless fillet strips that come cleaned and boxed because they are the easiest to work with and are generally uniform in thickness and size. They are also, alas, considerably more expensive than whole fish, which vary in thickness and may have both bones and skin.

The secret of this delicious dish is to soak the pieces of fish two to three days, turning several times and changing the water at least twice each day. A well-soaked piece of cod will be pale ivory in color and no longer stiff in the center. Be sure to use fresh rosemary, fresh bread crumbs, and very high-quality olive oil.

Makes 4 servings

1 pound 2 ounces baccalà (500 grams), thick center slices
6 tablespoons fresh bread crumbs
4 tablespoons minced fresh rosemary
½ cup high-quality olive oil
Spritz of white wine
Several grindings fresh pepper

Two or three days before serving, rinse the baccalà pieces well with cold water, then set in a large bowl filled with cold water. Refrigerate 2 to 3 days, turning the pieces several times and changing the water twice each day. The baccalà will be white and no longer firm in the center when it is ready. To check you can take a little taste to see if it still seems salty. Discard any bones or hard skin.

Drain the baccalà, rinse again under cold water, and cut into 8 equal pieces. Dry them on paper towels. Mix the bread crumbs, rosemary, oil, wine, and pepper together. Rub the mixture on both sides of each piece of fish and set them in a single layer in an oiled baking dish. Bake at 350°F until the bread crumbs are browned into a crunchy crust, about 20 minutes.

Fish seller, eighteenth-century engraving, Raccolta Bertarelli, Milan

Gnocchetti Tricolori al Salmone

Red, White, and Green Gnocchi Under a Smoked Salmon Sauce

Red, white, and green: The colors of Italy are blended into delicate gnocchi and then given elegant status beneath a smoked salmon sauce. The balance is perfect in this combination, but if you decide to try gnocchi in a different way, add nutmeg and onion to the spinach gnocchi and perhaps a bit of basil to the tomato gnocchi.

Makes 6 to 8 servings

5 large potatoes (2¾ pounds, 1¼ kilograms)
3 eggs
¾ cup (75 grams) grated Parmesan cheese
2 teaspoons salt
About 1½ cups (220 grams) unbleached all-purpose flour
1 tablespoon tomato paste
3 tablespoons frozen chopped spinach, thawed and squeezed dry

Bake the potatoes and let them cool enough that you can peel them. Rice the potatoes into a large bowl. Mix in the eggs, Parmesan cheese, and salt, then knead in all but 4 to 6 tablespoons flour until the dough is smooth and pliable. It should be a little sticky. Resist the urge to add much more flour or you will have heavy gnocchi.

Divide the dough into 3 equal parts. Leave one part as is; it will be the plain cheese-flavored gnocchi. Knead the tomato paste into the second part, adding another a tablespoon or so of flour to get the right smooth consistency. Add the spinach to the third part, adding 1 to 2 tablespoons flour to get a smooth pliable consistency.

Divide the dough into egg-size pieces, about 3 ounces each, and roll each one into a log 1 inch thick, about the width of a fat pen. Using a dough scraper or knife, cut each log into 1-inch pieces, like plump Chiclets.

To shape the gnocchi, set a piece on a lightly floured work surface and, using a fork, roll it against the back of the tines until it rolls all the way up the tines and over the top. You can catch it or just let it drop onto the table. Press gently as you roll the dough so that the gnocchi get a deeper indentation in the center than at the sides. Repeat with the rest of the pieces.

Bring a large pot of salted water to the boil. Drop in the gnocchi and cook until they come to the surface of the water. Cook a few seconds longer. Drain and serve with Smoked Salmon Sauce (recipe follows).

Salsa di Salmone Affumicata

~~~~~~~~~~~~~~~~~~~~~~~~~~~~~

Smoked Salmon Sauce

Smooth and fragrant with salmon, this sauce would be good on almost any kind of pasta. Don't buy the most expensive cuts of smoked salmon, since cooking will only obscure the delicate taste.

Makes 6 servings

1 small onion, finely chopped
4 to 6 tablespoons unsalted butter
1 pound (450 grams) smoked salmon, sliced and cut into small strips
1 tablespoon Cognac
5 tablespoons white wine
3 to 3½ cups heavy cream
1 peperoncino (dried red chile), seeded and finely chopped
Salt and white pepper
¾ cup chopped flat-leaf parsley

Sauté the chopped onion in the butter until golden. Add the smoked salmon and sauté very briefly. Bathe with the Cognac and wine and cook until they evaporate. If you want, puree half the smoked salmon mixture with a bit of cream and return it to the remaining salmon. Add the cream, chile, and salt and pepper to taste; cook about 2 minutes. Add extra cream if the sauce seems too dry. Spoon the sauce over the gnocchi and sprinkle with parsley.

Zuppa di Fasolan in Salsa Piccante

~~~~~~~~~~~~~~~~~~~~~~~~~~~~~

Spicy Clam Soup

Makes 4 to 6 servings

3 pounds (1⅓ kilograms) littleneck clams
6 tablespoons olive oil
1 onion, finely chopped
2 teaspoons finely minced garlic
1 peperoncino (dried red chile), seeded and finely chopped
1 can (28 ounces, 794 grams) Italian plum tomatoes, finely chopped or passed through a food mill to make about 1⅔ cups; save the juices
1 carrot, peeled and cut in long narrow strips
2 tablespoons finely minced flat-leaf parsley
Grated zest of ½ lemon
Salt and pepper

(continued)

Scrub and rinse the clams under running water and set them in a pot with 2 inches of water. Bring to a simmer, cover the pot, and raise the heat. Steam the clams until they open, 4 to 5 minutes. Transfer the clams to a bowl and let them cool. Strain the water several times through cheesecloth or paper toweling. Shuck the clams when cool enough to handle, chop each into 3 or 4 pieces, and reserve.

Warm the olive oil in a heavy pan or skillet. Add the onion and cook over medium heat until softened and pale golden. Add the garlic and peperoncino; warm them over medium-low heat but do not allow the garlic to burn. Stir in the tomatoes and carrot strips; cook 5 minutes over medium heat. Add 2 cups of the strained clam water, all of the juices from the tomatoes, the parsley, lemon zest, and salt and pepper to taste; cook 5 minutes.

Remove the carrot strips. Add the clams and heat only until warmed through or they will be tough and rubbery. Grind pepper on top and serve.

Risotto alla Ceraiola

Seafood Risotto

Prawns, squid, and clams marry in a great pot where risotto simmers, absorbing the fragrances and flavors of fish stock, garlic, and fresh to-matoes. To find fish from the sea permeating a risotto in landlocked Umbria is a sure sign that this is an extravagant dish meant for a great celebration. Extravagant it is, and it does take a bit of advance planning. Use trimmings, including the head, from halibut, bass, or cod for the cleanest-tasting fish stock. Make the stock ahead, but it is best to use it the same day. While the stock simmers, clean the squid and prawns and cook the clams so that you can look after the risotto as it cooks to its creamy finale.

Makes 8 to 10 servings

FISH STOCK

2 pounds (900 grams) fish trimmings, preferably cod, bass, or halibut
10 cups cold water
1 large onion, chopped
3 carrots, roughly chopped
10 fennel seeds
1 bay leaf
5 peppercorns
3 tablespoons chopped parsley
2 cups white wine

Cover the fish trimmings in a large pot with the cold water. Bring to a boil and skim off any froth. Turn off the heat, let rest, and skim again. Measure 5½ cups stock into a second pan and add the onion, carrots, fennel seeds, bay leaf, peppercorns, parsley, and white wine. Cook at a low simmer 30 minutes.

SEAFOOD

2 pounds (900 grams) prawns
2 pounds (900 grams) calamari
3 pounds (1200 grams) clams, scrubbed well

While the broth is cooking, peel the prawns and devein them. Clean the calamari. Cut both prawns and calamari into thin strips. Cover and set aside. Cook the cleaned clams in 2 inches water until they open. Remove the clams, let them cool, and shuck them. Strain the cooking water several times through cheesecloth until it is clear.

RISOTTO

¼ cup olive oil
¼ cup butter
1 onion, finely minced
2 cups Arborio rice
¾ cup white wine
½ peperoncino (dried red chile), seeded and finely chopped
2 cloves garlic, finely minced
4 tablespoons minced parsley
¼ cup water reserved from cooking clams
⅔ pound (300 grams) fresh tomatoes, finely chopped
Salt and pepper to taste

Heat the oil and butter in a large saucepan. Add the minced onion and sauté over medium heat until translucent, 4 to 5 minutes. Add the rice and cook just long enough to coat the grains, 1 to 2 minutes. Stir in ½ cup of the white wine and cook until it evaporates. Begin adding the boiling stock ⅓ cup at a time and cook, stirring constantly, over medium heat.

Meanwhile, in a separate pan sauté the peperoncino, garlic, and half the parsley very briefly over medium-low heat. Add the remaining ¼ cup wine and cook briefly. Stir in the calamari, prawns, and ¼ cup reserved clam water; cook only until the prawns turn pink and the calamari are tender. Five to eight minutes before the risotto is done, stir in the tomatoes, remaining parsley, the clams, and the seafood mixture. Finish with the last addition of stock. Season to taste with salt and pepper and serve immediately.

Spiedini Misti

~~~~~~~~~~~~~~~~~~~~~~~~~~~

Grilled Calamari and Prawns

What could be simpler or tastier than calamari and prawns rolled in flavored bread crumbs and grilled?

Makes 6 servings

1 cup fresh bread crumbs made from 4 slices of country bread
½ cup olive oil
½ cup minced parsley
1½ pounds (675 grams) calamari, cleaned
½ pound (225 grams) prawns, shelled and deveined
Lemon wedges

Mix together the bread crumbs, olive oil, and parsley. Dip the individual calamari and prawns into the bread crumb mixture—it won't adhere completely, but some will stick—and then thread on skewers. Cook on a grill over a hot fire to 2 to 3 minutes. Serve with lemon.

Conchiglie Mari e Monti

~~~~~~~~~~~~~~~~~~~~~~~~~~~

Seafood Salad Dotted with Mushrooms

Scallop shells full of the best of the sea and mountains; the Mediterranean and Adriatic provide the shellfish, while Italian mushrooms spring to life on plains and in mountain passes in the shade of trees.

Makes to 4 to 6 servings

1½ pounds (675 grams) mussels
1 pound (450 grams) clams
½ pound (225 grams) prawns
¼ cup olive oil
6 ounces (180 grams) mushrooms
½ cup good olive oil, preferably extra-virgin
2 tablespoons vinegar
1 tablespoon lemon juice
Salt and pepper
3 to 4 tablespoons chopped flat-leaf parsley

Scrub clean the mussels and clams and cook them separately until their shells open. Drain. Shell and devein the prawns and cook in 4 tablespoons olive oil very briefly until lightly colored, 1 to 2 minutes. Remove the mussels and clams from their shells and combine with the prawns in a bowl. Clean the mushrooms, slice them, and add to the seafood. Make a dressing of the ½ cup oil, the vinegar, lemon juice, and salt and pepper to taste. Add the parsley and pour over the seafood salad.

Fill scallop shells with the seafood salad and serve at room temperature.

Zuppa alla Ceraiola

xxxxxxxxxxxxxxxxxxxxxxxxxxxx

Zuppa Inglese, Gubbio Style

An inspired and delicious dessert that is a star turn on zuppa inglese, layers of sponge cake and pastry cream washed with the spicy Tuscan liqueur called *Alkermes*. Some say that this dessert comes from the English in Tuscany, who always had cookies with their tea. Enterprising servants took the leftovers and used them as a base for a creamy dessert. The Alkermes came from a jealously guarded secret Medici recipe. Leo X and Clement VII, both Medici popes, called it an "elixir for long life," and Maria de' Medici took it to France with her. Since Alkermes hasn't reached our shores yet, you can try to duplicate its flavors in the way indicated below. The crucial ingredient of cochineal, which gives it its red color, may be hard to find, so you might try substituting Marsala. It won't taste the same, but it will be delicious.

PAN DI SPAGNA

Makes 1 cake to serve 8

6 eggs, separated, room temperature
⅞ cup (175 grams) sugar
2 tablespoons honey
2 tablespoons rum
1 teaspoon vanilla extract
Pinch salt
1½ cups (200 grams) pastry flour
½ teaspoon baking powder

Beat the egg yolks, half the sugar, the honey, rum, and vanilla in a mixer bowl until light, creamy, and lemon-colored, about 5 minutes by hand-held mixer, 3 by standing electric mixer. Warm the egg whites in a bowl set in warm water for a few minutes, add the salt, and beat until soft peaks are formed. Gradually beat in the remaining sugar and continue beating until the peaks are stiff. Sift the flour and baking powder together and return to the sifter. Fold ¼ of the egg whites into the egg yolk mixture with a rubber spatula. Sift ¼ of flour mixture over the top and fold in. Continue folding in the egg whites and flour mixture alternately until all is incorporated. Butter and flour a 17 by 11-inch baking pan. Pour in the batter and smooth the top.

Baking. Heat the oven to 350°F. Bake until the cake springs back when touched lightly near the center, 40 to 45 minutes. Cool on a rack 5 to 10 minutes. Remove from the pan and cut horizontally into 3 equal pieces.

(continued)

P A S T R Y   C R E A M

> **4½ cups milk**
> **Strips of the zest of ¾ lemon**
> **2½ tablespoons coffee beans**
> **1 teaspoon ground cinnamon**
> **½ cinnamon stick**
> **8 egg yolks**
> **2 whole eggs**
> **¾ cup (150 grams) sugar**
> **¼ teaspoon salt**
> **¾ cup (100 grams) all-purpose or pastry flour**
> **2 tablespoons vanilla extract**
> **4 tablespoons butter**

Slowly heat the milk, lemon zest, coffee beans, ground cinnamon, and cinnamon stick in a heavy saucepan over low heat until it reaches a boil. Remove the lemon zest, coffee beans, and cinnamon stick.

Beat the egg yolks, whole eggs, 2 tablespoons of the sugar, and the salt until thick and golden, 2 to 3 minutes. Sift in the flour and all but 2 tablespoons of the sugar. Whisk ½ cup of the boiling milk mixture, 2 tablespoons at a time, into the egg mixture, then pour the egg mixture into the remaining milk mixture. Stir constantly over medium-high heat until thickened. When the pastry cream begins to boil, whisk it vigorously over low heat for 2 to 3 minutes to cook the flour. Remove from the heat and add the vanilla. Immediately smear the butter over the top so it doesn't develop a skin.

A L K E R M E S   (A Homemade Version)
My Adaptation of the Recipe of Paolo Petroni in Florence

> **2½ teaspoons (12 grams) cinnamon**
> **2 teaspoons (10 grams) ground coriander**
> **½ teaspoon (3 grams) mace**
> **½ teaspoon (2.5 grams) ground cloves**
> **1½ teaspoons ground cardamon or 10 pods**
> **1½ teaspoons (7 grams) cochineal, ground in a spice grinder or mortar and pestle**
> **1 teaspoon (5 grams) finely minced orange zest or dried orange peel**
> **½ vanilla bean**
> **2½ cups vodka (80 or 90 proof) or Triple Sec**
> **2½ cups water**
> **3 cups (600 grams) sugar**
> **6 to 7 tablespoons rose water**

Grind the spices together or pestle them. Cut the vanilla bean into pieces into the vodka and 1 cup water. Pour the mixture into a jar with a screw top and leave for 2 weeks, shaking at least once a day. After 2 weeks, dissolve 1 cup water and the sugar and add it to the mixture. Let it rest for a day. Finally, filter the mixture using cheesecloth or several layers of paper toweling, add the rose water, and let the mixture rest one final day. Store in tightly closed bottles.

ASSEMBLY

1½ to 2 tablespoons (10 grams) cocoa, preferably Dutch process

Set the first layer of cake on a flat serving platter, brush it well with Alkermes, and spread with pastry cream. Set another layer of cake on top, follow with more Alkermes and pastry cream, and finish with a third layer of ingredients. Sift cocoa over the top.

FESTA DEL RISO

RICE FESTIVAL IN VILLIMPENTA

Last Sunday in May

"Rice is born in water and dies in wine," say the Italians, who have invented hundreds of ways of eating rice and thousands of wines to serve it with. Once a year the inhabitants of the tiny town of Villimpenta celebrate their own special rice dish, which is more pilaf than risotto, in a simple rustic afternoon of eating. Theirs is a quiet festivity celebrating a traditional dish. Not for them the newer rice festivals electing Miss Rice Grain or risotto cookoffs held on the stages of old movie theaters.

Until twenty-five years ago, a rich network of canals and rivers nourished the rice fields that dotted the landscape near Mantua. The delicate green rice shoots were planted by hand and grew covered with a blanket of water that protected them from changes in temperature, night and day. From the countryside poor girls, like the one Silvana Mangano played in *Bitter Rice,* came to the farms to earn money by planting, cleaning the fields, and harvesting the rice. With bare feet and big straw hats on their heads, these *mondine,* whose name comes from the verb *mondare,* to clean, waded in the wet fields, cleared away the grasses that suffocated the rice plants, and then harvested the plants, one at a time. The rice then was given to the *pilotati,* the huskers who hulled it by cleaning away the outer skin. At the time of the rice harvest, the *pilotati* cooked riso in a special way that they invented, *alla pilota.*

It is this dish that is celebrated each May in Villimpenta, a frontier town on the border of what was once the dukedom of Mantua where it met the Venetian Republic of San Marco. The date for the *sagra* in

Villimpenta is set in conjunction with that of a nearby village whose *festa* serves catfish and carp from the canals. It comes at a time when the rice has just been planted in the few remaining *risaie*, but the event, overflowing the main piazza, really commemorates a bygone era when the people of the countryside lived on the milling of flour and rice. The wheel in front of the castle turned constantly, using water from nearby canals and rivers to clean the rice, as did similar wheels at handsome villas sprinkled around the area. The cleaning was done right in the central piazza. When the riverbed changed, rice became a much less profitable crop, and today most of the landscape around Villimpenta is dotted with tassels of corn and deep green fields of soy.

Once a year, however, the glory days of plentiful rice harvests are relived as the population of the entire town—no more than two thousand in all—masses under yellow and white striped canvas tents on the piazza where the Sunday market always takes place. People used to collect in the public gardens, and while one had to pay for a plate and glass, all the food was free. Now everything has a price, but it pays for all the activities of the community during the year. The *pièce de résistance* has always been the famous riso alla pilota, an unusual dish in risotto-crazed Italy, since the rice is added all at once to the boiling water. It boils in enormous copper cauldrons over great wood fires, and even on such a gargantuan scale the cooks use the same procedure as countrywomen at home do. They fill a cauldron with water, bring it to a boil, and then drop the rice from a great funnel (housewives make theirs from paper) so that it forms a perfect cone with the point just visible above the water. They shake the pot to distribute the rice and leave it to cook until most of the water has evaporated. At that point they extinguish the fire, cover the rice with heavy cloths, and let it steam under its warm blanket. Just before serving they mix in a delicious local garlic-scented pork sausage called *pesto,* and offer everyone bread made in nearby Ferrara to eat with it.

The same rice is transformed into ceremonial fare on the day they kill the pig. The cooks top it with grilled pork ribs and chops, making it into risotto col puntello (the bones of the chops are the handles, *i puntelli*). Other risotti are made with frogs' legs and tiny birds, a delicious combination of animals that lived in the *risaie* and the birds that fed on them. Risotto alla certosina, invented by a monk of the famous Charterhouse of Pavia, uses fish, frogs, and, if they can still be found, shrimp from nearby rivers. Rice remains the major source of income at the abbey, which was actually built using funds raised from water, since in the fourteenth century the ruling Visconti family gave the Certosa all the revenues it collected from taxing people living on the nearby Lambro River.

Rice stalk, nineteenth century

Weeding the Rice Fields,
engraving by Gian
Battista Spolverini, 1763

Rice is grown in much greater quantities from Pavia to Lomellina in Lombardy and around Novara and Vercelli in Piedmont, which produces a million tons a year. The air and climate encourage its growth, and the rivers Po and Ticino nourish the green countryside with its complex canal system. Four different types of rice are grown: *ordinario,* the shortest grain, used for puddings; *semifino,* medium-length round grain; long-grain *fino;* and long-grain *superfino,* such as Arborio or Vialone Nano, the finest of them all, preferred for riso alla pilota and perfect for most risotti because it absorbs a lot of liquid without ever breaking or becoming gummy. Americans are most familiar with Arborio, but Italians, always in search of the newest, the finest, the most chic and recherché, currently prefer Carnaroli because of its firm grain.

The Romans knew rice as a medicine, which they imported in tiny amounts from India. Rice didn't actually grow in Italy until the Arabs brought it to Sicily, and no one knows precisely how or when it found its way north. The Venetians loaded rice on their ships in the East and imported it during the Crusades. In the Middle Ages rice was served only to sick people who ate it *in bianco,* in broth. In *A Selection of Unedited and Rare Literary Curiosities,* which may be the oldest Tuscan prescription and recipe book in existence, Alessandro Falassi found a recipe that called for cooking rice "in water in which goat's feet have been cooked; add almond milk and sugar." The goat's feet in this case served both as ingredient and talisman. Dishes such as rice cooked in broth that were destined for convalescents were prepared by *pappini,* who got their name from making pappa and other simple soups. It wasn't until the 1500s, according to Falassi, that doctors actually considered rice fit for healthy people, thereby creating a tradition that remains a part of Tuscan gastronomy. Dishes from those early medieval days, like riso in brodo and minestrone with rice, are eaten by everyone today.

A Sforza duke of Milan gave the duke of Ferrara twelve sacks of rice in 1475. But it was only in the sixteenth century that it became popular, when Venetian women, who knew a good thing when they tasted it, created a whole cuisine around it. The ruling doges took it up and celebrated the feast in honor of San Marco (Saint Mark), the patron saint of Venice, by beginning the meal with risi e bisi, a thick risotto cooked with the delicate, sweet new peas of spring grown in the kitchen gardens of the nearby lagoon.

Two famous rice soups from Piedmont have similar names with similar ingredients, although the people of each town are vehement about the differences. The residents of Novara are dedicated to their paniscia, a rustic dish made with borlotti beans, delicate salame, and a vegetable broth, while the people of Vercelli make their very thick panissa using silky-skinned Saluggia beans and lots of meat or bean broth. These dishes, hearty enough to be an entire meal, are poor people's food par excellence, since they use only the ingredients that a rice farmer might have on hand: rice from the *risaie*, beans from the garden, and salame and lard from pigs raised in the stalls.

Riso alla Pilota

Rice in the
Style of
Rice Winnowers

In his novel, *Un matrimonio mantovano* (*A Mantuan Marriage*), Count Giovanni Nuvoletti describes a scene in which "the tureens of risotto were noticed with admiration, because in these towns, between the countryside of Emilia and Cremona, [riso alla pilota] was a rather exotic rare dish, coming from the eastern part of our province." The count is a novelist who also happens to be the president of the Italian Academy of Cooking, so he clearly knows whereof he speaks. The women of Villimpenta insist on using spring water, so I recommend doing the same. The local sausages called *pesto* that moisturize the mixture are easily re-created by combining tender pork tenderloin with pancetta, garlic, and lots of freshly ground pepper.

If the mixture seems rich, imagine when the workers made it in the great farmhouses in the centers of the *risaie* and used butter to sauté the sausage and sifted handfuls of freshly grated Parmesan into the final dish. I have actually reduced the cheese by half, removed the butter entirely, and can even imagine halving the amount of sausage. For the authentic dish sauté the meat in 7 tablespoons (100 grams) butter and sprinkle in twice as much cheese. During the winter, the same dish is called *risotto col puntello* (rice with handles) because it is served with grilled spareribs rising out of the dome of rice.

(continued)

Makes 6 to 8 servings

3⅓ cups spring water
Salt
2½ cups (500 grams) Vialone Nano or Arborio rice
7½ ounces (210 grams) freshly ground pork tenderloin
1½ ounces (40 grams) pancetta, ground or chopped as fine as possible
2 cloves garlic, pestled
Abundant freshly ground pepper
½ cup (40 grams) freshly grated Parmesan cheese

Bring the natural spring water to a boil in a 3- to 4-quart pot, preferably copper. Add a pinch of salt. Make a cone out of parchment or wax paper, fill it with the rice, and let it drop very slowly so that it forms a mountain peak in the center of the pan, with the point sticking very slightly above the water. If there is too little water, add more; if there is a bit too much, remove it with a bulb baster. When the water returns to the boil, very gently shake the pan so that the rice spreads over the bottom. Turn the fire down and cook the rice slowly until it absorbs the water, 7 to 10 minutes. Remove the pan from the fire and cover the rice completely with a tea towel while it is still in the pan. Leave it for 10 to 15 minutes.

Mix the ground pork, pancetta, garlic, and salt and pepper very well; and sauté until the ground pork is no longer pink.

Turn the rice out onto a serving platter, mix the meat mixture in well, and stir in half the Parmesan cheese. Serve, passing the remaining cheese at the table.

SAGRA DELLA FRAGOLA

STRAWBERRY FESTIVAL IN NEMI

Second Sunday in June

*A*nyone yearning to taste sweet juicy strawberries should come to Nemi on the second Sunday in June, when the little city celebrates their arrival with a charming, if slightly kitschy, festival. The rich volcanic soil and wooded green hillsides around Lake Nemi yield up strawberries known throughout Italy for their extraordinary flavor and sweetness. Fragoline del bosco, tiny wild strawberries, and larger cultivated berries grow in profusion in the area south of Rome high above the shimmering blue lake.

Twice during the day—once in late morning and again in the afternoon—teenaged girls dressed like the strawberry pickers of another era parade through the city, passing out samples of strawberries from baskets over their arms. The slightly off-key festival band tootles as it marches, announcing the arrival of a float pulled by a tractor and filled with children dressed as strawberries—little girls and boys looking like fat red fruits in green tights and a plump red papier-mâché ball slightly speckled with tiny black pips. Donkeys must have been the transportation when the festival began in the early 1900s, but if modern life has invaded in the form of a tractor, at least cars are prohibited in the city center, so everyone walks, admiring the view of the still lake and nibbling as many strawberries as a mortal could want.

The streets of Nemi are full of things to eat. Banks and baskets of strawberries spill over counters draped and garlanded with branches of golden broom and greens. Strawberries are eaten directly out of hand or

are turned into a splendid gelato alla fragola. There are a number of *norcinerie*, shops selling only products of the pig, including one with a ceiling of sausages and another, on a sloping side street, with a large outdoor display of salame, prosciutti, and sausages, with tastes provided. Everyone meanders around, admiring the berry displays and buying slices of porchetta on bread made in nearby Ariccia, famous for porchetta and chewy country bread baked in woodburning ovens. The vendor in Carlo Emilio Gadda's novel, *That Awful Mess on Via Merulana*, describes it exactly. " 'Get your roast pork here! Pork straight from Ariccia with a whole tree of rosemary in its belly! With fresh new potatoes, too, right in season! . . . The lovely pork from the Castelli! We sent the pigs out there to wet-nurse, raised in the country, on the acorns of Emperor Caligula himself! the acorns of Prince Colonna! The big prince of Marino and Albano! who killed the worst Turks on the land and sea in the battle of whatever it was. They still have the flags in the cathedral in Marino! with the Turk's crescent on them. Get your nice pig, ladies, roast pig with rosemary!' " All around the city people eat in restaurants that have moved out into the street for the day, or they picnic overlooking the lake.

Romans have been coming to Lake Nemi ever since Caligula built two ships for his pleasure and sailed them on its waters. When the ships sank they were preserved in the lake's depths for a thousand years and then sat in a nearby museum until the Germans blew it up during World War II. Over the centuries they have built villas in the shaded hills around Nemi, where cool breezes preserve them from the intense summer heat of Rome.

In mythic times, long before such summer escapes were dreamed of, a festival was held at Nemi on the thirteenth of August in honor of Diana. Torches blazed and a sacred perpetual fire was lit, perhaps foretelling the practice of lighting holy candles in churches. Young people participated in a purifying ceremony and drank wine and ate special food such as cakes served hot on platters of leaves and apples still on their their boughs. It seems that a variety of cities in Latium had joined against Rome in the name of Diana and built a temple to her. The woodlands became sacred to the goddess, and the still blue lake, enclosed in the green Alban hills, became known as the Mirror of Diana. It was in that sacred grove under an idyllic blue Italian sky that J. G. Fraser began *The Golden Bough*. Here wandered a figure who was both priest and murderer, a man whose time in the sanctuary was haunted by the reality that the priest of Nemi, who received his office by slaying its occupant, must himself be slain. In the wood was a tree with one branch, the Golden Bough, which a runaway slave could break off and use to fight the priest; if he could kill him, he then became the King of the Wood. It is said that this branch represented the bough that Aeneas used for his journey to the world of the dead and that these rites replaced even bloodier human sacrifices.

It is a long way from murdering priests to strawberries, although both have been nourished by the fertile soil of Nemi. The quiet grove was clearly a common place of worship for many of the truly ancient cities of Italy. As Fraser notes in ending *The Golden Bough* as he started it, at Nemi, the temple of Diana has vanished and there is no longer a King of the Wood to guard the Golden Bough. But the forests of Nemi are still thick with berries and gladioli, and the volcanic rocks shelter broom and viburnum. The chestnut woods host wild orchids, and the hothouses and cultivated fields at the bottom of the hill pour forth yet more berries and plants. Nemi is a lovely area beneath umbrella pines, far from the frenzied traffic of the roads leading from Rome, where the glorious wild taste of *fragoline del bosco* and the sweetness of cultivated strawberries are splendid reasons for a century-old *sagra*.

Pane di Ariccia

xxxxxxxxxxxxxxxxxxxxxxxxxxxxxx

*Rustic Country
Bread
from Ariccia*

Ariccia's famous rustic bread has a crunchy crust and a porous interior that is fragrant with the smell of wheat. You can make it two ways, depending on the timing you prefer. If you like to make bread with long cool rises that fit into a workday, cut the yeast back to ¼ teaspoon and leave the sponge to rise for a full eight hours while the *biga* flavors the dough. Then make the dough and let it rise four hours at room temperature or overnight in the refrigerator before shaping and baking it. The following method is more straightforward.

Makes 2 large or 3 medium loaves

SPONGE

¾ teaspoon active dry yeast or ¼ cake (4 grams) fresh yeast
½ cup warm water
3 cups water, room temperature
⅔ cup (150 grams) Biga (page 31)
3⅓ cups (450 grams) unbleached all-purpose flour
¾ cup (100 grams) whole-wheat flour

By Mixer. Stir the yeast into the warm water and let stand until creamy, about 10 minutes. Stir in the rest of the water and add the *biga*. With the paddle attachment mix the *biga* until partially dissolved. Add both flours and mix until you have a thick soupy batter, about 2 minutes. Cover with plastic wrap and let rise until doubled, about 2 hours. The batter will be frothy and very bubbly.

(continued)

DOUGH

**3⅓ cups (450 grams) unbleached all-purpose flour
1 tablespoon sea salt**

By Mixer. Add the flour and salt to the sponge and mix with the paddle until the dough comes together. Change to the dough hook and knead on low speed for 3 minutes, then on medium for another minute. The dough will be jiggly and Jell-O-like and will never come away from the sides or bottom of the bowl. Pour the dough out onto a lightly floured work surface, flour the top of it, and knead briefly to bring it together. Place the dough in an oiled container. Cover it tightly with plastic wrap and let it rise to 2½ to 3 times its original volume, 2 to 2½ hours.

Shaping and Second Rise. Pour the wet dough onto a well-floured work surface, flour the top of the dough, and shape into 2 large or 3 smaller rounds. Don't worry if it isn't perfectly or tightly shaped. The baker from Ariccia calls the dough languid and says that it should be as soft as a woman's breast. Cut 2 or 3 pieces of parchment paper, depending on how many loaves you are making, and set them on baking sheets or pizza peels. Sprinkle the paper with flour, set the loaves on them, then lightly dust the tops with a little more flour. Cover with towels and let rise until doubled, 1¼ to 1½ hours. Just before you are ready to put the loaves in the oven, dimple them gently with your fingers to keep them from splitting on top. Don't be afraid that you will deflate the dough; it is so springy that it will bounce back in no time and without the dimpling, it might well puff into a giant pillow.

Baking. Thirty minutes before baking, heat the oven with baking stones in it to 450°F. Just before baking, sprinkle the stones with cornmeal, turn the temperature down to 425°F, and gently slide the loaves onto the baking stones. Spray with water 3 times in the first 10 minutes. Bake until they ring hollow when tapped on the bottom, 30 to 40 minutes, depending on the size of the loaves.

Porchetta o Maialino di Latte

~~~~~~~~~~~~~~~~~~~~~~~~~~~~

Roast Suckling Pig for the Home Cook

Before it goes in the oven, it is known only as *maiale* (pork) but once cooked, this ceremonial beast ascends to the title of *porchetta* (roast suckling pig). *Non è festa se non è la porchetta.* "It's not a festival if there isn't a porchetta." Under those conditions every day is a *festa* in Ariccia, a town south of Rome famous for its giant roast pigs since they became a local industry in 1938.

Slices of the enormous roast pig are served as walk-around food. The rosemary, garlic, salt, pepper, and wild herbs from the hillsides that fill the interior of the pig are sprinkled on top of the meat to enhance its memorable taste. A porchetta may weigh about 130 pounds in the beginning, but once boned, it drops to about half that. The pig is cut down the center, laid open like a book, and seasoned. Oil is rubbed all over its body, the skin slashed to let out the fat, and then it is hung from a long iron pole that goes from one end of the beast to the other and rests on two tripods poised over a long narrow pan that catches the drippings. Of course no home oven is large enough for a genuine porchetta, but when roast suckling pig is treated like its larger relative, it is one of the great foods for a festive celebration. When you order a whole suckling pig weighing between 15 and 20 pounds, be sure that the butcher cleans its cavity well and has it ready for the oven. If you collect it a day ahead, you can salt the skin to bring out its flavor and leave it in the refrigerator overnight.

Makes 8 to 14 servings

1 suckling pig (15 to 22 pounds, 7 to 10 kilograms), ready to cook
4 to 6 tablespoons salt
1 tablespoon plus 1 teaspoon pepper
5 cloves garlic, finely minced
1 cup (100 grams) fresh rosemary, finely chopped
2 to 3 tablespoons fennel seeds, optional
1 cup plus 2 tablespoons olive oil
White wine for basting

Check the pig to be sure that no bristles or hairs remain; if they do, singe them over an open flame and then pluck them out. Mix together the salt, pepper, garlic, rosemary, optional fennel, and 2 tablespoons oil. Be sure that the cavity of the pig is well cleaned, its kidneys and other organs removed. Spread the herb mixture over the cavity. I also put whole onions inside to give the pig a nice round belly. Truss the opening with skewers about 2 inches apart and secure it well with string. To keep the legs close to the body, you can thread a butcher's needle and push it through the body and hind thighs in back, then through the legs and pig's throat in

(continued)

front. Or you can simply set the pig on its haunches and tie the legs together with string. Set a block of wood in the mouth so it will be open enough for a lemon when it's time to serve the pig. Slash the skin of the pig directly down the backbone and in parallel diagonal cuts about 2 inches apart to let the fat out. Rub olive oil over every bit of the pig's body—head, legs, ears, and tail. Put aluminum foil over the ears and the tail so that they don't burn.

Set the pig in a large roasting pan in the center of the oven. Heat the oven to 450°F and sear the pig 30 minutes. Turn the oven down to 350°F and rub the entire pig again with oil. Pour 1 cup wine into the pan to create some steam and put the pig back into the oven. Baste it with oil every 20 minutes and turn the pig at least 3 times during the cooking so that it browns evenly. Remember to handle it gently. Twenty minutes before the pig is cooked, remove the foil from its ears and tail to allow them to brown. The pig is ready when the internal temperature reaches 165 to 170°F and the skin is crispy and brown. The standard calculation for cooking a suckling pig is 15 minutes per pound, although I found that excessive; my 20-pound pig was thoroughly cooked in 3½ hours.

Serving. When the pig is done, slide it very carefully out of the oven onto a platter, put a lemon in its mouth, and let it rest 15 to 20 minutes. You can make gravy by skimming the fat from the pan juices, adding some wine, and cooking it over a medium flame. To crisp the skin once you have carved the pig, put slices of it back in the oven for 15 minutes.

INFIORATA

CARPETS OF FLOWERS IN SPELLO
Corpus Christi, the Third Sunday in June

*B*efore: Silent and elegant, Spello keeps to itself, a carefully tended medieval town with fine Roman gates, an amphitheater, and towers from the time of Augustus. Built of soft gray-pink stone quarried from nearby mountains, the tranquil city claims its hillside with a network of narrow streets that bend and turn and suddenly open with views onto the green and golden plain below. Here and there a small knot of teenagers lounge on the piazza. Ask any one of them how many shades of purple there are in a wild iris or of yellow in a wild lily, and an amazingly spirited discussion ensues.

After, but just briefly: it looks as if Raphael, Michelangelo, and even William Blake have paid a quick visit to this elegant Umbrian hill town, creating Madonnas and Last Suppers purely for the residents' pleasure. The paintings are glorious, but they are not made of oils and they aren't even frescoed on ancient walls. They are laid directly onto the main street on Corpus Christi Sunday, transforming it into a carpet of color made entirely of flower petals used as if they were pastel crayons. All eight thousand inhabitants are involved in creating the carpet, weaving patterns and pictures through Spello's only uninterrupted street, but it is the job of the oldest women to separate the flowers petal by petal into the most subtle gradations of hue. A single flower can have shades of lemon yellow, saffron, and amber with speckles of burnished gold and tiny dots of tangerine. By the time the petals have become part of incredibly complex designs, streams of spectators are walking uphill and down on the narrow

Infiorata in Genzano, from Antonio Jean-Baptiste Thomas, Un an à Rome, *1830, Paris*

bands of stone paving left on either side, amazed and delighted by variegated mosaics and plump Renaissance *putti* made entirely of flowers. Imagine the head of Michelangelo's Moses, nine feet across with finely shaded wavy hair all made of flower petals, or Masaccio's Adam and Eve being expelled from the Garden trailed by a coiled serpent, or the intricate pattern of a Gothic cathedral, constructed entirely of flowers.

Just collecting the flowers takes as long as two weeks. Most can be found in nearby valleys and plains, but some rare colors must be hunted down, so entire armies of Spello's fervent citizens raid gardens and fields and assault the shores of Lake Trasimeno or the hillsides of Monte Subasio. They go off to the mountains to find the blue flowers that disappear when grain takes over many of the fields. Pine needles, ivy leaves, pale chamomile, and wild fennel are ground up to make green; poppies are used for red, broom makes yellow, and white comes from marguerites and delicate elderberries that are picked at the last minute. Walnut flowers are dried in the oven and crumbled to a powdery black. Other colors that come from cyclamen, geraniums, and anemones are phenomenal: raspberry pink, saffron orange, periwinkle blue, a parchment hue as pale as onion skin. There are dark threads of green the color of sorrel, and flowers with petals as tiny as the pastine that float in broth. At the last moment on Saturday, teenagers race through the nearby fields, collecting the most perishable flowers, and add them to others already stored in cool stone caverns, *cantine,* and garages to preserve their freshness and color.

Teams of artists create their designs in secrecy and unveil them only as they go to work on the eve of the Infiorata. The luxuriant colors make the complicated designs more extraordinary: a Flight from Egypt, complete with pyramids, camels, and sphinx, along with Michelangelo's God; a huge abstract Kandinsky; a Daliesque Crucifixion with the Madonna at its base; a baptism of Christ set in the frame of a parchment scroll opened by two distinctly mischievous *putti;* the Holy Family floating in space beneath large letters saying CORPUS DOMINI in floral calligraphy. The themes are almost entirely religious, since Corpus Christi celebrates the miracle of transubstantiation. The petals themselves transform the city. Just as Jesus' blood became wine and blood again in the miracle that occasions the day, the petals are small drops of color briefly staining the street and turning it into a luxurious tapestry.

Sixty-five to seventy groups are given specific spaces on the street where, after tracing their overall designs, they lay out colored petals in numerous boxes and paper plates in a finely graduated spectrum of color. To make these designs, the young artists of Spello drip the petals from their fingertips and use the back of a spoon to pat them in place. They set the iris of an eye by tweezing a pinch of color and dropping it precisely where it belongs. Raphael's Holy Family is enthroned in a field of greens shading from jade to deep sorrel, announced by a transcendent ribbon of color made with ivory petals the color of vellum, accented with mustard, paprika, and tangerine. Entire carpets look like Missoni fabric or complex Roman mosaics fashioned entirely of pieces of flowers.

Each design must be at least thirty-six feet long and must follow the winding pattern of the medieval street. In the largest piazza with its fountain and plane trees young artists bring a powerful William Blake-like God to life on the dark pavement. Another piazza is designed like an enormous Navajo rug, and in a third a charming Madonna has a plump, adoring child on her lap. The three dimensionality in the chubby thighs and stomachs of the cherubs, the subtle mixture of colors, the gradations of color and shading are amazing, the fragility breathtaking.

The event starts in earnest at three o'clock on Saturday afternoon, when the main street is closed to automobile traffic. The groups of teen-aged artists lay out and make the designs under a protective superstructure draped with plastic sheeting. One year a rainstorm came up and gusts of wind blew away masses of petals, so no one takes chances anymore. And certainly no one goes hungry. The restaurants and *trattorie* send food out to the workers, making sure that a dinner of spicy pasta all'Amatriciana reaches everyone, which helps keep them going until the next morning. Caffès keep their doors open late in the night, offering free coffee and desserts to the hardworking artists.

Early Sunday morning, clusters of tired young people, running on pure nervous energy, are working against the clock to complete their designs by nine o'clock. Many finish by enclosing their designs in a richly patterned border made by dropping brilliant colored flowers into the compartments of a three-dimensional template. Once they are nearly done, the artists neaten the edges with a whisk broom and then spray a shot of water from an aerosol can to keep everything in place, since even a soft summer breeze can blow away hours of work. As each group rolls away the protective covering, revealing its design, a great cheer goes up. Bells ring out and birds wheel away overhead. The groups sit at the edge of the narrow street, protecting their designs from the crowd beginning to stream up the hill, for there is always danger that the trim edges will be smudged.

Long before visitors have come to see the Infiorata, the whole city of Spello is strolling and checking on the progress of the work. The bars and caffès are jammed with people of every age drinking cappuccino and eating maritozzi. Stepladders are set right in the middle of the street, making it easy to get a good aerial view of the scenes. In the same spirit, the people of Spello actually leave their front doors unlocked and invite visitors to climb up to their family apartments so they can look down to view the designs in their entirety. This change in perspective is remarkable. Pictures that are thirty-five or fifty feet long, much too big to be seen clearly at street level, coalesce and the designs open up into a complex third dimension.

A single long narrow tapestry of color winds from one piazza into the next; another turns the corner into the courtyard of a Gothic church. Branching off from the main street are tiny lanes, like the Via Arco di Augusto with its big pots of yellow flowers and tidy little houses, all framed by arches stretching across the street at the rooflines. Someone has spruced up a minuscule courtyard with an Oriental rug made of brilliant yellow broom edged with rose petals and dark green wild fennel. Red damask banners hang from windows; geraniums and impatiens sprout from terracotta jugs.

By eleven in the morning, the city is packed. The oom-pah-pahs of the band concert on the main piazza compete with the chanting of the mass inside the cathedral until the religious procession leaves the dark interior for the bright city streets. It is led by the bishop holding the host up high as he walks the length of the extraordinary carpet of flowers, the way all priests at one time walked into church on a carpet. Following the bishop are priests in yellow surplices swinging incense burners or carrying banners; behind them comes the band, a flood of people in their Sunday best, and somewhere in it all, the judges who have been carefully scrutinizing the designs. The procession makes a circuit of the lower part of town, scattering flower petals that are picked up by the currents of air, their scent and color crushed beneath heels and brushed out of doorways. The extravagant use of flowers is as ephemeral as it is beautiful; it lasts only a few hours before being scattered to the winds. It announces that the festival has such riches that it can afford to be extravagant with the transitory glories of nature.

No one knows who the winners of the judges' awards will be until a special dinner held later that night, but by then the designs will be gone, leaving only the scent of chamomile drifting on the air. The winners celebrate with prizes that include the local equivalent of an Oscar—a statue of Propertius, the Roman poet said to have been born in Spello. Every group that wins a prize gets money to use for a victory meal. Some spend it on a picnic to reunite the winning team and make plans for the next year, and others celebrate with a dinner for which the cooks are the town's mothers, not chefs, and the dishes are traditional tastes of Spello: bruschetta, slices of country bread rubbed with garlic and glistening with green extra-virgin olive oil; field mushrooms wrapped in tangles of spaghetti; slices of home-cured prosciutto; squab roasted on the spit; and a mixture of grilled meats.

The victory dinners are a far cry from the one at which the judges feast as they contemplate their decisions. That meal begins with what is called a rustic antipasto: bruschetta al pomodoro with a bit of Umbrian truffle shaved over the top, crostini of smoked salmon, a bit of liver pâté, and white beans sprinkled with a tiny hailstorm of black caviar. So much for rustic. They progress to risotto al profumo di bosco, a rice dish flavored with fresh porcini mushrooms and the pencil-thin wild asparagus that grows around Spello only during the month of June. Then comes a mixture of elegant pasta and butter lettuce stuffed with ham, mozzarella, and Gruyère cheese, covered with a besciamella sauce and baked until it turns

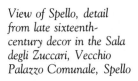

View of Spello, detail from late sixteenth-century decor in the Sala degli Zuccari, Vecchio Palazzo Comunale, Spello

golden: a mere prelude to the tacchino tartufato, a turkey in galantine with grated truffles on top. Dessert comes home to Umbria with la rocciata, the traditional nut- and fruit-filled apple strudel in a puff-pastry envelope.

By the time of the victory dinner, all the teams have been chosen for the following year and have met in deep secrecy lest any rivals discover what they have dreamed up. They have even sketched their designs in black and white since no one knows which flowers will bloom the next summer.

Infiorate have been a part of Italian tradition since the seventeenth century when flower designs were used to decorate altars on Maundy Thursday. In 1778 the city of Genzano, in the heart of the Castelli Romani, moved the flowers out of the church and laid the first carpet right on the street in honor of a papal visit. Genzano still enthusiastically creates its Infiorata on Corpus Christi Sunday when eleven groups of men, women, and children make eleven enormous pictures. Four tons of flowers transform the street into a carpet that covers the single main street from the Appian Way to the church at the top of the hill, a distance of almost a mile.

An Infiorata is an extravagant celebration of the flowers of the countryside with resonances of ancient spring festivals, perhaps connected with the worship of Aphrodite, the goddess of flowering plants, or with Adonis, whose gardens were tossed into the waters of the sea at the height of summer. In later times, instead of licentious Roman rites, young women in small towns used to go into the countryside to fill their baskets with wild roses and broom, and when the Corpus Christi Day procession arrived at its appointed spot, they showered petals upon the priest. Today, the young artists in Spello who lay down their flowery carpets share an intense experience, and for them and for everyone who sees Spello, the Infiorata is a moment of theater. And when all that is left is the fragrance of flowers and fragments of petals, poetic memories remain. The prizewinners' dinner re-creates the entire event two months later and while everyone celebrates by feasting, the teams plan the next Infiorata with even more extravagant pictures and designs.

Pasta all'Amatriciana

Spaghetti with a Chile-Spiked Sauce

Most experts say that this pasta gets its name from Amatrice, where it was made when that city still belonged to the province of L'Aquila in Abruzzo. Now the pasta is claimed by Latium, but its tangles of bucatini must still be flavored with guanciale, bacon made from the jowls of pigs that feast on acorns, which makes their flesh especially flavorful. Pancetta, salted and cured precisely the same way, is a perfect substitute.

Makes 4 servings

1½ to 2 tablespoons olive oil
4 ounces (100 grams) pancetta, cut in fine strips
1 peperoncino (dried red chile)
½ medium onion, finely sliced or chopped
¾ pound (340 grams) peeled tomatoes, chopped
Salt
10 ounces (300 grams) pasta, preferably bucatini or spaghetti
Abundant grated pecorino Romano cheese

Warm the olive oil over a low fire, stir in the pancetta, and sauté about 5 minutes. Add the peperoncino and continue to cook until the pancetta has browned. Add the onion and cook until golden. Stir in the tomatoes and cook until the sauce thickens, 10 to 15 minutes. Just before serving, season to taste with salt and remove the peperoncino.

Meanwhile, bring a large pot of abundantly salted water to the boil, add the pasta, and cook until it is al dente, about 10 minutes. Drain, mix right in the pan with the sauce, and toss well. Serve with the pecorino cheese.

Risotto ai Funghi Porcini

Wild Mushroom Risotto

This risotto is rich with the musky taste of the fresh porcini mushrooms that grow wild on the hillsides of northern Italy. Mushrooms with such intense flavor are hard to find in America, but if you can locate a supply of fresh boletus or cèpes—called *porcini* in Italy—by all means use them. Otherwise try cremini, a fresh mushroom with a hint of wild nutty flavor in its dark cap. Combining cremini with some dried porcini that have been soaked in warm water to release their flavor is one solution to re-creating the taste of fresh porcini.

(continued)

Makes 6 to 8 servings

1¾ pounds (750 grams) fresh mushrooms, preferably cremini
2 ounces (60 grams) dried porcini mushrooms
6 tablespoons unsalted butter
2 onions, finely sliced
About ½ (150 grams) fresh large tomato, finely chopped
Salt and pepper to taste
3 cups (750 grams) Italian short-grain rice, Arborio, Vialone Nano, or
   Carnaroli
½ cup plus 1 tablespoon dry white wine
9½ cups veal or meat broth, at a low boil
2 tablespoons heavy cream
½ cup freshly grated Parmigiano-Reggiano
2 tablespoons chopped flat-leaf parsley

Wipe the fresh mushrooms with a damp cloth and with a small brush or towel remove any dirt from the caps and stems. Slice them very fine. Soak the dried porcini in warm water to cover at least 30 minutes. Remove the mushrooms, pat dry, and chop fine. Strain the liquid twice through a sieve lined with cheesecloth and reserve for other use in sauces, soups, or stews. Melt half the butter in a heavy sauté pan, add the onions, and sauté over medium-low heat until limp and golden. Add all the mushrooms and cook over extremely low heat about 30 minutes. Add the tomato, salt, and pepper and cook 5 minutes.

For the risotto melt the remaining butter in a heavy-bottomed saucepan, stir in the rice, and cook over moderate heat until well coated with the butter. Add the wine and cook slowly until it is completely absorbed. Add the bubbling stock one ladle at a time, stirring with each addition until it is absorbed before adding more. Be sure to stir the rice frequently. Continue until the rice has absorbed almost all the stock.

After the rice has cooked about 15 minutes, add the cream and Parmesan to the mushrooms and simmer about 3 minutes. At the last moment, when the rice is almost ready to eat, stir the sauce into the risotto and blend well. Taste for seasoning and sprinkle with parsley. Serve immediately.

Spaghetti con i Turini

~~~~~~~~~~~~~~~~~~~~~~~~~~~~~~~

Spaghetti with Field Mushrooms

Makes 6 servings

3 to 4 tablespoons olive oil
1 small onion, finely diced
1 rib celery, finely diced
1 carrot, finely diced
1 peperoncino (dried red chile)
4 ounces (120 grams) pancetta, diced
1 pound 2 ounces (500 grams) field mushrooms, preferably cremini, cleaned and sliced
½ cup fresh basil, torn in small pieces
Salt and pepper
¼ cup chicken broth
14 ounces (400 grams) spaghetti
1 cup (100 grams) grated Parmesan cheese
1 cup (100 grams) grated pecorino cheese

Warm the olive oil in a heavy sauté pan and add the finely chopped vegetables, the peperoncino, and pancetta. When all are soft and golden, add the sliced mushrooms and the basil and sauté over low heat about 15 minutes. Remove the peperoncino and season to taste with salt and pepper. If the sauce seems dry, add the chicken broth.

Meanwhile, boil the spaghetti in salted water until al dente, about 10 minutes. Drain, add directly to the sauce in the pan, and toss well, stirring in most of the grated cheeses. Serve at table with the remaining cheese.

Rocciata

~~~~~~~~~~~~~~~~~~~~~~~~~~~~~

Fruit- and Nut-Filled Strudel

This is no ordinary strudel curling upon itself in the shape of a snail shell. Inside the fine dough hide figs, prunes and apples, hazelnuts and almonds, all coated with cinnamon. It is so delicate and full of flavor that no one should be surprised that it is claimed by a number of Umbrian towns, including Perugia and Assisi, Foligno at Christmas, and Spello during an Infiorata. This one is encased in a veil of flaky strudel dough, while others are often wrapped in puff pastry.

(continued)

Makes 2 strudels

STRUDEL DOUGH

1 egg, room temperature
1 tablespoon plus 1 teaspoon light olive oil
½ teaspoon lemon juice
¾ cup warm water
About 2¼ cups (300 grams) unbleached all-purpose flour

FILLING

About 5½ ounces (160 grams) prunes, pitted and sliced thin
About 5½ ounces (160 grams) dried figs, sliced
½ cup white wine, warmed
2 large or 3 medium (620 grams) Granny Smith apples,
  peeled, cored, and cut into ½-inch dice (about 3½ cups)
About 1 cup (125 grams) almonds, roughly chopped
About 1 cup (125 grams) hazelnuts, toasted, skinned, roughly chopped
½ cup (100 grams) sugar
½ teaspoon cinnamon
1 scant tablespoon lemon juice

FOR ASSEMBLING

1 cup melted clarified or unsalted butter
1 cup cookie crumbs, finely ground

Dough. Mix all the liquid ingredients together. Put the flour in a mixer bowl. With the paddle attachment in place add the wet ingredients slowly and evenly at medium speed until satiny smooth. You may need to add as much as ¼ cup more flour but do it slowly.

Knead the dough on a very lightly floured surface into a small ball with no seams so you will have no weak spots when you pull the fine veil of dough. The dough will be satiny smooth with tiny little blisters, very elastic, and springy. It should be warm, not cold.

Flatten the dough, being sure that it is entirely smooth, and brush off any excess flour. Brush the surface with a little oil to keep a skin from forming, moisten a plate with a little oil, and set the dough on it. Cover well with plastic wrap and set in a warm turned-off oven for 45 minutes.

Filling. Marinate the prunes and figs in the warm white wine about ½ hour. They will absorb all but 2 to 3 tablespoons of the wine. Move them to a large bowl and add the apples and nuts. Mix together the sugar and cinnamon and add them along with the lemon juice to the fruit and nuts. Mix well.

Stretching the Dough. Take off any rings on your hands. Set a bedsheet on the table on which you are making the dough and sprinkle it with flour. The dough must be slightly warm and have a silky smooth, unbroken surface with little blisters. Set it on the bedsheet and begin to work it by rolling it lightly with a rolling pin into a large circle. Relax the back of your hand and pick it up and drape it, letting it pull with its own weight. Keep moving it around while pulling delicately at the edges and smoothing it out, using a long gentle pull. Let it slip over the backs of your hands; the little tension in the drop will help pull the dough out. Never work in the same spot for long because you want to be careful not to tear it. Always work at the edges; inspect them and the dough so it stays even. As soon as you can get it over the end of the table, you can work against the table. Pull the dough out to about 42 by 40 inches. Once it is stretched into its great circular shape, trim off the thick outer edges all the way around. Let the dough dry until it feels papery, about 10 minutes.

Filling and Rolling. Brush the entire surface of the dough with melted unsalted butter. You will put the fillings for both rocciate on it, so sprinkle it evenly with the cookie crumbs to within about 2 inches of the edges but leave a path in the center for the separation between the 2 logs of filling. You can pull the cloth and continue buttering the dough without ever picking it up in your fingers. If your table is too narrow to have the dough lying flat at one time, reserve some crumbs to cover the part lying over the edge.

Spread the filling in 2 rectangles, about 16 by 6 inches each, at the end nearest you. Turn over the outside edge of the dough, pat the filling into place gently, and wiggle it to make it even. Press down on the center to seal the 2 rectangles off from each other. Once again roll it back and forth to distribute the filling evenly. Using the bedsheet roll the dough one turn, brush off any flour, and brush the exposed surface with melted butter. Continue to roll and brush to the end of the dough. After the final turn, cut the 2 edges so they are straight, then roll each log into a snail shape.

Baking. Put on parchment-lined baking sheets. Brush butter over the tops and prick holes in the dough with a skewer to allow steam to escape. Bake at 400°F 10 minutes, then turn the oven down to 350°F and bake another 35 minutes. Brush with melted butter every 10 minutes. Cut the ends off before serving.

FESTA DEI GIGLI

DANCE OF THE LILIES IN NOLA

June 22 or the First Sunday After the Summer Solstice

flood of people pours toward the center of town, drawn by raucous bursts of amplified music and the sight of an elaborately decorated tower as tall as a Gothic spire tottering from side to side. Eight of these gigantic constructions are moving in from every direction, their tops bouncing above tiled roofs and swaying through a tangle of streets that converge on the central piazza of the small southern town of Nola. Seventy-five feet high, taller than any house, taller even than the highest campanile and dome, the towers march across the stone streets, sending birds wheeling above them, holding the attention of spectators perched on every terrace and hanging out of every open window. They inch through dark, narrow passageways, brushing by balconies with barely a centimeter of space to spare, a death-defying act. And the noise! Trumpets blast and drums thump across the entire city, which is already vibrating with the energy of its people surging through the narrow lanes. Women bang tambourines and bounce to the music coming from orchestras that are actually sitting on the first level of each decorated tower, blasting out amplified Neapolitan tarantellas and Beatles tunes. The towers are I Gigli, the great lilies of Nola, four-ton wood and papier-mâché creations so massive that it takes relays of 90 to 120 men to hoist and parade them around town in a rite that has gone on since the fifteenth century.

Making these remarkable pieces of temporary architecture remains a special craft whose secret is passed from father to son. New Gigli are constructed each year, hidden behind canvas screens, until they grow taller than the highest building in town and are unveiled at last on the Saturday afternoon before the *festa*. An entire chestnut tree or poplar tree may be set down the center of a Giglio, forming its spine. The sturdy rectangular base has four strong feet and two chunky levels that rise about nine feet above the base, wide enough to accommodate all the participants. Each lily has a special motif, although its spire is always crowned with a statue of the saint. One theme may represent the gifts of the sea with octopus, urchins, and tropical fish, and another may be thick with pagodas and chopsticks and other exotic motifs of Japan. Years ago one Giglio re-created Pompeii and another represented the entire façade of Saint Peter's.

The men who carry the obelisk surround the first level, which is about four feet high, high enough for them to slide their shoulders under it without having to stoop much. On the level above them rides an entire orchestra complete with a single woman snapping her fingers, swinging her hips, and singing. The many rough pieces of wood that run the length of the lower section are nailed in place, since they maintain the equilibrium of the Giglio and keep it from rocking wildly or hitting the palazzi on either side of the streets. The wooden poles that run across the width of the Giglio are attached with ropes. Rows of men slide between them, like sailors on a galley ship, crouch, and then straighten up to shoulder the weight of the tower. Those poles not only move but can be removed. Sometimes twenty, thirty, even forty men must move away from the Giglio because they can't fit in the extremely narrow streets. Then poles and men join up later when the streets open again. Above the base the tower rises five full stories, each one progressively narrower and more attenuated, like the spire of a Gothic church. Underneath the veneer of beauty in a Giglio lies a statement of power, a rough, hand-hewn carpentry guided by muscle and sinew. The men who carry these enormous weights are proud masters for this one day. Like the Gigli, they can soar above it all, above poverty and the once proud city that is crumbling now.

Nola was once so powerful that the Romans allowed it to coin its own money. It claimed a huge territory that stretched beyond Pompeii to the sea. It may not be rich now, but that hasn't stopped the city from building new Gigli each year. Fund-raising begins in the late spring, when members of each Giglio committee visit stores and the houses of friends in search of donations. Each group gives sumptuous restaurant lunches, starting in early April and going on until June, and funds are collected to cover all the costs of the festival, including those of constructing and decorating each Giglio, which can run from $14,000 to $60,000. Like a potlatch, it encourages extreme outpourings of generosity from its participants in a kind of competition of conspicuous consumption, but it doesn't look as if any money is involved. There are no velvet costumes or showy processions as in most Italian festivals. The men are bare-chested and sweating, and the impressiveness of the event lies in its earthiness, its triumph over adversity. "The festival used to be for God and Faith, and every family had to sacrifice to bring it about," explained a retired businessman who began carrying the Gigli at thirteen. "It is a blessing to be able to carry the Gigli. That is what our strength is for."

The *festa* takes place on June 22 or the first Sunday after the summer solstice, but it always starts on a Saturday afternoon as each group proudly unveils its obelisk and parades it through town to show it off. Many people are in homemade costumes. Knights, shepherds, gladiators, boys in medieval dress, and pom-pom girls parade from neighborhood to neighborhood. Drums beat an incantatory rhythm that gets the blood flowing, encouraging the pairs of flag wavers whose banners crackle in the air and whirl end over end. As the crowd cheers and grows more enthusiastic, one group of teenaged boys hoists four girls on their shoulders and dances them around, like a human Giglio. Mothers push baby carriages, old people cast an appraising eye on this year's constructions, everyone visits the historical exhibit of past Gigli, and men and boys brag and swagger.

It seems as if the entire city is in the streets on this sultry afternoon, but everyone cools off with cups of icy lemon granita sold at little carts in almost every piazza. No formal eating is connected with the *festa*, but there is street food everywhere. Boiled or roasted corn on the cob is sold at street corners along with lupini beans, chestnuts, torrone, and slices of fresh coconut kept moist under little jets of water. Around dusk many people meander up to the traveling amusement park, where they buy

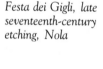

Festa dei Gigli, late seventeenth-century etching, Nola

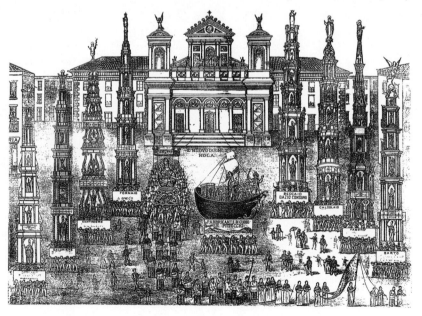

boiled pigs' feet and eat them sprinkled with salt and lemon. Everyone ends up in the piazza for a ceremony that begins with contests for the best costume and new song, and includes wild singing and dancing that go on until the sun comes up.

The Gigli festival celebrates the return of Saint Paulinus, who was elected bishop of Nola in the fifth century shortly after the Vandals sacked Rome and devastated the surrounding countryside, taking prisoner all the men of Nola and sending them to Africa in servitude. Paulinus had gone to Africa to save the only son of a poor widow by substituting himself for the boy, and then stayed on as caretaker of the king's gardens. He was eventually set free and allowed to return home, the liberator of all the men of Nola. The entire city turned out to welcome him, carrying what some say were huge bouquets of lilies, or perhaps candles decorated with flowers carried by the eight ancient master artisans of the town.

By the sixteenth century the holiday had become the high point of the year. The people of Nola carried a single very heavy candle decorated with sheaves of grain, set it on a bier in the city piazza, and lit it. Each year they collected money to pay for a new candle, and in time various trades—greengrocers, sausage makers, winemakers, bakers, shoemakers, butchers, tailors, and ironmongers—chose to make individual candles, decorate them with artisanal insignias, and parade them through the city. A ninth entry, a boat with a Moor aboard and a pirate swinging off the midsection, represents the vessel that brought Paulinus and the Nolese back from captivity, and it has the place of honor.

The columns and pilasters of the Gigli grew higher and more richly decorated over the years until they became much as they are today: eight obelisks, each weighing four tons and standing seventy-five feet high, the modern equivalent of the candles of the past. "A tower with motion," Sacheverell Sitwell said when he saw one. "A triumphal car, a juggernaut made from a pyramid . . ."

On Sunday exuberance and barely contained ecstasy take over. As firecrackers pop and bands play, the Gigli arrive from each part of the city and proceed into the piazza like enormous insects with many feet. Loudspeakers hanging off each one amplify the music that an eighteen-member band—all brass, cymbals, and drums—on the first-level platform plays so energetically that the Giglio bounces up and down like a trampoline while the top sways alarmingly back and forth. The discordant music of so many different bands blares louder and louder; the crackling noise is as raw and primitive as the brute force needed to raise the Gigli. Nine different lilies totter and dance through the narrow streets, arriving in the piazza at fifteen-minute intervals. They are so tall that people on the second- and third-floor balconies can reach out and touch them and shower them with flowers as they go by.

The cacophony mounts as the squawking music closes in for the morning "dance." More and more Gigli arrive in the piazza, with girls dancing around them and team followers singing behind, fists and arms swinging over their heads in rhythm. As each lily arrives in the piazza, it enters a fiercely felt competition to see who can keep the heavy structure in motion the longest. "The moment the wood lies on your shoulder and you hear the music and feel the tower above you, it is the moment for which you live!" an eloquent architect explained. For the people of Nola the Gigli seem alive in their movement, and the relationship between the men and the structures seems real, almost human.

The most moving event is the "raising" of the Giglio. Until you have actually seen a hundred or more men contract their muscles, trembling with the effort, and have actually heard the primitive force of their breathing, it is hard to imagine. So great is the weight of the Giglio that they must all lift it together. First the captain gives a signal, the band plays a short drumroll, trumpets blast, the captain raises his arms, then the group, with a collective intake of breath, prepares to hoist the lily. It shakes. It shivers. With a single fluid motion, the men raise the entire four-ton structure and dance with it, rocking with half-steps and then rolling forward as the band literally jumps up and down on their shoulders. The music begins slowly but the tempo speeds up as the obelisk is walked sideways to the town hall like a colossal many-legged beast. It makes a complete turn to the rousing rhythms of the March from Aïda, and after fifteen minutes backs to a resting spot in the piazza.

With hardly a pause, the next group arrives, moving briskly to melodies from Carmen. Each lily's supporters go berserk. They rush in from everywhere, taking over about a third of the enormous piazza, dancing to encourage their group. At the festival I attended the winning team kept its machine in motion for twenty-five minutes. Around and around they dance, bouncing up and down, rocking back and forth while the dancing continues in the streets and the piazze, and the trumpets and the brass bands fill the air.

When the Gigli are all in place, the bells of the campanile ring out and the doors of the cathedral open. Out comes the bishop followed by a retinue of ecclesiastics who accompany the shiny silver statue of Saint Paulinus, which is swathed in lurid red gladioli. The procession moves slowly as the bishop stops to bless each lily and people throw thick handfuls of confetti against the statue for good luck. Blessings completed, the statue is returned to the Duomo and everyone slowly leaves the piazza to go home for lunch or to a restaurant.

This bacchanalia celebrates not only a great religious festival but also the sense of community that brings the city together and calls home Nolese who have moved away to Rome, Milan, and even to the United

States. For a few days there is no class structure in the town as doctors
and carpenters work side by side, hoisting the huge lilies on their shoulders
and glorifying fifteen hundred years of the collective history of Nola.

For all its religious dimensions, it is likely that the festival must originally have been a pagan agricultural orgy, as Roman scholars have suggested, in which gifts were offered to a god of the fields at the time of
the wheat harvest. Just as Saint Paulinus, protector and savior of his
village, was in captivity in the darkness of Africa before he was released,
so the earth and the fields are in thrall to darkness before they release
new life when the sun is at the height of its powers. One glimpse of the
shape of the Giglio makes it easy to believe. As the day progresses, many
men bear the impress of the pole, which leaves a swollen lump on the
shoulder where it has rested. It is the mark of virility, and it proclaims
that for one day being a strong man is sufficient. During the space of the
morning and afternoon, the swellings rise perceptibly and as time passes
blood oozes through the skin and crusts on T-shirts. The men consider
the swellings important stigmata and bear them proudly and ostentatiously
as testaments of their physical strength and masculinity. Because this is
strictly a male ritual, the only women involved are the token females on
each Giglio, waving bouquets of flowers, swinging their hips, and dancing.

It used to be that the men stood at their Gigli and ate a hearty bracing
lunch. Each man was served braciole di maiale alla napoletana, rolled
pork stuffed with prosciutto, raisins, and pine nuts, with a Neapolitan
roll called a *carusella*, similar to the rosetta of Rome that puffed in the
baking and was almost hollow inside. Special foods are no longer connected to the festival, and no moment exists when the men eat together.

In the afternoon Gigli must make a circuit of the entire city in a
complicated choreography of turns. All of Nola follows their carefully
prescribed labyrinthine path through the densely packed streets, a memorable journey as each Giglio lurches forward, picks up momentum, and

bears down mercilessly on the spectators. Before and after each lily come members of its group, men dancing with men and women with women, clapping and singing and whirling. Confetti hangs in the air, and streamers loop over the edge of balconies and curl down into the dark streets. The town is so small and the route so cramped that the inevitable gridlock allows the members to rest, holding on to second-floor balconies while the bands serenade. The judges of the Gigli have their own balcony at a particularly difficult corner that slopes downhill, forcing the men to readjust the balance of the towers. *Chi non tocca, vince.* Whoever can turn these enormous Gigli around in the streets without touching the walls wins. The most difficult maneuver comes at the prison, where the surrounding walls have been painted with a wide white stripe to record the slightest mark. This is the trickiest part of the competition; half the Gigli are disqualified right here. By the end the men are so exhausted that it is only the exuberant rhythms of the March from *Aïda* that prod them to the finish.

The entire city lives the *festa* intensely. And when it is all over, and the dancing and the singing and the marching have come to an end, do people go home and collapse in delight? Absolutely not. The *festa* officially finishes at midnight, which is exactly when men turn up at city hall to start the long process of choosing leaders of each Giglio and thinking up new motifs to decorate the lilies that will dance again next year.

Braciole alla Napoletana

Stuffed Pork Rolls

A braciola is a pork cutlet rolled around a tangy Arab filling of capers, pine nuts, and raisins. It has been a traditional dish in Naples for centuries, but may have a double meaning in Nola, since the city was once jokingly known as the town of Fra Braciola, a resident monk who loved good food. These days no one serves any ritual food for the festival of I Gigli, and the men eat the Neopolitan pastas and sausages they eat the rest of the year. In the 1920s a special lunch was held near each lily for the men who carried the heavy obelisks. They ate only enough to give them strength: braciole, permeated with the rich flavors of long, slow braising, and a carusella, a traditional bread very much like the hollow-centered rosetta of Rome. So fortified, they set off with their great burdens through the dark, winding city streets.

Makes 6 to 8 servings

8 pork cutlets (about 2 pounds, 900 grams)
About 2 ounces (50 grams) raisins or currants
⅓ cup (50 grams) pine nuts
3 tablespoons plus 1 teaspoon (50 grams) capers, rinsed and drained
1½ tablespoons fresh bread crumbs
Salt and pepper
About 2 ounces (50 grams) prosciutto, thinly sliced
3 to 4 tablespoons olive oil
½ cup gravy left from a previous roast or ½ cup meat broth
1½ tablespoons tomato paste smoothed with a little warm water
1 peperoncino (dried red chile)

If you can persuade your butcher to pound the cutlets flat, definitely do so. They should be thin and quite square so they are easy to roll up. Otherwise you can buy pork chops, remove the bones, cut off all the fat, and split them horizontally like a book. If no accommodating butcher is in sight, pound the pork flat using a meat mallet or the side of a cleaver.

Soak the raisins or currants in warm water to cover 15 minutes. Drain and squeeze them dry in a paper towel. Chop together the raisins, pine nuts, and capers, then mix in the bread crumbs.

Lay each piece of meat on a work surface and salt and pepper them. Lay a slice of prosciutto over each piece. Sprinkle on the pine nut mixture, leaving room to fold in the edges. Roll each cutlet up and fasten it with a skewer.

Warm the oil in a heavy sauté pan and brown the pork rolls on all sides. Add the gravy or meat broth. Stir in the tomato paste dissolved in warm water and the peperoncino. Cover and cook over the lowest possible heat 1½ to 2 hours. Turn the meat every once in a while, adding water as necessary to keep the meat moist and watching to make sure that it doesn't burn. You can also cook the braciole tightly covered in a 325°F oven for 2 hours.

Remove the skewers, ladle the gravy over the braciole, and serve immediately.

Granita di Limone

~~~~~~~~~~~~~~~~~~~~~~~~~~~

Lemon Ice

Every garden and plot of land in Nola and the surrounding countryside seems to have at least one lemon bush. The lemons of Campania are famous for their flavor and fat skins, and in Nola they are particularly prized for making cool thirst-quenching granular ices called *granite*. During the afternoon course, the granita carts follow after the dancing Gigli just as bread ovens used to go off to battle with the armies in medieval times.

Makes 6 to 8 servings

1 cup (200 grams) sugar
2 cups water
½ cup juice from Meyer lemons (if available)
½ cup juice from regular lemons

Simmer the sugar and water 5 minutes. Add the lemon juice and stir. Strain and freeze in metal ice trays or a small metal baking pan. Stir the mixture when it gets mushy, after about an hour; return to the freezer and stir again after another hour. Serve when the mixture is grainy like shaved ice.

Drawing of a lemon by P. A. Mattioli, 1583, Venice

SAN GIOVANNI BATTISTA

FESTIVAL OF SAINT JOHN
THE BAPTIST

June 23 and June 24 in Grello, Rome, and Spilamberto

*I*f you go by the skies and astronomers' charts, Midsummer's Eve ought to fall on the summer solstice, the longest and most light-filled day of the year. Not in Italy. June 21 may be the turning point in the sun's course through the sky and the moment of its greatest strength, but Italians celebrate Midsummer's Eve three days later on June 24, which is also the Festa of San Giovanni Battista, the Feast of Saint John the Baptist. For millennia, festivals have been celebrated at decisive moments in the agricultural year, such as midsummer, which in Italy is still a time of frenzied activity, because the wheat harvest is being gathered in and workers are in the orchards picking the fruits of summer. In more agrarian times, people believed that there was a magical streaming together of events on Midsummer's Eve day. Processions of men wound through the fields carrying blazing torches to bless the crops, and they lit bonfires high on the hills and rolled burning wheels to the fields below, imitating the sun as it began its descent. Early pagan sun cults lit fires as magical gestures to stave off the decline of the sun by feeding it with a fresh source of strength. The ancient Romans worshiped the goddess of fortune, whose cult glorified fertility and whose symbol was a solar wheel of flames. The roaring flames and shimmering heat of all the pagan cults were undoubtedly also meant to allay anxieties about the uncertainties of life, since men understood they were defenseless before the coming darkness and cold, and even at the height of the summer, they knew they were caught in the unending waves that Marguerite Yourcenar calls "the rising and falling double helix" of the seasons.

Christianity simply grafted the pagan fires to the celebration of the Feast of San Giovanni. The prophet was born precisely at midsummer, just as Jesus was born six months later at the turning point of winter, two moments in the calendar that mark passage across a critical threshold. Bearded and dressed in animal skins, subsisting on honey and locusts, San Giovanni also resembles an ancient god of the fields, or the mythical King of the Wood who married the Great Goddess in dark midwinter. Six months later, the King of the Wood was put to death beneath a great sacred oak by his successor. So this sacrificial death, with its intimations of rebirth and renewal, was meant to encourage the fertility of the fields.

From the fertility of the fields to patron saint of love and friendship is not much of a jump. San Giovanni's Day was a time when young couples announced their engagements or set out to find romance. Girls who had not yet found a husband asked the saint about their futures by dripping egg whites, hot wax, or molten lead into a bowl of water and then reading the solidified shapes. A blob shaped like an oar suggested a sailor husband, while one looking like a pen might promise a writer, but of course the forms were as free as a Rorschach test, leaving a girl to see what she wanted to see. In Sicily and Sardinia, San Giovanni was when boys chose their *comare*, sweethearts. Fraser's *Golden Bough* describes the "gardens of Adonis," shoots of wheat and barley sown in a small pot and meant to grow quickly to fruition by the eve of the Feast of San Giovanni. In Sardinia a couple used to take the pot and break it against the church door; then they went down to the fields and settled down on the grass to eat eggs and herbs, drank wine, and later danced to the accompaniment of flutes. Sometimes blazing bonfires were lit, and sometimes the boy and girl thrust their hands quickly into the fire as a way of sealing their relationship.

Time is briefly out of joint when the strength of the sun is beginning to fade, so strange events can occur. Witches and other supernatural spirits were thought to gather for an annual meeting on Midsummer's Eve night, creating turmoil wherever they went. To keep them away, people sprinkled grains of coarse salt on their thresholds, barred the doors with a broom, and armed themselves with braids of garlic. They wove carnations into garlands and believed that herbs and nuts they collected on the solstice—lavender, chamomile, mistletoe, and walnuts—had curative and magical properties, just as the herbs and flowers in Shakespeare's *Midsummer Night's Dream* stirred up confusion between dream and reality and created passionate, if peculiar, attachments when rubbed on the eyelids. To this day Italians still begin making *nocino,* a walnut liqueur typical of Emilia-Romagna and the Val Padana, by going into the

Witches at work, from De lamiis et pitonicis mulieribus, 1489, Costanza

woods to collect walnuts on the night of San Giovanni when the shells are still green and soft. They gather them in multiples of twenty-one (the magical three of the Trinity multiplied by the seven of the cardinal virtues) and immerse them in alcohol with special spices or lemon rind, where they are left to sit for at least forty days—the same number John the Baptist wandered in the desert. Tradition says that green walnuts can be harvested only by women with bare feet who must use a wooden scythe, never a metallic one.

People who live along the ridge of the Apennines in Abruzzo still get up on the morning of June 24 to see the sun rise red as the blood of Saint John the Baptist, and to watch it shimmer in the water like the enormous golden platter on which Herod offered the Saint's head to Salome. The water is as important as the sun. Other people in small towns on the Adriatic dive three times into the sea on June 24, the day Saint John baptized Jesus. The baptism Saint John preached was an ancient rite marking a moment of dramatic passage in life, and scholars trace its origin to the Sumerian water god, Ea, who in the first days of Christianity was known as Oannes, or John. The festival's association with water probably explains why it is common to see bowls or barrels of water with bright yellow broom flowers, rose petals, and herbs set out on a windowsills or in a corner of the garden to collect the dew of Midsummer's Eve. The next morning, people wash their faces with the scented water to soak up the purifying powers (it is supposed to cure skin problems), and to cancel out any malignant effects from the witches flying about the night before. Country sayings connect the night to both fertility and the beginnings of fermentation in wine: *La notte di San Giovanni entra il mosto nel chicco,* literally, "The must [grape juice] enters the grape seed" on the night of San Giovanni, so that fermentation will begin.

It is hard these days to find a genuine celebration for San Giovanni, although the tiny hill town of Grello in northern Umbria has recently reinstituted an old *festa.* It is truly a small-town event that is unpretentious in the extreme. When we explained to the people of the town that we had driven from Todi, about an hour and a half south of Grello, they seemed stunned and behaved as if we had come from Como or Calabria, both many regions away. Rustic and naive the little festival may be, but it has all the hallmarks of the real thing.

The entire village—six hundred to seven hundred strong—turns out along with a number of visitors from neighboring towns. Most of the food in the piazza is carried there by girls or women from the kitchens of local houses. The menu is simple and genuinely Umbrian: bruschetta, saltless country bread rubbed with garlic and drizzled with extra-virgin green olive oil or topped with frutti del bosco, a mixture of wild mushrooms and tomatoes; pasta; sausages; pork ribs grilled over a big outdoor fire; and lots of bread and wine. People mill around or sit family-style at one of the tables in the piazza. The only other piazza in town stretches in front of the church, and it is full of people crowding around a big basket of panetti di San Giovanni, saltless rolls baked specially for the event, and a large barrel full of water in which broom flowers and rose petals are floating.

Once the sun has gone down, once mass has been said and the bread, firebrands, and water blessed, the fire festival begins. The main event is a race. Young boys, dressed in what look like fleecy lambswool togas, thrust forth firebrands (really straw brooms) that are lit by torches. Each boy, representing a neighborhood of little Grello, races three times around the old walls of the castle on the crest of the hill, holding his burning firebrand high, and then dashes back down to the piazza, where he lights an enormous pyramid of hay set on a wooden sled. Once the pile is ablaze, he and his five teammates set off at a dead run down the steep incline, pulling the heavy sled behind them. From the top of the hill we in town could see the burning haystacks flash through the fields as fans roared their approval. It wasn't long before the groups reappeared for the final sprint, panting and out of breath with their firebrands held high. Once the winning group had finished its sweep around the castle at the crest of the hill, the entire town rushed to congratulate them in a sudden maelstrom of cheering, yelling, and hugging. The winner lighted an enormous Midsummer Night's bonfire in the center of the piazza. A band arrived and the teenagers, who suddenly numbered in the hundreds (fires must bring them out from nearby towns), danced to rock music late into the night.

San Giovanni was once enthusiastically celebrated in Rome around the old basilica of San Giovanni Laterano, where the skull of the saint is buried. The emperor Constantine built the church to commemorate the triumph of the church over paganism, but the pagan spirit seems to triumph in the excesses of eating and drinking on the night of the twenty-third, the eve of the festival. Near the basilica today, strings of colored lights loop across the streets of the neighborhood. A great chunk of the population fills up the *osterie, trattorie,* and counters set out in the streets to feast on snails, lots of bread, and bottles of dry white wine from the Castelli Romani. The traditional snail feast, the *lumacata,* stems from a legend that people can take precautions against the Midsummer Eve witches and devils by eating snails. Why snails? Probably because their horns make them look like the devils that congregate along with vampires and witches on that night. For the dinner of San Giovanni, families used to carry pots overflowing with fat snails inside finely striped shells and gather in the green fields just beyond the basilica, singing, dancing, eating, and making an enormous rumpus to scare off the witches and devils. The big feast encouraged everyone to eat vast quantities, because the more snails they consumed, the fewer devils were left around to cause trouble.

Rome has almost no greenery anymore, but until the early part of this century, the entire neighborhood of San Giovanni Laterano was full of gardens and vineyards in which snails were common residents. Ada Boni, in her book *La Cucina Romana*, describes hawkers wandering through the streets with wicker baskets over their arms, lined with vine leaves and bread moistened with water, calling out, *"Da vigne le lumache,"* "Snails from the vineyards." To clean and cook them, the buyer left the snails for two days in a big basin full of water, a handful of salt, and a glass of vinegar, and kept changing the water until no more froth appeared. To this day the snails are prepared the same way, then boiled or braised in wine to make a thick, zesty sauce to which are added tomatoes, garlic, anchovies, and mentuccia, a field mint that grows in Lazio and Umbria.

At Ossuccio on the eve of San Giovanni, thousands of snail shells, emptied of their inhabitants, are filled with oil and tiny wicks and set to shimmer like candles on the waters of Lake Como. They light the way for a procession of boats bearing the relics of a martyr to a tiny island, Isola Comacina, where the ancient church of San Giovanni burned to the ground five centuries ago. The little flames are a reminder of the catastrophic fire, but they are also a symbol of San Giovanni, who is said to have come there once as a pilgrim.

The eating is a good deal more elaborate in Spilamberto, a small town in Emilia, near Modena, on the southern edge of the Po Valley. Each year as many as nine hundred producers enter a palio, a competition for which thirty trained judges sample entries in a contest devoted to aceto balsamico tradizionale, a rich, densely concentrated vinegar that is at least twelve years old and has more in common with wine than with the common condiment that gives it its name. Obviously this is no ordinary tasting. While bonfires burn on the hills around, the name of the winner is announced on June 24, the Feast Day of San Giovanni Battista. The lucky person whose vinegar has won the prize is honored in a sedate ceremony, then whisked off to a meal of bacchanalian proportions at a local restaurant, where throngs of enthusiastic eaters join in the fun.

Aceto balsamico is not made from wine, as most vinegars are, but from fresh grape juice (must) boiled and concentrated in a copper kettle. Nothing is added save for a tiny amount of very old strong vinegar before the mixture is aged in a series of small wooden casks for anywhere from twelve to one hundred years. Each cask is made of a different wood— chestnut, mulberry, oak, cherry, acacia, ash, and sometimes juniper. The casks rest in the heat of people's attics and each wood adds its flavor and color to the fermentation process until a deep ebony- or mahogany-colored, dense syrupy liquid is ready. Pungent, sweetly rich, and fragrant—aceto balsamico is more than a vinegar and more than a tonic. "To some [producers] it is art, passion, a way of life," writes Burton Anderson, an expert on Italian wine.

It is certainly a vinegar with a long and aristocratic history, worthy of celebration on Midsummer Night's Eve. Duke Boniface of Canossa presented a barrel of it to the Holy Roman Emperor Henry III in 1046. The Estes, the great ducal family of Modena and Ferrara, made gifts of it to important European heads of state, and served it as a balm and a cordial, much like a fine old brandy. Both Lucrezia Borgia and Gioachino Rossini swore by its healing properties. If wine was made by men, aceto balsamico was the province of the lady of the house and was usually included as part of a dowry. Until recently, it was never sold but made only for use at home and for giving to friends on special occasions.

Families still treat their rare vinegar with reverence and save it for special moments, although aceto balsamico has now been given official government recognition as a vinegar that is DOC, *denominazione di origine controllata,* just like wine, with prescribed methods of production and regional identification. The new groups and *consorzi* that oversee its manufacture are not without schisms, quarrels, and deviations, although peace of sorts reigns in Spilamberto on the night of San Giovanni for the contest judging the best balsamic vinegar of the year. Tensions and rancor dissolve in the medium that confers honor on food; course after course spills out of the kitchen, each flavored with the subtle, rich vinegar.

Witch, from an eighteenth-century wood engraving

Tagliatelle alla Boscaiola

~~~~~~~~~~~~~~~~~~~~~~~~~~~~~

Tagliatelle with Mushrooms and Olives

The tastes of the forests and hillsides of Umbria perfume this extraordinary pasta sauce. Mushrooms from the mountains and olives from the slopes of the countryside are wrapped around ribbons of delicate, freshly made tagliatelle. There is no trick to the very simple sauce. Just be sure to chop the olives very fine, since their rich, slightly salty flavor is essential— and use enough olive oil to coat the strands of the pasta.

Makes 6 to 8 first-course or 3 to 4 main-course servings

⅔ ounce (20 grams) dried porcini mushrooms
9 ounces (250 grams) fresh mushrooms
2 tablespoons (25 grams) butter
½ cup olive oil
Tagliatelle made with 2¼ cups unbleached all-purpose flour, 3 large
    eggs, and cold water (see instructions for making pasta on page 104)
About 4 ounces (100 grams) black olives, preferably oil-cured with
    herbs, pitted and finely chopped.
2 to 3 tablespoons chopped fresh flat-leaf parsley

Thirty minutes before you are ready to cook, soak the dried porcini mushrooms in warm water. Drain and save the water for another use. Put a large pot of well-salted water on to boil.

Wipe the fresh mushrooms with a damp cloth. Slice very fine, using a knife or food processor. In a 10- or 12-inch skillet heat the butter and half the oil. Add the fresh mushrooms and cook over medium heat until the mushrooms have released their juices and are soft, about 5 minutes. Add the drained porcini mushrooms and cook another 3 to 4 minutes.

Meanwhile, cook the fresh tagliatelle until done, about 1 ½ minutes. Take the pasta sauce off the fire and stir in the olives and parsley. Drain the pasta and toss it with the sauce and the rest of the olive oil.

Panini di San Giovanni

~~~~~~~~~~~~~~~~~~~~~~~~~~~~~~~~

Whole-Wheat Rolls

These whole-wheat rolls have a light, chewy crust, a soft interior crumb, and are full of the flavor of wheat. In Grello each one is stamped with an image of San Giovanni, but I like their surfaces lightly veined with flour.

(continued)

Makes 12 rolls

S P O N G E

1 teaspoon active dry yeast or ⅓ cake (6 grams) fresh yeast
1½ cups warm water
½ cup plus 2 tablespoons (150 grams) Biga (page 31)
About 1½ cups (200 grams) whole-wheat flour

By Hand. Stir the yeast into the warm water and let stand until creamy, about 10 minutes. Add the *biga*; stir vigorously with a wooden spoon and squeeze the starter between your fingers to break it up. Add the flour and stir well 2 to 3 minutes until you have a thick soupy batter. Cover with plastic wrap and let stand until very bubbly, about 1½ hours.

By Mixer. Stir the yeast into the water in a mixer bowl; let stand until creamy, about 10 minutes. Add the *biga* and mix with the paddle until it is broken up. Add the flour and mix well until you have a thick soupy batter. Cover with plastic wrap and let stand until very bubbly, about 1½ hours.

D O U G H

About 1½ cups (200 grams) whole-wheat flour
1 teaspoon (5 grams) salt

By Mixer. With the paddle attachment stir the flour and salt into the sponge; you may need to add 2 tablespoons flour to bring the dough together loosely. Change to the dough hook and knead on low speed 2 minutes, then on medium speed 2 minutes more. The dough is soft and sticky and never comes away from the sides of the bowl, although from time to time it looks as if it will. Finish kneading on a floured work surface.

First Rise. Set the dough in an oiled container, cover well with plastic wrap, and let rise until doubled, about 1 hour.

Shaping and Second Rise. Divide the dough into 12 equal pieces each about the size of a lemon. Shape each piece into a ball on a floured surface, then place them upside down on a well-floured surface about 3 inches apart. Cover with a towel and let rise until doubled, about 1 hour.

Baking. Thirty minutes before baking, heat the oven with baking stones in it to 400°F. Place the rolls floured side up on lightly oiled or parchment-lined baking sheets. Bake until lightly browned on top, 20 to 25 minutes. Cool on a rack.

Frittata al'Aceto Balsamico

~~~~~~~~~~~~~~~~~~~~~~~~~~~~~~~~~

Herb Frittata Drizzled with Balsamic Vinegar

Something magical happens to the taste of a simple frittata when aceto balsamico is drizzled over its surface. This recipe comes from Italo Pedroni, whose great-great-grandfather opened the Osteria di Rubbiara in Nonantola in 1862, and he and his wife, Franca, continue the family tradition.

Makes 4 servings

1 onion, finely sliced
4 tablespoons peanut or olive oil
10 eggs
1½ teaspoons chopped fresh rosemary leaves
2 fresh sage leaves, chopped
2½ teaspoons torn fresh basil leaves
½ teaspoon salt
1 tablespoon aged balsamic vinegar

Set the onion and oil in a 12-inch frying pan, turn the heat to medium, and sauté until the onion is translucent and becoming golden. In a bowl beat the eggs with the herbs and salt. Remove the onion from the pan with a slotted spoon, drain it well, and add it to the egg mixture.

Set the frying pan over medium-high heat and pour the egg mixture into it. As the edges begin to set, tilt the pan and lift the outer edges so the still runny eggs can run under. Turn the flame down to low and continue cooking until the eggs are golden brown underneath and quite well set on top, between 18 and 20 minutes. Put a large serving plate over the top of the pan and carefully invert the frittata. Slide it back into the frying pan, uncooked side down, and let it brown briefly 1 to 2 minutes to set on the second side. Remove to a serving platter.

Sprinkle the surface of the frittata evenly with the balsamic vinegar by holding the spoon about 6 inches above the frittata and tapping your finger against it as you move it uniformly over the top. Let the frittata sit a minute or two to amalgamate the flavors and serve.

Risotto e Pollo Al'Aceto Balsamico

Risotto and Chicken Flavored with Balsamic Vinegar

Here's an elegant and unlikely one-pot dish. Flavored by mushrooms and balsamic vinegar, the chicken cooks while the rice slowly becomes risotto.

Makes 4 to 6 servings

About 5 cups chicken broth
2 tablespoons olive oil
1 tablespoon butter
2 onions: 1 red, 1 yellow, finely sliced
1 young chicken, about 2½ to 3 pounds (1¼ kilograms), disjointed, in 8 pieces
10 ounces (300 grams) fresh mushrooms, sliced
4 tomatoes, peeled, seeded and chopped
2 tablespoons aged balsamic vinegar
1 pound 2 ounces (500 grams) Arborio or Carnaroli rice
Salt

Bring the chicken broth to a boil in a large pot.

In a heavy casserole heat the oil and butter and sauté the onions over medium heat until they are limp and translucent. Add the chicken and sauté until it is golden. Add the sliced mushrooms and cook over high heat for several minutes. Lower the flame, add the tomatoes, and cook until the chicken is about halfway done, 15 to 20 minutes. Add the balsamic vinegar and let it cook down to about half its original volume. Then add the rice, stirring and coating the rice grains thoroughly. Cook over medium heat as a risotto, adding a new ladleful of boiling broth as each previous one is thoroughly absorbed. Stir frequently to keep the chicken and rice from sticking to the bottom of the pot. Cook until the risotto is made, taste for salt, and serve.

Lumache di Vigna di San Giovanni

Snails for Saint John's Feast

For the eve of San Giovanni, people in Rome traditionally feast on mountains of snails served in a robust tomato sauce along with lots of country bread. This is no new passion. Columella wrote that the ancient Romans purposefully cultivated snails on the north walls of their farms where they fed on the moss. Cooks usually remove the garlic cloves when they add the anchovies, although I have chosen to leave them in. If you can find the small California *petit gris* snails put up by Enfant Riant, use them, as they are just right for this dish.

Makes 6 to 8 first-course or hors-d'oeuvre servings

4½ pounds (2 kilograms) fresh snails, or 2 cans (7 ounces each) small California *petit gris* snails (about 72); French snails are much larger; since 2 of the same-size cans hold 24 to 36 snails, you can halve them

½ cup olive oil

3 to 4 large cloves of garlic, finely minced

1 peperoncino (dried red chile), finely minced

1 full tablespoon anchovies beaten to a paste

¾ cup dry white wine

1 can (28 ounces, 794 grams) Italian plum tomatoes, drained, chopped, and liquid reserved, or 1½ pounds fresh tomatoes, peeled, seeded, and chopped

About 1 cup water

3½ tablespoons very finely minced fresh rosemary

3½ tablespoons very finely chopped fresh sage

Snails and a pot, nineteenth-century engraving

For the fresh snails: Purge the snails by setting them in a high-sided bucket with bran or cornmeal for 2 to 3 days, covered with a cloth. Then set them in a large pot of cold water with salt and vinegar for 2 days and change the water several times a day, always adding salt and vinegar, until there is no more froth. Wash them under running water and set the snails in a pan with cold water and salt and bring to a simmer over low heat. After about 5 minutes, turn up the flame and boil 10 minutes. Remove the snails with a slotted spoon, rinse again under cold water, and extract them from their shells.

If you are using canned snails start here: In a large heavy sauté pan warm the oil and lightly sauté the garlic and peperoncino over medium heat until the garlic is a pale golden color. Add the anchovy paste and cook about 5 minutes. Pour in the white wine and cook until it has almost evaporated. Stir in the tomatoes and enough tomato liquid and/or water to measure 1 cup. Simmer 45 minutes to 1 hour, stirring in additional water as necessary to keep the sauce thick but moist. Add the drained, fresh snails here, and cook at a very low simmer 20 to 25 minutes. Stir in the rosemary and sage and canned snails for the last 5 minutes. Serve immediately in bowls with lots of bread to dip into the sauce.

Coniglio al'Aceto Balsamico

Rabbit in a Balsamic Vinegar Sauce

Rabbit, wood engraving from Agricoltura volgare by Pietro Crescentino, 1511, Venice

Italo Pedroni and his wife, Franca Prampolini, of Nonantola have won the competition in Spilamberto for making the finest balsamic vinegar more frequently than any other contenders. Not only do they make the vinegar but they also create such delicious dishes as this rabbit luxuriating in its rich flavors.

Makes 4 to 6 servings

1 rabbit, 3½ to 4 pounds (1½ kilograms), fresh or thawed, disjointed
4 cups white wine
6 tablespoons plus 1 teaspoon white wine vinegar
¼ cup olive oil
1 onion, finely chopped
1 rib celery, finely chopped
About 3 or 4 fresh medium-sized (1 pound 2 ounces, 500 grams) tomatoes, peeled, seeded, and chopped, or canned Italian plum tomatoes
¼ cup (55 grams) butter
2½ cups meat broth
4 tablespoons finely chopped flat-leaf parsley
About 3½ tablespoons aged balsamic vinegar, or to taste
Salt and pepper

Five to six hours before you plan to cook the rabbit, marinate it in 2 cups white wine and the white wine vinegar. When you are ready to cook, drain and dry it well.

Warm the olive oil in a small frying pan and sauté the onion and celery over medium heat until limp and translucent. Add the chopped tomatoes, cook briefly, and set aside. Heat the butter in a large sauté pan and brown the rabbit pieces until they are golden. Add the remaining 2 cups white wine and boil until it has evaporated. Add the sautéed vegetables, enough meat broth to cover the mixture, and the parsley. Simmer about 35 minutes, then test to see if the meat is tender to the tip of a knife. How much balsamic vinegar you add depends on its strength. Add the initial amount and then start tasting; the mixture should be rich and flavorful, but the vinegar should never overwhelm the rabbit or call attention to itself. Simmer another 5 minutes and serve. You will probably have enough sauce to serve over pasta at another meal.

Insalata di Pane al Balsamico

~~~~~~~~~~~~~~~~~~~~~~~~~~~~~

Bread Salad Perfumed with Balsamic Vinegar

Here's a contradiction delicious to contemplate: a popular summer salad in Emilia-Romagna, humble in the extreme—made only of stale bread, tomatoes from the field, and simple country herbs—it gets its kick from balsamic vinegar, the food of kings. Why Tuscan bread for a dish from a region that is in the north? Because it was inspired by the Livornese dish called *troaio*.

Makes 4 servings

4 stale Tuscan rolls, split, or 4 thick slices stale Tuscan bread or any
    other rustic country bread
4 tomatoes, sliced very fine
2 tablespoons chopped fresh oregano
Salt and freshly ground pepper to taste
1 tablespoon plus 1 teaspoon aged balsamic vinegar
4 tablespoons extra-virgin olive oil

Soak the rolls or bread in water 15 minutes; drain and squeeze dry. Tear them into pieces. Put the bread in a bowl with the tomatoes, oregano, salt, pepper, vinegar, and oil and let them sit 1 to 2 hours so the flavors can mingle. Mix well and serve at room temperature.

Tortelli di Erbette

~~~~~~~~~~~~~~~~~~~~~~~~~~~~~

Pasta Filled with Ricotta and Swiss Chard

Legend has it that these tortelli, filled with greens and ricotta, have belonged to the midsummer Feast of San Giovanni in Parma since 1210, when they were served to celebrate a military victory over neighboring Casalmaggiore. Tortelli are sometimes called ravioli, but by any name they are still extremely popular and are served during dinners in the countryside on Midsummer's Eve. People used to stay at table outside long into the night, eating course after course. The tortelli are tradition-ally tiny and delicate, although I have eaten them as giant tortelloni. I must say it is much easier to make a few big ones than lots of smaller ones. You can serve them with melted butter and Parmesan cheese or with the tomato sauce included here.

(continued)

Makes 6 to 8 servings

FILLING

2 bunches fresh Swiss chard (1¾ to 2 pounds, 900 grams)
¾ pound (335 grams) fresh whole-milk ricotta, whirled in the food
    processor or put through a sieve
1 cup (100 grams) freshly grated Parmesan cheese
¼ cup (50 grams) unsalted butter, room temperature
1 egg
Large pinch freshly grated nutmeg
Salt and freshly ground black pepper to taste

Trim the chard, removing the thick stems, and wash the leaves very well.
Put them in a pot, using only the water that still remains on the leaves,
and cook until tender, 8 to 10 minutes. Drain and squeeze dry. Chop
the chard fine. Mix thoroughly the chard, the ricotta, Parmesan, butter,
egg, nutmeg, salt, and pepper. The filling should be thick. Be sure it is
cool before you use it. You can refrigerate it 4 to 8 hours.

PASTA

2½ cups (350 grams) unbleached all-purpose flour
Pinch salt
4 large eggs
A little cold water or milk if needed

By Hand. Combine the flour and salt and set in a mound on a work
surface. Make a well in the center, beat the eggs together, and pour into
the well. Work the flour into the eggs from the sides of the well with a
fork and knead until you have a soft dough.

By Processor. Set the flour and salt in the bowl with the steel blade and
pulse several times to mix. With the motor running, pour the eggs down
the feed tube and mix only until the dough has come together loosely
around the blade. If the dough is too stiff, add a little cold water. Remove
the dough from the bowl and knead on a lightly floured work surface
about 3 minutes.

Gather the dough into a ball, cover with plastic wrap, and let rest 15
to 30 minutes.

To roll out. Using a pasta machine, take a piece of dough about the size of an egg and roll up through the next to last setting. The pasta should be firm and silky but not extremely delicate, so the ravioli don't break open in cooking. Trim the sheet of pasta so that it is about 4 inches wide. If you are making tortelli, use 1 teaspoon filling and set 2 inches apart. If you are making tortelloni, use 1 tablespoon filling and set 4 inches apart. Just before covering with the second sheet of pasta, moisten all the edges on the bottom sheet with a pastry brush dipped in water. Roll out a second piece of pasta in the same way and cover the first. Cut between the mounds of filling with a knife or pastry wheel. Press down around the edges of each piece to enclose it tightly. Finish the process using all the pasta dough and filling. Put the ravioli on a tray or cookie sheet covered with a tea towel and make the sauce.

SAUCE

2 tablespoons olive oil
4 tablespoons butter
1 large red onion, very finely minced
Salt and pepper to taste
⅓ cup white wine
1 can (28 ounces, 794 grams) Italian plum tomatoes, finely chopped and
    well drained
Several sprigs fresh rosemary or sage leaves
2 tablespoons hot water, plus more if needed
⅓ cup heavy cream

In a medium sauté pan heat the oil and butter and sauté the onion very, very slowly over low heat until golden, about 20 minutes. Add the salt and pepper, then bathe with white wine and cook until it evaporates. Add the tomatoes, rosemary or sage, cover, and cook over low heat 35 to 40 minutes. Check the sauce from time to time as it cooks and add the initial 2 tablespoons water to keep it moist. It may be necessary to add a little more water. At the very end of the cooking remove the herb sprigs, stir in the cream, heat 2 to 3 minutes, and serve over the pasta.

Cooking. You can keep the ravioli in the refrigerator covered with a tea towel or plastic wrap for several hours. Otherwise they can be cooked immediately. Bring a large pot of water to the boil, add 1 tablespoon salt and the ravioli, and cook until tender, 3 to 5 minutes.

RACCOLTO DEL GRANO

WHEAT HARVEST
IN THE VAL DI CHIANA
The End of June

*I*n the agricultural drama of the year, the end of June is a time of transition as the grain is harvested. Men with scythes once sliced the sheaves to earth, then teams of white oxen pulled harvesting machines up the hills; but now motorized harvesters buzz and hum across the quiet landscape. The pattern of their tracks leaves whorls in the dry golden fields that look like giant thumbprints. Sheaves of wheat lie cut and fallen, ready for the thresher.

In days before machinery overtook ritual, men threshed the wheat stalks by hand on the *aie,* stone threshing floors, or courtyards of farmhouses. They beat them with thick sticks to separate the wheat from the straw. What became straw was piled in the fields around a thick central pole and formed like a cone standing higher than a man, or shaped like a small house from which farmers cut off wedges and chunks whenever straw was needed. What wasn't straw was the grain that they sieved to separate the wheat from the chaff.

While the men were busy threshing, the women were cooking an enormous dinner to celebrate the gathering in of the grain. Families went from house to house during the threshing time, helping each other as their grain fields were ready, so that sometimes an entire month was spent out of doors. When it was all over at each property, everyone sat down to a dinner consisting of many courses always based on geese, ducks, capons, and rabbits, no matter where in Italy the harvest took place. Often the women arrived in the fields balancing the dishes on their heads, but they didn't eat with the men and boys who had done all the work. Tables were set up in the fields and tablecloths thrown over them—for the fifty or sixty people who sat down to plunge their forks into many courses and drink vast quantities of wine. Wheels of country bread were placed right on the tables, a sign of the blessings of the earth. There was lots of singing, and sometimes a kind of rhyming contest in which people competed in making up relevant verses on an impromptu topic chosen that afternoon.

The gargantuan meals were a major reward for a major physical effort. During the actual harvest, they were often provided by the owners of the land. Usually, however, the meals came at the end of the harvest, when there was time for celebration. In the earlier part of the twentieth century families in the Val di Chiana of southern Tuscany brought forth similar meals. They were almost always based on young ducks and geese, raised only on the grain as it grew. There was fresh pasta, usually hand-rolled pici, tossed with a rich ragù of duck or goose. Next came an ingenious bit of charcuterie made by chopping the goose or duck liver, mixing it with carrots, onions, and garlic—sometimes even pistachio nuts—and then rolling it like a plump sausage into the skin of the neck. The ducks and geese were stewed or roasted and served with spinach, or salad, or fried artichokes and zucchini. Dessert was usually a simple tart made with a layer of homemade jam or fruit.

Today, once the grain harvest is over in Umbria, there are workers who move on to Abruzzo where there is more grain to be cut and then olives to be picked. But even as far south as Abruzzo, the meal barely changes: pasta alla chitarra, a fine egg pasta cut on the tensile strings of a local guitarlike culinary instrument, is served with a sauce made from duck. Next come grilled chickens, and for dessert there are amaretti the size of dinner plates to be dipped in wine, like biscotti.

Farther south yet, in Calabria, an abundance of rich food was a rarity in the lives of workers who needed strength for days of hard work. Sardines, stockfish, meat, and salad appeared infrequently, like mirages. The meat was usually goat, but it certainly wasn't veal, since an animal would have to be butchered especially for that meal.

Every early culture believed in the powers of a grain goddess who protected the fields and made them fruitful. In Greece Demeter's Eleusinian mysteries celebrated life growing in an ear of corn and a sheaf of wheat. The Romans looked on Demeter and on her daughter, Persephone, as emblems of fertile life and its barren, depleted underside. The goddess Diana of Ephesus, whose many breasts fell like a grape cluster from her neck to her waist, represented the Great Nourishing Mother.

When the Church was confronted with these pagan feminine forces, it assimilated and spiritualized them. Gradually the goddess of grain was

*Sheaf of wheat,
nineteenth-century
engraving*

The Grain Harvest,
copper engraving by Luigi
Doria Romano, from
Elementi della
coltivazione del grano,
eighteenth century

transformed into the Virgin Mary, protectress of fertility. When the Virgin appeared as a corn goddess, swathed in ears of corn, to a medieval merchant in Milan, he was so thrilled with her promise of abundance that he commissioned a painting of his vision to hang in the Duomo in Milan. At Montevergine, south of Naples, where a sanctuary of the Great Mother Cybele once stood, the Virgin was painted with a pomegranate, ancient symbol of abundance.

It was Mary's son, Jesus, who imitated the ritual cycle of growth, beginning with his sacrifice and ending with his resurrection from the soil. He was sacrificed like Osiris, who was cut into fourteen pieces and thrown into the earth, and from the flesh of Osiris wheat and vines and plants grew again.

Threshing and the *vendemmia,* the harvest of grain and grapes, are two great agricultural moments of the year, full of significance, in which are produced the bread and wine that are the symbols of Christianity as well as of Ceres' wheat and Bacchus' grapes. In Italy grain festivals are relatively few and seem not to include ritual foods, although the Sicilian cities of Agrigento and Aragona celebrate the Festa of San Calogero at the beginning of July with offerings of grain and bread. Earlier in the century six sets of white oxen pulled a carriage full of grain offerings through Agrigento. Nowadays when the statue of the saint makes its way through the streets, people throw at it hundreds of pieces of bread shaped like parts of the body—legs and arms, feet and heads, breasts and hands, all of them to be blessed by the priest and given to the poor or the faithful. These edible ex-votos recall the time of an epidemic when San Calogero made a circuit of the town in search of food for the sick. He asked people who were quarantined at home to toss breads right out of their windows, whereupon he collected them and fed them to the sick. In Aragona each year, bakers make fifty kilograms of ex-votos from white bread sprinkled with sesame seeds, instead of the traditional durum-flour loaves dotted with poppy seeds. In Foglianise, near Benevento in Campania, the harvest is celebrated by making immense sculptures of straw and sheaves of wheat and rolling them through the streets on flatbeds. These floats, the Parthenon, an entire Gothic cathedral, and Moses with the Ten Commandments, are images of abundance, consecrating and celebrating the fruits of the harvest, as well as magical invocations that are meant to pacify the forces that slumber in the darkness of the earth.

Collo di Anatra Ripieno
~~~~~~~~~~~~~~~~~~~~~~~~~~

*Duck Neck
Stuffed Like a
Sausage, from
Southern Tuscany*

The Tuscans, who waste nothing, invent ingenious charcuterie from unlikely scraps. When duck is the centerpiece of dinner, they save the skin from the neck, fill it with a rich mixture based on the liver, simmer it in broth, and serve it forth with warm boiled potatoes.

Makes 4 to 6 servings

Necks of 2 ducks
1 ounce (30 grams) bread
¼ cup warm milk
1 to 1½ tablespoons olive oil
½ onion, chopped
1 clove garlic, minced
1 duck liver
1 tablespoon chopped flat-leaf parsley
Nutmeg to taste
1½ teaspoons grated Parmesan cheese
Salt and pepper to taste
Chicken broth to cover

With a sharp paring knife, carefully remove the necks of the ducks from their skins. Save the skins as casings. Soak the bread in the warm milk. Warm the olive oil in a small heavy-bottomed sauté pan and slowly sauté the onion until it is pale and translucent. Add the garlic and let it soften, but be sure it doesn't brown or burn. Put the softened bread and the duck liver in a food processor fitted with the steel blade and grind the two together. Add the onion mixture, parsley, nutmeg, Parmesan, salt, and pepper; mix well.

Lay the skins from the duck necks on a flat surface, put half the stuffing mixture down the center of each duck skin, and close each with a skewer and string.

Bring the chicken broth to a boil in a medium-sized saucepan. Add the sausages and simmer 10 to 15 minutes. Remove the sausages from the pan, cut in slices, and serve with warm boiled potatoes.

Collo Ripieno dell'Oca

~~~~~~~~~~~~~~~~~~~~~~~~~~~~~~~~~~

*Stuffed
Goose Neck*

When goose was the center of the threshing dinner in southern Tuscany, it turned up in every course. Goose became sauce for the pasta, a roast for the main course, and pieces of it were even rolled into a sausage studded with pistachio nuts. Such elegant refinements appeared on the table at which Daria Lucherini of La Chiusa, in Montefollonico, grew up.

Makes 8 servings

1 goose neck
1 teaspoon olive oil
½ carrot, chopped
3½ ounces (100 grams) finely ground veal
1 goose liver, chopped
15 pistachio nuts, shelled
1 egg
Salt and pepper to taste
2 tablespoons grated Parmesan cheese

Remove the bone from the goose neck and use the skin as a container.

Heat the oil in a heavy sauté pan and sauté the carrot until it is cooked but still maintains a very slight crunch. Cool. Mix together the carrot, veal, goose liver, nuts, egg, salt, pepper, and Parmesan cheese. Fill the skin of the goose neck with this mixture, then close it with skewers and string. Poke it with a fork, so that it doesn't explode as it cooks.

Simmer it for 10 to 15 minutes in a broth of:

1 onion
1 carrot
1 rib celery
6 peppercorns
Enough water to cover

Serve sliced at warm room temperature with a mayonnaise-like sauce made with grated hard-boiled egg, pecorino, parsley, and olive oil.

Pici

Hand-Rolled
Spaghetti from
Southern Tuscany

*Sheaf of triticum wheat,
nineteenth-century
engraving*

Pici are a kind of homemade spaghetti as thin as the tips of shoelaces. I first encountered them in Montepulciano and Pienza, two small cities in southern Tuscany, where they used to be served during the wheat harvest. I learned how to make them from Ermendina Lorenzoni, a woman who learned from her mother and grandmother, and who still cooks them for a harvest dinner in July.

The dough for pici is soft and springy and easy to work with. After it rests, it can be stretched and pulled out to the desired length, just as if you were making breadsticks. Even so, making them is very time-consuming. Make pici with a friend or, although not traditional, try rolling the dough through the second widest setting of a pasta machine and then cutting it into thin strips on the fettuccine cutter. You will still need to stretch each noodle by hand to make it twice as long (and therefore half as thick). Signora Lorenzoni rolls out her dough with a rolling pin, although for this amount I just pat it into a 1-inch-high lump. She washes the top with olive oil and then sets a tea towel moistened with hot water on top and lets it rest for 40 minutes.

Makes 8 servings

3¾ cups plus 2 tablespoons (500 grams) unbleached all-purpose flour
1 cup water
⅓ cup olive oil
1 egg
Salt

Put all the ingredients in the bowl of the electric mixer and, using the paddle attachment, mix until the dough comes together. Change to the dough hook and knead 5 minutes on medium speed. The dough is silky smooth and resilient. Set it on a lightly floured work surface, flatten with your palm, wrap in plastic wrap or oil the top, and wrap in a tea towel moistened with hot water. Let it rest at least ½ hour.

Cut the dough in very thin pieces and roll each about 8 to 10 inches long and ⅛ inch thick. They must be very thin because they puff up in cooking. Roll them once, set them in a granular flour like Wondra, let them rest, and then roll them again. They will shrink back initially, but let them rest and roll to the desired thinness a second time. If you prefer to use a pasta machine, roll the dough twice through the next to thickest setting. Cut with a fettuccine cutter into thin ribbons. Immediately toss them with a granulated flour like Wondra and then separate them and pull each out to twice its original length. Cook in abundant well-salted boiling water with a splash of oil 3 to 5 minutes.

Pici con Ragù d'Oca

~~~~~~~~~~~~~~~~~~~~~~~~~~~~~

Pasta with Goose Ragù

This recipe begins with the drippings and giblets of a goose that has already been roasted, but you could also use stray chicken giblets and frozen drippings. Serve the goose, if you have it, for the main course, but use its drippings and its giblets to make an elegant pasta sauce.

Makes 4 servings

6 tablespoons olive oil
1 red onion, finely chopped
1 carrot, finely chopped
1 rib celery, finely chopped
Giblets from 1 goose, duck, or chicken, uncooked, excluding the liver
2 cloves garlic, minced
2 fresh sage leaves
6 fresh basil leaves
½ teaspoon fresh thyme or ¼ teaspoon dried thyme
1½ tablespoons chopped parsley
1 cup red wine
4 large ripe tomatoes, seeded and chopped, or 1 can (28 ounces, 794 grams) Italian tomatoes, drained
About ¾ cup drippings and gravy from the roasted goose or duck or chicken, previously cooked to thicken slightly and then degreased
½ recipe Pici (see page 111)

Warm the olive oil in a large sauté pan and add the onion, carrot, celery, and finely chopped goose giblets until they have browned lightly. Add the garlic and herbs and let them wilt but not brown. Add the wine and let it cook down over high heat until it has evaporated. Add the tomatoes and cook until they are thick. Add the drippings and gravy from the roast goose and cook 5 to 10 minutes. Serve over pici.

Geese and ducks, wood engraving from Agricoltura volgare *by Pietro Crescentino, 1511, Venice*

Ragù d'Anatra

Duck Sauce for
Pasta

and

Anatra
in Umido

Braised Duck

Two rich and deeply flavored dishes made in one pot from one duck produce the better part of dinner. Toss the pasta with the duck sauce to begin the meal and serve the duck for the main course.

Makes 6 to 8 servings

1 ounce (25 grams) dried porcini mushrooms
4 tablespoons olive oil (the original recipe calls for lard)
1 onion, finely chopped
1 carrot, finely chopped
1 rib celery, finely chopped
2 cloves garlic, finely minced
1 duck liver, finely minced, optional
1 to 2 tablespoons chopped flat-leaf parsley
2 fresh sage leaves, torn or chopped
1 duck, 4 to 5 pounds (2 kilograms), cut into 8 serving pieces
½ cup beef broth, heated
Scant ½ pound (200 grams) ground pork
½ peperoncino (dried red chile), minced, with seeds removed
⅔ cup white wine
⅔ cup red wine
2 to 3 drops vinegar
1½ cans (28 ounces, 794 grams each) Italian plum tomatoes, chopped
Salt and pepper to taste

Soak the dried mushrooms in a bowl of lukewarm water 30 minutes. When they have softened, drain the mushrooms and filter the water through paper toweling. Rinse the mushrooms and slice them. Heat 3 tablespoons oil in a heavy skillet over medium heat; add the onion, carrot, and celery and cook until they soften and turn pale and golden. Add the garlic, duck liver, parsley, and sage; sauté briefly until they are coated with the oil but not browned or burned. Remove the vegetable mixture with a slotted spoon and set aside. In the same pan warm the remaining 1 tablespoon oil and brown the duck well. Pour off as much fat as possible, return the vegetable mixture to the pan, pour in the heated beef broth, cover, and cook over very low heat about 1 hour. Turn the duck from time to time so that it cooks evenly. At the end of the hour, add the ground pork and peperoncino; cover and cook 20 minutes. Uncover, add both wines and the vinegar and cook until they evaporate. Add the porcini mushrooms. Add the tomatoes and cook 10 minutes, then cover and cook until the sauce is thick and rich. Season with salt and pepper and remove the duck. Serve the duck at room temperature for the main course and serve this sauce over Pici (page 111).

FESTINO DI SANTA ROSALIA

FEAST OF SAINT ROSALIA IN PALERMO
July 13, 14, 15

*I*l Festino, the great Feast of Santa Rosalia, was once one of the most elaborate events in all of Europe. It began as a three-day extravaganza that eventually stretched to five, even eight days of baroque celebration. It was so splendid, its pavilions and triumphal carts and great fireworks so magnificent, its promenade so gloriously decorated for the *passeggiata* of nobility that spectators couldn't get enough of it. In his account of an aristocratic childhood in Sicily, Fulco di Verdura wrote that for one evening vesper service, "the whole church appeared a flame of light, which reflected from ten thousand bright and shining surfaces, of different colors and at different angles, [and] produced an effect which, I think, exceeds all the descriptions of enchantment I have ever read." No wonder Francesco Domenico Guerrazzi, the nineteenth-century Italian patriot and writer, told travelers to "go to Switzerland for trout, to Lisbon to drink port wine, to London for horse races, and to Palermo to be part of the festival of Santa Rosalia."

While its current incarnation can hardly be expected to re-create those heady days, the *festino* still has traces of the great experience that lured travelers. Crowds still jam the streets of Palermo on July 13 to see the triumphal chariot, a modern copy of an original seventeenth-century cart, which looks like a great golden galleon set on a copper-colored seashell. It is ringed with life-sized images of prisoners tied to posts, reminders of cataclysmic battles with Turks in earlier centuries. Six horses pull the cart and inside it, in ascending rows, sits an entire orchestra of forty musicians in brilliant pink and lavender velvet costumes complete with tricorne hats, playing their music under the hot July sun.

Palermo itself is ablaze with a lacework of lights. Santa Rosalia, the patron saint of the city, clearly holds a special place in the hearts of the people, who have affectionately nicknamed her *La Santuzza,* the little saint. Once a year they celebrate her miraculous intervention that saved the city from the Black Plague. Legend says that Rosalia was the daughter of Duke Sinibaldo, Lord of the Quisquina and the Roses, who was a cousin of King William II of Sicily, who ruled over a sumptuous court. Like Saint Francis of Assisi, Rosalia turned her back on a life of ease and chose to devote herself to prayer and solitude. The legend says that in 1159 she retired to a hermetic existence in a remote cave on Monte Pellegrino, the rocky cliff high above the Bay of Palermo. Nothing was heard of her again until 1624, when the plague arrived in Sicily and decimated Palermo's population. The saints normally charged with protecting the city—Agata, Olivia, Christina, and Ninfa—were total failures at stopping its ravages.

Salvation came in the unexpected form of La Santuzza, who appeared in a vision to a hunter lost on Monte Pellegrino. "Don't worry," she is supposed to have said to him as he wandered buffeted by an enormous thunderstorm. "I will protect you and I will protect the city." She revealed to him the site of the cave in which she had lived as a hermit and told him to go back to Palermo and alert the archbishop and rulers of the city. The hunter did as he was told, and those leaders found her remains and paraded them through the streets of Palermo between huge candles and great masses of flowers. Within three days, says one version of the story, or six months, according to another, the plague ended, and she was proclaimed patron saint of the city.

Triumphal Cart of Santa Rosalia designed by Don Paolo Amato for the Festino of 1701, model for the current Triumphal Cart, eighteenth-century engraving

Triumphal Cart for the Festa of 1741, eighteenth-century engraving

The centerpiece of the celebration each year was a triumphal cart, a massive piece of elaborate architecture on wheels. In some years it was like an enormous warship with waves crashing over the prow, and angels and *putti* standing on top of columns balustrades, cornices, pedestals, pilasters, and garlanded columns. In other years the cart resembled a gigantic moving fortress, or even an enormous Sicilian cassata, which sometimes held an altar but always had an entire orchestra seated inside it. Patrick Brydone noted with amazement in 1773 that Santa Rosalia's triumphal cart was "a most enormous machine; it measures seventy feet long, thirty feet wide and upwards of eighty high, and, as it passed along, overtopped the loftiest houses of Palermo . . . the front assumes an oval shape like an amphitheatre, with seats placed in the theatrical man-ner. . . . Over the orchestra, and a little behind it, there is a large dome supported by six Corinthian columns, and adorned with a number of figures of saints and angels; and on the summit of the dome there is a gigantic silver statue of St. Rosalia. The whole machine is dressed out with orange-trees, flower-pots, and trees of artificial coral. . . . It ap-peared to be a moving castle and completely filled the great street from side to side. This vast fabric was drawn by fifty-six huge mules, in two rows, curiously caparisoned, and mounted by twenty-eight postillions dressed in gold and silver stuffs, with great plumes of ostrich feathers in their hats." The cart was so tall that it could catch balcony railings and tear them away from their buildings.

During the seventeenth and eighteenth centuries, the triumphal cart changed each year, growing larger and more elaborate. At one point it was so opulent that it was called "the little mountain of gold." By the nineteenth century, the cart had taken on some sort of subliminal con-nection with the culinary arts. An observer one year wrote with wonder that "the hulls looked like elegant silver sauce boats overflowing with spices of every color, shape, and type, and the top seemed like a huge wedding cake with layers sloping upward, sprinkled with floral decorations made of exquisite confetti and candied fruit." At the top stood a statue of the bride, for Santa Rosalia, all in white, was a little saint who looked like a second Madonna. The great wooden cart itself was so heavy that it took fifty white oxen to pull it along. Its iron wheels set off sparks that could take fire at any moment so brigades of men lined up along the streets throwing water at them to keep the heat under control.

For years the festival of Santa Rosalia was a sumptuous display of Palermo's supreme power over all the other cities on the island, but the event began to lose its popularity in 1860, when Italy was unified, and the authorities, leery of promoting any more Church power in the state, prohibited the construction of the triumphal cart. Even the efforts of Giuseppe Pitrè, Sicily's foremost ethnologist, to resuscitate the tradition in 1895 failed and Santa Rosalia's festival lost its popular following. Twenty-five or thirty years ago, when there weren't so many diversions, the festival was an important event in Palermo, but now there is grumbling that the city spends too much money on the event and that most of the people who line the streets are poor and ardent believers.

Although diminished from the days of its glory, the *festino* of Santa Rosalia provides an unparalleled opportunity for decorating Palermo with lights. The city is especially spectacular by night, when thousands of lights wheel across each street in completely different patterns: canopies of tiny white lights like thousands of raindrops arch across several blocks of the Boulevard Ruggero Settimo; the Via Maqueda is full of wriggly arabesques in hot Brazilian colors; the Piazza Politeama blazes with brilliant chunks of light that look like the jewelry of Russian empresses. The city is lit up for two major events of the holiday: the procession of the triumphal cart to the sea and the spectacular fireworks at the Foro Italico on the water.

People arrive from all over Sicily early in great numbers on July 13 to see the parade of the triumphal cart. During their wait and over the following days, they pass the time milling around, eating the traditional street foods of Palermo. Painted carts and counters are full of semenza and calia, nuts and seeds that together are called *passatempi* because eating them is a pastime in itself, especially since many require you to crack them between your teeth to extract the treasure within. The carts are painted to look like old Sicilian carts with folk motifs of Roger and the French paladins and one even has a winsome portrait of Santa Rosalia reclining dreamily above its wonderful display. She presides over pyramids of roasted fava beans, delicate nutty garbanzos, chunky pods of carob,

View of the Palazzo in Palermo with a reconstruction of the Campidoglio of Rome for fireworks display with Triumphal Cart in 1711, eighteenth-century engraving

lupini beans, salted pumpkin seeds, roasted hazelnuts, American peanuts, barley candies, and i cruzzidi, dried chestnuts to suck on. Food sellers used to have carts made especially for the Festa of Santa Rosalia. They were shaped like sailing ships, divided into compartments, and they were decorated with red, blue, and green flags that flew over the display of nuts and seeds. There were even triumphal carts made entirely of sugar that hung in pastry shops, but they have become relics now, memorializing a Palermo of the past. Here and there men sell acqua zammu, thirst-quenching water flavored with a few drops of anise, and offer watermelon, corn on the cob, and slices of coconut kept moist under little jets of water.

The current cart is nothing so grand as those of previous centuries, although in its great shiplike form it does echo those earlier incarnations. The parade itself begins near the cathedral, whose multiple architectural layers are a brief cultural history of the city. Begun as a basilica, later transformed by the Arabs into a mosque and then returned to Christian worship by the Normans, the cathedral sits in a great green open space, its lozenge-shaped majolica-tiled roofs sparkling in the hot summer sun. Inside, a great silver urn holding Santa Rosalia's bones is surrounded by worshipers who come to pray before it, by women who blow kisses to it and hold out their babies to touch it for good luck. It will travel along the arc of the Corso to the sea.

The procession begins. *Carabinieri* on horseback holding gleaming silver swords and representatives of the old maritime republics in Renaissance dress are followed closely by the cart of Santa Rosalia with the band busily playing music. It works its way along the broad Corso to the Quattro Canti, the dramatic piazza formed by four castles that meet at two richly ornamented crossroads. Their four façades are sculpted with balconies, cornices, windows, fountains, and niches that hold sculptures of the four female saints who were unable to save the city from the Plague. The parade progresses slowly to the sea, followed by masses of people, including faithful worshipers shuffling along on bare feet as a devotion to the saint. Soon people begin to leave, lured by the pastry shops and *gelaterie* all along the route. The parade ends with a band concert at the Porta Felice, and many people who have lasted long enough set off purposefully down the slight incline to the Marina.

More likely than not, they are in search of ice cream. The artisanal ice cream makers at the Foro Italico create the gelati that have inspired a veritable cult in the people of Palermo. Only two of the original makers remain, their shops set in what were once the stables of the Palazzo Reale. There, in the heat of summer, people sit at tables of the old caffès overlooking the sea (a huge amusement park and a highway full of fast-moving cars interrupt what was once a spectacular and romantic view) and eat ice cream that was set in a mold and cut into individual slices called *pezzi duri*, hard pieces. The most famous combinations include pezzo duro di giardiniera, a delicate, fresh-tasting combination of lemon and strawberry, and another that blends strawberries and cream. The ice cream flavors are incredible: black mulberry, jasmine with a tiny hint of cinnamon, even watermelon ice cream, which is as pink as bubblegum. Other specialties of the season include gelo di melone, which looks a bit like a naif artist's impression of a scoop of watermelon ice set into a little paper cup. Cold it may be, but an ice it is not. It is made by sieving watermelon pulp and mixing it with a little cornstarch so that it becomes as thick as pudding. Its delicate pink flesh tastes intensely of the fruit. Dot it with bits of unsweetened chocolate that look like seeds, sprinkle its surface with the pale green of chopped pistachio, chill it for several hours, and you have a refreshing, barely sweetened delicacy. The traditional dessert eaten during Santa Rosalia, gelato di campagna, more than makes up by assaulting the sweet tooth. Regardless of what its name suggests, it is not ice cream but a construction of multiflavored fondants resembling an ice cream cake with four layers: white (almond paste), brown (hazelnut paste), green (pistachio paste), and pink (strawberry paste), set in a mold studded with pistachios and with candied fruits folded in. It is a triumphant trompe l'oeil as well as a definite example of the Sicilian passion for excess.

Such ice cream was a bewildering discovery for the provincial Sicilians. Many first visited Palermo during the festival to fulfill a promise frequently made by husbands to bring wives to the *festino* within the first year of their marriage. A story is told of a Sicilian peasant, newly arrived in Palermo, who was so enchanted with his discovery of ice cream that he wrapped a bit in his handkerchief to eat when he returned home.

If the parade on July 13 is the high point of the *festino* for people who are devoted to Santa Rosalia, the fireworks on the night of July 14 draw thousands of spectators who come solely for the show. Everyone streams down to the sea, in groups of all sizes, until a wall of humanity makes it hard to proceed any further. People line the wide road along the waterfront, crowd into the narrower alleys and streets, and spill out of doorways. Families jam every balcony. They slowly eat babbaluci, garlic- and parsley-flavored snails so tiny that it takes a toothpick and great deal of patience to coax each one out of its shell.

The fireworks are called the *gioco dei fuochi*, the "play of fire." When Carlo Levi saw the fireworks in the 1950s, he was enchanted that there was nothing of "work about them, and nothing artful or artificial; they are, so to speak, aerial games, free movements of the soul, a spontaneous and tumultuous expression. . . ." He watched the thick mass of people below him, and then watched three competitive groups, each with a great reputation, compete against one another with fireworks displays to see who could make the greatest splash in the sky.

What he saw then, and what I saw years later, was an incredible exhibit of light and sound that exploded in patterns and crashing assaults of color and noise for almost two hours. The fireworks exploded all over the sky and lit up the sea where hundreds of boats bobbed on the water and exploded with sounds so loud that they sucked the breath right out of my chest. The rhythm of the explosions built to a crescendo. Levi wrote: "The glittering lights grew ever more compact, like an army of horses let loose in the overwhelming whirl of an avalanche. . . . archaic, fierce, barbarous, gory, this play of fire went on breathlessly, to its end, louder and louder, steadily increasing, endlessly multiplied, on and on, almost unendurable . . . to its grand final explosion."

Slowly the crowd came back to the actual world. Slowly people moved back to the streets, the sound of voices returning, sleepy-eyed children hanging on to their parents' hands, teenagers streaming across the broad roadway to the amusement park. The stream of humanity made its way home to whatever sleep it would find before the long solemn procession in the afternoon when the reliquary of the saint finds its way back to the cathedral and "her virgin bed."

The *festino* once ended with a procession of floats decorated with statues of saints and angels. There is no such charming finish to the current *festino,* although the procession bearing the great silver reliquary winds its way through the city of Palermo until the small hours of morning. By midnight I was very tired and confess that I crept back to my hotel room, stretched out on the bed, turned on the television, and watched the entire event come to a slow finish in the darkness of night.

Caponata di Melanzane

Eggplant Caponata

The Feast of Santa Rosalia occurs in mid-July, when the summer heat of Palermo is at its most intense. In midday the streets are empty, the piazze still and shadowless, while people make lunch of the traditional foods of the city. When the old rich families of Palermo went to the sea for the Festa of Santa Rosalia, they took with them this slightly piquant tomato-laced caponata. It is still a popular dish all year long. Because it isn't particularly appealing to look at, I like to give it some color by serving it on a bed of lettuce leaves or as an hors d'oeuvre on crackers topped with a sprinkling of chopped almonds.

No one is quite certain of the origin of the word *caponata*, although Giuseppe Coria suggests in *Profumi di Sicilia* that it comes from the Latin *caupo*, tavern, or *cauponae*, the Roman dives in front of inns that encouraged passersby to come in, so caponata becomes tavern food. Instead Mary Taylor Simeti believes that its beginnings were more nautical, since the vinegar that preserved the ingredients made it perfect oceangoing food.

Makes 4 to 6 servings

2 eggplants (about 2½ to 3 pounds, 1 kilogram, in all)
Salt
1 cup olive oil
2 ribs celery
⅓ pound (150 grams) green olives, pitted
5 tablespoons capers
1 large red onion, sliced
2 large fresh tomatoes, seeded and chopped
1 tablespoon tomato paste dissolved in ⅓ cup warm water
¾ tablespoon sugar
2 tablespoons red wine vinegar
3 tablespoons toasted almonds, chopped very fine

Peel the eggplants, slice into rounds, salt, and set them in a colander for an hour to drain off the bitter juices. Pat them dry, cut into dice, and sauté in ¾ cup oil until golden brown. Drain on absorbent paper. Set them aside. Meanwhile, cut the celery into 1-inch-long strips and boil them 5 to 6 minutes in salted water. Warm the remaining ¼ cup olive oil in the pan in which you sautéed the eggplant, add the celery and pitted olives, and sauté briefly. Stir in the capers, onion, tomatoes, and dissolved tomato paste; cook over low heat 10 to 15 minutes. Cool. Dissolve the sugar in the wine vinegar and add to the caper-tomato mixture.

Scoop the eggplant mixture into a large bowl and ladle the other ingredients over the top. Mix them together and correct the salt. You may refrigerate 24 hours. Serve sprinkled with the chopped almonds.

Babbaluci

xxxxxxxxxxxxxxxxxxxxxxxxxxxxxxxx

Tiny Garlic-
Flavored Snails

You need a toothpick and lots of patience to eat the tiny snails that everyone snacks on while waiting for the fireworks to begin at the Festa of Santa Rosalia. The snails are collected from the leaves of lemon and orange trees, boiled, and served in the shell with a delicious garlic and parsley sauce. They are easy to buy in Palermo, where canvas sacks are heaped high with them in great outdoor markets. The name *babbaluci* comes from the Arabic, and even today in Tunisia snails are called *babuci.* How traditional are they? A proverb, *Cu mancia babbaluci e vivi acqua, sunati li campani pirchi è mortu,* says that "for anyone without *babbaluci* and fresh water, you might as well ring the church bells because he is dead." And *Babbaluci a sucari e fimini a vasari un ponnu mai saziari,* meaning "Snails to suck [out of their shells] and women to kiss are two things you can never tire of."

Makes 4 to 6 servings

6 tablespoons olive oil
1 or 2 large cloves garlic, finely minced
3 dozen tiny fresh snails, ready to cook (see page 115), or 1 can (36
    snails) California *petit gris* snails, drained*
1 tablespoon chopped parsley
Salt and pepper
3 fresh tomatoes, about 1 pound, peeled and seeded, optional
Few sprinkles finely chopped peperoncini (dried red chile), optional

Warm the olive oil in a heavy saucepan and add the garlic, cooking it briefly and taking care that it doesn't brown or burn. Add the snails, parsley, salt, pepper, and tomatoes and pepper flakes if using. If you use snails in their shells, mix with a wooden spoon so the sauce finds its way into the openings and crevices of the shells. Warm over very low heat 5 to 8 minutes, only heating through the California snails and never letting them boil. Serve with toothpicks.

*Enfant Riant brand of California snails is available in gourmet shops.

Gelo di Melone

~~~~~~~~~~~~~~~~~~~~~~~~~~~~

Molded
Watermelon
Dessert

Rosy pink gelo di melone is the classic cooling dish of Palermo eaten during blazing mid-August. Looking like the watermelon from which it is made, it has tiny seeds made of chocolate and a sprinkling of pistachio nuts as green as watermelon rind, but the resemblance ends there. The chilled pudding, as tantalizingly exotic as its Arab beginnings, is made simply from sweetened watermelon pulp mixed with cornstarch and flavored, as Mary Simeti suggests, with the delicate taste of jasmine. Unless you are a gardener with a supply of jasmine flowers to steep, you will find vanilla an easy substitute.

Makes 8 servings

1 small ripe watermelon
½ cup (90 grams) cornstarch
½ cup plus 2 to 4 tablespoons (125 to 150 grams) sugar, depending on
    the sweetness of the melon
¼ teaspoon or large pinch cinnamon
Jasmine water made by steeping 2 dozen fresh jasmine flowers in 1 cup
    water for 12 hours or ¼ teaspoon vanilla extract
½ cup less 1 tablespoon (80 grams) chocolate chips, finely chopped
¼ cup (35 grams) candied citron, cut in very small dice
2 to 3 tablespoons finely chopped pistachio nuts

Cut the watermelon in thick slices, remove the rind and seeds, and press through a sieve or food mill or pulse in a food processor. Reserve 4¼ cups of the liquid. Set the cornstarch and sugar in a medium-sized saucepan over low to medium heat. Whisk in the reserved juice and continue stirring to remove all the lumps. Cook until the cornstarch is completely dissolved and the mixture comes to a boil. Continue cooking 2 to 3 minutes, then remove from the heat. Add the cinnamon and jasmine water or vanilla and let cool to room temperature. Stir in the chocolate and citron.

Assembly. Gelo di melone is usually made in individual molds or in small paper cups, although I have been told that for elegant Sicilian dinner parties it was once served in a single soufflé dish lined with a fine layer of almond paste. Dip the molds into cold water and drain. Fill and refrigerate several hours. Serve with the pistachio nuts sprinkled over the top.

FESTA DEL REDENTORE

FEAST OF THE REDEEMER
IN VENICE
July 19

*I*magine stepping onto a water taxi in Venice on a hot mid-July Sunday
expecting the slow, seductive rhythms and fragile Oriental splendor of
the city, and discovering a Venice electric with the energy of crowds
packing piazze and spilling onto tiny stone bridges. The golden evanesc-
ence of Turner's shimmering city that I expected was nowhere to be seen;
instead, there were Venetians at the lacy windows of the Gothic palazzi
where crystal chandeliers sparkled and reflected the sun. Even a remote
piazza, shaded by a single tree, and the thin veins of watery canals were
crowded with people. It was the Feast of Il Redentore (the Redeemer),
a festival of thanksgiving first celebrated in 1575 to mark the end of a
plague that had ravaged the city. To commemorate the event, Palladio
built a glorious church called Il Redentore on the Giudecca, a sliver of
an island across from Venice, and every year on July 19 masses of people
visit the church by crossing on a special, bobbing pontoon bridge put up
especially for the day.

At night they crowd on every inch of balcony and wall, they spill out
of every open window and perch on every rooftop, and they line the
embankment for what is the most spectacular display of fireworks put on
in a country famous for its fireworks. Handel's *Water Music*, composed
especially for the occasion in 1717, fills the air from small rafts that
surround an enormous barge decorated with flowers and flooded with
light. It is anchored in the Grand Canal as the staging ground for the
spectacular exhibit of consummate artifice, explosions of fire and light.

Every palazzo along the shore shimmers with colored lights that are reflected in the lagoon, creating a phantom Venice, a second city reflected in the water. Boats decorated with strands of tiny lights and colored lanterns bob up and down as people hop from one to the other, visiting friends. The boats come from myriad outlying canals and look like a new little city on the lagoon, filled with hundreds of Venetians at dinner parties, feasting on the ritual food of Redentore. Many dishes are served on these great moving feasts, but tradition calls for sfogi in saor, small fillets of sole from the Adriatic that are fried and then marinated in a sauce of onions and vinegar with raisins and pine nuts, a perfect dish for the heat of a Venetian summer; and anatra ripiena, domestic duck from the lagoons stuffed with a soft mixture of soppressata, Parmesan cheese, bread crumbs, and herbs. An old saying has it that *tutti i salmi finiscono in gloria,* "all the ragouts finish in glory." And indeed they do, for they are eaten just before the fireworks light up the sky.

The year that I went to the festival someone was selling thin phosphorescent tubes of plastic that glowed in the dark. People wrapped them like jewelry around their wrists and their necks, their ankles, and even their heads, and they glowed in the already magical atmosphere of Venice. For more than an hour, the sky was on fire with colored rockets and showers of stars, with wheels and umbrellas of reds, golds, and deep purples, followed by exploding disks of light. Fireworks that looked like paintings by Kandinsky and Frankenthaler stained the sky. The show was choreographed so that bouquets of exploding flowers were followed by great bold ribbons stretching in the night sky as far as one's peripheral vision could see. As each meteor was launched deep into the sky, the roaring booms seemed to make the very air shake like gunfire. And when the show was over, many of the Venetians floating on the canal went back to eating—this time to a ritual bowl of pasta e fagioli—before floating off to the Lido to wait for the sun to rise.

*The Festa del Redentore,
nineteenth-century
photoengraving*

Sfogi in Saor

~~~~~~~~~~~~~~~~~~~~~~~~~~~~~~~

*Marinated Sole
with Pine Nuts
and Raisins*

*How Novices Go in a
Gondola, nineteenth-
century engraving by
Franco Fornia*

Although this elegant dish hardly seems the stuff of picnics, Venetians eat it while bobbing on boats in the Grand Canal as they wait for the fireworks to start at the Feast of Il Redentore. The Romans discovered that pouring hot vinegar over fried fish preserved it, and the ancient method certainly resurfaced in the Renaissance, for the sixteenth-century Venetian cookbook *Il libro del cuoco* included a recipe that is virtually the same as one Venetians use today. *Sfogi* is Venetian for sole and *saor* comes from *sapore*, the Italian word for flavor. The slightly sweet-and-sour dish made with the small and tasty sole of the northern Adriatic used to be the centerpiece of the *sagra* of Santa Marta (Saint Martha), yet another Venetian celebration in July. Sole was fried in great pans set on the banks of the canal on the night of July 29 and again on August 1, when it was eaten in moments stolen from festive singing and dancing. This dish is made at least forty-eight hours before it is served.

Makes 6 servings

2 pounds (900 grams) fresh firm sole fillets
About ¾ cup (100 grams) all-purpose flour
About 3 cups vegetable oil
3 tablespoons olive oil
3 or 4 white onions, finely sliced
2 teaspoons sugar
1½ cups red wine vinegar
¼ cup (35 grams) pine nuts, toasted
¼ cup (35 grams) raisins, soaked in tepid water and drained

Cut the pieces of sole in half lengthwise, then cut again into 3- to 4-inch pieces. Pat them dry. Lightly coat each slice by dipping it into flour on a large platter. Heat enough vegetable oil in a heavy frying pan to come ½ inch up the sides, and fry the slices of fish until they are golden brown on both sides, being careful not to overcook them. Remove and drain on platters lined with paper toweling. Pour off the fat, warm the olive oil in the same pan, and sauté the onions over very low heat until they are limp and translucent, about 15 minutes. Sprinkle with the sugar and continue cooking another 2 to 3 minutes, then pour in the vinegar and cook until it has reduced by half.

Arrange the fish in a single layer on a serving platter. With a slotted spoon distribute the sautéed onions in a second layer and then pour over the vinegar glaze, trying to cover all the fish with it. Strew the pine nuts and raisins over the top. If you are going to serve the dish on the same day, cover and leave out at room temperature up to 12 hours. Traditionally the dish is kept for 2 days in a very cool spot or in the refrigerator before serving. It is often served with polenta.

Anatra Ripiena

Stuffed Duck

Venetians find their ducks close at hand in local lagoons and stuff them with this wonderful mixture of soppressata sausage, herbs, and mellow, slightly salty aged Parmesan cheese. The secret is to stuff and truss the ducks well, rub a bit of the herb mixture over the skin, and put them in a sizzling hot oven for a crispy-skinned bird. Venetian ducks are much less fatty than some of their American counterparts; lean ducks from Petaluma, California, are especially good for this dish. Roast a duck at this high heat without pricking its skin, and it will be crisp and crunchy without any of the usual greasiness. This stuffing is excellent in small squabs and large turkeys as well.

Makes 4 servings
1 duck, 4 to 5 pounds (2 kilograms), preferably fresh and lean

S T U F F I N G

2 ounces (50 grams) soppressata sausage
1 tablespoon plus 1 teaspoon very finely chopped fresh sage
1 tablespoon plus 1 teaspoon very finely chopped fresh rosemary
½ cup (50 grams) freshly grated Parmigiano-Reggiano cheese
½ cup plus 2 tablespoons (50 grams) freshly made bread crumbs
1 tablespoon butter at room temperature
Salt and freshly ground pepper
1 tablespoon butter
¼ cup olive oil

Heat the oven to 500°F.

Wash the duck very well and dry with paper towels. Remove any extra fat. Remove the liver and giblets to use in the stuffing.

Chop the soppressata in small dice, add 1 tablespoon each of the rosemary and sage leaves, and set in a mixing bowl. Stir in the Parmesan cheese, bread crumbs, and enough butter to barely hold the mixture together. Stuff the duck with the sausage mixture; truss and sew it up with string or needle and thread. Mix the remaining rosemary and sage with salt and pepper; spread over the skin of the duck. Heat the butter and oil in a large casserole. Sauté the duck on all sides until golden brown, about 15 minutes. Set it breast side up on a lightly oiled rack in a shallow roasting pan. Roast 50 minutes to 1 hour. When the tips of the wings and drumsticks begin to get dark, cover them with a little aluminum foil.

Remove from the oven and transfer the duck to a carving board. Allow it to cool 10 to 15 minutes before cutting. Use duck shears or a sharp knife to cut in half lengthwise and then to cut each half into 2 pieces. This dish is equally delicious at room temperature.

FESTA DEL CALDERON

FESTIVAL OF THE CAULDRON
IN ALTOPASCIO
July 25

*M*any centuries ago, beginning around the year 1000, poor, hungry, wandering travelers and pilgrims on their way to Rome knew that they could count on food and shelter when they arrived in Altopascio, a small medieval town not far from the city of Lucca, in Tuscany. The monks and lay brothers of the local confraternity, the order of the Cavalieri del Tao, made sure that no one would go hungry. They took their name from the Greek letter *tau*, which stood for the nearby river Teupascio, and their mission was to provide food and shelter to any who needed it. They went so far as to ring a bell every evening at sunset to alert any voyagers that it was time to collect inside the safe walls of their *ospedale*, lest anyone be forced to sleep within the nearby bandit-infested woods. The friars cooked a soup at the Badia twice a week and once a year, on July 25, they did even better. On the day of the local *sagra* when their gardens were full of vegetables, the monks took out a great earthenware pot, the *calderone* that gave the feast its name, and they cooked a steaming ribollita, a minestrone-like soup into which they tossed onions and tomatoes, zucchini, potatoes, carrots, garlic, and basil freshly pulled from the earth. Perhaps they added red wine to bathe the vegetables. It was ladled out free to anyone who came. The *calderone di Altopascio* was so well known that Boccaccio used it as a metaphor for the melting pot in his *Decameron*.

Altopascio still holds a *festa* on July 25, a historical commemoration in medieval dress, but the original minestrone is gone. In its place great cauldrons of pasta and sauce are cooked on the piazza and served with local wines. I've kept the spirit of the present-day recipe for the lemon-scented ragù, but I have added a small carrot for sweetness, garlic to heighten the flavor, and a bit of tomato. Don't be sparing with the grated cheese, since it binds and thickens the entire sauce.

Maccheroni con Ragù alla Contadina

~~~~~~~~~~~~~~~~~~~~~~~~~~~~~~~

Rustic Pasta with Lemon-Scented Ragù

Makes 4 to 6 servings

2 tablespoons olive oil
1 small onion, finely diced
1 small carrot, finely diced
1 rib celery, finely diced
2 or 3 cloves garlic, minced
1½ pounds (675 grams) lean ground beef
½ cup white wine
¼ cup water
4 tablespoons tomato paste
1 tablespoon minced lemon zest
1 teaspoon salt
Pepper to taste
1 pound spaghetti
½ cup (50 grams) freshly grated Parmesan cheese
3 tablespoons minced flat-leaf parsley

Warm the olive oil in a heavy frying pan. Stir in the vegetables and cook them slowly over medium-low heat until they are limp and lightly golden. Add the garlic and ground beef. When the meat loses its pinkness, add the white wine, water, tomato paste, lemon zest, salt, and pepper; let the mixture cook over a low flame 20 minutes. Add another tablespoon water if it seems dry.

Meanwhile, bring a large pot of salted water to a boil. Add the pasta and cook until al dente, about 10 minutes. Drain the pasta and add it to the pan full of ragù. Toss and mix well. Stir in the cheese, sprinkle the dish with parsley, mix well, and serve.

Large cooking pot, from Bartolomeo Scappi's Opera, 1625

PART TWO

Harvest

erragosto, the mid-August holiday, is the beginning of a mass exodus to the sea and the mountains. Businesses close, offices go dark, and the big cities look as if someone had locked the gates and abandoned them. Visitors, wandering around steamy Florence or Rome, can be forgiven for wondering if there has been a natural catastrophe of which they remain unaware. But no, it is only Ferragosto, when nothing gets done and traffic jams are monumental. At the beginning of August, *Corriere della Sera,* the biggest newspaper in Milan, prints a list of restaurants remaining open during the month. It fits into a couple of columns, although at any other time of the year it would probably fill an entire book.

August gets its name from *feriae augustae,* the holiday that the emperor Augustus declared as a civil festivity to celebrate the beginning of the month he claimed as his own in the year 8 B.C When the Christian calendar took over, August 15 became a religious day celebrating the Feast of the Assumption of the Virgin Mary, in honor of her death and ascension to heaven. This feast supplanted the August 13 festival of the pagan goddess Diana, who in her various incarnations was Queen of the Fields, Queen of Heaven, Earth, and Hell. The celebration came at a time when the fields were golden with wheat, trees laden with fruit, and grapevines almost ready to be picked. Until then, races and competitions were held in the quiet moments between periods of serious work in the countryside, but religious festivities soon replaced them.

August 15 became a day of paying homage to the Madonna in various extravagant displays. In Sassari teams of men carry Candelieri, enormous elaborately decorated columns of wood like the Gigli of Nola that they dance through city streets. In Messina faithful worshipers hoist La Vara, a pyramid more than sixty feet tall from which hang clouds and stars and sacred figures. The apostles, archangels, and cherubs were once live young boys who hung in the air from rings attached to La Vara; and a young girl, who represented the Madonna, actually freed a criminal as part of the ceremony. Now the heavenly figures are accompanied by I Giganti, two gargantuan papier-mâché figures, each twenty-seven feet high, representing the mythical founders of Messina. La Mata, the beautiful blond Giantess, is like Cybele, the Great Mother, while her black mate, Grifone the Saracen conqueror, resembles Saturnus, a king of the golden age.

Fields and orchards are full of fruit at the peak of ripeness. At the end

of the month prosciutto is celebrated in San Daniele del Friuli far to the north when the townspeople actually dress up to look like the aromatic cured hams produced from a rare breed of black pig in the Friulian hills. There is lots to buy and lots to sample.

In the seventeenth century, legend has it that fishermen in Naples fished up from the sea what they thought was a treasure, and it turned out to be a picture of the Madonna. Filled with religious fervor, King Carlo III constructed a church around it at the beach, and August 15 became the Festa della Nzegna, in which everyone, including the king, was tossed into the water. Food served on the occasion included a dessert that derived from eggplant alla parmigiana, although chocolate cream was substituted for the tomatoes, cream and basil took the place of Parmesan cheese, and raisins, citron, and cinnamon flavored the slices of eggplant. On the eve of August 15 a good Neapolitan ate only watermelon and bread.

During the late Renaissance the Piazza Navona in Rome was flooded on Ferragosto and successive Saturdays. An enormous fake fish splashed in the waters and young boys dove for coins that spectators tossed. Lights glimmered and tapestries hung from windows; at midnight, against the glorious backdrop of Bernini's fountains, Romans ate festive dinners called *sabatine,* little Saturday feasts.

Numerous Calabrian towns celebrate the Madonna on August 15, some with baskets of grain in gratitude for a good harvest, some with songs and parades and offerings of food. The next day, for the Feast of San Rocco, they offer up ex-votos of panpepato, spicy bread shaped like parts of bodies that need his intervention for healing.

On the tenth of September, Italians honor San Lorenzo (Saint Lawrence, official keeper of the books of the Catholic Church). He has a more than peripheral connection to food and cooking, since legend says he met his end by slow roasting on a gridiron over burning coals. It is out of respect for such a gruesome fate that believers refrain from cooking on his feast day and settle down to cold meals, as in Marradi, near Florence, where they eat watermelon, and in Imperia where dinner is an enormous salad made of tomatoes, cucumbers, sweet peppers, olives, and anchovies. In the fourteenth century, Florentines served cuts of pork and young sheep and a leek tart called *porrea.* On August 10, Florence used to have a big display of the work of bakers and pastrycooks in the Piazza San Lorenzo. Why Saint Lawrence should be the patron saint of cooks is fairly apparent, but he is also said to protect against burns of all kinds, a power granted, one assumes, in retrospective sympathy. In another gruesome food connection, Saint Bartholomew, who was supposed to have been flayed alive, became the patron saint of butchers. His feast day, August 25, was called the Feast of the Pig in Bologna, where a pig was carried through the streets, roasted, and distributed to the waiting crowds.

Come September, as grapes ripen on the vines, cheeses age, and mushrooms push their caps through the forest floor, the pace of festivals continues. On the first Sunday of the month, a colorful regatta with boatmen in medieval dress welcomes Venetians returning from their *villeggiature* in the country where they go to escape the heat of summer.

Numerous villages and towns have special celebrations on September 8 to honor the birth of the Virgin. Many of them shimmer with light, as if confirming the liturgical theme of the light that she brings to the world. Every house and farm in the Langhe in Piedmont has lights in its windows, and bonfires blaze on its hills, little points of light such as Pavese wrote about in *La luna e il falò*.

Alas, Piedigrotta, the great Neapolitan festival dedicated to the Madonna of Piedigrotta, is no more. In its days of glory, it was a splendid religious ceremony with a famous procession meant to pay homage to the Virgin. On one occasion, 350,000 people turned out to see the king in his gilded coach lead a cortege of forty more coaches drawn by many horses and attended by footmen wearing black velvet caps. Thousands came in from the country for the festive event; as with the Feast of Santa Rosalia in Sicily, some bridegrooms had to promise their new wives a visit to Piedigrotta during the first year of marriage. The *festa* was a gigantic explosion of eating, drinking, music, and sensual pleasures. Suggestions of its origins, a "September Saturnalia," in Harold Acton's description, point to priapic orgies. "The girls roll round in big motor cars on the Feast of Piedigrotta," Sean O'Faolain wrote, "all covered with flowers, swimming with wine and warm with love. In fear of it they pray to their saints or curse them, make silver eyes for Santa Lucia, silver teeth for San Appolonius, silver guts for some other saint, silver lights, livers, ears, noses, individually delicate hens, horses, dogs, all in an amazing medley of folly and faith, piety and paganism."

Booths and counters sold a profusion of sweets and fried fish, peppery and fennel-flavored taralli, prickly pears, and octopus. Eggplant cooked with Parmesan cheese, heaps of stuffed red and golden peppers, and bowls of pasta fed masses of Neapolitans. The music of guitars and mandolins filled the air along with songs, shouts, and yells, and streamers and handfuls of confetti pelted processions of grotesque figures on floats and parades. Piedigrotta began as a *festa* of the nobility, although King Ferdinand was happy to slide right in among the fishmongers and sell the fish he had caught. No one knows if he sold maruzze, the ubiquitous tiny sea snails always served for Piedigrotta. Even Garibaldi attended Piedigrotta but once Italy was unified, the event was without official pageantry. It was revived as a festival of Neapolitan song around 1880, when "Fun-

iculi, Funicula" became famous around the world. The *festa* became popular, but in the 1980s its expenses exceeded what the city was able to contribute, so now Piedigrotta is only a memory.

While Piedigrotta is gone, San Gennaro is not. Each September 19 the miracle of the liquefaction of the saint's blood is repeated before masses of believers in the jam-packed cathedral of Naples. O'Faolain again: "Inside and all around the porch the excitement had risen to a peak of paroxysm as a priest held around the *teca* [the vial holding the blood] to be kissed. The throng bore down on the altar like a rugby riot; police tore at them in vain; they shouted and implored this grace and that; a woman cried out wildly at the saint to cure her daughter of epilepsy; a man help up in his arms a child stricken with lupus; bambinos, terrified by the screams of the crowd, screamed with them."

Connoisseurs of *feste* who are fearful of the Neapolitan maelstrom can commemorate San Gennaro on a much smaller scale in Praiano, a tiny town on the Amalfi Coast. The piazza outside the Duomo twinkles with lights; the usual band, imported from Basilicata the year that I was there, and the usual church service are part of the event, which begins at dusk. A population of little girls in their white communion dresses, boys in their new suits, proud parents, and grandmothers in black parade behind the statue of the saint, which is draped with jewelry and many golden chains. Since the main street of Praiano is on the Amalfi Drive, San Gennaro causes traffic to stop for miles as the saint winds his way up the street and back, pausing for tributes at several preassigned spots. And when he returns to the church and the band has played its last, families go home to eat and young people dance in the piazza late into the night, while fireworks explode in the sky over the Bay of Naples.

In southern Italy, on the third Sunday of September, comes the festival of the Addolorata. In this celebration Mary is called *La Pecorella*, the little lamb, a name based on pagan sacrifice and traced to the Capuchins in the eighteenth century. The day is connected with the harvest of grain, and everyone eats the ritual dish of cuccia salata, grains of wheat berries cooked in meat broth and layered with goat or pork. The celebration ends with a raffle whose prize is a lamb, presumably referring to La Pecorella, meant to be eaten with friends after it has been boiled with onions and bay leaves, a savory way to exalt sheaves of wheat.

September 29 is the Feast Day of San Michele (the archangel Michael), and is also when farm contracts fall due in many regions. San Michele signals the autumm equinox and the end of summer, that first chill in the air. *Per San Michele il caldo va in cielo.* "For San Michele heat goes into the heavens." The autumnal harvest is ready. *Per San Michele ogni straccio sa di miele.* "For San Michele all the last fruits of the year are honeyed and ripe." People make predictions from weather conditions on

September 29. San Michele is the weigher of souls and therefore has become the patron saint of all trades using a scale, which means that he looks after pastry chefs and weighers of grain.

When October and the end of the agricultural year approach, *sagre* celebrate glossy chestnuts, the food of the poor, and elegant and expensive porcini mushrooms that add an autumnal taste to the dishes of the season. The harvest of chestnuts is celebrated all across Italy from Piedmont to Aritzo in Sardinia, where boys loop cowbells down the front of their pants like an enormous penis and dance around noisily. Surely this invokes continuing fertility just after the harvest, since the livelihood of the village depends on chestnuts all year long. In *L'Italie d'hier* published in Paris in 1894, Edmond de Goncourt described the roving vendors of castagnaccio, chestnut cake, dressed in dull faded clothes. They carried large pans of the cake resting on their thighs, selling their wares in the streets of Florence in fall and early winter. Castagnaccio is only one of many rustic sweets made from chestnut flour. A cake from the Tuscan countryside, it is seasoned with raisins, pine nuts, and sometimes with sprigs of rosemary, the "panforte of the poor," in Giovanni Righi Parenti's apt description. But there are other chestnut sweets: pattona is a chestnut-flour fritter from Emilia-Romagna; polenta dolce is made from chestnut flour; and necci are crepes cooked under hot embers in a special apparatus like a pizzelle iron, then filled with soft, fresh ricotta or pecorino cheese. Ligurians make a delicate pasta called *corzetti* from chestnut flour which they mark with their own personalized stamp. Many cities have vendors selling hot roasted chestnuts, but only in Piedmont are chestnuts transformed into Monte Bianco, a rich cake resembling Mont Blanc from which it gets its name. Made from fresh chestnuts that are cooked in milk, sieved, and flavored with chocolate, rum, and vanilla, the mountain peak is covered with a snowy coating of whipped cream.

This is the time of funghi porcini, the meaty mushrooms called *boletus* in Latin but named after little pigs in Italian. In the autumn they grow wild on the hillsides, and there are *sagre* and feste all over to celebrate them. When fresh, the caps are grilled and served like great beefsteaks. Dried, their musty flavor pervades sauces, risotti, and pastas all year long. The Apennine hills of Emilia, the Cisa Pass from Parma to the sea, the great Sila Massif in Calabria—these are but a few of the richest territories for these famous funghi, and there are particularly good *sagre* to prove it, where they can be tasted raw, marinated, fried with parsley and garlic, or stewed with wine and tomatoes.

A *sagra* celebrating the *tordo,* or thrush, of Montalcino lines up thousands of little birds to sizzle on grills as far as the eye can see. Brunellos and Montalcino reds, wines made from local grapes, are poured with abandon as intense conversations continue about the recent harvest col-

Mushrooms, drawing by P. A. Mattioli, 1583 edition, Venice

lected and crushed at the *vendemmia*. That brings two of the three mainstays of the Italian diet through the harvest—grain for bread and grapes for wine. Olives, the final piece of the triumvirate, must wait for November and December to be collected and pressed for oil.

Riso e Zucca

Creamy Pumpkin-Flavored Rice

Italians carve pumpkins for the annual pumpkin festival in Villastrada, near Mantua—they even set a candle inside each one just as Americans do at Halloween, but the resemblance ends there. The villagers carve pieces of pumpkin in the shape of fish, then fry and serve them as decoration on top of a creamy rice that is permeated with the taste of pumpkin. Making this dish is simplicity itself since the pumpkin (or squash) is merely boiled and then cooked with the rice, although I have reduced the amount of rice from the original. The magic comes in the mingling of tastes as creamy butter and cheese are stirred in.

Makes 6 servings

1 pound minus 2 ounces (400 grams) uncooked pumpkin or butternut squash, seeded
¾ cup minus 1 tablespoon (150 grams) Arborio rice
2 cups chicken broth
4 tablespoons (60 grams) unsalted butter, at room temperature
About ½ cup (50 grams) freshly grated Parmesan cheese
Salt and pepper to taste

Cut the pumpkin or squash in thick slices and cook in boiling salted water until a knife pierces the flesh easily. Drain, peel, and cut into small dice. Put the rice, diced squash, and cold broth in a pan. Bring to a boil, cover, and cook until the rice has absorbed the broth, about 15 minutes. Remove from the heat, stir in the butter and cheese, and serve immediately.

IL PALIO

PALIO IN SIENA

July 2 and August 16

The entire piazza is filled with dozens of long tables covered with white tablecloths and bright red napkins, but there are so many guests that more chairs and tables march out of the square and right up the hill, following the sinuous curves of street. Red and white flags flutter at the edges of stone palazzi, banners hang from the sills of windows, and bold red and white candelabra light up the darkness. It is the night before the Palio, the famous horse race steeped in pageantry, and the district of the Giraffe is celebrating with a good luck dinner in the streets.

Four or five hundred people are eating, drinking, and cheering at the top of their lungs. At one long table, fifty teenaged girls sing a special song that teenaged boys at a separate table answer with their own enthusiastic verses, tribal behavior a cappella. Everyone is wearing the red and white colors of the Giraffe, even the priest and the long-haired blond jockey, who is the object of the kind of rapturous attention usually reserved for rock stars. (A rumor goes round that should he win, the jockey can have his pick of young girls, willing sacrifices for the victor.) Everyone knows each other so well that all conversation is in the intimate *tu*, and when two ten-year-olds sit together and drink wine as if it were Coca-Cola, a couple of men keep a good-natured eye on them. Passionate speeches about victory in the race receive the delirious cheers of the crowd. Young boys, serving dinner off long wooden pallets that look straight out of Brueghel, pass plates full of salty prosciutto, spicy salumette, and chicken-liver crostini, then ravioli, roast beef, soppressata, and potato salad. The food may not be the finest in Tuscany, but it is abundant and it brings all the members of the Giraffe *contrada* together at table.

The people of Siena are divided into seventeen *contrade*, or districts, each with its own symbol, its own church and museum, its own motto and flag, its own patron saint, even its own fight song. Everyone is passionately loyal to his or her *contrada*, and these are the *contrade* that participate in the horse race called the Palio: the Giraffe, Panther, Leopard, Snail, Elephant, Porcupine, Forest, Tortoise, Owl, Unicorn, Conch Shell, Tower, Caterpillar, Dragon, She Wolf, Noble Goose, Wave, and Ram. Each is like a state within a state, a little fiefdom with intense loyalties and enmities that erupt on the occasion of the horse races that have gone on since the Middle Ages and, in the current form, for the last four hundred years. A *contrada* means as much as family to a Senese and is in fact like an extended family that embraces everyone. Its headquarters is like a home, where the kitchen is a center of warmth and sustenance used for organizing banquets and feeding its members. It looks after the children and provides sports facilities and activities for people of all ages. As a result, Siena has almost no crime, but it most definitely has deep loyalties and passionately felt hatreds. Members of Istrice (the Porcupine) may not want to have anything to do with anyone from Lupa (the Wolf) during the year, and people of Aquila (the Eagle) and Pantera (the Panther) may turn away when they meet, but come Palio time, those deeply held feelings are allowed free rein. The horse race provides an emotional outlet for the pent-up passions of a year.

The city's involvement in its Palio is scarcely imaginable by outsiders. I was once watching the pre-Palio parade from an apartment several stories above the Campo and was introduced to a man who was an expert on the race. "Signora," he said to me, profferring his palm, which he wanted

Palio of Siena, August 16, 1861, in a nineteenth-century engraving, Raccolta Bertarelli, Milan

me to study, not to shake. It was absolutely drenched in sweat. "It's the Palio," he said. "I'm so nervous and so excited, and my *contrada* isn't even running!" He explained that he was born during the war and as the time of his birth drew nearer, his mother, who had been evacuated to the countryside for her safety, got into the car and drove straight into town because it was unthinkable that a child not be born in the *contrada*, his true home.

The Palio itself takes place each year on July 2 and August 16, when the city erupts in a frenzy of emotion. The August Palio, the more solemn and important of the two, is run the day after the Assumption of the Sacred Virgin, patron saint and protector of the city. That doesn't make the emotional rite one iota less rancorous. It is a fanatical event so fraught with feeling that for the week of the Palio, husbands and wives often separate and return home to the *contrade* where they were born.

Pageant and paroxysm, the Palio is like a microcosm of the life and history of Siena. It "is a festival that has been many festivals," writes Alessandro Falassi, an engaging cultural anthropologist who has written several books on the Palio. It was a horse race like many others in Italy until the proud city fell in defeat to Emperor Charles V in 1555 and the Florentines. Falassi sees that moment as the turning point from which he traces the current furious competition between *contrade*. "Overnight the city lost its status and went into shock. Then it invested in a festival what it would have otherwise invested in real life: power, war, strategy. We had been a rich and famous city, and, by necessity, we turned our energies to abstractions, to an art form." What began as a simple horse race has become the essential event of an entire city.

One month before each race, lots are drawn for the ten *contrade* that will compete for the *palio*, a silken banner painted especially for each race (the same name is used for both the prize and the event). The week before the race, a track of ocher-colored earth from the countryside of Siena is laid around the edge of the Campo, the scallop-shaped piazza that Montaigne called the most beautiful in the world. For a brief time it becomes both piazza and racetrack. The horses are chosen in a lottery, so no one knows until three days before the race which horse will run for which *contrada*. The pairing is done by counters being pulled from an urn, as in a bingo game. Once the assignments are made the complex agreements between one *contrada* and another can begin in earnest. The *partiti* may technically be against the rules, but, says Falassi, everyone expects them. The palio is not just a simple horse race. "It is a tournament, a joust, and a battle," based on strategy and convolutions of diplomacy worthy of a Metternich. The *partiti* "represent man's attempt to control his fate through skillful diplomacy and manipulation." Since age-old enmities and friendships are deeply woven into the fabric of the city, one

The official emblems of the seventeen contrade *of Siena*

contrada will pay a rival *contrada* to defeat its great enemy; another will let the jockey it keeps on retainer ride under the colors of an ally. Such an act of self-sacrifice does not come cheap, but is part of the maneuvering necessary to win. There are offers and counteroffers in this "folk legal system," and a great deal of money changes hands. While it is true that only one team wins, any *contrada* wins when its enemy loses and it loses when its enemy wins. The other real loser is the *contrada* that comes in second. Its ignominy is so great that when the rest of the city is celebrating, that *contrada* literally turns out its lights and retreats into darkness.

The city is at a fever pitch for an entire week. It begins on the day that the horses are chosen and paraded to the Campo. Great groups of *contrada* members parade, arms linked, through the streets, singing songs to the horse. "*O bella, tu sei la stella,*" Caterpillar sings to its handsome chestnut. The song bounces off the dark stone buildings and leaves echoes, like motes of dust, dancing in the air. The brilliant colors of the *contrade* are everywhere—saffron yellows and oranges, cobalt blues with jagged red flames, forest greens with golden medallions, Matisselike designs rippling on silk flags and banners, on children and others who artfully tie scarves around their necks and hips as they parade through the city. The air is electric with songs and chants. Teenaged boys from the *contrada* of Istrice parade by, lustily singing their song, its lyrics full of pride in Istrice and contempt for its enemies. As the afternoon goes on, more and more *contrade* appear, singing their songs and serenading their horses, until it seems as if all of Siena is in the streets or in the Campo for the Prova, the running of six trial races.

The pace picks up. Every evening most of Siena is in the Campo, where the *alfieri*, flag wavers, practice tossing their silken banners high overhead, where the *tamburini* drum, and the archbishop, army leaders, and hordes of enthusiastic *contradaioli* come to watch. Late at night *contrade* run secret trials of the horses, and members watch carefully, noting idiosyncrasies and hoping for information that will help their jockey ride to victory. The August blessing of the *palio* begins with the Corteo dei Ceri e dei Censi, the procession of the candles and tributes, when the *palio* is escorted to the Duomo, where it remains until the day of the race. The ceremony is almost eight hundred years old, and it repeats the commune's entreaty to the Virgin, its patron in heaven, to bless its secular power. It was once the most important event in the city's life, for every town, every village and castle that Siena had conquered came on that day to pay tribute to the commune and repeat its oath of allegiance. Candles were the standard currency in such symbolic events, and so each representative carried a burning taper that he brought into the cathedral. All those candles represented wax in enormous quantities, wax that was collected below the vaults of the already magnificent cathedral, which was going to be expanded to be the largest in all the Christian world. Mountains of wax weighing more than ten thousand kilograms were amassed, and they, as much as the great procession of Siena's citizens, were a visible symbol of the republic's power and importance. Candles are still carried by representatives of the *contrade* and of the Palazzo Pubblico, but it is the *palio* banner itself that is the great cynosure of this parade. When it arrives, drums roll and trumpets blast as it is hung next to all the *contrada* flags. The flag wavers always thrust their flags at the *palio,* and then boys and men wad up their *contrada* scarves and toss them up at the *palio,* hoping that the mere touch of the sacred flag will magically give them good luck. Excitement is ratcheted to a new high.

On the night before the race, each *contrada* that is running has a good luck feast just like the one held in the streets of Giraffa. Thousands of people eat and drink on the curving streets long into the night, singing the special songs of the *contrada,* shouting out cheers at the top of their lungs, wishing victory for themselves and vile outcomes for their enemies. Passionate speeches by the prior and the captain of the *contrada* promise victory, and at one point the captain gets up, vaguely mentioning that there are still a few things left to do this evening, and the crowd instantly understands that a few more secret arrangements are still to be made, a few more deals, including perhaps payments to a rival jockey. It costs millions of lire (at least $120,000) to win a Palio.

On the day of the Palio, each horse is taken into the church of its *contrada,* where it is sprinkled with holy water and blessed with utmost seriousness by the priest, who ends by urging it to win, although that particularly addition is not part of the religious ceremony. The jockey merits a blessing as well but the horse is clearly the star. After all, a riderless horse can win the Palio, while a rider without a horse is out of luck. A steady stream of people begins to pour into Siena until by mid-afternoon more than sixty thousand are packed, body next to body, onto every conceivable piece of paving in the interior circle of the Campo. People fill up the wooden stands set up for the occasion, they are jammed on balconies, they crowd every window, perch on every rooftop, and claim every crenellation in a crush that leaves not an inch of space uninhabited. It looks like a pointillist canvas being painted with hundreds and then thousands of little colored dots filling the canvas until the colors take over and the background disappears.

Everyone is waiting for the historic pageant to wind through the city and arrive in the Campo. Its slow, stately progress contrasts sharply with the mounting frenzy preceding the race. After the track is cleared, the bell of the great Mangia tower begins to peal, announcing the arrival of the drummers, trumpeters, and musicians in fur-trimmed capes, pikemen in mail and armor, and centurions on velour-draped horses. Each *contrada*

Palio, the pageant of the contrade *in Siena, Vincenzo Rustici, sixteenth century, Palazzo Pubblico, Siena*

wears its colors which have been handwoven into velvets—chevrons of fiery red, undulating waves of sapphire blue, triumphal golden suns, emblems of spiky porcupines and aristocratic giraffes, yellows and deep forest greens emblazoned on silks and velvets and plates of armor—on bright particolored leggings and contrasting doublets, a gorgeous show of Renaissance splendor in a great medieval city. As the *contrade* encircle it, the entire Campo is ringed with great, brilliant banners flying high in the air, with *alfieri* furling their flags and sweeping them under their knees, snapping them behind their backs and over their heads, their shimmering silken patterns rippling on the wind. Then come the jockeys on horseback and little boys in red and white velour Renaissance costumes holding garlands of laurel leaves that loop between them. There are horsemen of the seven nonparticipating *contrade,* and then representatives of *contrade* that exist no longer, wearing fantastical helmets out of which rise coiled snakes, boars, and clenched hands. White oxen pull the float carrying the *palio,* and with its arrival a huge roar goes up from the crowd.

The endless flow of humanity into the center of the Campo finally stops, the bells cease, drums roll, trumpets play, and a mortar explodes as the horses and jockeys arrive for the race. Shouts and deep guttural roars of excitement rise up out of the crowd. As day fades into dusk, the great shadow of the Mangia tower falls across the piazza, and the horses arrive. The jockeys, riding bareback, are given small tight whips with which they are allowed to hit each other as well as each other's horses, all in the name of winning. This is the moment at which the order of starting is determined. The course itself undulates uphill and down and has treacherous slopes and sharp, tight corners. Mattresses pad the sharp turns, but sometimes half the horses go down at the famous San Martino corner, jockeys fall at the Casato turn, and occasionally a riderless horse speeds across the finish line first. The high-strung horses line up edgily, there are a number of false starts, but suddenly the race is on. The hysterical crowd, seething with energy, goes wild, shrieking with excitement, its entire being completely absorbed in the mad, passionate race and its outcome. So fast do the horses run, so quickly are the three circuits of the Campo completed that it is over almost as quickly as it began, a minute and a few seconds more and the victorious *contrada* swoops down on its jockey, hugs him into its collective grasp, and hoists him in victory.

The victory parade marches to the Duomo with the *palio* (in July the destination is the church of Provenzano) where a Te Deum of thanksgiving is sung as drums roll and flags wave and bells peal, and then members parade to their *contrada* headquarters and open their doors, offering wine to everyone who comes. On this one night, the winning *contrada* fountain flows with wine, not water. All night long bells ring and lights glow in the winning quarter, where songs and toasts and revelry continue until the last visitor leaves. In the Campo the *contrada* flag flies from the central window of the Palazzo Pubblico, alone in its glory.

A palio is, among other things, an excuse for members to meet at table. The *contrada* is like home, and the good luck dinners the night before the big race have entirely different menus each year. Most are planned and cooked by the best chefs and cooks in the *contrada*, some professional and some amateur. "If we relied totally on traditional dishes, this would be like a tourist event in no time," says Falassi. "We eat whatever is fashionable. It shows that the Palio is keeping up with the times. It isn't the survival of some archaic tradition. And regardless of what life serves us the rest of the year, there is always a huge amount to eat during the *festa*, a feeling of abundance and celebration." Menus include everything from a modest regional dish like zuppa frantoiana, a white bean soup usually served at the end of the olive harvest, to such exotic dishes as spaghettini del Maharaja, made with a curried besciamella sauce, or Mexican hors d'oeuvres. Tortellini alla panna, in a cream sauce, the traditional pasta of Bologna, has turned up at good luck dinners. Dishes may be inspired by medieval and Renaissance Tuscany (a sweet-and-sour pheasant from a medieval recipe, truffled veal roast, or a Medicean timbale), may be rustic food become chic (panzanella), or may simply be delicious dishes such as a rich lasagne or panforte ice cream. Whatever is served, the tables are jammed. It used to be that good luck dinners were small, but now there may be as many as one thousand people, depending on the size of the *contrada*.

Being at one of these dinners that claims the piazze and the streets is like being in a magic fable when everyone is united as a single family. In the old days, the whole city was at table for two to three days. And how do they pay for the Palios and for all this large-scale eating? By putting on yet other culinary *feste* in the streets or on big terraces behind houses, grilling the famous sausages of Siena and selling salame, prosciutti, and bread. There are games and a lottery, whose prize is likely to be some kind of food, an entire prosciutto perhaps. Everyone cooks and serves without pay; the *contrade* are the essence of nonprofit institutions. Most of the money raised goes for the Palio—there are jockeys to be bribed, deals to be made, dinners to be served. Running is expensive, and winning costs a fortune, since the *contrada* has to pay a great deal to the jockey and host a victory feast for thousands.

Not long afterward, in September, comes the banquet in the winning *contrada* when more than three thousand people may show up. A special *contrada* publication called *Numero Unico* is published, containing details of the victory, stories of the race, cartoons and caricatures and tales of heroism and how the victory was won. On Sunday afternoon a great parade winds through the streets, full of people wearing allegorical costumes showing the dejected enemy, and then hordes claim their seats in the streets under elaborate lighting devised just for the night. The year that the Giraffe won, red and white streamers draped the circumference of its piazza and banners marked all the tiny streets and *vicoli* of the *contrada*. Elaborately carved wooden torch holders were put into use for the night, and the Giraffe flag flew atop the church, surrounded by the flags of its three close allies. The running horse, the guest of honor at the victory dinner, is always placed in a special spot and fed a special dinner of oats and sugar. Humans fare considerably better. Once again, each *contrada* chooses and cooks its own menu. The year that the Giraffe won, the victory dinner began with a focaccia alla Senese flavored with herbs and included a risotto with wild mushrooms, spicy wild boar with polenta, a fillet of beef entitled *alla Truciolo* in honor of its winning jockey, and a timbale of artichokes. This last dish was called a *sformato alla fenosu*, a play on words, since Fenosu was the name of the horse, and although *sformato* in culinary terms means something cooked and then unmolded, it also means pulled out of shape, exactly what happened to the *contrada*'s opponents.

Sometimes, the day of the Palio begins with a meal of leftovers from the good luck dinner of the night before. Breakfast may be based on bread made into the traditional rustic Tuscan salad panzanella, for food at the *festa* must never be wasted. The members of the winning *contrada* eat together every night for thirty nights after winning a Palio.

A victory lasts long past the victory dinner, for there are many other ceremonial feasts. Only the participants from the winning *contrada* come to the Cena dell'Asta, the smallest and most intimate meal. At this dinner the captain is presented with the black-and-white pole from the two-sided *palio*, while his aides receive the tassels from the edges of the banner and the black-and-white canopy covering it. This dinner has no particular sacred nuances and may even take place at a restaurant outside the city.

Come January, there is the Cena del Piatto, when risotto is served out of the *piatto*, or round silver plate, which is fixed to the top of the pole that holds the *palio*. The winning *contrada* feasts on risotto right out of the plate, for grains of rice are like seeds or little eggs that symbolize abundance and the beginnings of life, and all the rice makes the feast like a wedding. It is a way, say Alessandro Falassi and Alan Dundes in *La terra in piazza*, their book on the Palio, of extending the triumph of the victory as long as possible. Once the dinner is over, the plate must be returned to the commune, engraved with the name of the winning *contrada* and the date of the Palio.

Since the celebrations do not end with the Palio itself, but last far into the winter, they carry the winning *contrada* through the darkness of winter and deep into the spring, sometimes even to the time of drawing lots of the next race. Palios are remembered and reenacted and become part of the life story of a *contrada*. It is always time after a Palio, says Falassi, or before a Palio. The year cycles round the Palio and is defined and measured by it. *Il palio dura tutto l'anno.* "Siena lives its Palio all year long."

Risotto Fratacchione

Risotto as Gourmand Monks Liked It

Although Palio food changes every year, a few dishes are part of ancient eating tradition in Siena. Risotto fratacchione takes its name from those searching rustic monks who often did penitence together at table, gulping down quantities of food and wine. The risotto is made with red onions, lots of fresh pepper, and the traditional Senese sausage. Every town in Italy thinks its sausage different, but Siena actually has a special breed of pigs called *cinto*, like a belt, the variety shown going toward the city in Lorenzetti's famous painting "The Effects of Good and Bad Government" in the Palazzo Pubblico in Siena. The meat from these pigs is made into a very lean, finely ground sausage seasoned with salt and pepper. Giuliano Bugialli has a recipe in *Classic Techniques of Italian Cooking*. Any mild Italian sausage, such as luganega, is fine if you add a pinch of red pepper flakes.

(continued)

Makes 5 to 6 servings

5 tablespoons olive oil
3 medium red onions and 1 medium yellow onion (14 ounces, 400 grams), finely sliced
1½ cups plus 2 tablespoons (320 grams) Arborio or Carnaroli rice
2 teaspoons white wine
4½ cups chicken broth, boiling
2 fresh mild very lean Italian sausages
½ peperoncino (dried red chile), finely minced, optional
1 tablespoon unsalted butter
3 tablespoons freshly grated pecorino or Parmigiano-Reggiano cheese
Salt
Lots of freshly ground pepper

Large pot, twentieth-century engraving

Warm 4 tablespoons of the olive oil in a heavy 2-quart sauté pan and cook the onions over medium heat until they are transparent, soft, and almost overcooked, 20 to 25 minutes. Add the rice, stirring often so that the grains become well coated with the oil and onion mixture, but being careful that they don't stick to the bottom of the pan. Add the white wine, then begin adding the boiling broth, ½ cup at a time. As each addition is almost completely absorbed, add another ½ cup, keeping the mixture at a constant simmer. Stir the rice frequently so it doesn't stick. Continue adding the broth until you have used it all up, about 18 minutes.

Meanwhile, film the bottom of a small frying pan with the remaining tablespoon of olive oil. Crumble the sausages and sauté them over medium heat. Add the peperoncino flakes just long enough to warm and toast them. After about 10 minutes of cooking, stir the sausages into the risotto mixture.

The rice is ready when it has absorbed the broth and is creamy. Just before it has finished cooking, stir in the butter and cook another 2 minutes. Stir in the freshly grated cheese, taste for salt, and grind lots of fresh pepper over the top. Serve immediately.

Focaccia alla Senese

~~~~~~~~~~~~~~~~~~~~~~~~~~~

Onion Focaccia

When made in Siena, these individual onion focacce cook in small high-sided molds that are only slightly larger than espresso saucers, and they rise a bit higher than regular focacce. The softness of the sautéed onions plays off against the crunch of coarse salt to make a particularly delicious focaccia.

Makes 12 to 14 individual focacce

2½ teaspoons (1 package) active dry yeast or 1 cake (18 grams) fresh yeast
1½ cups plus 2 tablespoons water: ¼ cup at warm temperature, the rest
    tepid or cold for the processor
4 tablespoons olive oil
3¾ cups (500 grams) unbleached all-purpose flour
1½ teaspoons sea salt
2 large onions, sliced
Coarse sea salt

By Hand. Stir the yeast into ¼ cup warm water in a large mixing bowl; let stand until creamy, about 10 minutes. Stir in the remaining water, 2 tablespoons oil, then the flour and salt. Knead on a lightly floured surface until smooth, soft, and elastic, 8 to 10 minutes.

By Mixer. Stir the yeast into ¼ cup warm water and let stand until creamy, about 10 minutes. With the paddle attachment in place mix in the rest of the water and 2 tablespoons olive oil, then mix in the flour and salt. Change to the dough hook and knead 5 minutes at medium speed until the dough is soft but not oozy. Turn it out onto a lightly floured table and knead it briefly into a ball.

By Processor. Stir the yeast into ¼ cup warm water in a small bowl; let stand until creamy, about 10 minutes. Place the flour and the salt in the processor bowl fitted with the dough blade and process briefly to sift. With the machine running, slowly pour the dissolved yeast, 2 tablespoons oil, and the cold water through the feed tube; process until the dough gathers into a ball. Process 40 seconds longer to knead. Finish by kneading 2 to 3 minutes on a lightly floured surface.

First Rise. Place the dough in a lightly oiled container, cover it tightly with plastic wrap, and let rise until doubled or slightly more, 1 to 1½ hours.

Shaping and Second Rise. Without kneading or punching the dough down, turn it onto a floured board and divide into 12 to 14 pieces. Shape each into a ball and let stand, covered with a towel, for a few minutes, then flatten each into a 3- to 4-inch disk. Set on oiled or parchment-covered baking sheets and let rise covered until almost doubled, about 1 hour.

Topping. Sauté the onions in the remaining 2 tablespoons olive oil until soft, lightly golden, and transparent.

Baking. Thirty minutes before baking, preheat the oven with the baking stone inside it to 400°F. Just before baking, press a spoonful of sautéed onions into the surface of each focaccia without deflating it and sprinkle with a pinch of coarse sea salt. Bake 15 minutes on the lower level of the oven, then move to an upper rack and bake 10 minutes more.

Cinghiale o Maiale con Polenta

~~~~~~~~~~~~~~~~~~~~~~~~~~~~~

*Boar or Pork
with Polenta*

Here is a hearty dinner for a cold winter's evening, based on the rich full flavor of boar or pork. Even though most boar in America is raised on ranches, the meat should still be marinated to tenderize it and give it a gamier flavor.

Makes 6 servings

Marinade (see page 165)
3 pounds (1⅓ kilograms) lean pork stewing meat with some fat, preferably from the shoulder, or boar meat, cut into 2-inch cubes
3 tablespoons olive oil, plus more if needed
2 cloves garlic, minced
1 rib celery, diced
2 carrots, diced
4 tablespoons finely minced flat-leaf parsley
20 juniper berries
2 sprigs fresh rosemary (about 1 tablespoon), chopped
1 bay leaf, chopped if fresh, lightly crushed if dried
½ teaspoon finely chopped fresh marjoram
3 tablespoons minced pancetta
1 cup red wine
½ cup beef broth
1¼ cups chopped canned tomatoes with their juices
2 teaspoons aged balsamic vinegar, optional
½ peperoncino (dried red chile), seeded and chopped
Salt and freshly ground black pepper

Place the meat cubes in the marinade, cover, and refrigerate 12 hours for pork, 28 to 48 hours for boar. Drain and pat dry.

Warm the olive oil in a large frying pan over medium heat and sauté the vegetables and parsley until they are pale and golden; add the juniper berries, rosemary, bay leaf, and marjoram. Add the meat and pancetta, with a little extra oil if necessary, and sauté until browned. Add the red wine and cook it down until it has evaporated. Add the beef broth and let it bubble until it has almost evaporated. Stir in the tomatoes, optional vinegar, and peperoncino; add the salt and pepper. Cover tightly and simmer until the sauce is thick and the meat is tender, about 1 hour for the boar, 1½ to 2 hours for the pork. Serve with polenta (page 357).

Sformato di Verdure

~~~~~~~~~~~~~~~~~~~~~~~~~~~~~

Artichoke Timbale

This creamy vegetable timbale is rich and filling enough to be a main-course dish. If you make it with any of the other vegetables that the Senese use—Swiss chard, fennel, or spinach—you will need only one pound.

*Artichoke seller, from
Lo Spassatiempo,
engraving by Borricelli*

Makes 6 servings

**6 medium artichokes (about 2 pounds), cleaned and trimmed of tough
outer leaves**
2 cloves garlic, peeled and slightly crushed but left whole
2 tablespoons olive oil
3 tablespoons finely minced fresh parsley
1 tablespoon finely minced fresh rosemary
1 tablespoon finely minced fresh sage
Salt and pepper
1 red onion, minced
3 to 4 tablespoons butter
2 cloves garlic, peeled and minced
½ pound (225 grams) chicken livers

B E S C I A M E L L A

3 tablespoons butter
1½ tablespoons all-purpose flour
1½ cups boiling milk
2 eggs
3 tablespoons grated Parmesan
Generous gratings of nutmeg
Salt and pepper
3 to 4 tablespoons fresh bread crumbs

Fill a saucepan with cold water, add salt, and bring to a boil. Add the
artichokes, whole garlic cloves, and olive oil and simmer until the leaves
are tender, about 30 minutes. Drain and set on a platter to cool. Scrape
the edible part of the leaves and chop the hearts to make about 2 cups.
Cool. Add the parsley, rosemary, sage, and salt and pepper to taste.

In a heavy sauté pan sauté the minced onion in the butter until
transparent. Add the minced garlic and the chicken livers and heat just
until the chicken livers set and the outside changes color. Cool.

Make the besciamella in a heavy saucepan. Melt the butter, whisk in
the flour, and cook until all the lumps disappear and the mixture is evenly
combined, 3 to 4 minutes. Over low heat add the boiling milk, stirring
until the mixture is smooth and thick. Remove from heat and cool slightly.
Whisk the eggs and Parmesan into the sauce along with substantial gratings of nutmeg and salt and pepper to taste. Let cool completely. Gently
mix in the artichoke and chicken liver mixtures.

Butter a 9- by 5-inch loaf pan and coat it with the bread crumbs.
Spread the mixture inside. Bake in a water bath in a 400°F oven until a
toothpick comes out clean, about 1 hour. Let it rest 15 to 20 minutes
before unmolding it.

TORTA DEI FIESCHI

CAKE OF THE FIESCHI
IN LAVAGNA
August 14

*B*eat together 4,000 eggs and 3,300 pounds of sugar. Sift 1500 kilos (3,300 pounds) of flour. Don't forget the 140 kilos of custard or the 120 liters of rum. Make the frosting from 110 pounds of almond paste. When cooked, the cake stands 21 feet high, is 9 feet at the base, and weighs over 2,650 pounds. Clearly this is no ordinary wedding cake but then, Count Opizzo Fieschi, the lord of Lavagna, was not after the ordinary. He wanted to celebrate the occasion of his wedding to Bianca dei Bianchi in 1230 in a memorable way.

In a gesture calculated to astonish the guests and reward the devotion of his subjects, Count Fieschi ordered the most enormous wedding cake imaginable—it was thirty feet high, according to medieval records—topped it with the nine-pointed crown of the Fieschi family, and served some to everyone. The size of the cake, he explained, was in direct proportion to the immensity of his love. It is written that "hills and dales learned of it, and everyone came to see the beautiful bride, the strong groom, and the imposing cake." A formidable trio.

It's easy to imagine why Lavagna continues to celebrate this romantic event on such an extravagant scale. It represents glamour and history. The Fieschi family was one of the most important in all of Liguria; it could count two popes, Innocent IV and Adrian V, seventy-two cardinals, and many other important personages on the branches of the family tree. Of course, there's the gargantuan cake itself, nineteen layers high, made of hundreds of little pieces wrapped and packaged in pairs and set in the shape of a gigantic pyramid in the central piazza. From a distance, the cake looks like an enormous badminton shuttlecock, although it is topped by the Fieschi crown instead of a red rubber tip.

The wedding is reenacted each year with a different young woman, who is part of a procession in medieval costume from the tenth-century Basilica di Santo Stefano to the central piazza. There are dramatic flag-throwing demonstrations, a fencing contest, a candlelight parade with squires and knights in costume, a band of horns and brass and drums, an orchestra, and lots of dancing, but what everyone in the big crowd really wants is a piece of the rum-spiked torta dei Fieschi. There's a game to be played first. Each participant gets a ticket that must be pinned on his or her clothes. The ticket is colored pink for women, blue for men and has on it a different fantasy name—for example, Franco and Franca, or Carlo and Carla—and each person must search through the crowd of fifteen thousand in the piazza to find someone of the opposite sex wearing the same name. Only when the two find each other can they have a taste of the cake, and then they must break open the cellophane and eat it together. With all this emphasis on romance and pairing couples who don't know each other, it's not surprising that love has been known to bloom and marriages come about as a result of a thirteenth-century wedding.

While many people go rushing around the crowded piazza, others eye the tantalizing windows of the pastry shops, which are full of cakes decorated with knights and swords and women in medieval gowns. It's not always easy to get to the big torta in the center of the piazza, so many people decide to stop right there, buy some cake, and eat it on the spot or take it home.

Lavagna is a picturesque village on the Mediterranean coast not far from Genoa, with buildings painted in a range of reds, dusty pinks, and burnt siennas. Like Camogli up the coast, it has so much *faux* decoration that a visitor is constantly doing double-takes at window frames, balustrades, and shutters that turn out to be painted on the house façades. Sometimes the undersides of eaves look as if they were made of fine wood, and sometimes a building, initially made of rough stone, is stuccoed to a smooth finish and then painted to look like rough stone after all.

Lavagna is also a wonderful town to eat in. There are a great number of food shops on the medieval Via Roma that are full of the specialties of Liguria: pandolce genovese antico, a low, crumbly predecessor of panettone genovese, which is softer, higher, full of dried fruits, nuts, and anise seeds; moist potato focaccine fragrant with potato; torta pasqualina, an Easter delicacy made of puff pastry filled with chard, ricotta, and hard-boiled egg; and of course the liqueur-flavored torta dei Fieschi itself. No wonder people come to Lavagna even if it isn't August 14.

La Torta dei Fieschi

~~~~~~~~~~~~~~~~~~~~~~~~~~~~~

*Rum-Flavored
Cake of Lavagna*

In Lavagna more than two tons of this cake are served in no more than two hours and then it is gone! The cake is essentially a soft sponge cake moistened with a wash of rum and layered with buttercream. On the very top lies a ribbon of almond paste that local bakeries decorate with the crest of the city and typical scenes of its history. The components look daunting but are really quite simple. None of the bakers was enthusiastic about parting with the details of the recipe, so this is my version, inspired by all that I learned. The torta dei Fieschi is very delicate and delicious and, believe it or not, tastes just as wonderful the second day.

Makes 1 cake, 8 to 10 servings

**Pan di Spagna (page 57), baked in an 8- or 9-inch round floured and
    buttered springform pan lined with parchment paper**
1 heaping tablespoon sugar
3 tablespoons hot water
2 tablespoons rum
1 tablespoon maraschino liqueur or additional rum

Assemble the cake on a circle of parchment paper the size of the spring-form pan in which it was baked. It is traditional to make 2 layers by cutting the cake in half horizontally, but it works very well if cut into thirds. Start with a layer of the cake and end with one.

Dissolve the sugar in the hot water, then stir in the rum and maraschino liqueur. Brush each layer thoroughly with the rum-sugar mixture.

BUTTERCREAM

⅔ cup (135 grams) sugar
2 teaspoons cornstarch
½ cup milk
4 egg yolks
1¼ cups (250 grams) unsalted butter, chilled
1 tablespoon plus 2 teaspoons vanilla extract
⅛ teaspoon almond extract
1 tablespoon rum

Mix the sugar and cornstarch and add to the milk. Heat the mixture until it is hot but not boiling. Beat the egg yolks until thick and creamy and add to the milk, cooking until thickened and almost boiling. Cool slightly. Whip the chilled butter until it is thick and fluffy. Add the egg mixture to it in the mixer and beat well. If the mixture is too soft, refrigerate it and then rebeat it. Add 2 teaspoons vanilla.

Flavor half the buttercream with ⅛ teaspoon almond extract and 1 tablespoon rum and spread it between the layers of the cake. Flavor the other half of the buttercream with 1 tablespoon vanilla and use it to frost the sides and spread a thin layer on top.

ICING

5 ounces soft almond paste, such as Odense or Blue Diamond
Confectioners' sugar

Work the almond paste with your hands until it is smooth and easy to manipulate. With confectioners' sugar on your work surface, roll almond paste out flat and then use a pastry brush to brush off any excess sugar. Using the bottom of the springform pan as a guide, cut paste in a 9½-inch circle and lay it carefully in place on top of the vanilla buttercream already on the cake. Pipe a little of the vanilla-flavored buttercream around the top edge of the cake.

Freeze any extra buttercream.

FIERA DEL CACIO

FAIR OF PECORINO CHEESE
IN PIENZA
First Sunday of September

*J*ust arriving in tiny Pienza is a celebration of sorts, for it is a handsome Renaissance town with a single main street and a single main piazza around which cluster four magnificent buildings all constructed by the Florentine architect Bernardo Rossellino within the space of three years. It sits in the disquieting landscape of the Val d'Orcia, whose earth is clean and raw and whose fields are ashen, marked by dry clods the gray color of elephant skin. The comb marks of the plow are etched in every furrow. A single tree sits atop a single hill. Some hills, made up of discrete dirt clods, are crowned with vines, others with a single farmhouse or minuscule towns. Umbrella pines outline the contours of the hills; cypresses punctuate the countryside. Sunflowers, their heads turned toward earth, are dry and sere.

When this little festival first began in Pienza more than a century ago, it was a simple commercial fair meant to sell whatever pecorino the cheese makers had left from their last production. Most of them lived on farms or in little houses in the countryside of the Val d'Orcia and came to town the day before the large fair, which concentrated on selling animals and hemp. They set out their round wheels of cheese in the cloister of the church of San Francesco and waited for buyers. It was easy to spot the cheeses that had just finished a six-month aging, because the rinds had been rubbed to a deep shiny red with sheep's blood; the same rich hue now comes courtesy of tomato sauce. There isn't any overproduction of pecorino anymore, and wheels and wedges of it are sold all year round, so the festival has become a celebration of the cheeses and the products of the countryside. It is also a nice way to see the town, and an opportunity to watch the game of *cacio al fuso* at the end of a Sunday afternoon.

In truth, the display of cheeses and foods that winds up the single street of Pienza may be more exciting than the spectacle of the game that crowns the lazy Sunday afternoon, and they may both pale slightly next to seeing this beautiful but usually empty town come to life with people meandering in its streets and tiny lanes, filling up its shops, and exploring the interior of its elegant civic and religious buildings. Sitting in a soft blue Tuscan haze, tiny Pienza came into being because Aeneas Silvius de Piccolomini, who became Pope Pius II, was born in the little village of Corsignano and he decided to transform it into a town worthy of being a subsidiary papal court. He renamed it Pienza in honor of himself, and commissioned Rossellino, who built the Palazzo Rucellai in Florence from Alberti's designs, to build the Duomo and the palazzi that edge the grand piazza in its center.

Even then sheep grazed on the herbs that grow in the clay soil that gives the name *crete senese* to this part of the landscape, but no one knows exactly when the area began specializing in the production of cacio pecorino. In his *Commentaries*, Pope Pius II does mention that he and his entourage were passing in the vicinity of the Val d'Orcia when a shepherd offered him some milk just produced by the sheep. The pope was evidently more touched by the gesture than the gift itself, but he doesn't indicate that the milk might have been intended to make cheese. He did, however, go to the monastery of Monte Oliveto and stop at the castle of Chiusuri, near the Val d'Orcia, and he remarked on the excellence of its cacio pecorino, mentioning that it was considered one of the best cheeses in Tuscany; so it is a fairly safe bet that pure sheep's cheese wasn't yet being made in this small area of southern Tuscany. There seems to have been a gap of two millennia between the time that the Etruscans produced cacio pecorino, perhaps even in Pienza where their influence extended, and the second half of the nineteenth century, when the pecorino of Pienza became recognized.

The cheese is produced in a landscape that looks more lunar than lush, a dry and bare contrast to the Tuscan countryside so familiar from the Annunciations and Resurrections painted in settings of green fields, ribbons of little rivers, and tiny hill towns crowning cones of land. Still, this is the countryside that produces the wormwood that give the sheep's milk and cheese their singular flavor. By tradition, the milk is curdled with wild artichoke (*Cynara cardunculus*), cooked, and molded into wheels. And in September it is pecorino cheese made from the milk of the sheep that graze in the nearby countryside, and are now often tended by Sardinian shepherds, which brings out the townspeople of Pienza and others from neighboring villages.

The festival begins with displays of food. Branches of bay leaves and great terracotta urns filled with sunflowers decorate the tables, and huge pumpkins and pale celadon-colored squash anchor the stands that are stretched out along the main street of Pienza. Many stands are piled high with rounds of the delicate straw-colored cheese that inspires the event. The youngest wheel, aged a mere three months, is creamy and soft with a lemony yellow rind; a smoky gray rind encircles a firmer-textured wheel that was aged for six months; the one rubbed with tomato to a rich, polished deep mahogany-colored rind is still older and more piquant. A huge boar's head complete with tusks rises above two tables, a sure sign there will be prosciutti (the legs still bristling with coarse hair) and other gamy products of the wild pig. Table after table also sports jars of honey, chests of dried porcini mushrooms, thick rounds of highly seasoned salame, and salty Tuscan prosciutto. Garlands of salame loop across old stone walls. Some of the displays are protected by an arbor made from poles topped with sunflowers and curving branches of bay leaves with screens of canvas slung over the top. Of course, there is porchetta, a lovely crunchy roast pig that weighed 120 kilos when it went into the woodburning oven, according to the man in charge of the stand. It took seven hours to roast it to crusty perfection; inside the porchetta lots of salt, pepper, rosemary, and whole cloves of garlic give it a memorable and compelling taste.

There are two strategies for dealing with all this food. You can buy lunch at the cloister of the church, where you have choices of pasta, gnocchi, rich sausages, or fagioli con le cotenne, beans with pork rind. Or you can make a picnic: Start with a sandwich made of porchetta slices rubbed briefly into the mixture of salt, garlic, and rosemary from its cavity; add to them slices of pecorino cheese in its every phase, from mild to pungent. Of course, you'll want to get some boar prosciutto and salame, and wedges of pecorino wrapped in thick slices of prosciutto and grilled over hot coals to a creamy softness. *Cacio serrato e pane bucarellato*, "tight-textured cheese and porous bread," make such a perfect combination that Tuscans use this phrase to describe a good match. Buy a bit of local wine, then sit down at a table in the cloister and have your picnic. For dessert slices of pecorino with a pear are considered so delicious that a local saying warns against telling farmers how good the combination is for fear they will keep all the cheese ever after. And when it's all over, there is still time to go back to the main street of Pienza and watch a man make croccante di pignoli, pine-nut brittle, starting with a sugary caramel-

Cacio pecorino cheese, twentieth-century photoengraving, from Il manuale del caseificio

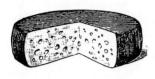

Wheel of cacio pecorino cheese, twentieth century, from La Gola

colored glob that hardens as he spreads it out with his cleaver in a tsunami of sugar.

The game of *cacio al fuso* is almost an anticlimax. First a band from San Gimignano, whose players range from an intent ten-year-old to an aged man with gnarled fingers, parades from one end of town to the other and back again, a ten-minute operation in Pienza, during which the conductor moves his hands so slowly and guardedly that their rhythms are almost invisible. Then, as the sun begins its descent and the piazza slides into shadow, it is time for the game. Garlands of bay leaves hung with yellow peppers, red apples, and lemons decorate the periphery of the playing field, the herringbone-brick square marked with concentric circles like an archery target. The entire town clusters around. The game itself is a slightly magnified edition of one played on quiet country evenings for which a nail is hammered into the kitchen floor. In the glorious Piazza Pio II, the nail is replaced by a fat spindle and each of the town's four neighborhoods has a team of five players. The rules are fairly simple: Roll a wheel of cheese directly into any part of the target and get points; roll it into the bull's-eye and get more points, but roll it so that it circles entirely around the back of the spindle before coming to rest in the center and get double or triple points. The players kneel on what looks like an Oriental carpet, pitch the wheel of cheese underhand, and hope for the best. The competition is intense—the men have been practicing for weeks—but good-natured. The winners get some good local wine and glasses to drink it from. After the game the crowds disperse slowly, loathe to leave such a *simpatico* event, and many wander down the hill, cradling wheels of cheese to take home as a reminder of the day.

Prosciutto e Pecorino

xxxxxxxxxxxxxxxxxxxxxxxxxxxxxx

Grilled Slices of Prosciutto and Pecorino

The trick of this simple and tasty hors d'oeuvre is to cut the prosciutto just thick enough that it will warm but not burn as the cheese inside melts. Since the traditional paper-thin slices of prosciutto would be much too thin, be sure that the meat is cut to about the same thickness as roast beef for a sandwich. The recipe is very similar to the ancient Roman dish formaggio al forno, baked cheese, a favorite of the poet Martial.

Makes 6 servings

12 slices prosciutto about ⅛ inch thick, preferably imported
12 slices pecorino or another young sheep's cheese about ⅓ inch thick
Olive oil

(continued)

Prosciutto e Pecorino (continued) Wrap a slice or two of cheese inside each slice of prosciutto, roll up, and close with a toothpick. Very lightly oil the outside and grill over coals or under a broiler about 1 minute a side, until the prosciutto is barely browned at the edges and the cheese is soft and melting. Serve immediately.

SAGRA DEL CINGHIALE

BOAR FESTIVAL IN CAPALBIO

Second Weekend in September

*I*n Italy, where half the population shoots at anything that moves to the point that songbirds have practically disappeared from the land, no one feels sentimental about hunting boar, the huge wild pigs with tusks, bristly hides, and fat pink snouts. The medieval town of Capalbio, set in the extreme southern part of Tuscany called the Maremma, is known as "the land of wild boar and Tiburzi," for a local brigand who was one of the most famous bandits of modern times. By all accounts he was every bit as wily and tough as the wild boar that shared the cover of the *macchia*, the virtually inaccessible dense thorny woods of the area. Tiburzi was seventy when he was tracked down in 1896 by the *carabinieri* in a cottage near Capalbio. A desperate fight took place, but Tiburzi was outnumbered, and when he fell to the ground, mortally wounded, he managed to whisper to the *carabinieri* bending over him, "Seek no further. I am Tiburzi, the King of the Macchia." He may be dead, but wild boar are still both targets and trophies of the chase. Hunters in the Maremma build a platform from which they can shoot down at the boar, while men in the nearby Chianti district shoot in the usual way. No matter which way they go at it, the beast is a formidable opponent, a challenge whose culinary rewards are great.

As exotic as it seems, boar meat appears in markets as well as in restaurants in southern Tuscany. In some years the boar themselves even appear in people's gardens. I was once a guest for lunch in a tiny cottage high above a town where the owners spoke about the hungry boar that had recently marched over the hillsides. The boar had terrorized their dogs and dug up their vegetable garden and grapevines, which provided a fine snack as it passed through on the way to more opulent feeding grounds. Some boar are fortunate enough to find and eat tiny truffles that grow at the base of oak trees as well as acorns and chestnuts, which give their flesh a particularly gamy flavor. Such tastes bring people to Capalbio, a handsome walled medieval hill town near which boar live in a large protected reserve in the surrounding hills. Once a year, when the herds are thinned out, the town puts on a big boar *sagra* to celebrate.

The festival starts on Thursday with the opening of the food stands, continues through a Saturday night dance—three thousand people turned up the year I was there—and ends Sunday night with concerts in the late afternoon and a bingo game with a million lire at stake. The cooking and eating, the main and continual events, take place in a parking lot converted to an outdoor restaurant, which is filled with long tables and shaded from the hot sun by a canopy woven of olive branches.

Boar is a rich and strong-flavored meat that tastes like a cross between beef and game. There are dozens of variations on dishes made with boar, and delicatessens are filled with hairy-legged boar prosciutto, coppa, and sausages, but at the *sagra* in Capalbio the choices are three: the meat is served grilled, *alla cacciatore,* or *in umido,* essentially boar stew with a robust tomato and rosemary sauce. With it come other such traditional dishes of the Maremma as polenta dei carbonei and a rustic soup called *acquacotta,* literally "cooked water," that used to be the daily food of itinerant shepherds and charcoal burners who were so poor that they had only a single pot in which to cook meals. They filled the pot with water and set it over a fire, adding only an onion, perhaps a bit of garlic, a piece of bread, and herbs from the fields, especially mentuccia, a delicate and aromatic wild mint. A local saying sums it up: *Mi manca la mentuccia, l'olio, e sale; farei l'acquacotta se ci avessi il pane,* which translates as "I don't have any mentuccia or oil or salt, but I'll make acquacotta if you

Boar, wood engraving by Jacques du Fouilloux, 1573, Paris

have the bread." The Capalbio version cooks onions, carrots, and celery together, and adds tomatoes, an embellishment that came later to the making of acquacotta. The soup itself has become more elegant, and in springtime it may contain fava beans and artichokes, while an autumn acquacotta might include sweet peppers or porcini mushrooms. Definitely not optional are the piece of grilled bread at the bottom of the bowl and the poached egg slid into its depths at the very last moment. When a fork punctures the yolk, the deep orange liquid oozes right into the soup. The charge for food at the *sagra*—the soup costs the equivalent of $1.50 and the boar about $3.50 in days when the dollar is strong—includes a half bottle of wine and a big wedge of saltless Tuscan bread, a perfect foil for the salty, spicy bite of the cinghiale.

The menu is prepared by the best cooks in the tiny town, and the large-scale cooking goes on in various open courtyards, piazze, and improvised enclosures. Even when the charm of Capalbio inevitably lures visitors away, smells from the food preparation mingle with the attractions of the narrow, winding streets. All lanes eventually lead to the massive crenellated tower at the top of the hill where the walls of the houses curve and bend tightly, leaving views only of fine slices of sky. It is a steep climb up the stone steps, past houses with little courtyards and past the *case pensile*, hanging houses, which are set right in the arches over the streets, and past a tiny white groin-vaulted church. On the way up you will inevitably come upon someone browning boar meat in a pan that is four feet across or someone else sliding dozens of eggs into deep tubs bubbling with the thick country soup. Take another winding alleyway and you cannot miss the *trattorie* and restaurants all featuring boar, for although the town contains only seven hundred people, in Capalbio eating clearly matters.

From the top of the town, the view is extraordinary. On one side rises the heavily forested mountain with its boar preserve, while on the other the land drops sharply away in an unbroken sweep to the sea. The landscape is as big and open as California, and there are even cowboys, called *butteri,* who round up large herds of cattle. This is the other Tuscany; it is a harsh countryside commanded by Siena in the early Middle Ages, when massive castles and menacing towers were military outposts and monastic orders inhabited ivy-covered abbeys in solitary sites. There are medieval towns here, but the Renaissance touched this area almost not at all. A few grace notes remain from the Etruscans, who made it the great mining center of their civilization, and while the Romans built the Via Aurelia, which slices its path along the seacoast, the Maremma has not experienced centuries of armies and popes, or the artists and architects who created the great city-states that gave Italy its refined urban spaces and cultivated countryside. The broad sweeping areas are uninhabited, for this land was marshy and malarial even into this century. When D. H. Lawrence came to the Maremma to write *Etruscan Places*, he learned that once Etruscan days were over, "great treeless tracts appeared, covered with an almost impenetrable low jungle of bush and scrub and reeds, spreading for miles, and quite manless. . . . And here the wild boar roamed in herds; foxes and wolves hunted the rabbits, the hares, the roebuck; the innumerable wild-fowl and flamingoes walked the sickly, stricken shores of the great pools and the sea."

Thus the country of the Maremma lay for hundreds of years until it was drained and cleared in the nineteenth and early twentieth centuries. When Lawrence came in the early 1930s, the game had gone to the hills. His driver's father "used to accompany the hunters in winter: they still arrive in winter-time, the hunters in their hunting outfit, with dogs, and a great deal of fuss and paraphernalia, from Rome or from Florence. And still they catch the wild boar, the fox, the *capriolo:* which I suppose means the roe deer rather than the wild goat. But the boar is the *pièce de résistance.* You may see its bristling carcass in the market-place in Florence, now and then, in winter. But, like every other wild thing, he is becoming scarcer and scarcer. Soon the only animals left will be the tamest ones: man the tamest and most swarming. Adieu even to the Maremma."

But not quite yet. Dense thickets of uncleared scrub still exist on huge farms where, here and there, one can see various configurations of hay, some rolled up like enormous carpets and others cut into cubes piled up ziggurat style. The forested sites are so rigorously protected that people aren't allowed to cut even a single tree branch without prior permission. And people there are, for hidden in the area around Capalbio are chic villas belonging to elegant families who come to live a bucolic existence near the sea.

Some of these people come into Capalbio for the *festa* when stands of snack food line the streets. The inevitable porchetta, domestic relative of the fierce boar, is ready to be sliced for sandwiches. It holds court on one sloping street while vendors in a sliver of piazza sell almonds, hazelnuts, chestnuts, peanuts, and very salty pumpkin seeds to strollers who walk uphill and down, munching nuts, drawn by the tiny medieval town on its cone of a hill.

Cinghiale in Umido

Boar Cooked with Herbs

"Boar may be easy to find in the Maremma," I said to the man in charge of cooking on the big piazza in Capalbio, "but not in America." "So," he said, shrugging, "substitute pork." Since almost none of the boar in this country are wild, adding *aceto balsamico* is my own invention, a bit of *fantasia* to make the dish taste rich and gamy. Here's a delicious snappy stew, perfect for a cold winter evening. If you have sauce left over, serve it on pasta.

Makes 6 servings

MARINADE

2 cups red Chianti wine, enough to cover the meat
10 juniper berries, crushed
1 bay leaf
2 cloves garlic, peeled and pressed with the side of a cleaver to release the oils
2 tablespoons chopped fresh rosemary
2 tablespoons chopped flat-leaf parsley

3 pounds (1⅓ kilograms) boar or pork stew meat, cut into 2-inch cubes

6 to 7 tablespoons olive oil
2 onions, finely diced
2 cloves garlic, finely minced
1 peperoncino (dried red chile), finely chopped
1 tablespoon finely chopped fresh rosemary
1 bay leaf
10 juniper berries, lightly crushed
1 cup canned Italian plum tomatoes, chopped
2 teaspoons balsamic vinegar, if using pork
Salt

Combine the marinade ingredients, mix well with the meat in a deep bowl, cover, and refrigerate. If you are using pork, marinate the meat 12 hours in the red wine with the juniper berries, bay leaf, garlic, rosemary, and parsley. For boar, marinate 24 to 48 hours.

When you are ready to cook, remove the meat from the marinade and pat it dry. Save some of the marinade for the stew. Brown the meat in 3 to 4 tablespoons of the oil. Set the meat aside, add the remaining oil, and warm it. Sauté the onions, and when they are lightly golden, add the garlic, peperoncino, rosemary, bay leaf, and juniper berries and cook very briefly. Return the meat to the pan and add the tomatoes, balsamic vinegar, and 2 to 3 tablespoons of the marinade. Cook covered until the meat is tender, about 1½ to 2 hours.

Acquacotta

~~~~~~~~~~~~~~~~~~~~~~~~~~~~~~~~

Vegetable Soup with Ribbons of Sweet Peppers

Acquacotta means "cooked water," but once you've tasted the sweet rich vegetable flavors of this country soup, you may well wonder why it got its name. For centuries it has been the everyday meal of shepherds and charcoal burners of the Maremma, who live off the land. Before tomatoes existed in Italy, shepherds used to crush unripe grapes and use them for flavoring. Some added wine if they had it or a bit of pancetta or stale bread from their sacks.

So much for pure and basic. There are numerous traditional variations on this soup. In springtime shepherds add fresh fava beans and peas; in the fall, slices of sweet red peppers, as I have in this variation on the Capalbio theme. They flavor it with nepitella, a local wild mint, but rosemary and sage are a fine approximation. In Grosseto acquacotta is made with fresh porcini mushrooms. Some people add garlic to the soup; others scramble the eggs with Parmesan cheese instead of poaching them. Everyone grates fresh Parmesan over the top. And some even use broth, instead of water, although that is clearly not what the name implies.

Makes 6 to 8 servings

3 large onions, finely diced
4 tablespoons olive oil
3 carrots, finely diced
3 ribs celery, finely diced
4 red peppers, roasted, peeled, seeded and sliced in long ribbons
1½ cans (28 ounces, 794 grams each) Italian plum tomatoes, chopped
1 teaspoon salt
Freshly ground pepper
4 cups water
1 tablespoon fresh sage and 1 tablespoon fresh rosemary, chopped
    together
1 egg per person
1 slice country bread per person, grilled or toasted and rubbed with
    garlic
Freshly grated Parmesan cheese

In a large sauté pan or Dutch oven, sauté the onions in olive oil until transparent. Add the carrots and celery and cook until they are soft. Add the red peppers, tomatoes, salt, and pepper and simmer over a very low flame, 20 to 30 minutes. Add the water and herbs and simmer 10 to 15 minutes. To poach the eggs in the soup, I break each one into a deep ladle and then slide it carefully right into the bubbling soup. When each egg is ready, ladle it and some soup into a bowl with a slice of grilled bread in the bottom. Serve with Parmesan cheese.

SAGRA DELL'OCA

GOOSE FESTIVAL IN MORTARA

Last Sunday in September

alk into the Lombardian town of Mortara from any direction on the last Sunday in September, and you will find booths decorated with sheaves of wheat, leafy green branches, ears of corn, and dozens of strange triangular-shaped salame. These counters appear regularly for a few days in late September to celebrate geese at a time when many of them have just ended up as salame or prosciutto. Dead or alive, they are the real stars of this event, and are very much in demand in the form of stubby-legged prosciutti, smoked goose breast, or blocks of crisp cracklings. People mill about and create culinary traffic jams as they stop for free tastes of the famous salame d'oca, the goose salame made only in Mortara.

Geese have been raised in the Lomellina area around Mortara at least since the time of the Sforzas, the dukes of Milan. Generations of the great ducal family loved the game from the country so much that they actively aided in raising geese, which lived in happy proximity to the region's rice fields. The Sforzas are long gone, but raising geese continues. Goose is still known as the poor man's pig because it is inexpensive to raise—it eats everything—grows to maturity in a mere six to seven months, and lives and reproduces happily on any kind of land, including court-yards, where chickens and ducks are raised. As with the pig, every part of the goose can be used, although pigs have no feathers to turn into precious goosedown.

Salame d'oca was first made in Jewish communities like the one in Mortara during the Middle Ages. Since eating pork was forbidden to Jews,

Geese, nineteenth-century engraving, from Oiseaux de Basse-Cour

they used goose to create salame that looked like tiny prosciutti. To this day the salame are made only from the end of August, when the geese have formed a little nut of fat under the wing, until the first of May. The meat is rolled inside the skin of the neck or breast, and you know that it's the real thing when you can see where the feathers were plucked out. There are still some pure goose products to be found, but country-people long ago made it clear that they didn't like the taste or texture of pure goose salame, so the salame makers, who had to earn a living, began adding pork. Nobody would think of giving away the local secrets (they would probably sooner sell their mothers), but the proportions are somewhere in the neighborhood of one third goose, one third lean pork, and one third pork fat or pancetta ground coarsely and then mixed with white wine and spices, including black pepper and coriander. The finest artisanal maker of these salame, Gioacchino Palestro, uses 40 percent goose meat, but he is alone in such largesse. The salame then hang for five or six days to dry before they are cooked for three to four hours in a cauldron full of barely simmering water and then hung again for one day. Once the meat is stuffed in the skin of the goose neck, the sausages are sewed tightly shut, leaving a strange object that looks like a plump pillow in the shape of an inverted funnel. The sooner it is eaten after being made, the mellower and fuller-flavored it is.

Live geese also have a starring role at the *sagra,* where over fifty cages of the birds in a variety of sizes and colors are displayed. The familiar white geese with orange bills and a big bump on the forehead are the most numerous, but there are black geese and gray geese, geese that look like ducks with long necks, geese the color of maple syrup, geese with wattles like a turkey, geese that have sprouted small red beaks, geese of the Nile that hiss, and geese that look to be right off a Chinese lacquer box. Like many current-day fairs, the exhibition in Mortara is a highly commercial event that provides a market for products as diverse as fax machines, furniture, and fur coats. Beyond them lies the gastronomy pavilion, offering tastes of rich, hauntingly flavored salame d'oca, cooked and raw; slices of goose liver; fried goose breast; and bites of cracklings called *ciccioli pressati.*

There is even a goose game. Members of various city neighborhoods take part in a competition based on *la gioca dell'oca,* a game that children play on a board rather like Parcheesi, only on this occasion it is played by grown men in Rennaissance costume who can move only after archers hit a target: A bull's-eye is worth twenty points, or twenty steps on the board, and lesser hits, five and ten points. There is the usual parade in historical costume, the usual band, the usual drum majorette group, but it is the food that is the focus of the day.

Food stands and caffès appear on the sidewalks and in streets that are closed off for the *festa*. The best stands offer smoked goose breast, foie gras, salame d'oca, cracklings, and salame sotto grasso, small fat salame buried in snowy white goose fat. These products are expensive even during the *festa*, since goose has more bones and fat than meat and loses a lot of its weight when cooked. Even so, everyone in the city seems to be out snacking on panini salame d'oca. During the day it seems hard to believe that Mortara gets its name from *mortis ara*, Latin for dead city, from the time when a raging battle between Charlemagne and Theodelinda virtually leveled it. There's nothing dead about the city during the goose *sagra*. Even the arcade under the newly painted city hall is full of shoppers buying local cheeses, fruits and vegetables, wines, and honeys. Tasters graze and people scoop up local specialties, including breads and ochelle—little buttery cookies in the shape of a goose.

Ciccioli

*Crunchy
Goose Cracklings*

Put these crispy hors d'oeuvres into a bowl and watch people pounce on them. Like peanuts they are extremely hard to stop eating after the first taste. Save a large handful to knead into a simple bread dough for the glorious flavor and texture they add.

You must have a goose to get cracklings. When you render the goose fat, cut it in ½-inch pieces, put in a pan, and add a glass of cold water. Put it over the fire and let it cook slowly, mixing it every once in a while. The little crunchy bits that form are called *ciccioli*; when they are golden, remove them with a slotted spoon and drain on a paper towel. Save the melted goose fat and use the crispy bits to serve as an hors d'oeuvre or to knead into bread dough. (Fresh pork fat may be rendered in the same way.)

*Goose, twentieth-century
engraving, from* La Gola

RASSEGNA DEI CUOCHI

CELEBRATION OF COOKS IN VILLA SANTA MARIA (ABRUZZO)

Second Weekend in October

*E*very little town in Italy may have its gastronomic festival, but only Villa Santa Maria in Abruzzo turns its rustic main street into an enormous outdoor buffet. It is said that half the cooks in Rome come from Abruzzo and that this particular remote mountain town, which calls itself *Il Paese dei Cuochi*, the village of cooks, has sent phalanxes of its residents across the world as chefs in restaurants, great hotels, and embassies. These "magicians of the whisk," as Vincenzo Buonassisi calls them, dream up feasts fit for kings, who in fact do get to eat them since they regularly employ chefs from the town.

A two-day *festa* in honor of Villa's culinary traditions sounded charming, and the town itself, set in a landscape of vertical cliffs pressed between huge outcroppings of rocks, is extraordinary to look at. Slabs and sheets of rock had erupted right out of the mountain at some time in the prehistorical past, so that the town's little stone houses and domed medieval church climb around them and rise and tilt with the cant of the land. Cars manage to drive up what look like vertical passageways. A river full of trout runs by. Ordinarily Villa Santa Maria is a very quiet place, but in mid-October trucks full of newly picked grapes rumble up the only road wide enough to accommodate them, and villagers stroll the main street, stopping in at the one-room museum celebrating the town's chefs. Its walls are covered with letters, pages from diaries, menus, newspaper clippings and testimonials to the skills of entire dynasties of chefs from Villa Santa Maria named Stanziani and Di Lello and Marchitelli, and others who have spread the fame of the city. They have cooked at the Connaught in London, at the Cipriani in Venice, at the White House, and in the embassies of the great cities of the world. They have cooked for Mussolini and Emperor Hirohito, for the king of Sweden, the shah of Iran, and for magnates like Gianni Agnelli, who once wrote out a check for eight million lire (tens of thousands of dollars) just to get back a chef who had left him to open a restaurant in New York.

The fact that Villa Santa Maria wasn't destroyed during the Second World War, when many other towns in Abruzzo were badly damaged, is due entirely to its cooks. Field Marshal Kesselring expressly spared Villa because he had eaten meals prepared by five of its chefs at the Excelsior Hotel in Rome, and reasoned that anyone who could make such good food in the face of incredible wartime shortages should have a town to go home to.

The town's commitment to cooking now extends to a movement, supported by a national delegation of chefs, to make the patron saint of the town, San Francesco Caracciolo, the patron saint of all cooks in Italy. His family first came to Villa Santa Maria from Naples in the sixteenth century because it was a cool mountain retreat in which to escape the heat of summer, and they brought with them not only a taste for good food and banqueting but the novelty of a cooking competition, a custom of Neapolitan nobility. The Caracciolos were especially keen on the wild game from the nearby woods, and they particularly liked the way the young men of the town cooked it for them. They began bringing the boys back to Rome and Naples to cook in the private homes of noble families. So the Villese tradition of chefs really began four centuries ago with fathers handing their secrets down to their sons, and today virtually a quarter of the little town consists of professional cooks. Every family has at least one or two. Whenever I asked I always heard a variation on "Oh yes, my grandfather and uncles are chefs and I have a cousin cooking in Winnipeg and a brother in Johannesburg." Cousins as well as fathers and brothers and sons were chefs. No wonder the town established a hotel school, which continues the tradition of teaching local young men to cook. What began as an attractive diversion has grown into a gastronomic embassy of Villese into the world.

Chefs from all over the world return home to Villa for the three-day *sagra*. They book passage from Vancouver and New York, from Switzerland and Australia to be part of the conclave that celebrates the town's attachment to food. Local chefs, returning or otherwise, and instructors at the hotel school may cook but they may not enter the invited competition with its very substantial cash prize for the good reason that they are acting as hosts. Competing would scarcely seem hospitable. It is charming, if ironic, that the town that sends its cooks all over the world

Cook, from Illustrazione Italiana, *nineteenth century*

celebrates by inviting different chefs from Italy to present its great feast. Only one of the fifteen participating cooks may actually come from Villa Santa Maria and avail himself of its splendid local ingredients. The year I attended, the chef fished crayfish out of the rushing waters of the Sangro River for a delicious pasta sauce, and the year before, his predecessor had grilled scamorza cheese and set it inside a nest of fried potatoes. So, of the fifteen chefs representing Italy, fourteen came from highly esteemed restaurants from as far north as Rovereto in Trento and as far south as Reggio Calabria and Catania in Sicily. Alongside them on the night of the dinner in the streets, retired chefs and other local cooks from Villa presented quantities of food that was available for everyone to sample and eat.

People from neighboring villages arrived for dinner on Saturday, the first night, to eat at tables set out in the biggest piazza. Students in toques and chefs' whites presided over enormous cauldrons bubbling on top of flames roaring out of gas jets set up at the far end of the street beyond the main piazza. The evening was billed as a Pasta Party, and pasta was definitely the star. It appeared in four entirely different dishes, ranging from spaghetti with clams the size of a fingernail to linguine with tastes of Magna Grecia: juicy tomatoes, capers, spicy chile peppers, fat black olives, and anchovies. It took 1,320 pounds of the famous DeCecco dried pasta from nearby Fara San Martino to feed the assembled crowds. A pasta expert named Peter Kubelka has described pasta as "architecture for the mouth, a language for the mouth, an icon for the mouth," an eloquent testimonial to the powerful impact of pasta on the lives of Italians. And crowds came to eat it. With two thousand people and seats for four hundred, there was also a crush for places, but everyone talked, laughed, and waited good-naturedly, drinking the Montepulciano d'Abruzzo reds and Trebbiano whites that flowed freely while music played.

As part of the official jury, I had a seat at the table of honor with all the other jurors. We dined in splendor, overlooking the expanse of silent green countryside with its sharp rocks and uncultivated landscape sliced through by the gray pylons of a newly built autostrada. Students from the hotel school served our pastas in courses as if we were in a fine restaurant, and with each course they poured a different wine. Nearby in the piazza stretched long tables full of people who had loaded up on pasta. Small children chased each other, boys ogled girls, husbands and wives lingered with friends, and grandmothers kept a proud, watchful eye on several generations. Many guests wandered up and down the street with plates of food in their hands. Over it all, standing on their balconies surveying the event like angels in a Renaissance fresco, hovered the residents of Villa Santa Maria. They had eaten their dinners at home, leaving space for the families that had come from the far reaches of Abruzzo and Molise.

After a morning church service in honor of San Francesco Caracciolo, the *festa* went into high gear late Sunday afternoon when the out-of-town chefs had chopped, sautéed, and roasted their entries in the single improvised kitchen. One made enough rice to cover a table the size of a front door, and another roasted two six-foot-long pigs that were destined to be hollowed out and used as the casings for a mosaic of three colors of cubed brioche dough, the biggest *nuova cucina* sausage in town. The refrigerator was a truck standing in the piazza, holding a variety of food and also a sculptural centerpiece of an enormous swordfish carved all in tallow, body arched and tail and sword pointing heavenward. It was a remarkable piece of work, even if it was not quite as extravagant as the tallow Lincoln Memorial from an earlier year.

Once the cooking was finished, the chefs embarked on transforming the rocky main street of this mountain village into a gigantic outdoor buffet. The chefs from the fifteen invited restaurants set up fifteen adjacent booths under swooping screens of green canvas. Complex feasts were displayed with great artistry and elaborate dishes filled tables that spread over one third of a mile. The entrants wore white toques and chefs' uniforms, but their presentations varied dramatically. Some were extremely restrained and showed only the finished platter with a simple display of the ingredients. For example, the Tre Vaselle restaurant from Umbria, which had cooked delicate sturgeon right on the plate, simply set out tiny cubes of lemon, miniature dice of tomatoes, fine threads of basil, plump capers, and a bowl of olive oil mixed with balsamic vinegar and lemon to accent the flavor of the fish. Others created elaborate fantasy landscapes for their entries. Particularly arresting were a galleon whose hull, port, and stern seemed to be made entirely of shrimp, clams, and crab legs; a tree sculpted of bread with globes of radicchio and eggplant hanging like ornaments; and the tallow swordfish *in excelsis*.

Cook, Illuztrazione Italiana, *nineteenth century*

Once the jurors had paraded by the *mise en scène*, we were seated at a special table in the adjacent piazza. The dishes were presented to us one at a time to refresh our memories and stimulate our taste buds. We ate restrained classical dishes like a Tuscan zuppa di farro, and tried tortelli neri con salmone al ragù di mare—black tortelli made with the ink of squid and stuffed with a brilliant pink salmon and clam filling. We plunged our forks into sea bass from Apulia beautifully cooked with tomatoes, and we lapped up baroque extravaganzas such as fish soup ladled into a bowl made entirely of bread and served with tiny breads shaped like the bass in the broth. We were dazzled by delicate smoked swordfish from Sicily. We ate and tasted and scored the dishes. Our ballots were collected, points were tallied, and the winner was announced.

It was not a popular choice among several chefs. One or two were certain they had the prize in the bag, others adamant that they should have won. Even food, it seems, can be political in Italy, and politics can dance on the taste buds and trip across palates. Tempers flared. Angry words were bandied about. I made a secret vow never to be on a food jury again.

None of this acrimony was apparent to the spectators. They saw all the dishes, bought tastes, and were also able to make dinner of many other dishes—quail, game, pastas, and breads prepared by chefs of the town who were not in the competition, although they had turned out lots of the food. All the dishes of the fifteen invited chefs were auctioned and everyone who wanted could buy the portions of their choice. Alongside those, one retired cook from Villa had duplicated the Roman Colosseum in bread and offered various local trout and shellfish from a creel made of bread. Another woman had made little cakes that looked exactly like peaches, and they too were for sale. The enthusiasm was palpable; energy surged through the crowd as it surged for its dinner. While everyone had to pay for their food, the wine was free. As I looked around at the rustic village, it seemed remarkable that a remote town in the far reaches of Abruzzo could produce such delicate and inventive food when elegant Tuscan Capalbio in another dramatic ancient landscape instead served hearty rustic dishes. In the singular Abruzzese village of Villa Santa Maria, full of chefs and cooks to the world, whole families ate extravagantly, drank splendid wines, saw old friends, and had a fine time.

Lingue di Passero alla Magna Grecia

Pasta in the Style of Southern Italy

A robust pasta full of the blended flavors of the Greek kingdom of southern Italy: fat juicy tomatoes, robust black olives, hot peperoncino, garlic, and salty anchovies pulled out of the waters of the Mediterranean. Lingue di passero are fine flat noodles as wide as the sparrows' tongues for which they are named. You can use spaghetti or tagliarini if lingue di passero aren't available.

Makes 8 servings

5 tablespoons olive oil
3 cloves garlic, finely minced
4½ anchovy fillets, mashed with the back of a wooden spoon
1½ cans (28 ounces or 794 grams each) Italian plum tomatoes, chopped
1½ teaspoons capers, chopped fine
4½ tablespoons Italian black olives, preferably Gaeta, pitted and cut in small pieces
1½ peperoncini (dried red chiles), seeded and divided into small pieces
6 tablespoons finely chopped flat-leaf parsley
1 pound (450 grams) lingue di passero, spaghetti, or tagliarini

Warm the olive oil in a 10- or 12-inch frying pan and lightly sauté the garlic and anchovies, being sure that the anchovies are well mashed and completely dissolved in the oil. Add the tomatoes, capers, half the olives, the peperoncini, and half the parsley. Cook over medium heat until the sauce is thick, 10 to 15 minutes. Cook the pasta in plenty of salted boiling water until al dente, 9 to 10 minutes. Just before draining it, add the rest of the olives and parsley to the sauce and cook briefly. Toss the pasta in the sauce, mix well, and serve immediately.

Spaghetti ai Gamberi di Fiume

xxxxxxxxxxxxxxxxxxxxxxxxxx

Spaghetti with Crayfish or Prawn Sauce

Crayfish are pulled out of the waters of the river Sangro in Abruzzo and turned into a delicious pasta sauce distinguished by the bite of hot peppers. Almost every dish in Abruzzo knows their heat, and, in case the peppers don't pack enough punch, most restaurants set a jar of chile oil on the table. This recipe was the entry of Antonio de Sanctis, chef of the restaurant La Ginestra in Villa Santa Maria. The sauce is a lovely departure from standard seafood mixtures; if you can't get crayfish, you can substitute prawns. The real trick is to have enough liquid to moisten the pasta, so flavorful fresh tomatoes are important. If the sauce looks too meager or too dry to moisten the pasta, add more liquid while you are cooking.

Makes 4 servings (the recipe doubles easily)

2½ pounds (1⅛ kilograms) crayfish or ½ pound (225 grams) medium or
  small prawns
4 tablespoons olive oil
2 large cloves garlic, finely minced
2½ tablespoons brandy
⅓ cup finely chopped flat-leaf parsley
4 basil leaves
9 ounces (250 grams) fresh flavorful tomatoes, cut in narrow slices
1 whole peperoncino (dried red chile), roughly chopped
Salt
14 ounces (400 grams) spaghetti

Ladle, *from Bartolomeo Scappi,* Opera, *1625*

It you are using the crayfish, cook them before shelling and deveining. Bring 2 quarts water to a boil in a large saucepan and cook the crayfish in two batches, about 5 minutes. Remove the crayfish and let them cool. Break the tail away from the head, peel the shell off the tail, and twist the vein out. Shell, clean, and devein the prawns.

Warm the olive oil and let the garlic stew in it without browning 2 to 3 minutes. Roughly chop the prawns and cook over low heat only until they turn pink. If you are using crayfish, chop and then warm them very briefly. Spritz with the brandy, flame it, and let it burn off. Add

(continued)

Spaghetti ai Gamberi di Fiume
(continued)

the parsley, basil, tomatoes, and peperoncino. Cook over low heat 5 minutes.

While the sauce is cooking, bring a large pot of salted water to a boil and cook the spaghetti 9 to 10 minutes. Drain and add the pasta directly to the sauce. Mix well and serve.

Sedanini all' Ortolano

~~~~~~~~~~~~~~~~~~~~~~~~~~~~~~~~

Pasta the Green-grocer's Way

Here's Italian ingenuity—vegetarian pasta alla carbonara made with crisp fried cubes of zucchini instead of pancetta.

Makes 6 to 8 servings

Salt
1 pound (450 grams) dried sedanini or small rigatoni or any fluted
   hollow pasta
3 cups olive oil
4 zucchini (about 1½ pounds)
4 eggs
½ cup (50 grams) freshly grated Parmigiano-Reggiano cheese
Salt and freshly ground pepper
½ cup basil leaves, cut in ribbons
¾ to 1 cup freshly grated Parmesan or pecorino cheese for serving

Fill a large pot with abundant water, add a tablespoon of salt, and bring to a boil. Set the platter on which you will serve the pasta right over the pot as it cooks, and it will be warm when it is time to mix the pasta. Begin to cook the pasta when you begin to fry the last batch of the zucchini.

Heat the oil in a deep frying pan to 400°F. As it is heating, clean the zucchini and cut them in ¼-inch disks. Stack and slice the disks in thirds. Pat dry, slide as many of them as fit comfortably into the heated oil, and cook until golden on both sides, 3 to 4 minutes each side. Repeat until you have fried all the zucchini. Use a strainer spoon to stir and mix constantly. Remove with a slotted spoon and drain on absorbent towels. In a separate bowl beat the eggs and Parmigiano-Reggiano well and season with salt and pepper.

Drain the pasta and toss with the eggs and cheese. Mix in the zucchini and basil, taste for salt and pepper, and serve with the extra cheese at table.

ERA DELL'UVA

.APE FESTIVAL IN GREVE
IN CHIANTI

September–October

n mid-September and the end of October, hundreds of kilos
heaped into carts and trucks and then transported from
illages and towns, where they are spilled out of baskets right
onto tables for tasting. All over Italy the festival called La Sagra dell'Uva
celebrates the sweetness and juiciness of table grapes and is followed
shortly afterward by the *vendemmia,* when grapes for wine are picked and
crushed. The most famous of all such *sagre,* the first in Italy, was the one
held in Marino, just outside of Rome, which Herbert Kubly described as
"sort of a wedding of the Virgin Mary with the grape god Bacchus followed
by a bacchanalia at which the municipal fountains flowed with wine
instead of water." Clusters of grapes arched over the streets to cover
terraces and doorways, and those streets were lined with food stalls heaped
with olives, mussels, clams, endless sweets, fruits, and nuts, to say nothing
of porchetta, the ubiquitous roast pig that appears at almost every festival.
Buses climbed into the little town square from Rome and all the nearby
hill towns, full of men anxious for the wine to flow. And flow it did. All
day long the fountain in the square poured wine and all day long the
men drank. Herbert Kubly describes a parade with a float carrying a lovely
virgin queen and her court sitting decorously in a sea of grapes. The crowd
set upon the float, pelting the girls with grapes, and so frightening them
that they jumped off and ran into the cathedral for protection.

Even today all along the roads of the Castelli Romani, inns still sport
signs or tin banners painted in red announcing that the new white wine

is available. If the carriages transporting the barrels of wine were once the umbilical cord connecting the towns of these Alban hills to Rome, nowadays Romans still make the voyage out to linger willingly at table, although the fountains flow with wine for only one hour during the *sagra*. There was ample historical precedent for turning on great spigots of wine in city squares. The first thing that Cola di Rienzo did when he was elected tribune of the people of Rome in 1347 was to order that from the nostrils of the bronze horse of Marcus Aurelius on top of the Capitoline Hill two streams should spout, one of water and the other of wine. Three centuries later, Pope Innocent X made sure that the lions of the Campidoglio spurted red and white wine. While men no longer drink from either of those sources, or even from their caps as they once did in Marino, they continue to sample the new wines in cool, dark grottoes. To this day bakers in Frascati make a gingerbready cookie shaped like a woman with three prominent breasts. While the cookie is undoubtedly modeled on Diana of Ephesus, whose breasts fell like a cluster of grapes from her neck to her navel, the people of Frascati swear that the middle breast is meant for wine.

Everything in the festival in Marino used to be on a mammoth scale —floats, parades, and especially the crowds, which even participated in the crushing of grapes in an enormous tub created for the event. They were celebrating the region's abundance the way their Roman ancestors had with the Vinalia, staged yearly for the harvest and featuring Lucullan meals and quantities of wine. The original festival in Marino was first held in 1571 to celebrate a famous naval battle at Lepanto when the Christian forces of Europe overwhelmed the Ottoman Turks.

Parades, music, and good food turn up everywhere in Italy. The considerable differences in grapes are more than underscored by the totally different local foods in each celebrating town. Moving from *sagra* to *sagra* to see those differences, I went from Greve in Chianti in the heart of wine-producing Tuscany to Quartu Sant'Elena, near Cagliari in Sardinia, and then to Merano in the extreme north, near the Austrian border.

In each town, food has a permanent and important place in the celebration; it is part of the town's identity and sense of self. The Fiera dell'Uva in Greve in Chianti plays upon familiar images and associations of landscape and history with the ancient red wines of Chianti and the foods of the region. During the fourteenth century, when the Florentines built fortified castles for use in their wars against Siena, they chose the symbol of a black rooster (*gallo nero*) for their defensive league; today the black rooster stands for the largest consortium of Chianti Classico producers, and the festival celebrates the five grapes of the area (Sangiovese, Canaiolo, Trebbiano, Malvasia, and Colorino) and the distinctive wines

they produce. Greve sits almost in the center of the growing region, which begins just south of Florence and stretches to the outskirts of Siena, and Greve's dark brick and stone *enoteca* sells a vast selection of the area's production. The landscape is familiar and evocative. Scattered across the hills of Chianti, wooded with oak, chestnut, cypress, and fir, are castles, great stone abbeys, villas, and farmhouses set in a rolling countryside that looks just like the backgrounds in paintings by Fra Angelico and Benozzo Gozzoli. Many of the olive trees that once dotted these hillsides were killed or severely damaged by the frost of 1986, and those that survived are returning as bushes that grow in thick, low clumps, giving the hills the look of a vast chenille bedspread dotted with the silvery green bushes. The vines that were once linked to mulberry, fig, or elm trees no longer stretch like garlands above plots of wheat, but instead have been planted in close-set rows that march in serried ranks like a well-disciplined army over the ancient hills of Tuscany.

If the countryside has changed, so too have its celebrations. The *sagra* at Greve has become a sort of market fair dedicated to the wines of the Chianti Classico district, so it is no bacchanalian revel, no opulent feast. Still, it continues to come to life in the beautiful funnel-shaped main piazza of this lovely Tuscan town. The piazza is arcaded on every side and lined with balconies full of geraniums and petunias. During the festival, when the green shutters of the houses are open, faces appear at every window. The *festa* goes on for five days and nights with concerts, dances, wine tastings, round-table discussions, and sporting events, but the biggest crowds arrive on the weekend for parades and dances and to sample the city's traditional pasta and sweets and salame. On Saturday night the year I attended, I saw the city return to the Middle Ages, full of people in both medieval and Renaissance clothes of lush velour in rich burgundy and deep brown, midnight blue and creamy parchment. Dozens of men, wearing the costumes of the Florentine soccer players, walk in the soft autumn air around and around the narrow streets of Greve, over stone paving worn smooth over the years, skirting the main piazza as they draw nearer and nearer and the blasts of horns and roll of drums grow louder and louder. The tension builds as the procession circles ever closer until finally it bursts into the piazza to the enthusiastic applause of excited waiting crowds. There are drummers in crimson velvet and warriors in pewter-colored armor, men in helmets that snap shut over their faces and nobles in black velvet gowns, even men carrying a cannon, which they set off with thunderous bangs: representatives of the Church, state, and army, all the members of medieval society walking the streets of Greve in Chianti. And for pure theater there are flag throwers, who hold their flags like tightly closed umbrellas, wooden handles up, until they toss them high in the air, where they snap open and flap in the breeze before turning over and plummeting earthward until caught with an authoritative snatch of the wrist.

An impromptu caffè set up in the triangular piazza sells tastes of Chianti wines along with such local antipasti as crostini, fat-flecked Tuscan salame, and thick slices of the regional prosciutto. A videotape running continuously outside the butcher shop is a very hot attraction, luring people in to buy sausages, polpettine, and boar sausage once they have seen how the Tuscan specialties are made. Families stroll behind small children on tricycles, while teenagers separate into tight groups. Most of the activity centers on sampling various dishes of Greve, among them the sensational desserts coming out of the pasticceria. Glossy africani, as light as eggy meringues, dissolve on the tongue; squares of schiacciata all'uva, made only at the time of the grape harvest, are moist with the juice of Sangiovese grapes that are baked under a crunchy cover of sugar. People file into the *enoteca* to buy their Chianti wines, and those who don't go home for dinner set off for a restaurant to eat such quintessentially Tuscan dishes as ribollita, a thick bean soup in which a fork might well stand up, and arista, a succulent pork roast veined with rosemary, garlic, and pepper. As darkness falls, the piazza fills up for jazz and rock concerts, and by midnight hardy survivors and an entire group of new arrivals go off to Castello di Montefiorale, a handsome medieval village above Greve, where they are rewarded with a second view of the parade by moonlight and free samples of pappardelle sulla lepre, wide noodles tossed in a sauce of wild hare, and consumed with quantities of red Chianti.

Festa dell'uva, twentieth-century photoengraving

Pappardelle
〰〰〰〰〰〰〰〰〰〰〰〰〰〰〰〰

You can't have pappardelle sulla lepre without the pappardelle, wide lasagne-like noodles with ruffled edges. Some people say they have to be freshly made; others, that dried lasagne noodles made from durum flour are the real thing. Still more controversy exists over the width of the noodles. Some say they should be 1¼ to 1½ inches wide, others insist that just under 2 inches is proper. For believers in the school of fresh pasta, this recipe seems just right.

Makes 2 pounds dough, 6 main-course or 8 first-course servings

3 cups (420 grams) unbleached all-purpose flour
½ teaspoon salt
3 extra-large eggs
1 tablespoon olive oil

By Hand. Put the flour and salt in a bowl and make a well in the center. Add the eggs and, using your fingertips, blend from the center out, gathering flour from the sides as you work. Do not worry if the mixture crumbles. When all the flour and eggs are mixed, add the olive oil and bring the dough together. Knead it on a lightly floured work surface until the dough is firm and smooth. If the dough seems too dry, add a bit more olive oil. Knead 10 to 15 minutes, until it is smooth and shiny. Cover and let it rest 45 minutes to 1 hour.

By Mixer. Set the flour and salt in the mixer bowl, and with the paddle attachment mix in the eggs and oil until a dough is formed. Continue mixing until the dough is smooth and shiny. Cover and let it rest.

By Processor. Set the flour and salt in the bowl of the processor with the steel blade in place. Pulse several times to sift. With the motor running, pour the eggs and oil down the feed tube and continue until a dough is formed. Cover and let it rest.

Roll the dough to silky fineness. If you are using a pasta machine, divide the dough into 8 pieces and roll each to the penultimate setting. Most machines turn out sheets of pasta that are 4 inches wide. Using a ravioli cutter or a pastry cutter to produce scalloped edges, cut each strip into three vertical sections, making noodles about 1¼ to 1½ inches wide about 1¼ to 1½ inches wide and 4 inches long.

Bring a large quantity of salted water to a boil in a stockpot. As soon as it comes to a boil, add the pasta and let it cook 1 to 2 minutes. Drain, transfer to a serving dish, mix well with the sauce, and serve with Parmesan cheese.

Pappardelle sulla Lepre

ᵚᵚᵚᵚᵚᵚᵚᵚᵚᵚᵚᵚᵚᵚᵚᵚᵚᵚᵚᵚᵚᵚᵚ

Wide Pasta with Rabbit Sauce

Eating this dish with its rich gamy tastes is a bit like spooning up autumn. Even if you can't find the wild hare that Tuscans use to make the sauce, a domestic rabbit will provide a hearty, full-bodied, and delicious dinner.

Makes 6 to 8 servings

1 rabbit, 2 to 2½ pounds (1 kilogram), cut into 8 pieces

M A R I N A D E

Red wine
2 tablespoons balsamic vinegar
3 long branches rosemary

2 medium red onions
½ rib celery
1 carrot
10 sprigs flat-leaf parsley
6 to 8 tablespoons olive oil
¾ pound (340 grams) lean ground beef
½ cup red wine
2 tablespoons tomato paste
1 pound tomatoes, about 3 fresh, or 7 canned Italian plum tomatoes
1⅞ cups (14 ounces) chicken broth
2 tablespoons chopped fresh basil
2 tablespoons chopped parsley
Substantial gratings of nutmeg
Salt and pepper
Pappardelle (see page 181) or dried lasagne noodles

If you can actually find a wild hare, marinate it in water to cover with ½ cup wine vinegar, 2 onions, and 3 long branches of rosemary for 8 to 10 hours to get rid of the strong gamy taste. Rinse under running water before you use it. Otherwise, 1 or 2 nights before you plan to cook, marinate a domestic rabbit in red wine to cover along with the balsamic vinegar and rosemary to approximate the wild taste of hare as closely as possible. Cover, and turn the rabbit 2 or 3 times to be sure it is marinating evenly.

Very finely chop the onions, celery, carrot, and parsley sprigs. Warm 4 to 6 tablespoons of the oil and add the vegetables. Cook them very slowly over low heat until the onion is pale golden, about 15 minutes. Remove the vegetables from the pan, add 1 to 2 tablespoons of olive oil, and sauté the rabbit until golden, 15 to 20 minutes. Remove it, add the ground meat and brown it. Return the vegetables and rabbit to the pan, add the wine, and let it evaporate slowly and completely, about 15 minutes. Add the tomato paste, tomatoes, and 1 cup broth; cook over very low heat about 2¼ hours. Remove the rabbit meat from the bones and either grind it or chop fine. Return it to the sauce, add the rest of the broth, the basil, parsley, nutmeg, and salt and pepper to taste. Cook over low heat another 45 minutes.

Serve the sauce over fresh wide pappardelle or lasagne noodles.

Schiacciata all'Uva

xxxxxxxxxxxxxxxxxxxxxxxxxxxxx

Tuscan Grape Harvest Sweet Bread

Wine cask, nineteenth-century engraving, from Enologia by Pollacci

All over Tuscany during the harvest of wine grapes, bakers make a sweet bread layered with Sangiovese grapes. Delicious as this bread is, it is always crunchy with grape seeds. In Greve in Chianti I was taken with the wit of the bakers at the Pasticceria Ferruzzi, whose briochelike schiacciata uses walnuts—the nutty crunch somewhat disguises the seeds of the wine grapes. In this country, Zinfandel or Corinth or Cabernet grapes are available to use in this sweet bread. If you don't like seeds, you can use seedless Red Flame grapes.

Makes one 16- by 11-inch bread

S P O N G E

2 teaspoons active dry yeast or ⅔ cake (12 grams) fresh yeast
¼ cup (50 grams) sugar
1 cup warm water
2 eggs
1¾ cups (250 grams) unbleached all-purpose flour

By Hand. Stir the yeast and sugar into the water and let stand until it is frothy, about 10 minutes. Whisk in the eggs, then stir in the flour in 2 or 3 additions. Cover tightly with plastic wrap and let stand until bubbly, 30 to 45 minutes.

By Mixer. Stir the yeast and sugar into the warm water in a mixer bowl; let stand until frothy, about 10 minutes. With the paddle attachment, beat in the eggs. Add the flour and mix well. Cover tightly with plastic wrap and let stand until bubbly, 30 to 45 minutes.

D O U G H

1¾ cups (250 grams) unbleached all-purpose flour
¼ cup (50 grams) sugar
1 teaspoon (5 grams) sea salt
7 tablespoons (100 grams) unsalted butter, warm room temperature

By Hand. Stir the flour, sugar, and salt into the sponge. Add the butter 1 tablespoon at a time and knead on a lightly floured work surface 6 to 7 minutes. The dough is soft and quite sticky; when you pinch the surface, the little peak you make should hold its point very briefly before it tips back over into the dough.

By Mixer. With the paddle attachment add the flour, sugar, and salt to the sponge. Mix in the butter. Change to the dough hook and knead on medium speed 3 minutes. The dough is soft and quite sticky; when you pinch the surface, the little peak you make should hold its point briefly before tipping back over into the dough.

First Rise. Set the dough in an oiled bowl, cover it tightly with plastic wrap, and let rise until doubled, 1¼ to 1½ hours.

TOPPING

3 cups (500 grams) fresh very ripe red grapes, preferably Zinfandel, Corinth, or seedless Red Flame
¾ cup (75 grams) walnuts, toasted and chopped
⅓ cup plus 1 tablespoon (75 grams) turbinado sugar
Strega liqueur, optional

Shaping and Second Rise. Turn the dough out onto a lightly oiled 16-by 11-inch baking pan and stretch it with your fingertips toward the edges as if you were making focaccia. You may need to stretch the dough and let it rest briefly before stretching some more. Sprinkle the grapes and walnuts over the dough. Cover with a towel and let it rise until puffy and doubled, about 1 hour. Sprinkle the top with the sugar.

Baking. Heat the oven to 400°F. Bake 15 minutes, then turn the oven down to 375°F and continue baking another 10 to 15 minutes. After 20 minutes of baking, tilt the pan and baste with the sugary juices and optional Strega liqueur.

Africani

~~~~~~~~~~~~~~~~~~~~~~~~~~~~~

*Delicate Golden
Cookies
from Tuscany*

Africani take their name from the glossy brown color they get in a wood-burning oven (although they are pale and golden when baked at home or in a pastry shop) and not from the brief Italian adventure in Ethiopia, as someone once suggested to me. They are a real country cookie from the tiny town of Greve in Chianti, where they were cooked in a brick oven at the very end of the day, after all the breads and sweets and custards were baked. As the temperature of the oven falls ever lower, the africani cook very, very slowly, which gives them their special texture. They are extremely delicate, with the crunch and hollow interior of a meringue and the eggy flavor of a ladyfinger. When Tuscan bakers make these by hand, just beating the yolks and sugar together can take a full hour. Fortunately, electric mixers speed things up immensely.

I first encountered africani when they appeared on the dessert platter at the Fiera dell'Uva in Greve in Chianti. This recipe comes from the Pasticceria Ferruzzi, whose very gracious bakers were extremely skeptical that they could be reproduced elsewhere in Tuscany, never mind America. The bakery makes a tiny box-shaped cookie paper, but I find mini-muffin paper cups a fine alternative. Are they light? Each one weighs about 3 grams, or ⅑ ounce.

Makes 44 cookies

8 egg yolks, warm room temperature
½ cup (100 grams) superfine sugar

Mix the egg yolks and sugar in an electric mixer at maximum speed about 4 minutes, until the sugar completely dissolves and leaves no gritty feel between your fingers.

Preheat the oven to 300°F. Fill mini-muffin paper cups slightly more than halfway, arrange them on a baking sheet, and bake 10 minutes. Turn the oven down to 275°F and bake 30 minutes. Once again, turn the oven down to 200°F and leave for an hour. No matter how curious you are, do not open the oven door! At the end of the cooking, turn the oven off and open the door, leaving the africani to cool very slowly for 2 hours.

SAGRA DELL'UVA

GRAPE FESTIVAL IN
QUARTU SANT'ELENA
September

To leave Tuscany for Sardinia is like leaving the sophistication of the Renaissance for a rugged landscape reminiscent of California in the 1850s. The festival in Quartu Sant'Elena in Sardinia is not really meant for tourists, and it is certainly not meant for those who identify Sardinia with sandy beaches and clear blue waters, prehistoric *nuraghe*, or uninhabited inland spaces, silent except for the bells of sheep and goats grazing on the hillsides. Quartu is rough and simple, a town of many raw cement and concrete-block buildings built in a hurry. On the big night of the festival, the minute all the tiny lights strung up in the piazza are turned on, the electricity immediately goes out all over town, plunging everyone into darkness for two to three hours.

This festival begins as a religious event for Sant'Elena (Saint Helena), the patron saint of Quartu, and only two days later does it take on the more joyful spirit of the harvest of the grapes, although to be truthful it never reaches the boisterous pace of other celebrations. It is a quiet Sagra dell'Uva, celebrating the famous muscat grapes called *zibibbo* that are as long as a date, as fat as a thumb, as golden as amber, and are perfumed by an unforgettable sweetness. Clusters are stacked high in the markets, and all along the town's narrow streets, people hang palm leaves at open garage doorways to indicate the boxes and baskets of grapes and wine they are selling. The grapes are dense and aromatic, perhaps because they grow on vines trained close to the ground where the heat of the strong Sardinian sun warms them and brings out their sugars.

The grapes are celebrated on Friday night with the presentation of the famous dolci of Quartu Sant'Elena, and again on Saturday when a simple procession of trucks and tractors draped with garlands of grapes is followed by a parade of women and children in traditional costumes. Wooden carts have been supplanted by machinery, and the costumes that used to be part of everyday life now are worn only for special events, but even while much of Sardinia looks modern, many young people belong to folklore associations that preserve passing traditions. Each village still has its special outfit and headdress; the women of Quartu, for example, have always worn long gold-edged scarves to cover their hair as a sign of modesty. Their elegantly pleated red velvet skirts with golden hems might have inspired Fortuny. The fanciest outfits have embroidered golden and black aprons and highly starched blouses with lacy pleated collars and cuffs billowing out from under velvet boleros. Extraordinarily fine filigreed golden buttons are shaped like fat berries or like lanterns and shovels; some are as convoluted as sea urchins, others as round as intricately worked Christmas tree balls, and it is not at all unusual for women to wear two kilos of gold jewelry, including brooches, necklaces, and as many as eighteen rings.

The *sagra* is a simple and unpretentious celebration of the original sweets that made Quartu the capital of dolci in Sardinia. Ironically, most of the sweets are based not on grapes but on the almonds that grow all over the island. On Friday night the girls of Quartu, dressed in glowing red and golden skirts, pass out samples of grapes and of the local pastries called *pabassinas*, made with zibibbo raisins, and *pirichittus*, which are like very delicate bignè perfumed with orange and lemon. To go with them they pour glasses of the strong aromatic Sardinian wines, like the Moscatos of Cagliari.

Restaurants, *trattorie*, and homes are filled with the fragrance of por-ceddu, milk-fed piglets roasted in woodburning ovens and then laid on beds of myrtle leaves. The porceddu are so sweet that you can still taste the milk they have fed on, and their skin is as crisp and crunchy as bacon, perfumed with lemony myrtle leaves. Myrtle grows near the sea all around the island. Its aromas give flavor not only to the ubiquitous pig, but in some places people lay myrtle down as a carpet so that when anyone walks over it the heady fragrance of the leaves is released into the air. Myrtle was once sacred to Aphrodite, so perhaps the erotic overtones once ascribed to the plant are part of the ambience of the island, and its perfumes still function as seductive aromas in the air.

Even so, it isn't food or fireworks but folk dancing that marks an end to the festival. Sardinian dances are deeply rooted in magic, in ritual, and in the religious feelings that were once evoked by dancing around a sacred fire. Now the fire is gone, but the main piazza is decorated with bright lights and the church is outlined by hundreds of tiny twinkling white bulbs. One by one, from nine until midnight, groups in local costume perform their centuries-old dances, with the dancers in a circle or interlacing in a cross. In one ritual performed with many precise little kicks, dance replaced the wrestling match once meant to end all disputes.

And then in the darkness of a cool Sardinian night it is over. Almost every *sagra* and festival in Italy builds to a big event on Sunday, but in Quartu there is nothing left to do but go to mass. While the city itself is so old that the "quartu" in its name means that it is four Roman miles from Cagliari, it seems like a newish suburb of the capital of Sardinia. Quartu sprawls and stretches, and much of it was built in the last few decades.

The few old houses that remain are built around outdoor courtyards where families sat at table for hours during festivals like the Sagra dell'Uva. Those houses have loggias with columns carved of juniper, richly patterned floor tiles of many colors, and ceilings painted with designs as intricate as Oriental rugs. Gardens in front of the courtyards are planted with brilliant red and pink hibiscus and hydrangea bushes full of pale lavender flowers. In the nearby village of Maracalagonis a restaurant in just such a house serves dinner with all the traditional specialties of this southern portion of the island. The waiters are boys in local costume who also perform Sardinian folk dances at the end of the evening, or serenade with traditional instruments including triangles and *launeddas*, cane pipes such as Pan must have played. Course after course arrives at the tables, but the *pièce de résistance* is paraded through the courtyard on long skewers: three bronze, crisp-skinned piglets, split in half and cooked on a spit over aromatic juniper or olive wood. Their interiors are milky white and, once served, they are eaten with cocoeddi, the traditional bread of Quartu that looks as if it has been created by an obsessed sculptor let loose with scissors. Hundreds of tiny cuts in the edges of dough make it look every bit as finely wrought as the filigreed buttons and jewelry of the Sardinian women.

Raisins drying in the sun, from Trattato dell'agricoltura, *Pietro Crescentino, 1561, Venice*

Pirichittus Vuoti

~~~~~~~~~~~~~~~~~~~~~~~~~~~~~~

Hollow Sardinian
Cream Puffs

There are two kinds of pirichittus in Sardinia: empty and full. The empty ones are like bignè glazed with a crunchy veil of sugar. Bite into them and you find a hollow center perfumed with the unforgettable fragrance of orange flower water. These are among the sweets of the grape harvest festival, the pride of the city of Quartu Sant'Elena.

Makes 26 to 28 pirichittus

1 cup plus 1 tablespoon water
½ cup (112 grams) unsalted butter or lard
1½ cups (210 grams) unbleached all-purpose flour
¼ teaspoon salt
7 eggs, cold
1 tablespoon sugar
2 tablespoons orange flower water
1 teaspoon lemon extract
Grated zest of ½ lemon
½ teaspoon vanilla extract
½ teaspoon baking powder

Bring the water and butter or lard to a boil in a heavy pan. Remove from the heat and add the flour and salt all at once, and beat until it is smooth and completely without lumps. Return pan to low heat and stir several minutes longer to dry the dough. Transfer to a mixer bowl with a paddle and cool briefly. Beat in the eggs one at a time, mixing very well. Do not add another egg until the previous one is well incorporated. The cold eggs will cool the dough to tepid. Beat in the sugar, flavorings, and baking powder and continue to beat several minutes more until the mixture is lighter in color.

Be sure the batter is cool before you attempt to pipe it. Fill a pastry bag with a plain ½-inch tip and pipe golf-ball–sized pieces onto parchment-lined cookie sheets.

Bake at 425°F until well puffed—they really double in size—and browned, 18 to 20 minutes. Turn off the oven, make a ½-inch slit in each piece, and leave them to dry in the warm oven, 20 to 30 minutes. Finish with crunchy sugary coating (page 192).

Cocoeddi or Coccoi

~~~~~~~~~~~~~~~~~~~~~~~~~~~

Fancifully Shaped Sardinian Bread

Cocoeddi used to be the golden semolina bread of festivals in Quartu Sant'Elena and Cagliari, but now people eat it every day. With its fanciful forms and extraordinarily fine flanges and fringes, it looks Byzantine, eastern, fantastical. It is easy to make and easy to shape once you start slicing into the dough and bending it where it is cut. Start by rolling out a rope of dough and bending it into a semicircle or an S. The blade of a dough scraper makes the tiny little cuts that give these breads such a distinctive look.

Makes 2 to 3 loaves

Scant 2 teaspoons active dry yeast or ⅔ cake (12 grams) fresh yeast
2⅔ cups warm water
3½ tablespoons (50 grams) Biga (page 31)
3¾ cups (500 grams) unbleached all-purpose flour
3¾ cups (500 grams) durum flour
2 teaspoons salt

By Hand. Dissolve the yeast in the warm water and let stand until creamy, about 10 minutes. Squeeze the *biga* into the water and yeast mixture through your fingers until it is stringy, then add the flours and salt. Knead on a lightly floured table until the dough is firm and resilient, 5 to 6 minutes.

By Machine. Dissolve the yeast in the water and let stand until creamy, about 10 minutes. Add the *biga*, flours, and salt. Combine them with the paddle until they form a firm dough; you may need to add a tablespoon of water. It is difficult to knead this dough in the machine. You will find it much easier to knead on a lightly floured surface for 5 to 6 minutes until it is firm and resilient.

First Rise. Set the dough in an oiled bowl and cover tightly with plastic wrap. Let rise until doubled, about 2 hours.

Shaping. Divide the dough in 4 pieces. Roll out each piece to a 14- by 8-inch rectangle by hand, or roll each piece through the pasta machine set at its widest setting 3 times. You may need to cut each of the 4 pieces in half if they get too long. Cover the pieces you are not using with a towel. Flatten each piece into a rectangle, then set two pieces together, one on top of the other. Flatten them together, pressing all the seams with your fingertips to seal them well. You may shape them in 1 of 3 ways:

* Starting at a long edge, roll the dough into a 16-inch-long rope and bend into a half circle.

* Roll the dough into a 16-inch-long rope and bend into an S shape, as illustrated at left.

* For a double size, roll the dough into a 18- by 12-inch rectangle and cut off three 1-inch-wide strips at the bottom. Roll the large piece of dough into a rope and shape as an S. With the 3 strips, make a braid and cut it into 2 pieces, ⅔ and ⅓. Set the larger braid on top of the S shape, bending it with the form, then center the smaller braid on top of the larger one (illustration at lower left).

With the edge of the dough scraper or a sharp paring knife, cut tiny little knife-thin cuts as shown in the illustration at the top of the opposite page. The larger cuts can be used to open the bread and make it possible to turn in new directions; the smaller cuts should be very close and are decorative. Sprinkle the tops with a fine veil of durum flour.

Second Rise. Set the shaped breads on a parchment-lined baking sheet, cover with a towel, and let rise until well doubled, about 1½ hours.

Baking. One half hour before you are ready to bake, set baking stones in the oven and preheat the oven to 450°F. Just before baking, sprinkle the stones with cornmeal, slide the breads onto the stones, and bake until they definitely sound hollow when you tap them on the bottom, 30 to 35 minutes.

Pirichittus di Cagliari

Lemon-Scented Bignè with Sugary Coating

Makes 24 pirichittus

5 tablespoons (60 grams) sugar
1¾ cup plus 2 tablespoons (250 grams) unbleached all-purpose flour
½ cup olive oil
1 tablespoon baking powder
½ teaspoon salt
½ teaspoon lemon extract
1 tablespoon orange flower water
1½ teaspoons vanilla extract
2 eggs
5 egg yolks

Put the sugar and flour into the bowl of a mixer. Add the olive oil, baking powder, and salt and blend with the paddle until the ingredients are well distributed. Add the flavorings and eggs and mix to a soft dough.

Shape into large walnut-sized balls and set them on buttered and floured or parchment-lined cookie sheets. Let them stand uncovered at room temperature 20 to 30 minutes. With a sharp knife slash a shallow 2-inch cut onto the top of each pirichittus.

Bake at 350°F 18 minutes. The pirichittus rise and split open as they bake. Dip each into the sugary coating that follows.

CRUNCHY SUGARY COATING

3 cups (600 grams) sugar
3 cups water
3 tablespoons orange flower water
1 teaspoon vanilla extract
Grated zest of ⅓ lemon

Set the pirichittus on a buttered cookie sheet, separating them so they don't stick together.

In a heavy saucepan cook the sugar and water together over medium-high heat until the sugar has dissolved. Add the flavorings and cook until a candy thermometer registers 280°F. Remove the pan from the heat and let it stand until the boiling stops. Wait to start ladling the sugar over the tops of the pirichittus until the white sugar crystals form in the foam. As the syrup thickens, you can reheat it slightly but do not add water. As it cools the syrup will turn opaque and crumbly. Eventually all the pirichittus will be iced in this white crunchy covering.

Candelaus

*Little Sardinian
Almond-Paste
Cookies*

Perfect testimony to Sardinian *fantasia,* these tiny candelaus are shaped from almond paste as if it were clay in the hands of a skilled potter. Bakers dream up any number of shapes—flowers, jugs, cups, hearts, boots, tiny shoes, little candles—and either leave them empty or fill them with the aromatic almond paste. It is important that they be very thin so as to really melt in your mouth.

Makes 24 cookies

2 cups (400 grams) sugar
1 tablespoon and 1 teaspoon orange flower water
3 tablespoons water
14 ounces (400 grams) peeled almonds, chopped very fine in a nut grinder
½ teaspoon lemon extract for the filling portion only
Confectioners' sugar for the work surface

GLAZE

1 cup water
2 cups (400 grams) sugar

Melt the sugar with the orange flower water and 3 tablespoons water over a low flame, cooking until it is clear and liquid, 15 to 20 minutes. Add the almonds and stir. Cook over very low heat, stirring with a wooden spoon every once in a while, until you have a mixture that has the consistency of almond paste. Remove from the fire and let cool. Set aside 1 cup of the filling.

Sprinkle your work surface lightly with confectioners' sugar. Take 24 walnut-sized balls of dough, dip each delicately in confectioners' sugar, and form into candelaus of any shape you want: round, oval, or heart. The Sardinians even form little shoes, pointed at one end and rounder at the other. The candelaus are hollowed out and then either left empty or filled. To hollow them, put your index finger gently in the middle of the form. Begin turning it carefully as if you were turning a pot on a potter's wheel and getting its sides higher and finer: Put your little finger inside the form and turn it slowly until it has fine sides. Don't be surprised if the shape looks somewhat like a shuttlecock. Put it on the table and gently stick your thumb inside to make a flat bottom. Pick it up with the fingertips of your left hand, then with your thumb still inside, turn again, making it thin and cuplike.

If you decide to bake the candelaus empty, you still need to glaze their interiors. Boil the sugar and water 15 to 20 minutes, then allow to cool slightly. Brush a light film of the glaze in the interiors. To fill the candelaus, first mix the lemon extract into the remaining almond paste.

(continued)

Candelaus (continued)

Scoop the filling inside the candelaus, being sure that it entirely fills the opening. Tamp it down evenly on top. Sardinians traditionally finish the candelaus by lightly brushing the glaze over the entire exterior and bottom. Let dry. Turn over and do the top. Be careful not to leave any blank spots or brush marks.

Bake on parchment-lined baking sheets at 275°F until pale golden, 35 to 40 minutes for the filled candelaus, 15 to 20 minutes for the unfilled.

Bianchini or Bianchittus

Sardinian Lemon-Scented Meringues

What gives these meringues their irresistible flavor? The crunch of toasted almonds and the fragrance of lemon.

Makes 5 to 6 dozen meringues

1 cup (250 grams) egg whites (7 or 8)
¼ teaspoon salt
2 cups (400 grams) superfine granulated sugar
Zest of 1 lemon
2 cups (200 grams) slivered almonds, toasted and chopped

By hand or using the highest speed of the electric mixer with the whisk attachment, beat the egg whites and salt until they are thick. Add the sugar 1 tablespoon at a time and continue beating until the mixture holds a firm peak. Grate the lemon zest directly into the mixture. Fold in the almonds.

Shaping. Oil a baking sheet or line it with parchment paper. You may either drop the meringue by tablespoons in a cone shape or make a base by dropping a tablespoon of the mixture, dip a spoon into water to flatten it, and drop a second cone on top. Set them 1½ inches apart.

Baking. Bake in a very low 250°F oven about 1¼ to 1½ hours. The bianchini dry out, but they must not change color or they will not be true to the white that gives them their name.

SAGRA DELL'UVA

GRAPE HARVEST IN MERANO
October

*A*rriving at the grape festival in Merano, a Tyrolean resort town in the northernmost Alto Adige, is like happening on an Oktoberfest with lots of beer drinking, wurstel eating, and countless military bands playing in the crisp mountain air. Suddenly Italy feels like Austria as beer meets wine at table and old Tyrolean costumes meet Italian customs. What a backdrop for a parade! There are trees and a river rushing over rocks in the very center of town, and just behind rise Italy's Alps, the dramatic Dolomites, all wooded and studded with small Alpine houses, castle spires, and sharp clear mountain crags. Here and there terraced vines define the contours of the hills, garlands of still unpicked grapes hanging heavy on their branches. The landscape is stunning with towns jammed into the steep mountain face. Red apples hang like Christmas ornaments in the trees of ubiquitous orchards, where men with red canvas bags slung across their chests cut them down with scythes, filling boxes in the fields and piling them at the road's edge. In the hills just outside of town, everyone strolls from castle to castle on the Tappeiner walk, stopping for a snack at one of many small wooden huts selling apples just picked from the trees, newly ripened chestnuts, cool juicy pears, plums, and freshly squeezed grape juice. This *sagra* occurs when the grapes are collected, squeezed to make juice, and then, two days later, combined with equal parts of barely fermented must. Of course many people come to Merano for its famous grape cure: What a lovely way to melt away an ailment.

If you come to Merano from anywhere else in Italy, you might well wonder if you ought to have a visa. All the signs are in German as well as Italian, the houses look Alpine, the roofs have great overhangs and are covered with brown tiles, geraniums tumble out of dark windowboxes, and the towers of brick and wood are squat and thickly proportioned. Even the people are thicker in figure. Most of them speak German, look Austrian, and eat dumplings called *knodel*, Austrian-style smoked prosciutto called *speck*, *gulasch* with sweet sauerkraut, and Viennese desserts like apple strudel. And no wonder: The South Tyrol was officially Austrian until the end of World War I when the Armistice made it Italian, so it was only a fluke of history that turned this into an Italian celebration. Fifty percent of the participants and viewers of the *sagra* are German, twenty-five percent are Austrian, and the rest come from the environs of Merano, although all its entertainments have been connected with the grape harvest for years.

In most Italian towns, life is lived in the streets and piazze; in Merano it is lived at the bandstands, the light-filled Kurhaus, and its theater. Even when Sunday is the big day of the festival, most Italian towns hum with activity all weekend long—restaurants are generally packed, piazze thick with people, *caffés* jammed long into the night. Not Merano, although there are more hotel rooms than residents of the town, and you can be certain that every one of them is filled during the *sagra*. The city is virtually empty on Saturday. The stores close in the afternoon, a few tourists straggle along the streets that are prettily decorated with shiny green crowns of boughs, and not a single food shop is open. Sunday brings an air of contained excitement. Fruit markets in Merano's two largest piazze sell huge plums, Jonathan and Golden Delicious apples, and seedless grapes with skins the deep burgundy of Concord grapes, although these taste much sweeter. Wooden baskets are filled with figs, with chestnuts just out of their prickly shells, and with fat honey pears. More serious eating goes on at several stands in the main piazza, although only one sells "Italian" food. The rest are Austrian in both language and cuisine. People drink beer and the juice of freshly pressed grapes, and eat in outdoor caffès near the river. All over town bands play polkas, waltzes, and pop tunes with lots of brass and the oom-pah-pah of tubas. Every seat and bench along the river walkway is filled with people listening to the music and watching the crowds that stroll by.

Given its origins and splendid grapes, it is not surprising that the city celebrates with the most meticulously organized parade in Italy. What was once a feast to thank God or nature for the grapes today has become a generalized harvest festival. People line the streets and fill the balconies, but there's no crowding, no pushing, and no one even crosses the streets between entries.

The procession begins with an Austrian military band, marching with precision in crisp gray uniforms with shiny silver buttons. There are more tubas and horns played in this one event than most people hear in a decade, but then there are more bands (180) than towns (140) in the Alto Adige. Thirty such bands alternate with groups that parade in the traditional costumes of their towns. The fabrics are thick wools, flat flannels, and heavy cottons in bold strong colors, unshaded by nuance except for the familiar gray-green lederhosen. The women wear pleated skirts using dozens of yards of fabric and bright red and green dirndls with embroidered white blouses and black bodices, while the men, walking in a forest of flags and standards, wear outfits in similar colors. Many of them are accompanied by the famous Palomino-colored Avellignese horses from nearby valleys.

The floats are glimpses into a rapidly receding past: an ancient wine-press transforms grapes into juice; a giant Della Robbia-like crown is made of green and yellow apples; and numerous grape clusters have been artfully woven into a single enormous oversized grape protected by a traditional folk figure holding sharp implements to scare away thieves of the field. A group of boys and girls in traditional country costumes wave woven sheaves of grain over their heads while miners dressed in black play military music. Finally there are the Schutzen, paramilitary defenders of the countryside, who are like vigilantes, although in Merano they are forbidden to bear the weapons they always carry in Austria and Germany.

Shortly after the Sagra dell'Uva, toward the end of October and beginning of November, after the grapes have been crushed, it is time to taste the new wines. People walk from house to house (or *mas* to *mas*, as they are known) in the countryside to eat speck, roasted chestnuts, apples, cumin-scented rye bread, and to drink new wine. The event is called Torggellan, from *torchio*, the word for wine press. Such meals are ritual connections to a rural past, to a time governed by the rhythms and agriculture of the season and the countryside.

Crushing the Grapes, from Trattato dell'agricoltura, *Pietro Crescentino, 1519, Venice*

Paarl

~~~~~~~~~~~~~~~~~~~~~~~~~~~~~~~~~~

Coarse Rye Bread Flavored with Fennel and Cumin

This slightly coarse textured rye bread with the haunting flavors of cumin and fennel is traditionally made in Valvenosta in the mountains above Merano. It is shaped into two balls that become attached as they rise. Its ingredients include a local blue clover that most farmers grow in their gardens. Residents brought the tradition to Merano when they came to the area from Yugoslavia. A bit of dried fenugreek is a fine substitute.

(continued)

Makes 1 loaf

STARTER

1 teaspoon (2½ grams) active dry yeast or ⅓ cake (6 grams) fresh yeast
1½ cups warm water
About 3¼ cups (350 grams) medium rye flour
½ teaspoon cumin seeds, crushed, or ground cumin

Stir the yeast into the warm water and let stand until creamy, about 10 minutes. Beat in the flour and cumin; cover and let sit at room temperature 18 to 24 hours.

DOUGH

1 teaspoon (2½ grams) active dry yeast or ⅓ cake (6 grams) fresh yeast
½ cup plus 1 tablespoon warm water
2 cups minus 3 tablespoons (250 grams) unbleached all-purpose flour
½ teaspoon cumin seeds, crushed, or ground cumin
¾ teaspoon fennel seeds
½ teaspoon dried fenugreek, crushed, optional
1½ teaspoons sea salt

Stir the yeast into the water and let stand until creamy, about 10 minutes. With the paddle attachment put the starter in the bowl of the mixer; add the dissolved yeast and stir. Mix in the flour, cumin, fennel, optional fenugreek, and salt and mix until combined, 1 to 2 minutes. Change to the dough hook and knead on low speed 2 to 3 minutes; the dough does not come away from the sides of the bowl. Knead briefly on a floured work surface and it will come together for a brief moment. It will become sticky again if you work it any longer.

First Rise. Set the dough in a lightly oiled container, cover tightly with plastic wrap, and let rise until doubled, about 2 hours.

Shaping and Second Rise. Divide the dough in half and shape into 2 equal balls. After shaping the balls, flatten them with the top of your hand to begin the process of their cracking open. Set them on lightly floured parchment paper so that as they rise, they will become attached. Flour the tops of the loaves well. Cover with a towel and let rise until they are overrisen, about 2 to 2½ hours. The dough must tear, especially at the edges, and it must slump somewhat, otherwise it will never get the typical pattern of cracks accentuated by flour.

Baking. Thirty minutes before you are ready to bake, set a baking stone in the oven and heat to 425°F. Just before you are ready to bake, sprinkle the stone with cornmeal. Bake 35 minutes, spritzing 3 times with water during the first 10 minutes.

Zuppa di Vino
~~~~~~~~~~~~~~~~~~~~~~~~~
Wine Soup

The first time I tasted this soup, I had no idea what gave it its haunting flavor. Since it was served during the grape festival and was a specialty of Merano, I should have guessed that the mystery ingredient was Riesling wine, but I was thrown off by the soup's subtle flavor, its smoothness and creamy cauliflower color. It is a lovely light way to start a meal.

Makes 6 servings

4½ cups meat broth, preferably homemade
6 egg yolks
½ cup heavy cream
½ cup Riesling wine
Good-sized pinch cinnamon
Salt
2 to 3 slices stale country bread

In a pot heat the broth over medium heat until well heated, but it must not boil. Keep it just below a simmer. Beat the egg yolks and cream together until they are thick. Mix in the wine, cinnamon, and salt. Add the egg yolk mixture to the broth, beating it continually until the soup is well mixed, creamy, and the color of cauliflower. Do not let it boil! In the meantime prepare crostini by toasting or grilling the bread, then cutting it into tiny dice.

Serve the soup hot and sprinkle a handful of the crostini over it or serve them on the side and let people help themselves.

Torta di Farina di Grano Saraceno
~~~~~~~~~~~~~~~~~~~~~~~~~
Buckwheat Flour Cake

When I ate this buckwheat cake in Merano, I loved the way its nutty, earthy flavor played against the sweet streak of jam in the center. The heartiness of the original is perfect for people working in the fields and orchards all day but perhaps a bit dense for more sedentary types, so I altered the proportions of flour to make a considerably lighter cake. All to a good purpose: Whenever I serve this cake, everyone wants more, although no one ever guesses what the wonderful mysterious taste is.

The traditional jam filling is made of berries known as *mirtilli rossi,* "red blueberries," so you can use red huckleberry, cranberry, bilberry, red currant, or even blueberry jams. Wild blackberry and raspberry preserves are delicious, too. *(continued)*

Torta di Farina di Grano Saraceno (continued)

Makes 1 cake

1¼ cups plus 2 tablespoons (300 grams) unsalted butter, at room temperature
1½ cups (300 grams) sugar
1½ tablespoons vanilla extract
3 tablespoons grappa
6 eggs, at warm room temperature, separated
¾ cup (100 grams) buckwheat flour
1½ cups (200 grams) unbleached all-purpose flour
1 tablespoon baking powder
⅛ teaspoon salt
12 ounces (335 grams) huckleberry, cranberry, red currant, raspberry, or any other berry jam
2 to 3 tablespoons water
Whipping cream sweetened with sugar and a little grappa, optional

Whip the butter with a wooden paddle or an electric mixer until it is white and creamy. Gradually beat in the sugar, vanilla, grappa, and egg yolks, one at a time. Keep mixing until the mixture is smooth and the sugar is completely absorbed. Sift the buckwheat flour, white flour, baking powder, and salt together, then add 1 tablespoon at a time to the butter mixture. Whip the egg whites to firm peaks, then fold them carefully into the dough.

Assembly. Spread in a 9- or 9½-inch buttered and floured springform pan.

Baking. Heat the oven to 325°F. Bake the cake about 1 hour. Do not open the oven during the first 30 minutes, but after that you can test for doneness using a toothpick. The tester need not come out absolutely clean. If the cake is slightly underdone when warm, it won't dry out too much as it cools.

As the cake cools, heat the jam with the water and stir until it is smooth. Cool. When the cake is completely cooled, cut it in half horizontally and spread the top of 1 layer with the jam. Set the other layer on top. It is up to you whether you put sweetened whipped cream on the top, on the side, or don't use it at all.

VENDEMMIA

WINE GRAPE CRUSH IN ALBA
AND TODI

September and October

*N*ot so very long ago, when the hillsides of Tuscany were still planted with grapevines looping above sheaves of wheat, the men who picked the grapes for wine sat at long tables in the middle of the vineyards, eating bowls of pasta and great platters of grilled meats as they rested from their labors during the grape harvest. Such a meal is rare today, although the grape harvesting goes on all over the country, on large estates as well as on tinier plots of land. On small family farms husbands, wives, children, and friends set out with baskets and plastic tubs to the fields, where they strip the vines and clip bunches of grapes with small scythelike cutters. They fill up the baskets and upend them into big wooden crates until they are overflowing with fat bunches of black grapes in one box, green in another, juices oozing from the pressure of their weight. Country people bring home the grapes and press and skin them, crushing them in a simple fashion, sending the frothy liquid to ferment with must in barrels. They may eat a light meal in the fields or come home at midday; often they wait for all the work to be over before they eat their hearty meal.

In some Sicilian families, the grape harvest is still a real family celebration, a coming together of generations. In his book *The Ten Pains of Death*, Gavin Maxwell tells how only the mother may knead the flour, salt, water, and oil for homemade maccheroni, using a special board for making pasta and bread. She cuts a cross into the dough as she says, "By the grace of God, I see that you are now dough." Then she and her daughters and her friends make the maccheroni by rolling out fine threads of dough, enclosing in each one a rough blade of grass, which then they very carefully extract, leaving the tube of pasta with a hole down the middle: this is pasta at its most rustic. Working at high speed, the women turn out hundreds of these, put them into baskets, and load them onto mules to be taken out to the fields. In the fields, the men work all morning, cutting grapes, tossing them into canvas sacks, and singing, but by midday, as the sun beats down, they stop to eat. "The pastry boards are laid out on rough benches," Maxwell writes, "and the women who have stopped to do the cooking have poured out the macaroni, tossed in tomato sauce, and sprinkled it with plenty of grated cheese. . . .

"The hurried meal lasts only a few minutes before the heads are raised from boards wiped almost clean: the people are bursting with laughter and gaiety, and their lips are red with sauce, so that they look like circus clowns." Such scenes still exist in Sicily, where wine is part of the most profound roots of the people's heritage. "Tradition here in Sicily is the same as it's always been," a peasant told Maxwell. "Christianity has taken away from us only the names of the old gods: their spirits live on as strong as ever in our hearts."

All over Italy the same harvest goes on, although the intense sense of connection to the earth and to past generations of ancestors may have diminished. When workers sit at tables out in the vineyard, drinking lots of wine, eating from platters heaped high with game, pork ribs, and great rounds of bread, it is probably when all the grapes have been gathered in and there is finally time to celebrate. In many areas wine has become big business. Mechanization and modern technology have changed the way men work. Since there are many more varieties of grapes, and huge amounts of money ride on the outcome of the crushing, there is unremitting pressure to get the grapes in.

Angelo Gaja, whose domain has been called the Romanée-Conti of Italy, stands in the supple, green rolling hills of Piedmont, a countryside more closed in than Tuscany but similarly laced with vines that sculpt the hills and the bowls of the valleys. It used to be that when people were hired from outside, winemakers gave them a thank you dinner at the end of the harvest, but no one does that during the actual picking and crushing of the grapes. In fact, wives often come by with small lunches so their husbands don't have to leave and go home. When Angelo Gaja does give a small dinner at the winery for the workers and their families at the very end of the vendemmia, it is to celebrate not only the harvest but the entire year. The meal usually comes in November at the end of the agricultural year, and typically begins with bagna cauda and chestnuts boiled with wild fennel, two ritual Piemontese dishes, and ends with the year's new Dolcetto.

Collecting the Grapes, from Trattato dell'agricoltura, *by Pietro Crescentino, 1519, Venice*

Elvio Cogno, another winemaker who has spent his entire life in the hills of the Langhe, remembers the *vendemmia* in his childhood as a real *festa.* Then, when country people came to buy grapes, they found it an excuse to *fare una bella mangiata,* "have a great feast." The women who helped pick grapes were less interested in money, according to Cogno, than in eating the grapes. Canny vineyard owners would go into piazze where the women were clustered in groups and ask them, one by one, if they could sing. The ones who said that they could were chosen immediately because the vineyardists knew that no one could eat grapes and sing at the same time. And everyone sang—up and down the hills from vineyard to vineyard as they picked grapes for the famous Barolos of Piedmont, and no day ended without contests to see who had sung best from hill to hill.

During the *vendemmia,* all sorts of relatives came to help pick the grapes, and everyone pitched in to make the bagna cauda. Two or three people peeled the cloves of garlic; others cooked the mixture of oil, garlic, and anchovies over a very low fire, and still others picked and cut the vegetables: cardoons, slices of the fleshy sweet peppers of Piedmont, Jerusalem artichokes, and cabbage leaves, tender and crisp from the first chill of winter. Families who could afford it used to dip slices of the extraordinarily lean beef called *razza piemontese* into the thick sauce as if it were a boeuf bourguignon.

Making the bagna cauda was a ritual that required time and patience, since the garlic must never take on any color. In some houses people ate standing up around the big copper or earthenware pot in which it was cooking, appetites prodded by the rich fragrances in the air. The bagna cauda might be cooked inside, but more likely it would simmer in the stone courtyard or under a portico, or cook over embers on the grill, its tantalizing aromas tickling the noses of everyone within range. And when everyone had eaten so much that all that remained was the oil, someone usually put the pan back on the fire, broke several eggs into it and scrambled them very, very slowly; at the very end, as an apotheosis of bagna cauda, they would shave slices of white truffle right over the mixture. And if any drops remained, slices of country bread dipped into the pan rescued them.

Somewhat to the south, in the Franciacorta region of Lombardy, famous for its champagne-style Spumantes, a mammoth *vendemmia* dinner is held at the Berlucchi winery for all the people who had anything to do with bringing in the harvest. It too occurs in November, after all the hard work has been done, and more than four hundred people celebrate in the cortile of the handsome brick winery. Red and green grapes spill over from the mammoth baskets that pickers once wore on their backs during the harvest. Goose prosciutto, a specialty of Lombardy, and delicately fried sage leaves are antipasti meant to *fare l'acqua in bocca,* "make mouths water" for the feast yet to come. People line up at long tables and find pumpkin gnocchi; more than nine hundred feet of grilled sausages called *strinu,* the dialect name for anything cooked until it is really black; an entire porchetta weighing close to one hundred pounds; and polenta grilled over a roaring fire along with the meat. Four hundred bottles of wine accompany this feast, which is presided over by Franco Ziliani, the owner of the winery, who remembers when he was a child eating the traditional *vendemmia* meal with his family in the fields. Each person had one fork and perhaps one plate and everyone dipped forks into common pots. Those people who could afford to served little birds as well, interspersed with a piece of lard, a leaf of sage, and a piece of chicken, pheasant, pork, or duck. They cooked on a revolving spit set up so the individual skewers fit into a large circle powered by an apparatus that caused it to rotate very slowly while a huge pan set underneath collected the drippings. The process took four and a half to five hours. Such equipment can sometimes still be found in Lombardy, in front of a fireplace, its pulley and heavy stone anchoring the revolving skewers, but it is not used much anymore. *Lo spiedo,* the word for the device, has remained in the language to describe someone who is slow-witted and picky, just like the long process to get those birds cooked.

Today, when such meals tend to be nostalgic remnants of a rural past, there are still a few people who continue the ritual. Piero Dorazio, the famous artist, and his wife, Giuliana, serve hearty meals to the twenty-five to thirty people who pick the grapes in their vineyard outside Todi in Umbria. The pickers start at seven in the morning, finish around six at night, and eat an enormous lunch that is served among the grapes: steaming platters of pasta made with chicken giblets and innards, pheasant and veal roasts and spareribs, turkeys stuffed with rosemary and pancetta, crisp diced potatoes cooked at high temperature with handfuls of fresh rosemary, great rounds of bread, a big bowl of salad greens from the

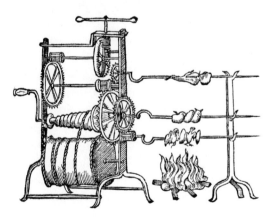

A spit for roasting meats with three skewers that turn mechanically, from Bartolomeo Scappi, Opera, 1670

Dorazios' garden, fruit, coffee, and, of course, wines. The simple foods of the countryside are cooked in woodburning ovens or grilled over the open fire and brought right to the table, where their flavors mingle with the crisp autumn air and the aroma of just-picked grapes. It is ample reward for all the hard work.

Bagna Cauda

Hot Bath of Olive Oil, Anchovies, and Garlic

Grape Harvest, fifteenth-century wood engraving

When the air in the vine-covered hills of Piedmont was thick with the aroma of newly made wine, workers once used to gather to share a pot of bagna cauda set over heat in the middle of a table. They would dip crisp raw autumn vegetables into the steaming garlicky mixture of oil, butter, and anchovies. This rustic dish is part of an authentic gastronomic tradition persisting to this day. Centuries ago feudal statutes required that a certain quantity of garlic be grown by each landholder, who was then taxed on it. (How wonderful that garlic should sustain the public order.) The oil for the bagna cauda was originally either hazelnut or walnut oil, but a light Ligurian olive oil would be just right today. Bagna cauda is eaten all winter long these days, usually as a first course served in individual pans. When the dip is almost gone, it is a tradition to break an egg or two into the dish and scramble it over low heat.

Makes 8 servings

3½ tablespoons (50 grams) unsalted butter
5 large cloves garlic, peeled and cut in thin slices
5 salted anchovies, boned and rinsed, or 5 anchovy fillets preserved in olive oil (100 grams), mashed
1 cup light extra-virgin olive oil,
2 or 3 eggs, optional, to scramble in at the end

Melt the butter in an earthenware pot if you have one or in a heavy saucepan set over a very low flame. Add the garlic and cook 3 to 4 minutes so that it becomes limp and soft but takes on no color at all. Add the anchovies and slowly drizzle in the oil, stirring almost constantly as the mixture cooks over a very low flame 10 to 15 minutes. It must always simmer, never boil, and is ready when the ingredients are well blended.

Serve with a basket or platter full of raw vegetables, including sweet red peppers, cardoons, celery, and any others that appeal—fennel, cabbages, arugula, or radicchio leaves, even leeks and Jerusalem artichokes.

Tacchino con il Rosmarino

xxxxxxxxxxxxxxxxxxxxxxxxxxx

*Roast Turkey
Scented with
Rosemary
and Pancetta*

It is rare now to come upon scenes of harvest dinners on Umbrian hillsides because machines have taken over the work of men, but Piero Dorazio, the well-known Italian artist, his wife, Giuliana, and their cook, Annetta Mannaioli, make sure that platters of food arrive for the workers to eat at midday after they cut the grapes from the vines and load them carefully into great wooden tubs. There is nothing complicated or arcane about this recipe, but the inspired addition of pancetta and rosemary transforms simple roast turkey into a dish fragrant with the smells and tastes of the Italian countryside. It is wonderful eaten cold the next day.

Makes 10 to 12 servings

1 turkey, 14 pounds (6 kilograms), ready to cook
Olive oil
½ pound (225 grams) pancetta, half cut into very small dice and the
    other half chopped in larger chunks
1 teaspoon fresh thyme
1 teaspoon minced fresh sage leaves
8 to 10 long sprigs rosemary; 4 tablespoons very finely chopped together
    with the diced pancetta, thyme, and sage, the rest left whole
2 large cloves garlic, peeled and roughly chopped
Salt and pepper
2 teaspoons finely chopped garlic
2 cups dry white wine

Rinse the turkey well inside and out and pat dry. Oil the cavity and put inside it the large chunks of pancetta, the long sprigs of rosemary, the roughly chopped garlic, and salt and pepper to taste. Truss and tie it well. Mix the finely chopped pancetta, rosemary, thyme, sage, and garlic together and season with salt and pepper. Loosen the skin of the turkey breast and slide some of the mixture all the way under the skin, getting it as far back as possible. Massage the filling in evenly. Spread a little olive oil on top of the skin and set the turkey in an oiled roasting pan. Bake at 350°F 3 to 3¼ hours, basting with white wine every 20 to 30 minutes. Serve with some of the fine pancetta, herb, and garlic mixture on every plate.

Patate al Forno con Rosmarino

~~~~~~~~~~~~~~~~~~~~~~~~~~~~~~~

Oven-Roasted Potatoes Sprinkled with Rosemary and Garlic

Some very lucky workers sit in Umbrian vineyards and eat tiny cubes of potatoes dusted with garlic and fresh rosemary and baked crisp and crunchy in a very hot oven. They eat them for lunch with turkey that has been roasted in a woodburning oven, during the *vendemmia*, but these potatoes are too easy and delicious not to make frequently.

Makes 6 servings

6 baking potatoes, peeled and diced into small cubes
2 tablespoons minced fresh rosemary
2 tablespoons minced garlic
½ cup olive oil
1½ teaspoons salt

Place the diced potatoes in a bowl. Add the minced rosemary and garlic along with the oil and salt, and toss with your hands, coating the potatoes well. Oil a roasting pan and spread the potatoes evenly over the bottom.

Heat the oven to 425°F. Bake until the potatoes are crisp and golden brown, about 45 minutes, turning them every 10 to 15 minutes with a spatula and and spreading them out in a single layer.

IL PALIO DEGLI ASINI E LA FIERA DEL TARTUFO

DONKEY PALIO AND TRUFFLE FAIR IN ALBA

First Week in October

iming is everything where festivals are concerned, but especially in Alba, in Piedmont, where for a brief moment at the beginning of October, Il Palio degli Asini, the Palio of Donkeys, overlaps the truffle fair. It can be a real opportunity to hit two birds with one fava bean, as they say in Italy, and a lovely example of going from the ridiculous to the sublime.

There's nothing serious about Alba's palio. Siena may have an elegant and emotionally charged race, with horses streaking around one of the world's most beautiful piazze, but Alba runs an anti-palio, a parody of a race, in which donkeys charge around a ring made of hay bales set up in the marketplace. It is prefaced by the usual handsome medieval-costumed parade with banners and flags snapping in the wind, horses and men in mail, armor, and velour, bells ringing and drums banging. The palio begins when the jockeys take a running start to land on the backs of their donkeys. Pandemonium breaks loose in the stands, with cheers and shouts and whistles. Some donkeys start out smartly, a few simply refuse to move, and others take off but then stop cold, tossing the jockey over their necks. One donkey might leave the track completely while another won't budge. At the palio I attended no amount of coercion could convince one stubborn donkey to change its mind. The jockey pushed from behind: nothing. He pulled and kicked and slapped its rump: not even the slightest acknowledgment of his presence. He went around to the front and pulled and tugged: still nothing. Another donkey made a short cut through the bales of hay and arrived in the center ring with the judges. A particularly promising animal was suddenly inspired to run at a fast clip around the ring, and the crowd cheered and shouted and jumped up and down until, without the slightest hint, the donkey came to a dead halt. It takes three heats to pick a winner, and by the end any number of riders have fallen off or have been left to sit stupidly on top of a motionless animal.

The event traces its origins to 1275 when, on the Feast Day of San Lorenzo, the patron saint of Alba, the people of nearby Asti leveled the area around his monastery. The Astigiani had a horse race to celebrate their victorious assault, and bestowed a silken banner, a *palio*, on the winner. The people of Alba may have had to give up the countryside, but they too held a palio, although it moved within the city walls. That palio went on until 1841. Finally, in 1932 it looked as if the people of Asti were finally ready to end their rivalry with Alba (feuds last for a long time in Italy); they invited the Albese to race in their palio. Horses were collected and riders prepared, but at the last moment, Asti withdrew the invitation and left the Albese out of the competition. And that is when someone dreamed up the idea of a Palio of Donkeys as a way to needle their enemies right under their noses.

Of course, there is a winner who gets a prize, which is treasured by the neighborhood of the city the donkey represents; and a celebrity guest is awarded a truffle the size of a golf ball. While there is a big meal at lunchtime, the real preoccupation with food goes into high gear only as the festival of truffles takes over Alba. It probably won't come as a surprise that the truffle celebration has its own history of conflict, only this time Alba fired the shot that launched the truffle war. It seems that when Asti organized its first truffle show in the 1930s, the head of the older Alba exhibition saw his opportunity. He collected all his co-workers and sent them to the preview with instructions to buy up everything in sight, so that when the fair opened in the morning there wasn't a single truffle for sale or for show.

The competition between the two cities remains strong, although from October through December truffles make Alba and the rolling hills of the Langhe the center of gastronomic geography in Piedmont for six to eight weeks. You know you've come at the right time when your nostrils are assaulted by a wild, intoxicating aroma that perfumes the air. It is the distinctive and mysterious fragrance of the white truffle, that extraordinary lumpy sphere that grows underground at the base of oak trees, limes, poplars, and willows. *Tuber melanosporum* ranges in size from a hazelnut to a melon, and can weigh up to a pound, although anything so big would be certainly the Hope Diamond of its species. There have been truffles in Italy since Roman times, but the first mention of pigs digging up white truffles in Italy comes in 1475 when Platina wrote about what he called a *trifola*. In 1524, thirty-seven dishes with truffles and capers were served in a single meal at the court of Ferrara. So far, no one has managed to cultivate a truffle, and so its origins still remain a mystery. Alexandre Dumas wrote, "You asked wise men what this tuber was, and after 2000 years of discussion they answered: We don't know. You asked the same tartufo and it replied: Eat me and adore God." Black truffles can be found in about half of Italy and in France, but the most famous and prized white truffles grow only around Alba. The best ones are the ones gathered when the weather is cold, for then they can be kept for a while. They are never cooked but always eaten raw, usually grated in a fine snowstorm to veil pastas and risotti, egg dishes, and meat. Reason makes sense of the old saying that a good year for wine is bad for the truffles, since grapes need sun while truffles need rain, since they grow, like mushrooms, isolated in the darkness of the woods.

On the first night of the truffle fair, there is a spectacular *passeggiata* down the main street of Alba. Everyone dresses up and strolls along the Corso Vittorio Emanuele before going out to eat the food "which awakens erotic and gastronomical dreams," as Brillat-Savarin once put it. During the season, restaurants grate truffles over almost everything except dessert, from handmade golden tagliatelle called *tajarin*, to risotto, to veal carpaccio, and Piedmont beef braised in Barolo. The menu of every restaurant offers gratings of tartufi (15,000 or 20,000 lire, or $12.50 to $16.00 extra), depending on the size of the truffle crop and the condition of the dollar. The truffle fair is especially lively during a weekend when the town is crowded with visitors.

During these few weeks, the main piazza becomes headquarters of the truffle hunters, who are normally a reclusive and competitive breed. For a couple of months these country people turn up for the market, dressed in their city clothes, carrying brown paper bags, which they open to show to knots of men clustering around. There are also a few women who carry little scales that hang from their thumbs to weigh the precious tubers that will bring them a major part of their annual income in a few short weeks. The men's hands shake—perhaps from excitement, perhaps from agitation—at being so removed from their regular lives, or perhaps from being in proximity to the kind of money the truffles bring. One morning when I was at the market, the gathering was broken up by the finance police checking to see that all the sellers were paying the value-added tax. Of course they weren't, so they snatched up their truffles and fled. In a matter of minutes, the crowded space was deserted. By Sunday they and their truffles were back, and it was just as difficult to edge into the thick crowds to hear the bargaining and get a glimpse of truffles or a whiff of their fragrance. Truffles are in evidence everywhere, not only in every

Truffles, Renaissance engraving

food shop but in the windows of other stores too. There are truffle graters in the hardware store, truffles displayed in bookstore windows. Truffles even turn up set discreetly in a corner of the window of a shop filled with ladies' lingerie, a rather startling conjunction considering their dark musky fragrance and taste.

I took a trip into the magical world of truffles with Cesare Giaccone, one of the most famous chefs in Piedmont, with his sixteen-year-old *sous-chef* and his truffle dog, Frida. After dinner, we drove in total darkness to a forested plot and immediately plunged without warning into a ravine full of fallen branches and thick roots and trees. Guided only by a single flashlight, we trod through patches of thick brush with tree branches slapping our faces, the dog leaping and sniffing out mysterious fungi at the bases of trees. It was a heady business. White truffles have a mysterious earthy smell that is like a primal narcotic for the senses. No wonder they fetch prices up to $2,000 a pound. The perfume remains in the nostrils as well as on the tongue for a long time, but never long enough.

No matter how wonderful Alba itself may be, everyone should drive through the countryside in autumn when it is time to celebrate the products of the earth: truffles, porcini mushrooms, hazelnuts and grapes, wild game like partridge and pheasant, wild hare and wild duck, hazelnuts and grapes—for these are the weeks of the *vendemmia*, when Dolcetto, Barolo, and Barbaresco grapes are being harvested. On small country roads, people sell baskets of apples, pears, and huge squashes whose interiors are the deep color of apricots. There are persimmons and pomegranates, sweet fleshy vegetables with thick interiors and seeds that hint of sexuality and birth and the lushness of the earth. And while visitors cannot go truffle hunting, they could learn how a *trifolau*, as a truffle hunter is known, searches for truffles with his dogs. Hunters usually venture out at night because the dogs' sense of smell is keener then, but also because it is harder for other truffle hunters to spot them at work.

I visited a famous truffle hunter, who greeted us in the army camouflage outfit he always wears to blend in with the countryside and throw off his competitors. His garden was full of apple trees, strawberry plants, rosebushes, and herbs growing in profusion. Truffle season was just beginning, and his face took on a decidedly baleful look as he described his pitiful findings, and shook his head dolefully about the prospects of the season. He went inside to his refrigerator and pulled out a couple of small beige lumps—truffles he had dug up earlier in the morning. He wrapped them in a handkerchief, tucked them into his pocket, and then took the dogs out into the garden beyond his house. A small demonstration: He took out his *zappa*, a special hoelike tool, and while the dogs weren't looking, buried the new truffles in the earth. He called them back from their romps and sure enough, after a bit of prancing and sniffing, one turned up the morning's catch with excited pawings at the earth. Point proved, the truffle hunter took off with his hounds. They disappeared completely a mere fifty feet beyond the garden, where the woods thicken immediately. The dogs sniffed around, and then, as they caught a scent, dug madly until their noses were deep in the earth. When they began to uncover a truffle, the hunter moved in quickly, pulling from his pocket tasty dog treats to distract them from eating the truffles.

In good years, thirty or forty holes full of truffles can open up in his fields, and some even pop through the crust of the earth. Fifty years ago grapevines marched along the rolling hills of the local landscape, each row marked with a willow tree at its head and its foot. Truffles grew luxuriantly under the trees and in the leas of the vines. Some were as big as a man's fist. This truffle hunter is so expert that he can look at a truffle and tell where it grew: a yellow one under a willow tree, a whiter one under a poplar; and those with a dark look and a gray interior beneath oaks.

During the festival, food stands serve all the specialties of Alba, which provide a perfect foil for the haunting taste of truffle. The menu reads like a roll call of foods of the Langhe: insalata di carne cruda, essentially veal carpaccio; lingua al verde, tongue with green sauce; tagliarini that are called *tajarin* and are as golden as hay; polenta e bagna d'infern, polenta with a peppery sauce; risotto con fonduta, a creamy fondue of three cheeses; beef braised in Barolo wine; three traditional cheeses called, depending on how long each has been aged, *toma, bross,* or *bra,* that range from young and frisky to old and powerful; and for dessert, rum-flavored custard known as *bonet,* the hazelnut pound cake called *la torta di nocciole,* and Alba's chocolate and hazelnut cookies, called *albesi al Barolo.* All these dishes can be eaten at a big improvised dining hall in the Cortile della Maddelena, or at various extraordinary restaurants in the area—La Contea, Da Guido, Il Giardino di Felicin. If you are very, very lucky, they can also be eaten at home, for every household has a *trifolia,* an instrument on which to shave a truffle into showers and fragments over melted cheese, risotto and pasta, and meats. During the season all who are able are sure to revel in the taste and perfume of the truffle. You can save truffles for a few days in a glass jar or a box of rice, which is perfumed in the process. But the very best way to keep a tartufo, says the truffle hunter, and he ought to know, is to eat it.

Tartra

Herb-Flavored Savory Custard

It is hard to imagine that this rich egg custard with its silky texture was once a common country dish in remote parts of Piedmont. These days it is an elegant first course, fragrant with fresh herbs and the subtlest hint of Parmesan cheese. Many decades ago it was probably made by poor people using the fresh milk and eggs produced on their farms to create a soup with the consistency of a pudding that they cooked in a fireplace. Giovanni Goria is certain that the name comes from *tarta*, Spanish for *torta* (pudding), whose Arab root persuades him of its ancient beginnings. This recipe comes from Claudia Verro in Neive, who is justly famous for her version. It is ambrosial under a hailstorm of fresh white truffle shavings.

Makes 10 servings

3⅓ cups fresh cream
1 cup plus 2 tablespoons milk
2 bay leaves
6 sage leaves
2 tablespoons chopped flat-leaf parsley
2 sprigs rosemary
2 tablespoons unsalted butter
1 onion, sliced
4 tablespoons grated Parmesan cheese
Grated nutmeg
Salt and pepper
6 eggs

Infuse the cream and milk with the herbs at least 1 hour. Melt the butter and sauté the onion over medium-low heat until it is transparent. Remove from the heat and cool. Remove the herbs from the cream and milk. Stir in the onion and cheese, a little nutmeg, salt, and pepper. Beat the eggs until they are thick and frothy. Add them to the cream mixture and beat them together well. Pour the mixture into buttered individual glass baking cups or into a 4- or 6-cup mold.

Baking. Heat the oven to 350°F. Put a water bath in the oven and set the molds into it. Bake until golden brown on top and firm to the touch, 20 to 25 minutes for the individual molds, 35 minutes for a 4-cup mold, and 50 minutes for a 6-cup mold. A tester need not come out entirely clean, since the custard sets as it cools. Serve hot or at room temperature. The tartra can be baked earlier in the day and reheated in a warm water bath in a 350°F oven about 10 minutes.

Tajarin delle Langhe

~~~~~~~~~~~~~~~~~~~~~~~~~~~~~

*Tagliarini from
the Langhe in
Piedmont, with a
Wild Mushroom
Sauce*

For more than 150 years the women of the Langhe hills have been making
these golden tagliarini, the only original pasta from Piedmont. Their
color comes from the incredible number of egg yolks absorbed by the flour
(in Italy yolks are almost orange), and their silky delicacy from being cut
almost as fine as strands of hair. During the truffle festival, they are always
served with paper-thin shavings of fresh white truffles over an already
rich and delicious sauce. Some people make them using 1 egg for each
100 grams (3½ ounces) flour, but the original recipe from Claudia Verro,
chef at La Contea in Neive, called for 30 egg yolks or 10 whole eggs to
2.2 pounds of flour.

Claudia once came to America and cooked in San Diego, where she
was asked to make pasta for two hundred people. "OK," she said, "I need
ten kilos of flour [twenty-two pounds] and three hundred egg yolks." The
chef looked at her as if she were crazy. "Very funny," said the look on
his face. "Impossible," is what he said. "Well," she said and shrugged,
"if you want me to make pasta. . . ." So they got the preposterous quantity
of eggs, and with the machine usually used for puff pastry she rolled out
the dough to its incredible fineness. When it was done, everyone came
to touch it. *"Com'è buona,"* they said in surprise. And it is so full of
flavor that people often think it must be made with a special freshly milled
wheat.

Makes 8 servings

PASTA

3¾ cups (500 grams) unbleached all-purpose flour
10 egg yolks
2 whole eggs, beaten
½ tablespoon olive oil
1 teaspoon salt

Put the flour in a mixer with the paddle attachment and add five of the
egg yolks one at a time. At midpoint slowly add the whole eggs. Continue
adding each of the five remaining egg yolks slowly but keep the dough
dry. When the dough has absorbed the eggs, add the olive oil. Put it
onto a lightly floured table and knead it, spritzing it with water from a
plant mister simply to keep it moist enough to be pliable. Divide the
dough in 3 parts, wrap in plastic, and leave to rest 20 to 30 minutes.

Roll the dough out through a pasta machine through the second-to-
last setting. It will be very fine and smooth and should be dry enough to
cut immediately. If it feels moist to you, hang the sheets of pasta on a
pasta or laundry rack. Cut to tagliarini width (in Italy, ½ centimeter or
¹⁄₃₂ inch wide) and if you are not using the pasta strands immediately,

put them on baking sheets lined with plastic wrap and sprinkle them with a granular flour like Wondra or semolina to keep the strands separated. It is important that the dough be dry or the pasta strands will stick.

Just before the sauce has finished cooking, bring abundant salted water to a boil and cook the pasta about 1 minute.

WILD MUSHROOM SAUCE

1½ ounces (40 grams) dried porcini mushrooms
¾ cup warm water
1½ tablespoons Marsala
3 tablespoons olive oil
2 tablespoons unsalted butter
2 onions, finely chopped
Giblets of 1 chicken, sliced very thin, and liver, optional
3 tablespoons minced flat-leaf parsley
2 sprigs fresh rosemary
2 sage leaves, sliced fine
2 teaspoons tomato paste, preferably double concentrate
2½ tablespoons red wine
1 to 1½ cups meat broth
Salt and pepper
White truffle, optional

Soften the dried porcini in the water and Marsala 30 minutes. Drain the mushrooms by putting them in a sieve lined with paper towels or cheese-cloth and save the liquid. Rinse the porcini well and slice them fine.

Melt the oil and butter together in a heavy sauté pan over medium heat. Add the onions and cook slowly until they are translucent. Add the chicken giblets and the herbs and continue to cook until the giblets look cooked on the outside, 5 to 10 minutes. Stir in the tomato paste. Add the mushroom water, red wine, and 1 cup meat broth; cover and cook over very low heat 30 to 35 minutes. If you are using the chicken liver, add it about 20 minutes before the sauce finishes cooking, 5 minutes before adding the mushrooms. If it looks as if the sauce is getting too thick add more broth. Season with salt and pepper and toss with the tajarin. Shave white truffles over the top, if you are lucky enough to have them, and serve immediately.

Torta di Nocciole

Hazelnut Pound Cake

This hazelnut pound cake is without doubt *the* dessert of Alba. It lines the shelves of every bakery in town and sits on almost everyone's table on the day of the Palio degli Asini. The famous hazelnuts of Piedmont have inspired elegant sweets, such as gianduja, but here in a humble and comforting incarnation, they make a cake perfect for breakfast or the end of supper. This recipe comes from Claudia Verro, who produces it daily at La Contea, her extraordinary restaurant in nearby Neive.

Makes 1 pound cake

½ cup plus 3 tablespoons (150 grams) unsalted butter, room temperature
1¼ cups (250 grams) sugar
3 eggs, separated, warm room temperature
1 teaspoon vanilla extract
1 cup (120 grams) hazelnuts, toasted, peeled, and finely chopped
2 cups plus 2 tablespoons (250 grams) pastry flour
1 tablespoon baking powder
Pinch salt

Cream the butter and 1 cup sugar with a wooden paddle or with the whisk of an electric mixer at medium-high speed until light and fluffy, about 5 minutes by hand or 3 to 5 minutes by mixer. Add the egg yolks, one at a time, beating thoroughly after each addition. Beat in the vanilla, then the hazelnuts. Sift the flour, baking powder, and salt together, then resift them over the batter and gently fold into the batter. In a separate bowl beat the egg whites until fluffy. Add the remaining ¼ cup sugar, 1 tablespoon at a time, and continue beating until the mixture is glossy and holds peaks. Change to the paddle attachment and, on the lowest speed, stir the egg whites into the hazelnut mixture in 3 careful additions.

Line a 9- by 5-inch loaf pan with parchment paper. Pour the batter into it.

Baking. Heat the oven to 350°F. Bake until a skewer inserted in the center comes out clean, 50 to 60 minutes.

Dog with truffle, twentieth-century engraving, from La Gola

Albesi al Barolo

Chocolate-
Hazelnut
Truffle Cookies
with Barolo

Take red wine made from Barolo grapes grown on the hills near Alba, grind intensely flavored hazelnuts from the Langhe, and add the famous chocolate of Piedmont to make these chocolate-hazelnut truffle cookies, an exceptional local specialty.

Makes about 48 double cookies

2½ cups (300 grams) hazelnuts, toasted and peeled
2½ cups (550 grams) sugar
½ cup plus 2 tablespoons (60 grams) unsweetened cocoa powder
1 teaspoon baking powder
½ cup egg whites
⅓ cup Barolo wine or other dry red wine
3 ounces (100 grams) semisweet baking chocolate
1 tablespoon butter

Grind the hazelnuts to a fine powder in a mortar and pestle, nut grinder, or food processor fitted with the steel blade. (If you are using a food processor, add 3 tablespoons of the sugar.) Mix the nuts and sugar in a mixing bowl. Add the cocoa, baking powder, egg whites, and wine and beat until the batter comes together smoothly. (If using the processor, add the rest of the sugar, the cocoa, baking powder, egg whites, and wine and process until they are a smooth cookie batter.)

Butter baking sheets or line with parchment paper. Drop the batter by teaspoonfuls at 3-inch intervals and let stand, uncovered, at least 3 to 4 hours, although you may leave them overnight.

Baking. Heat the oven to 350°F. Bake 18 to 20 minutes; the cookies should still be slightly soft inside. Cool completely on racks. While the cookies are cooling, melt the chocolate and butter together in the top of a double boiler over simmering water. Join each pair of cookies with melted chocolate. They should rest on their sides at cool room temperature for 2 hours or be refrigerated 15 to 30 minutes to set the chocolate.

Detail of the preparation of a country meal, eighteenth-century engraving, private collection

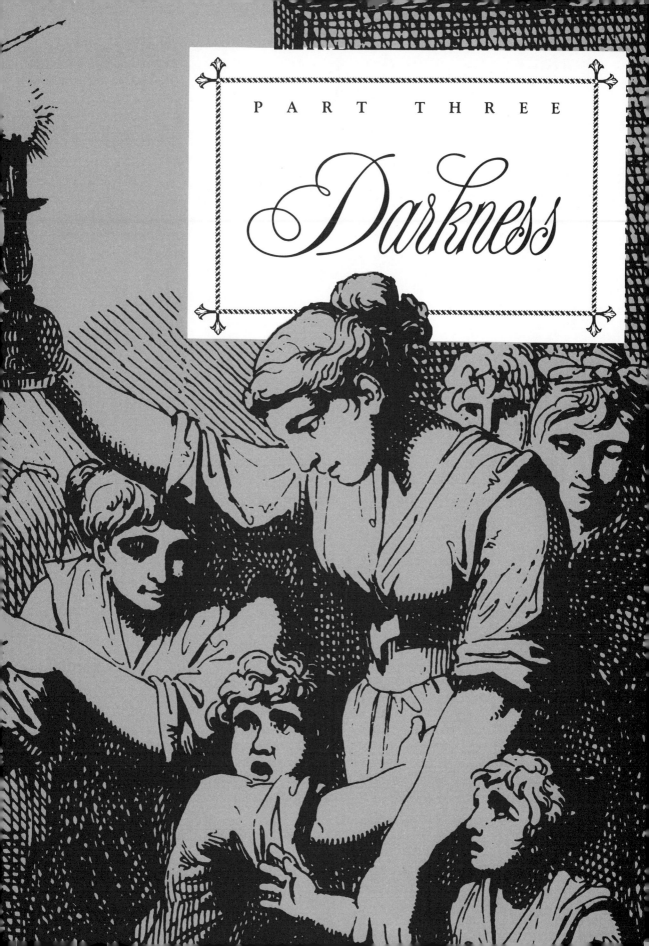

PART THREE

Darkness

rom November through January, the days cycle downward into the darkness of winter as the earth seems to die and seeds abide underground, where they must wait for spring and rebirth. It is a time when the dead feel an attraction to the living and hope to return for a visit, as they are said to do in Sicily, where families set the table for ancestors returning from their graves. In the Celtic calendar, November 1 was Samain, the feast of warriors and the first day of the New Year. In Italy it can be looked upon as what Mary Taylor Simeti calls "an alternative New Year," a moment in the agricultural year when, as the saying goes, "the wheat has been sown and the fruit all crated." The Celts believed that the dead returned to their homes through the brief fracture in time that opened up between one year and the next, a time of upheaval that permitted witches, demons, and other supernatural figures to reenter and walk upon the earth. It wasn't until the fifteenth century that the Church in Italy drew a veil of religion over the festival, which it christianized as Ognissanti, All Saints' Day. The festival commemorates the death of saints by celebrating death as birth into the Church and eternity. In the tenth century, Odile, abbot of Cluny, transmuted the Day of the Dead —what had been the Celtic feast of ancestors—into All Souls' Day, although in Italy it is almost universally referred to as I Morti, the Dead.

Tradition in Italy still has it that the dead return to earth between the first and second nights of November, and for Sicilians this means that it is departed relatives, not Santa Claus or the Befana, who bring presents. Not for them the convention of chimneys; instead, legend says that the dead rise up from their tombs on the night of November 1 and roister through town, plundering the best pastry shops and toy stores to bring gifts to children who have been good during the year. The children have already written letters to their deceased relatives, just as American children write to Santa Claus, and when they get up on the morning of November 2, they search throughout the house for the presents, which have been hidden, and shout out their thanks to a dead ancestor whenever they find something.

The presents are always heavily weighted with sweets, such as pupi di cena, tall, brightly colored dolls made entirely of melted sugar poured into a mold and painted. The most popular figures are almost two feet high and are shaped like the heroic knights from the puppet plays of Sicily, legendary heroes such as Roland and Tancred; also included are ballerinas, brides, and clowns as well as contemporary favorites such as Batman.

"Just at the time that the countryside turns in upon itself to nurse the dormant seeds and vines," Mary Simeti observes, "Palermo blossoms forth in an artificial flowering of marzipan, a cornucopia of fruit and vegetables molded out of almond paste. Each pastry shop works hard to outdo its competitors in realism—spiny prickly pears with all their prickles, pomegranates bursting with seeds, roast chestnuts tinged with the bloom of ashes—until the shop windows rival in miniature the variety and the color of the vegetable stalls in the marketplace." Baskets and individual pieces of the cunningly formed marzipan fruits and vegetables are given to the children too. These are the famous sweetmeats that Paolo Monelli saw in the 1930s, when he wrote that "all recipes come from convents where reclusive sisters clothe dreams and sighs in sugar and fine flour. Their hands caress the dough and candied fruits with maternal gestures. They confide ancient recipes like love letters. They imitate forbidden fruits with a wonderful almond paste." They taught the method to outsiders and today the pastry shops of Palermo call them "frutta alla Martorana"—after the ancient convent where they were first made.

On November 2 many families in Sicily go to church and to the cemetery, where after spreading a tablecloth they lay out a banquet at the family tomb, complete with chrysanthemums, the Italian flowers of the dead, as centerpieces of a bouquet set on the grave. Unlike the Romans, who honored their dead ancestors in February, during Parentalia, the nine-day passage between winter and spring, the Sicilians do not drip milk and honey on the lid of the sarcophagus, although they do eat favas, the emblematic dish of death. The Greeks saw the black spot on the petals of the fava plant as the stain of death and used the beans in funeral ceremonies, but refused to eat them. Pythagoras thought that their hollow

La Canzone de'Morti,
fourteenth-century
engraving

stems reached down into the earth to connect the living with the dead, and that therefore favas might contain the souls of those who had died. The Romans honored their connection with death but they cooked and served the beans as the most sacred dish at funeral banquets. When the monks assembled at the abbey of Cluny, in Paris, in the tenth century for the first Christian celebration of I Morti, they were confronted with the problem of what to do with the pagan beans. They proceeded to boil enormous batches of them and offer them up for the souls of the dead. The Church allowed the custom to continue of placing tubs of favas and boiled garbanzos at street corners and everyone, especially the poor, came to take liberal helpings. In some places, *farro* is served on the Day of the Dead, for grains are like eggs in the vegetable world, containers of new life. Perhaps that and its shape help to explain why *fava* in the Tuscan dialect is the word for penis.

"Folk culture," explains Piero Camporesi in a startling chapter called "Sacred and Profane Cannibalism" in his book *Bread of Dreams*, ". . . had a healthily ambiguous relationship with death: naturally 'equivocal' because it believed that the ambivalent 'death-life' rhythm constituted the obscure but powerful principle of human life. The 'other world' dwelt within the world of the living, constituting the other side of human existence."

So who can be surprised that Italians eat ossi da morto, bones of the dead, sweets made of finely chopped almonds, egg whites, and sugar shaped like tibia and skeletons, along with fave dei morte, little cookies formed to look like fava beans. Even sweets shaped like human figures, in the form of pupi di cena, are to be eaten on the Day of the Dead. Sicilians still make special ritual breads for the dead, including one called *armuzzi*, dialect for souls of the dead, shaped like two hands crossed on a breast, the fingers spread wide.

Elsewhere in Italy, chestnuts have a close connection to the dead. In regions as far removed from each other as Val d'Aosta, Calabria, and the Marches, chestnuts are sprinkled with sugar and grappa and served flaming, so they take on a dark, funereal color. The chestnuts served with sweet potatoes in Verona for I Morti are a wild variety known as *maroni matti*, crazy chestnuts, which are supposed to prevent colds and flu. Ligurians eat both dried favas and fresh chestnuts while in Piedmont the dish served for I Morti is called *cisrà*, a soup made of ceci beans and various parts of the pig. In the Veneto, where sweets are the ritual food of the day, the people of Verona eat a polenta cake called *tressian* or *pan dei morti*, bread of the dead, while in nearby Treviso, everyone expects ossi da morto, bone-shaped biscotti made out of bread dough sweetened with honey and flavored with anise. Once upon a time, goose was the traditional dish in the Italian countryside, tied as it is to sexual symbolism and life, but today it is eaten for Ognissanti, All Saints' Day, only in the Lomellina section of Lombardy; in Romagna, the Marches, and Umbria.

San Nicola and Santa Lucia, two more bearers of gifts from the other world, arrive on December 6 and 13 and then it is time for the twelve days and nights that separate Christmas from Epiphany. At this time there are so many celebrations that for a few years the Italian government moved Epiphany from January 6 to the closest Sunday before it because everyone was treating the entire two-week period as a holiday. And in truth Christmas *is* only the beginning of the celebration. December 26 is a full holiday in the Italian calendar, dedicated to Santo Stefano (Saint Stephen). December 31, New Year's Eve, the "pagan" island in a series of religious days, ostensibly belongs to San' Silvestro (Saint Sylvester), the pope who baptized the emperor Constantine. January 1 marks the beginning of the New Year, and January 6, Epiphany. These holidays, with the long bridges connecting them, are a continuum of festivals, full of great feasts of food, blazing fires, and rituals to drive out the old year.

The twelve days between Christmas and Epiphany concern the closing of one year and the opening of another, and are a time of transition used to read omens and prognostications. Country people forecast the coming season by observing the weather between Christmas and Epiphany (or from December 13, Santa Lucia, to Christmas), and with each day corresponding to a month they take a reading to predict the weather for the outcome of the next year's crops. On the night of Epiphany, animals are said to be able to talk, a belief that probably arises from the legend of the donkey and cow keeping the baby Jesus warm all night with their breath, but their owners take no chances and feed them well, lest they gossip about bad treatment. Fountains and rivers in Calabria are said to run with olive oil and wine, and everything turns briefly into something to eat: the walls into ricotta, the bedposts into sausages, and the sheets into lasagne.

Foods, like ricotta or lasagne, that are ordinary on most days take on a deeper importance in the context of festivals. Simple favas, grains, and ceci beans become communications from the ancients and symbols of death. On New Year's Day, the ancient Romans offered the god Janus grains of *farro* mixed with salt, and proffered *ianual*, a focaccia made with cheese, flour, eggs, and oil, for his help in providing good harvests. Later, on January 17, for the Feast of Sant'Antonio Abate, when a pig is slaughtered, people eat dried chestnuts, invoking fertility at the precise time the greatest source of plenty has been slaughtered. Whoever finds the black bean cooked into a sweet focaccia becomes King of Epiphany, and although he is destined to be dethroned, he no longer meets the fate of the King of the Wood, who was sacrificed in the forest.

Winter may be a time to drive out the bad spirits and ghosts that haunt the world in the fragile days of transition, but it is also the time to harvest the olives that will be turned into the olive oil that flavors much of the food eaten in Italy. Men have been picking olives in Italy since Romulus and Remus were born under an olive tree, symbol of their divine nature. Virgil sang the praises of the olive tree and its fruit in the *Georgics,* and Horace wrote that "olives nourish me." Romans anointed their kings with olive oil and reserved the burning of olive wood for the altars of the gods. The harvest varies by region. In Sicily the picking starts in November as soon as the workers have finished with the grapes. It goes on in November and December in Tuscany and Umbria, while in Calabria, the olive harvest may start in January, and in Campania it may even wait until spring. In Liguria, Molise, and Apulia, nets are strung from tree to tree to catch the fruit as it falls, while in Tuscany and Umbria men climb ladders and comb the branches with wooden tools or pick each olive by hand without the safety of nets. The old people in Tuscany are so practiced and skilled that it is said that they can pick 100 kilos (220 pounds) a day! In *Honey from a Weed,* Patience Gray describes the men spreading a fine plastic net and then climbing into the trees, while women pick the freshly fallen olives off the ground. It is arduous work, and at night they carry heavy sacks filled with the olives to a large studio, where they pick out leaves, twigs, and stems that would mildew or ferment, and then pack the olives off to a *frantoio,* the village olive oil press. Until this century the stone wheels of the *frantoio* were turned by donkeys. Now electricity powers the mills and workers are no longer paid in sacks of olives.

Olive oil terracotta orcia, *from Bartolomeo Scappi,* Opera, *1670*

Wherever olive oil is produced, it is traditional to celebrate the harvest with bruschetta, thick slices of country bread grilled over a fire, rubbed with garlic, and drizzled with pungent fresh green olive oil. Bruschetta is named from Roman dialect for the word *bruciato,* burned, a logical term for a great wheel of rustic, chewy crusted bread toasted or grilled over a charcoal fire. The same dish is called *fett'unta* (oiled slice) in Tuscany and *soma d'ai* (dialect for brushed with garlic) in Piedmont, although in Piedmont it is not bread but fat wands of crisp grissini called *rubatà* that are dipped in a shallow bowl of olive oil and then rubbed with garlic. Olives are frequently accompanied by glasses of wine, a fitting companion, since cultivating olives almost always includes planting vineyards. Peasant wisdom has it that the father who plants a vineyard for his sons plants an olive grove for his grandsons, because olive trees begin to bear years after the vines but once well rooted, may survive for centuries.

Cisrà

*Garbanzo and
Vegetable
Minestrone
from Piedmont*

This winter minestrone is substantial and nourishing, a hearty mixture of the earthy tastes of Piedmont. The trick of shaking the beans in flour and oil comes from Giovanni Goria, an expert on Piemontese cuisine who researched the ancient secrets of this particular soup. Don't be surprised when it froths up a bit during the cooking. I like to make the soup a day or two ahead so that the flavors can mingle. It needs to be served with garlic-rubbed country bread in the bottom of the bowl and a fine drizzling of extra-virgin olive oil, sprinkles of Parmesan cheese, and substantial gratings of pepper on top. The soup is so deeply rooted in the culinary history of Asti that it was once traditional to leave a spoonful or two outside the window on November 1 so that ancestors, returning to earth for a visit, could help themselves on the eve of I Morti.

Makes 8 to 10 servings

4 cups (600 grams) dried garbanzo (ceci) beans
1 teaspoon baking soda
¼ cup good-quality extra-virgin olive oil
2 tablespoons flour
Scant ½ pound (200 grams) pork rind, boiled for 20 minutes and cut
    into thin strips, or prosciutto rind, optional
8 to 10 cups water
¼ cup (50 grams) lard or olive oil
1 onion, finely chopped
2 cloves garlic, finely chopped
3 sage leaves, chopped
1 branch rosemary, chopped
Tender leaves from the tops of 2 ribs celery, chopped
1 large baking potato, peeled and cut in half
2 carrots, peeled and sliced
3½ ounces (100 grams) broccoli rape, chopped
2 ribs celery, chopped
2 leeks (white part only), sliced
4 or 5 cabbage leaves, cut into ribbons
Salt and pepper

Twenty-four hours before you intend to cook the soup, soak the garbanzos in tepid water with 1 teaspoon baking soda to soften the hard outer layer of the beans.

Next morning drain the beans. Put them in a large deep pot with the extra-virgin olive oil and flour, cover the pan, and shake the mixture vigorously. If you want to add the pork or prosciutto rind, do so now. Cover the mixture with water and cook 1½ hours over medium-low heat; you may need to skim off the foam.

Sauté the onion, garlic, sage, rosemary, and celery leaves in the lard or olive oil over a low flame about 10 minutes. Add them to the pot of garbanzos after the first 1½ hours of cooking, then add the remaining vegetables in the order listed above. Bring to a boil and simmer another 1 to 1½ hours, skimming as necessary to remove any froth that comes to the surface. If the soup becomes too thick, add a little water. It is done when the garbanzos are tender and the potato disintegrates in the liquid. Season with salt and pepper.

Serve in deep soup bowls with slices of grilled bread rubbed with garlic, with freshly ground pepper, good extra-virgin olive oil, and grated Parmesan cheese.

Zuppa Frantoiana
xxxxxxxxxxxxxxxxxxxxxxxxxxx
White Bean Soup

Imagine the crisp, cold air of Chianti as you make this thick white bean minestrone, which is traditionally cooked during the olive harvest. The harvest itself is a high point of the Tuscan year, but making the soup must wait until the olives have been carefully hand-picked and laid on long wooden trays, individually inspected, and then transported to the *frantoio*, the ancient stone mill where olives have been crushed for centuries. As the great wheel turns, rich deep-green oil runs out of the spout to be collected in immense terracotta jars called *orce*. But first there is fett'unta to be made with the fruity oil and then this white bean soup, which depends on the first pressing of oil and is served at room temperature, layered with the fett'unta in a deep bowl.

Makes 8 servings

14 ounces (400 grams) dried borlotti or pinto beans
10 to 12 cups water
Salt
6 to 8 tablespoons extra-virgin olive oil, plus additional for serving
1 onion, finely chopped
1 carrot, finely chopped
1 rib celery, chopped
1 tomato, peeled, seeded, and chopped
1 clove garlic, minced
2 medium bunches (about 1½ pounds) kale, chopped
3 zucchini, chopped
2 potatoes, peeled and roughly chopped
2 carrots, sliced
½ to ¾ tablespoon dried thyme

(continued)

5 or 6 fennel seeds
8 slices country bread
1 clove garlic, cut in half
About 4 to 6 tablespoons extra-virgin olive oil
Freshly grated Parmesan cheese for serving

The night before, soak the dried beans in cold water to cover. The next day drain the beans and cook them in a large deep pot with 10 to 12 cups salted water. Simmer until the beans are tender, at least 1 hour. Drain but reserve the cooking water.

In a deep heavy frying pan or Dutch oven, warm the olive oil and sauté the chopped onion, carrot, and celery in the oil until they are soft and translucent, about 15 minutes. Add the tomato and cook another 5 to 10 minutes. Set aside 4 tablespoons of the cooked beans and puree all the rest. Add the pureed beans to the frying pan with about 8 cups of the cooking water and bring to a boil. When it is boiling, add the garlic, all the vegetables, and the herbs. Cook over medium heat ¾ to 1 hour, adding water if necessary. The soup is quite dense, and it will thicken more as it cools to room temperature.

Just before you are ready to serve the soup, add the remaining whole beans. Cut the bread in slices, grill them, and rub them with garlic. Put half the bread in the bottom of a soup tureen and drizzle with 2 to 3 tablespoons of oil. Add half the soup, then the remaining bread, the remaining soup, and finish with drizzles of 2 to 3 more tablespoons of oil. Serve with Parmesan cheese.

Fave Dolci

xxxxxxxxxxxxxxxxxxxxxxxxxxxxxx

Bean-Shaped
Clove- and
Cinnamon-
Spiced Cookies

These crunchy nut-sized cookies for All Souls' Day may get their name —"sweet fava beans"—from being shaped just like the beans of the dead, but that doesn't mean that each tiny bite isn't full of almonds, spices, and the slight intoxication of rum.

Makes 42 cookies

1 cup (100 grams) unpeeled almonds
½ cup (100 grams) sugar
Grated zest of ½ lemon
1 egg
1 tablespoon rum
½ teaspoon cinnamon
¼ teaspoon ground cloves
½ cup (70 grams) unbleached all-purpose flour

Grind the almonds to a coarse powder in a nut grinder and pestle them with the sugar, or grind nuts with 2 to 3 tablespoons of the sugar in a food processor fitted with the steel blade. Add the remaining sugar and process to a very fine powder. Transfer to a large bowl and mix in the lemon zest, egg, and rum; mix until blended. Add the spices and flour and stir until the dough is well blended.

Divide the dough into 4 pieces. Flour a work surface very lightly and roll each piece into a log the width of a finger. Cut into 1½-inch pieces and flatten them slightly. Place 1 inch apart on oiled or parchment-lined baking sheets.

Baking. Heat the oven to 350°F. Bake just until barely browned, 16 to 18 minutes.

Fave dei Morte

Dead Men's Cookies

Italians eat these tiny sweets called dead men's cookies on All Souls' Day, when they are shaped to look like fava beans, the emblem of the dead in ancient Greece and Rome. The grappa in this Venetian sweet gives the cookies a distinct and slightly bitter edge. The same cookies are made in Rome without pine nuts or grappa by reducing the almonds to a fine powder, adding a tiny bit more butter, and flavoring them with cinnamon.

Makes about 5 dozen cookies

About 1½ to 1¾ cups (250 grams) blanched almonds
½ cup (100 grams) sugar
¾ cup (100 grams) unbleached all-purpose flour
1½ tablespoons (25 grams) pine nuts, coarsely chopped
1 tablespoon grappa
Grated zest of 1 lemon
1 tablespoon (15 grams) butter
1 egg
1 egg yolk
1 egg white for glaze

In a food processor fitted with the steel blade or with a sharp knife, chop the almonds into fine grains but not a powder. Move them to the bowl of an electric mixer or to a large mixing bowl and add the sugar, flour, pine nuts, grappa, lemon zest, butter, egg, and egg yolk. Mix on the lowest speed in the electric mixer or stir together by hand. The dough initially seems very dry but does eventually smooth out and come together. If you are really having trouble, add egg white, a teaspoon at a time.

(continued)

Shaping. Butter and flour baking sheets or line them with parchment paper. Divide the dough into several pieces. On a lightly floured work surface roll each one into a long narrow log about ¾ inch wide. Cut into 1-inch segments, about the size of a fava bean. Roll each one slightly to smooth out the edges, then press a small indentation in the center, so that the cookies really do resemble the fava beans for which they are named. Set on the baking sheets. Whip the egg white until it is frothy and brush a little bit on each cookie.

Baking. Heat the oven to 300°F. Bake until the cookies are a pale gold color, 20 to 25 minutes. Cool on racks.

Scarpetta di Sant'Ilario

Saint Hilary's Shoe

When Sant'Ilario crossed the river into Parma, he lost one shoe, which is why cookies that look like his low-heeled boots appear all over the city on his feast day. Spicy with cinnamon, nutmeg, and cloves, scented with cocoa, and slightly crunchy, these cookies are such favorites that they reappear for All Souls' Day in the shape of a tibia.

Makes about 3 dozen cookies

¾ cup (100 grams) hazelnuts, toasted and peeled
¾ cup (100 grams) almonds, toasted
1¼ cups (250 grams) sugar
1¾ cup plus 1 tablespoon (250 grams) unbleached all-purpose flour
Pinch salt
1 tablespoon plus 1 teaspoon cocoa
1 teaspoon cinnamon
½ teaspoon ground cloves
½ teaspoon freshly grated nutmeg
7 tablespoons (100 grams) unsalted butter, at room temperature
1 egg
2 egg whites
1 teaspoon vanilla extract
Grated zest of 1 lemon or ½ teaspoon lemon extract

I C I N G

1 cup (100 grams) confectioners' sugar
1 egg white
1 teaspoon lemon juice

Grind the nuts to a coarse powder in a nut grinder or process them with 2 tablespoons of the sugar to a coarse powder in a food processor fitted with the steel blade; if you are not using the mixer, add the remaining sugar and process to a fine powder.

By Hand. Place the nut and sugar mixture, flour, salt, cocoa, and spices in a bowl and stir to mix. Cut the butter in small pieces and cut it into the flour mixture until the mixture resembles coarse meal. Slowly stir in the egg, then the egg whites, mixing thoroughly. Then stir in the vanilla and lemon zest. Gather the dough together and knead it briefly on a lightly floured surface until it comes together.

By Mixer. Cream the butter and the remaining 1 cup and 2 tablespoons sugar in the mixer bowl with the paddle until pale and creamy. Add the egg, egg whites, vanilla, and lemon zest, one at a time, mixing thoroughly after each addition. Add the flour, salt, ground nuts, spices, and cocoa and mix until the dough comes together.

By Processor. To the ground nut and sugar mixture in the processor bowl add the flour, salt, spices, and cocoa. Cut the butter, which must be chilled, into small pieces and scatter over the top of the flour mixture. Process with 4 to 6 pulses until the mixture resembles coarse meal. Mix the egg, egg whites, vanilla, and lemon zest and with the machine running, pour the egg mixture down the feed tube and process only until the dough comes together. It does not even need to collect on top of the blade.

Chilling. Wrap the dough with plastic wrap, set in a bowl, and chill 1 to 2 days.

Shaping. Let the dough stand at room temperature 30 to 45 minutes. Knead it very briefly on a lightly floured surface, then roll it out ¼ to ⅜ inch thick with a rolling pin. Cut cookies into the shape of a low boot, about 4 inches long and 2 inches high; you could also use a 2-, 3-, or 3½-inch round cookie cutter, if you don't feel the need to be traditional. Place the cookies 1 inch apart on buttered and floured or parchment-lined baking sheets.

Baking. Heat the oven to 350°F. Bake 15 to 18 minutes, only until the cookies are slightly brown at the edges. Don't let them become crisp in the oven and don't worry if they are slightly soft when you take them out of the oven. They become crunchier as they cool on racks.

While the cookies cool, make the icing. Sift the confectioners' sugar into a bowl. Stir in the egg white and lemon juice and mix until smooth. You can brush it onto the cookies, draw shoelaces, outline the sole or the shape of the boot, or you could just give it a little free-form decoration.

Pan co'Santi

~~~~~~~~~~~~~~~~~~~~~~~~~~~~~~~~~~

*All Saints'
Day Bread*

From the end of October to the middle of November, people in Siena eat pan co'santi, All Saints' Day bread bursting with walnuts and raisins. In the countryside they go right on eating it until Christmas, when it is time to switch to panforte; but, no matter what, it is imperative to have a loaf on the table on November 1 for All Saints' Day. This bread makes wonderful toast and is the food of choice to have with the first Vin Santo and young Chianti Classico produced at the last harvest. Some bakers sprinkle their loaves with substantial grindings of black pepper; others include a handful of figs, a bit of lemon zest, or anise. Of course in Tuscany, they already have the bread dough, so they just knead everything else right into it, let it rise, and put the bread in the oven. During the winter season when the pig is slaughtered, people add cracklings to pan co'santi. If you decide not to use lard, you can substitute olive oil, although the bread will lack the smooth taste that lard gives.

Makes 2 round loaves

About 1¾ cups (300 grams) raisins
1½ cups tepid water
2½ teaspoons active dry yeast or 1 cake (18 grams) fresh yeast
1½ tablespoons (25 grams) sugar
3 tablespoons (35 grams) lard or olive oil
3¾ cups (500 grams) unbleached all-purpose flour, plus 2 to 3
    tablespoons for the raisins
1½ teaspoons (8 grams) sea salt
⅛ teaspoon (1.25 grams) freshly ground pepper
1 cup (100 grams) walnuts, toasted and roughly chopped
1 egg yolk for glaze

Soak the raisins in the tepid water at least ½ hour. Drain the raisins, but reserve 1⅓ cups water. Warm the raisin water to 105° to 115°F for the dry yeast, 95° to 105°F for fresh. If using the processor, warm just ¼ cup and refrigerate the remaining water until cold.

By Hand. Stir the yeast and sugar into the raisin water in a large mixing bowl; let stand until foamy, about 10 minutes. Stir in the lard or olive oil. Mix the flour, salt, and pepper and stir the flour mixture, 2 cups at a time, into the yeast mixture. Knead on a lightly floured surface until the dough is firm and silky, 4 to 5 minutes.

By Mixer. Stir the yeast and sugar into the raisin water in the mixer bowl; let it stand until foamy, about 10 minutes. Stir the lard or oil in with the paddle. Add the flour, salt, and pepper and mix until the dough comes together. Change to the dough hook and knead until firm and silky, 2 to 3 minutes.

By Processor. Dissolve the yeast and sugar in ¼ cup warmed raisin water in a small bowl and let it stand until foamy, about 10 minutes. Place the flour, salt, and pepper in the food processor fitted with the dough blade and process with several pulses to blend. Stir the lard or oil and the cold raisin water into the dissolved yeast mixture. With the motor running, pour the yeast mixture down the tube as quickly as the flour will absorb it and process until the dough gathers into a ball, adding another tablespoon of water if necessary. Process 30 seconds longer to knead. Finish by kneading briefly on a floured work surface.

First Rise. Place the dough in a lightly oiled bowl, cover tightly with plastic wrap, and let rise until doubled, 1¼ to 1½ hours.

Filling. Turn the dough onto a lightly floured surface. Without punching it down or kneading it, pat it gently with your palms into a 14-inch circle. Pat the raisins dry and toss with 2 to 3 tablespoons flour. Work them and the walnuts into the dough in 2 additions.

Shaping and Second Rise. Cut the dough into 2 pieces. Shape each piece into a round, tucking the ends of the loaf in and trying to keep the raisins and walnuts under the taut surface of the skin. Set each loaf on a lightly floured peel or a parchment-lined baking sheet. Cover with towels and let rise again until doubled, 1 hour to 1 hour 10 minutes.

Baking. Heat the oven to 425°F. If you are using baking stones, turn the oven on 30 minutes before baking. Sprinkle the stones with cornmeal just before sliding the loaves onto them. With a razor or a sharp dough scraper, slash the dough with 2 horizontal and 2 vertical cuts. Brush the loaves with the egg yolk and bake 5 minutes. Reduce the heat to 400°F and bake 30 to 40 minutes more.

Torcolo di Santa Costanza

ᴡᴡᴡᴡᴡᴡᴡᴡᴡᴡᴡᴡᴡᴡᴡᴡᴡᴡ

Sweet Bread for the Patron Saint of Perugia

Eat this anise-flavored fruit and nut bread on January 29, the feast day of the patron saint of Perugia, and if Santa Costanza (Saint Constance) winks, you'll be married within the year.

Makes 3 round loaves

1¾ cups (400 grams) newly refreshed or fresh Biga (page 31)
1 cup water, room temperature
1¾ teaspoons active dry yeast or ⅔ cake (12 grams) fresh yeast
½ cup warm water
Scant 1 cup (200 grams) sugar
6 tablespoons olive oil
4½ cups (600 grams) high-gluten bread flour
1½ teaspoons sea salt
1 cup plus 3 tablespoons (200 grams) raisins, soaked briefly and
    squeezed dry
⅔ cup (100 grams) chopped candied orange peel
1½ cups (150 grams) toasted pine nuts
2 tablespoons plus 2 teaspoons anise seeds
3 to 4 tablespoons flour
1 egg yolk for glaze

By Hand. Mix the starter with 1 cup room temperature water until smooth. In a separate bowl stir the yeast into the warm water and let stand until creamy, about 10 minutes. Stir the sugar, dissolved yeast, and oil into the starter. Mix the salt into the flour and add 1 cup at a time until you have a smooth dough. Knead on a lightly floured surface 8 to 12 minutes.

By Mixer. Mix the starter with 1 cup room temperature water until smooth. Stir the yeast into the warm water and let stand until creamy, about 10 minutes. Using the paddle add the dissolved yeast, sugar, and oil to the starter. Add the flour and salt and mix until the dough comes away from the sides of the bowl. Change to the dough hook and knead at medium speed 5 to 7 minutes. Finish by kneading the strong elastic dough on a floured working surface.

First Rise. Set the dough in a lightly oiled container, cover it well with plastic wrap, and let rise until doubled, about 2 hours.

Shaping and Second Rise. Mix together the raisins, chopped candied peel, pine nuts, and anise. Divide both the dough and the filling mixture into 3 equal parts, and keep covered the parts of the dough you are not working on. Toss each fruit and nut mixture with about 1 tablespoon flour. Flatten 1 piece dough into a rectangle, strew the nut and fruit mixture over its surface, tuck in the sides, and roll up from one end to the other. Roll into a rope about 18 inches long. Pinch closed along the seam. If the rope gets too springy, let it rest under a kitchen towel 5 minutes, then return to shaping it. Repeat with the other 2 pieces dough. Set each rope of dough onto a parchment-lined baking sheet or peel, connect the ends to make a circle, pinch them together tightly to seal, cover with a towel, and let rise until doubled, 1½ to 2 hours.

Baking. Thirty minutes before you plan to bake, set baking stones inside the oven and heat it to 400°F. Just before baking, cut a five-sided polygon into the center of the dough at the top and open the cuts well. You may brush the loaves with beaten egg if you wish. Sprinkle your baking stones with cornmeal and slide the bread into the oven. Bake 30 minutes. Turn the heat down to 375°F and bake 10 minutes longer. If the top gets too brown, cover it with aluminum foil.

SAN MARTINO

SAINT MARTIN'S DAY

November 11

hat timing! The saint's day arrives just when it is time to bottle and sample the new wine of the year. The French launch their Beaujolais Nouveau on Saint Martin's Day, but in Italy bottles are dispensed with and everyone gathers to sample the wine right out of the casks. The celebration truly marks the end of the agricultural year when the hard work of many months is finally over and all has been harvested. The weather is often so warm and mild for the Feast of San Martino that *l'estate di San Martino* is the Italian expression for Indian summer. San Martino used to be celebrated with great quantities of food and wine, with fairs and fires and general carousing. In Calabria boys used to go out banging old tambourines and ringing cowbells on the night of San Martino. In some places boys and men did lots of drinking, and put on masks when they went out carousing, so nobody knew who was drinking and dancing and serenading the girls. The great early twentieth-century anthropologist Pietro Toschi, who grew up in Faenza, in Emilia-Romagna, remembered boys sneaking out with paints and brushes under their coats to draw enormous cuckold's horns on the houses where they were deserved. In Abruzzo they would scoop out a pumpkin, light a candle inside, plant two red peperoni-like horns on top, and set it outside the door of the man with the most lascivious wife in town.

Why such carryings on for San Martino? November 11 was once an important day on the Italian calendar, a kind of new year when schools and parliament opened, municipal elections were held, leases signed, and

236

farm contracts renewed. If leases and contracts weren't renewed, November 11 became moving day, which happened so frequently that *far San Martino* is the expression for packing up and moving on. San Martino was very important to children as well, since he brought presents like the Befana and arrived via the chimney. In Piedmont people hoarded geese, chestnuts, and wine for San Martino. It is easy to understand chestnuts and wine, since they are seasonal products, but geese? Alfredo Cattabiani suggests that San Martino is like the Celtic New Year celebrated for ten days at the beginning of November, in which geese played their part as symbolic messengers to the other world. Domestic geese, sacred and untouchable, accompanied pagans and pilgrims to their sanctuaries. A curious destiny to become the centerpiece of the feast, although wild geese, migrating south at the time, are targets for hunters and domestic geese are killed in early November.

The importance of Saint Martin of Tours in the Italian calendar came about early in the Christian era. Born in Hungary in 316, the young boy joined the Roman army and became a professional soldier, which is why he is usually depicted on horseback. He converted to Christianity, founded the oldest monastery in Europe, and was the first nonmartyred saint to be worshiped; his basilica, called San Martino ai Monti, remains on the Esquiline Hill in Rome. During the Middle Ages he was the most popular and charismatic saint. In France he is still a major religious figure whose tomb attracts people who come to be healed as at Lourdes. He became the patron saint of the French monarchy and also of churchgoers, innkeepers, grape growers, and winemakers, and in some places he is also the protector of drinkers. Many stories about him involve wine. Perhaps the most famous tells of his rescuing a drunken man, then whipping his own cape from his shoulders, using his sword to cut it in half, and wrapping the man in it to protect him from the cold.

The legends surrounding San Martino have strong overtones of pagan New Year festivals. One in which he is said to have transformed a river of water into wine sounds remarkably like the Roman Martinalia, a festival

Making wine casks, Renaissance engraving

Praising Wine, from
Trattato dell'agricoltura,
Pietro Crescentino, 1519,
Venice

for which Bacchus turned water into wine, long before Jesus performed his first and similar miracle.

This *festa* seems like a mini New Year or Carnival, which often starts by casting out all kinds of bad things. Perhaps those boys and men with their painted evidence of cuckoldry are casting out the evil of an old year so as to start the new one fresh. One scholar made the suggestion that such announcements of sexual license may be a subtle way of indicating abundance at a time of year when the products of the earth have been collected. Another likens it to Mardi Gras, the last fling before the end of Carnival's excesses, when a group acts out the sins and peccadilloes of villagers in clever rhymes and scenes.

There are very few places where people still eat ritual foods for San Martino. It is mostly old people who continue to roast turkey and chestnuts in Apulia and Abruzzo and in Sicily (does the saint's great cape suggest feathered birds?). Waverley Root quotes a Venetian saying: *La paeta gù un destin che finisse a San Martin,* meaning, "The turkey has a destiny which ends on San Martino's Day." In Nereto, near Teramo, in Abruzzo, a turkey *sagra* is held on November 11 for which the turkeys have been raised on walnut shells, which hardens their meat and eliminates the fat. A special dish, tacchino in porchetta, is turkey cooked the way a whole pig is, except that halfway through it is cut in half and put back in the oven so that even the interior becomes golden.

Venetians eat a buttery cookie shaped like the saint on horseback, complete with a quince medallion sprinkled with gold and silver confetti. The biscotti di San Martino eaten in Sicily are flavored with anise and cinnamon or orange and cooked not twice but three times. No wonder they are as hard as a stone. They are a direct descendant, says Sicilian food expert Pino Correnti, of food served at the Thesmorphoria, the harvest festival of thanksgiving to Demeter when people paraded with focacce in the shape of genitalia. These Sicilian cookies were originally phallic in form, an irreverent reminder of the member of San Martino, and they are still made that way in a few places, but they are also shaped as spirals or rings, although many biscotti di San Martino are distinctly breast-shaped. Giuseppe Pitrè, the famous nineteenth-century ethnologist, described the biscotti as being decorated with rococo flourishes. All these cookies are meant to be dipped into new Moscato wine. A Palermo chronicle of 1876 noted the use of Moscato, *biscotti di rito,* ritual biscotti, and turkey. The sweets eaten these days in Sicily for San Martino are called *sfinci,* bigne made of mashed potatoes and flour, fried, and drizzled with honey. Nobody, it seems, follows the old ritual of eating cicerchiata, a wreath made of tiny dice of sweet dough drizzled with honey. Cicerchiata still appears for New Year in many parts of Italy, but it has disappeared from the Feast of San Martino.

Tacchino alla Porchetta

ıllıllıllıllıllıllıllıllıllıllı

Herb-Scented Roast Turkey from Nereto

Crispy-skinned and fragrant with herbs, this turkey is cooked in the small Abruzzo town of Nereto as a tribute to San Martino in an event called a Sagra del Pitone—turkeys are also called *piti* in various regions of Italy. When turkey first appeared in the Veneto, it was known as *gallo d'India* (Indian chicken) or *pitto.* At the beginning of this century a rich chicken farmer in Padua made so much money that he built himself a villa that local wits referred to as the Palazzo Pitti.

I don't know why cooking a turkey like a porchetta should make it so delicious, but the combination of the herbs—do not use a light hand with the rosemary or garlic—and cutting the turkey in half during the cooking seems to be the secret. Roasting just half a turkey doesn't seem to achieve the same results.

Makes 8 servings

**1 turkey (10 to 11 pounds, 5 kilograms), cleaned
Salt and pepper
6 cloves garlic, roughly chopped
⅓ to ½ cup chopped fresh rosemary
2 bay leaves
¼ cup olive oil or lard
4 cloves garlic, roughly chopped
¼ cup fresh rosemary leaves, loosely packed
1 bay leaf
2 cups dry white wine**

Clean the turkey well, removing the giblets. Salt and pepper the cavity and the interior of the neck. Chop together the first amount of garlic, rosemary, and bay leaves and place it in the cavity and interior of the neck. Skewer and truss the turkey and set in a well-oiled baking pan. Rub the turkey with the olive oil or lard. Rub some of the second amount of garlic, rosemary, and bay-leaf mixture into the skin, but let some fall to the bottom of the pan. It will make the juices delicious.

Baking. Heat the oven to 450°F. Set the turkey to cook at high heat 15 to 20 minutes, turn the temperature to 350°F, and continue roasting for 2¼ to 2½ hours. After the first half hour, pour half the white wine over the top of the turkey and baste every half hour, adding additional wine as needed. At midpoint in the cooking, remove the turkey from the oven, take out the skewers, and cut it in half. Return the turkey to the oven skin side down, baste well with the cooking juices, pouring them into the now-available cavity as well as over the skin. Continue roasting and basting the turkey until the leg wiggles easily, 1¼ to 1½ hours later. Let it rest 15 minutes and serve with the basting juices.

SANTA LUCIA

SAINT LUCY'S DAY IN SICILY AND LOMBARDY

December 13

*I*n Italy, there are no fireworks in the cold of winter for Santa Lucia, no bands playing or great revelrous feasts, but that isn't to say that torches aren't lit for nighttime processions or that there aren't special foods charmingly linked to her legend. In Sicily in fact, Palermo and Syracuse contend for the honor of being the site of the miracle she wrought in 1582 by bringing food to a famine-stricken people. So powerful is her presence that the entire island still changes its diet on the day of her festival.

People usually think of Santa Lucia as the Swedish saint dressed in a diaphanous white gown, wearing a wreath of lighted candles in her hair and long red ribbons streaming down her back. Such a romantic image presents a prettier picture than the original Santa Lucia, a virgin who came from Sicily, where she is still revered as the patron saint of sight. She became an early Christian martyr when an admirer was captivated by her eyes. Just hearing his flattering words compelled her to pluck those eyes right out of their sockets and send them to him on a platter. It was an extreme and dramatic response that made sure that she would resist succumbing to the temptations of love.

In one telling of the story, her suitor denounced her as a Christian to the Roman authorities, who retaliated by sentencing her to live in a brothel and when she refused, ordered her executed. Another legend says the Romans tried to drag her out of the temple where she had been imprisoned, but she wouldn't budge. Even a fire built around her had no effect, and when she refused to leave, she was condemned to death. She is always shown carrying her eyes on a plate. The walls of many churches are hung with little oval silver or wax masks with ruffled edges and incised eyes staring out of the middle. They are used as ex-votos against eye disease, although people keep them at home as well, hanging them on the wall next to the bed or in a wardrobe. All over Sicily Santa Lucia's eyes are also made out of bread or even appear as biscotti to be eaten as a way of partaking of her protection and perhaps tasting the enlightenment she brings.

December 13, Santa Lucia's Day, used to coincide with the winter solstice, the shortest day of the year, which linked the saint with the promise of light and the reappearance of the sun after the long, dark winter. Even though she herself lived in perpetual darkness, Santa Lucia has a natural connection with light, since her name comes from *lux* and *lucis,* the Latin words for light. In Sicily on the night of the thirteenth, people once lit bonfires that burned brightly in the dark, in Syracuse they marched in torchlight processions from the church with her name, and in Realmonte they heaped up logs of wood in front of every house and lit them at night to make it seem that the whole town was in flames. The fires not only commemorated the time when Santa Lucia withstood the flames but also marked the day when the sun was at its weakest, and lighting fires was a way of encouraging the sun to return to its power and warmth.

Sicilians still commemorate Santa Lucia's intervention during a severe famine in 1582. Food was in desperately short supply. As if by magic a flotilla filled with grain appeared in the harbor on the thirteenth of December. The people of Palermo claim the ships came to *their* harbor, while in Syracuse they insist the boats arrived there. People were so hungry that they couldn't even wait to grind the wheat into flour but boiled the grains immediately. To this day Sicilians honor the memory of Santa Lucia by refusing to eat anything made of wheat flour on December 13, which means forgoing pasta or bread, the usual staples of their diet. Instead they eat potatoes or rice in the form of arancine, golden croquettes shaped and fried to the color of the little oranges for which they are named and filled to bursting with chopped meats. During most of the year, sellers of panelle make flat cakes out of ceci flour, which are then fried and tucked inside a golden semolina roll, but on December 13 every street vendor sells the fritters to be eaten plain without any bread at all. In Palermo everyone eats cuccia, a surprisingly tasty penitential dessert made of whole-wheat berries cooked in water, then mixed into sweetened ricotta flavored with tiny dice of candied orange and shavings of chocolate. In earlier times and other places, such as Realmonte, the cuccia was flavored with honey or grape must, or even stirred into roasted fava beans. Cuccia rhymes with Lucia; its origins are Arabic even though

S LUCIA

the name is dialect for chicchi, wheat berries or grains. The grains are like seeds, holding the promise of abundance at the next harvest. This dish is made to thank the saint for one's having been saved from starvation, which may explain why peasant women in their religious fervor often thought they saw traces of the saint's passage in the pan where the cuccia was cooked.

Today Santa Lucia's fame has spread far beyond the borders of Sicily. Goose is eaten to commemorate the saint in a small area of Lombardy. In the Veneto and several parts of Lombardy, it is she, instead of Father Christmas or the Befana, who gives out presents to children. She travels on a donkey on the eve of December 13, when children hang bunches of carrots or hay and leave bowls of milk outside their windows to attract the hungry donkey and to make sure that Santa Lucia will stop to leave them some presents. In Bergamo and surrounding countryside, children once left their shoes on the kitchen windowsill along with a little hay for the donkey, and the next morning they found tiny sweets the size of a coin tied to the tips of their shoelaces. Children in Bergamo still get all their presents from Santa Lucia, many of which come from the brightly lit market in town where during the week of the thirteenth the streets are filled with tables bearing gifts and toys and sweets. They drop letters to Santa Lucia in a special mail box and then eat frittelle as they wander from table to table gazing hungrily at the tempting displays. From Lodi to Cremona and the area around Mantua children open their presents on the morning of Santa Lucia, while those who live in Verona receive special cookies shaped like piglets or ponies or flowers from Santa Lucia.

Cuccia

Ricotta Pudding for Santa Lucia

Remembering Santa Lucia is a delicious event in Palermo because the entire city eats tender whole-wheat berries folded into a ricotta cream that tastes very much like the filling of cannoli. It is a surprisingly delicious and healthful dessert. Sicilians evidently have no trouble finding soft white winter-wheat berries, but you may need to find a store with a large grain selection. Be sure not to buy the dark hard winter-wheat grain; even if it softens during the cooking, the grains will toughen up unforgivingly the next day. Sicilians know they have to plan ahead and soak the grains three days and so should you, but there's no work other than that bit of advance preparation. Recipes in Palermo call for equal amounts of wheat berries and sheep's milk ricotta, but since American wheat berries triple in the cooking, I have changed the proportions to keep the mixture creamy. To approximate sheep's milk ricotta, mix in a little fresh goat cheese. It isn't traditional, but a little cinnamon is a lovely addition to cuccia.

Makes 10 to 12 servings

1 pound 2 ounces (500 grams) soft white wheat berries
Pinch salt
2 pounds 2 ounces (1 kilogram) fresh ricotta or 2 pounds fresh ricotta
    and 2 ounces fresh goat cheese
1¼ cups (250 grams) sugar
¼ teaspoon vanilla extract
⅓ cup (50 grams) candied orange peel or citron, cut in tiny cubes
A few chocolate chips

Three days before you plan to serve the cuccia, soak the wheat berries by covering them with water and changing the water twice a day. On the fourth day drain the berries and set them in a large pot. Cover with lightly salted water, bring them to a boil, and simmer over the lowest possible flame until they are soft and almost bursting, anywhere between 3 to 6 hours. Remove from the fire, cover with a lid, and let them stand 6 to 8 hours.

Meanwhile, press the ricotta through a sieve into a mixing bowl and stir it well. Add the sugar and vanilla and beat until creamy. Let it sit at least 2 hours, then press the mixture through a sieve again. Drain the wheat berries extremely well, squeezing out all the excess water, and add them to the ricotta cream. Stir in the orange peel or citron. Serve in little cups or bowls as they do on the streets and in the houses of Palermo, and strew a few shavings of chocolate or tiny chocolate chips on top.

Panelle

Garbanzo Bean Fritters

Steaming garbanzo bean fritters are sold all over Palermo by vendors who fry them in little trucks right on the street. The fritters are folded immediately in panini made from durum flour every day of the year except December 13, when they are eaten plain out of respect for Santa Lucia. Sicilian panelle are extremely reminiscent of Ligurian panizza and Tuscan cecina, which are made by boiling garbanzo bean flour until it thickens like polenta, letting it cool, slicing it, then frying it to a pale golden brown. I like to cut my panelle into small squares and serve them as hors d'oeuvres or part of an antipasto, but they are also delicious on a larger, more filling scale. Sicilians used to give them a variety of names including *pisci-panelle,* because they were once shaped like fish.

Makes 6 to 8 servings

3¾ cups (500 grams) ceci (garbanzo bean) flour, sifted after measuring
6 cups cold water
2 to 2½ teaspoons salt
3 tablespoons minced fresh flat-leaf parsley
3 tablespoons grated Parmesan cheese, optional
Sunflower or safflower oil for frying

Gradually whisk the sifted ceci flour into the cold water in a 6-quart pot, being sure to avoid lumps. Add the salt and cook over a medium fire, stirring almost nonstop as for polenta, until mixture comes away from the sides of the pot, about 15 minutes. At that point stir in the parsley and cheese. Working quickly, spread the mixture ¼ to ½ inch thick on a moistened marble surface or wet baking sheet. Leave to cool. Cut the panelle into rectangles 3½ by 2½ inches.

Frying. Heat the oil in a deep pan to 365°F. Slide in several panelle, being sure they are not crowded and can move freely, and fry until golden brown on each side, about 5 minutes. Drain on absorbent paper and serve immediately.

Bottaggio

~~~~~~~~~~~~~~~~~~~~~~~~~~~~~~~

*Goose Braised
with
Savoy Cabbage*

Goose braised with Savoy cabbages appears on the night of Santa Lucia in a little pocket of southern Lombardy around Piacenza. It is simply a variation on the traditional Milanese cassoeula, which takes a miscellany of pork cuts and cooks them with cabbage. The trick with the goose is to cut away as much fat as possible. Brown the goose, and then braise it very slowly so the meat becomes rich and tender. Fine cooks in Italy search out cabbages that have iced over in the ground because their crispness and sweetness subdue some of the rich taste of the goose. This recipe is closely inspired by the one Franco Colombani served on the night of Santa Lucia at his splendid restaurant, Il Sole, in Maleo. If you can't get a goose, you could certainly use duck in this dish.

In parts of Lombardy, in Umbria, the Marches, and in the countryside of Romagna, goose is also served for All Saints' Day, when it is eaten with roasted chestnuts and bread made with crispy little bits left when the fat is rendered (see page 169). It is eaten with polenta from mid-November to mid-December after the harvest of corn.

Makes to 6 to 8 servings

1 goose, 11 pounds (5 kilograms)
White wine to cover
3 carrots, roughly chopped
3 ribs celery, roughly chopped
1 onion, roughly chopped
9 tablespoons olive oil
1 tablespoon butter
14 ounces (400 grams) celery, very finely diced
14 ounces (400 grams) carrots, very finely diced
1 onion, diced very fine
1⅓ cups dry white wine
2 tablespoons tomato paste dissolved in ⅔ cup warmed broth
5 cloves
10 whole allspice berries
¼ cup finely chopped flat-leaf parsley
Salt and pepper to taste
About 3 cups broth
3 Savoy cabbages, cut in quarters

The night before you plan to serve the bottaggio, use a cleaver or a poultry shears to cut the goose into serving pieces. It is easiest to start by cutting away the backbone, then cut into pieces. Marinate the goose overnight at room temperature in white wine to cover. Around it strew the carrots, celery, and onion, all roughly chopped.

Next day, just before you are ready to brown the goose, pull away all

(continued)

the loose fat, being especially sure to remove all you can from the haunches. That means not only the loose fat, but also the fat under the skin. You can render it and use it for preserving goose or making a confit. Warm 4½ tablespoons of the oil and brown the pieces of goose. Remove them to a platter. In a large heavy roasting pan, warm the remaining oil and the butter over medium heat and sauté the finely diced celery, carrots, and onion until they are soft. Return the goose to the pan. Pour in 1⅓ cups white wine and cook over medium-high heat until it evaporates. Add the tomato paste dissolved in warm broth, cloves, allspice, parsley, salt, and pepper. Pour in enough broth to come halfway up the roasting pan, cover, and let the goose cook slowly over low heat or in a 325°F oven about 2 hours. Mix and turn the goose every once in a while. Wash the cabbage leaves. In a separate pot, boil 2 inches of water, add the cabbage, and cook 8 to 10 minutes. Transfer the cabbage leaves to the pan with the goose and cook another hour, mixing every few minutes, until tender. Degrease the pan juices, add more broth, if necessary, and boil to concentrate the liquid into gravy; serve on the side.

NATALE

CHRISTMAS

December 25

The Italians say: *Natale con i tuoi; Pasqua con chi vuoi.* "Christmas with your family, Easter with whomever you like." At Christmastime whole families come together to celebrate in the intimacy of the home. Fat logs burn in the fireplace and rooms are scented with the dried rinds of mandarin oranges that have been tossed into the flames. Rome is the place to be at this time, since the pope is at St. Peter's, and even the gypsies are dressed extravagantly for midnight mass at Santa Maria in Aracoeli, where the huge wooden Christ Child in the crèche wears a crown of jewels and is swathed in golden and silver cloth. "A little wooden doll, in face very much like Tom Thumb, the American dwarf," said Charles Dickens.

By the middle of December you can smell Christmas in the crisp air, in the chestnuts roasting at street corners, and in the steamy fragrances spilling out the doors of bakeries and restaurants. You can feel it in the sharp drop of temperature as fountains frost over, leaving tritons and nymphs riding on icicles. You can hear it in the mournful tunes played by the *zampognari*, Italy's bagpipers, shepherds who have come down from the Abruzzo mountains dressed in crisscrossed leather leggings that reach up to the knees, shaggy sheepskin vests worn sheared side out, and slouchy felt hats. The keening sounds of their bagpipes and rough rustic flutes swirl eerily through the streets, a melancholy poetry that is as familiar to a Roman as Santa's sleighbells are to an American. The *zampognari* walk slowly in twos and threes up and down the Via Condotti and the Via della Croce and the other elegant shopping streets below the Spanish Steps, where, startling reminders of the shepherds at the manger in Bethlehem, they play their ancient instruments in front of rich window displays of furs, leathers, and silks. The *zampognari* arrive some days before Christmas, but they used to arrive much earlier and always charged a set rate for a nine-day serenade to the Madonna called a *novena*. Now they merely hold out their hats and everyone drops in a few coins or bills.

Romans also know the Christmas season has come when a blaze of flowers appears in terracotta pots and window boxes, warming the walls of dark stone buildings. Strings of tiny white lights whorl and swoop, wheeling across the Corso and other shopping streets in exuberant patterns. Crèches begin appearing everywhere—the Spanish Steps look like an opera stage, with a life-sized Nativity scene set up at midlevel, but there are numerous other crèches (*presepio* in Italian) in churches and piazze, and even in store windows and restaurants.

Many Roman families continue to set out crèches with figures collected and added to over the years. Some make simple displays and put them on a mantelpiece or table, and others design enormous scenes that fill half a living room, "like a dollhouse but a hundred thousand times more enchanting: the doll is the Baby Jesus," wrote Barbara Grizzuti Harrison in *Italian Days*. The crèche is placed in a landscape that is detailed and specific. Goats and oxen are guarded by shepherds on a chain of mountains or a hilly rise. In the valleys sheep are eating their fill of grass, and perhaps even lower down there is a hut inside which shepherds are milking their sheep and then heating the milk to make cheese. Here and there farmers are at work in the fields. Shepherds carry gifts of bread, ricotta, lamb, and greens to the grotto, where a baby lies in a manger with donkeys and oxen on their knees and Mary and Joseph, of course, and above it all an angel is suspended against a sky glowing with tiny stars. Saint Francis made the first crèche in the little town of Greccio in 1223 as a way of dramatically telling the story of the birth of Jesus. He created a manger in the straw and surrounded it with the full cast of characters: shepherds, cattle, and donkeys, the Magi, Mary, Joseph, and Jesus. In the centuries that followed, his innovation became one of the strongest, most endearing parts of the Christmas celebration. Ordinary people saw scenes of the familiar story with ordinary villagers going about their daily lives while the miracle of the birth was taking place.

The most dramatic crèche scenes were created in baroque Naples during the reign of the Bourbon king Charles III, who built a huge *presepio* filled with one thousand shepherds—they were his subjects, after all. His *presepio* launched a great competition, so the Neapolitan nobility not only followed his example but opened their palaces to the public, allowing them to compare the lavish Nativity scenes. Today in Naples, the shep-

herds' market has everything for Christmas, especially the clay figures for the manger, and in three or four winding alleys off Spaccanapoli you can see artisans hard at work making figures that are shipped all over the world.

In Rome many windows are filled with beautifully rendered fantasies of a small village in Jesus' time. Landscapes are painted so that the story of the miracle in Bethlehem looks truly natural to Italians, especially since all the terracotta figures are dressed in Italian clothes. Particularly charming scenes show Jesus born under the covered loggia of a crenellated castle tower, and bakers, butchers, and fruit vendors, dressed in medieval outfits, are depicted selling Italian specialties along winding streets lined with medieval and Renaissance buildings.

Natale con i tuoi; Pasqua con chi vuoi. By the twenty-fourth of December most of the population has departed for family homes elsewhere. The city becomes so quiet that it is actually possible to cross a street or drive a car without imminent peril to life and limb. Those who are still in residence ought by then to have snatched up seasonal temptations on display in the food shops: rounds of pangiallo crammed with fruit and nuts, and darker, peppery panpepato, cigar-shaped mostaccioli, and many kinds of panettone, including some with a hood of chocolate icing arching over a crèche scene set on the top of the sweet bread. From other parts of Italy come foods for celebration: the buttery cheeses of Apulia wrapped in green reeds; black and white truffles; smoked bottarga, the tasty roe of Sardinian tuna; marinated eel; and lots of nuts such as ones the ancient Romans ate at holidaytime to ensure a fertile year. Windows are full of dried and candied fruits, fat Malaga grapes and creamy pignoli, sultanas, and sugared and candied orange halves.

In some areas the Christmas season starts with the celebration of the birth of San Nicola, the original Saint Nicholas, on December 6, or on the Feast of Santa Lucia, December 13, but in Rome Christmas begins on December 8, the Feast of the Immaculate Conception, when the pope leaves the Vatican for the Piazza di Spagna to drape garlands of flowers around the statue of the Madonna. Since the statue stands high on top of a column, the pope cedes his right to place the wreath to the fire department, whose ladders are long enough to reach.

December 24 and 25 are the most important days of the holiday. Christmas is a two-day feast, a traditional celebration whose unchanging menu and form satisfy a deep longing for permanence. While each region has its own tastes and ritual dishes, ever since the Church imposed the penitential rule of *mangiare di magro,* everyone eats fish on holiday eves to purify the body and get it ready for the big feasts that follow.

Until very recently Christmas in Rome began in earnest with a visit to Cottio, the wholesale fish market that was opened to the public just once a year, from two A.M on December 23 till dawn the next day. Into the stone building on a street lit by pinwheels of light came tens of thousands of pounds of fish to be scrutinized, prodded, and poked. Romans bargained seriously for the creatures that would form the centerpieces of their Christmas Eve dinner. The market was open by invitation only, but the milling crowds grew larger and larger each year, and there were always as many people there out of sheer curiosity as there were those grudgingly spending the few coins in their pockets. The name *Cottio* probably comes from the verb *quotare,* to bid—and the stone building rang and echoed with the noisy voices of sellers praising the fish and calling out descriptions of them while buyers bargained with such intensity that they actually came to blows. The wholesalers used to fry little fish in a gargantuan pan that was seven feet wide and hand them out like hors d'oeuvres with glasses of white wine from the local hills. The tradition ended only recently in the 1980s, dealing a real blow to both bargains and tradition.

All over Italy, eel is the traditional centerpiece of the Roman *cenone,* as the big Christmas Eve dinner is known. The banquet seems to have originated in the fifth or sixth century when the pope said three masses on Christmas Eve; wherever he went for the mass, they set out a banquet. Romans have an enormous fondness for eel, which they bought at the fish market at the Portico d'Ottavia, the gate that now forms part of the Jewish ghetto. Columella wrote of eel, and Apicius included recipes for it in his *De re coquinaria.* The eel certainly comes from a pre-Christian cult, a water snake that was known and consumed during the time of the

Etruscans; now it is a ritual food in which the sacred and profane meet. Eel is always sold live and wriggling at the markets so the buyer is sure of its freshness. It is still alive when it is beheaded, and also when pieces of it are dropped into boiling water and bend like a snake. Like a serpent of the lake, guardian of life and immortality, the eel seems alive even as it dies. It resembles the snake that renews itself by sloughing its skin, like the festival that returns anew each year. The female eel, much tastier than the male, is called *anguilla* when young and small, and becomes *capitone* when it gets bigger, weighing in at about eleven pounds and measuring four feet long. The eels that appear at the Christmas Eve table are the larger ones. They are laid on a log, heads and tails cut away, the pieces separated with a knife and then skewered together and spit-roasted or grilled well seasoned with olive oil, vinegar, garlic, and salt. Sometimes they are stewed with white wine and peas (*in umido*), roasted in the oven, or pickled in vinegar, oil, bay leaves, rosemary, and cloves.

Even though Cottio is not open every year, anyone can go to the outdoor market at the Campo dei Fiori on Christmas Eve day and see dinner swimming and wriggling before his eyes. At the far end of the piazza, finger-sized eels slither in the big basins of water, next to others as fat as a man's arm. There are buckets of bright red gamberoni, baskets of tiny sea snails and clams the size of a thumbnail, iridescent mullet, and shiny cod. An entire porchetta with bows and ribbons around it is displayed at the other end of the piazza. There are mountains of vegetables—broccoli and the thornless artichokes grown only around the Roman plain—and fruits that include Sicilian blood oranges and the pale yellow bumpy-rinded citron whose candied rind finds its way into the traditional Christmas pangiallo.

Our family spent a traditional Roman Christmas Eve with a family of sixty people, three generations ranging from six brothers and sisters in their sixties and early seventies to babies; they were a varied lot, including Catholics, Jews, and a wonderful Berber woman. The family have always had Christmas together in their big house in the center of Rome, but the year we joined the group, the aunt in charge of the vast preparations

Eel, sixteenth-century copper engraving from Aquitalium Animalium Salviati *by Beatricetto Nicolo*

wasn't well enough to superintend them. So the middle generation, husbands and wives in their twenties and thirties with a dozen kids among them, took over. They certainly weren't going to allow the traditional Christmas Eve to change. The children stood up on a table and sang Christmas songs and recited poems. One year, all the aunts and uncles climbed onto the table and did the same! The uncles put coins on the table after each performance so the kids would have a little money with which to play *tombola,* a bingolike game that is always played between the end of dinner and midnight mass, a tradition that reaches back to the Roman Saturnalia, when the game was played with dice. In *tombola* the counters are dried beans—food seems to enter into everything—and the game is exciting and noisy. This particular year the older generation was slightly restrained. Although the dinner itself showed no hint of holding back. Course after course poured forth, all built around fish. This *cenone* began with beautiful red shrimp, smoked salmon, and insalata russa, and progressed to fettuccine with smoked salmon and bavette al tonno, pasta with tuna. Eel was served roasted, but was uniformly spurned by the two younger generations. "Uggh," said the little kids, making faces. Old traditions are dying fast, but huge meals are certainly not going out of style. Out of the kitchen in rapid succession came spigola al forno (baked bass) and grilled salmon, both steaming on their big white platters. Next came a combination of fried broccoli, artichokes, zucchini, and cubes of ricotta, a dish once known as *pezzetti,* little pieces, fried in batter. A *meta tavola tirano fuori il fritto,* "At the midway point they bring out the fried dish," according to an old saying. Baccalà, asparagus, apple slices, other products of the season are sometimes included.

My favorite dessert was the cassola made by an aunt named Maria, who shrugged modestly when I told her it was the best cheesecake I had ever eaten. Next to it sat panpepato, a relative of panforte, and a Roman pangiallo along with a phenomenal selection of fruits, including fresh kiwis, now an important Italian crop, and lichees—an impressive display of *primizie,* first fruits, in December.

Once, every Roman table had to have spaghetti alle alici, with anchovies; marinated eel, which is still sold and eaten all over Rome; spigola (bass); pieces of broccoli; and for dessert, both pangiallo and torrone. And afterward, before midnight mass, if they didn't play *tombola,* they played *gioco dell'oca,* the goose game, invented in honor of the geese that saved the Campidiglio from invasion by northern Gauls.

And then there's Christmas dinner at midday. We hardly had time to rise from the table on Christmas Eve, pocket our winnings from *tombola,* go to mass, come back for a taste of pangiallo, and sleep briefly before we had to confront yet another massive meal. This time we ate with friends in their apartment near the Piazza Navona, in a more regionally

mixed group—Roman, Umbrian, Milanese, and Neapolitan. Many Christmas dinners start with pasta in broth, and in Rome we had cappelletti in brodo di cappone, "little hats" filled with a variety of chopped meats, cheese, eggs, and spices. Everyone is required to eat at least a dozen. Some Romans say it isn't Christmas without gallinaccio brodetato, chicken broth with onions, prosciutto, egg yolks, and a goodly spritzing of vino dei Castelli Romani, but at this meal we had instead a Christmas soup from the Marches, a region northeast of Rome, where lemon-flavored gli straccetti, similar to the Roman soup stracciatella, is obligatory. Next we had capon rubbed with crushed garlic, sage leaves, and lemon juice, and a turkey bursting with pancetta, eggs, bread crumbs, and Parmesan cheese. Instead of frankincense and myrrh, friends had brought a variety of traditional sweets. Mostaccioli represented Rome; struffoli came from Naples; fig-filled buccellati came from Sicily; cavallucci from Siena; and panettone, by now practically the national Christmas sweet bread, was the gift of the Milanese at the table.

Our friends set their presents under a decorated Christmas tree, but the real Christmas tree in Italy is the ceppo, the Yule log burned in the fireplace during the twelve nights at the end of the year. The burning log gives heat and light, just as the sun does, and is probably a remnant of worship of the gods of the forest, a magical attempt to influence the events of the year. During the Agonalia, celebrated for the god Janus as one year dissolved and the next came into being, the ancient Romans ate enormous focacce, great disks of bread as round as the sun.

In Siena the Yule log was a piece of wood, sometimes shaped like a four-wheeled carriage pulled by two beasts, and it was whisked out of sight at an early hour only to reappear later to the delighted screams of the children. The young members of the family received presents from their grandfather in front of the Christmas log and then watched as their father lit it and left it to burn all day long.

Christmas is a holiday that is a barely disguised eating orgy. During the rest of the year, meals for Italians were often meager, but Christmas, with its abundant platters and bowls of food, has always stood in extravagant contrast to ordinary life. To be ready for it, workers in the cities had a sort of Christmas Club arrangement with local shopkeepers, whereby they paid a small sum of money each week and at the end of the year were rewarded with a big basket of foodstuffs for the holidays.

Christmas Eve is called La Vigilia, the eve. In the south it is when the big meal of the holiday is served, while in the north Christmas Day food tends to be more important. No meat is served at nighttime, but that hasn't deterred the north from devising a remarkably rich cuisine. Cappon magro, the specialty of Liguria, is a fantasy of the nobility that may sound abstemious (magro means lean), but it is lavishly composed of such expensive fish as lobster and shrimp, individually poached, elaborately molded, and held together with a delicious rich sauce. Some penitence. In Piedmont lasagne della Vigilia was made with sheets of pasta as wide as a man's palm and sauced with lots of butter and anchovies, a whiff of garlic, spoonfuls of Parmesan cheese, and grindings of fresh black pepper. Wider than the usual lasagne, the noodles evoked the swaddling clothes that wrapped Jesus in the manger. Paolo Monelli, a journalist who traveled from one end of Italy to the other recording its culinary traditions, wrote about a Christmas Eve dinner in Parma in the early 1950s. It started with spicy, slightly sweet chestnut-filled tortelli, which were followed by a layered pasta called *manica di frate,* monks' sleeves, and fried cod with pine nuts, raisins, garlic, and parsley. Two candles burned during dinner, and the leftovers were left for the souls of the dead. Some people believe that if they don't eat that ritual meal, the head of the house will die— certainly a compelling reason for finishing dinner.

In the south the richest Christmas Eve eating traditions exist around Naples, where the holiday used to go on for four days. The city becomes unnaturally quiet as life moves indoors, although the nearby tiny village of Ciminna isn't quiet at all, because a raggedly dressed, wrinkle-faced doll called *La Vecchia di Natale,* the Old Woman of Christmas, comes out, followed by children blowing pipes, banging pots and pans, and ringing cowbells. She is like the Befana, and in some places she changes form, turning into an ant or a bird. Before departing, she always leaves fruits and sweets as presents. In Naples, however, everyone is inside eating enormous dinners. On family tables there is a sauté of broccoli and of frutti di mare; "drowned" baby octopus, sold in the markets already prepared; vermicelli with anchovies or with tiny Neapolitan clams; eel fried or roasted (the typical Neapolitan used to eat half a meter of eel on Christmas Eve); lobster or baked fish or "pastette" di baccalà, little pieces of baccalà fried in a soft batter of leavened dough; caponata; and a salad made of cauliflower, black olives, anchovies, capers, and pickled vegetables in oil and vinegar that is called *rinforzo* because Neapolitans eat it daily from Christmas to Epiphany and add to or reinforce it each day. It's the sweets, though, that dazzle: struffoli, pyramids of fried dough glazed with a spicy honeyed syrup; sweet wreaths called *rococò;* marzipan; rafaioli, fingers of pan di Spagna stacked up like cordwood and iced; croccante; apostrophe-shaped susamielle, once made with the sesame seeds and honey that gave them their name; and sciosciole, dried fruits strung like a necklace.

In Abruzzo, where tradition prevails, people prepare Christmas Eve meals with the required seven or nine dishes—seven for the seven virtues and the seven sacraments, and nine for the Trinity multiplied by three, an extremely powerful number. Courses include fedelini with a sauce of anchovies or sardines, roasted eel, and various fish that are fried, roasted, marinated, or served in broth. (Baccalà, the quintessential fasting food, appears as well.) In the regions of Italy that once were part of Magna Grecia, the ritual number is thirteen, for Jesus and his twelve disciples, and it applies to fruits and nuts offered at the end of the meal, which must include nuts, figs, olives, watermelon, and mandarin oranges.

Christmas Eve dinner in Apulia varies from city to city, although certain dishes always appear: eel, baccalà, or shellfish; young fennel cooked with garlic and anchovies; and cardoons. Once again the sweets capture the imagination. They include curly ribbons of dough called *le cartellate*, which symbolize the sheets of baby Jesus; *calzoncielli*, the pillow on which he laid his head; *latte di mandorla*, the Virgin's milk; *dita degli apostoli*, fingers of the apostles; *pettole*; and *frittelle. I calzoni di San Leonardo*, the specialty of Molfetta, represent the cradle. When they are made, the last piece of fried dough is broken and an Ave Maria said over it, before it is tossed into the fireplace for good luck.

In Sicily every household, no matter how poor, had little altars called *le cone*, which were often hung with green leaves and encircled by oranges, mandarin oranges, and lemons. Families competed to see who could make the most beautiful altars, surrounding them with highly polished apples, enormous pears, medlars, chestnuts, figs, and colored eggs that swayed gently in the heat given off by candles. Today Sicilian fish markets still sell oysters and lobster, triglie (red mullet), trout, and silvery cod, but eel is the ritual food in Sicily as elsewhere, although some people eat salted swordfish. Food shops display enormous pyramids of prosciutto and columns of cheeses, and I have even read of a crèche made of butter or lard. Fruit vendors set dried figs into hearts or crowns made of silver and gold papers, even turn them into a star with a tail like the comet that guided the Magi. There are big burlap bags full of the hazelnuts that were used instead of marbles in traditional Christmas games.

That is just Christmas Eve. Every region, every city, and every country town has ritual foods for Christmas Day as well. All over Italy, Christmas lunch almost invariably begins with stuffed pasta, usually in broth. Pellegrino Artusi, the great gastronomic writer at the turn of the century, who addressed his cookbook to the middle class of the newly unified Italy, came from Romagna, and in his Christmas menu the cappelletti were served in capon broth. There were men, he says, who bragged of eating one hundred of these cappelletti, and since each was 2½ inches in diameter that clearly was no small gastronomic feat. It's not Christmas in Bologna without tortellini cooked in capon broth—while farther south, in Gubbio, cappelletti are more like huge tortelloni stuffed with veal, turkey, prosciutto, Parmesan cheese, and nutmeg. Elsewhere in Umbria tagliatelle dolce, flavored with sugar, cinnamon, walnuts and a bit of lemon rind, are a ritual dish similar to a Venetian Christmas lasagne layered with the same ingredients.

In northern Italy the next courses dispense with fish, but while the feasts may be wild the meats are not. Traditionally they feature the most domesticated fowl available—turkey, goose, and capon. Capon turns up boiled or roasted with potatoes, and the broth made from the bird is used for the first-course soup. Capon used to be a special Christmas dish all over Italy, although turkey is also extraordinarily popular. In Rome pancetta, bread crumbs, eggs, and Parmesan cheese fill the cavity, while in Milan chestnuts, apples, pears, prunes, and walnuts are chosen. Turkey arrived in Italian kitchens in the mid-sixteenth century when it seemed so exotic that it was called *gallo* or *pollo* or *pavone d'India* (Indian rooster or chicken or even peacock). Today it is not exotic at all and it is eaten throughout the whole country, sometimes stuffed and sometimes not, but never quite as elaborately prepared as the stuffed dishes served at the Gonzaga court in Ferrara, when a boar was served inside a stag and so on, like the Russian dolls that nest one inside the other.

The city hall in Milan used to offer an enormous meal to its resident street sweepers, who were famous for big appetites. They ate turkeys, chickens, squab, capons, and hare that were raised on rice in Mantua to make their flesh especially tender. In Piedmont numerous antipasti preceded a roast turkey stuffed with chestnuts, sausages, eggs, cheese, and chopped pork. In Friuli duck is the chosen dish, while in Brianza, north of Milan, it is grilled kid.

In the south an old saying has it that "Anyone who doesn't make Christmas a meatless day is either a Turk or a dog." Dinner is the big feast, and fish is often the only choice. In some families in Apulia, the number of dishes is set at nine and eel must be one. In Calabria the ritual number of dishes for Christmas is always either nine or thirteen or twenty-four, depending on the area. The table is left set even after the meal is over, because Calabrians believe that the Madonna will come with the baby to visit and taste the food, much as the Romans believed that the gods presented themselves at table. What she would find is stockfish, trout or red mullet, cabbage, and sweets, including fried cream puffs called *zeppole*, or dried fruits, walnuts, hazelnuts, and chestnuts.

Churchgoers in little Sicilian towns used to take food with them on their way to church, where they would settle down right in the pews to eat roast sausage, fried pork chops, pastries with eel, snails, cauliflower, onions, and many kinds of fruit. It was a sort of holy picnic, much discouraged by Church authorities over the centuries, but no longer a worry since the custom has died out.

After the Christmas log has burned slowly for twelve days, its ashes are collected and sprinkled on the earth to make it fertile for the year to come. During the Christmas season, according to Alfredo Cattabiani, people used to say that "tomorrow is the day of bread," which is why every town and village had its own special Christmas bread, a symbol of abundance that people hoped would continue for the year. In the Christian tradition, Jesus became bread incarnate on the night of the Nativity, the occasion for giving special Christmas breads to one's entire family and friends—panettone and pandoro, pangiallo and pandolce.

Bakers made many of these ritual Christmas breads, pane di Natale, by enriching the bread of everyday with lard, oil, or butter, adding eggs, and kneading in nuts, raisins, dried fruits, and clean sweet-tasting candied fruits. Scholars trace the ancestors of panettone to the end of the fourteenth century, when Florentines folded walnuts, pine nuts, dried figs, dates, and honey into Tuscan bread dough, making pan co'santi. By the seventeenth century, the historian Vincenzo Tanara wrote that the citizens of Emilia-Romagna made pan di Natale by rolling raisins, black pepper, and honey-candied pumpkin right into ordinary bread dough. These low, dense Christmas breads, bursting with nuts and fruits, were nothing like the delicate, high-domed panettone that has become the famous Christmas bread of Milan. The more recent versions were invented in the 1920s, when Angelo Motta founded a company that used natural yeast and tall cylindrical forms to turn out a rich, porous, high-sided panettone. Studded with raisins and bits of candied orange and citron, the new panettone was such a popular success that Motta's friend Gioacchino Allemagna opened a competing business the next year, and in the decades that followed panettone gradually became the Christmas bread of Italy. Nowadays panettone weighs one, two, or three pounds, while rustic panettone was traditionally made in enormous six- to ten-pound rounds. It was once a real status symbol for immigrants who came to Milan and felt that they had arrived when they could set a panettone on their Christmas table.

Many Christmas sweets have the word bread in their name—pane speziato, spice bread; panforte, strong bread; and pan ricco, rich bread —but they are not really breads at all. They are made not by bakers with bread dough but by pastry chefs, inheritors of the tradition of the speziale, apothecaries and herbalists who sold spices for culinary as well as medicinal purposes, and made special dolci with them. It is easy to taste the medieval beginnings of panforte in the honey and cloves, the coriander, cinnamon, and white pepper that flavor them. In the Tuscany of the Middle Ages tiny panforte were hung from the Christmas tree boughs as presents for babies; by the sixteenth century, panforte had already become a traditional Christmas present in Siena. Just the name panpepato—peppery bread— evokes the fragrance and pungent taste of pepper, of the flavors of cinnamon, nutmeg, ginger, and cloves. Spicy Tuscan panpepato filled with

S. GIO. BATTISTA

Pesci di pasta, fan da Zuccherini, Con ingredienti buoni, rari, e fini.

S. MARIA NUOVA

Fan Mortadella in fette tanto piane, Che sembra vera, ed è di Marzapane.

almonds, hazelnuts, walnuts, pine nuts, and candied fruit rind has been called the true panforte of Siena. In Ferrara a low, round panpepato crammed with fruits and nuts is covered with a fine coating of chocolate, indicating that it was first made after 1600, when chocolate arrived in Italy. Cloistered nuns made it to give to dignitaries of the Church, and bakers gave it to their clients with ceremony. (It is still eaten in Ferrara on Christmas Day.) In Umbria chocolate is folded right into the panpepato, which countrypeople originally made during the time of the wheat harvest.

Before the seventeenth century, there was no formal division between simple breads and the sweets made at home, although many pastries were made by either the apothecaries or the nuns, who were the great pastry cooks of Italy. Today during the Christmas season the tradition splits into breads made by bakers and specialties turned out by pastry chefs, who make the panforte of Siena, the spongata of Emilia-Romagna, and the buccellato of Palermo. Bakers have always made sweet risen breads and they still take charge of panettone; pandoro of Verona and natalizia, its denser predecessor; and pandolce genovese. The Piemontese version of panettone was invented seventy years ago by a baker in Pinerolo who covered the fragrant dough with a crunchy glaze of hazelnuts, sugar, and vanilla.

In *La scienza in cucina e L'arte di mangiar bene*, Pellegrino Artusi included on his Christmas menu pane certosino di Bologna, an enormous pan di Natale spiced with raisins, candied pumpkin, and pepper, the same or similar to one Tanara mentioned in his book of 1644. No matter what they are called, many Christmas breads and sweets share a wealth of walnuts, almonds, and hazelnuts, symbols of abundance and fertility, and like Roman New Year sweets contain honey as a talisman that the coming year may be sweet.

Some traditional sweets have fallen victim to industrialization and to an accelerated pace of life, although in small towns and at special bakeries dolci are still made as they have been for centuries: low, dense pandolce (as well as higher, airier versions) in Genoa; in Verona, natalizia, the ancestor of today's pandoro; Brescia's panforte-like pan di morte; fruit- and nut-filled zelten from Alto Adige; and panon, a chestnut focaccia filled with walnuts, hazelnuts, raisins, and dried figs from Sondrio in Lombardy. The busolai of Trieste and the bussola of Brescia and Friuli are ring-shaped ciambelle, first called *buccellati* from the Latin *buccellatum*, which means a ring, but from which came *boccone*, a morsel. The ciambelle began as biscotti, military bread for soldiers and sailors, while in medieval times a buccellatus was a sweet, delicate, ring-shaped bread that country people gave the lord of the land for Christmas. It is a true pan di Natale, which to this day can be found as far south as Palermo in fig- and almond-filled buccellato. Chewy almond torrone first surfaced in 1260, when the French count of Valois brought it to Benevento. He defeated Manfred there and torrone came and stayed. It is still made and given for Christmas almost everywhere in Italy, from little mountain villages to towns deep in the Sicilian interior, a truly unifying taste of Christmas.

Cappellacci di Zucca

Cappellacci Stuffed with Pumpkin

You can eat these pumpkin-stuffed treats almost any day in Parma, where they go by the name of *tortelli,* but go to Ferrara and suddenly they are known as *cappellacci* and are always served as the first course for Christmas Eve dinner. The name comes from their shape, which looks like the pointed hat an Alpine climber wears. Cappellacci have been around at least since Lucrezia d'Este's cook gave the recipe to a fellow Ferrarese for a cookbook he published in 1584. It is no surprise that they are stuffed with zucca, a type of pumpkin that closely resembles our butternut squash. The people of Ferrara have been called *magnazoca,* pumpkin eaters, for a very long time.

Makes 8 servings

PASTA

4 cups (540 grams) unbleached all-purpose flour
1 teaspoon salt
5 extra-large eggs

In a food processor fitted with the steel blade, combine the flour and salt. Pulse several times to sift. With the machine on, add the whole eggs, one at a time, to form a soft dough. If the dough isn't quite moist enough, add a few drops of water. Turn out onto a lightly floured surface and knead briefly until it forms a smooth ball, about 1 minute. Cover and let rest at least 30 minutes.

FILLING

2½ pounds (1⅛ kilograms) pumpkin or butternut squash, cut into large
**   chunks, seeds removed**
½ cup (112 grams) unsalted butter, cut up, room temperature
1 egg yolk
Heaping ¾ cup (85 grams) freshly grated Parmesan cheese
1 teaspoon salt
¼ teaspoon freshly grated nutmeg
¼ teaspoon freshly ground pepper

Preheat the oven to 350°F. Put the pumpkin or squash chunks on a lightly oiled baking sheet and bake until tender, 30 to 45 minutes. Cool and remove the skin. Press through a ricer or a coarse sieve, or process briefly in a food processor just until smooth.

Transfer the puree to a bowl, add the cut-up butter, the egg yolk, Parmesan cheese, the salt, nutmeg, and pepper. Mix well until the puree is firm and holds together well. If it is too soft, add a little more Parmesan cheese.

Divide the pasta dough into pieces the size of a lemon. Roll out through a pasta machine through the next to last setting. Set the sheets of pasta on a well-floured surface and cut with a 3-inch round cookie cutter. Cover the dough with plastic wrap or a towel to keep it moist.

Spoon a heaping teaspoon of squash filling on the center of each circle of dough. Moisten the edge with a bit of water and fold in half to form a half-moon shape. Press with your fingertips to seal the edges firmly. Shape into little hats by bringing the 2 ends together, overlapping the points and pressing them firmly together. Repeat with the rest of the dough. (If you are not going to cook them immediately, arrange on a cookie sheet lined with parchment paper, cover with plastic wrap, and set aside at room temperature up to 1 hour. Or refrigerate for longer, until you are ready to cook them.)

FOR SERVING

½ cup (112 grams) unsalted butter, melted
1 cup (100 grams) freshly grated Parmesan cheese

In a large pot of boiling salted water, cook the cappellacci until they float to the surface, about 5 minutes. Be careful not to overcook or the filling will ooze out. Drain and transfer to a warm serving dish. Pour the melted butter over the top, sprinkle with Parmesan, and toss gently. Pass the rest of the cheese separately.

Straccetti

~~~~~~~~~~~~~~~~~~~~~~~~~~~~

Christmas Soup with Bread and Cheese Strands

Christmas lunch in the Marches region of Italy always begins with a delicate soup flavored with strands of bread crumbs and Parmesan cheese bound together with egg yolks. It reminds Romans of stracciatella and natives of Modena and Bologna of soup with passatelli, although this version has a fine lemony flavor found nowhere else.

Makes 4 to 6 servings

4 egg yolks
Heaping ¼ cup (30 grams) freshly grated Parmigiano-Reggiano cheese
⅓ cup (50 grams) fine fresh bread crumbs
Freshly grated nutmeg
Salt
Grated zest of 1 lemon
8 cups chicken broth, preferably homemade
Extra Parmesan cheese to pass at table

Blend together the egg yolks, cheese, bread crumbs, nutmeg, salt, and lemon zest until they form a firm mixture. Place the broth in a large saucepan and bring to a simmer. You may either whisk in the mixture, stirring to break it up well, or press it through a ricer directly into the broth. Simmer 3 minutes. Serve immediately with extra grated cheese.

Sorbir d'Agnoli

~~~~~~~~~~~~~~~~~~~~~~~~~~~~

Stuffed Pasta in Wine-Spiked Broth

Christmas lunch in Mantua begins with stuffed agnoli, little disks of pasta floating in a red-wine–spiked broth. The Mantuans use as much red wine as broth, but I think the wine overwhelms the delicate pasta and the flavorful broth, so I prefer to use just a splash of spritzy Lambrusco.

Makes 8 servings

The recipe has 3 parts: pasta, filling, and broth. Begin with the pasta filling, which can be made ahead and left overnight.

FILLING

2 ounces (50 grams) pancetta
About 2 ounces (60 grams) pork sausage or soft salami with little fat
2 ounces (50 grams) prosciutto
2 ounces (50 grams) ground lean pork
2 to 3 tablespoons olive oil
A few drops broth, if needed
1 egg
Scant ¾ cup (70 grams) freshly grated Parmesan cheese
Freshly grated nutmeg

Chop the pancetta, sausage, prosciutto, and pork very fine, combine, and cook the mixture slowly in olive oil about 20 to 30 minutes without allowing it to brown. If it sticks or feels too dry, add a little broth.

Remove the pan from the fire and transfer the contents to a bowl. When cooled, mix in the egg and Parmesan cheese and grate a good dusting of nutmeg over the top. Cover and leave for several hours or overnight.

PASTA

1½ cups (200 grams) all-purpose flour
2 eggs
2 teaspoons oil
Salt

To mix the dough, see page 104.

Shape the pasta by rolling the dough through the finest setting on your machine. Divide the dough in half and cover the portion you are not using so it doesn't dry out.

Use a 2-inch cookie cutter to cut the dough into rounds. Moisten the edges with water. For agnolini, put ½ teaspoon filling on the center of each round, fold it in half, and pinch the edges firmly together with your fingertips to close them well. You also may shape the pasta as tortelli (page 103) or as round ravioli by laying one on top of the other and pressing them firmly together so they won't open during cooking.

BROTH

9 cups broth, preferably homemade, either all beef or veal or half meat
    and half Capon Broth (page 265)
½ cup Lambrusco wine

Bring the broth to a rolling boil, then turn it down slightly when you slide the agnoli into it so they don't break up or cloud the broth. Cook until they test done, about 3 minutes, turn off the heat, and let them sit for a minute or two so the flavors of the broth and pasta can mingle. Add the Lambrusco and serve immediately.

Lasagne della Vigilia

Christmas Eve Lasagne from Piedmont

There used to be a strong Christmas Eve tradition in Piedmont of eating lasagne made at home from huge sheets of pasta that were as wide as the sheets that swathed the Christmas child, wider even than the palm of a man's hand. This dish, which isn't at all like the many-layered baked lasagne of Bologna, is a wonderful combination of unlikely ingredients. Just be sure to mash the anchovy fillets to a paste and be generous with the pepper. The lasagne noodles should be short; if you use commercial ones, cut them in half crosswise.

Makes 6 servings

½ cup (112 grams) unsalted butter
8 anchovy fillets preserved in oil, drained and finely chopped
2 large cloves garlic, finely minced
1 pound lasagne noodles (450 grams), preferably fresh and cut 6 inches long and 3½ inches wide
1 cup (100 grams) grated Parmesan cheese
Lots of freshly ground pepper

In a large enameled skillet melt the butter slowly over medium-low heat. Add the anchovies and garlic and warm them in the butter about 5 minutes, using a wooden spoon to mash the anchovies as thoroughly as you can.

In a large pot of boiling salted water cook the pasta. Fresh lasagne noodles will cook in about 1 minute, dried in about 10. Remove with a slotted spoon, drain them very quickly, and toss immediately in a large bowl with ¼ cup of the Parmesan cheese to coat their slippery surfaces. Quickly transfer the noodles to the anchovy sauce, grind a lot of fresh pepper over the top, and toss well. Serve everyone a few lasagne noodles on well-warmed plates. Pass the remaining Parmesan cheese on the side.

Brodo di Cappone

~~~~~~~~~~~~~~~~~~~~~~~~~~~~

Capon Broth

How do you get capon broth? By cooking a capon, of course. And what do you do with the capon? You make it the centerpiece of Christmas lunch. And what do you do with the broth? Make it the first course with some filled pasta floating in it. Capon may be a rarity the rest of the year, but it turns up all over Italy as the ritual bird at Christmastime. Capon is richer than chicken, fuller flavored than turkey, and once you have tried the broth it produces, you'll wonder how you ever got by without it.

Makes 3 quarts

4½ quarts (18 cups) cold water
2 tablespoons coarse salt
1 medium yellow onion, cut in quarters
2 carrots, peeled and cut in quarters
2 medium-sized ribs celery, without leaves, roughly chopped
16 to 20 sprigs flat-leaf parsley
1 capon, about 5 to 6 pounds (2½ kilograms)

Bring a stockpot with 4½ quarts cold water to a boil, add the salt, onion, carrots, celery, and parsley. When the water returns to a boil, add the capon and cook, uncovered, over a medium-low flame 2 hours, skimming off foam as needed. Remove the capon and save for Christmas lunch or for serving separately. Strain the broth and refrigerate it. When the fat congeals on the top of the cold broth, carefully lift it off and discard.

Arancia Candita

~~~~~~~~~~~~~~~~~~~~~~~~~~~~~~~~~

Candied
Orange Peel

Many Italian sweet breads, cookies, and cannoli owe some of their vibrant taste to the intense flavor of candied orange peel. Alas, the translucent waxen cubes that are sold in American grocery stores bear no resemblance to the real thing, so it is really worth the effort to make your own. Since the process takes time, I like to candy a large amount and keep it on hand for all of my baking. Once candied and rolled in sugar, the peels will last for months. Save the orange-flavored syrup to use as a fruit syrup or to brush on layers of pan di Spagna or sponge cake. Make the candied peel at least one day before you plan to use it.

Makes 54 to 72 pieces

9 thin-skinned navel oranges*
2 cups water
4 cups (800 grams) sugar
4 tablespoons corn syrup
Granulated sugar

Wash and dry the oranges. Cut off tops and bottoms of the oranges and cut them vertically into 6 to 8 pieces and remove peels. Set the peels in a large heavy saucepan, cover well with cold water, and cook slowly over medium-low heat 45 minutes to 1 hour. Drain. Cover with clear water and let sit 1 hour or overnight. You may also make the sugar syrup and let the orange peels sit in it overnight before cooking.

Pour 2 cups water into a 3- or 4-quart saucepan. Stir in the sugar and corn syrup, mix to blend, and bring to a boil. Add the orange peels, cover the pan partially, and cook over very low heat about 2 hours, using a candy thermometer to make sure that the temperature rises to 212° to 218°F but stays below 220°F. You may need to add water periodically to keep the sugar from becoming concentrated, but it is important to cook the syrup slowly so that it can penetrate the peels. After 2 hours, remove the lid, turn up the heat slightly, and let the temperature of the syrup rise to 230°F to evaporate the water. Turn off the heat and let the peels stand until the liquid stops bubbling. Carefully remove the pieces of orange peel with a slotted spoon and transfer them to a rack set over a baking sheet. Leave them until they are cool, 1 to 2 hours. Roll each piece in granulated sugar and let dry on the rack. You can also put the peels in a paper bag with sugar and shake them around. They keep very well in a covered plastic or metal container.

*This same procedure works for citron, grapefruit, lemon, and tangerine peels.

Cartellate

~~~~~~~~~~~~~~~~~~~~~~~~~

*Honeyed
Christmas
"Roses"
from Apulia*

Ribbons of sweet dough rolled to look like roses are a special Christmas delicacy in Apulia. Though some versions are filled, and many are made with a dough composed only of flour, olive oil, white wine, and egg, these are yeast-raised spirals of delicate, crunchy pastry, a perfect way to finish a feast. To make purciduzzi, cut the dough in little pieces and shape them on the back of a grater like gnocchi. Fry and glaze just as directed for cartellate.

Makes about 16 to 20 "roses"

2½ teaspoons (1 package) active dry yeast or 1 cake (18 grams) fresh
    yeast
1 cup plus 3 tablespoons warm water
3¾ cups (500 grams) unbleached all-purpose flour
¼ teaspoon salt
6 tablespoons Marsala or white wine
3 tablespoons olive oil
Zests of 1 lemon and 1 orange, cut in strips; peels should be heated in
    the olive oil to give it flavor, then the oil cooled and the peels
    discarded
Olive oil for deep frying
Honey or mosto cotto (page 273)
Superfine sugar
Cinnamon

By Mixer. Stir the yeast into the warm water; let stand until it becomes creamy, about 10 minutes. In the mixer bowl with the paddle attachment, mix in the flour, salt, Marsala, and oil until the dough comes together, 1 to 2 minutes. Change to the dough hook and knead at low speed 2 minutes until the dough is soft, velvety, elastic, and very smooth. Knead very briefly on a lightly floured work table.

First Rise. Set the dough in an oiled bowl, cover it tightly with plastic wrap, and let rise until doubled, about 2 hours.

Shaping and Second Rise. Roll the springy dough out very thin, no more than ⅛ inch thick. Using a pizza or ravioli cutter, cut out ribbons of dough about 20 inches long and 2 inches wide. Cover whatever dough you are not working on. Using a pastry brush, moisten one edge with wine or water. Fold each ribbon in half so that it is 1 inch wide. Pinch the dough together along its length at 1-inch intervals by placing your fingertip on the dough and pinching the dough on either side of it. Roll up the dough in a spiral. As you roll it, pinch the outside of the dough already turned into a spiral with the inside of the part you are rolling up so that it looks like a rose. Let the "roses" rise covered until half risen,

(continued)

about 40 minutes. While they are rising, heat 2 to 3 inches olive oil in a heavy deep-sided pot to 375°F.

Cooking. Slide each "rose" into boiling oil headfirst so that the oil in the little folds of dough will drain off immediately. Fry until they are golden brown, then remove with tongs or a slotted spoon and drain upside down on a rack set over absorbent paper toweling.

Glaze. Heat the honey or mosto cotto in an enameled pan, and when it starts to boil, delicately slide the fried "roses" into it, 1 or 2 at a time, letting them absorb the honey or mosto cotto for a few minutes, first on one side, then on the other. Carefully lift them out with tongs or a slotted spoon and set them on a rack over waxed paper or a cookie sheet to drain. Sprinkle them with superfine sugar mixed with cinnamon.

Pangiallo

Roman Christmas Bread

I want to start a movement to bring back pangiallo, the Christmas bread of Rome. Contrary to what its name suggests, it is neither golden nor bread, like the panettone or pandoro to which fashionable tastes have migrated these days. No matter. The extraordinarily dense collection of raisins, nuts, and freshly candied peels is spiced with cinnamon, cloves, coriander, allspice, and ginger, rolled into a ball, and baked under a sugary glaze. This version, which comes from Ugo Farsetti, a wonderful Roman baker, is simplicity itself. Just toss all the ingredients into one bowl, mix them together, and leave them for as long as 24 hours. Pangiallo was such a Christmas ritual that Roman bakers made it in at least two forms, with yeast or with baking powder, with eggs or without. Pastry cooks had their own variation, for which the best nuts and seedless raisins were folded inside and the top glazed with a sugar syrup.

Makes 7 rounds

SPONGE

2½ teaspoons (1 package) active dry yeast or 1 cake (18 grams) fresh
  yeast
½ cup warm water
1 scant cup (125 grams) unbleached all-purpose flour

Stir the yeast into the warm water and let stand until creamy, about 10 minutes. Whisk in half the flour, then stir in the other half until the dough forms a ball and comes away from the sides of the bowl. Cover well with plastic wrap and let rise until doubled, about ½ hour.

DOUGH

Scant 3 cups (450 grams) golden raisins
2 cups plus 2 tablespoons (300 grams) whole almonds, toasted
6 ounces (175 grams) pine nuts
2 cups (250 grams) whole hazelnuts, toasted and skins removed
10½ ounces (300 grams) apricot jam
2 cups (300 grams) candied fruit, preferably orange peel and citron, chopped
2 eggs
½ teaspoon cinnamon
5 shakes ground allspice
Pinch ginger
⅛ teaspoon ground cloves
⅛ teaspoon ground coriander
Pinch dried sage, optional
Pinch pulverized dried bay leaf
2¼ cups (300 grams) unbleached all-purpose flour

While the sponge is rising, soak the raisins in tepid water to cover, 20 to 30 minutes. Remove the raisins and squeeze dry. Set the sponge in a large bowl. Using a mixer with the paddle attachment, add all the ingredients except the flour and mix slowly. Add the flour at the end using the slowest speed until the mixture comes together as a rough dough. Leave in the bowl or set in an oiled container, cover with plastic wrap, and let rise overnight. The dough will only rise slightly. Divide into 7 equal pieces and shape into rounds. Set on parchment-lined or oiled baking sheets.

GLAZE

2 tablespoons honey
2 tablespoons water
2 tablespoons confectioners' sugar
1 teaspoon unbleached all-purpose flour

Baking. Heat the oven to 375°F. Just before baking, mix the glaze ingredients and brush over the top of each pangiallo. Bake until the tops are the color of hazelnuts, 30 to 35 minutes. Remove to a rack, brush the warm pangialli with a bit more glaze, and let cool completely.

Spongata

ssssssssssssssssssssssssssssss

*Honeyed
Christmas Nut
Cake from Parma*

Imagine a honeyed, chewy nut cake bursting with walnuts, raisins, pine nuts, and orange zest, like a panforte that is wrapped in two disks of pastry and baked in the oven. The spongata was such a favorite at ducal tables that Francesco Sforza, duke of Milan, received one as a Christmas present in 1454, and the people of Parma and Reggio have claimed it as their traditional Christmas pastry for centuries.

Makes 1 large or 2 smaller cakes

P A S T A   F R O L L A

3¾ cups (500 grams) unbleached all-purpose flour
½ cup (100 grams) sugar
½ teaspoon salt
1 cup (230 grams) unsalted butter
2 eggs
2 tablespoons white wine
1 tablespoon vanilla extract

By Hand. Place the flour, sugar, and salt in a bowl and stir to mix it. Cut the butter into small pieces and cut it into the flour mixture with a pastry blender or 2 knives until the mixture resembles cornmeal. Slowly stir in the eggs one at a time, mixing thoroughly. Stir in the white wine and the vanilla. Gather the dough and knead it briefly on a floured surface until it comes together.

By Mixer. In a mixer bowl with the paddle attachment, cream the butter and sugar until pale and creamy. Add the eggs, wine, and vanilla, mixing thoroughly after each addition. Add the flour and salt and mix until the dough becomes consistent but is still soft. Be careful not to overmix or you will have a tough pastry crust.

By Processor. Put the flour, sugar, and salt in a food processor fitted with the steel blade. Cut the cold butter into small chunks and scatter over the flour. Process with 4 to 6 pulses until the mixture resembles cornmeal. Mix the eggs, wine, and vanilla and with the machine running, pour them down the feed tube; process only until the dough comes together on top of the blade. Do not process until it gathers into a ball or the pastry will be tough. Knead the dough briefly on a lightly floured surface just until it comes together and is no longer sticky.

Roll out the dough and divide to make 2 flat disks in ⅓ and ⅔ pieces. Chill in the refrigerator at least 1 hour.

FILLING

½ cup (80 grams) raisins
½ cup (80 grams) pine nuts
½ cup (80 grams) candied orange rind
½ cup (80 grams) candied citron
1⅔ cups (200 grams) walnuts, toasted
2 tablespoons lightly toasted bread crumbs
½ teaspoon ground cloves
1 teaspoon cinnamon
½ teaspoon nutmeg
1 cup honey
1 egg white, beaten, optional
1 egg, beaten

Using a sharp oiled knife, chop the raisins, pine nuts, orange rind, citron, and walnuts. Mix them together in a large bowl and add the bread crumbs and spices. Use a wooden spoon or your fingers to combine them well. Melt the honey in a double boiler, then stir into the nut and spice mixture, mixing quickly to distribute it evenly. Set it aside while it cools.

Assembly. Butter 2 low-sided 9-inch pie pans or 1 deep 9½-inch springform pan. Be sure to divide the *pasta frolla* into ⅔ and ⅓ pieces; if using the 2 smaller pans, divide each of those pieces in half. Roll out one of the larger pasta frolla pieces ⅛ to ¼ inch thick. Leave considerable excess so the dough droops over the pan. Slip the dough into the pan. Put half or all the filling on the dough. Collect the dough over the filling so that it covers almost ⅔ of the mixture.

Roll out one of the smaller *pasta frolla* pieces ⅛ to ¼ inch thick so that it fits exactly over the filling and comes to the edge of the pan. Using a pastry brush, wash the exposed edge of the bottom dough with a little bit of water or egg white. Cover the bottom dough with the top disk of dough and press the edges firmly into place so that no seam shows. Brush the top with the beaten egg and pierce it with a skewer to allow steam to escape. Repeat with the other pieces of dough and filling if making 2 cakes.

Bake at 400°F 30 minutes, then reduce the heat to 350°F and bake 15 minutes.

Panpepato

~~~~~~~~~~~~~~~~~~~~~~~~~~~~~~~~

Spicy Chocolate-
Flavored
Christmas Bread

Walnuts, P. Mattioli,
Venice, 1583

Translated literally, *panpepato* means peppered bread, and this Christmas treat is the direct descendant of medieval sweet breads that were crammed with nuts, raisins, and all manner of spices. During the Renaissance, bakers made panpepati like these to give to the nobles for whom they worked, a tradition carried on by the Umbrian countrywoman from whom I learned how to make this rich robust sweet flavored with chocolate and a little espresso. It was her Christmas present to the family for whom she works, and I was lucky enough to be offered a piece at a big Christmas dinner in Rome.

Makes 5 panpepati

⅔ cup (80 grams) raisins
1 cup (120 grams) walnuts, toasted
½ cup (60 grams) hazelnuts, toasted and peeled
½ cup (60 grams) almonds, toasted
¼ cup (40 grams) pine nuts
3½ ounces (100 grams) semisweet chocolate, grated
½ cup (80 grams) candied orange peel, chopped
2 tablespoons strong brewed espresso coffee
6 tablespoons (100 grams) honey
2 to 3 tablespoons water
¼ cup (50 grams) mosto cotto*
Substantial grating of nutmeg
Grated zest of 1 orange
¼ teaspoon salt
6 to 12 grindings pepper
1 cup (140 grams) unbleached all-purpose flour
Orange syrup (page 266) or melted apricot jam
Confectioners' sugar

Soak the raisins in warm water to cover 30 minutes. Drain and squeeze dry. Chop together the walnuts, hazelnuts, and almonds. In a big bowl mix the chopped nuts, pine nuts, raisins, chocolate, candied orange peel, and espresso coffee. Melt the honey in 2 to 3 tablespoons water. Mix it and the mosto cotto well into the nut mixture. Add the nutmeg, zest, salt, and pepper. Reserve 2 to 3 tablespoons of the flour and add the rest, a bit at a time, mixing with a rubber spatula and using only enough to get the mixture to hold together. It isn't a dough.

*Mosto cotto is juice squeezed from fresh grapes and cooked down to about a third its original volume in a thick jellylike consistency. If you don't have fresh grape juice, substitute grape or red currant jelly.

Shaping. Divide into 5 equal balls. Flour the work surface very lightly and incorporate the reserved flour into the mixture. Roll each piece into a round that looks like a hamburger patty. Set on a buttered and floured baking sheet.

Baking. Bake at 350°F until firm, 15 minutes. Brush the top of each with a little of the syrup from the candied oranges, melted apricot jam, or with a little cooked mosto cotto if you have it. Continue to bake another 5 minutes. Let cool briefly and sieve confectioners' sugar over the tops.

Cassola

Zia Maria's Christmas Cheesecake

Cheesecake for Christmas? Custardy cassola is a traditional Jewish dessert, perfect for an ecumenical celebration and irresistible whatever denominations are at table. Deep and creamy, it is a velvety cheesecake flavored with flecks of vanilla bean. It can be baked early in the day and served at room temperature, but it is at its best still warm from the oven.

Makes a 9½-inch cake

2 pounds 2 ounces (1 kilogram) ricotta, as fresh as possible
5 eggs
1½ cups (300 grams) sugar
Pinch salt
½ fresh vanilla bean, pulverized

Preheat the oven to 400°F. Sieve the ricotta into a mixing bowl or process with several pulses in a food processor fitted with the steel blade until smooth. Beat the eggs, sugar, salt, and pulverized vanilla together until creamy. Beat into the ricotta 1 tablespoon at a time.

Baking. Butter a 9½-inch springform pan and line the bottom with parchment paper. Pour the filling into the pan. Set in the oven, turn the temperature down to 350°F, and bake 30 to 35 minutes. The cake will set around the sides but remain jiggly like Jell-O in the center. Turn off the oven and let the cake continue baking slightly 10 to 15 minutes. Open the door and let it cool and set another 15 minutes. This cake is so delicious served warm that it seems a shame to eat it any other way.

Pandolce Genovese

xxxxxxxxxxxxxxxxxxxxxxxxxxxxx

*Christmas Sweet
Bread
from Genoa*

Every city has its own Christmas bread: Milan has panettone; Verona, pandoro; and Genoa, pandolce, literally "sweet bread." In its rustic form pandolce is a low, dense bread, thick with raisins, candied fruits, pistachios, and pine nuts, without any of the softness or light, airy quality of its Milanese or Veronese relatives. Perhaps that explains its current unfashionable status and makes sense of why there are two kinds of pandolce, the old-fashioned countrified round and a lighter, softer sweet bread more pleasing to contemporary tastes. When this pandolce arrives at the Christmas table surrounded by bay leaves, its low, round form is a reminder of its medieval origins, for it is scented with such Near Eastern flavors as orange flower water and fennel seeds. If you want to be really traditional, allow the youngest member of the family to cut the first slice, wrap it in a napkin, and offer it to the first poor person who passes. It is wonderful with a sweet white wine.

Makes 2 loaves

SPONGE

4 teaspoons active dry yeast or scant 1⅔ cakes (30 grams) fresh yeast
1 cup plus 6 tablespoons warm water
2½ cups plus 2 tablespoons (355 grams) unbleached all-purpose flour

Stir the yeast into the warm water and let stand until it is creamy, about 10 minutes. Mix in the flour, cover with plastic wrap, and let rise until well doubled, about 40 minutes.

FIRST DOUGH

½ cup plus 3 tablespoons (150 grams) unsalted butter, very soft
¾ cup (150 grams) sugar
½ cup plus 2 tablespoons Marsala
2 tablespoons milk
1 tablespoon orange flower water
1 teaspoon orange extract
3 tablespoons fennel seeds
1½ teaspoons salt
1¾ cups (250 grams) unbleached all-purpose flour

By Mixer. Put the sponge in the mixer bowl and with the paddle attachment mix in the soft butter in chunks until it is smooth and well mixed. Add the sugar, Marsala, milk, orange flower water, extract, fennel seeds, and salt; mix slowly until smooth, 3 to 4 minutes. Change to the dough hook, add the flour, and mix on the lowest speed until the dough is smooth and elastic, about 3 minutes. The dough will be soft and sticky.

Turn it out onto a well-floured board and knead briefly. Don't worry if it is too soft and sticky to form a ball.

First Rise. Set the dough in an oiled container, cover it well, and let rise until doubled, about 3¼ hours.

FILLING

3 tablespoons (30 grams) pine nuts
3 tablespoons plus 1 teaspoon (40 grams) pistachios
½ cup (75 grams) raisins, soaked in tepid water for 1 hour, drained, and squeezed dry
⅔ cup (100 grams) candied orange peel, chopped

Shaping and Second Rise. Pour the delicate, very soft dough out onto a well-floured board. Flatten it into a long rectangular shape and, leaving a 1-inch border all around, sprinkle the top with the pine nuts, pistachios, raisins, and candied orange peel. Pat them in well. Fold in the borders all around and pat well again before rolling the dough up into a ball. Cut the dough in half and make a ball of each piece. Set the dough to rise on parchment paper-lined baking sheets, cover with a towel, and let rise until doubled, about 1½ hours.

Baking. Preheat the oven to 400°F. Just before baking, use a razor blade to cut the shape of a cross or a triangle in the center of each loaf. Set in the oven and bake 45 to 50 minutes.

Roast chestnut seller, detail of an engraving by Bartolomeo Pinelli

Natalizia

vvvvvvvvvvvvvvvvvvvvvvvvvvvvvv

*The Original
Christmas Bread
of Verona*

Before Verona became famous for its pandoro, everyone ate natalizia, a delicate lemon-flavored sweet bread with a Christmas star cut into its domed top. This pattern gave rise to the star-shaped mold in which today's pandoro is baked. While the natalizia is not as buttery or as delicately porous as its famous descendent, it is a delicious celebratory bread whose top is washed with Marsala and sprinkled with the crunch of pine nuts. It is wonderful at breakfast, teatime, or dinner, and makes the best toast in the world.

Makes 2 tall domed loaves

SPONGE

2½ teaspoons (1 package) active dry yeast or 1 cake (18 grams) fresh
  yeast
1½ cups warm water
⅔ cup (90 grams) bread flour
¼ cup (40 grams) unbleached all-purpose flour

Stir the yeast into the water in a large mixing or mixer bowl and let stand until creamy, about 10 minutes. Whisk in both flours. Cover well with plastic wrap and let rise until doubled, 20 to 30 minutes.

FIRST DOUGH

2½ teaspoons (1 package) active dry yeast or 1 cake (18 grams) fresh
  yeast
3 tablespoons warm water
2 eggs, room temperature
2 cups (270 grams) unbleached all-purpose flour
¼ cup (45 grams) sugar
2 tablespoons (25 grams) unsalted butter

Stir the yeast into the warm water and let stand until creamy, about 10 minutes. Add the dissolved yeast, eggs, flour, and sugar to the sponge and stir well. Add the butter and beat well until the dough is smooth and elastic, about 3 minutes at medium speed on the mixer, 5 minutes by hand. Cover with plastic wrap and let rise until well doubled, 2 to 2½ hours.

SECOND DOUGH

2 egg yolks
3 eggs
¾ cup (150 grams) sugar
3 cups (420 grams) unbleached all-purpose flour, plus ½ cup for
  kneading

1 teaspoon salt
2 teaspoons vanilla extract
1¼ teaspoons best-quality lemon extract
Grated zest of 1 lemon
½ cup plus 2½ tablespoons (145 grams) unsalted butter, room
    temperature

By Hand. It is much easier to make this dough in a mixer, but it is possible to make it by hand. Add the egg yolks, eggs, sugar, flour, salt, vanilla, lemon extract, and lemon zest to the first dough and stir until blended. Stir in the butter gradually and beat well to be sure it is thoroughly incorporated. Knead on a floured surface, sprinkling with ½ cup additional flour, until the dough is soft, sticky, and delicate.

By Mixer. Add the egg yolks, eggs, sugar, vanilla, lemon extract, and lemon zest to the first dough and mix with the paddle on medium speed until blended. Add the butter gradually, then the flour and salt. Change to the dough hook and knead at low speed 6 to 8 minutes, gradually sprinkling in 6 to 8 tablespoons flour. The dough will never come away from the sides of the bowl; it is soft, sticky, and delicate and must be handled with some care.

First Rise. Place the dough in a buttered straight-sided container, cover tightly with plastic wrap, and let rise until tripled, about 3 hours.

Shaping and Second Rise. Flour the table and turn out onto it the soft, sticky, velvety dough. Lightly flour it on top and divide it into 2 pieces. Gently shape each into a ball. Place each one in a buttered 1½-quart mold. With a sharp razor blade, cut a tic-tac-toe pattern onto the top and pull open the right angle at each of the outer edges of the four corners so that the pattern looks vaguely like a Christmas star. Cover with a heavy towel and let rise to the tops of the molds, about 2½ hours.

TOPPING

2½ tablespoons pine nuts
1 tablespoon Marsala
1½ tablespoons turbinado sugar

About 15 minutes before you are ready to bake the breads, soak the pine nuts in the Marsala. Recut the Christmas star pattern if it has closed up. Sprinkle the pine nuts over the tops, brush the excess Marsala over the surfaces, and finish by sprinkling with the turbinado sugar.

Baking. Heat the oven to 375°F. Bake 10 minutes. Reduce the heat to 350°F and bake until a tester comes out clean, about 35 to 45 minutes longer. Let breads cool completely in their forms before removing them.

Panettone Piemontese

~~~~~~~~~~~~~~~~~~~~~~~~~~~~~

*Panettone
from Piedmont*

This little-known Piemontese variant of the classic panettone of Milan is lower and somewhat less airy than its relative but only because it is baked in a shallower form. The baker in Turin who let me in on his secrets uses natural yeast, so his panettone has richer, more complex flavors and keeps longer than one made with commercial yeast. Please use the mixer if you decide to follow his lead, because dough made with natural yeast is sticky and hard to handle. Making the dough that way can fit easily into a busy life. Make the sponge–first dough combination in the morning and let it rise during the day; come home from work, make the second dough, shape it, and let it rise in a cool kitchen during the night. Get up the next morning and the panettone is ready to go into the oven where it will dome dramatically. Be certain to use fresh or very recently refreshed natural yeast that has not soured.

Makes 2 panettone

SPONGE

2½ teaspoons (1 package) active dry yeast or 1 small cake (18 grams)
   fresh yeast or 1 cup (250 grams) fresh or recently refreshed Natural
   Yeast Starter (page 32)
⅓ cup warm water
½ cup (70 grams) unbleached all-purpose flour

Stir the yeast into the warm water in a small bowl; let stand until creamy, about 10 minutes. Whisk in the flour. Cover well with plastic wrap and let stand until doubled, 20 to 30 minutes. If you use the natural yeast, squish it into the water through your fingers until it is fairly well mixed. Whisk in the flour, cover well with plastic wrap, and let stand until doubled, about 1¼ hours.

FIRST DOUGH

2½ teaspoons (1 package) active dry yeast or 1 small cake (18 grams)
   fresh yeast or 1 cup (250 grams) fresh or recently refreshed Natural
   Yeast Starter (page 32)
¾ cup minus 2 tablespoons warm water
4 egg yolks, room temperature
1 cup plus 1 tablespoon (150 grams) high-gluten bread flour
½ cup plus 1 tablespoon (80 grams) unbleached all-purpose flour
½ cup (100 grams) sugar
7 tablespoons (100 grams) unsalted butter, room temperature

By Hand. Stir the yeast into the warm water in a mixing bowl; let stand until creamy, about 10 minutes. (If you use the natural yeast starter, squish it into the water until it is fairly well mixed.) Add the sponge and beat together thoroughly. Add the egg yolks, both flours, and the sugar; mix very well, about 5 minutes. Stir in the butter by mixing very thoroughly. Cover with plastic wrap and let rise until doubled, 3 to 3½ hours or overnight for dough made with natural yeast.

By Mixer. Stir the yeast into the water in a mixing bowl; let stand until creamy, about 10 minutes. (If you use the natural yeast starter, squish it into the water until it is fairly well mixed.) With the paddle attachment add the sponge, egg yolks, both flours, and the sugar; mix well on medium speed 3 to 4 minutes. Add the butter and mix until the dough is soft, golden, and bubbly, about 3 minutes. (Dough made with natural yeast is wetter and stickier than that made with active dry yeast, and it falls in ribbons from the paddle, like buttercream.) Cover with plastic wrap and let rise at warm room temperature until doubled, 3½ hours for dough made with fresh or active dry yeast or overnight for dough made with natural yeast.

SECOND DOUGH

5 egg yolks
6 tablespoons (100 grams) honey
½ cup plus 2 tablespoons (125 grams) sugar
1½ teaspoons vanilla extract
Grated zest of 2 oranges or 1 teaspoon best-quality orange extract
½ cup plus 1 tablespoon (125 grams) unsalted butter, room temperature
2½ cups (350 grams) unbleached all-purpose flour
¾ teaspoon salt

By Hand. Place the first dough in a large mixing bowl, add the egg yolks, honey, sugar, vanilla, and orange zest and mix well. Add the butter and stir until smooth. Stir in the flour and salt and keep stirring until smooth. The dough will be soft. Knead gently on a well-floured work surface with well-floured hands until it is smooth, soft, and buttery.

By Mixer. Add the egg yolks, honey, sugar, vanilla, and orange zest to the first dough and mix thoroughly with the paddle. Add the butter and mix until smooth. Add the flour and salt in 2 additions. Mix very slowly until the dough comes together, stopping the machine as needed to push down the dough as it climbs the neck of the shaft. Mix vigorously until smooth. Change to the dough hook and knead until smooth, soft, and lightly elastic, 2 to 3 minutes. Finish kneading on a lightly floured work surface, using a little extra flour if necessary.

(continued)

FILLING

2 cups (300 grams) chopped candied orange peel
⅓ cup (50 grams) chopped candied citron

Combine the candied orange peel and citron. Pour the sticky velvety dough out onto a floured surface and dust the top with flour. Cut the dough in half. Pat each piece of dough into an oval, about 11 by 9 inches, and sprinkle each with half the filling. Roll each into a ball.

Shaping and Second Rise. Slip each ball of dough into a well-buttered 2-quart soufflé dish, springform pan, or charlotte mold lined with a buttered parchment-paper circle on the bottom. Lightly oil the tops of the dough, cover with plastic wrap and a heavy towel, and let rise 6 hours or overnight in a cool kitchen.

TOPPING

3 egg whites
3 tablespoons (35 grams) sugar
¼ cup (35 grams) hazelnuts, toasted and coarsely chopped
½ cup (70 grams) whole unpeeled almonds
3 to 4 tablespoons confectioners' sugar

Beat the egg whites until they form soft peaks, then begin adding the sugar gradually until the mixture is stiff and glossy. Stir in the hazelnuts. Spread over the surface of each bread, but be careful not to seal the edges or you will have a terrible time freeing the panettone. Dot each loaf with whole almonds, then finish by sifting a heavy layer of confectioners' sugar over the tops.

Baking. Heat the oven to 400°F. Bake 10 minutes on the lowest rack of the oven, reduce the temperature to 375°F and bake 10 minutes, then reduce to 350°F and bake until a tester comes out clean, 25 to 35 minutes more. If the top gets too brown, cover it with aluminum foil.

Cavallucci

*Spiced
Christmas Cookies*

At Christmastime in Siena everyone eats two cavallucci and one piece of panforte. Everyone knows that panforte is a highly spiced dessert dating from medieval times, but the lesser-known cavallucci, medium-hard white cookies once made with an image of a horse imprinted on the top, are no upstarts. They too are perfumed with spices—anise and coriander, cinnamon and clove—and in the classical version they too offer bites of candied orange and walnuts. According to Giovanni Righi Parenti, cavallucci were mentioned in a 1559 collection of Florentine carnival songs of the time of Lorenzo de' Medici. The sweets were then known as *biriquocoli* from the name of the men who drove two-wheeled carts. Such carts used to stop at certain *osterie* in the countryside where these sweets were always sold, not only because they were tasty but also because they were filled with so many spices and so much pepper that everyone got thirsty. Righi Parenti says this is why they were called *cavallucci*, the cookie of the *cavallari*, horse drivers. And because they need something thirst quenching, they also turn up on All Saints' Day in Siena, which is when everyone tastes the new wines, especially that year's Vin Santo.

Makes about 2 dozen cookies

1 cup plus 2 tablespoons water
1¼ cups (250 grams) sugar
⅓ cup (50 grams) candied orange peel, chopped
⅓ cup (50 grams) walnuts, toasted and coarsely chopped
1 teaspoon anise seeds
1 teaspoon ground coriander
½ teaspoon (2.5 grams) baking powder
½ teaspoon (2.5 grams) cinnamon
½ teaspoon (2.5 grams) ground cloves
1/16 teaspoon white pepper
2½ cups (350 grams) unbleached all-purpose flour

To make these cookies, work quickly and have all your ingredients at hand. Bring the water and sugar to a boil. Immediately add the other ingredients in order, keeping the flour until last. The less you boil them, the softer the cookie remains. Mix well. Cool briefly.

Shaping. Turn the mixture while it is still warm onto a floured work surface, flour the top, and roll into a rope. Pat the top to flatten it evenly. Divide the dough into two equal halves and cut into individual pieces that are 2 inches long and at least ½ inch thick. Turn each cookie so the cut side is up. Flatten the top with the fleshy part of your thumb, using force so that it leaves what is supposed to be a horselike shape, to be true to its name, although the shape is really vague at best.

Baking. Heat the oven to 350°F. Bake on buttered and floured parchment-lined cookie sheets about 30 minutes; they must not turn golden or take on color at all. These cookies harden once they are out of the oven, so be careful not to overdo the baking.

Mostaccioli Romani

Spicy Nut and Fruit Pastries

Romans love this pastry with its finely ground nut filling spiked with sweet candied orange and spiced with cinnamon, cloves, and nutmeg. It is a bit like a Fig Newton without the figs. The ancient Romans made them from cooked grape must (mosto cotto; the Latin name for the cookie was *mustaceum*) mixed with almonds, flour, pepper, and other spices, and served them for wedding feasts and Saturnalia.

Later in the Rome of the popes the pastries were known as *mostaccioli*. When Saint Francis became sick in Rome he asked especially for them. They were spiced with cinnamon and even later, sometimes covered with chocolate and arabesques of sugar. Mostaccioli used to be ritually served at Christmas all over southern Italy and can still be found in Calabria and Basilicata, where they are very hard and crunchy. Present-day Roman mostaccioli come in a highly spiced chewy cookie form as well as wrapped in a light pastry crust. You must make the first filling the night before.

Makes 12 four-inch mostaccioli or 16 three-inch mostaccioli

FIRST FILLING

1⅓ cups plus 1 tablespoon (165 grams) almonds
1¼ cups (250 grams) sugar
1 cup plus 2 teaspoons (250 grams) honey
½ teaspoon cinnamon
¼ teaspoon cloves
¼ teaspoon grated nutmeg
⅓ cup (50 grams) candied orange peel, cut into tiny pieces
¾ teaspoon vanilla extract
About ¼ cup (40 to 50 grams) unbleached all-purpose flour
About 4 ounces (125 grams) cookie crumbs; fruit or nut cookies are
    particularly good but use whatever you have on hand

Toast the almonds in a 350°F oven for 10 minutes and grind into a flour in a nut grinder or blender.

In a heavy saucepan cook the sugar and honey together until they have melted. Add the almonds, then the other ingredients in the above order, mixing in the nuts first. Stir well and remove immediately from the fire. Cool and leave overnight.

PASTRY

Makes 3 pounds 6 ounces (1530 grams) dough

4½ cups (600 grams) all-purpose flour
1¼ cups (250 grams) sugar
¼ teaspoon salt

1 cup plus 2 tablespoons (250 grams) unsalted butter
4 eggs
2 teaspoons vanilla extract

Follow the directions for Pasta Frolla on page 270, omitting the wine.

By Processor. If your processor takes less than 7 cups of dough, you will need to divide the recipe in half and do it twice.

Chilling. Wrap the dough with plastic wrap and chill at least 1 hour but no more than 1 day in the refrigerator.

SECOND FILLING

2 cups (250 grams) whole almonds
5½ ounces (165 grams) semisweet chocolate
1½ cups minus 2 tablespoons (325 grams) quince or apricot preserves
1¼ teaspoons cinnamon
⅛ teaspoon white pepper
⅛ to ¼ teaspoon ground cloves
¼ teaspoon grated nutmeg
¾ teaspoon vanilla extract
1 tablespoon plus 1 teaspoon rum
½ cup (75 grams) mixed candied fruits, cut into tiny dice
¼ cup plus 1 tablespoon (50 grams) unbleached all-purpose flour

Next day make the second filling. Toast the almonds and grind to a coarse powder in a nut grinder or blender. Melt the chocolate over a double boiler and cool. Melt the jam in a heavy saucepan over moderate heat until it comes to a boil, then cook it for several minutes, being sure to stir out any lumps. Stir in the cinnamon, pepper, cloves, nutmeg, vanilla, and rum, then the candied fruits and almonds, and finally the cooled chocolate. Stir in the flour and mix well with a rubber spatula or wooden spoon. Let the mixture cool.

Stirring the 2 filling mixtures together by hand takes a little effort. You can also beat the two mixtures together with the electric mixer. The first mixture is as thick as almond paste but denser and stiffer. You may add part of an egg white to loosen it up, although I just mix it, a bit at a time, into the second filling with a wooden spoon. The mixture remains stiff and dense.

Shaping. Let the dough stand at room temperature 30 to 45 minutes before rolling it out. Knead it briefly on a lightly floured surface to loosen it and make it supple enough for shaping. Cut the dough into 12 four-ounce

(continued)

pieces or 16 three-ounce pieces. On a lightly floured work surface roll each piece out to a circle about ¼ to ⅛ inch thick and set each in a buttered 3- or 4-inch tartlet pan. The larger mostaccioli take about ½ cup filling, while the smaller ones use a little less than ⅓ cup. Mound the filling in the pastry shell, pull the dough over the top, and close it well, making sure that there are no holes or openings to permit the filling to escape.

Baking. Preheat the oven to 350°F. Set the pans in the oven and bake until lightly golden brown, about 30 minutes. Cool well on racks.

Icing. The Roman baker who gave me this recipe dips the mostaccioli into melted milk chocolate or fondant chocolate, but I can't imagine wanting to add anything more.

Buccellato Siciliano

~~~~~~~~~~~~~~~~~~~~~~~~~~~~

Fig-and-Nut– Filled Christmas Wreath

Think of mince pie shaped in a wreath, and you have a picture of this Sicilian Christmas dessert, bursting with figs, raisins, and nuts. Buccellato is a wonderfully rich cake that is traditional for Christmas, but now can be found in Palermo all year long. Its name comes from the Latin *buccellatum*, which means a ring or a wreath, although I have seen one as long and flat as a flag and others that are bite-sized pastries. Its nickname in Palermo, *ammarra-panza*, means a full stomach or a stomach stopper, clearly a tribute to its irresistibility and richness. Once upon a time it was dipped into a sweet syrup—an Arabic custom—when it was sold, although that, of course, cost extra. You must start the fillings at least 12 hours ahead.

Makes 1 wreath or 60 to 65 individual buccellati

PASTRY

2 cups (275 grams) unbleached all-purpose flour
Pinch salt
⅓ cup (75 grams) sugar
7 tablespoons (100 grams) unsalted butter or lard
1 egg yolk
3 to 6 tablespoons water or white wine
1 teaspoon vanilla extract
¼ teaspoon grated lemon zest

Make the pastry according to the directions for Pasta Frolla (page 270).

FILLING

8 to 10 (250 grams) dried figs, preferably Calimyrna
¾ cup (75 grams) apricot jam
¾ cup red wine, plus 1 to 2 tablespoons more as needed
Scant ⅔ cup (75 grams) raw almonds, toasted and finely chopped
½ cup (50 grams) walnuts, finely chopped
⅓ cup (50 grams) sultana raisins
¼ teaspoon cinnamon
¼ teaspoon cardamon
⅛ teaspoon ground cloves

TOPPING

1 egg, beaten
2 to 3 tablespoons pistachio nuts, finely minced

Filling. Cut each fig into 12 pieces. Heat the jam and wine together to a boil. Add the figs and let them cook for 2 minutes. Add the nuts, raisins, cinnamon, cardamon, cloves, and finally the figs. Cook 5 to 10 minutes, until everything is well mixed. Remove from the fire and stir well until the filling is neither too hard or too soft. You can refrigerate it at this point and keep it for as long as a week.

Large Wreath. Roll out the pastry to a 12- or 14-inch round, a bit larger than a large dinner plate. Make a ring of the filling about 2 inches in from the outer edge, then turn in the edges of the pastry, enclosing the filling. Use an espresso saucer or large teacup to cut out a small hole in the exposed center of the pastry. Moisten the edges, then close up the wreath by pinching the edges of the dough firmly all around the inside edge of the wreath. Make perpendicular cuts around the interior of the ring and a few around the exterior. Use the tines of a fork to perforate the top of the pastry like the spokes of a wheel. Egg wash the pastry and sprinkle the minced pistachios over the top. Bake in a 350°F oven until golden brown, 30 to 35 minutes.

Cookies. When the filling and pastry are ready, take 1 tablespoon of pastry, flatten, and fill it with a similar-sized piece of filling. Roll the pastry dough around the filling, making sure that the filling is well covered. You can gather the pastry at the top like a drawstring purse or roll it into a ball that looks like a fat walnut. Seal the edges well. Pierce the pastry lightly with a fork. Bake in a 350°F oven until lightly golden, 20 to 25 minutes. Cool on racks. Sprinkle with confectioners' sugar.

Dita degli Apostoli

Apostles' Fingers

This traditional Christmas dessert in Apulia starts with little vanilla-flavored omelets that are filled with chocolate- or espresso-flavored ricotta and rolled up as slender as fingers.

Makes 12, enough to serve 6

FILLING

1 cup plus 2 tablespoons (11 ounces, 300 grams) ricotta, as fresh as possible
½ cup plus 2 teaspoons (110 grams) superfine sugar
1½ teaspoons unsweetened cocoa powder, preferably Dutch process, or 1 to 1½ teaspoons instant espresso powder
⅛ teaspoon cinnamon

OMELETS

8 eggs
2 teaspoons vanilla extract
Pinch salt
2 tablespoons oil

TOPPING

2 teaspoons confectioners' sugar
Large pinch cinnamon

For the filling, press the ricotta through a wire-mesh sieve into a mixing bowl. Add the sugar, leave for an hour, and sieve again. Mix in the cocoa or coffee and cinnamon and blend so well that you can't sense any granularity at all.

For the omelets, beat the eggs with the vanilla and salt. Heat 2 teaspoons of the oil in a 6-inch nonstick frying pan. When the pan is hot, pour in enough batter to cover the bottom of the pan and swirl it around quickly. Once the omelet has set and become lightly golden, quickly turn it over and cook the other side very briefly. Slide it onto a plate lined with paper towels to drain. Repeat with the rest of the batter.

Spoon 1 to 2 tablespoons of the filling on each warm omelet and roll up into a cannoli or cigar shape. Sift confectioners' sugar mixed with cinnamon over the tops of the omelets and serve immediately.

CAPO D'ANNO

NEW YEAR

December 31 and January 1

"No matter what else we eat, you can be sure that there will be lentils and raisins in our New Year's Eve dinner," my friend Giovanna promised. "Last year Roberto was devastated when we went out and there wasn't a single lentil in any course. He couldn't talk about anything else when we got home. No lentils! He was convinced that our money would run out or that we'd have some dreadful financial disaster in the coming year."

Since lentils and raisins look a bit like coins, Italians eat them for their promise of prosperity in the New Year. Tuscans eat lentils with cotechino, a big pork sausage sliced like coins, and people in Bologna and Modena eat them with zampone, the same sausage mixture stuffed into a boned pig's trotter. Umbrians eat the deep brown lentils of Castelluccio, while Abruzzeze eat lenticchie di Santo Stefano, tiny orange-tinged lentils whose deep taste comes from local soil rich in minerals. In Piedmont little grains of rice mean money, so New Year's Eve menus always used to feature risotto in bianco with creamy fonduta on top, and—for double luck—a big plate of boiled beef and chicken would be served later in the meal with spinach and lentils.

We went to visit friends in Tuscany for New Year's Eve, driving north from Rome past fields full of tiny baby lambs born during Christmas week. All along the way the land was the pale green of winter wheat. Pollarded poplars with swollen nodes and fine, thin branches stood in ghostly files against hillsides. Gnarled vines, spiny trees, simple stone houses out of a Morandi painting, cypresses defining the swell of the earth: at the end of the year this landscape sculpted by the low winter light is an unfamiliar vision of the countryside in which luxuriant vine and olive usually define the swell of land.

On the day of New Year's Eve, we stopped for lunch by the shore of Lake Trasimeno just beyond Perugia, and were treated to a meal full of symbols of money and good luck. We sampled lentils and cotiche (pork rind), followed by an enormous carp, called *regina del lago,* queen of the lake, cooked on skewers set before a roaring fire. Dessert was as sweet as it was symbolic: Torciglione, the traditional Umbrian cake shaped like a coiled snake, and made of almonds, sugar, and egg whites, was undoubtedly served because snakes shed their skins to renew themselves, just as time renews itself as one year passes into another. Chiacchiere, tiny balls of dough that look exactly like little sweet lentils, are drizzled with honey, so that the coming year may be sweet.

No matter where a New Year's Eve dinner is served, regional differences dictate its menu. Our Tuscan friends began with the ritual lentils and cotechino. The next courses, tagliarini with lobster sauce and a leg of veal stuffed with an artichoke frittata, were contemporary contributions to the elegance of New Year's Eve. We knew that raisins would find their way into dessert and indeed they danced through the schiacciata di zibibbo, a traditional Tuscan sweet served with cremetta al mascarpone, a relative of crème anglaise that had crossed the border and introduced itself to Italian mascarpone cheese.

Slightly before midnight, we were each given a small bunch of grapes to dip into the glasses of champagne that magically appeared in one hand, and we were told to hold at least two coins in the other. The savvy businessmen among us had wadded various currencies—yen, francs, and dollars as well as lire—in their palms, but we were content with a couple of gold-and-silver-layered five-hundred-lire coins and a few lire notes, hoping they would multiply and promise us more holidays in Italy. While talking and waiting for the arrival of the New Year, we had a panoramic view of fireworks outside the window, thundering rockets in brilliant oranges and reds and silvery whites pinwheeling in the sky. At the stroke of midnight huge Roman candles went off, the antique clock chimed, we drank toasts with the champagne, ate the grapes we had dunked in it, and exchanged kisses.

Italians make it clear that they hope the New Year will bring new things by tossing old, useless possessions out the window at midnight. It is an energetic, if symbolic, way of getting rid of the bad accumulated during the past year. On New Year's Eve day, Americans are used to seeing pages of old calendars drift out of office windows and flutter slowly to the streets below, leaving the financial districts of many big cities buried under a blizzard of white paper, but in Italy what comes out the windows is anything from a used bar of soap to shoes, old glasses and terracotta dishes, even couches and refrigerators, and they come flying like missiles. With fear and trepidation do Italians walk about on that night, pressing as flat as they can against the walls of buildings, never knowing when something will come whizzing by. Cars are not exempt from assault. Sometimes so many objects land on an automobile that its owners have to wait for the street cleaners to unearth it. Newspapers carry long articles detailing the carnage: 500 INJURED AND THREE DEAD the headlines read one year, all casualties of what they call "toasts with blows." The crashing sounds of broken pottery are often accompanied by loud firecrackers or shots or the popping of champagne corks—noises expressing high spirits like those of the Romans centuries before, with the added intention of driving away evil spirits.

In ancient times Romans gave friends a glass jar full of dates and dried figs in honey, along with a bay leaf branch so the coming year would be as sweet and full of good fortune as the gifts. Neapolitans still wrap dried figs in laurel leaves and exchange them at New Year's. They treat the gifts as a kind of insurance of abundance all year long. Romans called their gifts *strenne* from the Sabine goddess of prosperity, Strenia, and she in turn gave her name to the laurel boughs that were cut from a wood sacred to her. From *strenne*, the word for those branches, the word became used for all gifts given at the New Year (predecessors of presents now exchanged at Christmas). At that time New Year was still celebrated at the spring equinox, when branches of bay leaves were discarded and new ones put in their place before the temple of Vesta. Those branches, Cattabiani tells us, were themselves connected with the great Cosmic Tree, which offered its powers to the earth at the beginning of a new year.

The Romans moved New Year to January 1 in 153 B.C, and they dedicated the month to Janus, the god of beginnings, who with his two

New Year celebration in Naples, nineteenth-century watercolor engraving

faces looks back toward the old year and forward to the new. They celebrated New Year for a full six days of carousing and rejoicing. Citizens picked boughs and decorated their houses with garlands of greenery like holly and mistletoe, magical plants that bore fruit in a dead season. They hung lights and set out tables full of fine food, eating and drinking on an epic scale. Present-day Romans have not lost their interest in celebrating, although planked fish and stuffed capons and turkeys have replaced more traditional dishes, and today the real Roman ritual is a plunge into the chilly waters of the Tiber, a bracing immersion in the New Year.

Until recently groups of children and adults in Sicily went around singing "*La Strenna*," wishing everyone a Happy New Year and asking for presents. This custom was similar to trick-or-treating on Halloween; everything was fine as long as raisins, cookies, or dried figs or fruits or nuts were forthcoming. But let a person refuse, and curses and bad omens were sung along with a threatening verse meant to sting the holdouts into producing the desired food. The groups were accompanied by musical sound effects. They might only be cowbells, although sometimes men played the flute, violin, and contrabass, and younger boys played tin cans and beat old pans with pieces of iron. These door-to-door visits continued until church bells rang out at midnight. Then it was time for a big feast of such sweets as mustazzola, pine-nut–studded pignolate, ring-shaped cuccidate, and biscotti della regina covered with sesame seeds, with intermediate courses of sausages and pork chops. Eating and drinking in honor of both new and old years went on until dawn.

New Year's Eve may have all the raucous features of a fine pagan feast, but it is officially known as San Silvestro, since it falls on the Feast Day of Saint Sylvester, who was pope when Constantine declared Christianity the official state religion. Even so, the day was fraught with such riotous implications that the Church didn't get around to recognizing the holiday until the sixth century, and then in the 1970s turned it into the Feast of Mary. It is said that every year San Silvestro liberates the village of Poggio Catino near Rieti, in Latium, from the grip of a dragon who lives in a cavern 365 steps deep into the earth, one for each day of the year. In exorcising both the pagan monster and the old year, San Silvestro is like a Christian Janus who closes the door on one year and its pagan ceremonies and opens it on a new one in a Christian era.

New Year's in Sicily brings out ritual breads. Baked on Christmas Eve and eaten on New Year's is a big, round bread, cannizzu, which gets its name from the dialect word for the reed basket in which it is baked. The two-tiered bread has a little bread ladder connecting the bottom to the top, where bits of dough are shaped to look like tiny grains of wheat. The ladder is a symbol of good luck, and the grainlike dough set in a little circle becomes a magical incantation for filling the granaries of the

Caricature of New Year, nineteenth-century engraving

household. Two half-moons or horns of bread, yoked together with a cord of pasta, are called *'uoi,* short for *buoi,* or oxen; they are eaten at New Year's lunch, and lucky are the children for whom the cord is saved. The yoking surely invokes the fertility yearned for as one year passes into darkness and the next one arrives as a great unknown.

In Molise every family offered a bowl of lessata, a soup of beans, garbanzos, and grain, and the town of Campodipietra made a cake with three little flying birds on top. Once they were real birds that had been stuffed (New Year must have been a splendid time for taxidermists), but now fortunately they are made of sugar and are eaten with the cake at midnight between bouts of singing and dancing.

New Year's desserts have been made with honey since Roman times, but some are more complicated than others. Neapolitans almost need the talents of an architect to construct the ornate confection of caramelized dough with tiny almond pieces called *il croccante.* It is an elaborate triumph of the pastrymaker's art, a *fantasia* meant to inspire toasts and then to be eaten little by little over a series of days, so that when Epiphany finally arrives, the New Year's dessert has completely disappeared.

In many cities the traditional lunch served on New Year's Day once required lasagne as one of its courses. Tradition may have changed, but a codex of the fourteenth century, discovered in the University of Bologna, gives a recipe for lasagne more or less as it is made and eaten today. In Sicily lasagne were made with wide noodles that had to be bought, not made at home, and only the ones with ruffled edges would do. They were sauced with ricotta, other cheeses, and the dark tomato ragù left from stew, an appearance that gave it the memorable name of *lasagna alla cacata,* which Mary Taylor Simeti gracefully translates as *lasagna a la merde.*

Elsewhere in Italy, happily, the food of the New Year is lentils, raisins, and oranges, symbols of riches, good luck, and the promise of love.

Lenticchie col Cotechino

Lentils with Cotechino Sausage

On New Year's Eve, everyone from Rome north eats lentils cooked with delicately spiced cotechino sausage. It is a perfect dish with which to start another year, since lentils symbolize money and sausage represents the container that will hold it. In Emilia-Romagna, especially around Modena, New Year's Eve dinner is unthinkable without zampone, which is the very same sausage meat packaged more spectacularly—in a pig's foot.

Makes 6 servings

1 cotechino sausage, about 1 pound (450 grams)
1 pound 2 ounces (500 grams) lentils
3 cups broth
¼ cup (60 grams) olive oil
1 small onion, finely chopped
1 rib celery, finely chopped
1 carrot, finely chopped
2 cloves garlic, finely minced
8 fresh sage leaves, chopped
3 tablespoons tomato paste diluted in a little water
Salt and pepper

Soak the cotechino in cold water for 2 hours. Clean the lentils well by soaking them briefly and changing the water at least once. Put them in cold water, bring to a boil, and cook until not quite done, 45 minutes to 1 hour.

Wrap the cotechino in cheesecloth and pierce it with a fork in several places. Boil very slowly in broth over low heat about 50 minutes, skimming off the fat from time to time. When it is cooked, remove it from the broth, unwrap it from its casing, and let it cool briefly.

Warm the oil and sauté the onion, celery, carrot, garlic, and sage leaves in the olive oil until the onion is transparent and the vegetables limp. Be careful not to burn the garlic. Drain the lentils, saving a bit of their water, add the chopped sautéed vegetables, salt, and pepper, and mix in the tomato sauce with a wooden spoon. Bathe with about 3 ladlefuls of broth from the cotechino. Slice the cotechino and serve next to the cooked lentils.

Tagliarini all'Aragosta

Tagliarini with Lobster Sauce

What better way to bring in a new year than with ribbons of silky pasta wrapped in a rich lobster sauce? This combination comes from the seaside town of Ostia. Although Italian lobsters are different from our Maine variety—they don't, for instance, have claws—this pasta is wonderful made with East Coast lobster.

Makes 6 servings

2 lobsters, 1¼ pounds each
Salt
1½ tablespoons extra-virgin olive oil
2 large cloves garlic, peeled and slightly crushed but left whole
½ to 1 teaspoon peperoncino (dried red pepper), seeded and finely chopped
½ cup dry white wine
¾ cup heavy cream
3 very ripe tomatoes, peeled, seeded, and chopped (about 1¼ pounds) or 1 can (16 ounces) Italian plum tomatoes, drained and chopped
1½ pounds fresh green or egg tagliarini or dried linguine

Bring a large pot of water to a boil. Add the lobsters and cook 10 minutes over high heat. Remove the lobsters and let cool. Reserve the water for cooking the pasta and salt it well. Remove the lobster meat from the tails and claws and chop into fine pieces.

In a large flameproof casserole heat the oil over moderate heat. Add the garlic and the red pepper; cook until the garlic cloves are golden all over, about 5 minutes, then discard the garlic. Add the white wine and cook over medium-high heat until it has almost evaporated. Reduce the heat to low and stir in the cream. Cook the mixture over low heat until just hot, about 5 minutes. Add the tomatoes and cook 5 minutes longer. Off the heat, add the lobster meat to heat through.

Bring the reserved lobster water to a boil, add the pasta, and cook until tender but firm, about 2 minutes for fresh, 8 minutes for dried. Drain the pasta and add directly to the sauce. Cook, tossing, for a minute or two to blend and heat through. Transfer to a platter and serve immediately.

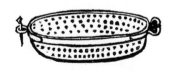

Risotto con Fonduta

Risotto with Fondue

This delicate risotto enfolding a creamy fonduta became a New Year tradition in Piedmont after it was accidentally invented by Cavour's cook in Geneva who had meant to make a soufflé base. This is what he turned out instead, and the dish, which crossed the border during the years of the Risorgimento, has since become part of Piemontese tradition. Shavings of white truffle over the top only make it taste better.

Makes 4 main-course or 6 first-course servings

7 ounces (200 grams) Fontina cheese
½ cup lukewarm milk
1 tablespoon olive oil
2 tablespoons butter
1 garlic clove, finely minced
1 bay leaf
2 cups plus 2 tablespoons (400 grams) Arborio rice
½ cup plus 1 teaspoon dry white wine
4¼ cups beef broth
1 tablespoon flour
1 egg yolk, well beaten
Salt and white pepper

Cut the Fontina cheese in ½-inch cubes and put in a small bowl with the lukewarm milk. Heat the oil and butter in a heavy pot or flameproof casserole over medium heat. When the butter has completely melted, add the garlic, bay leaf, and rice and sauté 3 to 4 minutes. Add the wine and let it cook until it has evaporated.

In a separate saucepan heat the broth to a boil. Start adding it to the rice a half cup at a time, stirring continually, until the rice has absorbed all the broth, 16 to 18 minutes.

In the top of a double boiler set the Fontina and milk with the flour over barely boiling water and stir until the cheese has melted. At this point add the egg yolk and mix well. Taste for salt and pepper.

Turn the rice out onto a platter in the form of a nest and put the fonduta in the middle.

Torciglione I

///////////////////////////

*Almond-Paste
Snake Coiled into
a Cake*

This slightly chewy, chunky-textured almond-paste cake looks like a charming snake, with coffee beans for eyes and a thin slice of candied orange peel for a tongue. Snakes were part of Etruscan iconography, and while that mysterious civilization has disappeared, it left behind a motif that lives on in this delicious cake.

Makes 1 cake, enough to serve 8

2¼ cups (250 grams) peeled almonds
¾ cup plus 2 tablespoons (175 grams) sugar
¼ cup plus 1 tablespoon (40 grams) candied citron or orange peel, finely minced
1 to 2 egg whites
Confectioners' sugar
9 blanched almonds
2 coffee beans or 1 amarena or maraschino cherry
1 sliver candied orange peel

Grind the almonds to a flour in a nut grinder. Transfer to the bowl of a mixer and add the granulated sugar, candied fruit, and egg white and mix with the paddle attachment until you have a sticky almond paste.

On a table lightly floured with confectioners' sugar, roll the mixture into a log that is thicker in the center than at the edges. Use a rubber dough scraper to help with the sticky paste. With scissors cut 9 parallel cuts along the top and then do the same along the inner edge at a 180-degree angle, forming an X. It will look somewhat like the markings of snakeskin. Put a whole almond in each cut along the back, so the almonds march down the back of the snake. Set the almond-paste snake on a cookie sheet lined with parchment paper and bend into a loose half circle so it looks like a snake. Use 2 coffee beans for the eyes or cut an amarena or maraschino cherry in half and press into place. Set a thin slice of candied orange peel to look like a tongue.

Baking. Heat the oven to 325°F. Bake 5 to 10 minutes, then turn the oven down to 300°F and bake until it takes on color, about 25 minutes.

Torciglione II

~~~~~~~~~~~~~~~~~~~~~~~~~~~~~

Snake-Shaped
Almond Cake of
Perugia—the
Easy Version

An easy shortcut that uses store-bought almond paste.

1 pound 2 ounces (500 grams) almond paste
2 to 3 tablespoons egg white, essentially half an egg white
⅓ cup (50 grams) candied citron or orange peel, finely chopped
Confectioners' sugar
9 blanched almonds
2 coffee beans or 1 amarena or maraschino cherry
1 thin slice candied citron or orange peel

Beat the almond paste, egg white, and candied citron together in the electric mixer fitted with the paddle attachment. Do not use the food processor for this step. Proceed as in the recipe for Torciglione I, page 295.

Baking. Heat the oven to 250°F. Bake 20 minutes, then turn oven to 325°F and continue baking until it is lightly golden, about 15 minutes longer.

Crema Mascarpone

~~~~~~~~~~~~~~~~~~~~~~~~~~~~~~~~~~~~

Creamy Mascarpone Sauce

As smooth as crème anglaise, as haunting as zabaglione, this rum-scented dessert sauce is perfect for poached fruits and buttery cakes. I have eaten it as the creamy dessert at the house of friends in Tuscany and as a sauce at Il Sole in Maleo when Franco Colombani served it at the end of a phenomenal meal. (Though I thought I was full, I discovered I wasn't.) It tastes like dessert for a celebration, and indeed it was originally served only at Christmastime in Lombardy, in a tiny sliver of the region that runs from Maleo to Melegnano. You can make the sauce ahead if you wait to beat and add the egg whites 1 to 2 hours before serving.

Makes 6 to 8 servings

3 eggs, separated
3 tablespoons superfine sugar
3 tablespoons rum
⅔ pound (300 grams) mascarpone, as fresh as possible
¼ teaspoon cream of tartar
12 to 16 amaretti, optional

Whip the egg yolks with the sugar and rum. Press the mascarpone through a sieve and add it to the egg yolk mixture. (Can be made ahead up to this point.) Beat the egg whites with the cream of tartar until they hold a soft peak. Fold in the egg whites until the sauce is smooth. Refrigerate for an hour or two. To make a creamy mascarpone dessert bathe the amaretti with the rum and proceed as directed, but omit the rum in the first step. Put a layer of the crema in the bottom of a serving bowl, cover with the amaretti and top with the rest of the crema. Refrigerate before serving.

EPIFANIA

EPIPHANY IN TARCENTO

January 6

If Christmas is the first in a thick cluster of holidays, Epiphany, coming twelve days later, is the last, sweeping them all away in its wake, just as the expression promises:

> *E l'Epifania*
> *Tutte le feste porta via.*

It started with the three Magi traveling to Egypt, following the star. They were priests or astrologers, the first to worship at the manger, the first to recognize the divinity of the baby in the crib, and the first to bring gifts. Which is why the Italians traditionally don't get presents on Christmas but on January 6 at the Feast of Epiphany, when they are brought by a toothless old woman named *La Befana.* She is the Italian equivalent of Santa Claus, a kind of good witch who is said to live in the interiors of chimneys and to fly around on her broom on Epiphany Eve, leaving presents. When she finds shoes or stockings that children have hung by the chimney, she fills them with toys and with sweets that are sometimes called *befanini.* If children are bad, they get garlic and lumps of *carbone,* but the charcoal, miraculously, is made of sugar, so what looks dark and forbidding is a sweet, sugar-filled warning. The story is told that the three Magi came by the Befana's house and invited her to accompany them on their voyage to see the Savior, but the old lady turned them down, saying she had too much housework to do. Ever since, she has regretted her decision, and each year she sets off with a big bag full of gifts, stopping to distribute them at every house in case children should live there. The name *Befana* comes from *befania,* a corruption of the Greek word *epifania,* which means apparition or manifestation, since this was the day on which Jesus appeared to the Magi, giving the first evidence of his divine birth.

The Befana sounds motherly and comforting, but in Tuscan nursery rhymes, she appears as an aggressive old bogeywoman. It is said that Florentine children who had anything on their consciences were terrified that the Befana wouldn't leave toys or sweets for them, but instead would poke holes in their stomachs. At dinner they filled up on bread and braised fava beans to present a strong abdominal defense, and some even covered their stomachs with a terracotta griddle.

The good and bad sides of the Befana are like the good mother/bad witch of fairy tales, two aspects of a single person. The Befana may bring wonderful presents, but she can also be a grotesque woman with a sinister black face, associated in some accounts with Hecate, Queen of the Night.

Of course, it is not this dark side of the Befana that brings hundreds of children to the Piazza Navona on the night of January 5, where dozens of booths of gifts and toys and the target-shooting at the end of the Christmas cycle have always been part of this holiday season of noise, games, and prodigious feats of eating. "On the night of January 5," one guidebook writer explained, "the show becomes really an exceptional one, with its stacks of merchandise for gifts, pyramids of toys, and mountains of sweets to suck, to lick, to crunch."

The toys and candies are still there, although they have become commercialized and a bit tawdry. In the piazza you can also find political kiosks to enroll party members; Santa Clauses, a new addition, looking trimly Italian in their little red suits (*la bella figura* extends even unto Santa); darts to throw at balloons; and bottles to knock over with baseballs.

Epiphany may be the end of the Christmas season, and it is certainly the most popular holiday in the countryside, but it is also regarded as the beginning of Carnival, when every joke and trick is allowed, so celebrating has always been energetic and intense. In times past in Tuscany a man used to dress up like a witch and surround himself with *befanotti,* shrewd and desperate low-life characters wearing false beards, and inside-out jackets, with faces smeared with grease. In Rome, the streets were illuminated with torchlights set on red and yellow poles, and amid a great uproar people exploded out of the Piazza Navona, down the narrow streets, which were made even more crowded with stands selling toys and games, and into the center of the Piazza dei Caprettari and Piazza Sant'Eustachio, which were full of enormous booths. To attract a clientele, vendors dressed young boys like women, blackened their faces, set caps on their heads, put a long reed in their right hand and a lantern in the left, and hung baskets of oranges and golden pine cones.

Even now, a procession including three children, dressed like the Magi and carrying a pole with a golden star on top, goes through the little towns at night during the week before Epiphany, stopping at houses and singing *pasquelle*, little songs about the coming of the Magi. (The word *pasqua*, which means Easter, the most important holiday in the Catholic calendar, is also used for other major holidays; Epiphany is called *Pasqua Epifania* and Christmas is sometimes referred to as *Pasqua Natale*.) Often the members of the procession ask for small good luck presents or food. Sometimes they are given money, which is spent for a communal meal. In Sabbio Chiese, near Brescia, dinner is based on taragna, a polenta of finely ground buckwheat and corn. Elsewhere, in the Marches or Abruzzo, traditional gifts of sausages, bread, eggs, dried figs, and wine become dinner, or are taken home and eaten later.

In Roman times whoever got the good luck bean baked inside a cake was made master of the Saturnalia revels. By the fourteenth century beans were still being baked into cakes; but now this was for Epiphany, called the Festa del Re, the Festival of the King, and lots were drawn for a focaccia in which were hidden three white fava beans, one for each of the Magi, and one black one. Whoever found the black bean in his slice of cake was made king and could choose his queen and rule the banquet. The custom is still honored in Piedmont with a single bean, although it may be replaced by a tiny porcelain jug or a baby or a little fish. *Trovare la fava nel dolce*, "to find the fava in the cake," is an expression that means making a fine discovery. Bakers in Piedmont used to present focacce to their best customers on Epiphany, and families always left a focaccia for the Befana next to the fireplace.

Most festivities were rustic, and of these only a few remain. Some towns in Piedmont and the little village of Rivisondoli, near L'Aquila in Abruzzo, still have a living crèche on Epiphany Eve and reenact the Nativity with the last baby born in the town taking the role of Jesus.

Other communities required a public announcement of engagements on Epiphany and often devised a sort of parody. All the bachelors and spinsters were paired by lot—the underlying message was that everyone is meant to be part of a couple—and any girl without a partner was given the title of Befana for the entire year.

Epiphany in Friuli, a slice of land tucked into the foothills of the Alps between Venice and Trieste, is celebrated in a particularly evocative way. Families at home gather around the warmth of fires in a special raised hearth called the *fogolar*, where the big Christmas log finishes burning at the end of the twelve days. The *fogolar* sits in the middle of the room, where the flame burns freely under an onion-shaped hood that carries the smoke up into a chimney. Fires have burned on the eve and night of Epiphany for centuries, even when Friuli was menaced by barbarians and armies from other regions, for they are magical flames to light the way for the three wise men going to see the baby Jesus. In some places the fires are called *pan e vin,* bread and wine, and in others they are called *vecja,* old one. While the fires burn, boys run through fields with burning brands and jump across the fires using long poles. In some parts of Friuli, groups of young men roll burning wheels called *cidulis* down the hill, shouting out the names of their fiancées as a way of announcing the engagement for the first time. The ashes from their wheels will be added to the remnants of the bonfires that burn all over Friuli to fertilize the earth and assure a good harvest.

Numerous conquerors gave Friuli a rich early heritage and left it with three capitals: Aquileia, which was Roman; Cividale, which was Lombard; and Udine, which was and remains Venetian in look and influence. The Celts, who were here first, ranged along the arc of the northern Carnic Alps, leaving the plain free for the Romans, who made an alliance with the Venetians, founded colonies, connected them with roads, and settled the city of Aquileia in 181 B.C Friuli may be bound by Venetian culture, but on a clear day you can see Yugoslavia, which is close enough to give a Slavic slant to some of the food of the region.

The Epiphany procession in the town of Tarcento, which is not far from Udine, reenacts the coming of the three Magi. Many of the towns-people, including farmers who bring produce to present to the baby Jesus, are in medieval clothing, while the three kings from the East and the man carrying the star are dressed in striking biblical costumes. The proces-

The Befana, etching from Bartolomeo Pinelli, 1825

sion begins in the last rays of daylight and proceeds in the growing darkness from the piazza in Tarcento along the city streets to a slightly elevated site upon the hill where one of the Magi lights the *fogolar*.

The parade is always led by the oldest man in the community. The three kings and all the costumed participants carry torches, but there are many children, bundled in sweaters and jackets against the cold, holding candles that are lit one at a time. The black winter night envelops everyone, and those who remain at the bottom of the hill can watch the procession ascend only by following the pinpoints of flickering candles as they serpentine to the top of the hill. It is a long climb to the remains of the medieval castle of Cojo and the *pignarul*, a pyramid as thick as a haystack in a Brueghel painting, composed of sheaves of corn, brambles of brushwood, and pine branches. As hundreds watch from the bottom of the hill, the oldest man in the parade holds up a lit firebrand. He touches it to the "mother" *pignarul*, which roars into flames. Two enormous firecrackers explode, fireworks burst in pinwheels of color across the sky, and bells ring throughout the town. The flames are said to light the way for the Magi, but they also foretell the coming harvest, and it is always the oldest man who reads their meaning. If the smoke blows to the east, where the sun rises, then it will be a year of abundance, but should the smoke blow to the west, where the sun sets, it is a bad omen for the crops. Later, when the flames are out, some people remove the embers with a big fork to fertilize their fields, although folklore says that each spark is thought to change magically into a sack of wheat.

All these ceremonies are festive and exciting, and they are also a signal to all people to light their own fires. I stood in the garden of a family in Tarcento whose haystack was at least twelve feet high. A straw figure of the Befana crowned the top. As soon as the *pignarul* at the top of the hill burst into flame, one of the men in the garden lit a firebrand and touched it once, twice, three times to the haystack and it took the fire in a great whoosh. Sparks flew everywhere. Quickly the men drew a large circle in the earth to keep the flames from leaping out of control. The fire roared and warmed us all, and when we looked up we could see fires all over the countryside, lighting up the plain and the mountain, and shimmering on the shoulders of the hill.

In some parts of lower Friuli, young boys run along the edges of fields with sheaves of burning reeds, and elsewhere, when the fire is about to go out, they throw chestnuts on it and roast them, not only because they are delicious, but because they are a symbol of fertility. Epiphany brings engaged couples together for the first time in public. At the party I attended the family set fire to the straw effigy of the Befana, with her hunchback and enormous feet. Because she represents the end of the season, burning her gets rid of the old year.

As we stood in the reflected light of the fires, we kept warm drinking vin brulé, a hot mulled wine that is traditional on this evening, and eating pinza, a rustic sweet bread made only for Epiphany. There were no beans hidden inside it, but it is clearly related to a sweet pizza or *focaccia*—its name is as close to pizza as its origins. Pinza is filled with raisins and pine nuts and figs, spiced with fennel seeds, and is sometimes made with corn flour, sometimes with a mixture of rye and wheat. It can be shaped into a simple round or made to look like a Greek epsilon with three arms of equal length, perhaps to represent the three Magi. The sweet bread was once cooked under the embers and eaten by the adults while small children paraded from house to house announcing the end of the season and the beginning of Carnival. It is still considered good luck to eat pinze made by seven different families.

The fires lit, people now stream to the piazza in the center of town for a *sagra* serving the traditional foods of the region. They are cooked on a big *fogolar*, which can hold dozens of musetti, the cotechino-like sausage that gets its name from the snout of the pig, one of the ingredients. Other, and even lesser, parts of the pig are added, all finely diced and spiced with cloves and cinnamon, coriander, peppers, nutmeg, and sweet white wine. The sausage is stuffed and left to hang for a month in the *cantina*, and after being cooked, it is served with brovada, sweet-and-sour turnips marinated for forty days under the grape skins left over from winemaking until the turnips turn violet and taste like very sharp sauerkraut. Other dishes include grilled local sausages, beefsteaks, and pinza served with the splendid wines of Friuli.

The tastes of those dishes were wonderful, but tastes were all I was allowed, since I was taken off to a traditional party at a local *trattoria*, where it seemed that every specialty of the region was served for dinner. A holiday spirit prevailed at the tables, which were full of large groups of celebrating Friulani. We ate frico, the onomatopoeic crunchy fried local cheese; gnocchi alla zucca with ricotta affumicata, pumpkin gnocchi with shavings of smoked ricotta; gnocchi alle susine, filled with prunes; baked veal osso buco with a wild mushroom sauce; and a parade of desserts that began with strucolo, Friuli's version of strudel, wandered through torta di mele, stopped briefly at biscotti to dip in chocolate sauce, and ended, finally, with pinza. Everyone cracked jokes, sang Friuli folk songs, and wandered from table to table, greeting friends. Laughter erupted constantly as people took turns telling elaborate, funny stories while consuming enormous quantities of Merlot and Tocai, Pinot Grigio and Cabernet. Even the normally elusive sweet golden Picolit, the prestigious dessert wine of Friuli, was on the table.

My companions were a group of Friulani who had been honored earlier in the afternoon when five outstanding citizens of the region were presented with special awards. The auditorium was jammed with people of all ages for an event that has only grown more meaningful since an earthquake devastated the area in 1976. No matter that many Friuliani have long since departed for other homes—*emarginato,* left to the side, by the greater importance of Venice to the south and Trieste to the east. No matter that one recipient of the prize had been in Australia for decades, so his brother accepted it for him, and that another returned from Rome to receive his recognition. For the Friulani this ceremony rekindles the fires of tradition and it is a reminder of a way of life that will be kept alive as long as the celebration lasts. Theirs is a countrified culture with rituals and traditions that are tied to the earth. As each of the winners spoke, their love of the land—their Friuli—was palpable and its values clearly permeated their sense of self. Tears flowed. Men hugged and kissed each other on both cheeks. In this ceremony the Friulani were celebrating their allegiance to this region with its star-shaped fortress town, its vineyards, its villas and houses with great fireplaces that are centers of family life, its simple country cuisine, and its tradition of hospitality.

Gnocchi di Zucca

xxxxxxxxxxxxxxxxxxxxxxxxxxxxxx

Pumpkin Gnocchi with Shavings of Smoked Ricotta and Sage Leaves

Amber-colored pumpkin gnocchi light up cold January nights, but only if they are delicate and finely flavored. The trick is to bake the squash so it doesn't get waterlogged and absorb quantities of flour. Do not puree the squash in the food processor; use the grating disk or press it through a ricer instead. These lovely gnocchi from Udine, in Friuli, are flavored with lemon, nutmeg, and brandy, and are served with a sprinkling of Parmesan cheese, grated smoked ricotta, and sage leaves slightly wilted in butter.

Makes 4 to 6 servings

1 pound 2 ounces (500 grams) pumpkin or butternut squash weighed
    before baking; it should measure about 1 cup grated or riced
2 eggs
Grated zest of 1 lemon
Pinch sugar
2 teaspoons brandy
¼ teaspoon freshly grated nutmeg
1 teaspoon salt
Pepper
1½ cups (200 grams) unbleached all-purpose flour
3½ tablespoons (50 grams) unsalted butter, very soft

3 or 4 sage leaves

¼ cup (30 grams) shaved smoked cheese; ricotta is best but smoked mozzarella is delicious too

Heat the oven to 375°F. Cut the pumpkin or butternut squash in large chunks and remove the seeds. Bake on an oiled sheet until chunks are tender when poked with a fork. Cool them enough to handle comfortably and peel them. You may either press the squash through a ricer or set the squash in a food processor fitted with the grating disk. Do not puree it in the processor or your mixture will be too smooth.

With the paddle attachment on an electric mixer or by hand, stir together the squash, eggs, lemon zest, sugar, brandy, nutmeg, salt, and pepper. Stir in the flour and mix vigorously until well blended. The mixture should come away from the sides of the bowl and hold together. You may need to add 1 to 2 extra tablespoons flour so that the dough is not too soft.

Bring a large stockpot of salted water to the boil. Scoop out balls of the dough by the half teaspoon and drop them into the boiling water, immediately sweeping them from the bottom so they don't stick. Cook until the gnocchi float to the surface, 2 to 3 minutes. As soon as the gnocchi are cooked, remove them with a slotted spoon, drain on paper towels, and put in a well-buttered warm baking dish. In a small sauté pan melt the butter and wilt the sage leaves briefly. Serve the gnocchi immediately tossed with the butter and sage leaves and with the smoked cheese shaved right over the top. The gnocchi can also be reheated in a 350°F oven.

Pinza
della Befana

~~~~~~~~~~~~~~~~~~~~~~~~~~~~

*Epiphany Polenta
and Fig Bread
from Friuli*

A rustic cornbread flavored with fennel and anise, nuts and raisins, pinza is the traditional sweet bread eaten in Friuli at Epiphany. An essential part of the festivities for centuries, it starts with polenta that is transformed into a fruit-filled country loaf.

Makes 2 loaves

1 cup plus 6 tablespoons water, plus up to ½ cup to loosen the mixture
    as it cooks
2 bay leaves
1 scant tablespoon fennel seeds
2 teaspoons anise seeds
¾ cup (115 grams) stone-ground cornmeal or polenta
Heaping ¼ cup (60 grams) sugar
3 tablespoons (40 grams) unsalted butter
2 tablespoons active dry yeast or 2⅓ cakes (42 grams) fresh yeast
1 cup water, warm
About 3½ cups (450 grams) unbleached all-purpose flour
1½ teaspoons sea salt
1 cup minus 1 tablespoon (150 grams) sultana raisins, soaked in cool
    water, drained, and squeezed dry
1 cup plus 2 tablespoons (225 grams) figs, preferably Calimyrna,
    chopped the size of the raisins

G L A Z E

1 egg
1 to 2 tablespoons turbinado sugar

Bring to a boil 1 cup plus 6 tablespoons water flavored with the bay leaves, fennel, and anise. Add the cornmeal or polenta and cook slowly, 5 to 6 minutes for the cornmeal, 8 to 10 for the polenta. Add up to ½ cup water to loosen the mixture as it cooks. Remove the bay leaves and add the sugar and butter. Cool to 100°F.

By Mixer. Stir the yeast into 1 cup warm water and leave until creamy, about 10 minutes. Using the mixer with the paddle attachment, add the cooled polenta mixture, flour, and salt and mix 1 to 2 minutes at medium speed. Change to the dough hook and mix at medium speed 3 to 4 minutes, adding up to 2 tablespoons flour. The dough won't come away from the sides of the bowl and will seem soft and sticky when done, but it comes together immediately when kneaded briefly on a lightly floured surface.

First Rise. Put the dough in a lightly oiled bowl, cover with plastic wrap, and let rise until doubled. It will happen in a brief 30 to 50 minutes because of the warm polenta.

Shaping and Second Rise. Flour the table well. Toss the figs and raisins with 2 to 3 tablespoons flour. Drop the extremely soft and plump dough out of its container onto the floured table, flatten it gently, and spread the figs and raisins on top, leaving about a 1-inch margin all around. Cut the dough in half and make 2 rectangular loaves. Place in well-oiled or parchment-lined 9- by 5-inch loaf pans. Cover with towels and let rise 45 minutes to 1 hour, till doubled and well over the top of the pans.

Baking. Preheat the oven to 400°F. Just before baking, egg wash the tops with beaten egg and sprinkle with turbinado sugar. Bake at 400°F 10 minutes, then turn down the heat to 350°F and continue baking 30 to 40 minutes more.

Corn, for polenta

Pinza Friulana
~~~~~~~~~~~~~~~~~~~~~~~~~~~~~~~~~~

Epiphany Bread
from Friuli

This pinza, made with sifted cornmeal, Marsala, and pine nuts, is a recent refinement of the earthy country loaf. I went to a party in Cividale on Epiphany Night, and after we had drunk vin brulé to keep warm while watching great bonfires roar on every hillside, we set off for a massive dinner. At the end we were each handed our very own pinza, which tasted just like this.

Makes 2 round loaves

SPONGE

1 tablespoon plus ¾ teaspoon (1½ packages) active dry yeast or 1½
   cakes (27 grams) fresh yeast
1 tablespoon sugar
1 cup plus 1 tablespoon milk, warmed to 105°F
1 cup plus 1 tablespoon (150 grams) unbleached all-purpose flour

Stir the yeast and sugar into the warm milk and let stand until foamy, about 10 minutes. Beat in the flour to make a batter. Cover with plastic wrap and let rise until doubled, 20 to 30 minutes.

DOUGH

2 tablespoons Marsala
2 to 3 tablespoons milk
1½ cups plus 3 to 4 tablespoons (235 grams) unbleached all-purpose
   flour
1 cup plus 1 tablespoon (175 grams) regular cornmeal, sieved in a small
   strainer
1 cup (100 grams) sugar
Scant 6 tablespoons (80 grams) unsalted butter
1 teaspoon salt
1¼ cups (200 grams) raisins, plumped in tepid water, drained, and
   squeezed very dry
⅔ cup (100 grams) pine nuts
⅔ cup (100 grams) candied orange peel or citron, chopped

GLAZE

1 egg, beaten

By Mixer. Using the paddle, mix the Marsala and milk into the sponge. Add the flour, cornmeal, sugar, butter, and salt and mix until well blended. Change to the dough hook and knead 2 to 3 minutes on medium speed. The dough is sticky, but knead it briefly with 1 to 2 tablespoons additional flour on a work surface and it is silky and smooth.

First Rise. Place the dough in a lightly oiled container, cover tightly with plastic wrap, and let rise until doubled, 3 to 3¼ hours.

Shaping and Second Rise. The dough is soft, pliable, velvety. Turn the dough out of its container onto a floured work surface and flatten it gently into a big round. Add the raisins, pine nuts, and candied orange peel in 2 additions. Sprinkle half over the surface, pat them in well, fold in the edges, and roll it up toward you. Let the dough rest 5 to 10 minutes. Flatten the dough as well as you can, sprinkle the rest of the nuts, raisins, and orange peel over the top, pat them in well, and roll it up again. Cut the dough in half and form into 2 rounds. Set on parchment-lined baking sheets, cover with towels, and let rise until doubled, 1½ to 2 hours.

Baking. Preheat the oven to 400°F. Just before baking, cut a 6-pointed asterisk or star into the top and glaze with the beaten egg. Bake 10 minutes, then turn down the oven to 350°F and bake 35 to 45 minutes more. If the top browns very deeply, cover it with aluminum foil or continue to turn the oven down.

Vin Brulé

~~~~~~~~~~~~~~~~~~~~~~~~~~~~~~~~

Hot Mulled Wine from Friuli

On the night of Epiphany as bonfires blaze on the hillsides of Friuli, people stand in their gardens or on their terraces, watching the flames and keeping warm by drinking vin brulé.

Makes 16 servings

2 bottles red wine, preferably Cabernet or Merlot from Friuli
6 cloves
2 apples, peeled and cut in small chunks
1 cinnamon stick
½ cup sugar

Bring all ingredients to a boil. Flambé and serve.

SANT'ANTONIO ABATE

FEAST OF
SAINT ANTHONY THE ABBOT
January 17

*N*ot long ago if you had asked children what the best day of the year was, they wouldn't have answered first communion or Epiphany," the chef-owner of a small *osteria* in Friuli told me. "They'd all have told you that it was the great Festa del Porco, the day the pig is killed." Unlikely (not to say unpleasant) as it sounds, the day promises an orgy of eating on an epic scale, courtesy of the pig, who provides dish after dish of sausages, ribs, and risotti, even breads with crisp cracklings kneaded right into the dough. For centuries in the countryside this bacchanalian feast was often the only day when people could eat all the meat they had dreamed of the rest of the year.

All country people used to keep pigs at home and fatten them on tasty scraps from the table, herbs that grew wild on hillsides, acorns that ripened on oaks, and grains and corn sprouting in nearby fields. Sometime after the first frost of winter, they called for the *norcino*, the special pig butcher, who arrived with his knives. In many parts of Italy the brief moment between the end of the old year and the sowing of seeds for the new coincides with January 17, the Feast of Sant'Antonio Abate, white-bearded Saint Anthony the Abbot, who is always pictured with a rosy pink pig at his side.

The saint is the protector of domestic animals, so on his feast day all kinds of beasts are blessed in the church. From Lugano in the north to Reggio Calabria in the south, horses and donkeys, courtyard geese and ducks, even dogs and cats and monkeys and parrots, arrive at the doors of the church on foot or carried in the arms of their owners. When Goethe was in Naples he was amused to discover that on the Feast of Sant'Antonio Abate "horses and mules, their manes and tails gorgeously braided with ribbons, are led up to a small chapel, detached from the church proper, and a priest, armed with an enormous brush, sprinkles them with holy water from tubs and buckets in front of him." The custom continues, even in the middle of Rome. These days the animals are apt to be on leashes, in baskets or birdcages, and while many may be garlanded with flowers and ribbons, they are no longer decorated with plumes and elegant accoutrements mentioned by early travelers. Alas, the intrusions of modern life are now recognized by some priests, who actually include automobiles in their blessings as the current incarnation of beasts of burden.

As protector of animals, Sant'Antonio is always accompanied by his pig. In many towns in southern Italy, the citizens buy a pig that belongs to the community and let it run around the countryside and wander freely in and out of houses. A notch cut in its ear or a bell tied around its neck identifies it as the pig of Sant'Antonio, which means that everyone must give it food and drink and allow it to sleep wherever it stops. This luxurious life goes on for an entire year as the pig grows ever fatter and sleeker, although fate finally catches up in catastrophic form with a lottery in early January. Whoever wins the pig takes it home and turns it into sausages and other tender cuts that are served up on Sant'Antonio's Day. The price the animal fetches goes toward paying the expenses of the festival. A new pig is immediately chosen to take its place for another

Saint Anthony and his pig, Biblioteca Estense, Modena

year, until it too is immolated, just like the pregnant sow that the pagan Romans and Celts sacrificed to Ceres and Mother Earth as a way of guaranteeing the fertility of the earth during the darkness of winter.

Some Italians are lyrical as they reminisce about Sant'Antonio's Day and the spectacular riches that are created in the kitchen. They remember leaping out of bed at daybreak, dressing in a hurry, and rushing to watch the proceedings as the pig was dispatched in the courtyard. The women kept huge pots of water boiling so they could wash the pig down and brush it hard to take off its bristly hairs. (These days a blowtorch is a welcome shortcut.) However, there are also those who recall rushing back to bed and pulling the pillow down hard over their ears to blot out the shrieks of the pig. That sound, says Giovanni Goria, a scholarly expert in all things gastronomical, is the immutable prelude to the great "Day of the Pig, when the mass of pig [is transformed] into mountains of exquisite delicacies, ritual foods of this meal in the countryside."

These are no little roseate pigs. They weigh in somewhere between 275 and 325 pounds, with haunches large enough to provide sizable prosciutti. Farm families have always taken turns helping each other, moving from place to place every few days, and participating in a great feast at the end of the arduous work. The women use their fists to mix the meat in wooden tubs, wash sausage casings in vinegar, and dry them with corn flour, but it is often the men who stuff the sausages and tie them with twine. They hang the links in a warm room with a fireplace for the first week and then send them to a cellar for longer drying. "I still remember the smell of my grandparents' room," one man told me. "It was tiny, the warmest place in the house, so the sausages always hung there at first. We had to make them during a waning moon to be sure they would turn out, and I used to find all sorts of excuses to go there just for the smell."

There is a specific ritual to the killing of the pig. The *norcino* himself seems as precise as a surgeon as he cuts the body in half or quarters, tossing the innards into a big basket. Then he sections the legs, separates the lard, pancetta, and shoulder, cuts away the rib and shoulder, the *lombata,* and the fillet, the loin, and sirloin, separating out the meat that will be aged as prosciutti, pancetta, salame, salsicce, and cotechini. No part of the animal is thrown away: not the spleen, the stomach, the cheek, the muscles, or even the snout. The aromas that escape from the cooking pots flavor the air of the courtyard and whet appetites: crispy cracklings, the freshest possible chops and livers wrapped in bay leaves are laid on the grill. Some meats are minced and turned into fat sausages that are spiced, moistened with wine, and flavored with garlic before being stuffed in their wrappers and hung up to dry while others are preserved in snowy white lard to keep them soft and fresh for months to

come. Other fresh sausages are made to be eaten that day. The spicing is absolutely determined by regional tradition and is one of the strongest expressions of local identity. Tuscan finocchiona sausage, for instance, is flavored with seeds from the fennel that grows wild on the hillsides; Calabrian coppa is spicy with hot pepper; the sausage of Lecce tastes of cinnamon and cloves, while the lively Friulian mixtures were influenced by the Cramars, traveling merchants who distributed Venetian spices until the end of the nineteenth century.

Whatever cannot be salted, cured, or smoked and put aside for the rest of the year is cooked and eaten immediately. Before the industrial age, when hunger was widespread, people lived out a fantasy of extravagant eating in the few celebratory days of the year and none offered more promise than the Feast of the Pig. Then as now, the dishes included sanguinaccio, blood pudding, a finely spiced delicacy whose name may put off modern city dwellers. Farm families know better, for under many regional names it is enjoyed all over Italy. It is called *migliaccio* in Tuscany, which is how Boccaccio referred to it in *The Decameron; biroldo* in Pistoia, where the day's dinner is called a *biroldata; baldon* in the Veneto; *burleng* in Romagna; *mulis* in Friuli; and *sanceli* in Sicily, where chocolate and pistachios add to the taste. In Piedmont they mix the blood with fresh milk, sautéed onions, raisins plumped in Marsala, brains, salt, nutmeg, and pepper, then they turn the mixture into little sausages, boiled and served on a bed of sautéed leeks or a round of polenta. Blood pudding is always eaten with the final piece of a salame left from the previous year. Every region has its own recipe—some use red wine instead of milk, add bread crumbs and pine nuts, and a bit of sugar—but it is almost always one of the major dishes in a meal.

The meal has always been a *festa della famiglia,* an occasion when family and friends gather for a huge *mangiata* called a *maialata* since it is all based on the pig. Its regional variations are many. In Piedmont the feast begins with fresh sausages made with red wine cooked for several hours and eaten with braised cabbages or lentils. There is always a grand fritto misto, mixed fry, that includes liver and lungs; a crisp heart cut in strips; a piccata of pork loin breaded and dipped in egg; little chunks of sausage;

breaded and fried brains; and pieces of liver chopped and seasoned with juniper berries and bay leaves before being wound into a casing and fried or grilled between bay leaves. And in Piedmont it wouldn't be Sant'Antonio without a dish called *batsoa* (from *bas de soie*, silk stockings), pig's trotters cooked with vinegar and seasoned with cloves and red wine. In Friuli and in Lombardy the Sant'Antonio Day meal often begins with a huge wheel of polenta sauced with the heart and the liver, still marbled with its fat and wrapped in bay leaves. Next come le ossa bollite, meat still on bones that have been boiled with coarse salt; a creamy risotto made with sausage crumbled into tiny pieces; and ribs roasted in the oven, served with borlotti beans boiled with cotenne, soft pork rind. Cassoeula is made with several cuts of pork and Savoy cabbage. In Friuli radicchio isn't chic or part of *nuova cucina*; it is a classic winter vegetable, usually eaten with shoulder chops for dinner. All the leftover fat from the pig —and there is a lot—is melted down and conserved in jars; some goes into the sausages, some filters out as tiny crispy bits known as *ciccioli*, which are baked into bread; and the rest is kept for use in cooking the remainder of the year.

The food of Sant'Antonio's Day, especially in northern Italy, is celebratory and joyful, but there is a darker side to the feast. The pig is sacrificed, perhaps to ask the favor of the gods, and the sacrifice is indicated in dishes of beans, vegetables symbolizing death through their connection with the underworld and the darkness of the earth. That is why borlotti beans are cooked with the soft pork rind called *cotenne*, and why ceci (garbanzos) are flavored with onion and strips of pig skin, perfumed with sage and rosemary, and mixed with a little green olive oil and a sprinkling of Parmesan cheese. Now a second shadow falls across the day, for Italians are beginning to be so concerned about cholesterol and their weight that lard is rarely used, and fat pigs, once thought to bring good luck, are no longer prized.

In Umbria the sausage makers are so good that Norcia, a small city to the east of Perugia, gave its name to the *norcino* who kills the pig and to *norcinerie*, delicatessens filled only with pork products. In Norcia large and powerful black pigs sniff around the base of oak trees, drawn by the dark intoxicating aroma of truffles, and they eat acorns that fall to the ground. No wonder they grow large, healthy, and flavorful, until they are turned into an entire new configuration of products. Part of the original pig may then be gone, part of it eaten, and the rest preserved and set aside for the remainder of the year. It reappears as a prosciutto that is much saltier than the prosciutto of Parma or San Daniele (all the better to eat with the saltless bread of Umbria); as garlicky, peppery sausages hung to dry on fragrant hillsides; as salame, and as specially cured capocollo, which is ready to be eaten at Eastertime with focaccia al formaggio (cheese bread), hard-boiled eggs, and a glass of good local white wine.

Nowhere is the celebration of Sant'Antonio and the pig more dramatic or opulent than in Abruzzo. Carnival actually once began on Sant'Antonio's Day with a ritual feast called a *panarda*, a pantagruelian banquet with thirty to forty local dishes. The *panarda* became a marathon meal in which people finished off last year's food supply in a blaze of conspicuous consumption. The meal began on the eve of Sant'Antonio and went on until long past midnight and far into the morning hours. When the restaurateur Paolo Scipioni was invited to one such feast in the Abruzzo town of L'Aquila, he recorded it in its entirety; even with a limited description of the dishes, the account goes on for forty pages. Hors d'oeuvres included smoked herring with roe like fine caviar; smoked eel and anchovies; crayfish caught that morning by the host; and tiny fire-red lobsters. The dinner that followed included a fritto misto—a fried mixture of baccalà, cauliflower, anchovies, and slices of apple—and a salad of tuna, onions, and white beans. There was a brief pause before a parade of dishes cooked by neighbors and friends arrived: huge frittate, fragrant with garlic, parsley, and peperoncino; vegetables, including wild asparagus from local gardens; local cheeses preserved in oil, served with crunchy crusted, chewy homemade dark bread baked in a woodburning oven. Glasses were constantly refilled with vast quantities of homemade red wine fresh from the *cantina*. The wine may have added to the energetic dancing, laughing, story and joke telling that went on until midnight when everyone thought it must now be time for some fruit and splendid rustic desserts.

But no. It turned out that dinner was just beginning. Now that the eve of Sant'Antonio was over, with its commandment to eat no meat, the real *festa* could roll. Now began the true *panarda* of L'Aquila, which the writer Gian Gaspare Napolitano at the end of the nineteenth century called "the Arab phoenix of the Abruzzese table: a meal that begins again just when it seems to be finished, starting over every time that it arrives at the end." So, from the top once again, only this time with *piatti grossi*. Out came trays full of prosciutto and the famous Abruzzese mortadelle made with pork liver and studded with citron, orange peel, and pistachio nuts. Those made with honey were called *fegato dolce*, sweet liver, while the devilishly hot ones with lots of peperoncino were known as *fegato pazzo*, crazy liver, and the two were meant to be eaten in alternating bites. At a famous nineteenth-century *panarda* one diner announced that he was really too full to go on, and perceived at once that his host was offended. Pointing to his hugely distended stomach, the guest pleaded for mercy. The host leaned over and whispered in his ear, "Either you eat or I'll kill you."

Undoubtedly he plunged his fork enthusiastically into the next course, maccheroni alla chitarra, homemade pasta cut on an instrument with strings as fine and tensile as a guitar's. Next at the more recent *panarda* came a timbale of egg lasagne filled with meatballs, chicken, and the famous scamorza cheese of Rivisondoli, lightly sauced with tomatoes. Other L'Aquila specialties rolled right along: a cardoon soup with tiny rounds of veal, liver, and bits of fried bread floating in its depths; boiled meats with salads and sauces and broccoletti soffocati, a winter vegetable harvested from beneath the snow and cooked in a copper pot under a heavy weight to bring out its natural juices and flavors.

A brief pause in the proceedings gave everyone a breather before the arrival of a platter of fried brains with lamb chops and a green salad meant to refresh the palate. If the diners were tired, the women in the kitchen were not. Next arrived great earthenware pots heaped high with tracchiulella e panuntella, pork cutlets and a spiral of sausages on homemade bread moistened with cooking juices and peperoncino-scented oil. The vegetable: the tiny dark brown lentils of Santo Stefano di Sessanio, tasty from growing in iron-rich soil.

Wine flowed and toasts tumbled off the diners' lips, but the group was silent for a moment before bursting into applause with the arrival of " 'his majesty, the goat,' *il capretto incaporchiato,*" suckling kid roasted to perfection and enthroned by potatoes. Who could resist the next course composed of the famous cheeses of Abruzzo? There was caciotto; pecorino con la "lacrima"; the delicate scamorza of Rivisondoli; caciocavallo dolce, tiny forms of ricotta from Bazzano; and a rustic sheep's milk cheese called *marcetto.*

As the clock struck three, the dinner had already gone on for seven hours and the desserts were only just about to arrive. Every woman had made her specialty: almond sweets and ferratelle, fine batter cooked in a special pincer-shaped hot iron and filled with pastry cream; chewy mostaccioli made with honey and cooked grape must; fried sweet ravioli bursting with ricotta; sfogliatelle; and tocchetti with chocolate or pastry cream inside. There were also crostate filled with quince and various jams, and the famous multilayered torte of Abruzzo, much lubricated with liqueurs.

The diners were also well lubricated with hearty local wines. Those who could manage to find room for coffee drank it for the quick jolt it provided, and then set off for another wing of the house, where newly made sausages, salame, mortadella, and prosciutti hung from the ceiling like edible stalactites. There, in a large room with flames roaring in a giant fireplace, the guests sat on great wooden benches and watched two sizable women with impressively muscled forearms cook paniccio, the traditional dish of Sant'Antonio, a polenta made of millet. The women stirred the massive cauldron of polenta with giant wooden paddles and chipped a wheel of pecorino into chunks that they mixed into the polenta. Toasts with hip-hip-hurrahs (pronounced *eep-eep-urra*) were drunk to the

The Temptation of Saint Anthony, nineteenth-century woodcut

host, Don Nicola, whose response was to cast yet more wheels of cheese into the immense cauldron of polenta. The women continued to stir until the dark, creamy mass was ready for the priest to bless and the assembled guests to eat. It was the traditional centerpiece of the celebration, the symbol of the "ferocious" hospitality of the Abruzzo countryside. And, in this case, it was the final taste in an endless meal.

There is something puzzling about a humble and ascetic monk being honored with a gargantuan feast, and it is especially curious that Sant'Antonio was chosen to protect men from devils and witches, since he himself was beset by the demons of desire. Perhaps this is yet another example of the way in which the Church disguised a pagan myth by creating a saint out of the ritual of a country culture. So the rosy pig that is always by Sant'Antonio's side is probably a transmutation first of pagan ritual and later of temptation, since pigs are perfect symbols of luxury and temptation. Sant'Antonio, like John the Baptist, who renounced luxury to retire to the desert in fasting and prayer, was repeatedly assaulted by the Devil. Paintings by Bosch and Grünewald portray his torment. Many tales tell of his struggles. In Abruzzo men and boys once went from house to house on the eve of Sant'Antonio singing songs about the saint's combat with the Devil. Then they asked for contributions of wood for a huge bonfire.

On the eve of Sant'Antonio it was common all over Italy to light enormous fires at crossroads, in courtyards, or church piazze. In Fara Filiorum Petri, in Abruzzo, they still tie thousands of reeds into bundles called *farchie* that rise sixty feet high, while elsewhere vine branches are lashed together and mounded in a pyramid. The bonfires on the night of Sant'Antonio, meant to encourage warmth so seeds will grow again, have become like sacred fires, and their ashes are sometimes spread on crops in the depths of winter to encourage their growth.

In preindustrial Italy, when work in the countryside had seasonal celebrations with parallels in the liturgical year, the day of January 17 often began with the pig, sleek and fat in the farmyard, and ended as it was turned into a glorious panoply of salame and prosciutto, coppa, and sausage. Dead he was, but resurrected shortly thereafter to provide an abundance of delicious flavors and preparations that lasted the whole year. For millennia Italians have passed down secrets of how to salt, preserve, flavor, smoke, and cure the pig so his fleeting days on earth could be extended into a new incarnation, and families could be fed the rest of the year with *le delizie del divin porcello*, "the delicacies of the divine pig."

Pane di Sant'Antonio

~~~~~~~~~~~~~~~~~~~~~~~~~~~~

Bread for the Feast of Saint Anthony

Sant'Antonio is the patron saint of all four-footed creatures, and his celebration is a wonderful day for man and beast. It is traditional to make a special bread, which the priest gives out after he blesses the animals. Sometimes the bread is made only for the animals, but in some cities, like Milan and Padua, Sant'Antonio is also the patron saint of bakers. In Perugia lucky humans can eat this wonderful rough and chewy country bread made with natural yeast. Luigi Faffa, a very talented baker in Villavalleceppo, a bit outside the big city, uses a special stamp to cut a tic-tac-toe–like pattern on top, but I cut the shape right into the dough with a razor. Although Umbrian bread is traditionally saltless, a little bit of salt seems to make the bread taste better. These loaves are full-bodied and taste intensely of wheat, especially if you use natural yeast, and even with the addition of salt, they keep for several days.

Makes 5 rectangular loaves, each about 8 by 4½ inches

1 scant teaspoon active dry yeast or ⅓ cake (6 grams) fresh yeast
3¼ cups warm water
2 cups (450 grams) Natural Yeast Starter or Biga (page 32 or page 31), at least 2 days old
6¼ cups (850 grams) unbleached all-purpose white flour
1 cup plus 1 tablespoon (150 grams) whole-wheat flour, stone-ground
1 tablespoon salt

By Mixer. In the mixer bowl dissolve the yeast in the water and let stand until creamy, about 10 minutes. With the paddle attachment add the starter and mix well. Stir in the flours and salt on low speed. The dough is immediately elastic and responsive. Change to the dough hook and mix on low speed 2 minutes, then on medium speed 2 minutes. The dough is very, very wet when made with the natural yeast.

First Rise. Put the dough in a large oiled container, cover it tightly with plastic wrap, and let rise at warm room temperature until well doubled, 3½ to 4 hours. Dough made with *biga* will take about 3 hours.

Shaping and Second Rise. The dough is very wet, and you will need a fair amount of flour on your work surface. Pour out the dough and flour the top of it as well. Cut the dough into 5 equal pieces and begin the shaping using a dough scraper. Shape each one firmly into a rectangle by rolling it tightly toward you, using your thumbs as a guide. Let the dough rest on a lightly floured surface under a towel 10 minutes, then reshape it tightly again before you stretch it to an 8- by 4½-inch rectangle. Let the bread rise seam side up on well-floured parchment paper until it puffs and rises to about double its original volume, about 1 hour.

Baking. Thirty minutes before baking, preheat the oven to 425°F and set a baking stone inside. Just before baking, sprinkle the stone with cornmeal so the loaves won't stick. Turn the loaves over and with a razor slash a tic-tac-toe grid pattern, with 2 lengthwise cuts and 3 across. Set the loaves well apart on the baking stones. Immediately after putting them into the oven, turn the temperature down to 400°F and bake 35 minutes.

Pane con i Ciccioli

Bread with Pork Cracklings

When pigs go to their reward in the cold days of winter, country people save the crisp bits left over after the lard is rendered and knead them into a rustic loaf. If you don't have cracklings on hand, pancetta is a delicious substitute. This makes spectacular sandwich bread.

Makes 2 loaves

1 teaspoon active dry yeast or ⅓ cake (6 grams) fresh yeast
1⅓ cups plus 2 tablespoons warm water
5 ounces (150 grams) pancetta, chopped in fine dice, or cracklings from rendering lard (page 169)
2 tablespoons reserved fat
A heaping ⅓ cup (75 grams) Natural Yeast Starter or Biga (page 32 or page 31)
3¾ cups (500 grams) unbleached all-purpose flour
Black pepper
1 tablespoon sea salt

By Mixer. In the bowl of the mixer stir the yeast in the water and let stand until it is creamy, about 10 minutes. While it is dissolving, sauté the pancetta until crisp or prepare the cracklings. Drain on paper towels and cool. Save 2 tablespoons of the fat. With the paddle attachment add the starter and fat to the yeast, then the flour and salt; mix 1 to 2 minutes until a dough is formed. Change to the dough hook and knead 3 minutes on medium speed. The dough is sticky, elastic, and strong, but it never quite comes away from the bottom or sides of the bowl. Finish by kneading briefly on a lightly floured surface and it will come together easily.

By Processor. Refrigerate the starter until cold. Stir the yeast into the warm water; let stand until creamy, about 10 minutes. Add the starter and the reserved fat. Place the flour and salt in the bowl of a processor fitted with the steel blade and process with several pulses to mix. With the machine running, pour the starter mixture down the feed tube and

(continued)

process only until it starts to come together. You may be able to process 15 to 20 seconds, but the dough will not come together and may tax the motor on your machine. Finish kneading on a floured surface, adding sprinkles of flour as necessary, 4 to 5 minutes. The dough will remain soft and sticky.

First Rise. Set to rise in an oiled container, well covered with plastic wrap, until doubled, 1½ to 2 hours. It may take longer, depending on the strength of the natural yeast. If things are proceeding slowly, set the container in a bowl of warm water.

Shaping and Second Rise. Turn the dough out onto a lightly floured surface and shape into a rectangle. Pat the cool well-drained pancetta or cracklings over the surface, grind a bit of black pepper, tuck in the edges, and roll up. Flatten the dough with your palms and let it rest under a towel 5 to 10 minutes. Divide the dough in half and shape each piece into a taut, springy round. Cover with a towel and let rise until well doubled, about 1½ hours.

Baking. Thirty minutes before baking, heat the oven with a baking stone in it to 425°F. Just before baking, spread a little oil over the tops of the dough. If you are using cracklings, sprinkle a bit of sea salt as well. Sprinkle the baking stone with cornmeal. Bake 20 minutes, then turn the oven down to 400°F and bake until the tops are a lovely deep golden color, 25 to 30 minutes longer.

Cooking bread outside, Biblioteca Estense, Modena

Taralli al Finocchio

****

Fennel-Flavored Bread Rings

Taralli, little rings of braided bread, are sold in Naples and the surrounding countryside whenever it is festival time. Counters are stacked high with taralli flavored with cracked pepper, fennel, or almonds, and vendors hang big oval baskets of them over their arms as they make their way through the crowds. Taralli appear at the entrances to cemeteries for I Morti and I Santi on November 1 and 2 and turn up again on January 17, the Feast Day of Sant'Antonio Abate. Flocks used to be brought to church to be blessed on that day, and pigs were once garlanded with wide necklaces of taralli. These tasty wreaths of bread disappear in four or five bites and are best eaten the day they are made. They are so appreciated in Naples that the expression *i taralli per che non ha denti,* "taralli for someone without teeth," is used when someone has something pleasurable but doesn't have the means to enjoy it.

Makes about 2 dozen wreaths

2½ teaspoons (1 package) active dry yeast or 1 small cake (18 grams) fresh yeast
1⅓ cups warm water
3¾ cups (500 grams) unbleached all-purpose flour
⅓ cup (40 grams) fennel seeds
1 teaspoon sea salt
1 or 2 egg whites

By Hand. Stir the yeast into the water in a large mixing bowl; let stand until creamy, about 10 minutes. Stir in the flour, fennel seeds, and salt until well blended. Knead on a floured surface until firm, solid, and elastic, 8 to 10 minutes.

By Mixer. Stir the yeast into the water in a mixer bowl; let stand until creamy, about 10 minutes. With the paddle attachment mix in the flour, fennel seeds, and salt. Change to the dough hook and knead 3 minutes on low speed, stopping to push down the dough if it climbs up the shaft, until the dough is firm, solid, and elastic.

By Processor. Stir the yeast into ⅓ cup warm water; let stand until creamy, about 10 minutes. Place the flour, fennel seeds, and salt in a food processor fitted with the steel blade and process with several pulses. With the machine running, pour 1 cup cold water and the dissolved yeast through the feed tube and process until the dough gathers into a ball. Process about 40 seconds longer to knead. Finish kneading briefly by hand on a lightly floured surface. The dough should be elastic and firm.

First Rise. Set the dough in a lightly oiled container, cover tightly with plastic wrap, and let rise until doubled, 1¼ to 1½ hours.

(continued)

Shaping and Second Rise. Set the dough on a lightly floured work surface and flatten it into a rectangle approximately 12 by 8 inches. Cut it crosswise into cylinders ¾ inch wide, about the width of a finger. Roll or stretch each piece to about 24 inches long, then cut into three 8-inch pieces. Twist or braid three pieces together, wrapping them tightly around each other, then shape them into a circle and press tightly where the ends join. Set on lightly oiled or parchment-lined baking sheets, cover with a towel, and let rise until doubled, about 1¼ hours.

Baking. Heat the oven to 375°F. Just before baking, brush the taralli with beaten egg white. Bake until golden, about 20 minutes. Cool on racks.

A variation calls for bringing a large pot of water to boil and dropping in the risen taralli one at a time. Allow them to come to the surface, drain immediately, and set on oiled baking sheets. Bake until just golden, about 15 minutes.

Another variation: To make pepper-flavored taralli, use 1¼ cups water and ½ cup (100 grams) lard or olive oil and substitute 2 teaspoons (10 grams) of pepper for the fennel seeds.

L'Jumacche Fellate di Sant'Antuon

Broccoli-Flavored Polenta Layered with Sausages and Cheese

On Sant'Antonio's Day in the mountainous Abruzzo region, dinner begins with polenta flavored with broccoli and layered, like lasagne, with sausages, pork ragù, cheeses, and dried hot peppers. This dish, originally made with dried fava beans pestled into flour, came to Abruzzo from ancient Greece via Sicily. Its name comes from the verb *ammaccare*, to crush, which is precisely what happened to those favas. Later on in the town of Villa Santa Maria in Abruzzo, it may once have been a poor person's dish, but today it is rich and substantial, a perfect one-course meal. For a festival in honor of Sant'Antonio, however, it is but the first of many dishes based on the meat of the pig. This recipe and those of the rest of the Abruzzo dinner come from Antonio Stanziani, one of Villa Santa Maria's great chefs and director of the chef's school. I have made the dish with broccoli instead of the traditional broccoletti di rape (although use rape if you can find it); the taste really makes the polenta something very special. If you can find scamorza cheese, wonderful—if you can't, use imported provolone. If imported provolone is unavailable, try grating domestic Auricchio provolone for a sharp and creamy taste.

Makes 8 servings

11¼ to 12 cups water
1 peeled potato
1 pound to 1 pound 2 ounces (500 grams) broccoli flowerets or broccoli
 rape, weighed, then trimmed
1 tablespoon coarse salt
2½ cups (400 grams) freshly ground cornmeal or polenta
4 fresh pork sausages
1 to 2 tablespoons olive oil
6½ cups Pork Ragù (page 325)
Pinch hot pepper flakes
1 cup (100 grams) grated scamorza or ½ cup (50 grams) imported
 provolone and ½ cup (50 grams) Auricchio, grated or finely diced
Scant ½ cup (50 grams) freshly grated pecorino cheese
3 tablespoons butter

Put 11¼ cups water and the potato in a deep heavy pot, bring water to a boil, and cook until the potato is tender. Rice the potato and return it to the cooking water. Add the broccoli and salt and cook 1 to 2 minutes. Now add the cornmeal by dropping it in a steady fine stream into the pot. With a wooden spoon or long-handled rubber spatula stir constantly to get rid of any lumps. Don't worry about the broccoli pieces; you can stir them vigorously along with the cornmeal because they are meant to break down, and will end up looking like little green peppercorns in the finished polenta. Cook 20 to 30 minutes, or until the polenta comes away from the sides of the pot, adding a little water if necessary so the polenta doesn't get too dry. Be careful not to let it stick to the bottom of the pot or burn. Turn the mixture out onto a lightly oiled baking sheet, taste for salt, let it cool, and form into the shape of a brick.

Cook the sausages in a pan barely filmed with olive oil; when they are lightly browned, remove from the pan, remove casings, and slice. Cut the polenta in ¼-inch-thick pieces. Spread a very fine layer of the pork ragù on the bottom of a buttered deep baking dish. Build up the dish as if you were making lasagne: a layer of ragù, a layer of polenta slices, sliced pork sausage, pinch of hot pepper flakes, more ragù, scamorza, and so on. Finish with the ragù, pecorino cheese, and flakes of butter. Bake in a 375°F oven 1 hour.

Salsicce e Faciuol d'Pane

Sausage and Red Beans as Good as Bread

Give a country cassoulet made of beans and sausage an Italian twist, and you have an idea of this thick, tasty dish. Even though it is served as a vegetable in the Sant'Antonio Abate Eve dinner at which pig is the star, it could easily be the centerpiece of a meal served with crunchy, crusty rustic bread and a glass of hearty red wine.

Makes 6 to 8 side-dish servings

About 8½ ounces (250 grams) red borlotti beans; you can substitute pinto beans
2 pounds 2 ounces (1 kilogram) fresh sausage made with fennel and red pepper
2 tablespoons olive oil
1 onion, chopped
½ pound (200 grams) fresh Italian plum tomatoes (about 5), chopped fine
1 or 2 basil leaves, chopped
½ peperoncino (dried red chile), seeded and chopped fine

The night before making the dish, rinse the beans, cover them with water, and let them soak overnight. Leave the sausages uncovered in the refrigerator overnight or up to 18 hours so that they dry out a bit. Turn the sausages over once or twice so their entire surfaces will be exposed to the air.

The next day drain the beans, put them in a large pot, cover with cold water, bring to a boil, and cook 2 hours or until tender. Keep them warm over low heat (either over barely simmering water in a double boiler or on a hot tray).

Meanwhile, cut the sausages so each person gets 2 pieces. Put the sausages in a heavy skillet large enough to hold them all, and with just enough olive oil to film the bottom, sauté them about 5 minutes. Remove the sausages to a plate, add the chopped onion to the pan, and sauté until golden. Return the browned sausages to the skillet, add the chopped tomatoes, basil leaves, and peperoncino, and cook over medium-low heat 20 minutes. Finally, add the beans and let everything cook over low heat 30 minutes, adding a little water now and then if the mixture gets too dry. Serve hot.

Ragù di Maiale

━━━━━━━━━━━━━━━━━

Pork Ragù I

This rich and flavorful ragù from Abruzzo is what kept people going when they worked on cold winter days. It gets its subtle flavor from the whole pork shoulder that cooks in it. Use the sauce for Polenta (page 357) or for pasta; you can save the pork shoulder to serve as a main course. The sauce is best cooked ahead, because it should be carefully degreased before it is served. If you want to make this dish with lamb, add a couple of ounces of pecorino cheese to the mixture spread on the inside of the meat.

Makes about 1½ quarts

3½ pounds (1½ kilograms) boned pork shoulder
2 small cloves garlic, minced
⅔ cup minced flat-leaf parsley
2 tablespoons fresh bread crumbs
½ cup olive oil or prosciutto fat, chopped
1 onion, finely chopped
Pinch hot pepper flakes or ½ dried peperoncino, seeded and chopped fine
6½ cups Abruzzo Tomato Sauce (page 327)
Salt

Open up the pork shoulder like a book, spread the interior with the garlic, half the parsley, and the bread crumbs, then roll it up like a fat salame, lacing it closed with skewers and string. Wipe the meat dry. Heat the olive oil or prosciutto fat in a heavy skillet or large fireproof casserole dish and sauté the pork shoulder over medium heat until it is lightly browned all over. Add the chopped onion, remaining parsley, the pepper flakes, and tomato sauce. Simmer over low heat uncovered about 2 hours, stirring every 20 minutes. Season to taste with salt. Remove the piece of meat and serve at in a later course or at a different meal.

Sweet in the form of a pig, nineteenth-century engraving

Ragù di Maiale

~~~~~~~~~~~~~~~~~~~~~~~~~~~~~~~

Pork Ragù II

In these cholesterol- and diet-conscious days, even the citizens of Villa Santa Maria are thinking about lighter cuisine, and this is their modern solution to pork ragù. Use sausage meat instead of a whole piece of pork shoulder and carefully skim off all the fat before serving. This sauce is usually cooked at sausage-making time when all the fresh scraps of piglet can be ground together.

Makes about 2½ quarts

½ cup olive oil
2 medium onions, chopped
1½ pounds (600 grams) pork sausage
⅔ cup finely chopped flat-leaf parsley
2 bay leaves, torn in half
Good pinch hot pepper flakes or ½ dried peperoncino, seeded and
    chopped fine
1 cup red wine
6½ cups Abruzzo Tomato Sauce (see opposite page)
2 tablespoons tomato paste
Salt

Warm the olive oil in a heavy sauté pan and cook the chopped onions over medium heat until they are golden. Add the crumbled sausage and cook until it is no longer pink; add the parsley, bay leaves, and pepper flakes and cook over low heat just until the parsley is limp. Add the red wine, stir well, and cook until it evaporates. Add the tomato sauce and paste, cover, and cook over low heat for 2 hours, stirring frequently, until it is thick and is reduced to about 2½ quarts. Season to taste with salt.

Pigs, drawing by P. A. Mattioli, 1583, Venice

Pomodoro Cotto e Passato

~~~~~~~~~~~~~~~~~~~~~~~~~~~~~~~~

Abruzzo
Tomato Sauce

In Villa Santa Maria in Abruzzo people preserve huge quantities of this sauce when tomatoes are in season and then use it all winter long.

Makes 6½ to 7 cups

6 tablespoons olive oil
3 onions, finely chopped
6 pounds (4 kilograms) fresh, very ripe Italian plum tomatoes, chopped,
    or 8 cups (four 28-ounce cans) canned tomatoes
2 tablespoons fresh basil leaves, torn into pieces
Pinch hot pepper flakes (peperoncino)
Salt to taste

Warm the olive oil in a large heavy skillet and sauté the onions over medium heat until they are golden. Add the tomatoes, basil, and pepper flakes and simmer over medium heat 10 to 15 minutes. Add the salt during the last minute or two and be sure that it dissolves in the sauce. Press the mixture through a food mill and cook briefly to reduce it slightly.

PART FOUR

Rebirth

arnival is celebrated in Italy with elaborate parades, masked balls, elegant horse races, and gargantuan feasts. "When Carnival arrives," writes Jeanne Carol Francesconi, Italy's expert on the food of Naples, "a contest of lasagna heats up. At least once a year every family must eat it and until Ash Wednesday it is a continuous subject of discussion. . . . Once Carnival is over no one thinks about this extraordinary dish the rest of the year." And there is a reason. Only at Carnival, when the social situation is temporarily topsy-turvy, can such a monumentally rich food be a dish for everyone.

If Carnival bids farewell to the old year with bonfires, Candelora ("Candlemas" in English) on February 2 declares the end of winter with processions of blazing candles. Forty days after Christmas, it commemorates Mary's bringing Jesus to Jerusalem to enlighten the people. Yet one more year-end festival, Candelora has resonances of Imbo, the Celtic celebration of the passage of winter at the same time of year, an event sacred to a goddess with a light-filled crown, who sounds like Santa Lucia or Sant'Agata with her candles. It also has resonances of Groundhog Day, when the day's weather is used to predict if the season will be fierce or fair before the coming of spring.

The day that Lent begins depends on the date of Easter, which is determined by the spring equinox, so it can be observed any time between February 4 and March 11. Ash Wednesday makes it clear that the excesses of Carnival are over and that the season of penitence and contrition has arrived. The priest draws the sign of the cross on the foreheads of believers, using black ashes, a reminder that death is always near, and a suggestion that it is better to die in a state of grace than not.

The dates for these occurrences have changed over the centuries. Initially Italy used the Julian calendar, which was introduced by Julius Caesar in 45 B.C. It was based on a solar year of 365¼ days, with a leap year whose extra day came from the quarter days collected every fourth year. The calculation was not exact, and by the sixteenth century, astronomers determined that an eleven-day difference existed between the Julian calendar and the solar year. Enter Pope Gregory, who introduced the Gregorian calendar in 1582 to erase the discrepancy by canceling the eleven extra days. Almost all of Italy accepted the revision and began the new year on January 1, although there were holdouts. In the Roman calendar, March 1 had marked the beginning of the New Year, and the

Venetians clung to that date, while Florence continued to celebrate on March 25, which became the birth date of the Christian world with the Annunciation, which is still celebrated on March 25, more or less the spring equinox. Easter was initially celebrated at the first full moon of springtime until A.D. 325, when the Church decreed that it should be observed on the first Sunday (day of sun) following the first full moon after the spring equinox.

Before there was Easter there was Passover, which the Italians call *Pasqua Ebraica*, Jewish Easter. The seder, the ritual meal eaten around the world, is distinctly Italian as cooked in the Jewish Community Center in Rome. The entire ceremony is chanted, and while ritual eating begins with the traditional dish of hard-boiled eggs and the shank bone of a lamb, the meal itself is Roman. It starts with hors d'oeuvres of bresaola, air-dried beef served with hard-boiled eggs, and carciofi alla giudea, literally "artichokes cooked the Jewish way," enormous Roman artichokes without chokes that are fried until they look like autumn chrysanthemums and are exquisitely crisp on the outside with creamy interiors. Roman seders often begin with risotti containing asparagus, artichokes, or fresh peas, or with tomatoes stuffed with basil- and garlic-flavored rice. Scacchi, a Sephardic dish similar to lasagne with layers of meat and sautéed vegetables alternating with matzoh, takes the place of pasta. Every seder serves haroset, a mixture of raw fruits and nuts chopped to a fine paste to represent the mortar that the Jews used while they were slaves in Egypt; but none is as rich and full-flavored as the conserve that Roman Jews make with nuts, fruits, and red wine, cooked as thick as preserves.

Lamb must be served on the second night of the festival as a reminder of the Passover sacrifice, so Romans eat roast lamb or lamb with artichokes or agnello brodettato, lamb flavored with eggs and lemon. Chickens stuffed with rosemary and garlic are roasted in the oven, and may be served with spinach, pine nuts, and raisins, with fresh fava beans stewed with lettuce leaves, or even with carciofi alla romana, artichokes stuffed with wild mint, garlic, and parsley and braised. Desserts must be made without regular flour, for Passover commemorates the time when the Jews had to flee Egypt so quickly that they could not let the bread rise, but had to bake it immediately, making unleavened matzoh, called *azzime* in Italian. Instead there are amaretti, macaroons made with almonds or coconut; delicate bocche di dama; or pizzarelle, little rounds fried like French toast but with crumbled matzoh beaten with eggs, cinnamon, nutmeg, grated orange rind, raisins, pine nuts, and sometimes even a bit of haroset. It is a splendid meal, amazingly delicious, a Jewish tradition in the Roman idiom.

Springtime brings Ascension Sunday and Pentecost as well as Passover. It is a time of country *sagre* celebrating the first artichokes of the season in the Roman *campagna*, asparagus in Piedmont and the Veneto, and fava beans and peas. Marzolino, the first sheep's milk cheese of the year, is made in March, when sheep are nursing their lambs, so there is a limited production. April 25, the Feast Day of San Marco, the patron saint of Venice, was celebrated with risi e bisi, creamy rice cooked with the first fresh peas from the kitchen gardens of the Venetian lagoons. On April 23, the Feast of San Giorgio, the patron saint of dairymen, is celebrated with pan di mei, originally a coarse, rustic millet bread but now made with corn flour sweetened with sugar and flavored with light anise taste of sambuco, the elderberry plant. Until recently dairy workers whose contracts ran from April 23 to April 23—or from San Giorgio to San Giorgio, as they said—celebrated the day by eating pan di mei with rich country cream.

Minestra di Carciofi

Artichoke Soup

Artichokes in the area around Rome have inspired special *sagre* called *carciofolate*, big artichoke feasts, which celebrate one of the great contributions of Roman cooking. One such feast in Sezze Romano celebrates the *violetta* artichoke, which is named for the purple tinge of its leaves. It is medium-sized, conical, and has neither thorns nor choke. Some are now being grown in California and Oregon. If you can find them, by all means use them, because they permit you to slice the entire artichoke without removing the choke and milling the leaves. But if you have to use the more readily available variety of artichoke, this rich-tasting soup is still worth the effort. To concentrate its taste I have used broth instead of water and have cooked the artichokes to extract as much flavor as possible.

Makes 6 to 8 servings

8 medium artichokes
1 lemon
2 cloves garlic, crushed but left whole
4 tablespoons olive oil
Salt
9 to 10 cups chicken broth
1 clove garlic, minced
1 peperoncino (dried red chile), seeded and chopped
1½ large fresh tomatoes, seeded and chopped, or 3 to 4 canned plum tomatoes, chopped
2 eggs
6 to 8 thin slices of stale bread, grilled or toasted   *(continued)*

Clean the artichokes by snapping off any stiff leaves and carefully trimming their tops. Put artichokes in water acidulated with lemon until you are ready to use them. Cook in water flavored with 2 cloves garlic, 1 tablespoon oil, and salt; water should come ⅔ of the way up the artichokes. Drain and cool. Save the hearts and slice into strips. Scrape the edible part of each leaf from the bottom and add to the hearts. Set aside. Put into a food processor fitted with the steel blade; pour in enough chicken broth to make a coarse mixture and process. Then place the mixture in a food mill and set over a wide-mouthed bowl. Pour more chicken broth over the pulpy mixture and mill the leaves to get as much liquid as possible out of them. The result will be a relatively small amount of dark green liquid.

Put 3 tablespoons olive oil in a large heavy saucepan and very carefully warm the minced garlic and peperoncino. Do not allow either to brown or burn. Add the tomatoes, let them cook over medium heat 3 to 4 minutes, then add the artichoke liquid. Add 6 cups chicken broth, bring to a simmer, cover, and let the mixture simmer about 1 hour. Add reserved sliced hearts and leaf trimmings after about 45 minutes. Just before serving, break the eggs right into the mixture. Stir, but never allow it to boil or the eggs will scramble. Set a slice of toasted or grilled bread in the bottom of each soup bowl and ladle the soup over it.

Asparagus, Roman mosaic, Vatican collections

Scacchi

~~~~~~~~~~~~~~~~~~~~~~~~~~~~~~~~

*Layered Vegetable
Dish for Passover
in Rome*

This multilayered torte uses matzohs like lasagne noodles to make a filling one-dish centerpiece for the Passover dinner. It is reminiscent of complicated tarts baked in the Renaissance, when sumptuary laws decreed a maximum of three dishes for a meal, inspiring clever gourmands to wrap many vegetables inside a single dish. The trick is to use thin matzohs and to pour over them enough broth and egg mixture to moisten the dish sufficiently. Although the instructions look long, it is only because each vegetable is sautéed individually before being layered in the baking dish. This is also delicious made without meat.

Makes 8 to 10 servings

12 thin matzohs

1 tablespoon olive oil
1 pound (450 grams) chopped sirloin
Salt and pepper

1½ pounds (675 grams) onions, thinly sliced
4 tablespoons olive oil

4 artichokes, cleaned, chokes and fibrous leaves removed, cooked in
    water with lemon juice, and sliced thin
4 tablespoons olive oil
2 cloves garlic, minced
¾ teaspoon minced rosemary
¾ teaspoon minced sage
1 teaspoon salt

2 large bunches spinach (about 1 pound, 450 grams), cleaned, stemmed,
    and cooked 4 to 5 minutes in a pot with only the water left on the
    leaves, then squeezed dry
4 tablespoons olive oil
2 cloves garlic, minced
1 peperoncino (dried red chile), seeded and minced
½ teaspoon freshly grated nutmeg
¼ teaspoon salt

1 pound (450 grams) mushrooms, sliced
4 tablespoons olive oil
2 cloves garlic, finely minced
½ teaspoon salt

6 eggs
½ cup lemon juice
About 1 cup beef broth

(continued)

Cover the matzohs with water and let sit until wet and almost crumbling. Warm the olive oil and sauté the chopped sirloin, stirring, until it is no longer red. Add salt and pepper. Sauté each of the vegetables separately over very low heat: The onions are sautéed alone; the artichokes with the minced garlic, fresh rosemary, sage, and salt; the spinach with garlic, peperoncino, fresh nutmeg, and salt; and the mushrooms with the garlic, added after 3 to 4 minutes, and the salt.

Assembly. Oil a large, deep baking dish and cover the bottom with the sautéed chopped sirloin. Cover with a layer of 3 matzohs and cover them with the onions. Layer 3 more matzohs on top, and so on, using the individual vegetables. Finish with vegetables, not matzohs. Beat together the eggs and lemon juice and pour over the top of the mixture, shaking the pan to be sure that the liquid reaches the various air pockets left between vegetables. Pour over enough broth to moisten the mixture well. Cover loosely with foil.

Baking. Heat the oven to 400°F. Bake until the mixture is set and cooked through, about 30 minutes.

Haroset

vvvvvvvvvvvvvvvvvvvvvvvvvvvvvvv

Haroset for Passover in the Jewish Community of Rome

Haroset is traditionally served at Passover dinners all over the world as a symbol of the mortar used by Jewish forefathers when they were slaves in Egypt. This Roman version tastes not of melancholy but of triumph; the rich, moist mixture of fruits and nuts is cooked together until it is as thick as jam. Children decorate it with pine nuts, which represent the straw used to make the bricks.

Makes 15 to 20 servings

1½ cups plus 1 tablespoon (180 grams) walnuts
⅓ cup plus 1 tablespoon (45 grams) hazelnuts, skinned
1 cup (150 grams) almonds
⅓ cup (60 grams) raisins, coarsely chopped
6 or 7 (75 grams) pitted prunes, coarsely chopped
9 or 10 (75 grams) dates, coarsely chopped
4 (75 grams) figs, coarsely chopped, optional
1 pound (450 grams) cooking apples, peeled and coarsely chopped
1 pound (450 grams) cooking pears, peeled and coarsely chopped
¾ cup (150 grams) sugar
¾ teaspoon cinnamon
½ teaspoon freshly grated nutmeg
½ cup kosher red wine
1 tablespoon (15 grams) pine nuts for garnish

Toast all the nuts in a 350°F oven 10 minutes. Using a food processor fitted with the steel blade or a sharp knife, coarsely chop them. Combine the dried fruits, apples, pears, and nuts in a heavy-bottomed saucepan. Stir in the sugar, cinnamon, and nutmeg and pour over the wine. Cook over very low heat 2 to 3 hours, until the mixture is as thick as preserves. Stir frequently to keep the mixture from sticking to the bottom of the pan. You may need to add 2 to 3 extra tablespoons of red wine during the cooking. Serve in a dish and decorate with the pine nuts.

Carciofi al Forno

Baked Artichokes

Artichoke, twentieth-century engraving, from La Gola

I'd never thought of baking artichoke until the cooks of Sezze Romano demonstrated how easy and tasty it was. The Romans have a delicate wild mint call *mentuccia;* a combination of rosemary and sage leaves gives a fine approximation of its taste.

Makes 6 servings

6 medium artichokes, preferably *violetta* variety
1 lemon
6 tablespoons finely minced fresh rosemary
6 tablespoons finely minced fresh sage leaves
½ to 1 peperoncino (dried red chile), minced, optional
Salt and pepper
Olive oil

Snap the bottom outer leaves off each artichoke and discard. Put the artichokes in water acidulated with a few drops of lemon juice to keep them from discoloring. Using a small sharp knife, trim the stems to their tender cores and cut the tops off the leaves. Spread the leaves and scoop and scrape out the choke and any prickly inner leaves with a spoon. To make the filling, mix the herbs, peperoncino if you are using it, salt, pepper, and a little olive oil. Divide the mixture evenly and pack it in the artichokes. Stand them in a single layer in a baking pan filled to 1-inch height with equal amounts of water and olive oil. Sprinkle olive oil liberally over the tops. Heat the oven to 350°F and bake until tender, about 45 minutes. Serve hot, at room temperature, or cold.

Bocca di Dama

~~~~~~~~~~~~~~~~~~~~~~~~~~~~~~~~~~

Almond
Sponge Cake

Bocca di dama, a delicate sponge cake well known all over Italy, becomes part of the traditional Passover meal in Rome, where its flavor is enhanced with almonds and a hint of lemon.

Makes one 9½- or 9-inch cake

1⅓ cups plus 1 tablespoon (175 grams) blanched almonds
¾ cup plus 2 tablespoons (175 grams) sugar
4 egg whites
Pinch salt
6 egg yolks
½ cup (50 grams) matzoh meal; if you are not cooking for Passover, you
    may substitute 7½ tablespoons (2 ounces, 60 grams) potato starch
    and ¼ cup plus 1 tablespoon (2 ounces, 60 grams) unbleached all-
    purpose flour
Grated zest and juice of 1 lemon
¼ teaspoon lemon extract, optional
Confectioners' sugar

Chop the almonds fine in a food processor with ⅓ cup of the sugar. Beat the egg whites and salt until stiff. Beat the rest of the sugar and the egg yolks together until they are lemon-colored and creamy, 5 minutes by electric mixer, 8 to 12 minutes by hand. Gradually mix in the chopped almonds, matzoh meal, and the lemon zest, juice, and extract. Fold in the egg whites very carefully.

Baking. Heat the oven to 350°F. Line the bottom of a 9½-inch springform pan or a 9-inch cake pan with parchment paper. Butter or oil the sides and spread the batter in it. Place the cake in the oven, turn the heat down to 325°F, and bake until a toothpick inserted in the center comes out clean, 35 to 40 minutes in the springform pan, 45 to 50 in the 9-inch cake pan. Cool completely on a rack before turning out of the pan. Serve with confectioners' sugar sieved over the top.

SAN BIAGIO

FEAST DAY OF SAINT BLAISE
February 3

ander around almost any part of Lombardy at the beginning of
February, and it looks as if Christmas is back. Bakery shelves are once
again full of panettone, but this time two can be bought for the price of
one. Some people still believe that eating a piece of panettone on February
3, the Feast Day of San Biagio, patron saint of the throat, will protect
them from a sore throat (or worse), but they no longer bother to save a
piece from December 25. Bakers routinely gear up for the second coming
of panettone, turning out whole shelves of them or selling off stocks left
from the holiday season.

San Biagio, the saint who occasions all this eating, was originally an
Armenian physician who became the bishop of Sebastea. He was already
well known as a healer when he miraculously saved the life of a small
child who was choking on a fishbone caught in her throat. By the 700s,
a cult had grown up around him, and there are still a few small towns in
Italy that celebrate his feast day with special baked breads and sweets
connected to his protection of the throat. In Serra San Bruno in Calabria,
a cookie called an *abbacolo* is baked in the form of a question mark or
bishop's scepter, depending on who is telling the tale. The young men
of the little town offer one to their fiancées. The most romantic story
says that if the girl breaks it in two, returning the main part to the boy
and keeping the other for herself, it is a sign that they will marry very
soon. Sicilians make tiny breads called *panuzzi* or *cavadduzzi* or *miliddi*,
which are as white as snowflakes and shaped like intricately stylized

grasshoppers, to recall a miracle when the saint freed the town from an infestation of them. The connection of all these breads with San Biagio may come from the fact that his name resembles the word for wheat (*blé* in French; *biade* means "crops" in Italian) and his day, February 3, fell just before spring planting began.

San Biagio is still celebrated every year in Taranta Peligna, a small community high in the sparsely settled green hills of the Maiella, in Abruzzo, the mountainous region directly east of Rome. Shepherds once kept thousands of sheep in this high valley during the summer and then herded them down to their winter pastures on the plain of Apulia. As they waited out the warm months they made wool for themselves, using special clay from the riverbanks to cleanse and thicken the cloth, and then they set off throughout southern Italy, slowly building up an industry of woolen cloth.

They chose San Biagio as their patron saint after he was martyred on the table used for combing out wool, and then flayed with the prickly metal comb that removes tiny stones in the wool and opens up knots in its tight fleecy texture. For centuries February 3 brought forth celebrations in Italian towns where wool was worked—Milan; Biella, in Piedmont; Prato, in Tuscany; and Maratea, in Calabria—but since 1536, only Taranta Peligna has baked special votive breads in the same unusual shape.

Even now the townspeople begin making bread four days before the actual event, setting the sponge dough to rise. Two days later, the only remaining wool company closes and all the workers and a variety of old people set off to make the panicelle. The men collect the risen sponge, which is made with natural yeast, and pummel the mountain of stiff dough—three to four hundred pounds of it—so firmly that it is imprinted with an outline of their knuckles. When they finish, at one in the afternoon, church bells ring out, calling the women to finish the process. The women settle along both sides of a long, narrow, scarred wooden table to roll the dough until it is supple and pliable enough to be shaped like an open hand with four fingers. Perhaps this shape was chosen to offer friendship in the sign of religious faith. It almost certainly symbolizes the cooperation between the four kinds of wool workers—dyer, spinner, weaver, and finisher.

Before the Second World War destroyed much of the village, a town crier went through the streets of Taranta Peligna on the morning of February 1, calling out the name of the person who had opened his house for the day to make the bread. There was so much singing, dancing, eating, and drinking as the little breads were formed that it literally took the house apart, and no one is willing to offer such hospitality anymore. Instead, everyone goes to a community building. As more people arrive, the men help the women, who set the four fingers of dough next to each other, scoring them for authenticity with three joints or knuckles on each finger. The women cover the little breads with rough pieces of cloth and leave them to rise in a room that warms up as crowds arrive to sing, drink, and dance. Once the panicelle have risen a bit, the men stamp them with an image that shows San Biagio, the mother and child with the fishbone caught in her throat, and San Rocco, the city's other patron saint. The stamping recalls an ancient rite when the woolen cloth of Taranta Peligna was stamped with the town's special mark to guarantee its provenance.

When the dough is ready in the evening, all the breads are hoisted onto great wooden boards, covered with cloth, and carried by the women on their heads. Torches light their way through small village streets to the baker's ovens, which are roaring and hot, ready for the first of dozens of batches. The breads are baked as they always have been, on the first night of February for use two days later, but everyone arrives at the back door of the bakery to taste them hot out of the oven, gathering in the steamy bakery, where the fragrance of the sourdough perfumes the air, as part of the ritual. Besides, it is well known that the breads will be hard and dry by the time they are given out at the church on February 3, fine for a ritual but not for eating. On February 3 the faithful line up in front of the priest, who rubs a bit of oil on their throats to strengthen them against sickness and then hands out the breads at the church door. Everyone in town has already tasted the panicelle. Now they are seriously honoring San Biagio and hoping to stay well for the year that stretches ahead.

Panicelle di San Biagio

xxxxxxxxxxxxxxxxxxxxxxxxxxx

Sourdough Rolls

Makes 12 rolls

1¾ cups plus 2 tablespoons water
1¼ cups (300 grams) Natural Yeast Starter (page 32)
7½ cups (1 kilogram) unbleached all-purpose flour
1 tablespoon salt

By Hand. Add the water to the starter. Make a well of the flour and salt and work the water-and-yeast mixture in with your hands. Do not be discouraged because the dough is very stiff and hard to work.

By Mixer. With the paddle attachment stir the starter and water together in the mixer bowl. Add the flour and stir until a stiff, dry dough is formed. Change to the dough hook; it is difficult to knead the dough. After an initial brief kneading, take the dough out and knead by hand, just as they do in Taranta Peligna.

(continued)

Kneading. Break the dough into 4 pieces and knead them alternately; if one piece gets too stiff, cover it and set it aside and work on a more relaxed one. After 4 to 5 minutes per piece the dough will be very smooth, satiny, white, and very dry. Do not worry if the surface is somewhat broken and blistered.

First Rise. Stack the 4 pieces on top of each other, set in a lightly oiled container, cover with plastic wrap, and let rise until very puffy and doubled, about 24 hours.

Shaping and Second Rise. Punch down the dough and divide it into 12 equal pieces. Roll each piece into a 20- to 24-inch log and let it rest under plastic about 30 minutes; be certain not to leave it so long that it develops a skin. You may either cut each log into 4 equal segments and set them next to each other, or you may fold it back and forth on itself 3 times so that you have a piece of dough with 4 parallel coils. Use a knife to cut through ends where they connect. The roll should look like a four-fingered hand, so it's fine if the fingers are a bit uneven or tapered. Use a dough scraper to score 3 parallel sets of lines across the dough, like the knuckles on a hand. Lay the rolls on a baking sheet lined with parchment paper, cover first with plastic wrap and then with a heavy towel, and leave until the dough is puffy, almost doubled, and the 4 pieces of each roll are well attached to each other, about 2 hours.

Baking. Thirty minutes before baking, place a pizza stone or baking tiles in the oven and set the temperature at 425°F. Bake 30 minutes, until golden brown. These rolls are wonderful when they are fresh from the oven, but they get progressively tougher to chew as they age, which is why you should do as the natives of Taranta Peligna do and eat them as soon as possible. The taste will still be wonderful the next day, but your teeth may get a workout.

CARNEVALE

CARNIVAL IN ITALY

*R*omantic myth would have us believe that the classical world was a paradise filled with people enjoying unlimited sexual ecstasy until the Church came along and spoiled it all. Once the Church imposed restraints that made people feel guilty about their instincts, it was only at Carnival that they could abandon themselves and, disguised behind masks, give in to sexual abandon and a variety of other excesses, the last indulgence before the retrenchment of Lent. Carnevale literally means good-bye to the flesh (*carne levamen*), since it is the last chance to eat meat before Lent, but it also refers to the gastronomic orgy of the wintertime that exhausted the entire supply of meat before the spring.

The Roman festivals that were the precursors of Carnival were full of such libertine moments. Saturnalia, with its anything-goes reversal of roles, as slave and master changed places and men dressed as women and women as men, took place in December. Next came Bacchanalia, drunken orgies dedicated to Bacchus, followed in February by Lupercalia, when priests, called *luperci*, offered up two goats and a dog, animals known for lusty sexual appetites, smeared their own foreheads with blood from the sacrificial knife, burst into uproarious laughter, and ran naked through the streets snapping goat thongs at women to call forth fertility. Even earlier, the Greeks celebrated the passage from winter to spring with a three-day holiday devoted to Dionysius. On the first day, they opened jars holding the new wine and drank themselves into a euphoric state in a kind of communion with the god. On the second day, a parade featured

Dionysius, grape clusters in hand, enthroned between two flute-playing satyrs and riding on a *carrus navalis*, a great ship that traveled on wheels and gave its name, some say, to the festival. People wore masks (from *masca*, a nocturnal apparition), which symbolized the dead arising from the newly fertilized earth. They acted like buffoons, terrifying the people around them and creating a fracas as they went about destroying the old year, engaging in mock battles that sometimes turned serious as personal jealousies were acted out in public. February, the month dedicated to purification and the cult of the dead, got its name from the Sabine word *februo*, to purify.

When I went to Carnival celebrations in Italy, I did not expect to find Roman priests killing the two scapegoats that symbolize the evil of the past year, nor did I expect to see them running nude through the streets. But I did wonder if I would find dances and dalliances and piazze awash in wine and delicately fried pastries, *le bugie*, little lies as they are called in some places. An old year was dying, a new one was being born, and Carnival was the last great party, the land of milk and honey become reality for a brief time. The end of Carnival has long been an occasion for masked balls, processions, and feasts, magical rituals to assure the abundant harvests on which they depended, although there were also reminders of death, for Saturnalia once celebrated the passage from one season to the next.

To hear about Carnival in Italy in the early Middle Ages, when wine and food flowed freely, when there were obscene songs and erotic dances and games of chance set up on church altars, when masks guaranteed anonymity, and palios were run with only an old man, a baby, and a woman as a parody of the flight into Egypt—to know about these excesses does set up certain expectations. The celebrations often ended in an orgy, for the obscene singing and sensual dancing were intended to stimulate the earth to produce abundantly. All this abandon was an invocation of good luck for the seeds sleeping in the earth and for the children growing in their mothers' wombs.

What we might call fat city, the Italians actually called fat week, *la settimana grassa*, with Giovedì Grasso (Maundy Thursday) and Domenica Grassa (Fat Sunday) and Martedì Grasso, or Mardi Gras (Shrove Tuesday), which is the last day of Carnival before the rigors of Lent set in. Bonfires still burn all over Italy on Martedì Grasso, and a doll representing the King of Carnival is consumed in the flames. Sometimes Carnival itself is tried and condemned to the gallows or led to the pyre.

At its height, Carnival lasted for six months in Venice, although most celebrations extended only from Sant'Antonio Abate in mid-January, when meat was plentiful, to Ash Wednesday, when eating meat was forbidden. In Bergamo and Brescia, Carnival started the day after Christ-

Banishment of Carnival, eighteenth-century woodcut

mas: *Dopo Natale è subito Carnevale,* while elsewhere it began either on New Year's Eve or right after Epiphany. Celebrations expanded and retracted, depending on plague, famine, and local conditions. Instead of bread and circuses, the authorities kept order with *festa, farina, e forca,* festivals, flour, and the gallows. During the good times, people thronged to pageants and parades and waged vicious battles with oranges, eggs, or bran. Today with one exception the pageants tend to be less explosive and flour has been replaced by shaving cream, which is sprayed everywhere, leaving everything and everyone veiled in white.

Of the few wild, battle-filled Carnival celebrations still left in Italy, the one in Ivrea is the most fascinating. A lovely town in the green Canavese valley in the northernmost part of Piedmont, Ivrea sits at the entrance to Val d'Aosta. Today the valley is full of ski resorts, but two thousand years ago it guarded strategic mountain passes with castles, some of which are still standing among vineyards terraced on the rocky hillsides.

Ivrea may pull out all the stops for Carnival, but it also boards up all the windows. And with reason. The main event is a violent battle of oranges that occurs on three separate days as squads of fighters hurl tens of thousands of oranges at each other. Five piazze in the medieval section of town become combat zones. They are guarded by two teams of two to three hundred foot soldiers called *arancieri,* who wait to do battle with other warriors passing through on thirty or more horse-drawn carts. Each cart carries ten men, heavily padded and wearing helmets with mesh over the mouth and mere slits for the eyes. Sometimes the players in the carts hurl oranges unremittingly at the heads and faces of the team players below them, and sometimes an intense battle erupts between two people, but usually there is general mayhem, juice spraying and pulp flying, splattering on the fan-shaped stones that line the streets of Ivrea. The teams on the ground have no protection for their faces or bodies, and even though the riders are heavily padded, the oranges wedge under the neck guards, fly into the mouth openings, and smash into the eyepieces, making vision almost impossible. Is it claustrophobic? So they say. Is it painful? That too. And is it fun? "I'd never give it up," said one twenty-two-year-old who has been on the front lines since he was thirteen.

All the events of the week wrap around three battles on Sunday, Monday, and Tuesday afternoon, in which oranges are thrown like the stones that medieval fighters once tossed in deadly games played out in city piazze. But oranges? Since no oranges grow in Piedmont, an entire train carrying sixty tons of blood oranges arrives each year from Sicily, paid for by the people of Ivrea so they can be hurled and squandered in an extravagant display of conspicuous consumption. They are used only as weapons, never as food. Not a single orange is squeezed into juice or transformed into a ritual dish.

For three days the entire city becomes perfumed with oranges. Tiny atoms of juice hang like motes of dust in the air. Oranges are everywhere: split and whole, trampled in the streets, wedged in closed shutters, splattered against the boarded-up fronts of shops, smeared in the city streets. Gutters run red with the juice of Sicilian blood oranges. Children ski down the wet streets sliding on juice and orange peels from one piazza to the next.

Anyone who wants to stay out of the path of the flying oranges must put on a special red knit cap that declares its wearer a noncombatant. It is the same conical red cap that French revolutionaries wore as a sign of their freedom from tyranny, and from Saturday night through Tuesday the entire town is a sea of red, men and women in the headgear of liberty, which makes Ivrea looks like a gigantic costume party.

In classical times, people threw everything from flowers to fruit at masked paraders. There are Renaissance accounts of *putti* throwing oranges, and Brazilians pelted each other with the very same fruit during Carnival, so perhaps the tradition came to Italy from Spain. In fifteenth-century Palermo, people did battle with common oranges that were good only for making juice or polishing copper. By the end of the seventeenth century the Milanese threw not only confetti (sugar-coated almonds) but pellets of plaster confetti, and used slings or catapults to propel them a long distance. After these were outlawed, the Milanese turned to coriander seeds that they rolled in flour or plaster and left to dry, so perhaps these forerunners of paper confetti resemble oranges as projectiles. Carnival, writes Barbara Grizzuti Harrison, "was a peculiar mixture of glamor and cruelty. . . . In the eighteenth and nineteenth centuries, revelers wore little wire face masks in order to escape being hit in the lovely crossfire of confetti (sugared almonds), oranges and nosegays."

In Ivrea the oranges are said to replace the beans that the feudal lord distributed free to the poor once a year. The gesture evidently wasn't enough to compensate for their wretched state on the remaining 364 days, and according to legend, one year they tossed the beans into the street

Trial and Confession of Carnival, from the popular press, nineteenth century

to show what they thought of his generosity. A chronicler in 1872 wrote that the well-to-do of Ivrea threw such quantities of confetti, candies, and beans that the poor collected enough to live on for the rest of the year. Oranges had already become part of the festivity by then, although no one has been able to trace when and why they replaced the beans. Revelers in nearby Turin once threw caramels along with an occasional orange, since oranges were very precious. Oranges actually inspired two major invasions of Italy by dazzling northern rulers such as Charles V into visions of conquering paradise. "Oranges were the fruit of the gods," John McPhee explains in *Oranges*, ". . . the golden apples of the Hesperides."

This complicated Carnival celebration goes on for almost a week. It is a rarity, since it is based on real people and a real rebellion that took place in the late twelfth century against two hated local overlords and the taxes they exacted both from marriages and the milling of grain. It celebrates the town's freedom from tyranny and makes a star of La Mugnaia, the Miller's Daughter, who was about to be married. In a popular version of the tale, the two tyrants became one and the two taxes were condensed into the single and singularly infamous "right of the first night," the *jus primae noctis*, which allowed the local lord to sleep with a bride on her wedding night. Violetta, the miller's daughter, went off to the castle on the eve of the wedding, but when she was alone with the despot, she took out a knife from under her clothes, stabbed him to death, and cut off his head. She went to the window and held up the severed head for all the people to see, then threw it in the nearby Dora River and set fire to the castle. The populace battled for three days before winning their freedom.

Carnival begins when fife and drum wake Ivrea on the morning of Epiphany, but the celebration starts in earnest on Maundy Thursday. La Mugnaia, the Miller's Daughter, is presented to the crowd at the stroke of nine on Saturday night. Shortly afterward the rest of the cast assembles: the marchese who helped her start a rebellion; her attendants in brocade wimples and velour capes and mantles; squads of armed fighters; and the fife-and-drum corps whose evocative music swirls through the city streets until Carnival is over. At her side throughout the event sits a general in full French uniform, a holdover from the era when Napoleon captured the region of Piedmont. He reinstated Carnival and appointed a general, charging him to make peace between the city's five feuding neighborhoods, which each held its own festivity. La Mugnaia and the General lead a lengthy medieval cortège in a colorful torchlight parade of, among others, historical figures, knights in armor, drummers, and flag wavers snapping their brilliant banners in the cold night air. At the end march the *arancieri*, singing team songs at the top of their lungs. Many teenagers stream behind them, their faces painted in outrageous patterns in the colors of their teams.

There are so many dances, outdoor feasts, pageants, parades, and fireworks that much of Ivrea gives up sleeping altogether and grabs naps for an hour or two when it is possible. People dance in the streets, the piazze, and in the discos. Half the town jams into bars and caffès to drink everything from rich hot chocolate to jolting grappas made in the nearby hills. A cake for three hundred disappears almost as soon as it is set on the table. Dinners include an annual feast given by the local confraternity of gourmets devoted to such traditional foods of Ivrea as zuppa canavesana, thick cabbage soup, and sweet-and-sour onions. Great cauldrons of beans cook on the main piazza on Saturday night, sending up clouds of steam in the cold night and warming the curious and hungry. At around two in the morning, masses of people begin to make their way to the Piazza Gioberti on their way from one party to another so they can get a preview taste of the beans that will be served early next morning. The people of Ivrea are curious to see how the beans are faring—and to taste them— as they simmer slowly over enormous fires.

The beans that were once given to citizens by their tyrannical overlord inspired the monumental *fagiolate*—literally big bean feasts— that are held all over the city for three weeks. The biggest feast takes place early on Sunday morning. Forty men and women cook a dish called *tofeja* in thirty-four huge pots over continually stoked fires. In the space of a few hours, 1½ tons of beans and 440 pounds of salame become part of a thick, rich, and filling wintertime soup. The entire undertaking is financed by a committee that collects products from farmers and donations from everyone else. Since pigs are killed just before Carnival, various pieces of pork are easy to find, as are the silky Saluggia beans grown and sun-dried in nearby fields. Everyone is bundled up against the cold, but the only ones who are warm are the cooks standing next to roaring fires and the teenagers who scurry back and forth, passing out bowls to the hungry crowd. People stop to feed small children, to hug and fuss over babies in their mothers' arms, and many dance to the music. A great cheer goes up when the Miller's Daughter and the General arrive, sample the beans, and drink a toast from an enormous brandy snifter. In the Middle Ages confraternities distributed beans free to the poor; now the Miller's Daughter ladles them into bowls in the garlanded piazza. A ton of chocolates and cheeses are part of an entire meal given to the poor citizens of Ivrea. Everybody drinks red wine before following the mayor through sloping medieval streets to the bridge over the river from which he hurls a piece of brick pulled from the old castle, just as the marchese's head was thrown centuries earlier.

The last and fiercest battle of oranges is fought on Martedì Grasso in the afternoon in piazze decorated in the colors and insignias of the defending squads. When it is almost over, the participants are virtually marinated, with their dripping hair and sopping shirts. They are singing and laughing, looking jubilant if a bit dazed. Nasty-looking bumps and bruises and black eyes are commonplace (when the city returns to normal the next day, it turns out that those black eyes to belong to bank clerks, bakers, greengrocers, and pharmacists). At the end of the last battle all the carts and players are on hand, squishing across the main piazza on pavement that is still slippery, the crimson juice dripping down the face of the *arancieri*. It takes great courage for a group of men to stand on the balcony of city hall and announce the winners of the best horses and team, for the minute they deliver the news shutters clang shut and within seconds, hundreds of oranges thud against the buildings.

It is the last explosion of violence, for when everyone returns at sundown for the funeral of Carnival, swords and oranges will have been exchanged for torches. Early on Monday morning, in preparation for this moment, the most recently married couple in each of five neighborhoods has scooped out the first trowelful of earth to make a hole in which *scarli*, poles as tall as trees, have been planted. Then, on Tuesday evening, garlands of heather and juniper are wound around them all the way to the top. In the central piazza, La Mugnaia raises her unsheathed sword high above her head and young boys touch their torches to the tall pole wrapped with greens. As flames leap high, the juniper and heather hiss and sparks flicker in the air. If the flames reach the banner planted on the top, the next year will be full of prosperity and weddings. A procession walks from neighborhood to neighborhood to burn the *scarli*, as a single fifer plays a mournful tune that signals the death of Carnival. At the last stop, across the river, the General slips a foot out of his stirrup, slides down from his horse, unsheathes his sword, and walks in a slow and melancholy gait, dragging the sword along the stone pavement. Darkness is falling. There is no sound save for the rasp of the sword scraping across the cobblestones. Carnival is dead, and the entire city walks slowly behind the General, a cortege following its leader along the arc of the streets.

The lugubrious ending makes way for Ash Wednesday and the beginning of Lent, but penitence has to wait for one last feast. Preparations for this started a full six days earlier. Salt cod soaked for four days and bathed in fresh changes of water every twelve hours was drained on door-sized tables before the cutting and trimming that began on Sunday night. On Monday, men cleaned 1,200 pounds of the fish and chopped over 175 pounds of onions. For many years, Olivetti, the main employer in Ivrea, closed down for the entirety of Carnival, freeing dozens of vol-

Crazy Carnival, engraving by Giuseppe Maria Mitelli, late seventeenth century

unteers to slice the onions by hand all day long. Now machines have replaced the workers, who have to stay on the job, and a small group of neighborhood men oversees the preparations. They begin to fry the cod at six o'clock on Tuesday evening, and they finish by ten-thirty the next morning. Groups work separately making two sauces, one red and the other a besciamella that uses more than 500 pounds of flour, 300 quarts of olive oil, and 250 liters of wine. The two sauces are layered as in lasagne with the cod and onions. Early next morning, on Ash Wednesday, the whole town turns up to eat the dish. A squad of polenta makers arrives from nearby Val d'Aosta with six enormous cauldrons that each hold 150 liters of water, and their arms are given a powerful workout stirring enough polenta to feed an army. People literally assault the food on Monday night when they stop by between dances and dinner to get their first tastes. By Wednesday morning, they arrive with pressure cookers and pails and pots. Some can survive for a month on what they take home. Others stock their freezers, then send their sisters, cousins, and aunts to bring home more.

Carnival in Italy is still a time when anyone who is hungry eats. Italians eat to exhibit power, to affirm themselves, to exorcise hunger and death. Carnival banishes hunger in great style, and while the gamut of the sweets served during the festival varies from town to town, you can find light, fragile ribbons of fried dough veiled with vanilla-flavored powdered sugar everywhere. Each city or region gives them a different name and scents them with a different liqueur; they are called *chiacchiere* (gossips) in Milan; *crostoli* in Alto Adige, where they are flavored with acquavit; *galani* in Verona; *bugie* (lies) in Piedmont; *cenci* (rags) in Tuscany, where they are made with Vin Santo; *lattughe* (lettuces) in Emilia-Romagna; *sfrappe* in the Marches, where they are flavored with anise seeds; and *nastri delle suore* (nuns' ribbons) in many other places. They are known as *tortelli* when filled with jam or thick, sweet grape must and honey. In Trieste it is a point of honor to serve krapfen, an apricot-jam–filled pastry like a jelly doughnut. Almost every town and village serves frittelle, fritters sprinkled with powdered sugar. Frittelle are filled with raisins or cream in Venice, become friceau in Piedmont, and castagnole (chestnuts) in Romagna and the Marches. A pyramid of tiny dice of sweet dough, fried and piled high atop one another, are called *cicerchiata* in Umbria and Abruzzi and become *pignolata* in Sicily. *Fare le frittelle* has always been another expression for observing Carnival and having a good time. The ingredients and form of the frittelle (flour, sweetener, and the frying fat) have not changed in centuries. Grustoli, a lesser-known sweet made from a square of frittelle dough that swells as it fries, leaving four sides that look like the rays of the sun, reminds us that in a short time the sun will no longer be held hostage to the cold days of winter.

At one time, people at Carnival made *salsicce di sterco*, sausages of *merde*, according to Folco Portinari, an irreverent carnival joke. Certainly Sicilians have served *lasagne alla cacate* at New Year for centuries. This name did not deter people from eating the dish with enthusiasm, because it was real lasagne made with a delicious ragù, mozzarella, ricotta, and fine Parmesan cheese. Perhaps it is no accident that the typical sweet of Carnival in Naples is sanguinaccio, blood pudding, although today the pudding is made with cocoa, chocolate, and milk, instead of fresh pig's blood. If food such as the sausages really once existed, it has been gentrified and in its place now are sweet sausages and chocolate salame.

At Carnival people eat everything left in the larder, but they also dip into fresh sausages and meat because tradition requires one eating mountains of meat and sausages, drinking rivers of wine, and ending every meal with frittelle, sweet pastries that were once fried in lard. (In these days of concern about cholesterol and waistlines, frittelle are either fried in lighter oils or baked fat-free).

All this goes on while people are masked and costumed, which guarantees their anonymity while they are luxuriating in excess. Venice is famous for revels and balls in the piazze, for it permitted masks to be worn and licentious private parties to be held in palazzi while others did not. (Disguised nobles used to recognize each other by the jewelry they wore.) By the seventeenth century, the Venetian celebration was full of private and public events. It was resplendent with parades of nobles dressed in gold and silver, floats carrying drunken bacchantes singing the praises of the god of wine. No wonder thirty thousand visitors came in 1687 to participate. By the eighteenth century, a masked procession on the Grand Canal was followed by a ride to the Giudecca to eat frittelle, and on the last day, a meal of lasagne and raw eel. Even when masked parades became less popular, the balls continued until Mussolini outlawed masks, then Carnival in its entirety. When the Venetian Carnival was revived in 1979, it succeeded so brilliantly that now buses are turned back after eight in the morning and footbridges become one-way.

Martedì Grasso, Shrove Tuesday, is the last feast before Carnival's death. In Calabria it was so important to eat pork on that day that people sold their front doors to get it. Giovanni Goria, a great expert on the history of the food and culture of Piedmont, recently re-created a feast for the last day of Carnival at which he served an antipasto called *Piatt' del Crin pen-a-massa*: an earthenware terrine of beans, leeks, and potatoes with fresh pork rind cooked at very low temperature for a long time, followed by the blood pudding of Asti with fried cabbages; cotechino sausages with puréed potatoes and spinach; batsoa, pig's trotters, with fried polenta; roasted pork spareribs with rosemary; a platter of fritto misto, including pork loin, coppa, sausages, diamonds of sweet semolina and

Cabbage, drawing by P. A. Mattioli, 1583, Venice

pork shoulder rolled with sage, pepper, and parsley, dipped in eggs and Parmesan cheese, then fried. And that was just the antipasto! Next came agnolotti stuffed with three different roast meats and a puréed garbanzo bean soup. A main course would have been unthinkable, so a hot savory pie enclosing melting Piemontese cheeses was served up next. Desserts, hard even to imagine after such a meal, included a pumpkin pie, zabaione, and bugie, traditional fried ribbons of dough.

In Rome in 1787, Goethe was highly taken with a very different finale of the *festa*, especially the dramatic candlelight procession on Shrove Tuesday. He wrote: "The darkness has descended into the narrow, high-walled street before lights are seen moving in the windows and on the stands; in next to no time the fire has circulated far and wide, and the whole street is lit up by burning candles.

"The balconies are decorated with transparent paper lanterns, everyone holds his candle, all the windows, all the stands are illuminated, and it is a pleasure to look into the interiors of the carriages, which often have small crystal chandeliers hanging from the ceiling, while in others the ladies sit with coloured candles in their hands as if inviting one to admire their beauty.

"*Sia ammazzato chi non porta moccolo.* 'Death to anyone who is not carrying a candle.' This is what you say to others, while at the same time you try to blow out their candles. . . . The louder the cries of *Sia ammazzato*, the more these words lose their sinister meaning, and you forget that you are in Rome, where at any other time but Carnival, and for a trifling reason, the wish expressed by these words might be literally fulfilled. . . .

"No one can move from the spot where he is standing or sitting; the heat of so many human beings and so many lights, the smoke from so many candles as they are blown out and lit again, the roar of so many people, yelling all the louder because they can not move a limb, make the sanest head swim."

With such tumult and the shimmering of thousands of candles did Carnival in Rome come to an end. The rumble of human noise was almost loud enough to rouse the seeds buried in the earth. The light and heat of thousands of candles mimic the sunlight and warmth of spring, which will soon liberate nature so that plants may break through the earth's cold crust and pour forth an abundance of grains, fruits, and vegetables, food for another year.

Fricandò from Ivrea

Spareribs and Sausages Braised with Wine Vinegar

Spareribs, sausages, potatoes, and vegetables—a wonderful robust dinner for a cold winter evening. It's the meat and potatoes of Ivrea. Some say another dish with the same French-sounding name went to France with Catherine de' Medici and then made its way back to Milan and Piedmont at the end of the eighteenth century. Others insist that it was brought by Hagy, Napoleon's omnipresent Egyptian cook, who opened a restaurant in Milan when the emperor's fortunes went into decline. That dish, made of veal larded with prosciutto, was reserved for great occasions, while this fricandò is a rustic dish cooked at home for family and friends.

Makes 6 servings

2½ tablespoons (40 grams) butter
3 carrots, finely chopped
2 onions, finely chopped
2 ribs celery, finely chopped
4 tablespoons olive oil
3 mild Italian sausages
3 pounds (1⅓ kilograms) baby backribs, cut into 2 rib sections
6 cloves
2 bay leaves
2½ tablespoons red wine vinegar
2 tablespoons tomato paste
1¾ cups water
Salt and pepper
4 potatoes, peeled and cut into 8 to 10 pieces

Warm the butter in a heavy pot and sauté the carrots, onions, and celery until they are soft. Remove to a plate. Film the pan with the olive oil, prick the sausages, and add them to the pan along with the ribs. Sauté until brown. Drain off the fat. Add the cloves and bay leaves. Add the vinegar, raise the heat, and let it bubble until it evaporates. Add the tomato paste diluted in 1¾ cups water. Return the vegetables to the pot, season with salt and pepper, cover, and cook over a medium-low flame 1½ to 2 hours, turning the sausages and ribs every so often. You may need to add water if it gets dry. Add the potatoes and cook another ½ hour, turning them over so that they absorb the sauce and cook evenly.

This dish tastes even better the next day.

Zuppa alla Canavesana

~~~~~~~~~~~~~~~~~~~~~~~~~~~~~~~

Thick Bread and Cabbage Soup with a Crunchy Cheese Crust

This substantial soup is so thick you could almost eat it with a fork, perfect for the cold days of winter. It is a traditional sturdy zuppa from northern Piedmont, where winters can be very cold indeed. Grilled garlic-scented bread is layered with cabbage braised in butter, then bathed with broth flavored with onions and garlic. Its golden crust of well-aged cheese reminds me of the onion soup that used to be served around Les Halles in Paris. If you want to make the soup into a whole meal, just add a few sausages at the last moment.

Makes 4 to 6 servings

1 pound (450 grams) Savoy cabbage
4 cloves garlic
½ cup (112 grams) butter or ¼ cup butter, ¼ cup olive oil
8 slices stale country bread
2 pounds (900 grams) onions, thinly sliced
Salt
4¼ cups meat broth
4 to 6 Italian sausages, optional
⅓ pound (150 grams) strong well-aged Fontina or toma cheese, shredded
¼ cup (25 grams) grated Parmesan cheese, plus additional as needed
Pepper
Large pinch ground cloves

Parboil the cabbage leaves 1 to 2 minutes, drain, and dry. Peel and flatten the garlic with the side of a cleaver. Melt 5 tablespoons butter in a small heavy skillet and add the garlic. Dip the slices of country bread into this mixture and sauté over medium heat until they are lightly toasted. You may also brush them with the butter-garlic mixture and bake them in a 375°F oven until they have become golden and dried out, 20 minutes. Warm 3 tablespoons butter in a heavy-bottomed casserole, add the onions and salt, and cook over very low heat 45 to 60 minutes, stirring occasionally. After the onions have cooked, they will be somewhat browned and reduced in quantity; stir in the broth and scrape up any bits that have stuck to the bottom of the pan. If you are using sausages, prick them with a fork and add to the onions after 45 minutes. Cover and continue cooking for 15 minutes. Mix the 2 cheeses together.

Assembly. If you use sausages, cut each into 3 or 4 pieces. In a high-sided earthenware tureen make a layer of cabbage leaves, strew several pieces of sausage, then put a layer of bread over them and season with grindings of fresh pepper and a sprinkling of ground cloves. Sprinkle additional Parmesan cheese lightly over the top. Bathe the layers with a couple ladlefuls of broth and onions. Continue with the layering process until you have used up all the ingredients. Finish with cheese, then add the final ladlefuls of broth.

Baking. Heat the oven to 375°F. Bake until the broth has largely been absorbed and the cheese on top has formed a golden crust, at least 2 hours. The trick is to be careful that the crust doesn't burn or get brown too quickly; if you find that it is, simply set a piece of foil over the top of the pot.

Serve the soup in warmed bowls, being sure to divide the crusty cheese topping among them.

Carnival, from
Bartolomeo Pinelli, 1825

Tofeja

~~~~~~~~~~~~~~~~~~~~~~~~~~~~~~~~

*Traditional
Carnival Dish
from Ivrea*

*Mangia bene, engraving,
1690*

At its most rudimentary tofeja is a thick, rich soup made of silky-textured beans and tasty pieces of pork. It is simple "innocent" food made of basic and easily gotten ingredients, a return to the countryside of a rustic past. The soup is cooked in a *tofeja,* a squat four-handled terracotta pot that gives the dish its name. Women used to take their pots to the baker, who put them into his woodburning oven after he had finished baking bread. The oven was just warm enough to cook the beans over a twelve-hour period as the temperature gradually fell. Delicate and tender Saluggia beans are a mottled creamy color with deep pink markings, and, although they look like cranberry beans, they are much silkier and seem to have no skins at all. If you can find butter beans, by all means use them. Otherwise try white cannellini beans. At one time tofeja was made with the pig's ears, snout, and feet, but these days whole ribs are often used. There were little salamini in the tofeja of Ivrea, but other cooks in that city add cotechino. The plump rolled pieces of pork fat are named *preive,* priests. Each Sunday morning of Carnival, crowds delightedly gather around when the preive are first offered to the local bishop so they can watch him bite right into the "priests." Because the pork pieces are so fatty, I have cut back on their number and have added cinnamon as a little zing for the taste buds. Although it isn't authentic, I like to use the whole pork ribs. If you decide to substitute cotechino sausage for the rolled pieces of pork fat, cook it separately and add it during the last 5 minutes of cooking. Sauté all the herbs called for with the onion.

Makes 6 servings

14 ounces (400 grams) dried beans, either butter or cannellini
5 or 6 leaves sage
2 branches rosemary
2 bay leaves
½ peperoncino (dried red chile), seeded
2 cloves garlic
**3 ounces (100 grams) fresh pork fat, pork back fat or the fat just
   beneath the rind of a ham**
2 teaspoons cinnamon
Salt and pepper
1 pound (450 grams) pork spareribs
2 tablespoons olive oil
1 onion, finely chopped
6½ cups broth or water
½ pound (225 grams) cotechino sausage, optional

The night before, soak the beans in tepid water. Next day drain them and cover with fresh water.

Finely chop the sage, rosemary, bay leaves, peperoncino, and garlic. Divide the mixture so that ⅓ is reserved for the pork fat and ⅔ for the onion. Take the pork fat and flavor it with cinnamon, salt, and pepper. Cut it into strips about 2¼ by 1¼ inches. Sprinkle a bit of the finely chopped rosemary, garlic, bay leaf, and sage mixture on each piece, roll the strips into cigar-shaped pieces, and tie them with string. Cut the pork ribs into 2-inch pieces.

Warm the oil in a skillet or earthenware pot and sauté the onion until translucent. Add the larger portion of the chopped herb and garlic mixture and cook it slowly until golden. (Use the entire mixture if you decide not to do the pork rolls.) Add the rolled pork fat, the ribs, and drained beans. Cover with broth or water and salt lightly. Bring to a boil, cover tightly, and cook over a very low flame until the beans are done, 2 to 3 hours. You may also start the tofeja in a 350°F oven and cook slowly by reducing the temperature over the next 2 to 3 hours. If you add cotechino sausage, prick its skin with a skewer, wrap it in cheesecloth, and cook in slowly boiling water to cover for 1 to 2 hours. Drain, slice, and add to the tofeja about 5 minutes before you are ready to serve it.

Serve very hot with country bread that has been rubbed with garlic.

Polenta Valdostana

Creamy Polenta with Cheese

Polenta makers from Aosta arrive in Ivrea bringing their own enormous cauldrons to make this cheese-laced polenta on Ash Wednesday morning.

Makes 10 to 12 servings

9 cups water
1 tablespoon salt
3 cups (450 grams) regular-grind polenta or yellow cornmeal
10 ounces (300 grams) Fontina cheese, diced
¼ cup (55 grams) butter
Salt and pepper

Bring the salted water to a boil in a large pot and sprinkle in the polenta in a thin stream, cooking and stirring constantly with a wooden spoon 15 to 20 minutes. When the polenta comes away from the sides of the pot, after about 30 minutes, it is ready. Stir in the cheese, butter, salt, and pepper and continue mixing until they are completely absorbed.

Merluzzo e Cipolle

~~~~~~~~~~~~~~~~~~~~~~~~~~~~~~~~~~~~

Salt Cod and Onions, Layered with Two Sauces Like Lasagne

In Ivrea one neighborhood makes enough merluzzo (baccalà, or dried cod) for the entire town. When the cooks begin soaking it four days in advance, the aroma floats across the river and up through the medieval streets, letting everyone know that Ash Wednesday is not far off. To visit the storeroom where the fish is soaking is a jolt to the nostrils—over one thousand pounds are in tanks with running water, which is changed twice a day for each of those four days. When the dish is served, one would swear that the delicate mixture of white fish and red and white sauces had been cooked at a fine restaurant. I have made one major change. The besciamella in Ivrea is made with olive oil instead of butter and with wine instead of milk. I have opted for a traditional white sauce that tastes delicious. This recipe may be doubled easily and makes the work worthwhile.

Makes 6 servings

2 pounds (900 grams) baccalà
2 to 3 medium onions, thinly sliced
3 to 4 tablespoons olive oil

Since there are several different salt cods available that vary in saltiness, size, and moisture, it is difficult to give precise directions. I prefer to use small boxes of boned baccalà because the pieces are all the same size. Soak baccalà 3 days to remove excess salt and to rehydrate it. Turn it over every few hours and change the water twice a day. You will have to try a small sample to see if it is still too salty. Drain and sauté in olive oil. Remove from pan and sauté the onions in the same oil until translucent.

S A U C E

1 rib celery, finely minced
1 carrot, finely minced
2 cloves garlic, finely minced
3 tablespoons olive oil
2 leaves basil, torn in pieces
¼ cup finely chopped parsley
1 teaspoon chopped fresh rosemary leaves
2 or 3 sage leaves, finely chopped
2 bay leaves, finely chopped
¼ cup white wine
1 cup canned Italian plum tomatoes, chopped, 1 cup juice reserved
2 tablespoons tomato concentrate
¾ cup water

Sauté the celery, carrot, and garlic in the oil until golden, being careful not to burn the garlic. Add the basil and parsley and sauté briefly. Add the rosemary, sage, and bay leaves, cook for a minute or two, then stir in the wine and cook over medium heat until it evaporates. Mix in the tomatoes, tomato concentrate, and the water and cook about 10 minutes, adding the juice from the tomatoes as the mixture thickens.

BESCIAMELLA SAUCE

4 tablespoons (55 grams) butter
6 tablespoons (50 grams) flour
2 cups boiling milk
½ teaspoon salt
Nutmeg

In a heavy saucepan melt the butter and when it bubbles whisk in the flour, stirring gently until it is a thick creamy mixture. Add a little of the hot milk and stir vigorously, adding more as it is absorbed until you have used it all up. Season with salt. The sauce should be smooth and creamy, but you must cook it another 15 minutes or so to rid it of its floury taste. Grate a little nutmeg over it.

Assembly. On the bottom of an oiled or buttered ovenproof dish set a layer of baccalà, a layer of onions, a layer of red and a layer of white sauce. Continue layering baccalà, onions, and sauce until they are used up. Finish with the sauce. Bake in a 350°F oven 1 hour. Serve with sliced Polenta (page 357).

Cipolline in Agrodolce

Sweet and Sour Onions from Ivrea

Ivrea is famous for its cipolline, tiny yellow onions the size of a walnut, which are cooked until they are almost a conserve. This makes a delicious sweet-and-sour side dish.

Makes 4 to 6 servings

2 to 3 tablespoons olive oil
30 cipolline, little yellow onions, peeled
2½ tablespoons red wine vinegar
1½ teaspoons sugar
Salt
¾ cup broth

(continued)

Warm the oil in a large skillet or pan that can go into the oven, then add the onions and sauté them until they are lightly browned all over. Add the red wine vinegar and let it cook until it has evaporated. Add the sugar and salt, cover with broth, and bake in a 350°F oven 1¼ to 1½ hours. The onions will be well done and the sauce must be dense.

Eporediesi al Cacao

XXXXXXXXXXXXXXXXXXXXXXXXXXXXX

Chocolate- Hazelnut Cookies from Ivrea

This is a dark, chewy macaroon made of hazelnuts and chocolate with a slightly cracked top under a light powdering of sugar. These crunchy cookies that get their name from the citizens of Ivrea aren't made anywhere beyond the city limits. They are best eaten fresh, since, unlike macaroons, they dry out after a day or two.

Makes about 36 cookies

1¾ to 2 cups (200 to 250 grams) hazelnuts, toasted and peeled
1 cup (200 grams) sugar
2 egg whites (50 grams)
1 cup plus 1 tablespoon (230 grams) sugar
⅓ cup water
2 tablespoons light corn syrup
½ cup plus 2 tablespoons (50 grams) unsweetened cocoa powder
Confectioners' sugar

Grind 1¾ cups (200 grams) toasted hazelnuts with 1 cup sugar in a food processor until they are a chunky mixture. Add the egg whites and mix until well combined into a hazelnut paste. Separately cook the 1 cup plus 1 tablespoon sugar, the water, and corn syrup over a medium flame until the mixture is clear and reaches 240°F on a candy thermometer. Do not cook it any more or it will harden. Leave it to cool completely, then add it to the hazelnut mixture and mix in the cocoa. As the dough cools, it will stiffen up. If, when the dough is totally cool, it is still soft, add up to ¼ cup chopped toasted hazelnuts. Drop by heaping teaspoonfuls at 3-inch intervals on parchment-lined or buttered and floured baking sheets. They spread considerably as they bake. Flatten the tops with the back of a moistened spoon and sift a little confectioners' sugar over their tops.

Baking. Heat the oven to 350°F. Bake 18 to 20 minutes. The cookies look slightly cracked when they are baked.

Polenta Dolce

*Sweet Polenta
Cake from Ivrea*

Every bakery and pastry shop in Ivrea sells this rustic polenta cake in sizes ranging from a bite-sized cookie to a great two-pound cake. Sometimes it is perfumed with vanilla, sometimes with a little lemon, and sometimes, as in this particular one, with rum-soaked raisins.

Makes one 9½-inch cake

6 eggs
1 cup (200 grams) sugar
2 cups (240 grams) whole-wheat pastry flour
3 tablespoons plus 1 teaspoon (35 grams) potato flour
⅓ cup (50 grams) finest-grind cornmeal
2 teaspoons baking powder
Pinch salt
½ cup (80 grams) raisins, soaked in ¼ cup rum, drained but rum
 reserved
3 tablespoons (20 grams) chopped candied orange peel or the grated zest
 of 1 orange
1 tablespoon and 1 teaspoon (20 grams) honey
½ cup plus 1 tablespoon (125 grams) unsalted butter, melted, cooled,
 sediment at bottom discarded
Grated zest of 1 lemon or ½ teaspoon lemon extract
Grated zest of 1 orange or ½ teaspoon orange extract

Whisk the eggs and sugar together over low heat until they are tepid. Remove from heat and keep beating in a mixer or with a whisk until the mixture is thick, lemon-colored, glossy, and can hold a ribbon for 3 seconds. You'll know it is thick enough when you can write your initials and they stay there for 3 seconds. Pour the mixture—it will pour in ribbons—into a wide-mouthed bowl, so you can sift in the flours without deflating the dough.

Sift together the flours, cornmeal, baking powder, and salt. Return to the sifter and gently sift them over the egg mixture in 3 additions, folding them in very carefully, trying to deflate the mixture as little as possible. Add the raisins and candied orange peel and when they are well incorporated, the honey, melted butter, rum, and the lemon and orange zests or flavorings.

Butter a 9½-inch springform pan, line the bottom with parchment paper, and coat the sides with cornmeal or with polenta. Gently pour the batter into it.

Baking. Heat the oven to 350°F. Bake until the cake is lightly golden, 35 to 40 minutes.

Bugie

~~~~~~~~~~~~~~~~~~~~~~~~~~~~~~~~~~

*Fried Ribbons of
Dough
for Carnival*

All over Italy delicate strips of sweetened fried dough are eaten to celebrate Carnival. The strips are known generically as *nastri delle suore,* nuns' ribbons, although they have all kinds of regional names: *chiacchiere* (gossips) in Lombardy, *chiacchiere di suora* (nun's gossip) in Parma, *bugie* (lies) in Piedmont, *lattughe* (lettuces) or *sfrappole* in Emilia-Romagna, *cenci* (rags and tatters) in Tuscany, *crostoli* in Trieste and Friuli, *galani* in the Veneto, and *frappe* in Umbria. *Frittelle piene di vento,* "fried treats full of wind," is how they were described in a sixteenth-century book published in Venice.

Makes 70 or 80 ribbons

1½ cups (200 grams) unbleached all-purpose flour
1½ tablespoons (20 grams) unsalted butter, room temperature
1½ tablespoons (20 grams) sugar
Scant 1 tablespoon liqueur, rum, Cognac, grappa, or Grand Marnier
1 large egg
Pinch salt
Grated zest of 1 orange
1½ teaspoons vanilla extract
3 to 4 tablespoons milk
4 cups olive or sunflower oil
Confectioners' sugar

By Hand. Set the flour in a mound in a large bowl or on a work surface and make a well in it. Set the butter, sugar, liqueur, egg, salt, orange zest, and vanilla in the center and mix them together. Slowly incorporate these ingredients into the flour, a little at a time, adding whatever amount of milk is necessary to make a dough. Knead until the dough is smooth and firm, 10 to 12 minutes. Cover with a tea towel and leave 45 to 60 minutes.

By Mixer. In the mixer bowl with the paddle attachment, combine the flour, butter, sugar, liqueur, egg, salt, orange zest, and vanilla, adding enough milk to get a dough that is firm enough to roll out very fine. Cover with a tea towel and let it rest 45 to 60 minutes.

With a rolling pin roll the dough out very fine on a lightly floured work surface until it is ⅛ to ¼ inch thick. Using a ravioli cutter or a knife, cut the dough into ribbons about 4 to 5 inches long and 1 to 1¼ inches wide. In some places it is customary to tie a knot in the center or twist the ribbon twice and pinch it closed in the center. Elsewhere bakers cut the dough into rectangles and make two parallel short cuts in the center.

Heat abundant oil in a heavy deep-sided frying pan to 350°F and fry a few of the ribbons at a time very, very quickly—20 seconds at the very most. Drain on plates lined with absorbent paper towels and sprinkle well with confectioners' sugar.

Krapfen

Jam-Filled Doughnuts

Jam-filled puffs of dough are traditional for Carnival, but the fillings are determined by where they are being made. Rum flavors the krapfen of Friuli, aquavit is used in Alto Adige, and lemon zest or vanilla is more common in Lombardy.

Makes 12 puffs

SPONGE

2 teaspoons active dry yeast or ⅓ cake (12 grams) fresh yeast
½ cup warm water
¾ cup (100 grams) unbleached all-purpose flour
½ teaspoon salt

Stir the yeast into the warm water and leave until creamy, about 10 minutes. Stir in the flour and salt and cover well. Let rise until doubled, about 45 minutes.

DOUGH

2 teaspoons (10 grams) sugar
2 tablespoons (30 grams) unsalted butter, room temperature
1 egg yolk
1 teaspoon rum, aquavit, marsala, vanilla extract, or grated lemon zest
¾ cup (100 grams) unbleached all-purpose flour

FILLING

8 to 10 tablespoons apricot jam or an equal amount of pastry cream or
    whipped cream flavored with vanilla and sugar

Milk
Oil for frying

Stir the sugar and butter into the sponge. When they are incorporated, add the egg yolk and rum and finally the flour. Mix together well 2 to 3 minutes.

Second Rise. Cover and let rise until the dough is elastic but not doubled, about 30 minutes. *(continued)*

Shaping and Rise. With a rolling pin roll out the dough until it is ⅜ inch thick. You are making a dough sandwich with jam on one piece. Cut out 3½-inch rounds using a cookie cutter or wineglass. Put 1 to 2 teaspoons jam in the center of half the rounds; wash their edges well with milk and then put a plain disk on top of a jam-studded one. Pinch the edges closed very firmly; you don't want the jam to leak out in the frying. Set on a parchment-covered cookie sheet, cover, and let rise under a moist tea towel about 45 minutes. Be careful that the krapfen don't develop a skin.

Frying. Heat the oil to 325° to 350°F. Just before frying, reseal each krapfen. If you take a slightly smaller glass or cookie cutter and press down lightly on it, you can make a smaller interior circle that domes up in the cooking and effectively seals the jam in. Fry 7 to 8 minutes over medium-high heat; when one side becomes golden brown, turn over, and cook the other side. You may also bake these in a 350°F oven for 35 to 45 minutes. Brush them well with melted butter before putting them on buttered baking sheets, leaving 2 inches between them.

Berlingaccio or Berlingozzo

Tuscan Sweet
Bread
for Carnival

There are lots of pleasures at Carnival time and surely one of the best is berlingaccio, a delicate orange-scented sweet bread. It is one of the oldest breads in Tuscany where it is made for parties on Giovedì Grasso, Fat Thursday, the week before Carnival ends. Its name comes from the Tuscan dialect for Giovedì Grasso, which, in turn, comes from the verb *berlingare,* to chatter idly (especially when one is full of food and drink). The Florentines were once called *i berlingatori,* and on Fat Thursday when everyone goes overboard eating tasty foods and giving no thought to tomorrow, they were called *i berlingozzi.*

Makes 2 loaves

SPONGE

3½ teaspoons active dry yeast or 1⅓ cakes (24 grams) fresh yeast
¾ cup warm water
¾ cup (100 grams) unbleached all-purpose flour

Dissolve the yeast in the warm water in a mixing bowl; let stand till creamy. Stir in the flour, mix well, and cover the bowl with plastic wrap. Let rise until doubled, 20 to 30 minutes.

½ cup (50 grams) sugar

3½ tablespoons (50 grams) unsalted butter, well mashed

¾ cup (100 grams) unbleached all-purpose flour

By Mixer. Leave the sponge in the mixing bowl and, using the paddle attachment, add the sugar and well-mashed butter. When sugar and butter are incorporated, add the flour and mix well. Cover with plastic wrap and let rise until doubled, 45 minutes to 1 hour.

SECOND DOUGH

7 tablespoons (100 grams) unsalted butter, room temperature and well mashed

½ cup (100 grams) sugar

¾ teaspoon salt

3 eggs

½ teaspoon cinnamon

Pinch freshly grated nutmeg

⅛ teaspoon vanilla extract

Grated zest of 1 orange

2¼ cups (300 grams) unbleached all-purpose flour

Leave the dough in the mixing bowl and with the paddle beat in the well-mashed butter, sugar, salt, eggs, cinnamon, nutmeg, vanilla, and orange zest. Mix them well and add the flour, beating on low speed until it forms a well-mixed dough. It will never come entirely away from the sides or bottom of the bowl. Change to the dough hook and knead 3 to 4 minutes on medium speed, stopping every once in a while to push the dough down if it has climbed up the shaft. The dough is very soft, silky, velvety, and always slightly sticky.

Shaping and Rise. Divide the dough in half. It is a gooey briochelike dough and will need 3 to 4 tablespoons flour on the work surface when you work it. It will be sticky, so flour the surface well and use a dough scraper to handle the dough initially. You may shape the dough into 2 free-form rounds or as 2 ring-shaped breads and set them on parchment-lined baking sheets. Although it is not traditional, you can make 2 loaf shapes and set them in greased 9- by 5-inch low-sided glass baking pans. Cover with towels and let rise until doubled, 1½ to 2 hours.

GLAZE

1 egg, beaten

1 to 2 tablespoons turbinado sugar

(continued)

Baking. Heat the oven to 400°F. Just before setting the loaves in the oven, brush the tops with the egg and sprinkle with sugar. Bake 10 minutes, then turn the oven down to 350°F and continue baking until the loaves are done, about 25 minutes. Cool on racks. If you baked the bread in loaf pans, turn out immediately onto a rack.

Cannoli

Cannoli with a Creamy Ricotta Filling

Forget all those heavy cannoli, dotted with a maraschino cherry at each end, that line the shelves of Italian bakeries in America. Cannoli made in Sicily are filled to order, and the creamy interior sings with the flavor of sheep's milk ricotta, almost custardy in texture and slightly spritzy in taste. With very few exceptions—Paula Lambert of the Mozzarella Factory in Dallas, Texas, has a small production of ricotta di pecora—even the best ricotta in America starts with cow's milk so the taste just isn't the same. In adding a little fresh goat cheese to fresh cow's milk ricotta, I am following the excellent invention of Nicholas Malgieri, a teacher and cookbook writer.

Cannoli are such an essential part of the Carnival celebration that families in Palermo used to send no fewer than a dozen to friends and relatives. The cannoli in this recipe are modeled on those made by Costanzo Corrado, an extraordinary pastrymaker in the baroque Sicilian city of Noto. His secrets include making an extremely light pastry shell by rolling the pastry dough to 1/32 inch, slightly thinner than a shirt cardboard, and by sieving the ricotta mixture not once but twice. He makes so many cannoli that he uses a special machine for sieving the ricotta, although such an exotic piece of equipment is not necessary for this recipe. Most kitchenware stores sell the metal cannoli tubes needed to make the pastry shells.

Makes about 2 dozen cannoli

RICOTTA FILLING

2 pounds 2 ounces (1 kilogram) freshest ricotta cheese
About 3 ounces (75 grams) fresh mild goat cheese, optional
½ teaspoon cinnamon
¾ to 1 cup (150 to 200 grams) confectioners' sugar (use the smaller amount if you omit the goat cheese)
½ cup (75 grams) finely chopped candied orange peel
2 ounces (55 grams) semisweet chocolate, chopped fine
Chopped pistachio nuts
Confectioners' sugar

Press the ricotta through a sieve or whirl in a food processor with the steel blade until smooth. Beat in the goat cheese and cinnamon. Sift in the confectioners' sugar and mix until smooth. Refrigerate at least 2 hours or up to 24 hours.

CANNOLI SHELLS

1¾ cup plus 2 tablespoons (250 grams) unbleached all-purpose flour
1 tablespoon sugar
Pinch salt
1 tablespoon plus 1 teaspoon (20 grams) lard
7 to 8 tablespoons Marsala or white wine
1½ quarts vegetable oil for frying

In a large bowl or the bowl of an electric mixer, mix together the flour, sugar, and salt. Cut in the lard and slowly add the wine until the mixture comes together and is no longer dry, although it may be a bit dimpled and lumpy. Be especially careful not to get the dough too wet. Gather into a ball and knead on a lightly floured surface until the dough is smooth, about 2 minutes.

Shaping. To roll the dough to ¹⁄₃₂ inch, you can use a rolling pin, but it is much easier to use a pasta machine. Cut the dough into 4 pieces and cover the ones that you are not working on with a towel. Flour each piece, flatten it, and run it through the pasta machine with the rollers set at the widest opening. Dust the dough lightly with flour, fold it in thirds like a business letter, and pass it through the machine again at the same position until the dough is finally smooth and elastic, about a dozen times. Gather into a ball, set it on a lightly floured surface, cover with a towel, and repeat with the other pieces of dough. Let the dough rest 1 to 2 hours.

To roll the dough to its ultimate fineness, take each ball, dust it lightly with flour, and roll it once again through the pasta machine with the rollers set at the widest position. Now begin decreasing the width of the rollers, so that the dough becomes progressively finer, until you reach the second narrowest setting; if that seems just too difficult, the third narrowest setting is acceptable. Set each ribbon of dough on a lightly floured work surface and using a 4-inch round cookie cutter, cut out circles. Save the scraps, reroll, and cut them in 4-inch rounds. Roll each circle out to a slightly thinner and larger oval, about 5 to 6 inches.

Center a cannoli form lengthwise on a disk of dough, roll one end of the dough over the top of the tube, lightly brush the far edge of the dough with water, and gently roll up so the edges overlap. Press lightly to create

(continued)

a good seal so the shell won't open during the frying. Repeat with the other disks.

Frying. While you are rolling the dough on the cannoli tubes, set the oil in a deep Dutch oven or heavy saucepan and start heating it to about 375°F. You probably won't have enough tubes for all the dough you have made, so you can fry the cannoli shells a batch at a time. That way the tubes will have time to cool briefly and be ready for use again. Do not wash the tubes; just wipe them off and use them again.

Gently lower no more than 3 or 4 shells into the hot oil, being very careful not to crowd them. They will puff up and turn golden brown in about 3 minutes. Pick them up with the tongs, allowing any excess oil to drain back into the pan, and set them on a platter lined with absorbent paper. Let them cool briefly, then very carefully remove the cannoli shells by grasping one end of the tube with a potholder or wooden tongs (be careful, they are very hot!) and use the potholder or a towel to hold the pastry and gently work the tube loose. Finish frying the other shells and let them cool to room temperature.

Assembly. About 20 to 30 minutes before you plan to use it, take the filling out of the refrigerator, sieve it again by hand or in the food processor, and stir in the candied orange peel and chocolate chips. Scoop the filling into a pastry bag fitted with a ½-inch plain tip. Pipe the filling into each end of the cannoli shell. Finish by sprinkling a little of the chopped pistachio nuts at each end and dusting a little confectioners' sugar over the top. Serve immediately. Until you eat one, you can't believe how wonderful freshly made cannoli can taste!

Cannoli shells keep in an airtight container for 2 to 3 days and freeze well.

VENERDÌ GNOCCOLAR

GNOCCHI BACCHANALIA
IN VERONA
Last Friday of Carnival

Baccanale dei Gnocci, nineteenth-century engraving, Raccolta Bertarelli, Milan

*G*nocchi Friday in Verona is also known as the bacchanalia of gnocchi, and doesn't that conjure up visions of a gargantuan feast with mountains of gnocchi and wine flowing freely through streets and piazze? Not long ago voices shouting out, *"Gnocchi, gnocchi, gnocchi,"* called to people all over the city and brought them running to great bubbling cauldrons on the square in front of the church of San Zeno, where they would wait for huge spoonfuls of gnocchi to be heaped high on their plates. These days the celebration is quite a bit tamer, and the only racing through the streets is a well-organized procession. If there is more bacchanalia than gnocchi, it is simply because the gnocchi are in rather scarce supply. The event has become a parade that goes on for two full hours during which seventy-five floats pass by, interspersed with bands and drum majorettes from a variety of northern Italian cities. Il Papa del Gnocco, the Pope of Gnocchi, is king for the day as he parades through Verona in his red and white suit—white for the gnocchi and red for the sauce—his scepter an oversized fork on which is impaled a single enormous gnocco. The floats are full of references to various local foods: one is dedicated to pastissada di caval, the sauce of the city; another to herring, the traditional Lenten dish; others to strawberries and local wines; and one to the delicious little fish from the Oglio and Adige rivers. The gnocchi themselves are actually served in the beautiful piazza at a stand that also offers sausages and polenta with herring.

Clearly the celebration has fallen off from the legendary event on the

Piazza San Zeno in 1530 when Tommaso da Vico, a local doctor, is said to have made gnocchi for the entire city. At that time the people of Verona were caught in the war between the French, Spanish, and Germans, who were carving up the country, leaving thousands to starve. Da Vico decided to divert the beleaguered Veronese, and on Friday before Carnivale, he distributed thousands of gnocchi. They were made entirely of flour and water; Columbus hadn't returned from America bearing the potatoes with which everyone makes gnocchi today. To make the sauce, Da Vico butchered a few horses, and made the ragù known as *pastissada*. To this day it is a specialty of the city. The Veronese speak of it with real enthusiasm and offer the recipe without the slightest provocation. Fortunately the gnocchi are also served with butter, sage leaves, and handfuls of Parmesan cheese, so tradition can be accommodated without having to eat horsemeat.

Local lore has it that the *festa* was started to calm the people by feeding them gnocchi on an epic scale, but the spectacle is clearly a Carnival event with all its inflections of abundance and overeating. With a fork big enough for a giant, Papa Gnocco is the masked figure of Verona—as Gianduja is Turin's and Pulcinella is Venice's—and a joky invocation of fertility and the abundance of nature. A Falstaffian figure, who looks like a big gnocco himself, he is dressed in a bright jacket the color of steamy red sauce. Mounted on a donkey, he was for years a sort of Sancho Panza figure, although these days he looks more and more like Santa Claus. His sidekick Bacchus turns up wearing a tunic the color of pressed grapes with a crown of vine leaves askew in his hair and he showers the assembled crowd with candies just as he must once have freely poured wine.

As the parade snakes its way through medieval Verona to the square in front of San Zeno, one of the most beautiful churches in all of Italy, people follow, ready to plunge into a *scorpacciata*, a big eating blowout before the restraint of Lent is imposed. Or at least that was once the case. Tommaso da Vico didn't really make those first gnocchi in the sixteenth century, nor did he finance the festival from a bequest, although he has become the famed progenitor and gnocchi have always been the symbol of the festival. In the nineteenth century, gnocchi were given out free in the piazza, after a long procession of floats sponsored by various arts and trades paraded through the city. Among the floats was a cart of abundance pulled by white bulls from which breads were thrown, followed by another one showing the making, cooking, and preparation of gnocchi, which were then served with great amounts of wine. Many of the carts had some connection with eating, and from most of them various kinds of food were launched into the assembled crowds: oranges, dried figs, breads, colored hard-boiled eggs, cheese, meats, cookies, even live pigeons. In some years the floats were full of political satire. In others, when finances didn't permit, there was no bacchanalia at all. The current parade is slightly kitschy, and the ceremony and its food small and intimate, since it belongs to the neighborhood of San Zeno where it takes place. But no matter what, tradition requires that there be gnocchi on every table in Verona on Venerdì Gnoccolar, the Friday before Carnival's end.

Gnocchi

*Eating Maccheroni, by
Tifi Odasi, 1521, Venice*

Although there are at least a dozen kinds of gnocchi in Italy, those of Verona are famous for being especially delicious. Perhaps it is because the Veronese invented this particularly delicate mixture of potatoes and flour and have a special skill in making them, or perhaps the gnocchi evoke memories of the platterfuls that used to be served free at Carnivaltime to the entire city. Like so many dishes based on the simple ingredients of the poor, gnocchi were originally made only with flour and water and perhaps with some leftover bread crumbs. Potatoes weren't even eaten in Italy before the eighteenth century. Though pasta was called *maccheroni*, the dough was treated just like gnocchi; it was rolled in long logs and cut into small pieces that were shaped by being pressed against the front of a grater and rolled against the thumb.

All traditional recipes for gnocchi in Verona start by boiling the potatoes, but when Vincenzo Corrado in 1801 added a whole section to his book *Il cuoco gallante* (*The Gallant Cook*) that included gnocchi, he chose to bake the potatoes. I learned to do this from a wonderful Tuscan woman in San Francisco and strongly recommend that you do too, so the potatoes don't absorb so much flour that they become gummy. The traditional Veronese gnocchi recipe uses an egg, although incredibly light gnocchi can also be made leaving it out. The trick of making delicate gnocchi (with or without egg) is adding as little flour as possible. I have the greatest success when I mix in only a cup of flour, but if that seems too little to keep the dough together, use a bit more.

Makes about 12 dozen gnocchi, enough for 4 to 6 servings

2¼ pounds (1 kilogram) baking potatoes (about 4 large)
1 teaspoon salt
1 egg
1 to 1½ cups (135 to 200 grams) all-purpose flour
10 cups water

(continued)

S A U C E

8 to 10 tablespoons (100 to 125 grams) unsalted butter
A few fresh sage leaves, torn

1 cup (100 grams) freshly grated Parmesan cheese

Bake the potatoes until the point of a knife enters them easily. Cool the potatoes, peel them while they are still warm, and rice them into a large bowl. Mix in the salt, the egg, and as little flour as possible to make a soft, smooth, consistent mixture. Roll out into logs about the width of a finger and cut into ¾ to 1-inch segments. To get the characteristic shape of gnocchi, hold them between thumb and forefinger and roll them lightly and quickly against the front of a hand-held grater.

Bring 10 cups water to the boil in a large pot and cook the gnocchi until they rise to the top, 1 to 3 minutes. Meanwhile, melt the butter in a small heavy saucepan, and wilt the sage leaves in it briefly. Remove the gnocchi with a slotted spoon, drain, and serve immediately with the sage and butter sauce. Pass the Parmesan cheese at table to sprinkle on top.

The gnocco, copper engraving by Giacomo Vittorelli, from Rime, *1784, Bassano*

POLENTATA

POLENTA CELEBRATION IN TOSSIGNANO

Last Tuesday of Carnival

*I*t is easy to be enthusiastic about the excesses of Carnival when they include a meal of creamy polenta pasticciata. The tiny village of Tossignano in Emilia-Romagna is not secretive about its famous specialty, so it is no wonder that cars full of people determined to attend this gargantuan feast loop up the winding road carved out of a chalky cliff. More than a dozen expert cooks wearing yellow jackets, floppy berets, and white gloves hover over copper cauldrons lined up in the center of a big outdoor piazza. Set over roaring wood fires, the pots are filled with water that must boil energetically before the cooks sift in 440 pounds of polenta. The fires roar and shimmer with dizzying heat, but that doesn't deter the cooks from stirring with wooden paddles the size of an oar. They trace huge circles in the golden mass, stirring continuously for thirty minutes or even more in the same direction so the polenta will be smooth and free of lumps. There is enough polenta to feed the entire town several times, and of course the town population does show up several times during the course of the day. The cooking begins just after early morning mass, and the first plates are ready to be served just around noontime.

Distributing the polenta is no easy task. The crowd gets progressively thicker as the aroma swirls out into the air. A town band plays music with big banging drums and tootling horns, there are martial tunes and celebratory music, and there is even music for dancing. As each cauldron is ready, the chefs hoist it onto their shoulders and pour out the polenta, like an enormous lake, onto a table the size of a barn door. They smooth out concentric circles of ripples with their paddles, then cut the polenta into slices, which they lay in the bottom of an enormous wooden drawer that is lined with metal to keep in the heat. This is no ordinary baking or serving dish! The drawer looks as if it had been pulled out of a giant's dresser. On top of the layer of polenta goes a thick wash of ragù sauce made in the dainty quantities of 220 pounds of sausage, 66 pounds of ground beef, 44 pounds of pancetta, and 55 pounds of Parmesan cheese, previously grated. Many hands quickly assemble the polenta pasticciata like a enormous lasagne by adding another layer of polenta and sauce and strewing handfuls of Parmesan cheese over all.

No one goes hungry today, although famine occasioned the original polentata in 1622, when Tossignano was the capital of a feudal state that extended to Imola ten miles away. In that year, when war created great shortages and left people hungry, Mastroantonio da Farneto, the duke of Alternis, gave orders that there be polenta and wine in abundance served in the piazza on the last day of Carnival. The government opened the storehouse where the supplies were kept and made certain that there was enough polenta to feed the entire town. The event has taken place ever since, save for a very few interruptions during subsequent wartimes. Otherwise, everyone can fill himself up on portions of the creamy polenta, served on special ceramic plates made with a different design each year in faience-famous Imola.

People used to open their doors and offer wine to friends and foreigners alike, and the town held sack and donkey races, there was a greasy pole to climb for a prize, and even some sort of conveyance pulled by a goose. It was certainly very friendly when I was there, but there wasn't an open door that I was aware of, the old entertainments had disappeared, and while I heard about another polentata where special visitors and guests were presented with one of the gigantic stirring paddles, I think that the cooks held on to their wooden spoons. To find games you must drive to Borgo Tossignano at the bottom of the hill, where a maccheroni *sagra* that happens simultaneously has been going on since 1900.

The people in Borgo had to get permission to start their *sagra* from the mayor of Imola because they knew what the authorities of Tossignano would say to their cries of *Viva i maccheroni! Abbasso la polenta!* (Long live pasta! Down with polenta!). The streets of the town are full of fairway games like bumper cars and target-shooting. The place is a great deal more crowded than the smaller *sagra* at the top of the hill, and the food is harder to find. More than 4,000 pounds of cooked pasta are sauced with a mixture of beef, sausage, and creamy white back bacon, and served under a blizzard of 330 pounds of grated Parmesan cheese, but for pure pleasure and a purer festival, the top of the hill is the feast to see.

Polenta, from popular Milanese print of 1860, Raccolta Bertarelli, Milan

Ragù

~~~~~~~~~~~~~~~~~~~~~~~~~~~~~~~~

A Bold Ragù from
Tossignano's
Polenta Festival

Makes 8 servings

1 small carrot, finely chopped
1 small onion, finely chopped
1 small rib celery, finely chopped
4 to 5 tablespoons olive oil
1 small clove garlic, minced
1 pound 2 ounces (500 grams) pork sausage
⅓ pound (150 grams) lean ground beef
6½ ounces (200 grams) pancetta, diced
Salt and pepper
Gratings of nutmeg
½ cup red wine
Scant ½ cup tomato paste dissolved in ½ cup warm water
2 tablespoons finely chopped parsley
1 cup chopped Italian plum tomatoes
Optional: ½ to 1 ounce (15 to 30 grams) dried porcini, soaked in warm
    water at least ½ hour, drained, and chopped
Salt and pepper

Sauté the carrot, onion, and celery in 4 tablespoons olive oil until the onion is golden and lightly transparent. Add the minced garlic clove and warm it in the oil briefly, never allowing it to brown or burn. Add a little more olive oil if necessary and brown the sausage meat, ground beef, and pancetta over medium heat. Season with salt, pepper, and a few gratings of fresh nutmeg. You will need to tilt the pan and press down with a spoon to help drain off the fat. Use a bulb baster or carefully pour off the accumulated fat. Pour in the wine and cook until it evaporates. Add the tomato paste dissolved in water, the parsley, tomatoes, and porcini if using; cook about 30 minutes over a moderate flame, adding a little water if the sauce gets too thick.

Polenta Pasticciata

////////////////////////////////

Layered Polenta Pie

Creamy polenta is layered like lasagne with a rich, full-flavored ragù sauce.

Makes 8 servings

P O L E N T A

Follow the recipe on page 357, using 6 cups water and 2 cups (300 grams) polenta. Turn the polenta out onto a marble surface and spread it with a wet spatula to a ½ inch thickness. Let it cool while you prepare the sauce. Prepare the ragù on page 375.

1 cup (100 grams) Parmesan cheese

Cut the polenta into pieces 4 inches long and 3 inches wide. Butter a wide shallow flameproof dish. On top of a layer of polenta spread some ragù and follow with 2 more layers of polenta and ragù. Finish by sprinkling the Parmesan cheese over the top. Set in a 375°F oven until the crust is golden and bubbly, 25 to 30 minutes.

Polenta, engraving, from Quattro elegantissime Eloghe Rusticali, *1760, Venice*

PRANZO DEL PURGATORIO

ASH WEDNESDAY PURGATORIAL
LUNCH IN GRADOLI

*C*ome to Gradoli, a tiny town near Lake Bolsena reached over a winding back road from Orvieto, and discover a gigantic feast that celebrates the beginning of Lent. Never mind that Ash Wednesday is the first day of abstinence, when everyone is supposed to pare back on the pleasures of the flesh and get along without meat, eggs, or any of the delicious dairy products that grace the Italian table. During the period called Quaresima, from the Italian word for forty, the number of days Christ wandered in the wilderness, people are supposed to grow in spiritual strength through the hard work of renunciation. Even if the Church no longer requires strict fasting, and renunciation mainly means giving up meat, it still seems extraordinary that Gradoli celebrates with six abundant and tasty fish courses that pour one after another out of the kitchen and onto the tables for almost two thousand people. This is the annual Pranzo del Purgatorio, an expiatory lunch that has been held in the town for five or six hundred years.

What began all those centuries ago as a ritual feast, bringing together members of a confraternity in memory of the souls of the dead, is now an enormous blowout cooked entirely by the men of the very same religious group. Its members do good works in the town of Gradoli, and, with an organization worthy of the military, they put together a banquet for 3,000 lire, a bit more than $2.50 per person, based entirely on fish. For it they have fished quantities of tiny tench and almost a ton of *luccio*, pike, from the waters of nearby Lake Bolsena. They use 660 pounds of baccalà, 220 pounds of rice, and twice that amount of silky-skinned puntassoli beans, soaked, cooked, and served with lots of pepper and very good green extra-virgin olive oil.

They arrive at five in the morning of Ash Wednesday to start the fires for cooking, warming the cold stone rooms for the people who clean fish, chop vegetables, and make elaborate and complicated stocks and sauces. In one room cauldrons are set in a circle over burning stacks of wood, and as the cooking proceeds, the space heats up to such temperatures that the chefs, in shorts and goggles, look like creatures out of a circle of Dante's Hell; the Pranzo del Purgatorio is cooked in heat worthy of the Inferno.

Drumrolls reverberate under the vast tin roof at noontime, calling the hungry celebrants to eat at tables extending the entire length of the barnlike space that serves as the *cantina* and wholesale fruit and vegetable market the rest of the year. While the pots bubble in the impromptu kitchen, young boys serve forth the lunch to the assembled multitudes. Many of the guests come from Gradoli and its countryside, so they know to bring their own knives and forks and glasses, their own wine, and even their own bread. The same rules applied when the *pranzo* originally took place in the Palazzo Farnese with its Sangallo frescoes and its handsome light-washed rooms. Then it was an occasion for neighbors to offer each other bread and wine, the elemental foods of life, as well as a way to make up quarrels. Angry disputes and furious rifts were commonplace in a time when resources were limited and disappointments and jealousies flourished easily. During the recent refurbishment of the palazzo, architects discovered that the Farnese disposed of their enemies by tossing them into a great hole that fed into channels carved in the earth and filled with water. The hole now contains an elevator, but arguments and altercations are still part of daily life in Gradoli, and the Pranzo del Purgatorio remains an opportunity to patch them up. Many neighbors break bread with estranged friends and pour wine that they have brought from their homes. Only two tables set for guests provide the normal impedimenta of silver and glassware as well as wine for the meal.

And what a meal it is! It begins with an extraordinary and slightly spicy fish soup first made by the Etruscans. By the time it was known to the Romans it was called *iusculum* by Tacitus, and Cato referred to the soup as *iuscumme*. By any name it is extraordinary, based on fish broth with the addition of a number of secret flavorful ingredients such as fish eggs, peperoncini, anchovies, and tuna. It is made only in Gradoli, and after watching the complicated proceedings, I could understand why. Not only are pike and tench cooked separately, sieved, and simmered but they are added to finely diced vegetables along with wine, tomato paste, an-

Fish tub, from Bartolomeo Scappi, Opera, 1625

chovies, and tuna. Rice is cooked in the usual way and added to produce a piquant soup with amazing taste.

It is hard to understand how food for eighteen hundred people can be so delicious, but the cooks in the makeshift kitchen, with its gigantic pots simmering over great bundles of wood, produce splendid dishes like pesce in umido, pike cooked in broth and served in a creamy concentrated sauce. First garlands of garlic cloves are braided into whole ribs of celery, and the two are then sautéed together. Parsley, olive oil, a bit of anchovy, and tomato paste are added, along with a splash of sauce from the fish soup.

Next come fried fish from the sea, cooked to delicate perfection, and even the final dish, the baccalà in bianco, is delicious. I admired the ingenuity of the cooks who soaked the dried fish right in their wooden packing crates, leaving them to soften for three full days and nights with numerous refreshings of water. I was astonished to see them carefully lower the baccalà, still in crates, into the simmering water. After a few minutes, they hoisted crate after crate out of the water, twisted off the metal fastenings, and pulled out perfectly cooked baccalà. To finish the dish, they added a lot of garlic, green extra-virgin olive oil, Italian parsley, and freshly ground pepper before serving them to the multitudes.

Of course, wine flowed freely, and at the end of the long lunch, whole groups of men broke into song, swaying slightly as they sang verse after verse. They began to wander around the huge space, searching out friends and hugging them, reminiscing. According to stories I heard, people used to drink a great deal more, sing many more songs, and stay long past the afternoon and into the evening. Even so, it was almost five by the time I had drunk my last toast with the mayor of Gradoli and with my host, who presented me a bottle of local Aleatico wine as a souvenir. The young foot soldiers in the confraternity who waited tables looked very tired, the chefs removed the goggles that they had worn to cook the purgatorial lunch, and a new crew arrived to attend to stacks and stacks of pots and cooking pans. And the chefs? They could look forward to the special confraternity dinner on the next day. Would it be a reprise of the dazzling array of fish specialties? Absolutely not. This may be Lent, but these chefs and the members of the hardworking confraternity could all sit down to a meal of lamb.

The feast is a reward for all their hard work that began the previous week with a fund-raising questua dei Incappucciati. Members of their brotherhood, wearing their black hoods, knocked on all the doors in town, asking for money or contributions. Most people donated money, although some gave what they had on hand in oil, wine, liquor, sausages, or cheese that could be used in the lunch or sold at auction that very afternoon.

The butcher donated a lamb and the florist gave flowers. Once the funding is in place, it takes the men a week just to clean the market and turn it into the dining room where lunch is served.

Food and feasting seem to be the point of the Ash Wednesday celebration. There are no announcements, no prayers, no songs, no words from civic or church officials about Ash Wednesday or the history of the feast. It is assumed that everyone knows it is time for a gargantuan meal.

The city itself is surrounded by fields of bright green wheat, by plots of silvery gray olive trees, and by soft hills sculpted with grapevines. It is not unusual to meet shepherds in blue jeans herding their flocks over this lovely landscape, many with baby lambs that are undoubtedly destined to become the centerpiece of Easter, a mere forty days away. The sheep may be sacrificed for that great meal, but on Ash Wednesday, the penitential day par excellence, everyone in Gradoli partakes of great bowls and platters of fish whose very plenty makes a delicious contradiction of penitence.

Minestra di Tinca

Fish Soup

This piquant fish and rice soup with its silky broth may have Etruscan beginnings, but it is now made only in Gradoli near Lake Bolsena, from which tench and pike are fished. Tench—*tinca* in Italian—apparently doesn't exist in America, but carp is a fine substitute. Even so, it is not always easy to find pike and carp. I get my fish from an Asian fish market that has silver carp swimming in tanks. When pike isn't available, white bass would be an excellent substitute, with halibut as an acceptable second choice. Ask for carp with roe; the eggs add an excellent flavor to the dish.

The recipe looks daunting, but the two fish broths are made exactly the same way. Once the broths are cooked and sieved, they are combined with anchovy, tuna, and red pepper flakes and rice is stirred in at the end. It takes a bit of planning, but when you are finished, you will have a whole dinner, since you can use the pike that isn't part of the broth in luccio in umido, a flavorful and wonderfully moist braised fish.

Makes 6 servings; the recipe doubles easily

PIKE BROTH

6 tablespoons olive oil
2 onions, chopped
3 cloves garlic, minced
1½ carrots, minced
2 ribs celery, minced

3 tablespoons minced flat-leaf parsley
Heads of 4 pike
½ cup dry white wine
¼ cup tomato paste
5 to 6 cups water

CARP BROTH

¼ cup olive oil
2 onions, chopped
3 cloves garlic, finely minced
1½ carrots, diced
2 ribs celery, diced
3 tablespoons minced flat-leaf parsley
1 whole carp or 2 silver carp (about 4 pounds, 1¾ kilograms), cleaned
   and cut into 4 pieces (reserve the egg sacs if there are any)
½ cup dry white wine
¼ cup tomato paste
3 to 4 cups water
1 tablespoon canned tuna fish
1 tablespoon anchovy paste
1 peperoncino (dried red chile), finely chopped
Salt and pepper

RICE

About 5 cups water
3 tablespoons olive oil
1 medium onion, finely chopped
2 cups rice, preferably Arborio or Carnaroli
Coarse salt

To make the pike broth, heat the oil in a deep casserole over medium heat. When it is warm, add the chopped vegetables and sauté until the mixture is soft and the onion translucent, about 10 minutes. Add the pike heads, pour in the white wine, and cook until the wine has evaporated. Stir in the tomato paste and enough water to cover the fish entirely, about 4 cups. Cook over low heat 1 hour, then add another 1 to 2 cups water and cook another 45 minutes to 1 hour.

While the pike broth is cooking, start the carp broth. Heat the oil in a deep casserole over medium heat. When it is warm, add the chopped vegetables and sauté until the mixture is soft and the onion translucent, about 10 minutes. Add the carp and sauté over medium heat until the skin is lightly golden, about 10 minutes. Pour in the white wine and cook until it has evaporated. Stir in the tomato paste, the roe if you have it,

(continued)

and enough water to cover the fish entirely. Cook over medium-low heat until the fish crumbles easily into little pieces, 20 to 30 minutes. Remove from the heat. When the pieces of fish are cool enough to handle, strain the broth to separate it from the fish and vegetable mixture. Press the fish mixture through a sieve into a clean bowl, checking constantly that the carp bones do not get through the fine mesh of the sieve. Add the sieved fish, the tuna, anchovy paste, and peperoncino to the broth. As the broth cools, skim off any oil that comes to the top.

About 25 minutes before you plan to serve the soup, bring the water for the rice to a boil. Heat the olive oil in a deep saucepan and sauté the onion until it is pale and translucent. Stir in the rice, being sure that the grains are coated with the oil. Add the water and cook until the rice is al dente, about 16 minutes. Meanwhile, combine the soup broths and bring to a low simmer, stir in the rice, add salt and pepper, and taste carefully to be sure that the soup is slightly hot and peppery.

Fish, twentieth-century photocomposition, from La Gola

Luccio in Umido

Braised Pike

In Gradoli where this dish is made for eighteen hundred people and still manages to taste delicious, the pike is braised in gigantic cauldrons and served not only with its own sauce but with a dollop of extra broth from the fish soup, which has boiled down to a deep concentrate.

Makes 6 servings

6 tablespoons olive oil
3 cloves garlic, minced
¼ cup minced flat-leaf parsley
½ cup white wine
¼ cup tomato paste, preferably double concentrate
1 or 2 pike (about 5 pounds, 2¼ kilograms, total) or 4 whole lake bass, scaled, gutted, rinsed in cold water, and sliced
Salt and pepper
About 2 cups water
Optional: about 6 tablespoons concentrated broth from the Minestra di Tinca (page 380)

Choose a sauté pan that can accommodate all the fish slices in a single layer. Heat the olive oil over medium-low heat and warm the garlic until it is a light golden color, being sure that it does not burn. Add the parsley, stir once or twice, add the white wine, and cook for a few minutes. Add the tomato paste and cook 5 to 6 minutes, stirring briefly from time to time. Add the slices of fish in a single layer. Add salt and pepper and enough water to cover the fish. Turn the heat down to medium-low and cook about 5 minutes. Turn the fish over and cook another 5 minutes or until the slices are done. Serve with the juices from the pan and a bit of concentrated sauce from the minestra, if you have it.

QUARESIMA

LENT

$\mathscr{T}$he Church was serious about Lent: Anyone who ate meat during the designated days was kept from communion at Easter by decree of the Council of Toledo in 653. Charlemagne actually condemned such miscreants to death. Even so, if Lent hadn't existed, they would have had to invent it. Until relatively recent times, food supplies were at an all-time low at this time of year. Winter provisions were exhausted and the harvest was far off. The lambs still grazing in the fields were far too tiny to be eaten. The pigs had all been slaughtered, and what hadn't been eaten fresh had been preserved as prosciutto, salame, and sausage. What was left in the winter larder was mostly pasta, dried beans, and such salted fish as herring and anchovies. Even sweets had to be made without eggs or lard, but no matter: Italian ingenuity dreamed up sweets called *maritozzi romani*, buns bursting with raisins; *quaresimali* and *tozzetti*, glossy nut-studded biscotti cooked to a crunchy bite; *pan di ramerino*, rosemary-scented sweet rolls from Florence; *corollo*, a little anise-flavored bread made in Tuscany; and *pazientini*, cookies whose name means "little bits of patience," which is just what one needs at Lent.

Although abstinence is the theme of Lent, a profusion of special meals and events thread through the season. In Udine Ash Wednesday was like a continuation of Carnival. In the afternoon everyone used to go to the town of Vat in the nearby countryside and toss oranges along the street. They bought walnuts and dried chestnuts from vendors in the open green fields, and ate salad in the *osterie*, where they also drank lots of wine and feasted on herring plump with eggs, since they had been fished during spawning season. The Carnival of Borgosesia, near the rice center of Vercelli, keeps going right through Wednesday. It isn't enough to have eaten quantities of buseca, tripe with local greens, or to have tossed numerous mandarin oranges at each other, so the people in town just keep on celebrating through Mercu Scurot, Wednesday Obscured, a day that undoubtedly gets its name from all the drinking that has gone on before. It isn't until Thursday that anyone gets around to the ritual meal of salted sardines (although the fact that the sardines are so salty provides a perfect excuse to keep on drinking).

The figure of a fat jolly old man hung with sausages often represents Carnival, but in many parts of Italy a thin, hagridden Old Woman (La Vecchia) is the personification of Lent. In Sardinia she is made out of bread and has seven legs or she appears as a baby with seven fingers, for the seven Sundays of Lent, and as each week passes, a leg or finger is broken off. In Abruzzo La Vecchia is a doll with seven feet or seven black feathers, and each Sunday one of those feet or feathers is snapped off. In Basilicata seven dolls dressed in black are displayed on the piazza, and each Sunday one is snatched away. On the first Sunday of Lent, a game called *pentolaccia* is still played in a few towns in southern Italy. Clay cooking pots full of sweets, dried fruits, chestnuts, and any number of toys and presents are hung out in the piazza and everyone tries to crack them open, loosing an abundant cascade of tasty treats. And once they are empty, what could make fasting more obvious than breaking all the cooking pots?

At times the Old Woman is a puppet reminiscent of the Befana, dark and wrinkled but generous, especially when she is wearing a necklace of dried fruits and chestnuts or when she is filled with raisins, dried figs, dried apples and pears, and cotognata, little rounds of dried quince. Often she is called *Segavecchia* (Saw-the-Old-Lady) because she is literally sawed in half to release the treats she contains.

Fires are lit across Italy at midpoint in Lent, often as a kind of capital punishment for the Old Woman, who may also appear as a witch, gathering in all the cold and sterility of the midwinter period. When La Vecchia is burned in the main piazze of Treviso and Bergamo, it is as if death itself were being killed, and the light and warmth of the fires are meant to encourage the return of life. Sometimes La Vecchia is a dry old tree, as sterile as a witch, which crumbles when it is put into the flames, producing in death the ashes that will nourish the earth and encourage its fruitfulness in spring. Alfredo Cattabiani, a scholar of festivals and their rites, talks of burning Segavecchia as punishment for the gastronomic orgy of Carnival. Lent not only celebrates deprivation—if that is not an oxymoron of sorts—but it tells us about penitence and it reminds us of

Engravings of The Contrast of Carnival and Lent, *1550*

death, all dressed up as La Vecchia, a rite of passage parading as a dark character.

In a few places Ash Wednesday was celebrated with a peculiar rite in which turkeys, not witches, became scapegoats for the sins of the community and everything bad that had occurred during the year. Torre, a tiny village outside Goito, near Mantua, as well as Tonco, near Asti, and Palo del Colle, Bari, all held festivals whose centerpiece could only be called turkey bashing. The people of Torre used to bury the turkey in the sand with only its head left above ground as a clearly visible target. Men on horseback rode toward it at great speed with scythes extended, intent on killing the bird by slicing off its head. Today, in a somewhat more humane version, they hang a dead turkey about six to eight feet up in the air, and the horsemen ride toward it, holding a thick club or sword to sever the turkey's head. Whoever succeeds in doing so wins a (different) turkey. This peculiar event is a startlingly pagan ceremony for Ash Wednesday, but a big crowd shows up to watch. No one eats anything special that day—I imagine they've lost their appetites—but the next week, Lenten food includes a frittata with crayfish, fried local fish, and freshwater pike from the nearby Mincio River served with polenta.

Many of these events used to happen at Mezza Quaresima, halfway through the six weeks of Lent. They provided a break in the long period of abstinence, splitting the period at midpoint, just as sawing the Old Woman cuts her in half. In Florence La Vecchia was a huge wooden doll hung on the face of the loggia in the Mercato Nuovo and sawed in half on the night of Mezza Quaresima, producing a shower of delicacies. It was probably in the early Renaissance that the Romans held a ceremony in the Campo Vaccino, where cattle once fed among the ruins of the Forum. They made a figure of an old woman from rags, filled it with the dried fruits and oranges that were available during Lent, and then proceeded to draw and quarter it. One half of the foods were given to the people in charge of the event and the other half were left for the famished mobs to fight over. The people of Brescia made an enormous Vecchia, filled it with dried fruit, sawed it in half, then participated in a free-for-all when everyone fought over the spoils. This event ended with a contest to see who could eat the most spaghetti in the shortest time; nearby Bergamo served cauldrons of polenta. The tradition lives on in Sant'Ippolito, in the area around Prato, where everyone is served spaghetti with tuna sauce (ingredients and procedure are closely held secrets) for Carnevalino, as the first day of Lent is known in Tuscany. Nearby, Vernio celebrates with polenta made from chestnut flour served with baccalà and roasted herring. Until the middle of the eighteenth century, in Palermo the Old Woman was condemned to death in a public ceremony, transported to the scene of her execution in a huge carriage pulled by oxen, and was attended by members of a confraternity whose heads were covered with large baccalà.

Today the only things on people's heads are the ashes of repentance. And even they are modestly confined to a small cross on the forehead. Many treat the prohibitions of Lent like New Year's resolutions, and give up drinking or eating fattening foods as a gesture toward self-improvement. Some of the special dishes of the period are still cooked only at Lent, but many are available all year long, and deprivation seems to be optional these days.

Quaresimali Toscani

xxxxxxxxxxxxxxxxxxxxxxxxxxxx

Orange-Flavored Chocolate Cookies for Lent

Children in Florence look forward to these chewy chocolate cookies, which are shaped like alphabet letters during Lent.

Makes 21 to 24 alphabet cookies about 3 inches tall

2½ cups (250 grams) confectioners' sugar
¼ cup (30 grams) cocoa
1½ cups (200 grams) unbleached all-purpose flour
Grated zest of 2 oranges
2 teaspoons vanilla extract
4 egg whites

Sift together the sugar, cocoa, and flour. Stir in the orange zest and vanilla. Add the egg whites, beating slowly, either by hand or at the lowest speed on the electric mixer, until the batter is thick and smooth.

Assembly. Butter and flour baking sheets or line them with parchment paper. Spoon the batter into a pastry bag fitted with a ½-inch plain tip. Pipe out the batter in the shape of alphabet letters, about 1½ inches apart although they spread only very slightly.

Baking. Heat the oven to 300°F. Bake the cookies until the tops have set and are slightly cracked but they still feel slightly soft, 10 to 12 minutes.

Croccante Quaresimale

zzzzzzzzzzzzzzzzzzzzzzzzzzzz

Crunchy Hazelnut Cookies for Lent

These authentic Lenten cookies from Umbria are nicknamed *cazzotti quaresimali* (Lenten Punches) because, like biscotti, they are so hard they pack a real punch. Sweet and crunchy with the flavor of hazelnuts—you may choose to make half these cookies chocolate—there's nothing remotely penitential about them.

Makes 24 cookies

Scant 1 cup (120 grams) hazelnuts, toasted and peeled
1 cup (200 grams) granulated sugar
¾ cup (100 grams) unbleached all-purpose flour
3 egg whites, plus 1 tablespoon if needed
⅓ cup (40 grams) unsweetened cocoa powder, optional
Confectioners' sugar
⅓ cup (40 grams) whole peeled hazelnuts

I C I N G

1 tablespoon egg white
3 tablespoons confectioners' sugar, sieved

Grind 1 cup hazelnuts to a powder in a nut grinder or process them with ¼ cup of the granulated sugar to a fine powder in a food processor fitted with the steel blade. Add the remaining granulated sugar and the flour and process until finely ground. Place the nut powder and the egg whites in the food processor or in the bowl of an electric mixer; process or mix until the dough is the consistency of a firm, slightly sticky almond paste.

If you want to make some chocolate cookies, divide the dough in half. To the half in the processor or mixing bowl add the cocoa powder and mix in well. Sift confectioners' sugar over a work surface, keeping a mound of extra sugar nearby, and place the plain dough on it. Knead in half the whole peeled hazelnuts. Although you may be tempted to do the kneading in a machine, don't, because the hazelnuts break up too much. Work the rest of the hazelnuts into the cocoa-flavored dough. The dough should be firm; if it seems sticky, scrape your hands and the table clean and sprinkle both with more confectioners' sugar.

Assembly. Sprinkle the work surface well with confectioners' sugar. Pat each part dough into a fat log about 2 inches wide, about the width of 3 fingers. The trick is to make sure that the dough is firm enough to keep its shape when it bakes, but not so hard that it's inedible. If the dough seems too sticky, add a little extra flour. Flatten the top with your palm and pat out dough until it is 16 to 18 inches long. Be sure to even the edges. I like to use a dough scraper to keep them neat. Do not worry about mistreating the dough when you bang and flatten it because it can take anything. Cut into chunks about 3 inches long. Set on parchment-lined baking sheets. Mix the icing and brush it over the tops. Don't worry if it drips over the edges. Leave uncovered at room temperature about 15 minutes.

Baking. Heat the oven to 325°F. Bake until firm, and in the case of the nonchocolate croccante, lightly golden, about 30 minutes.

Corolli

\\\\\\\\\\\\\\\\\\\\\\\\\\\\\\\\\\

*Anise-Scented
Sweet Bread*

*Prudent Lent, late
seventeenth-century
engraving by Giuseppe
Maria Mitelli*

Tuscans have it easy. They just go to the baker, buy 500 grams of Tuscan bread dough, and bring it home, where they add sweetening and flavors and shape the bread. We have to make the dough from the beginning, although I've combined a couple of steps with no change in the final result. To be authentic, use lard in the dough. If you want, you can divide the dough and make half of it into corolli (remember to put the anise seeds only in the corolli part of the dough) and the other into a loaf of Pan co'Santi (page 232) by mixing 1½ cups (250 grams) raisins and 1¼ cups (125 grams) walnuts into the second piece of dough.

Makes 16 medium sweet bread rings

1¼ teaspoons active dry yeast or ½ cake (9 grams) fresh yeast
1⅓ cups warm water
1¾ cup (400 grams) freshly made or refreshed Natural Yeast Starter or
    Biga (page 32 or page 31)
½ cup (100 grams) sugar
½ cup (100 grams) lard or unsalted butter, room temperature
3¾ cups (500 grams) unbleached all-purpose flour
⅛ teaspoon salt
1½ teaspoons (8 grams) anise seeds
1 egg yolk, beaten

By Hand. Stir the yeast into the water in a large mixing bowl; let stand until creamy, about 10 minutes. Stir in the starter, sugar, and lard and mix until the starter is broken up. Add the flour, salt, and anise and stir until the dough comes together. Knead on a lightly floured surface until soft and slightly sticky but elastic.

By Mixer. Stir the yeast into the water in a mixer bowl; let stand until creamy, about 10 minutes. Add the starter, sugar, and lard and mix with the paddle until the starter is broken up. Add the flour, salt, and anise and mix until the dough comes together. You may need to add an extra

(continued)

tablespoon of flour. Change to the dough hook and knead at low speed about 3 to 4 minutes, until the dough is soft, elastic, and slightly sticky.

First Rise. Set the dough in an oiled bowl, cover tightly with plastic wrap, and let rise until doubled, 1 to 1½ hours.

Shaping and Second Rise. The dough is soft, springy, and easy to work with. Flour the work surface and set the dough on it. Divide it into 16 even pieces. Stretch each piece to about a 6-inch rope; the dough is so elastic that it pulls very easily. Join the ends to make a ring, pat the top flat, and pinch the ends together well so that they stay joined. Set on buttered and floured or parchment-lined baking sheets. Let the corolli rise until well puffed, about 1 hour. I've also seen them in the Maremma shaped like fat little bones about 1½ inches wide and 4 to 5 inches long.

Bake. Heat the oven to 400°F. Just before baking, brush each one with beaten egg yolk. Bake on the middle rack of the oven until lightly golden, about 25 minutes.

Quaresimali Romani

Orange and Almond Biscotti

It is hard to imagine why these delicious biscotti flavored with crunchy almonds and sweet candied orange peel should be considered penitential eating, but they are reserved for Lent in Rome.

Makes about 3 dozen bars

7 tablespoons (100 grams) unsalted butter, room temperature
½ cup plus 2 tablespoons (125 grams) sugar
1 egg
2 egg yolks
½ teaspoon vanilla extract
1 scant cup (125 grams) unbleached all-purpose flour
1 teaspoon cinnamon
1 teaspoon baking powder
¼ teaspoon salt
1 cup (125 grams) almonds, toasted and roughly chopped
About ½ cup (75 grams) finely chopped candied orange peel
Grated zest of 1 orange

Cream the butter and sugar in a mixer bowl until light and fluffy. Beat in the egg, one of the egg yolks, and the vanilla. Sift the flour, cinnamon, baking powder, and salt over the mixture, sprinkle with the nuts, candied orange, and orange zest, and gently fold in. If the dough seems too soft to shape, cover and refrigerate 1 to 1½ hours.

Shaping. Transfer the dough to a lightly floured surface and roll into a 12- by 10-inch rectangle. Roll up the dough on a rolling pin and unroll it on a buttered and floured or parchment-lined sheet. Repair any tears with your fingers. This is very forgiving dough. Beat the remaining egg yolk and brush over the dough. With the tines of a fork make a pattern of serpentine squiggles.

Baking. Heat the oven to 375°F. Bake until shiny and blond but not golden, 10 to 12 minutes. Remove from the oven and reduce the temperature to 325°F. To make these biscotti cut the rectangle diagonally into 2-inch-wide strips, then cut into ¾- to 1-inch long bars, and return them to the oven for another 10 to 15 minutes, until they are golden. Cool on racks.

The Triumph of Lent, oil on canvas by Romeyn de Hoodghe, late eighteenth century

SAN GIUSEPPE

SAINT JOSEPH'S DAY

March 19

*I*t is a long time from January 6, when the Befana sweeps away all the holidays, to March 19 when San Giuseppe brings them back with an orgy of eating in the middle of Lent, just when everyone is ready for some relief. San Giuseppe may be the patron saint of the family (he was Mary's husband, after all), but he also looks after orphans, unwed mothers, the needy and homeless, all the dispossessed who are the underside of family. "Between God, the Madonna, and the saints," the scholar E. Sereni explains, "the Sicilian country has made a hierarchy of sons. Christ is more important than God, Maria is more important than Christ, and San Giuseppe, universal father, more important than all three taken together." An overstatement perhaps, but a definite indication of his status in Sicily. To celebrate his feast day and gather in all the community, families in Sicilian villages fulfill a vow to create an altar and a ritual meal, a *cena di San Giuseppe*, to thank the saint for helping them recover from an illness, escape an accident, or for protecting a family member from some calamity or misfortune. In some villages the entire community is in charge of a single table, while elsewhere an extended family does it all. Whatever occasioned the vow, come March 19, the group must make good on it and provide an enormous banquet for their families, neighbors, and friends. At home the centerpiece is an improvised altar set in a homemade sanctuary. The altar is laid with the finest linens and decorated with bowls of fresh flowers and hundreds of decorative breads in the shape of almost everything in God's creation.

All over Sicily in small villages and larger towns such altars and tables are built and filled with food in prodigious quantities, and while the banquet and ritual celebration may vary from place to place the food always spills out of simple kitchens on dozens of platters. In Borgetto and Salemi, in Sommatino, in Ribera and Valguarnera, women collect ingredients and donations from friends and neighbors, and they prepare tables with an abundance of dishes.

I spent the feast (and never was a term more accurate) of San Giuseppe in Salemi, a hill town in the Belice Valley southwest of Palermo, where glorious breads and foods filled entire tables and decorated homemade sanctuaries. One woman told me, "We make one hundred dishes, or fifty, or even thirty-five," meaning surely that they aim for one hundred, but are content with fewer as long as the tables are overflowing. And because San Giuseppe is the patron saint of pastry cooks, many dishes are sweet. Most important, in Salemi each family sets a table in front of the altar for the *virgineddi,* the little virgins, a girl and two boys chosen to represent Mary, Jesus, and Joseph. At one time the *virgineddi* were three poor children chosen to eat to their heart's desire on this one day of the year, and their principal role was to receive the meal of unbelievable extravagance, but these days, I was told, it is hard to find poor children, so friends and relatives are often selected. In some places the Holy Family is played by an old man, a young orphaned girl, and a boy, sometimes even wearing simple costumes in biblical style. In Salemi the three preadolescents were dressed in nice clothes (Mary wore a sweater with CANNES embroidered on it) and were served a prodigious meal by the father of the household, with some help from his daughters and wife.

The twelve or fourteen Salemi families each began their preparations for a San Giuseppe's table at least two weeks before the event. The banquet occasions major expenditures of cooking and cash, so whoever is doing the table asks friends, neighbors, and family to pitch in. The women make the breads and do the cooking; the men transform a room in the family house or turn part of their garage into a small sanctuary constructed with a latticework that they cover with branches of green myrtle and glossy bay leaves. More branches swoop from the sides to the center of the ceiling, where a special box, garlanded with greens, holds the light that illumines the altar. Onto this framework they hang oranges and lemons and golden breads in the shape of moon and stars, flowers and fruits, birds and baskets. The women first shape the small decorative breads called *le vastedde,* then the panini and other breads served at the meal, and finally the breads called *cuccidatti,* huge devotional rounds for the altar itself.

It takes fifteen women working the equivalent of ten full days to make all the ornamental breads. At the height of the preparation that I observed mothers, grandmothers in black, aunts, cousins, friends, and young women with small children sat at a long, narrow table sculpting the dough with the youngest at one end and the most experienced old women at the other. A couple of women made the dough in the mixer using a tiny bit of homemade yeast and very little salt. Two others kneaded it in long, thick ropes, rolling it back and forth between their hands for as long as two hours to get it as soft and as malleable as clay. The dough is so stiff that in some communities the women stomp on it and knead it with their feet. When it finally reaches the right consistency, it is fed through the widest rollers of a pasta machine several times and then cut into strips. The next contingent of women cuts and shapes the basic dough and decorates it. Their only tools are simple everyday objects: a ravioli cutter with its fluted edge, a paring knife as tiny as a nail file, a plastic thimble, a comb ordinarily used in looming cloth, scissors, needles, and a thin dowel. To make a simple flower they use a fat plastic thimble to cut out small disks of dough; they press each disk on a simple implement that looks like the old-fashioned wooden paddle used to make butter balls to create a series of decorative ridges; they roll out a little stem of dough and dip its tip into sesame seeds; then they set the disks in concentric circles around the stem, building up several layers like little petals.

What else do they create with this cold, hard dough made entirely of the golden *grano duro* wheat of Sicily? Wicker baskets overflowing with flowers, fat pears ripe for the picking, thorny prickly pears, the sun and the moon and the star that showed the way to Bethlehem. Women turn the dough into jasmine flowers, angels sounding trumpets, pods bursting with fava beans, great birds, and a peacock, the symbol of eternity, spreading its impressive tail. There are little roses and fish, and bunches of grapes destined to become wine, the blood of the Savior. The small breads have a handle of dough so they can be hung on the leaf-covered

The Fryer, by Bartolomeo Pinelli, detail of engraving of 1815

latticework like Christmas tree ornaments. Larger breads for the bower enclosing the altar include roosters that let the world know about the birth of Jesus, sheaves of wheat to indicate the abundance of the earth in the springtime, hazelnuts, bouquets and wreaths of flowers, birds making love, and more angels sounding trumpets, some with ridges of chocolate or sesame seeds decorating their gowns and their shoes.

Two expert old women took large lumps of the dough and cut and shaped them into three breads weighing between eight and ten kilos (sixteen to twenty pounds) each. These enormous wreath-shaped ritual breads measure about eighteen inches across. In the past some of the breads were so gigantic that they couldn't be baked in a regular home oven without removing some of the bricks around the oven door. Today they fit handily in bakery or home ovens. The *pane grosso,* big bread, for San Giuseppe is shaped like the saint's staff, which is said to have burst into bloom when he was chosen to be Mary's husband. Mary's is in the shape of a date palm, for it is believed that when she went to Egypt, God made the date palms blossom with fruit. She uttered a little "oh!" when she saw the miracle and that is why the Madonna's mark is a little O, a microscopic dot, inside each pit. The bread for Jesus is a great wreath with an interior in the shape of a star, for he represents the light of truth.

While the two old women rolled and bent and snipped at the dough, turning outside slices into fronds and cutting and shaping it on a large scale, others were making tiny flowers and fruits, animals and angels to ornament the surfaces like appliqué. Still others had begun to shape panini, little golden rounds that would be scored, decorated, and set on the second tier of the altar.

Once the women had finished, they left the breads under blankets and towels for about three hours. I could hardly believe that the dough would actually respond. It had been beaten and thumped, rolled through a pasta machine, and formed into many intricate shapes. It had been sitting at a very cool room temperature for hours without budging a millimeter. But rise it did. After the women removed the heavy cloths, I could see that the dough had puffed. There were bubbles and tears in the little breads that had been decorated with a cross-hatching of cuts. Before baking, each one was brushed with a wash, made from twenty-one eggs combined with the juice of two lemons, and then set in a steaming oven. The loaves more than filled every shelf. A second shift had already formed, with a waiting line of breads carried by the men who were in charge of the public celebration that would be held in the city hall. A thousand people were expected, many brought from neighboring communities on big tour buses.

Each family's altar is decorated on the Saturday before the event. The three enormous breads are set on the first tier: the one for Mary on the right, the one for Joseph on the left, and the one in the center for Jesus. Little ornamental breads connected with each of them hang in the same positions on the frame: Mary is invoked in scissors and in an elaborate script letter M; San Giuseppe in loaves shaped like such carpenter's tools as a saw and pliers, and a long, narrow loaf like his beard. Jesus' breads are shaped as nails, a hammer, the crown of thorns, and the lance used to pierce his side.

On Sunday friends and relatives arrive at each house to view a *mise en scène* of great charm. If the three children playing the roles of the Holy Family represent a kind of *commedia dell'arte,* then the theatrical backdrop is the altar with the enormous breads on the first level; flowers, crystal pitchers of wine, and panini on the second; a monstrance, on the third, the cup for the Host completely decorated in bread; and on the very top a picture of the Holy Family. A colorful throw rug covers the floor on which sit large glass bowls swimming with goldfish, and in front of them, as if she had just stepped out of them, lie the Madonna's slippers rendered in bread, size 36 written freehand in the instep, the upper piece of the slipper attached to the sole with cloves.

Bread may be a metaphor for the magical ritual of mixing grain and water with the wild yeasts of nature to create and sustain life, but it is also a gift, a talisman, and an offering. The shapes of the breads are survivals of ancient agrarian rites and rustic traditions relating to the pre-Christian sun and moon and earth. San Giuseppe is celebrated at the spring solstice, and his day is a feast of bread that invokes the powers of fertility and riches of the earth. It comes at a critical moment when a blast of cold air or a sudden frost could ruin the patient work of many months, so the ostentatious display and excess is meant to appease the capricious powers governing the destiny of the crops.

In Salemi the table of San Giuseppe is a gigantic buffet. The twelve or fourteen families putting on similar lavish *cene* allow their addresses to be printed on circulars distributed all over town and open their doors to anyone who appears. There is no formal table. Everyone mills around, eating at one remove, since the meal is initially intended for the three *virgineddi.* Once the priest has blessed the altar, and once the father and mother of the house have washed the hands of the three by pouring water from a basin, the young people tuck their napkins under their chins and look forward to the task at hand. The boy in the button-down shirt who represents Jesus is thrilled by all the attention he is getting, and Mary, a substantial and self-contained girl, looks up to the challenge of the food on the tables.

Dishes served at the *cene* vary from village to village. In Salemi the first plate is always three orange sections sprinkled with sugar and the last one is pasta con la mollica, spaghetti sauced with garlic, a pinch of sugar, cinnamon, and crumbs grated from the interior of golden Sicilian bread. San Giuseppe isn't the patron saint of children and pastry chefs for nothing; his famous sweet tooth is clearly being indulged. Servings of each dish come in three pieces, for the three members of the Holy Family. In some towns the rule is that each vegetable and fish must be prepared three different ways. In some parts of Sicily legumes are part of the meal, but not in Salemi. Everywhere the message of the opulent display is, see we have so much that we can afford to make more than we need, even to waste it, and certainly to redistribute it.

Between the beginning and end of the meal, an enormous variety of dishes arrives. In truth, one hundred or so dishes tends to be a bit overwhelming not only in concept but in execution. Who can think of so many different things to prepare? The requirement tends to stretch people in *fantasia* as well as finances, so it isn't surprising that among the elegantly decorated platters are some boxes of Italian snack food and candies for children as well as a few commercially produced cakes. There was meat in at least one form at almost every house I visited, either prosciutto mixed in various fillings or slices of ham rolled up as an offering. These are clearly post-Vatican II San Giuseppe meals. Whether one hundred dishes or fifty, it is still an extraordinary achievement.

The three *virgineddi* must eat a bite of every one of them. They each develop a strategy: Joseph has a taste of some artichoke frittata, then puts some on a piece of bread and hands it to a friend who wolfs it down. Mary makes an hors d'oeuvre of each course by putting a bit on some bread before she eats it; the boy representing Jesus spears a piece with his fork, takes a bite, then hands it on to friends. Each dish is served on trenchers made from the small pale golden breads on the second tier of the altar. Even at the end, after a stupefying amount of food has come their way, the three are still at it, although they have piled desserts and leftovers on plates to take home. It looks like Halloween trick-or-treat booty on a scale yet undreamed of in America. All the little decorative breads and much of the food that is left over is given to guests at the end of the day to eat or to keep as souvenirs. Some pieces are eaten days after the festival, or they are saved by the family who organized the celebration.

Once the first dozen dishes have been offered to the *virgineddi*, the women of the house pass whole platters of food to the milling guests as if they were at a giant cocktail party. Here is an abbreviated list of the dishes served:

> *Sarde fritte come sogliole,* sardines fried like sole, marinated in vinegar, then dipped in flour and eggs and fried; *calamari ripieni,* fried calamari, stuffed with garlic, bread crumbs, and parsley; *crocchette di merluzzo fresco bollito,* fried croquettes of fresh cod mixed with besciamella,

Parmesan cheese, and sprinklings of fresh parsley; *baccalà fritto*, bite-sized pieces of fried baccalà; *gamberetti fritti*, fried shrimp with fine slices of lemon; *arancini*, rice croquettes the size of a tennis ball with a filling of fresh spring peas and ragù.

A whole category of vegetables cooked as if they were fish, such as: *Pesci di funghi*, mushrooms dipped first into egg, then into bread crumbs before being fried; *pesce d'uova*, a mixture of bread crumbs, garlic, parsley, and egg shaped to resemble a small fish, then fried; *polpette di finocchio selvatico*, wild fennel boiled, chopped, mixed with garlic, eggs, parsley, and cheese, and formed into little balls the size of a silver dollar.

Stuffed artichokes; stuffed sweet peppers; stuffed tomatoes decorated to look like mushrooms; *frittate* of every early spring vegetable available, such as wild asparagus, cauliflower, artichokes, wild greens, fennel, favas, and peas; even eggs fried sunnyside down.

Half the tables seemed to be filled with desserts:
All manner of fresh fruits, including strawberries and prickly pears, the *primizie* or first offerings of the season; endless tortes; *cenci; cannoli; spergi or pesche* (peaches), which look like peaches but are actually balls of dough filled with ricotta sweetened with sugar, cinnamon, and grated lemon peel—two of them are put together like the halves of a peach and one side is rolled in sugar and washed with peach jam, while sprinkles of green coat the other side; lacy *frittelle* sandwiched together with a sweet ricotta cream; *pignolate*, tiny logs of fried sweet dough dipped into honey; *cassateddi*, half-moons of sweet dough filled with a lemon-scented ricotta filling and fried; *tiramisù*, the chic dessert found all over Italy these days, a sure sign that San Giuseppe has room for innovation and is keeping up with gastronomic trends.

Until a few years ago, the Feast of San Giuseppe was a national holiday, but now it is only optional. The table of San Giuseppe started in the south, not only in Sicily but also in Apulia and Abruzzo, where it is still celebrated and known as *La Mattredda*, from the *madia*, the deep wooden chest in which women make the bread dough. The numbers of *cene* are diminishing, but the day itself is still marked all over the peninsula by bonfires lit in honor of San Giuseppe. At one time people who had neither food nor shelter could celebrate the saint by collecting cuttings, old fishing boats, broken chairs, and tree trunks and burning them in a piazza. Since San Giuseppe has nothing to do with fire, why would anyone honor a carpenter by burning wooden furniture? Probably the fire was originally meant to propitiate the sun and invoke its warmth before the coming of spring.

The feasting persists. Special sweets are prepared all over Italy, and although their names and shapes may differ from region to region, they come both empty, as frittelle and zeppole, and filled, as bignè di San Giuseppe, zeppole again, or sfinci in Sicily. Many are filled with sweetened ricotta or custard cream, but now that greater attention is being paid to cholesterol and calories, bakers have discovered a way around frying by adding extra eggs to make a softer dough and baking these sweets in the oven.

The zeppole eaten in Umbria, Florence, and eastern Sicily are made of rice, while those of Sardinia, Lazio, Campania, and points south are based on flour. When the pastries are filled they sometimes change their name to frittelle, confetti or bignè. In Rome mountains of frittelle are fried in the streets of the Trionfale district, between the Tiber, the Vatican, and Monte Mario. In Florence huge frying pans once bubbled in the Piazza Santa Croce where men fried frittelle di riso.

Every region has its own story of the pastrymaker who dreamed up these hot delicate fritters, although the ancient Romans made them of flour, cheese, eggs, sliced apples, and grated lemon rind, and offered them to Bacchus and Silenus for Le Liberalia, a festival held on March 17 near their temples. Women wearing crowns of ivy in their hair set up improvised frying shops for the day and dedicated the frittelle to the old gods of wine. The term *zippula* used in Sicily is thought to come from the Arabic *zalabiyah,* which means a soft dough made with other ingredients and fried in oil; *sfinci* comes from the Arabic *sfang,* a fried pastry. A young woman from Palermo described the zeppole of San Giuseppe as a rich

The Cooking of Fritelle,
by Abraham Bosse

dough that virtually explodes in the hot oil into a bignè that is hollow but soft inside, crisp and golden on the outside. Instead of filling the puffed dough, the Sicilians spoon sweetened ricotta over the top, and while it is slightly awkward to eat, the combination is exquisite.

Romans say that bignè filled with pastry cream were invented in the nineteenth century by the keeper of a coffeehouse in the Piazza Pasquino who split them open to use up his leftover whipped cream. Neapolitans claim zeppole as a sweet from the early Middle Ages, and point to a recipe, from the Neapolitan cookbook *La cucina casareccia* published in 1800, for making zeppole with a creamy mixture of flour, a little salt, and white wine (flavored with rosemary), then fried in oil and sprinkled with sugar.

It is not only towns that celebrate. Southern Italian immigrants have transplanted the table of San Giuseppe to Italian-American communities in New York, Philadelphia, New Orleans, Los Angeles, San Jose, and San Francisco, among others. In America the festival has become like a giant potluck, with its social aspects more important than strict fidelity of the dishes served at the banquet. At a recent San Giuseppe's Day banquet in San Francisco, the men did all the cooking, although one woman baked anise-flavored breads shaped like the saint's beard and staff and crown to set on the altar. Some of the dishes were exactly what I ate in Sicily—pasta con la mollica, asparagus frittata, stuffed calamari, fennel picked wild in the fields—and some were local innovations, ranging from eggplant parmigiana to Jell-O molds, definitely an American addition. No one was allowed to leave without a bit of bread, an orange, and a single fava bean, because tradition says that with one such bean, you can never be broke.

One bean may be enough symbolically to keep plenty at hand, but in Sicily excess triumphs. The tables in Salemi were out of a folk tale, for every time a platter became empty, a full one immediately appeared in its place. There was so much food that all of it could not possibly be eaten, even by the crowds that pressed into the house, so midway through the afternoon, family members loaded up a car and delivered food to neighbors who were unable to come. In Salemi the table of San Giuseppe overflows with a touching abundance of food: The father of the Holy Family provides.

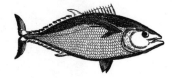

Maccù

~~~~~~~~~~~~~~~~~~~~~~~~~~~~~~~

*Fava
Bean Soup*

This bean soup is thick enough to eat with a fork. Favas and lentils and peas are cooked together until they form a thick puree (the word *maccù* comes from *ammaccare,* to crush), flavored with fennel and the cucumber-like herb borage. If you don't have any borage, you could substitute half a chopped cucumber and no one will ever know the difference. If you can't find the dried chestnuts, simply omit them.

Maccù is traditionally served in western Sicily for San Giuseppe's Day, right in the middle of Lent, but it really dates from ancient celebrations of the spring solstice. This end-of-the-year dish is meant to use up everything left in the pantry before the first crop of new vegetables makes its way into the kitchen. Such soups are common throughout Italy, although in cool mountain-shaded Abruzzo the equivalent of maccù turns up at the beginning of May, while Gubbio's imbrecciata is made on New Year's Eve, literally the end of the year. The Sicilian version is especially rich and delicious.

Makes 8 servings

About ½ pound (200 grams) dried chestnuts
¾ pound (300 grams) dried fava beans
About ½ pound (200 grams) dried split peas
¼ pound (100 grams) dried garbanzo beans
⅓ pound (150 grams) dried borlotti or kidney beans
¼ pound (100 grams) lentils
⅓ cup fresh borage, chopped, or ½ cucumber, peeled and chopped
2 teaspoons (8 grams) fennel seeds
2 tablespoons chopped leaves of wild fennel
1 medium onion, sliced
2 dried tomatoes, about 2 tablespoons, chopped
3 ribs celery, sliced fine
Salt and pepper

Soak the chestnuts and all the beans, except the lentils, in water overnight. Next morning drain them and squeeze off the skins from the fava beans. Put all the beans and peas along with the lentils in 9 to 10 cups salted water, bring to a boil, and simmer about 1½ hours. Add the herbs, onion, tomatoes, and celery; continue cooking another 1½ to 2 hours, until the beans are well cooked and the entire soup is thick and rich. Add a bit more water if you need it. Season with salt and pepper.

Pesce d'Uova di Salemi

~~~~~~~~~~~~~~~~~~~~~~~~~~~~

Little Croquettes in the Shape of a Fish

You could call these tasty little fritters "poor man's fish," since that's a rough translation of their name. They look like the little fish sold from the small trucks that park right on the streets of Salemi, only these are made out of well-flavored bread crumbs, grated cheese, and eggs. The mixture is a ubiquitous part of San Giuseppe's table in Salemi, when it is used as a stuffing for artichokes, zucchini, sardines, etc. So much for facts. The surprise is that the fritters taste so light and flavorful and make a wonderful side dish at lunch or dinner.

Makes 6 servings

1 tablespoon olive oil
3 tablespoons finely minced garlic, about 6 cloves
3 cups fresh bread crumbs, preferably from Sicilian Bread made from durum flour (page 425)
6 tablespoons (35 grams) grated pecorino cheese, preferably studded with peppercorns
1½ teaspoons sea salt
Pepper, if you aren't using the pepper-studded cheese
2 tablespoons finely chopped flat-leaf parsley
Pinch sugar
5 eggs, beaten
Olive oil for frying

Heat the 1 tablespoon olive oil in a small sauté pan and lightly warm the garlic, never allowing it to brown. Place the bread crumbs, cheese, salt, parsley, and sugar in a medium-sized bowl. Add the garlic and mix well. Stir in the beaten eggs and mix until the mixture holds together well. Set a cup of water on your work surface. Moisten your hands and roll small pieces of the mixture into logs about 3 inches long and 1 inch across.

Fill a deep frying pan with olive oil about 1½ inches deep. Heat to 375°F and fry logs until they are a light golden brown. Drain on absorbent paper towels and serve immediately.

Cassateddi

~~~~~~~~~~~~~~~~~~~~~~~~~~~~~~~~

*Sweet Ricotta-
Filled Turnovers*

The first cassateddi I ever tasted were still so warm that the sweet ricotta filling literally melted in my mouth. More than a dozen women were making these sweet ravioli-like pastries in a primitive cave-like kitchen barely illuminated by a single naked light bulb. They sat in groups of four, with squares of wood resting like tables on their knees. At the first table two women worked the pasta machine—one held it steady and the other cranked the dough through. A third woman cut it into rough squares and the fourth scooped ricotta onto the pieces. She then passed it to table number two, where two women gave the cassateddi a definite shape and the other two cut around the dough with a ravioli wheel, making a fat half-moon filled with the sweetened cheese. More women then fried them in pans bubbling with oil and then rolled them afterward in cinnamon sugar. Be sure to eat cassateddi while they are still hot, or at least warm, and you will understand why they are one of the most exquisite of the traditional dishes essential to the celebration of San Giuseppe.

Makes 3 dozen turnovers

DOUGH

3¾ cups (500 grams) durum flour or all-purpose flour
¼ cup (50 grams) sugar
Pinch salt
5 tablespoons (75 grams) unsalted butter
2 eggs plus dry white wine to measure 1 cup

Follow the directions for making Pasta Frolla on page 270.

FILLING

1 pound 2 ounces (500 grams) fresh ricotta
1 cup (200 grams) sugar
Grated zest of 1 lemon
2½ ounces (50 grams) chocolate chips, optional

Vegetable oil for deep frying
Cinnamon sugar

Press the ricotta through a sieve. Stir in the sugar and grate the lemon zest directly into the bowl. Leave for about an hour. Before using, put the entire mixture through a sieve again, then stir in the chocolate chips if using.

Shaping. When you are ready to use the dough, set it on a floured work surface, divide into several pieces, and put each piece through the first

(continued)

3 settings on a pasta machine. Keep the dough lightly floured and cover the pieces you are not using. As long as you flour the work surface and the dough, there is nothing to worry about. The dough is smooth, silky, and extremely forgiving. If it tears going through the machine, just fold it over and put it through again. If there are a lot of scraps, press them together and put them through the pasta machine.

Cut the dough into 4-inch squares. Put 1 to 2 tablespoons filling on the center of each square, moisten the edges with a little water, and fold the dough over to make a triangle. Press firmly with your fingers to seal the edges. You can use a fluted ravioli cutter if you have one to cut a half-moon–shaped pastry, or you can simply trim the triangular pastry neatly and press it firmly around the edges so no filling leaks out during the frying.

Frying. Fill a deep-sided pot with about 3 inches of oil and heat it to at least 375°F. Slide several cassateddi into the oil and fry them until golden. Drain on paper towels and turn onto a plate sprinkled with cinnamon sugar. You must eat these while hot, or at least warm, so the ricotta literally melts in your mouth.

Sfinci di San Giuseppe

Fried Puffs for Saint Joseph's Day

I like the fact that Sicilians eat these deep-fried sweets as a kind of devotion on San Giuseppe's Day. They are filled with a ricotta cream, and in Palermo a bit of the cream is spread on the outside as an elegant finishing touch. This recipe comes from a wonderful home baker in Palermo, although the same sfinci are made at Scimone, a fabulous *pasticceria* in that city, using durum flour, ¼ cup lard instead of the much larger amount of butter, and nine eggs. The puffs swell dramatically to almost triple their original size; even in this version the dough swells amazingly.

Makes about 2 dozen puffs

1 cup plus 2 tablespoons water
½ cup plus 3 tablespoons (150 grams) unsalted butter
Pinch salt
1¾ cups (250 grams) all-purpose flour
5 or 6 eggs
About 6 cups vegetable oil for frying

1 pound 6 ounces (625 grams) freshest ricotta, sieved
½ cup plus 2 tablespoons (125 grams) superfine sugar
1 teaspoon vanilla extract
5 tablespoons chocolate chips, roughly chopped
4 tablespoons minced candied orange peel

TOPPING

24 fine slices candied orange peel
Sprinkling pistachio nuts

Bring the water, butter, and salt to a rolling boil in a saucepan. Sift in the flour and stir until the mixture is thoroughly combined and does not stick to the pan. Remove from the heat and set aside until cool.

Put the mixture in the bowl of an electric mixer with a paddle attachment or in a mixing bowl. Add the eggs one at a time, mixing thoroughly so that each egg is well incorporated. Continue to beat until the dough is smooth.

Heat the oil in a deep-sided heavy pan to 375°F. Drop spoonfuls of the dough from an oiled tablespoon into the oil and fry the puffs until the tops are fairly dry and full of tiny holes. Do not disturb them or the pastry will split and tear. Since the fritters puff up greatly as they cook, be sure not to cook too many at one time. Cook until golden. Drain on paper towels. Cool.

Combine all ingredients for the filling. Split open the cooled sfinci and fill with a bit of the ricotta cream. Finish with a smear of ricotta cream on top and decorate with thin slices of candied orange peel and a sprinkling of pistachio nuts.

Zeppole di San Giuseppe

~~~~~~~~~~~~~~~~~~~~~~~~~~~~~~~~

Italian Doughnuts

Fritelle made with zibibbo grapes, eighteenth-century engraving by G. Zompini

Neapolitans claim that zeppole were invented in Naples sometime in the Middle Ages, when they were made with a little white wine and a branch of rosemary. They had a whole new incarnation in the nineteenth century, when a certain Don Pasquale Pintauro presented the waiting world with sweet zeppole for San Giuseppe's Day. These light-as-air doughnuts are made of bignè dough, fried, then filled with a delicious pastry cream and each one topped with a single amarena, the preserved wild cherry of Italy.

Makes 18 to 20 zeppole, or 5 to 8 zeppole and enough dough for 1 recipe of Frittelle di San Giuseppe (page 407). Each zeppola weighs about 2 ounces (50 to 60 grams).

2 cups water
1 cup (225 grams) unsalted butter, room temperature
1¾ cups plus 2 tablespoons (250 grams) unbleached all-purpose flour, measured and then sifted
9 or 10 eggs
Vegetable oil for deep frying
2 to 3 tablespoons Pastry Cream (page 58) for each zeppola
Confectioners' sugar
18 to 20 amarena cherries

Bring the water and butter to a boil in a 3-quart pan. Add the sifted flour in 1 addition and mix vigorously with a wooden spoon over the fire until the mixture is really dry and comes away from the sides of the pan and the mixing spoon. It will take 5 minutes or even a bit longer, and you can almost hear it hissing as it cooks. The mixture must be dry to make light zeppole.

Let the mixture cool about 5 to 10 minutes, then add the eggs one at a time, being sure that one is well incorporated before adding the next.

Shaping. Put the dough into a pastry bag fitted with a ½-inch number 6 fluted or plain tip. Pipe into fat circles like doughnuts about 3½ inches in diameter right onto parchment paper.

Cooking. Heat the oil to 325° to 350°F. Test fry a piece of dough to see how it cooks and how long it takes. The zeppole should cook about 8 minutes; they will reach a certain definite brownness and then suddenly stop getting any darker outside while they continue cooking inside. Drain them on paper towels and let them cool. Pipe 2 to 3 tablespoons pastry cream into each zeppola, sift confectioners' sugar over the top, and finish with an amarena on top.

In Milan these are called *tortelli*, are flavored with vanilla, lemon, cinnamon, and rum, and are cooked first in oil heated to 250°F until they swell, and then are transferred to a second oil, boiling at 350°F. After they puff up dramatically, they cook as above. They are not filled.

Frittelle di San Giuseppe

Rice Fritters for Saint Joseph

What a perfect way to celebrate the patron saint of the frying pan: puffy, light, creamy rice fritters with the fragrance of lemon and orange and the crunch of sugar on top.

Makes 12 to 14 fritters

2 cups plus 2 tablespoons milk
Pinch salt
Strips of zest of 1 lemon
½ cup plus 2 tablespoons (125 grams) Arborio rice
7 ounces (200 grams) Zeppole dough (opposite page)
Grated zest of 1 lemon
Grated zest of 1 orange
Sunflower oil, preferably, for deep frying
Granulated sugar

Combine the milk, salt, and lemon strips and bring to a boil in a medium-sized heavy saucepan. Stir in the rice and reduce the heat to very low. Simmer covered, stirring occasionally, until all the liquid is absorbed. Spread the rice on a dinner plate to cool and discard the lemon strips. To the cooked rice add the zeppole dough and grated zests.

Line baking sheets with parchment paper. Scoop the mixture into a pastry bag fitted with a number 6 fluted ½-inch tip and pipe out a rectangle 2 inches wide and 4 inches long onto the parchment paper.

Heat the sunflower oil to 325° to 335°F in a heavy deep-sided pot. Cut each frittella on its own piece of parchment into a separate square and slide each one into the boiling oil. You can remove the paper after a few minutes of gentle stirring. The *frittelle* will puff up a lot, then lose some volume as they cool. Cook about 8 minutes; they will take on color quickly but won't get too brown, and they need time to cook inside completely. Drain on paper towels, cool, then cover with lots of granulated sugar.

PASQUA

EASTER IN SICILY

Natale con i tuoi, Pasqua con chi vuoi. Italians solve prickly dilemmas with the formula of spending Christmas with their families and Easter with whomever they please, but I was in Sicily at Easter and family was not the issue. The confusingly rich variety of observances was. Almost every village and town has its own extraordinary celebration complete with ritual foods, and it was hard to choose between Good Friday processions with hooded men and re-creations of the Passion. I wondered about Easter festivities in which streets were decorated with wheels of bread, and villages where devils with chains shook down visitors for contributions and taunted Death dressed in a yellow jumpsuit.

In Sicily Good Friday is more about Mary's intense suffering than about Jesus' death, and its ceremonies focus almost exclusively on the pain of a mother's loss and the mystery of death. In much the same way, Easter is less about Jesus' Resurrection than a joyful celebration of their reunion. The rhythms of the event, like darkness chased away by sunlight, recall the despair of winter followed by the promise of springtime.

These observances are rooted in celebrations older even than Rome. The Church was not the first to celebrate the darkness before the explosion of light, but the Catholicism of Sicily is particularly dramatic. Influenced by the flamboyant Spanish who ruled the island for more than four hundred years, the highly theatrical religious processions are marked by the baroque expression of extreme emotions. What Sicilians prefer, according to Leonardo Sciascia in *Le feste religiose in Italia,* is "an aspect of the Passion rather than the joy of the Resurrection. It is related to the Sicilian feeling of aloneness and betrayal and by an interest in the image of the Mater Dolorosa. They love death, express themselves in mourning, the end of possibility. They prefer contemplating death, but no one is looking to the Resurrection. The interest in death is for itself, as opposed to the Catholic meaning of death. . . ."

I decided to go to Trapani for Good Friday, partly because its famous procession is especially stark and dramatic and partly because it is easy to get to the port city at the western edge of Sicily, where dazzling white salt flats protrude into the Mediterranean. In ancient times sailors used to put in at Trapani and head straight up the hill to the little town of Erice with its temple devoted to the worship of Aphrodite. The goddess had been born here on the waves of this sea and carried to shore by nymphs. The erotic rites on the cloud-covered heights of Erice were instrumental in making her an important figure (she had been a mere village goddess before). Although the temple is gone now, its ruins subsumed within the crumbling stones of the Saracen and medieval castle, Erice remains an enchanting and elegant little town. With a bit of good timing, I managed a glimpse of Erice's intimate Good Friday procession as it climbed vertical streets whose soft gray paving is banded by lozenge-shaped ivory-colored stones. It stopped at the Romanesque cathedral whose ceiling looks like the Book of Kells written in white icing, but the freezing winds and dark, muffling fogs that whip around the top of the hill added a chilling note and sent me off without regret to the much more dramatic parade in the port of Trapani which goes on without interruption for a full twenty hours.

For four centuries men in Trapani have carried the "Mysteries," twenty groups of life-sized wooden sculptural groups portraying scenes of episodes in the Passion of Christ. The Mysteries are borne on platforms with handles by which the men carry them out of the church and throughout the town at a slow, mournful pace during the afternoon and into the darkness of night, when they take on even greater dramatic effect. The bearers pause and then continue their voyage through the streets of Trapani until the procession ends on the morning of Holy Saturday.

The sculptures of the Mysteries were carved with great realism in the artisans' workshops that flourished in the city in the sixteenth, seventeenth, and eighteenth centuries. They are carried to this day by men of the trade guilds, representing butchers and bakers, fishermen and salt workers, gardeners, pasta makers, and pastry chefs. They hoist the heavy scenes onto their shoulders and carry them so that the events they portray appear to be happening before the viewers' eyes. The drama is reflected in the emotional intensity of the suffering Jesus, in the eyes of the Roman soldiers that blaze with fury, in the malicious grins and furious gestures of the scourgers, the wrought-up expression on Pilate's face, and the anxiety and grief of the Madonna. Real men still enact these scenes in nearby Marsala—this event is doubtless a descendant of medieval Passion Plays, the itinerant performances of sacred events—but in Trapani heavy sculptures of betrayal, capture, and death, illuminated by the flickering light white tapers, create the theater in the streets.

I missed Trapani's warm-up events on Tuesday and Wednesday, when two Madonnas, the Madonna del Popolo and the Madonna of the Workers, move alternately through the city streets, searching in vain for Jesus. Each is accompanied by phalanxes of tearful women mourners dressed all in black and by a band playing lugubrious music, but of course neither grieving mother finds the object of her search. At one moment these two representations of the mother of Jesus actually meet before they must return to their respective churches, each having failed in her mission. One of them is a black Madonna whose dark skin and features recall a wonder-weaving pagan fertility goddess transformed or assimilated into a sacred Christian figure. Millennia ago, spring fertility rites were the supreme celebration of the pagan year just as Easter later became the climax of the religious calendar. Especially in Sicily, where Persephone was abducted from her mother by the lord of the underworld, both the rites and Easter focused on mothers whose sacred children rose from the darkness of death to become goddesses or gods of immortal life. People used to make their way to the temple of Demeter, high on the rocky cliffs of Enna at the center of the island, where they celebrated the return of Persephone from her rule over the realms of darkness six months of the year. Her release announced the return of life to the earth made barren by her grieving mother, for when Persephone was released Demeter allowed the land to flower again, and seeds sprouted once more as fruits and flowers, trees and grain.

To this day Trapani celebrates the sprouting of pale shoots of wheat and lentils on Thursday evening, when the entire town takes to the streets, voyaging from church to church to see the *lavureddi*, the "sepulchers" of grain. Fine white linens cover several tiers of altar, which are decorated with pots. Six weeks before, women set pots of sprouted grain to germinate in the darkness and then they carry them into the church on Maundy Thursday. The shoots are pale, larval, newly released from dark vaults and tombs, looking bleached and exhausted, barely grown into fragile stalks. They are memories of the "gardens of Adonis," seeds cultivated by Greek women in clay pots and bowls in the heat of summer. The blazing sun scorched and withered them so that they went through the entire life cycle in a mere eight days, after which the women tossed them into the sea in yearly ceremonies held to honor the death and rebirth of Adonis, who was the lover of Aphrodite, born in the foam of waves such as lap at the shores of Trapani.

These pale shoots sit in the place of honor in the church, surrounded by bright silver candlesticks holding tall white candles. All around stand vases filled with white flowers, with lilies and filmy stephanotis, with callas rolling sensuously around their golden stamens, with carnations and Gerber daisies. The spacing, the different heights, the softness and whiteness of the flowers are ravishing. In one hushed church the floor in front of the altar was covered with vases full of flowers, with banks of flickering electric candles, and with the tops of shoeboxes set out for contributions. The only sounds were the low whispers of the crowd pressing forward and the steady clinking of coins being tossed as if this were some sort of sacred carnival.

The narrow streets of Trapani were crowded with people making their way from church to church, but the real crush was at the door of the church of the Collegio, where people pushed to get inside and see the Mysteries. Services are no longer held in the church and the groups of statues are stored here while they are being decorated. Crews of people cover their bases with flowers and greens, creating entire landscapes with stacks of irises and roses, white lilies and birds-of-paradise. It is a gardener's dream in the midst of an extraordinary outpouring of community spirit, an event as joyous as Christmas Eve. People work at it for two full days, going without sleep to make the Mysteries beautiful. Electric candles flicker at their bases. Freshly shined silver haloes and swords and breast-plates gleam, and brightly colored feathery plumes rise from the soldiers' helmets, but it is the flowers that dazzle. A blanket of orchids covers the the ground where the Madonna sets her feet. Pale pink and white an-therium thrust out of the orchids. Here she seems sensuous, yielding, like Bernini's ecstatic Santa Teresa.

The procession itself begins at two o'clock on Friday afternoon, when blasts of trumpets and drumrolls announce the departure of the groups of statues from the church. First comes the confraternity of San Michele, the keepers of the Mysteries, wearing shiny red satin tunics and sinister white hoods with small slits for the eyes. They look frighteningly like members of the Ku Klux Klan, but these hooded men are members of a secret society that reaches back to medieval times. Behind them follow the Mysteries, decorated with flowers and flickering lights.

Unlikely as it seems, the Church has very little to do with the event. No priests officiate and few prayers are said, save for a nighttime mass in the streets as the huge sculptures rest in the piazza between the old and new parts of town. The trade guilds sponsor the event, and each guild takes care of one episode, parading the group through the city streets. Fishermen, for example, are in charge of the statues showing the Washing of the Disciples' Feet, fruitgrowers Jesus in the Garden of Gethesemane, butchers the Sentence by Pilate, and carpenters the Crucifixion. The anthropologist Fatima Giallombardo suggests that in some cases the guilds

are relevant to the episode they portray, but that doesn't explain why the pasta makers sponsor Jesus in his tomb or why Mary, the focus of the entire procession, is carried by waiters, chauffeurs, and pastry chefs.

The story of the Passion, starting with the Separation from Mary and progressing through the Judgment before Herod, the Betrayal, the Crucifixion, and the Deposition, passes before us until Jesus' body appears wrapped in white linen inside a glass coffin. At the very end, too far away to see her son in death, comes the Madonna. The procession winds through the narrow, curving streets of the medieval part of the old port town, past the Liberty-style buildings that thread through the city, their sinuous art nouveau curves set against the swellings of the baroque and the cool stone façades of the Middle Ages. Dirges announce each group, for there are twenty bands, selected from various Sicilian cities and twenty confraternities, each member wearing a black tunic and a brilliant-colored hood, preceding each group. The other men are in black suits or in tuxedoes and black leather gloves.

The bearers of the Mysteries dance the heavy sculptures on their shoulders in a special rolling motion reminiscent of a mother rocking a child to sleep. It has a surprisingly fluid and graceful rhythm, since it takes from six to twenty-four men to hoist and carry the heavy platforms. A captain directs each Mystery using a set of wooden clackers on his fingers. When he claps them together, they make a clacking rattle like castanets or the dramatic beats of an anxious heart. Echoes of the clackers reverberate through the streets all day and all night, for they give the signal to the bearers when they may set down the heavy weights they are carrying and when they must pick them up again.

The Madonna is preceded by dozens of women wearing black dresses and black lace scarves on their heads; many have a picture of the Madonna pinned to their breasts. Dejection marks their faces. The Madonna herself, sad and bereft, looks amazingly real as she is borne down the street. All around her are clumps of huge burning tapers wrapped with black ribbons. A canopy embroidered with golden threads billows above her head.

The streets are lined three or four rows deep, and many of the people stand absolutely still as they wait for her arrival. There is a brisk sale in Madonna pictures as advance ranks of her group arrive with postcards and pictures, pass baskets for contributions, and send them up the face of buildings on ropes. The crowd is hushed and still. As the Madonna moves by, people cross themselves, blow her kisses on the wind, and watch her smooth passage. Once she has gone everyone rushes to follow her. All the food vendors race with their stands, full of candies and nuts, tiny pinwheels spinning like the windmills at the edge of the salty sea, balloons bouncing in the air.

All night long Mary searches for her son. Candles flicker in the darkness. The air is thick with the perfume of flowers. For some people Good Friday is a deeply moving voyage inward, a mystical experience. If in medieval times frescoes on cathedral walls made the Bible real for people who could not read, how much more dramatic are these groups that pass by at eye level, their emotional impact real and compelling as the cataclysmic events they portray sink into the hearts of the crowd.

As the procession leaves the old city for the modern part the mood changes. Via Fardella, as broad as a boulevard, fills up with people strolling arm in arm, sampling pastries and licking ice cream cones. Restaurants are jammed with revelers eating couscous and spaghetti sauced with tuna roe. Some even sit at a window and watch the Deposition and the Crucifixion go by while eating pasta made black in a sauce of squid ink. On Good Friday, people are expected to fast or eat lightly and simply. *Anche gli uccelli digiunano.* "Even the birds fast." Fish or pasta is often the preferred dish. In Trapani many eat couscous in fish sauce, while in Agrigento the dish of choice is pasta con le sarde, pasta with fresh sardines, which they call *pasta alla milanese* because of the saffron it contains. As the procession stops for a two-hour rest, the action on the street picks up and energy surges. The Bar 900 seems like the epicenter of the crush, as dozens of people jam in to taste cannoli and miniature cassatas, to buy chocolate Easter eggs and gelato.

Later, the procession sets off again in the dark and the emotional power of the scene intensifies. Slow funereal music fills the air. In the early hours of morning, the Mysteries progress slowly on their final homeward journey to the Church of the Purgatorio. The bands' sad cadences echo off walls and vibrate in the narrow streets. By midmorning every window is jammed, every balcony filled. One emotional scene after another passes before us. The bearers make a slow rhythmic turn as the music grows louder and they begin their final journey into the interior of the church. Their jackets are covered with wax from the candles that lit the Mysteries during the night, and their bodies are hunched with fatigue in the morning light. They move closer and closer, but can't quite give in, so they rock the Mystery back into the sunlit morning. Back and forth they move, their hesitation palpable, until finally they make the decision to enter the dark interior.

Now all heads turn, tensing to see the Madonna. It is her grief and her ordeal that concentrate the feelings of the crowd. She is preceded by a young girl of about twelve, dressed exactly like the Madonna and looking remarkably like her, holding a silver heart in her hand. She has walked with the Mysteries since she was three years old, when her mother vowed that she would join the procession in devotion to the Madonna if her heart condition did not worsen. And here she is, solemn, tired, the heart still held out in her hand. Behind her come the women in black, some of whom have walked these twenty hours, some still holding the hands of the children and grandchildren with whom they began their devotional march. Now many stand at the edge of the crowd watching, tears rolling down their cheeks, as the Madonna approaches, her rhythmic gait slower and slower in its inexorable movement. From balconies and from the high bell tower of the church, masses of red and white flower petals cascade down upon her, a few catching in her halo, others resting on the bearers' collars. A roar goes up from the crowd. The rocking continues. The men's faces are inutterably sad. She too looks profoundly dejected, as if the experience of searching vainly for her son has marked her. Her movement is hesitant.

Back and forth, turning with excruciating slowness, she grows ever closer to the final commitment to enter the doors of the church. She is not certain her son is inside the church and she knows that once she enters she cannot come out again. Some years the equivocation lasts 45 minutes, even an agonizing hour, as she sways back and forth, rocking nearer and nearer the door before she declines the final commitment and backs slowly away. Although everyone knows she will eventually enter, we all hold our breath. This year the agony is comparatively brief, for after ten minutes she slowly rocks closer to the dark interior and finally decides that the long search is over. She disappears to the insistent rhythms of the band, the last bearer waves, and the door is closed. I am amazed to find tears in my eyes, for I haven't realized that the drama of her ordeal has carried me along so powerfully. Now she has entered the church, it is over. No more music, no more drama. The crowd dissolves in a minute, leaving almost no residue of the event. Suddenly we all are in the streets, along with the vegetable vendors and men selling fish from beds of ice in their little three-wheeled vans. *La festa è finita.*

HOLY WEEK

Easter begins almost as Good Friday ends. The church bells that were muffled and silenced by bonds of black cloth are loosed so they can ring over the countryside. The time for joy approaches, and with that in mind I went to see the triumphal arches decorated with breads and fruits in San Biagio Platani, a tiny village in the Sicilian interior high above Agrigento.

The only road to San Biagio loops through a country landscape, climbing past almond trees, grapevines, and brilliant green wheat fields. I discovered that coming to San Biagio Platani on the Saturday night before Easter is a bit like arriving at Cinecittà in Rome during the construction of a movie set. Half the town was busily hammering or sawing. Forklift trucks were hoisting enormous decorative medallions made of bread into place; women were threading oranges and lemons, bay leaves, and branches of rosemary into the latticework edging the street; and little vans rumbled up the stone streets bringing supplies to groups of hardworking men. One of the organizers explained that the tradition of the arches began sometime in the beginning of the eighteenth century to decorate the main piazza, the setting for the Incontro, the meeting of mother and son. The Incontro is the heart of Easter in many Sicilian villages (although not in Trapani or towns with similar Good Friday observances) where the same scene is played out again and again as Mary, the sorrowing mother, searches the streets. She leaves her church still dressed in a black gown of mourning, while Jesus approaches from the other side of town; they circle, each unsuspecting that the other is near. In San Biagio Platani, the statues of Mary and Jesus are automated by internal ropes, which make their actions a bit jerky. There is Mary, rushing down the street once she has sighted him, arms flapping and pumping as she hastens toward the yearned-for embrace. In her joy she drops her gown of mourning, letting it slide to the ground with an almost coquettish shrug, revealing an embroidered gown of virginal white. Mother and son embrace as they meet. (In some towns, doves fly forth at this emotional moment.) In his hand Jesus holds the gifts of this plentiful land: sheaves of grain, fava bean pods, and an eel from the Platani River, all symbols of fertility.

When the ceremony began in the early eighteenth century, the village decided to split into two rival groups, the *Madunnara* (named for the Madonna) and the *Signurara* (named for the Lord). Ever since, everyone must belong to one group or the other, and although there is no bad blood between them, it does make one wonder what the Church thinks of this particular competition—not to mention the Easter soccer game between the two teams, even if it does seem to combine the two religious passions of the country. In the beginning the two groups squared off to see who could create the most beautiful arches for the sacred meeting place of Mary and Jesus. Then they decided to extend the arches by embellishing the street leading up to the great meeting place, weaving reeds and branches of split willow into screens that edge the street and decorating them too. The arch at the piazza is the triumphal proclamation of Easter, while the arch at the far entrance represents the front of a church; the avenue between the two is the nave. Plans for their construction, decoration, and form are shrouded in secrecy until Saturday night, when the wraps come off.

These preparations take time. There are breads to be baked, rosemary, palms, dates, oranges, and bay leaves to be collected, and reeds and willow branches to be woven into screens. And the amounts! More than 1,800 pounds of oranges, 400 pounds of sugar, and enough flour to make more than 10,000 pounds of decorative breads. There is still a sense of rural tradition in this homemade celebration, a respect for the rituals of the earth and dazzling imagination as well. One year the women created a mammoth gate almost as tall as Ghiberti's Baptistery doors in Florence with biblical scenes sculpted in bread. This year fifteen bread medallions, each three feet in diameter, reproduced Adam and Eve and the snake in their last fateful moments in Paradise, a moving Pietà, as well as portraits of the Madonna and Jesus and enchanting depictions of the four seasons.

Of course the entire town of San Biagio Platani makes its *passeggiata* along the streets on Saturday night, admiring the arches and comparing the two teams' work. There are no prizes, but popular opinion weighs heavily. The year before, one team had made a rather disappointing showing, occasioning much discussion. To make up for it they got started on the next year's project as soon as Christmas was over. Men took leaves of absence from their jobs and engineers were brought in to configure special constructions.

What they had done was extraordinary. In the center of the two-block corridor, along which exotic arches curved like the vaulting of a church, delicate onion domes, constructed of an airy latticework of wicker and reeds, rose thirty feet above the street, making this part of San Biagio Platani look like something out of the Arabian Nights. Whole trees of rosemary and bay leaves marked each end of the street. Lanterns woven of palms and decorated with an ornamental fringe of dates illuminated the scene. Columns crowned with capitals of bread marched down the edge of the street, alternating with decorative arches outlined in glossy laurel leaves and filled with oranges, lemons, and dates.

Not to be outdone, the rival team took its own two-block corridor and created a cathedral-like space with Gothic arches, columns, a cupola, rose window, and vaulting. To decorate its walls, they sculpted thirteen mammoth breads in the form of events of the Passion. Imagine the Stations of the Cross created in bread, each eight feet high and baked onto screens as large as a door and then hung like giant pictures. They were created by five women, none of them bakers, but each a phenomenal artisan in working an extremely stiff breadlike dough made of water, flour, and salt. Each year five or six different women from each group also make hundreds of small shiny golden breads to hang on the walls. A simple dough is transformed into all manner of flowers and plants, into prickly pears, butterflies, lady bugs, oranges, crocodiles, and suns and moons and trees. Until a few years ago, these breads were blessed at the moment of the meeting of Madonna and Jesus, and were then distributed to friends, neighbors, and the poor of the town. But now that many visitors come to San Biagio Platani at Eastertime, the arches are left up for two weeks and the breads are too weatherbeaten to keep.

Each street meets the piazza with a triumphal arch shaped to look like the front of a church. To decorate the top part, the Madonna's team created a picture of Madonna and child of tiny pasta shells and of dried peas and beans, while across the piazza the huge arch of the Signori team showed the meeting of Mary and Jesus in a mosaic of dried beans and pasta set within a frame of oranges. Under the lunettes both also have a dark background of baked breads shaped in pinwheels and rounds. The dark breads are called *cudduri* and they are overlaid with *marmurati*, breads named for their dazzling white color. The dough is made without leavening, is then baked, brushed with egg whites, dusted with powdered sugar, and put back into the oven so the brilliant white color bakes into its crust. The breads are formed as peacocks and doves, as angels and stars, as palms and flowers, as roosters to announce the morning, as a two-headed Hapsburg eagle to represent the state from days of Spanish rule, and the church itself with rose window and bell. Around the arches appears the legend VIVA MARIA SANTISSIMA written in dried lentils on a golden background of tiny pastine. And beneath the arches, the interior of the structure is decorated with woven canes and cords reminiscent of the nets for eel fishing that families wove in the wintertime while they sat in front of the fire.

Every Italian festival has its market. While such ambulatory stores of food and goods once featured tables piled with garlic, glass, copper, and tinware, or with fruits and vegetables, fish in oil, brilliant-colored candies, toys, and lots of small items, now most are overrun with objects imported for the event. The year that I was there, many of the stands in San Biagio Platani were full instead of authentic local wares. There were displays of dozens of woodburning ovens, the town's principal product, and a charming food stand decorated like a tiny museum with old implements for making ricotta, tools for the wheat harvest, and hoes for the fava crop. The man who went to all this trouble sold not the implements but walnuts and pistachios from local orchards, figs he had dried himself, herbs from the hillsides, and wild asparagus as fine as wheat stalks. The air was perfumed with these fragrances and with the aroma of street foods like panelle, fried garbanzo bean croquettes served inside a roll of golden durum bread.

Traditional breads and sweets are an essential part of the festivities of Easter in Sicily. Pitrè says, "It is possible that a Sicilian might not help at religious ceremonies, it is easy to imagine that he would not take part in any Holy Week practice, but it is not possible to think that he would be indifferent to the sacrosanct practice of offering Sicilian food. You can skip over the boiled meat and chicken, even the lamb that is always on the table." But, says he, even old proverbs point out that no one can be without cassata on Easter.

Certainly not in Palermo, where every bakery and shop window proudly displays the traditional Easter cake. Cassata combines the tastes brought by the Arabs with the pan di Spagna of the Spanish. While some say it gets its name from the Arabic *qas'at,* the deep, round bowl or pan in which it was made, others believe its name came no later than the fourteenth century from the Sicilian word for cheese, *casù* or *caseata,* for it is bursting with sweetened ricotta, which is delicately flavored with tiny dice of candied pumpkin and then enclosed in alternating squares of sponge cake and almond paste colored green to look like the pistachio paste with which cassate were originally made. The cake is iced and decorated in a flourish of baroque extravagance with ribbons of candied pumpkin sweeping around a candied half orange set in the center, and it is dotted with glacéed cherries and sprinkled with silver sugar balls. In some Sicilian towns the holiday was actually called the Easter of the Cassata. This may explain why the scandalized ecclesiastical authorities in Mazara del Vallo prohibited its production during the Holy Week once they realized that the nuns were so busy making cassate that they didn't have time for their devotions.

I couldn't believe people actually ate le pecorelle, the enchanting Easter lambs made of almond paste seen in pastry shops all over Sicily. Almost all of them are seated on a carpet of grass, with a little red flower at the neck, and hold a red flag to symbolize the Resurrection. I have seen them with a little moustache of greens, with tiny chocolate hooves, with delicate pink noses, and with fierce penetrating eyes, but the most charming of all were made by Maria Grammatico, a remarkable baker in Erice who learned her métier in the fifteen years she spent being schooled by the nuns in the convent at Erice. Like most *pasticcieri,* she presses the almond paste into a plaster of Paris mold, but she fills each lamb with delicious citron preserves, and then decorates them by piping out fluffy marzipan fleece, setting in place perky ears, four little legs, a little red tongue, and two soulful eyes edged in chocolate. I thought these little works of art were much too charming to be eaten, but discovered that not only were they served at Easter dinner, but that people drove great distances in order to get them. Corrado Costanzo, a noted pastry chef in Noto, agrees that lambs are the universal Easter present, with one exception: Girls give their fiancés almond-paste hearts covered with icing, decorated with tiny balls of sugar, and with a message elegantly written in a script of white icing.

These Easter dolci could very well be the finale of the holiday, a glorious send-off for the sweet tooth, but they are not. At least as big a holiday as Easter itself is Pasquetta, or Little Easter, as Easter Monday is known, a *festa* whose entire reason for being is to allow people to eat themselves into a stupor. Everything stops while the population of Sicily goes off for a ritual picnic. Entire cities empty out; newspapers don't even publish.

Families used to hitch up their brilliantly painted carts and set out for the fields. While cars have supplanted the horse-drawn transportion, families still arrive in the countryside with many picnic dishes already cooked, so they spread out tablecloths, deal plates as if for a hand of cards, and settle in for a *grande bouffe,* Italian style.

In *On Persephone's Island,* her book about Sicily, Mary Taylor Simeti speaks of the roasted artichokes that are traditional for Pasquetta lunch around Palermo. They are made, as she says, by holding the stem and pounding the artichoke with enough force to open up the leaves and make an opening for a mixture of garlic, salt, pepper, and mint. Then enough olive oil is rubbed inside the artichoke so it stays a bit moist as it is roasted on ash-covered coals for about forty-five minutes, until the outer leaves are charred and black and the heart and tips are soft and creamy. At the Pasquetta picnic I attended, pyramids of these artichokes were stacked on the table, the way Middle Westerners in America heap corn on the cob for the Fourth of July, and we just kept reaching for more, pulling the creamy tips off the leaves with our eager teeth.

The picnic table overflowed with food. A huge platter held the fritedda, a frittata of the wild asparagus that we could see growing in a hedge just beyond in the fields. We tore off hunks of crusty country bread made of Sicily's golden durum wheat, and onto them we put slices of young sheep's cheese called *tuma.* The fire yielded up lamb grilled under the embers. Tonino, host and father of the family, pulled cipolline lunghe, spring onions, right up by their roots and added them to the fire until they were charred on the outside but soft and sweet when peeled. The salad of wild greens came from the fields of neighbors who were hosting their own, much larger Pasquetta picnic—cooking more than 125 pounds of beef and pork and an entire sheep, and roasting 100 artichokes for phalanxes of guests. But they didn't have the delicate sheep's milk ricotta that we spooned up like porridge, still warm minutes after the shepherds brought it, as golden and soft as the softest scrambled eggs. We ate black olives warmed by the sun, drank the vino della casa, and tumbled on the grassy earth for a little rest before tackling a platter full of sweets made by the nuns at the convent of Santo Spirito in Agrigento.

The sweets were in fact my gift to the family, since I had been fortunate enough to visit the convent. Like the Prince on a visit to a similar convent in Lampedusa's *The Leopard,* I liked the "humble simplicity of the parlour . . . its double gratings for interviews, a little wooden wheel for passing messages in and out." He liked the look of the nuns "with their wide wimples of the purest white linen in tiny pleats gleaming against the rough black robes." And the Prince enjoyed "the pink and greenish almond cakes which the nuns made up from an ancient recipe. They crunched satisfactorily." As indeed did the ones I found. The nuns' sweet couscous is famous all over the island, as well it might be, but I was really crazy about the bocconcini di dama, little sweets made of almond paste that had crystallized like maple sugar. They were flavored with lemon, studded with thick chips of peeled almonds, and topped with whole pistachios—they were among the most memorable tastes I carried home from Sicily. And I have to admit I couldn't stop eating le conchiglie, shell-shaped almond-paste cookies stuffed with pistachio cream, although I left some room for a taste of the little almond-paste Easter lamb stretched out on a green lawn.

The Pasquetta picnic is meant to last the whole afternoon, so one can lie drowsy in the first warm sun of the year and feel spring humming in the earth, see the herbs and plants returning to life. If, as Cicero says, Demeter is the mistress of Sicily, her joy in the return of her daughter is palpable today. The desperate mother who cast a blight on the land and caused the wheat to stop growing has been restored to her beneficent and generous self.

EASTER FOOD BEYOND SICILY

Flocks of baby lambs begin to appear in the fields as spring arrives, just in time to become the succulent centerpiece of Easter dinner. Lamb is one of the great delicacies of a pastoral culture, but as a symbol of innocence it is also the sacrificial dish par excellence. Since 1500 the food of Easter has been the food of the Last Supper, the ultimate meal in gastronomy and history: lamb (the symbol of Christ), bread (from grain, the gift of Demeter), and wine ("the blood of the earth," Dionysius' contribution).

In Rome today everyone eats abbacchio, baby lamb, which is a mere thirty to sixty days old, weighs no more than thirteen pounds, and has been fed only upon mother's milk, so its flesh is tender and succulent, delicately veiled with a fine layer of fat. Abbacchio may get its name from the stick used to kill the lambs, for in ancient times *abbacchio* in the Roman dialect meant killed, as in "sacrificed," with a particularly compassionate nuance when used to refer to nursing lambs, tender symbols of innocence. In the early days of the twentieth century, shepherds used to bring their flocks into Rome so people could select their tiny victims. No matter where in Italy the meal is served, the lamb is likely to be flavored with rosemary and garlic, roasted in the oven or on a spit; cooked in a fricassee with egg yolks, lemon, and parsley; served in a cacciatore sauce; or made into a sauce for pasta.

The dishes of the holiday tend to be shaded with the fresh green of springtime. In Piedmont people eat torta di riso con erbette, rice tart with the first greens in the fields. Liguria is famous for torta pasqualina,

Selling Easter goats, detail of an 1831 engraving by Bartolomeo Pinelli

a savory vegetable tart originally made only with beet greens, a local ricotta-like cheese called *prescinsena*, onions, marjoram, and eggs. Thirty-three layers of dough stretched as fine as phyllo pastry, one for each year of Jesus' life, enfold the vegetable filling, but before it is baked small holes are scooped out of the filling to hold eggs, which will become hard-cooked during the baking. These days it is rare to find thirty-three layers of paper-thin pastry—twelve to eighteen are more usual—and artichokes and Swiss chard often replace beet greens. But even in its modified form the tart is a wonderful delicacy.

In early times, hard-boiled eggs were eaten to break the fast of Lent. In Italy they were not dyed until around 1400, when Italians gave them color by wrapping them in herbs and flowers; onion skins turned them golden, for example, and the petals of violets gave them a lavender hue. Taking *fantasia* further, the Italians made chocolate eggs as tiny as a sparrow's, others larger than a child could hug, wrapped them in colorful foil papers, and decorated them with elaborate bows and ribbons. The eggs are hollow and always have a present or surprise inside. Some hold very simple trinkets; others are created by special commission. Love knows no bounds at Eastertime, when lucky recipients are likely to find diamond rings, airplane tickets, an expensive wristwatch inside the fine shell of chocolate. The Peyrano family, the great *chocolatiers* in Turin, remember when the firm was robbed just before Easter, for word had somehow gotten out that great valuables were being enclosed in their handmade chocolate eggs. Imagine those thieves sitting in a hideout somewhere, cracking open chocolate eggs with their hammers, scooping out rings and necklaces,

Eggs in basket, nineteenth-century engraving

bottles of fine perfume, promises of a yachting trip on the high seas. These eggs are big business: In 1987 it took ten million pounds of chocolate just to make the Easter eggs. Many are so large and so expensive that shops sell chances on winning a chocolate Easter egg.

People all over Sicily give *la pupazza con l'uovo*, the doll with an egg, as a traditional Easter gift. Often referred to by its dialect name, *púpi cu l'óva*, it is made of savory dough wrapped around one or more hard-boiled eggs. Poor people used to make it with bread dough, while anyone with money sweetened and enriched it, then shaped it as a doll, a heart, a little purse with a handle, a wreath, a dove, or even a porcupine. Every town has its own version, so what is called *canniléri* (candlestick) at San Biagio Platani becomes *cannatéddi* in Erice and *cannatunni* at Prizzi and Salemi. And you can count on the fact that the bigger it is and the more eggs it holds, the more important its recipient. One can measure how much affectionate feeling and respect lies behind the present, which is why the father of a family traditionally received his púpi cu l'óva with at least one more egg than anyone else's.

Since eggs are the emblem of beginnings, of seeds of life flowering within a delicate shell, they are an obvious symbol for Easter, which occurs after the spring equinox. Philosophers spoke of "the egg of Orpheus" when they wanted to refer to the secret forces of fertility in the earth, for according to the Orphic mystery religion, the world was created when the Great Goddess, appearing in the form of a snake, coupled with the sacred serpent that encircled the world in a symbol of eternity. The rays of the growing sun began to warm the egg the goddess had laid, and when it hatched at the spring equinox, the world came into being. With Christianity, eggs became images of resurrection, the tangible symbol of hope, of the triumph of light and warmth over darkness. Eating an egg at the end of Lent was the visible proclamation of the end of a period of abstinence, so eggs baked right into Easter sweets proclaim the rebirth of life and a new world.

Eggs were eaten for good luck, to ensure eternal life. Ancient Romans cradled eggs to celebrate the goddess Demeter as they paraded to her temple, but by the fourth century, the Church transmuted these ceremonies of resurrection and the major Sunday was called Pasqua dell'Uovo, the Easter of the Egg. Believers exchanged eggs as a symbol of hope and faith in a spiritual rebirth; the eggs were blessed in church on Saturday so they could be eaten on Sunday after the long days of Lent during which they were prohibited. To this day in small villages and country towns housewives still do a thorough spring cleaning in the week before Easter and invite the priest to come in and bless the house. They then sit down to hard-boiled eggs, slices of prosciutto or capocollo, pizza di pasqua, bread with cheese, and pizza dolce di pasqua.

In the south of Italy egg-filled breads were the common Easter specialties. No matter what shape they took—round wreaths, horses, babies, birds, or as doves—eggs were always inserted in the dough. In the small town of Ofena in Abruzzo eggs were set as breasts in doll-shaped breads. And, although today it is hard to find the Sardinian Easter bread called *angulla,* shaped like the snake for which it is named, it too once wrapped around a bright red hard-boiled egg.

Easter is also the time when love is announced to the world. In Venice fiancés declared their true intentions by presenting their loves with a rich buttery focaccia shaped like a dove with an egg planted precisely at its heart. In Florence fiancés were on the receiving end of colombine, dove-shaped sweet breads decorated with bright red eggs, the dove being a symbol of love and red, the color of passion. Calabrian girls had to bring their beloved a basket with Easter ciambelle, egg-studded bread wreaths, while in Apulia they gave cuddura with twenty-one eggs (the mystical seven times three).

Lombardy claims la colomba, a delicate panettone-like sweet bread shaped like a dove. It has become the national Easter bread of Italy and is made industrially and shipped all over the country. Even so, many local specialties remain.

The dove, a pagan symbol of the coming of spring as well as the sign of the Holy Spirit in Catholicism, is the inspiration for a sweet called *moscardini* (*muscardinu*) in Palermo, *pasta raffinata* in Noto, and *caneddate* in Syracuse, where it is shaped like a dove sitting with little candies at its base. It tastes nothing like la colomba, for it is made of pasta forte, a mixture of sugar, flour, and water spiced with cinnamon and cloves; some bakers add finely pestled almonds. In Noto it is shaped into little rhomboids scored lightly with designs; elsewhere it looks completely different depending on local fantasy and tradition, and may even be sprinkled with tiny colored sugar balls. Verona is home of broade, a doughnut-like sweet whose spiky edges make it look like the crown of thorns. A baker told me that he mixed the dough in the mixer for one and a half hours in the morning, boiled and drained it in the afternoon, cut it the next morning into tiny pieces the size of gnocchi, and then set them into the oven with enormous amounts of steam where they expanded to ten times their original size. Broade, whose name comes from a dialect word for crown or wreath, are extremely delicate; each seems to weigh about a gram.

In the countryside of Tuscany it wouldn't be Easter without a fat risen sweet bread called *la schiacciata di Pasqua,* made with a dough enriched with an astonishing number of eggs and scented with Vin Santo and anise seeds. Slightly south in Umbria and Lazio, a similar bread that domes even higher is called *la pizza di Pasqua* and is flavored with grated lemon peel and orange liqueur. In small towns around Lucca people eat pasimata, a golden bread flavored with saffron and anise. Casatiello, the spicy ring-shaped cheese bread of Naples, has eggs baked into the top under crossed bands of dough. Pastiera is an elaborate Neapolitan tart made of wheat berries soaked in milk and then cooked into a ricotta custard flavored with lemon rind, orange flower water, and spices. Pastiera was once a springtime sweet, made with tender grains that were sacred to Demeter. Grain, the symbol of fertility and abundance, was the focus of her cult, and in her Eleusinian ceremonies a grain of wheat was given to the faithful. In Apulia la scarcedda, a sweet bread shaped like a heart, a star, a horse, or a bird is covered with jam or chocolate, while pudhica always has at least one egg woven with strips of dough onto its surfaces. The sweet may be shaped like a doll, a rooster, or a big ring, but it can be eaten only after the church bells have rung. Whoever finds the hard-boiled egg hidden inside it will have good luck in the coming year. In one town the pudhica had to be covered with sesame seeds for good luck, while Lecce required an uneven number of hard-boiled eggs in its decoration.

> Pasqua, Pasqua viene correndo
> che i bambini vanno piangendo
> vanno piangendo con tutto il cuore
> perche vogliono le scarcedde con le uove.

> Easter, Easter it comes flying
> So the babies go off crying
> Go off crying with all their heart
> Because they want their scarcedde full of eggs.

In Sardinia pardulas are bite-sized sweets shaped like a rising sun filled with lemon-scented ricotta and encircled by rays of dough. They are quite reminiscent in appearance and taste of the fiadone of Abruzzo, ritual Easter sweets bursting with ricotta.

On Easter Monday entire cities become deserted. No matter what else appears on people's plates, it is traditional to eat a simple antipasto called *il piatto benedetto*, consisting of a hard-boiled egg, salt, and local bitter greens like arugula or radicchio, fennel, or sarset, the deliciously tart leaves grown in Piedmont. It is very similar to the dish included at the start of the Jewish Passover Seder to remind participants of the bitterness of exile in Egypt and elsewhere and to keep those memories alive. There are other dishes too that the women have cooked days ahead to bring to the country on Easter Monday, although now barbecues and grills are taken along and pasta is cooked in the great outdoors.

Pane Siciliano

Sicilian Bread

Sicilians have been growing golden durum wheat for millennia, so it is no wonder they can make a fragrant, crunchy-crusted country loaf with a porous, chewy interior. This is the bread I ate at an Easter Monday picnic outside Palermo, but it should definitely not be confined to holidays. It is the stuff of glorious everyday meals.

I learned how to make the bread at an immensely popular truck stop outside the Sicilian city of Syracuse, where bakers turn out hundreds of loaves and sell them as sandwiches or as delicious snacks. The latter are made by drizzling olive oil mixed with peperoncino on a piece of bread, sprinkling on lots of coarse salt, crumbling fresh oregano leaves over the top, and then eating out of hand.

Bakeries keep a natural yeast going all the time, but the bread can be made very well with a *biga*, in which case the rising times will be cut almost in half.

Makes 2 large loaves

SPONGE

1 cup (225 grams) Natural Yeast Starter, preferably made of durum
 flour, or Biga (page 32 or page 31)
3 cups warm water
3¾ cups (500 grams) durum flour

Mix well and let rise until soupy, frothy, and bubbly, 2 to 3 hours. If you use a *biga*, let rise about 1½ hours.

DOUGH

2¼ cups (300 grams) unbleached all-purpose flour
1 tablespoon sea salt

In a mixer with the paddle attachment mix the flour and salt into the sponge and beat 1 to 2 minutes. Change to the dough hook and knead at medium speed 4 minutes. The dough never comes away from the sides or bottom of the bowl. Sprinkle 2 to 3 tablespoons flour on a work surface and pour the dough out onto it. Sprinkle another tablespoon flour on top of the dough. It is very, very soft, moist, and floppy to work with initially, with a velvety smooth texture. Use a dough scraper to help knead it briefly so it becomes malleable.

First Rise. Set in an oiled container, cover tightly with plastic wrap, and leave to rise until doubled, 3 to 4 hours, depending on the strength of the starter. If you use a *biga*, the dough takes about 2 hours to rise.

(continued)

Pane Siciliano (continued)

Shaping and Second Rise. Pour the dough out onto a floured work surface, lightly sprinkle it with a bit more flour, and divide into 2 pieces. You will see many bubbles under the surface and hear them pop under your fingers as you shape the dough into 2 fairly long ovals. Set 2 pieces of parchment paper onto pizza peels, wooden cutting boards, or cookie sheets, sprinkle them with durum or regular flour, and set the dough onto them, seam side up. If you are nervous about the eventual problem of inverting such a wet dough when it is time to bake it, simply flour the parchment paper and strew flour lightly over the top of the dough and leave it to rise. Cover well with towels and let rise and spread until doubled, about 1 hour.

Baking. About 30 minutes before you are ready to put the bread into the oven, set baking stones in place and turn the oven on to 450°F. Just as you are ready to bake, sprinkle the stones with cornmeal to keep the bread from sticking. You may just slide the floured loaves onto the stones right on their paper or you may carefully turn the breads over onto the stones so that the flour-veined surfaces are up. If some of the parchment paper sticks, trim it so it doesn't hang over the edges of the baking stones, and peel it off 20 minutes later. Bake until the bottom rings hollow when tapped, about 35 minutes.

426 CELEBRATING ITALY

Cannatéddi or Cannatunni

Easter Sweets with an Egg Braided In

Decorated eggs, twentieth-century design from La Gola

Though there are many special Easter pastries in Sicily, this is the one enclosing a whole egg in the shell. The sweet is called *cannatéddi* in the town of Prizzi, where two devils and Death swoop down on visitors, demanding payment for drinks as the price of freedom; some escape, but everyone gets a lyre-shaped pastry enclosing an egg. Sometimes the egg is colored; sometimes it is brown, sometimes white, but it is always hard-cooked by the end of the baking. The Sicilians use lard in making cannatéddi or cannatunni. I experimented with butter and margarine, and discovered that they make a much blander and more crumbly sweet. In Sicily the pastry is also made into a wreath with the eggs set at equal distances around the circumference, held firmly in place with crisscross lattices of dough.

Makes 6 cannatéddi

2 ounces (60 grams) best-quality lard
¼ cup plus 2 tablespoons (75 grams) sugar
1 egg
½ cup milk
1¾ cups plus 2 tablespoons (250 grams) unbleached all-purpose flour
1 teaspoon baking powder
⅛ teaspoon salt
6 raw eggs in their shells, preferably brown or dyed
Confectioners' sugar

Cream the lard and sugar in a mixer bowl until they are light and fluffy. Gradually add the egg and milk and continue mixing until well blended. Sift the flour, baking powder, and salt over the batter and mix until smooth.

Shaping. Cut the dough into 6 equal pieces. Using the palms of your hands, roll each piece on a lightly floured work surface to a 12-inch-long cylinder. Cut off two ¼-inch strips from each cylinder. Because of the delicacy of the operation, you may prefer to move the dough to a parchment-lined baking sheet at this point. Bend the remaining piece into a U shape, and set an egg horizontally in the interior at the base of the U. Roll the two ¼-inch strips so that they are long enough to crisscross the egg and attach to the dough on each side, holding the egg in place. Proceed in the same way with the remaining cylinders of dough, setting the pastries 1½ inches apart on the parchment-lined baking sheets. Bend the tips outward slightly and, using the blade of a dough scraper or a rubber spatula, score the dough lightly every inch or so as a decorative motif.

Baking. Heat the oven to 375°F. Bake the cannatéddi 20 minutes or until golden. Cool on racks and sprinkle with sifted confectioners' sugar.

Pane di Cena
~~~~~~~~~~~~~~~~~~~~~~~~~~~~~~~~~

Sweet Milk Bread
Rolls for
Easter Week

While I was wandering deep in the interior of Sicily, I was overcome by the need to see a newspaper and found a tiny town called Vallelunga. On my way to the only shop selling the news of the day, I passed a bakery in which five or six women were clustered around a woodburning oven. The patriarch of the family was sliding special Easter buns into its cavernous interior. Behind him a young woman was snipping little Xs on the tops of the risen rounds of dough. I couldn't resist going right in to taste these breads, made only once a year. I suspect that the little cuts on top are a slight twist on the traditional cross cut for religious festivals.

Makes 10 to 12 sweet rolls

SPONGE

1 teaspoon active dry yeast or ⅓ cake (6 grams) fresh yeast
2 teaspoons sugar
½ cup milk, warmed to 105°F
¾ cup (100 grams) pastry or unbleached all-purpose flour

Stir the yeast and the sugar into the warm milk and let sit until foamy, about 10 minutes. Stir in the flour. Cover well with plastic wrap and leave until it is frothy and bubbly, 1 to 1½ hours.

DOUGH

2 egg yolks
½ cup milk (cold if using the food processor)
2 teaspoons vanilla extract, optional
½ cup plus 1 tablespoon (125 grams) unsalted butter, lard, or
    margarine, room temperature (cold if using the processor)
3⅓ cups (465 grams) pastry or 3 cups (420 grams) unbleached all-
    purpose flour
½ cup (100 grams) sugar
1 teaspoon salt

GLAZE

1 egg white, beaten

By Hand. Stir the egg yolks, milk, and vanilla into the sponge. Mix in the butter. Add the flour, sugar, and salt in 3 additions, stirring about 3 minutes. Knead on a lightly floured board, adding as little flour as possible, until silky and elastic, 5 to 6 minutes.

By Mixer. Put the sponge in the mixer bowl with the paddle attachment, add the egg yolks, milk, vanilla, and butter, and mix about 1 minute. Add the flour, sugar, and salt and mix on low speed. Change to the dough hook and knead about 3 minutes on medium speed. The dough doesn't entirely come away from the sides or bottom of the bowl. Knead briefly on a lightly floured work surface.

By Processor. Put the flour, sugar, and salt into the processor fitted with either the dough blade or steel blade. Pulse 2 or 3 times to mix. Place the sponge and cold butter, cut into 8 or 9 pieces, on top of it. Mix the egg yolks, cold milk, and vanilla in a cup and, with the motor running, pour it down the feed tube. Process until the mixture forms a dough. Process 30 seconds longer to knead.

First Rise. Put the dough in an oiled container, cover tightly with plastic wrap, and let rise until doubled, 2 to 2½ hours.

Shaping and Second Rise. Divide the dough into 10 to 12 pieces, form each into a round, and set on oiled or parchment-lined cookie sheets. Cover well with towels and let rise again until they have about doubled, about 45 minutes. Just before baking, imagine a cross in the centers of the rolls and snip little V-shaped cuts in each quadrant so they will open up.

Baking. Heat the oven to 400°F. Brush the tops of the rolls with beaten egg white and bake 20 to 25 minutes. The Sicilians frost these with boiled white icing and decorate them with sprinkles. I prefer them plain or with a dusting of turbinado sugar over the egg white glaze.

Abbacchio Brodettato Pasquale

Easter Lamb in Sicily

Easter lamb, nineteenth-century engraving

If lamb is the quintessential Easter food, then this is the dish to celebrate the holiday with. The tastes of spring sing from the creamy lemon sauce enfolding the meat. When I ate this at Regaleali, a great Sicilian wine estate in the interior of the island, I wanted to fly into the kitchen immediately and learn its secrets. I restrained myself long enough to eat an extraordinary dinner and drink wonderful wines, and then Mario Lo Menzo, the family cook, gave me the recipe and showed me how he had made the dish.

Makes 8 servings

2 tablespoons olive oil
1 onion, minced
4 pounds (1¾ kilograms) boneless lamb stewing meat, cut in large chunks
2¾ cups meat broth or enough to cover the lamb thoroughly
6 egg yolks
Juice of 4 lemons
1 pint heavy cream
1½ to 2 tablespoons potato starch for every 2 cups liquid
Salt and pepper

In a large casserole warm the oil and sauté the onion until it is translucent. Add the lamb pieces and cover with broth. Cook over medium-low heat until the lamb is tender, 35 to 45 minutes. Remove the lamb from the broth and keep it warm. Degrease the broth. (The recipe may be done ahead to this point; you may want to chill the broth and remove the fat when it has solidified. You can reheat the lamb in a 350°F oven for 30 minutes.)

Warm the broth. Off the fire whisk in the egg yolks and lemon juice and mix well. Over a very low flame whisk in the cream bit by bit. Turn the fire up to medium and slowly stir in the potato starch, whisking it well to prevent lumps from forming. As the sauce thickens, add the lamb, season with salt and pepper, and serve immediately.

Capretto al Forno

~~~~~~~~~~~~~~~~~~~~~~~~~~~~~~~

Roast Kid

The people of Palermo traditionally have eaten kid at Easter. In elegant houses an entire baby goat is boned, stuffed with herbs and pistachio nuts, and basted with Marsala. Most families, however, sit down to a platter full of meat baked with rosemary-flavored potatoes. Because this dish is so simple, its success depends on using the best-quality kid, which should be as white and tender as veal. If you can't find kid, you can make the dish with lean lamb, as the people of Agrigento do, in which case you might want to add some chopped tomatoes.

Makes 8 servings

6 pounds(2½ kilograms) kid, preferably from the forequarters, cut into
    stewing pieces
2 medium onions, sliced
4 medium (1 kilogram) baking potatoes, peeled and diced
Salt and freshly ground pepper
4 to 6 tablespoons minced fresh rosemary
3 tablespoons minced fresh flat-leaf parsley
2 to 3 cloves garlic, minced
2½ ounces (75 grams) best-quality lard
1¼ cups olive oil

Rinse and dry the meat well. In an oiled baking pan large enough to hold all the ingredients in a single layer, distribute the meat, onions, and potatoes. Sprinkle the salt, pepper, rosemary, parsley, and garlic over the top. Rub the lard into the meat and moisten both meat and potatoes well with the olive oil, using your hands to turn and coat the surfaces.

Baking. Heat the oven to 400°F. Bake until the meat is tender, about 1 to 1¼ hours, turning the meat and potatoes 2 or 3 times during the course of cooking. Serve with slices of lemon.

Tagano

~~~~~~~~~~~~~~~~~~~~~~~~~~~~~~~

Easter Monday Dish from Aragona

Pino Correnti calls tagano the "Easter bomb of Aragon," although the recipe in his *Golden Book of the Foods and Wines of Sicily* has a mere ten eggs, while the one I learned from Salvatore Schifano, a chef from Agrigento with a passion for researching traditional dishes, calls for almost four dozen more. Hardly the thing for cholesterol-conscious eaters, but surely the epitome of Easter when eggs represent the return of fertility to the earth. Still, in the interests of health, I have opted for the lower number—essentially two eggs for every 100 grams of pasta. Those who want to live dangerously should try the more daring quantity.

(continued)

A charming, if apocryphal, story attributes this dish to a poor woman who had sold all the family lambs and goats to get food for winter. When Easter came, she didn't have any of the traditional food so instead she used ingredients she had on hand, a vast quantity of eggs from her hens and cheese freshly made from sheep's milk, to create a new dish. *Tagano* is the name of the terracotta container in which the dish is cooked. The unusual flavorings of saffron, cinnamon, and mint make this a lovely and haunting pasta dish. It is made on the Saturday afternoon before Easter, although it is meant to be eaten at the Easter Monday picnic. It has the rare advantage that it can be made ahead and served later at room temperature or reheated slightly before eating.

Makes 6 to 8 servings

10 eggs, beaten
2¾ cups chicken broth
Salt and pepper
½ cup finely chopped flat-leaf parsley
2 teaspoons finely chopped mint
1 teaspoon cinnamon
1 large pinch saffron dissolved in 2 tablespoons chicken broth
1 pound or a bit more (500 grams) rigatoni
1 pound or a bit more (500 grams) sheep's milk cheese, such as
   lachesos, thinly sliced
10 slices stale bread or 1 pound ground pork, optional

Oil the bottom of an oval baking dish, preferably terracotta.

Beat the eggs with the chicken broth, salt, pepper, herbs, cinnamon, and saffron. Cook the pasta in a large quantity of salted water until al dente, drain, and place in layers in the baking dish, alternating it with the slices of cheese. If using bread, set it on the bottom; if using ground pork, sauté lightly and distribute with the cheese as you construct the tagano. Pour some of the egg mixture over each layer of cheese and pasta and, when you have finished the layering process, pour whatever remains over the last layer of cheese so that it fills all the air pockets left in various lower strata.

Baking. Heat the oven to 350°F. Bake 1 hour.

Frittata di Verdure
~~~~~~~~~~~~~~~~~~~~~~~~~~~~~~
Vegetable Frittata

Before I went to Sicily I had never thought of a frittata as portable picnic food, but now I know differently. First I watched women make many kinds of frittate for Saint Joseph's Day—spinach, artichokes, pencil-thin wild asparagus, broccoli, fava beans, fried potato slices, and wild fennel —which they served at room temperature to dozens of guests. On Easter Monday, many Sicilians carry frittate with them when they picnic in the country. A note of caution: Don't try to double the recipe and cook it in a larger pan. It doesn't work. A frittata may be made for two, three, four—five at the outside—but beyond that it is best to make two frittate.

Makes 4 servings

2 cups (about 1 pound, 450 grams) vegetables: wild fennel greens,
    broccoli, asparagus, spinach, fried potato slices, or eggplant
¼ cup olive oil
8 eggs
¼ cup freshly grated Parmigiano-Reggiano or caciocavallo cheese
Pinch salt
Pepper
A few basil leaves and slices of young sheep's milk cheese, such as
    caciotta or pecorino dolce, if you are using eggplant

If you are using any of the greens, boil them in salted water until they are tender but still slightly crunchy. Drain completely and slice into bite-sized pieces. If you use eggplant, slice it, sprinkle it with salt, and set in a colander to drain for about 1 hour, then pat the slices thoroughly dry with paper toweling. Warm the oil in a 10-inch frying pan and cook the vegetables over low heat until they have absorbed the oil.

    Beat the eggs, cheese, and salt and pepper together in a small bowl and pour over the vegetables. If you are using eggplant, add a few basil leaves and 2 to 3 slices of young sheep's milk cheese. Cook over the lowest possible flame until the top is set, 16 to 18 minutes. Set a dinner plate over the top of the frittata and, holding it firmly with one hand, carefully invert the frittata onto the plate. Slide the frittata, cooked side up, back into the pan and cook 2 to 3 minutes longer, until set. Slide onto a serving platter. Slice and serve immediately, or cool the frittata and serve at room temperature.

Pizza di Pasqua Ternana

vvvvvvvvvvvvvvvvvvvvvvvvvvvvv

Easter Bread from Terni

A dramatic domed sweet Easter bread, similar to panettone although delicately flavored with liqueur, comes from the Umbrian city of Terni.

Makes 2 loaves

S P O N G E

2½ teaspoons active dry yeast or 1 cake (18 grams) fresh yeast
¾ cup warm water
¾ cup (100 grams) unbleached all-purpose flour

Stir the yeast into the warm water in a large bowl and let it stand until creamy, about 10 minutes. Stir in the flour and mix well until it is a smooth batter. Cover tightly with plastic wrap and let rise until doubled and very bubbly, 1 to 1½ hours.

D O U G H

½ teaspoon active dry yeast or ⅙ small cake (3 grams) fresh yeast
⅓ cup warm water
⅓ cup Curaçao
1½ cups (200 grams) bread flour
3¼ cups plus 1 tablespoon (450 grams) unbleached all-purpose flour
½ teaspoon salt
2 whole eggs, at room temperature
4 egg yolks, at room temperature
¾ cup (150 grams) granulated sugar
3 lemons
½ cup plus 3 tablespoons (150 grams) unsalted butter, room temperature

T O P P I N G

1 egg white, beaten
2 to 3 tablespoons turbinado sugar

By mixer. Stir the yeast in the warm water and let stand until creamy, about 10 minutes. Add it to the sponge and beat with the paddle. Beat in the Curaçao. Add ⅓ of the flour and the salt and beat until smooth. Mix in 1 egg, then add the next ⅓ of flour and beat well. Add the second egg, mix well again, and add the final ⅓ of flour. Beat in the yolks, one at a time. Mix in the granulated sugar. Grate the zest of the lemons directly into the bowl so that none of the oils are lost. Beat in the butter, 2 tablespoons at a time. With the paddle still attached, beat the mixture at low speed 4 minutes, then at medium speed 4 minutes. You may want to turn the machine off once or twice to make sure the motor doesn't overheat. Switch to the dough hook and knead at medium speed 2 minutes; the dough does not come away from the sides of the bowl. It is very elastic, the color of buttercream, and comes out of the bowl in thick, fragrant ribbons.

First Rise. Set the dough in an oiled container, cover tightly with plastic wrap, and let it rise until doubled, about 3 hours. If you are working in a cold room, set the bowl in a larger container with warm water.

Shaping and Second Rise. Flour the work surface lightly and slide the dough onto it. With your dough scraper divide the dough in half and shape into 2 round loaves. Place in 2 well-buttered 2-quart soufflé dishes or charlotte molds. Cover with a towel and let rise until puffy and well risen but not doubled. The dough will have lots of bubbles under the surface, but it will not quite double or fill the baking dish. Don't worry; later it will puff dramatically in the oven.

Baking. Heat the oven to 400°F. Just before baking, brush each loaf with beaten egg white, then sprinkle it with turbinado sugar. Bake about 40 minutes, covering the top with aluminum foil if it begins to get too brown. The dough will puff dramatically as it bakes. Let the loaves cool in their forms 15 to 30 minutes before unmolding them, although they can cool completely without any danger.

Bon Hom

~~~~~~~~~~~~~~~~~~~~~~~~~~~~~~

Delicately Sweetened Easter Bread

Children love this lightly sweetened milk bread shaped like a man with an egg under each arm. I also like to make it into a wreath and decorate it with a lattice of dough that holds the eggs in place. The eggs are uncooked when they go in the oven and hard-cooked when they come out—another miracle of Easter.

Makes 2 loaves

S P O N G E

1 teaspoon active dry yeast or ⅓ cake (6 grams) fresh yeast
½ cup plus 2½ tablespoons milk, warmed to 105°F
½ cup plus 5 tablespoons water
Pinch salt
3¾ cups (500 grams) unbleached all-purpose flour   *(continued)*

By Mixer. Stir the yeast in the warmed milk in the mixing bowl; let it stand until creamy, about 10 minutes. With the paddle attachment add the water, salt, and flour on low speed. Change to the dough hook and beat 1 minute on low speed and 3 minutes on medium speed.

First Rise. Cover and let stand until doubled, about 1¼ hours.

DOUGH

About 5 tablespoons (65 grams) unsalted butter, room temperature
¾ cup milk, at warm room temperature
3 tablespoons (35 grams) sugar
1¾ cups (250 grams) unbleached all-purpose flour
Pinch salt
¾ teaspoons vanilla extract, optional
6 whole eggs in their shells
1 egg, beaten

By Mixer. With the paddle attachment beat the butter into the sponge. Add the milk, sugar, flour, salt, and optional vanilla and mix well. Beat on medium speed 4 to 5 minutes until firm but silky. Cover the dough with a towel and let it rest 15 minutes.

Shaping and Second Rise. Divide the dough in half. Roll each piece out to a 24-inch-long fat cord. Cut a 2- to 3-inch strip off each piece, then shape the remaining dough into a circle. Set on greased and floured or parchment-paper–lined baking sheets. Put 3 eggs at equidistant points on each. Cut each small strip of dough into 6 pieces. Roll out each piece so that you can crisscross a pair of strips over each egg to hold it in place. Cover with a towel and let rise until doubled, about 1 hour.

Baking. Heat the oven to 375°F. Brush the beaten egg over the loaves. Bake for 35 minutes, until very golden brown. Cool on racks.

Pardulas or Formagelle

Saffron-Scented Ricotta Pastries

Pardulas look like little golden suns risen especially for Easter in Sardinia. There is something particularly charming about the way the dough wraps around the saffron-scented ricotta filling. It suggests a pastry chef's vision of the glowing sun. People who don't have a sweet tooth are especially fond of pardulas because they contain very little sugar and the saffron gives them a slightly tangy edge.

Makes 20 to 22 pastries

PASTRY DOUGH

7 tablespoons (100 grams) lard, unsalted butter, or margarine
3 tablespoons (40 grams) sugar
1¾ cup plus 2 tablespoons (250 grams) unbleached all-purpose or
    durum flour
1 teaspoon lemon extract
6 tablespoons egg whites

Cut the lard or butter completely into the sugar and flour. Add the lemon
extract and egg whites and mix until you have a smooth dough.

FILLING

9 ounces (250 grams) ricotta, as fresh as possible
Scant ½ cup (50 grams) confectioners' sugar, sieved, plus more for
    garnish
3½ tablespoons (40 grams) unbleached all-purpose flour
¼ teaspoon baking powder
Pinch of powdered saffron
Grated zest of 1 lemon
Grated zest of 1 orange
1 egg yolk

Press the ricotta through a sieve into a wide-mouthed bowl. Sift the
confectioners' sugar into it, stir in the flour, baking powder, saffron, lemon
zest, orange zest, and egg yolk. Mix together until they are smooth and
well incorporated.

Shaping. Roll the pastry as fine as tagliatelle, about ¹⁄₁₆ inch thick. Use
a 3-inch cookie cutter to cut out circles the size of a teacup. Keep a little
bowl of water near you as you work. Moisten your fingertips and palm
and scoop up a full teaspoon of the ricotta filling, roll it into a ball the
size of a walnut or drop it from a teaspoon, and set it in the center of
the dough. Dip a pastry brush or your finger into water and moisten the
edge. Gather up the dough over the filling, leaving about ⅓ of its surface
exposed and pinching the dough at 6 equidistant points so the pastry
looks like a sun. You can begin by pinching the dough at 4 corners, then
finish by pulling the dough out at the center of each side. Pinch each
corner firmly so the pastry won't separate from the filling during the
baking. Set on oiled and floured or parchment-lined baking sheets.

Baking. Bake at 400°F 18 minutes, until the center is not quite firm,
although the crust is lightly brown and the top is just beginning to take
on a brown color. Cool slightly, then sift confectioners' sugar on top.

OF MEALS AND MYTHS

*A*t their best, festivals in Italy are like a collective return to rites of another time, when the "carnal·delights and golden crops" that Lampedusa describes in *The Leopard* still characterized the country. The festivities stir memories of a past when nature, agriculture, and cultural tradition met in harmony, and because this is Italy, celebrations have a way of beginning or ending at table. The kitchen becomes a steamy sanctuary full of the good smells of food as families collect to cook for their celebrations or citizens bring forth dishes that are offered to the entire community. It is not only the pleasure of the food and the warmth of the company that call everyone together, for sacred and ceremonial meals offer more than mere nourishment. Their special dishes are a language that communicates the emotions connected with the elusive ghosts of a golden past, the cultural roots of the country. Cooking becomes a "voyage in time in search of roots, of irremediably lost origins; an attempt to recuperate through the mediation of the dinner table (talisman and magic object) . . . a universe of lost smells and flavors that restores—in an illusory fashion, as with all drugged liturgies inevitably destined to alter the relationship of time and space—the ghost of a lost culture." So says Piero Camporesi, an unorthodox historian who uses food to probe the dreams and underside of the country in *Alimentazione, folclore, società.* So enlightenment and wisdom, which we are used to thinking of coming through science and speculative reason, may come as well through taste and thirst, primitive and essential ways of taking everything in. Eating is a very powerful activity, a way of consuming and assimilating and even becoming.

Religious festivals and important moments in the agricultural season have always had a special menu or dishes. The Romans saw food and drink as a gift of the gods: Bacchus gave the juice of the fermented grape and Demeter taught humankind how to eat holy grain. Wild drinking and intoxication were encouraged as a means to ecstatic communion with the divine; eating grain, the fruit of life in Demeter's Eleusinian mysteries, gave participants a taste of immortality. Like the Etruscans and Celts, Romans decorated tombs and served a funeral feast to their dead ancestors, communicating with them through food. They offered flour mixed with salt, served a bread to be dipped into wine, and ate cooked fava beans, the ritual funereal plant whose petals were marked with the black stain of death and represented a direct connection with the underworld. Nineteenth-century Sicilians prepared fruits and nuts—figs, apples, walnuts, chestnuts, hazelnuts, and favas—as gifts for the dead, and to this day Sicilians arrive at the cemetery for a meal with their ancestors at the beginning of November, set a table at the tomb, and invite their spirits to rejoin the family.

Most festivals began as celebrations rooted in the rhythms of nature. They offered both consolation and reward, magical moments of release from the anxieties of daily life. In acknowledging that humans live at the mercy of powerful forces governing the earth, the celebrations included ceremonies to propitiate the gods at which special foods were served. Rice, grains, eggs, and beans invoked abundance and fertility during those times of the year when the earth was dormant; honey was meant to make a new year sweet; lamb and grain were sacrificial offerings.

In ancient times major festivals always fell on the equinoxes, when the sun is at its highest and lowest points in the sky, and at the spring and autumn solstices, critical midpoints in the passage of the sun. These are thresholds in that passage, the four points of the compass of the festival year. They are as well perilous moments that are full of anxiety and uncertainty, for as the sun grows weaker, cold settles into the earth and seeds lie dormant, waiting for spring and the return of warmth. Observances always marked such interruptions, for the world trembled with barely contained violence as the earth was said to open up, allowing the dead and the demonic brief passage to walk upon the earth.

Christmas, for example, falls at the winter solstice. It is the shortest day of the year, which is why it was once considered the birthday of the sun. By the time the solstice festival was observed in imperial Rome, it had become the Saturnalia, a boisterous event that lasted from the seventeenth to the twenty-fourth of December. Saturnalia was held in honor of Saturnus, the first king of Latium, a legendary ruler who introduced agriculture in an early golden age. Bonfires blazed for seven days, drunken revelry and feasting were encouraged, and a king, called the Lord of Misrule, took charge of the rowdy festivities. Anarchy ruled. All distinctions between master and servant were turned upside down, so that servants wore their masters' clothes and sat at their tables and ridiculed them while the masters did their bidding. In a public ceremony on the first day, a young pig was sacrificed, and sometime later a virile young man was chosen to play the role of a king like Saturn. At the end of his reign the young man became a sacrificial victim much like the pig. His throat was cut on the altar, and his blood flowed into the soil to encourage its fertility and to restore life to nature in the days following the darkness of winter.

The Saturnalia orgy was not tamed until the fourth century, when the Catholic Church became the official religion of Rome and Jesus took over from the Lord of Misrule. In the preceding years, Christianity had been in fierce competition with a pagan religion centered upon Mithras, a Persian god who was so identified with the sun that his worshipers called him "The Unconquered Sun." December 25 was Mithras' birthday; it celebrated the birth of the sun, the victory of light over darkness, and the renewal of life. Like Jesus, Mithras had a virgin birth in a grotto attended by shepherds, and he was visited by Magi, who came on January 6. The Church recognized the competition of the powerful Mithraic cult and saw a way to counteract Christians' participation in the birth of the sun. They simply transferred the Nativity feast from January 6 to December 25. One way of reading the myth then is to view the sun, the giver of life, as being supplanted by a son who gave his life.

In Roman and early Christian times great foccace and breads as round as the sun were served as magical foods at Christmas, when the sun was at its weakest and in need of help. In the Middle Ages, risen Christmas breads such as pandolce and panettone were also meant to pacify the forces of darkness and invoke fertility, while smaller rounds of medieval panpepati and panforte were equivalents on a more intimate domestic scale.

In every religion food is woven into myths and ceremonies, for food is metaphysical—meant for the soul—as well as nourishment for the body. Divinities eat consecrated meals with their faithful disciples, and gods even make a meal of their sacrificial victims. Perhaps the archetypal sacrificial meal was served by the Persian god Mithras, who plunged a knife into the primeval bull. Out of the bull's body grew all the healthy herbs and plants of the earth: From its marrow came grain, from its blood the vines, and finally seeds, which were collected by the moon. Its blood drenched the earth, but it also turned magically into grain, life created and fed by sacrifice. Mithras then sealed his friendship by sharing his feast with the Sun in the cool recesses of a grottolike Cosmic Cave, symbolic meeting place of the soul and the universe.

Jesus communicated his life in terms of a meal with his brotherhood, so that now Easter, the feast served to believers, consists of lamb, bread, and wine, symbols of sacrifice and of divinity become food. To eat God in the Eucharist was "a kind of audacious deification, a becoming of flesh that fed the world," in Bridget Ann Henisch's startling description in *Feast and Fast*. For millennia, bread and sweets have been made in the image of the gods, and eating them sacramentally has been a way of incorporating the gods' power. In a similar, more secular way, the people of Siena, where a famed horse race, the Palio, is a transfiguring experience, once ate the totem animals of their *contrade* as a way of ingesting their virtues. Eighteenth-century celebratory menus actually featured porcupine, wolf, owl, turtle, and other heraldic beasts. To this day, Italians create breads and sweets in the shape of the virtues associated with saints—the eyes of Santa Lucia, the breasts of Sant'Agata—and shape breads as religious amulets into ex-votos of legs, arms, and other parts of the body needing a saint's healing.

Italians have always celebrated abundance at the time of the harvest. Great moments in country life such as threshing the wheat, crushing the grapes, and killing the pig brought people together to help each other. And when the hard work was finished, they all sat down to a table heaped high with food. The meal was never more abundant than after the death of the pig, sacrificial animal par excellence. Chopped, spiced, and re-configured, it turned up as sausages, salame, ribs, roasts, and rich ragùs at the *panarda*, a gigantic thirty- to forty-course dinner held in Abruzzo for the Feast Day of Sant'Antonio, which coincides with the killing of the pig. Although there are no indications that the orgy of food stimulates a sexual orgy, the atmosphere of excess probably encourages it, as one scholar has commented, just at the time when fertility could use some encouragement. The Sant'Antonio celebration offers the first fruits of the farm. Pigs had always been common—almost every family had one—and they became familiar symbols of sacrifice. The pig's body grew quickly, and its soft fat must have seemed like the earth itself, so the animal became sacred, a symbol of death. It was sacrificed ceremonially, tossed into a pit spaded out of the earth, and left there like an enormous seed to sprout into a new life. In eating the pig, participants essentially partook of the sacrificial offering and shared in the meal of the gods. If we are what we eat, then those diners in some way became the god and his blessings became theirs.

In ancient times when festivals began, there were no visible barriers between the natural and the spiritual worlds. The rituals of the pagan world referred to the forces of nature that determined men's lives, so fires were burned in midwinter to help the sun pour its diminished warmth into seeds lying in the earth. Christmas falls at the winter solstice, while midsummer is at the summer solstice, when the sun begins its inevitable descent toward winter, an unending double spiral of darkness and light, heat, and shadow. The winter and summer equinoxes come during the shortest and longest days of the year when, in Christian symbolism, Jesus and John the Baptist, gods of sun and water, are the keepers of the gates. Fires are lit in winter to reverse the darkness as if by magic and to make light out of the night. They help the weak winter sun burn away the old season in a collective exorcism. Come summer, the apex of the year, the flames of the fires help the skies prepare for the approaching darkness of winter.

Italians celebrate these natural phenomena through a narrative that tells of Mary, a virgin mother, whose son was born, suffered, died, and returned to life. The narrative is similar to others in earlier cultures, for in their need to explain the bewildering forces that determined their lives, people have created myths portraying gods as spiritual illustrations of the forces of nature, signs through whom revelations of the universe can be understood. They have dramatized the stories through rituals that borrow from the agricultural cycle in which plants and animals are born, grow and die in an repetitive cycle, in which every month brings its work, and the seasonal rotation of crops means that nothing really dies but returns to the earth as matter and waits for another spring. These are rituals repeated year after year in a rhythm of expectation and release or sacrifice and redemption.

Perhaps Persephone is the archetypal goddess of the festivals. In her myth the beautiful daughter of Demeter, goddess of agriculture, was abducted by Pluto while she collected flowers by the shores of Lake Pergusa in the center of Sicily. Pluto, King of the Underworld, wanted her to be his queen and stole her away, leaving no trace. When Demeter realized her daughter was gone, she tried without success to track her down, and in her grief vowed no plant would grow until Persephone was restored to her. And so the earth became barren and not a single ear of corn or blade of wheat pierced the dark crust of the soil. Demeter pleaded with Zeus to free her daughter and finally secured his promise, but just before Persephone left the underworld, she ate a pomegranate, whose seeds are little containers of fertility and rebirth. For partaking of the food of the gods, Persephone was forced to return each year and spend six months in Hades, just as her abduction in November into the underworld was followed by her freedom and the resurrection of plant life in the spring.

Ceremonies celebrated at Demeter's temple at Enna in Sicily culminated in the showing of "that great and marvelous mystery of perfect revelation, a cut stalk of grain," in the words of Joseph Campbell, who compares this stalk to the host in the Eucharist, the holy wafer made of grain, physical nourishment become spiritual food. Persephone's myth was transmuted by Christians to the story of Mary and Jesus, the sorrowing mother whose child dies and rises again in the springtime.

Even before Persephone and Demeter, there were similar figures in other cultures, although in some cases, it was the son who suffered, who was sacrificed, who died, then was reborn to be reunited with the Great Mother. Tammuz, a Sumerian shepherd, the son and spouse of Inanna, was sacrificed to the underworld, where he suffered and was reborn; Osiris was killed, and Isis, his mother and lover, cast a blight upon the earth and made it barren until he was returned to her; Adonis, son and lover of Aphrodite; Attis and Cybele: These are the pagan ancestors of Jesus and Mary, gods and goddesses absorbed into the Christian retelling. Each god dies violently, is buried in the earth, and is mourned by a grieving wife/mother until he is resurrected in the yearly cycle of renewal.

The Church essentially christianized the rites of Attis and Adonis and turned them into Easter. The sacrifices made by those gods are much bloodier—Adonis was gored to death by a wild boar, and Attis' priests flagellated and mutilated themselves, spattering blood upon the altars in what E. O. Jones called "a wild dance to unite their blood to the Mater Dolorosa, sorrowing for her dead lover." The intense mourning continued at night, and on the morning of March 25, during the festival celebrating the reappearance of the sun, Attis' tomb was found empty, marking the god's triumph over death, and he was resurrected and reunited with his goddess mother, Cybele. She is the source of the moon, which dies and rises in a known rhythm, the mother of the sun/son, who is born, dies, and rises again glowing with life. Each becomes a symbol and a channel to the great mystery of death and resurrection.

The cast of characters is large, but the Mother Goddess, Mother Earth in whatever guise, is always the same. Sometimes she split herself in two, as in Mesopotamia, where she was Inanna, Queen of Heaven, and Eresh-kigal, Queen of Hell; or in Egypt, where Isis searched both land and underworld for Osiris' body; or in the Eleusinian mysteries, where as Demeter she was the goddess of grain on earth, and as Persephone, the goddess of the darkness. Even the Virgin Mary has her dark underground aspect in the form of the Black Madonna, a wonder-working source of fertility and delight.

Look deep enough and it is still apparent that Italian festivals celebrate the forces that direct and determine life: sun, moon, tides, and rain. From these elements plants grow, animals flourish, and the year cycles round. The earlier rituals of fire, of foods invoking fertility, of consecrated meals calling upon unseen powers and asking the blessings of fate were repeated year after year in a rhythm of expectation and release. Today Italian celebrations are still deeply rooted in the soil of myth and in the cyclic calendar, bound to seasons and harvests. If saints have replaced gods in the rituals, there are still more than faint traces of Demeter's grain and Bacchus' grapes in the wheels of bread and barrels of wine that Italians consume as part of the celebrations.

COOKING FROM THIS BOOK

*A*nyone who has ever traveled in Italy knows that Italians celebrate at the slightest provocation. Every village and every city has a saint who has a feast day and a dish that goes with it, so it is hardly an exaggeration to say that there seems to be a food for every festival and a festival for every food. When I discovered a festival celebrating lard, I knew that the Italians could celebrate anything. The moments in the year when the wheat is threshed, the grapes are brought in, even when the pig is killed and turned into prosciutto, salame, and sausages, are times of hard work that stimulate ferocious appetites. And they are rewarded. Lazier events, like country *sagre* celebrating the fruits and vegetables of the countryside, may offer games of chance and an accordion player, but there is also a grill with meats sizzling on it or tables with wheels of local cheese, large pots of pasta, or heaps of sweets produced for the day. Religious holidays like Christmas and Easter bring forth platters full of specialties that vary not only from region to region but from city to city.

At festival time, desserts appear in abundance. Pastry cooks were part of a religious corporation in medieval times and rare and expensive ingredients—eggs, flour, sweetener, nuts, and candied fruit rinds—were perfect for folding into the special dishes of a celebration. The ancient Romans also made sweets in special forms and offered them as sacrifices to the gods and goddesses who controlled their fates. To this day almost every festival has a special cookie or sweet and some, such as the feast day of San Giuseppe, the patron saint of fryers, are celebrated with multiple forms of the same sweet. The frittelle—fritters—cooked for San Giuseppe in Milan are entirely different from those of Naples or Palermo, but that is the fun of Italy. Just when you think you have caught on, you discover that you have barely tasted any of the seemingly unending variations the country provides. Many of the recipes for the most traditional festival sweets and sweet breads are in *The Italian Baker,* my earlier book, which is why recipes for Christmas panettone and pandoro, Easter colomba and gubana, New Year's veneziana, and the panforte of Siena are not included in this book. But you will find twenty-seven new breads—from crunchy rustic rounds to delicate sweet breads for Easter, Christmas, and various holidays throughout the year. And there are over forty celebratory cookies and pastries, most of which will be new to Americans.

I have arranged this book by the calendar, starting in summertime, with its abundance of fruits, and progressing through the year. Each chapter describes a single festival and is followed by special recipes of the day. I have included such classic dishes as cotechino and lentils, which almost every Italian eats for good luck on New Year's Eve, as well as more regional recipes that may be made in only one tiny village one day of the year. Although a great many of the recipes are traditional tastes of the festivals, some may derive from special juried events tied to a particular holiday. I couldn't resist including recipes from the annual contest judging the best aceto balsamico, and I loved the pasta with crayfish made at a recent festival celebrating the chefs of the small town of Villa Santa Maria in Abruzzo. The organization of the book is clear, but cooks in search of specific recipes or looking for ideas in structuring a meal or dreaming up a dinner with which to entertain friends may need some help. To spare endless thumbing between index and chapters, use the Recipes by Category (page 449), organized from first course to dessert.

You might decide to invite guests for a dinner with a Palio theme, or for a meal celebrating the threshing of the wheat in the countryside of Tuscany, and create a spectacular evening that people will remember for years. But when making dinner for your family or a few casual friends, you don't want to order a suckling pig or worry about having the time to make a fruit-and-nut strudel. There are many easy and delicious dishes connected with festivals that can become part of your everyday repertoire. Here, for instance, are a few menus that might inspire you:

Gnocchi di Zucca: Pumpkin Gnocchi with
Shavings of Smoked Mozzarella and Sage Leaves

Tacchino alla Porchetta: Herb-Scented
Roast Turkey

A salad of arugula and other greens

Cassola: a creamy vanilla-scented cheesecake

Acquacotta: Vegetable Soup with Ribbons of
Sweet Peppers

Polenta with pork

Cipolline in Agrodolce: Tiny Sweet and
Sour Onions

Torta di Farina di Grano Saraceno: Buckwheat
Flour Cake with a Jam Filling

Spaghetti con i Turini: Spaghetti with Field
Mushrooms; or Tagliarini with Mushrooms
and Olives

Spiedini Misti: Grilled Calamari and Prawns
on Skewers

Baked artichokes with herbs

Baked fruit served with mascarpone sauce

Riso e Zucca: Creamy Pumpkin-Flavored Rice

Arrosto di Agnello alla Ceraiola: Garlic and
rosemary-studded leg of lamb

Pesce d'Uova: Little Croquettes in the Shape of
a Fish

Granita di Limone: Lemon Granita; and *Eporediesi:*
Chocolate-Hazelnut Cookies

Sedanini all'Ortolano: Pasta the
Greengrocer's Way

Tacchino con il Rosmarino: Roast Turkey Scented
with Rosemary and Pancetta

Caponata di Melanzane: Eggplant Caponata,
served warm

Fruit and Lemony Cookies from Cocullo

Li Straccetti: Lemon-Flavored Soup with Bread
and Cheese Strands

Coniglio in Aceto Balsamico: Rabbit in a Balsamic
Vinegar Sauce

Oven-roasted Potatoes Sprinkled with Garlic
and Rosemary

Quaresimale Toscani: Orange-Flavored
Chocolate Cookies

Minestra di Carciofi: Artichoke Soup

Risotta e Pollo all'Aceto Balsamico: Chicken and
Risotto Flavored with
Balsamic Vinegar

A green salad and a crunchy crusted
country bread

Bocca di Dama: Almond sponge cake, served
with mascarpone sauce

There are lots of hearty dishes that are perfect one-dish meals:

Fricandò: Spareribs, Sausages, Potatoes, and Vegetables

L'Jumacche Fellate di Sant'Antuon: Broccoli-Flavored Polenta Layered
    with Sausages and Cheese

Pappardelle sulla Lepre: Wide Pasta with a Rabbit Sauce

Tagano: Easter pasta dish that can be cooked ahead

Polenta Pasticciata: Baked polenta layered with a bold-flavored ragù

Risotto Fratacchione: Risotto, sausage, and cheese—As Gourmand
    Monks Liked It

Cisrà: Garbanzo and Vegetable Minestrone

Salsicce e Faciuol d'Pane: Sausage and Red Beans

Tofeja: Traditional Bean and Pork Carnival Dish

Sformato di Verdure: Artichoke Timbale

One word of caution: Many of these recipes call for peperoncini, dried
red chili peppers, which should be seeded and chopped. *Please* wear rubber
gloves when you do so. The seeds and volatile oils still in the peppers
are very strong and can migrate to any cuts you might have. I learned
the hard way. Once when I removed my contact lenses, the oil from the
dried peppers still on my fingertips permeated the lenses immediately.
My eyes stung for a long time and I had to throw the contact lenses away.
Please don't repeat my experience.

I have tried to give straightforward directions for recipes that include
texture and tastes of the foods to encourage everyone to try them. I hope
that the flavors and aromas will send people to their kitchens and perhaps
inspire journeys to the festivals themselves. To make that easier, a Traveler's Calendar (page 455) lists numerous festivals and their special foods,
which are served in the piazze and great halls in many areas to everyone
who comes to enjoy the special day.

RECIPES BY CATEGORY

APPETIZERS

PASTA AND SAUCES

RICE, RISOTTO, AND POLENTA

SOUP

FISH AND SEAFOOD

MEAT AND POULTRY

DESSERTS

*F*or travelers who might want to go to a festival or two, the trick is to be in the right place at the right time. Aldous Huxley recognized the problem when he wrote about coming upon little market towns in his travels and finding feasts and celebrations "that were orgiastic like the merry-making in a Breughel painting," and wondered how he would ever remember the date, and even then, how to arrange to be in the same place at the right time.

An excellent question. This fragmentary calendar contains only the tiniest sampling of Italy's rich heritage of feasts and festivals. I am certain that thousands of Italians will be furious that the *feste* or *sagre* of their towns have been neglected, but this is not an encyclopedia. I have tried to highlight celebrations that serve some sort of ritual food as well as country feasts that are focused around food, although I admit that I have included a few of Italy's most important festivals where food is not a focus. For every *festa* listed in this book, there must be hundreds more. After all, every village and country town in Italy has a patron saint who rates a celebration, and there are dozens of *sagre* devoted to mushrooms, chestnuts, peaches, seafood, and fava beans, to name only a few. I actually made a list of every ingredient in the Italian diet and could find a festival or *sagra* serving almost every one.

I have tried to be accurate, but since events in Italy change without warning, I cannot guarantee that a festival has not been moved to a new spot on the calendar or vanished entirely. Just as an example, I once went to a festival in Calabria after confirming the date, but as I drove down the curving road to the sea, I noticed how few cars there were and saw how easy it was to park. Hunting down the man in charge of the event confirmed my worst fears: the town had moved the festival to a later date because the national elections in the previous week had been so tiring. Hardly consoling for someone who had come hundreds of miles for the event, but a lesson to be remembered.

Feste and *sagre* that were part of the calendar ten years ago may have disappeared by now or lost their sparkle, while new ones have popped up, launched by tourist agencies or local authorities hoping to bring tourists to the town. A guidebook of Italian festivals published before the Second World War confirms that many no longer exist: no more can you celebrate the melons of Brindisi, the capons of Morozzo, or the various fish of Chioggia. The city of Casalvecchio has given up having a contest to see who can eat the most maccheroni di ricotta using no implements but one's mouth. I hope I am not adding to the confusion. By including the Infiorata in Spello, a charming and beautiful town, I do not mean to neglect Genzano, where the tradition started and continues today. Some festivals like the ancient Corpus Christi celebration in Orvieto are dying out, and some may soon come to an abrupt halt for political reasons. In 1987 it was touch and go whether Noiantri, the famous festival of Trastevere in Rome, would be held once party politics entered the fray. "It is the festival of the historical center of Rome and there are 160,000 inhabitants; it is time to arrange ourselves," the newspaper quoted the president of the cultural commission as saying, but there were eleven votes against the festival, five for, and two abstentions. The next day the cultural commission reconsidered the vote, tossed out the president, and saved the porchetta, Coca-Cola, and counters of food and wine. The *sagra* went on.

Be prepared for the fact that almost everything, except bars, restaurants, and souvenir shops, closes down on festival days. Traffic can be jammed and parking very difficult. Wear comfortable shoes and be prepared to walk long distances. And remember that when a national holiday such as Christmas falls on a Thursday or Friday, it is very likely that stores and restaurants will remain closed on Saturday and Sunday as city authorities make a "bridge" to the next working day, thereby creating a very long weekend. It happens not only at Christmas and New Year, but again for the Feast of Saints Peter and Paul on June 29, when *everything*—offices, banks, stores—closes. Public transportation is dramatically reduced at these times. Needless to say, there are long lines of traffic returning to the cities on Sunday night.

As protection against the unexpected, it is worth checking newspapers and magazines to be sure that *feste* and *sagre* are still being celebrated on their posted dates. And it is definitely worth turning off the road when you see a sign for a *sagra* or hear a band playing. You may come upon a simple celebration in a village, with old men drinking and women dancing and children playing games. You may find food being served in the piazza or on an old country road, where chickens, ribs, and sausages are grilled over an immense fire as townspeople, even nuns, fill your plate. You may find also that the pasta and crostini are served on the hydraulic lift in a local garage usually given over to fixing Fiats. Men and women in white aprons and hats all dusted with flour may be frying big vats of frittelle in the church courtyard, and you could decide to stay until night falls and the dancing starts. Trying to find your car by the light of the moon is one more part of the adventure of Italy, where *feste* and *sagre* occur every day of the week, and especially on Sundays.

January 2

CASTIGLIONE D'ASTI (Piedmont) For a bean festival that has been celebrated in this town since 1200, cauldrons of silky-skinned white beans bubble on the main piazza. Once cooked, they are distributed free to everyone.

January 5 · Eve of Epiphany

FASSA, PALÙ, SABBIO CHIESA, AND MITTERBERG (Alto Adige) These towns, among others, celebrate the eve of Epiphany with ritual visits by the three kings and with special songs; in some places, dinner is offered to the group. It includes polenta taragna, buckwheat polenta with layers of melted Gorgonzola, young, unaged formaggelle cheese, and butter.

ROME (Latium) On the last day of the holiday season the Piazza Navona is full of counters selling toys and sweets of every variety, including the famous *carbone,* black sugar made to look like the coal that goes into the stockings of bad children.

January 6 · Epiphany

FERENTILLO (Friuli) A *sagra* offers sausages and the white polenta of Friuli.

PIANA DEGLI ALBANESI (Sicily) Women in Greek Orthodox costumes are part of an elegant procession to the church for the Feast of Lights and the Oriental rites connected with the baptism of Christ. Oranges are blessed, then distributed to the community as a symbol of prosperity for the New Year.

TARCENTO (Friuli) A costumed procession precedes a torchlight parade to the top of the hill for the burning of a great bonfire called the *pignarul.* Traditional foods grilled on the *fogolar* on the main piazza as part of the celebration include local sausages called *cotechino* and beefsteaks. See page 303.

CIVIDALE AND GEMONA (Friuli) Spectacular masses are celebrated in the ancient churches of these two towns. In the one held in the basilica in Cividale a deacon wearing a warrior's helmet uses a sword to bless the faithful during a mass that was instituted by a ninth-century ruler, the warlike Patriarch of Aquileia.

NARDO (Sicily) celebrates the Feast of Sant'Elia by demonstrating how ricotta is made and then serving it on tagliatelle.

First Saturday in January

FAENZA (Ravenna, Emilia-Romagna) In the deep cold of winter, the people of Faenza light a large bonfire on which they burn Il Niballo, a figure named for the Carthaginian general Hannibal. Afterward they eat roast sausages and traditional sweets, and drink Italian mulled wine poured from jugs made of the world-famous local ceramics.

January 13 · Feast of Sant'Ilario (Saint Hilary)

PARMA (Emilia-Romagna) celebrates the festival of its patron saint, Sant'Ilario, a Christianized Cinderella, with cookies baked in the shape of the shoe he lost while crossing the river to Parma.

January 16 and 17 · Feast of Sant'Antonio Abate (Saint Anthony the Abbot)

VOLONGO (Cremona, Lombardy) A fire made of branches pruned from trees in the Po Valley burns on Sant'Antonio's Day while housewives make a crumbly mint-scented cake called *torta dura*. It is much like torta sbrisolona and is made of a mixture of corn and wheat flours.

VILLAVALLELONGO (Abruzzo) Fava beans are cooked in large cauldrons on the piazza, tossed with olive oil and herbs, and distributed to everyone with le panette, anise-flavored focacce.

FARA FILIORUM PETRI (Chieti, Abruzzo) Thousands of branches are made into huge pyramids that are set afire, and then everyone goes from house to house for wine and dessert. Many other small towns in Abruzzo, such as Alfedena, Pescocostanzo, Introdacqua, and Collelongo, celebrate with bonfires, processions, and food.

SUTRI (Latium) Country people bring horses with richly decorated bridles to be blessed in the main piazza, but they also participate in special games. Costumed processions precede a competition in which riders galloping on horseback must use a lance extended arm's length to cut loose a star hanging from a thread. This event is followed by dancing and feasting on such local products as sausages, beans cooked with pork rind, cheeses, sweets, and wine.

NAPLES (Campania) The bonfires of Sant'Antonio are built out of discarded household objects and are burned at many street corners. In the neighborhood dedicated to the saint, vendors pass through the streets selling soffritto, or zuppa forte (strong soup), made of giblets, and lesser parts of the pig cooked in tomato sauce and served with spaghetti or ladled on grilled bread.

DORGALI (Sardinia) Fragrant rosemary is set ablaze in a bonfire on the piazza, and i pistiddu, a local sweet, is served with the first wine of the new year.

LILLIANES (Val d'Aosta) Delicate sweet tortelli made with butter from the Alps are covered with honey or sugar and eaten with the best wine of the valley.

NOVOLI (Lecce, Apulia) It takes more than a month to collect the branches and vine cuttings that build a pyre as high as the façade of the town Duomo. A sheaf of wheat and orange branches crowns the top. Once it is lighted, animals are brought to be blessed, processions and games begin, and platters of turcinieddi, bits of highly seasoned lamb giblets, wrapped in casings of intestines and cooked over a smoldering fire, are served.

VILLASTRADA (Lombardy) The country restaurant Nizzoli serves a traditional *maialata,* the dinner of the day the pig is killed. Bowls full of crispy ciccioli are followed by a pâté made of lard pestled with garlic, onions, and parsley spread on sliced grilled polenta. The meal of steamy risotto, with newly made sausages, livers, pigs' feet, even sanguinaccio, is served on long wooden boards and on trenchers while Lambrusco flows freely.

PINEROLO (Piedmont) The Feast Day of Sant'Antonio Abate is celebrated with focacce colored gold with saffron and seasoned with salt and pepper. The foccace are not meant to be eaten but kept as talismans until needed to aid a sick animal.

Third Sunday in January

TUSCANIA (Latium) A *sagra* of cauliflower frittelle, fritters cooked in huge frying pans, takes place during a traditional gathering of local cowboys.

Last Thursday in January

CANTÙ (Como, Lombardy) A figure representing winter is burned, after which everyone settles down to a meal of risotto e luganega, rice and local sausage, with lots of Parmesan cheese.

Last Saturday in January

ALBAVILLA (Como, Lombardy) At the ceremony of the burning of winter a simple rustic fried bread called *cotizza* is served. The snack, common around Lake Como, is made of a sweetened dough that is fried and then sprinkled with vanilla sugar.

Last Sunday in January

BADIA DI DULZAGO and *BELLINZAGO NOVARESE* (Piedmont) A *fagiolata*, a great celebration of beans, is an old rustic custom for which freshly picked beans are cooked in seven copper cauldrons and distributed to everyone present.

January 30 and 31 · Fair of Sant'Orso

AOSTA (Val d'Aosta) A crafts fair is held in honor of Sant'Orso, an Irish monk who lived in the Aosta Valley in the sixth century. He was a very able carver who turned out quantities of wooden sandals that he distributed to the poor. To this thousand-year-old fair craftsmen bring articles carved of wood, such as the *grolla*, a many-spouted cup for sharing wine, along with such cooking implements as mortars and pestles, ladles, whisks, capacious flour scoops, and special instruments for removing cream from the top of milk. Fine lace and woolen fabrics are sold next to farm tools, household furniture, and delicate sculptures, but the selling occurs only on January 31. Local restaurants serve regional specialties that include moceta, leg of chamois cured like prosciutto; zuppa alla valdostana, cabbage soup glazed with melted Fontina cheese; polenta rich with Fontina; and the local buttery Fontina and toma cheeses.

 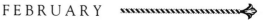 FEBRUARY

Sometime in February

SAN SECONDO (Parma, Emilia-Romagna) A select group of fewer than two hundred people is invited to dinner in the town hall to taste approximately fifteen different kinds of culatello. Silky culatello, the "heart" of prosciutto, is made from the center of the rump, and the meat is both precious and rare. This dinner honors the fine artisans in several nearby villages who cure and produce it. Two juries of experts award a prize to the best of the best in a ceremony in which the president of the confraternity, dressed in an ermine-trimmed velvet robe, invites the winners to kneel, touches a sword to their heads, and makes them swear they will always make an equally fine product.

First Thursday and Friday in February

GERGEI (Sardinia) The night before the ancient *sagra* of the *sassineddu* —for which a big arbor of braided reeds is decorated with flowers, oranges, apples, mandarin oranges, candies, and little cookies—a great dinner is held on the piazza at which sausages and game are cooked on a huge grill and local Malvasia wine is poured.

First to Second Sunday in February

AGRIGENTO (Sicily) A weeklong festival is held in honor of the flowering almond trees. In Phrygian myths the almond tree was considered the father of the world, perhaps because it was the first tree to flower in springtime and in Greek myths the almond was the nut of immortality. Nowadays this festival, heralding the arrival of the first fruits of spring, is combined with an International Folklore Festival with exotic instruments, uninterrupted singing, and processions and performances. All kinds of Sicilian sweets made with almonds and almond paste are served along with almond ice cream.

RETORBIDO (Lombardy) Polenta, which is known as the meat of the poor, and salame are distributed with good wines from the region.

February 3 · Feast Day of San Biagio (Saint Blaise)

TARANTA PELIGNA (Abruzzo) After mass, sourdough breads shaped like four-fingered hands are distributed at the church door. See pages 340–341.

SERRA SAN BRUNO (Calabria) A special mostaccioli-like sweet called an *abbacolo,* shaped like a bishop's scepter or a question mark, depending on the view of the beholder, is baked this one day of one year for a young man to present to his fiancée. If she breaks it and keeps the round piece at the bottom, it means they will be married soon. Even people who aren't engaged eat abbacoli, which are also known as *nzuddi* and reappear in November for All Souls' Day.

SALEMI (Trapani, Sicily) Tiny snow-white breads called *cavadduzzi* are intricately formed to look like grasshoppers and baked to commemorate San Biagio's intervention during a plague of the insects.

February 3–5 · Feast of Sant'Agata (Saint Agatha)

CATANIA (Sicily) "Long live Sant'Agata," shout the people of Catania as 11 twenty-foot-high wooden eighteenth-century bell towers called *cannalore,* decorated with sculptures, flowers, candles, and embroidered banners, are "danced" through the streets. Bearers carry the *camalore* as they make courtesy calls on the city's churches and visit the shrine of Sant'Agata, who was martyred for refusing to yield to the Roman consul Quinziano in 251. The ritual food connected with Sant'Agata is a sweet cake shaped like one of the Saint's breasts and filled with almond paste. See page 11.

Carnival

Carnival has many expressions in Italy. Among the most fascinating are:

IVREA (Piedmont) The battle of oranges. See pages 345–350.

BAGOLINO (Lombardy) Young girls in beautiful headdresses and costumes dance in the streets, while other celebrants carry heavy wooden cradles with children or dolls in them, rocking and cuddling them as symbols of the New Year.

ROMARZOLO (Trentino) A procession followed by hearty eating precedes the burning of winter in the form of a tree covered with bay leaves and chains of colored paper and garlanded with oranges, sausages, dried bread, and eggshells.

TERMENO (Trentino) The Festa dell'Egetmann is celebrated every four years with a procession featuring the wedding of Egetmann Hansel, a straw doll that is carried through town with his fiancée on a carriage. The procession stops at every fountain, where tall horned figures with crocodile heads jump around as marriage banns are read. At each fountain, one of the creatures is "killed" with a butcher knife.

ORISTANO (Sardinia) The Sartiglia, from *sortija*, the Spanish word for ring, is an extraordinary race and medieval joust in which riders wear elegant costumes, finely carved wooden masks, and top hats as they gallop at full speed toward a silver star and thrust their swords through a ring. An ancient rite that belonged to the aristocracy until fairly recently, the Sartiglia is preceded by a beautiful procession, and followed by offerings of Carnival sweets—amaretti and *zippulas*, as the fritters called zeppole are known in Sardinia.

MAMOIADA (Sardinia) Carnival in Mamoiada is really a lugubrious anti-Carnival featuring twelve men called Mamuthones who are dressed in animal skins and wear mournful wooden masks and clusters of heavy brass bells. They are treated like scapegoats by onlookers, who chase them out of town in four ritual performances. At the end of the day the town explodes in a joyous festival.

VIAREGGIO (Tuscany) Huge floats, many spoofing current political and entertainment figures, make their way through crowded streets for one of Italy's most famous Carnival celebrations. The event is televised to an enormous viewing audience, some of whom may be waiting to hear the results of the big lottery held on the day.

VENICE (Veneto) The most beautiful Carnival in Italy is also the most famous. People wearing masks and costumes carouse in the silvery Venetian light.

RONCIGLIONE (Latium) A riderless horse race through the streets of this tiny town is followed by free platefuls of maccheroni.

Last Friday of Carnival (Venerdì Gnoccolar)

VERONA (Veneto) holds a bacchanalia of gnocchi at which the Pope of Gnocchi leads a parade of people dressed in fifteenth-century costumes. When the procession reaches the Piazza San Zeno, in front of the church with its beautiful doors, steaming gnocchi are available. See page 369.

CASTEL GOFFREDO (near Mantua, Lombardy) The election of a different "pope" and distribution of gnocchi are highlights.

Last Monday of Carnival

SANTHIA and *BIELLA* (Piedmont) A bean festival is held in the towns' public gardens or on their main piazze.

Last Tuesday of Carnival

TOSSIGNANO (Emilia-Romagna) At the same time a festival serves polenta layered with sausage and Parmesan cheese in a little town at the top of the hill. See page 373.

BORGO TOSSIGNANO (Emilia-Romagna) A *festa* serving maccheroni con ragù is held in the little village at the bottom of the hill from Tossignano: polenta versus maccheroni, north versus south. Lots of carnival rides and a parade complete the day. See page 374.

Ash Wednesday

GRADOLI (Latium) An expiatory lunch the Pranzo del Purgatorio serves six delicious fish courses to more than 1,800 people. See page 377.

IVREA (Piedmont) A gigantic meal of merluzzo e polenta includes polenta grassa, prepared in Val d'Aosta fashion, layered with slices of Fontina cheese and well lubricated with butter. See page 349–350.

BORGOSESIA (Piedmont) Il Mercu Scurot says farewell to Carnival early in the morning with bean feasts in each district of the town. Men wear the traditional dinner jacket and top hat and have a ladle hanging from their necks. In the evening, wine is distributed to everyone.

CASTEL D'ARIO (near Mantua, Lombardy) A counter-Carnival held as consolation for what was once a year-long Lenten existence, this huge culinary blowout called a *bigolata* serves homemade spaghetti formed by a special press that extrudes the pasta. Platters of it are served with a sauce of anchovies and onions. The original meal was polenta and a single herring, slapped at the polenta or dipped into it briefly.

February 12 · Feast of San Bello

BERBENNO (near Sondrio, Lombardy) This popular celebration recalls a historical event around 1466 when a friar, Fra Benigno of the Order of Humility, arrived in the Valtellina and identified himself as Ippolito de' Medici of the Florentine family who had come to found a monastery. The townspeople renamed him San Bello and celebrate his memory with risotto, chicken, salame, and wine.

Third Sunday in February

SPELLO (Umbria) A celebration of the olive harvest features bruschetta, country bread rubbed with garlic and drizzled with newly pressed extra-virgin olive oil. A group of olive pickers parades from the countryside into the town singing folk songs and carrying branches cut from olive trees. Joined by the townspeople, they proceed to three taverns, one for each neighborhood of the city, which that day serve hot mulled wine, roast pork, and grilled sausages, white beans, and polenta.

Third Week of February

NORCIA (Umbria) is perfumed with the smell of the black truffles that grow in its woods. Counters on the street sell the truffles and other local products.

March 6

MONASTERO BORMIDA (Piedmont) A gigantic polenta festival called a *polentonissimo* is linked to the memory of the generous Marchese Rovere who saved some starving coppersmiths when they were trapped by a sudden snowstorm. He fed them polenta and a frittata, and to this day, more than 180 years later, a mountain of polenta covered with a sauce of sausage and salame and an onion frittata weighing more than eighty pounds are cooked and served on the main piazza of the town.

First Sunday in Lent

GOITO (Lombardy) On this day a game is played that focuses on a ritual turkey bashing, as if the bird were a *piñata*. Seven days later a feast of fish from the nearby Mincio River is served.

SANT'IPPOLITO DI VERNIO (Tuscany) A centuries-old *sagra* features chestnut-flour polenta served with herring, and spaghetti with tuna sauce. The spaghetti is cooked in big pots on the piazza, then everyone eats, sings, and dances.

March 19 · San Giuseppe (Saint Joseph's Day)

CASTELL'ARQUATO (Lombardy) To honor San Giuseppe, tortelli, baked or fried, are distributed from numerous kiosks.

LEZZENO (on Lake Como, Lombardy) Various sections of town vie to see which can build the biggest bonfires in a contest that has its roots in the Middle Ages. The celebrations end with tastes of tortelli—everyone's reward.

ROCCA SAN CASCIANO (Emilia-Romagna) Two adjacent villages have a contest to see which can light the longest-lasting fire. Celebratory foods include tortelloni alla lastra, salame, pecorino cheese, and piadine, the tortilla-like bread of Romagna, along with lots of wine.

SANTA MARGHERITA LIGURE (Liguria) Frittelle made of fish, apples, sweets, and much wine are offered to everyone while bidding good-bye to winter with a great bonfire. The neighboring Genoese used to make limone fritte, frittelle with fresh lemon leaves in the dough, for San Giuseppe.

ROME (Latium) The Trionfale quarter is hung with lights, all the better to celebrate with the traditional frittelle for San Giuseppe.

FABRIANO (the Marches) Mountains of frittelle are fried in the Piazza del Commune.

TORO (Molise) The ritual lunch of San Giuseppe has thirteen courses. They begin with pasta con la mollica (the bread signifies the saint's beard) made with a thick pasta called *reginella*. Next come pasta with anchovies; rice cooked in milk; baccalà baked with bay leaves; fried baccalà; fried fish; boiled turnips; beans; a sweet-and-sour vegetable dish; and calzoni, puff-pastry cakes filled with chick peas that have been boiled and mashed, sweetened and flavored with spices.

SAN MARZANO, MONTEPARANO, AND LIZZANO (Apulia) serve meals that have thirteen peppery dishes and very sweet desserts. *MOLA DI BARI* serves lasagne with two sauces, a white one made with almonds, anchovies, and toasted bread crumbs, and a red one made with tomatoes.

NAPLES (Campania) Frittelle are fried at stands and bakeries all over the city.

ALCAMO, BORGETTO, AND SALEMI (Trapani); *SANTA CROCE CAMERINA AND SOMMATINO* (Caltanisetta); *RIBERA* (Agrigento); *VALGUARNERA, CANOPEPE* (Enna); *CAMPOBELLO DI LICATA AND BURGIO* (Agrigento); *SCORDIA* (Ragusa); *AND BARRAFRACCA* (Catania) in Sicily hold traditional San Giuseppe's meals with intricately shaped breads and many platters of food. See pages 392–398.

Almost every Italian town prepares special fried sweets for San Giuseppe's Day. Their names may vary from region to region, but they are usually called *zeppole, frittelle,* or *bignè di San Giuseppe,* depending on the area. They may be creamy rice fritters or like cream puffs that are either fried or baked. They come plain or filled with custard or whipped cream.

March is the time for marzolino, an oval sheep's milk cheese made during March, the month when lambs are being nursed, so there is very little available.

Last Sunday in March

RETORBIDO (Lombardy) holds an enormous polenta festival.

Good Friday

TARANTO (Apulia) The day before, Holy Thursday, begins with a procession of men in white hoods and tunics who walk barefoot while visiting the sepulchers of the city. The penitential pilgrimage continues the whole day, and gives way to a second procession that lasts through the night during which a man holding a wooden board with four iron knockers beats out the rhythm for its agonizingly slow progress. By early morning on Good Friday a procession of the Mysteries continues at the same torturous, sad pace along streets lit only with torches and lanterns. Other such processions occur at *CHIETI* and *SULMONA* (Abruzzo); *GUBBIO* (Umbria); and *TRAPANI* and *CALTANISETTA* (Sicily).

SAN MARCO IN LAMIS (Apulia) Dozens of bonfires made of *le fracchie,* tall pyramids of branches, light the way for a procession in which the Virgin Mary begins to search for her son.

TRAPANI (Sicily) The Procession of the Mysteries. See page 409.

Easter

PRIZZI (Sicily) The devils' dance, *abbullu di li diavuli,* features two gap-toothed devils with shaggy sheepskin manes and Death dressed in a yellow suit. The devils pounce upon local citizens and pull them into an improvised bar where they are compelled to pay a sizable sum for a drink. Cannatuni, local Easter sweets made with dough enclosing an hard-cooked egg, are given to guests who arrive before Death and the devils are finally chased away. The Madonna in her blue gown can embrace her risen son, represented by mechanical figures that are carried separately through town until they meet triumphantly.

SAN BIAGIO PLATANI (Sicily) Arches of bread line two full blocks of the village in a glorious display of the fruits of the earth. A meeting of the Madonna and her risen son occurs in the piazza where the streets meet. See page 339.

PIANA DEGLI ALBANESI (Sicily) Easter is celebrated according to traditional Byzantine rites, after which red-dyed eggs are distributed to all visitors.

TREDOZIO (Emilia-Romagna) A comical battle is fought with hard-boiled eggs as weapons. The winner is the first contestant to hit his opponent's egg and break it.

FLORENCE (Tuscany) A cart called the *Brindellone* is drawn to the Piazza del Duomo by garlanded white oxen. Inside the Duomo, at the moment when the Gloria is said, a paper dove begins to descend along a steel wire crossing the length of the nave and continues its downward trajectory out of the cathedral into the piazza, where it hits the Brindellone and sets it on fire in an explosion of color and noise. Traditional Easter fare in Florence once included herbolati e agnelli benedetti, vegetable tarts and lamb that had been blessed, and the ritual lunch served to the corporal and soldiers who escorted the cart included two dishes with ceci (garbanzo beans), baccalà in zimino (fried cod served with fresh bread crumbs and garlic), cacio pecorino, and a half flask of wine per person.

Easter Monday

FONTANELICE (Emilia-Romagna) celebrates the Festa della Piè Fritta. The unleavened piadina cooked on a griddle is the traditional country bread of the region, "smooth as paper, round as the moon."

First Sunday After Easter

FENIS (Val d'Aosta) The first elimination round is held in the battle of the queen of milk cows, a contest that will be decided late in October. Traditional foods of the Aosta Valley are featured: polenta layered with Fontina cheese made from the milk of those local cows, grilled sausages, and spezzatino, a veal stew. The people of the valley say of fresh cheese like the young Fontina in the polenta, "Fresh cheese has three virtues: It sates hunger and thirst and it cleans your teeth."

Second Sunday in April

TEOLO (Veneto) Thousands of pounds of potatoes are turned into gnocchi for the six thousand people who come here to eat them.

BUBBIO (Piedmont) A golden coin is concealed inside an enormous polenta made on the main piazza. Everyone gets to eat the polenta, sausages, and frittata, and drink Barbera wine, but the finder of the coin receives a special prize.

April 23 · Feast of San Giorgio (Saint George)

MACCASTORNA (Lombardy) Fried frogs' legs are served in all the *trattorie* of the area. These were common fare in Lombardy when frogs by the thousands used to be fished out of the rice fields where they lived. San Giorgio's Day is a pastoral rite that was originally linked with turning the flocks and herds out to new pastures. The Roman poet Ovid wrote of sprinkling both sheep and people with water, cleansing and sweeping the animals' stalls, and lighting fires to purify the fields. In Lombardy until the end of World War II, farm contracts, traditionally signed on the Feast Day of San Giorgio, were said to run from San Giorgio to San Giorgio. Everyone ate pan di mei, which used to be made out of millet, but is now a lightly sweetened cornbread served with thick cream.

April 25 · Feast of San Marco (Saint Mark)

VENICE (Veneto) San Marco, the patron saint of Venice, was celebrated by the doges with risi e bisi, a creamy rice dish made with fresh spring peas from the kitchen gardens of the lagoon. During the years of the Republic of San Marco, the banquet held in the Palazzo Ducale on the Feast Day of San Marco was relatively modest, so the rulers could keep a low profile and suggest that theirs was a government based not on oligarchy, but on the will of the people. In keeping with that philosophy, a mere twelve to fourteen courses were served instead of the usual seventy to eighty. The menu always began with rice terrines and a dish called *bisi col persutto*, peas with prosciutto; the scholar Massimo Alberini surmises that when the two dishes got mixed, risi e bisi was the result. The doge had the first taste, and while the doges are no more, risi e bisi is still served.

LEI (Nuoro, Sardinia) In honor of San Marco, protector of the fields, breads baked in the shape of a Greek cross with leaves, flowers, and plants appliqued on top are passed out to bless the countryside. Their extreme whiteness is a sign of their purity.

Last Weekend in April

BOMARZO (Latium) The town that is famous for a garden of stone monsters celebrates its patron saint, Sant'Anselmo, with an anise-flavored ciambella that was once eaten by countrypeople and shepherds. Bands and a parade with floats that show the making and cooking of the dough precede the actual eating and drinking. Ciambelle are often dipped into wine.

SEZZE ROMANO (Latium) The enormous round artichokes called *cimaroli* and the cone-shaped violet-leaved *violetta* variety of the Rome countryside, both tender and without thorns or chokes, are cooked six different ways and served with the famous breads of Sezze. Especially renowned are carciofi alla romana—seasoned with garlic, salt, pepper, and mentuccia, a delicate herb of the mint family—and carciofi alla giudea, cooked in the Jewish style. The latter are fried until they are crispy outside, creamy inside, and look like a large autumnal chrysanthemum.

PONTI (Piedmont) This town holds a polenta *sagra* that dates back to 1650, when a group of hungry and tired coppersmiths from Cosenza in Calabria came to the ruling de Carretto family and asked for help. They commissioned the smiths to fashion an enormous copper pot for cooking vast quantities of polenta, which was served along with a huge frittata of eggs and codfish. The festival remains faithful to its origins.

BUSCEMI (Syracuse, Sicily) A *sagra* of ricotta, made from the milk of local sheep, celebrates this cheese, which is slightly piquant and as delicate and custardy as the softest scrambled eggs.

MAY

May 1 · Calendimaggio

ASSISI (Umbria) The return of spring is heralded with parades in medieval costume, games, and a competition between the lower and upper parts of the city in singing ballads of love. The traditional dish of the festival is porchetta.

TERAMO (Abruzzo) The Sagra delle Virtù, once celebrated on the piazza in front of the cathedral, has now moved into restaurants. The food of the day is a minestrone called *le sette virtù,* a thick soup whose ingredients merge leftovers from the old year with the fresh vegetables of the new.

May 1–3

CALATAFIMI (Sicily) A spring festival in honor of the sacred crucifix occurs only once every six years. Armed with rifles, the men of the village walk in a procession carrying an ancient wooden crucifix. They are accompanied by thousands of faithful pilgrims, each group with its insignia of agricultural products. Dozens of men on horseback or riding in carriages toss breads, made specially for the festival, right into the crowds.

May 1–4 · Feast of Sant'Efisio (Saint Efisius)

CAGLIARI (Sardinia) For the *sagra* of Sant'Efisio, people from every city on the island of Sardinia arrive in Cagliari in their traditional costumes and jewelry. In an opulent procession through the city, they follow the image of the saint as it sets out on its annual pilgrimage to Pula, a tiny town about fifteen miles away, where the saint was martyred. Once

Sant'Efisio reaches the city limits, the procession stops, he trades his glorious seventeenth-century costume for a much plainer outfit, and is transferred to a lighter cart. Most of the elegantly dressed Sardinians leave the procession at this point, but the saint persists through night and day, and once he has participated in the religious ceremonies in Pula, he returns to Cagliari for a whirlwind celebration full of music, sport, and banqueting.

May 1 · Sagra

VILLAIOLA (Emilia-Romagna) A celebration of Parmigiano-Reggiano, the queen of Italian grating cheeses, includes a demonstration of the process of how it is made using the implements of another era.

Pentecost and the Following Two Days

ACCETTURA (Basilicata) Two trees, the *maggio* and the *cima*, which symbolize the male and female, are brought from two local forests to the piazza, where one is mounted upon the other to make a tree that is more than ninety feet tall. Teams of men then try to shake loose money hidden in the leafy branches, and everyone feasts on taralli, zeppole, and wine.

May 1–10 · Sagra of San Francesco (Saint Francis)

LULA (Sardinia) This is a serious religious festival for which shepherds have traditionally borne gifts of food to friars praying at the foot of the sanctuary. The ritual food is called *filindeu*, vegetable soup made with cheese, and *cordula*, tiny pieces of lamb giblet and innards wound with lamb intestine as fine as ribbon into long strips, and then grilled. It is a traditional food of the shepherds' culture. The friars prepare rustic tables with food and wine in the shade of olive trees. On May 10 the faithful enter Nuoro, a large nearby city.

First Thursday in May · Feast of San Domenico (Saint Dominic)

COCULLO (Abruzzo) This town is noted for a religious festival in honor of San Domenico, who, like Saint Patrick, drove snakes out of the village. Special sweet wreathlike cakes shaped like snakes biting their own tails are made for the bearers of the town standard. See page 21.

First Sunday in May

PRETORO (Abruzzo) To celebrate a miracle in which San Domenico transformed poisonous snakes into fragrant bread, the women of Pretoro follow a celebratory procession carrying rounds of bread shaped like snakes.

May 7 · Feast of San Nicola (Saint Nicholas)

POLLUTRI (Abruzzo) This festival, with its picturesque parade of deco-rated carts, commemorates the great spirit of charity in the life of San Nicola. During a terrible famine he crossed the sea to procure food for his people; today taralli are distributed in memory of this act.

BARI (Apulia) The Sagra of San Nicola, patron saint of Bari, began when the Turks menaced the city of Mari in Asia Minor in 1807, compelling sailors from Bari to bring the saint's relics (then in Mari) back to their city. The event begins with a picturesque parade through torchlit streets as the statue of the saint is carried to a floating altar set on a fishing boat. Three days of celebration follow, and then the faithful return home. The myths and religious elements of the festival connect sea and land, although no traces remain of the May Day celebrations that once took place at around this time. The food of pilgrimages is usually the food of the poor, such as olives, cheese, or bread—and San Nicola's *sagra* is no different. The bread is said to derive from a miracle he performed in bringing grain to the starving people of Mari during a famine. The hospice attached to his order once gave out three meals a day, but they were reduced in 1929 to one roll, two eggs, and a glass of wine. Now the roll is all that is offered, and it has become a simple tarallo. See page 321.

First Sunday in May · Sagre

BASSANO DEL GRAPPA (Veneto) White asparagus, grown under straw to keep it from turning green, is judged in a contest. Local restaurants cook it in traditional dishes.

SESSAME (Piedmont) An exceptional group of cooks prepares a gigantic risotto made, according to an old recipe, with meat that has marinated in wine. The *sagra* dates back to a famine in the thirteenth century when the Marchese del Carretto opened his warehouse and presented people with a great quantity of rice. There is only one catch: in order to have a taste of risotto, everyone must buy a hand-painted ceramic plate from the town.

CAVALLINO (Veneto) In the evening, after an afternoon regatta of canoes and catamarans, people eat asparagus with hard-boiled eggs.

Second Sunday in May · Sagre

CAMOGLI (Liguria) A fish festival on a gigantic scale fries up small fish. See page 37.

CILAVEGNA (Lombardy) Here is a chance to eat the famous asparagus of Cilavegna and to watch a pig palio in which each animal represents a different street in the town.

CESSOLE (Piedmont) According to a legend of the seventeenth century, some Ligurian merchants arrived in Cessole to sell salt and oil, but were stuck in a snowstorm when winter arrived unexpectedly. A local count offered them some flour, milk, and eggs; the dough that they made and then fried in boiling oil became known as *frittelle*. For the *sagra*, cooks prepare the frittelle, which are distributed by girls in period costumes, bands play, and folk dancers whirl around the piazza.

SELVA DEI MOLINI (Bolzano) The day before the festival, young men bring onto the piazza a tree that is almost one hundred feet tall, and put at its crown a doll called *sagra milch*. On Sunday every family brings homemade sweets, including wonderful krapfen, and once the tree is auctioned off, the proceeds are used to prepare a mammoth dinner that goes on far into the night.

May 15 · Corsa dei Ceri

GUBBIO (Umbria) See page 43. Specifically gastronomic events include a Colazione di Magro for those who participated in the Procession of the Saints, which takes place at 9:00 A.M on May 15. The menu is fixed:

> *Antipasto di magro misto*, mixed lean antipasti
> *Baccalà arrosto alla ceraiola*, roast codfish
> *Merluzzetto lesso con salsa verde*, cod with green sauce
> *Frutta fresca*, fresh apples and raw fennel
> *Vini locali*, local wines
> *Asti Spumante Cinzano*

After 1:30, the city officials, Ceraioli, and guests sit down to a formal banquet called *La Tavola Bona*, which serves about one thousand people.

Second Half of May

PORTO CESAREO (Apulia) A *sagra* of fish and wine serves some of the best foods of Apulia.

Third Sunday in May · Sagre

SANTENA (Piedmont) is famed for its asparagus, which grows in the brief season from San Giorgio (April 25) to the end of June. At the *sagra*, steamed asparagus is served to everyone who comes, and restaurants and *trattorie* cook it in traditional ways such as with melted butter, Parmesan, and fried eggs; in oil or with vinaigrette; or with traditional sauces.

SATURNIA (Tuscany) This Tuscan *sagra* celebrates pecorino cheese. Tastes of it and other local products are offered, with a demonstration of how milk is transformed into pecorino cheese.

OLBIA (Sardinia) This coastal town celebrates the riches of the sea with a *sagra* of mussels.

Third Sunday in May

MARTA (Latium) This ancient *festa*, La Barabbata, features a procession of farmers and fishermen representing the old guilds, their products—grains, vegetables, and fish—and the implements they use. Preceded by drum rolls, they pass three times in front of the church door, each time drinking some wine. Simultaneously the priests offer ciambelle, twists of bread whose snakelike shape is linked to pagan spring festivals.

GUBBIO (Umbria) In alternate years Sansepolcro (Tuscany) and Gubbio, a lovely town that seems virtually unchanged since the fifteenth century, host a medieval crossbow competition for which participants dress in historical costume. The contest is followed by a costumed procession through torchlit streets.

Last Sunday in May · Sagre

VILLIMPENTA (Lombardy) The tiny town celebrates the rice huskers by serving a dish of their invention, riso alla pilota. See page 63.

CASALE MONFERRATO (Piedmont) Frittate made with spinach, asparagus, and cheese are offered with local wines to everyone in the main piazza.

MALALBERGO (Emilia-Romagna) The Romans loved asparagus, and Italians today love it, too. The town holds a *sagra* with asparagus, which is served in restaurants and on the piazza.

DORGALI (Sardinia) A Sardinian city puts on a colossal fish fry.

Sometime in May

TONNARA DE CAPO VICO (Campania) A celebration of the harvesting of tuna takes place in May or June at one of the most famous *tonnare* (tuna fishing grounds) in Italy.

SAN GIOVANNI IN BERSIGETO (Bologna, Emilia-Romagna) Two hundred and sixty members of culinary brotherhood celebrating the salame of the region meet Sunday night at long tables under the wisteria where they eat piadina, the flat bread of the region, stuffed with salame, and drink Lambrusco.

J U N E

First Sunday in June

MAROSTICA (Veneto) Marostica grows cherries that are famous in the region, and distributes them in abundance in the piazza of the castle along with Asiago cheese and Breganze wine. The pope used to serve his cardinals cherries at the sacred meal on Holy Thursday. When the fruit was not in season, he had the cherries ripened artificially on the slopes of Vesuvius. No such problem now.

COMACCHIO (Emilia-Romagna) It is not spawning time, so the famous eels of Comacchio are not in the grip of the amorous frenzy that drives them to the sea to reproduce. But no matter: the town celebrates anguille anyway in the beginning of summer.

CHIESANUOVA DI SAN CASCIANO DI VAL DI PESA (Florence) A *sagra* commemorates pine nuts, which were once the principal source of income of this tiny town. Now tables are set out between olive trees and vines as people eat pesto crammed with pine nuts and a pasta sauce called *boscaiolo,* made with a bit of boar meat and lots of porcini mushrooms and pine nuts. Pine cones, bursting with the little nuts, are an enduring symbol of fertility in early Italian paintings, so perhaps all this food is auspicious as well.

NEMI (Latium) A celebration of strawberries, wild and cultivated, in this town by the shores of Lake Nemi includes a parade of teenaged girls dressed in typical costumes of strawberry pickers from earlier times. See page 65.

June 6

VICO DEL GARGANICO (Apulia) The Feast of Saint Valentine celebrates oranges by decorating the church and statue of the saint with bay leaves and thousands of oranges from the town's fruit trees. The *festa* represents a propitiation of all the forces that may be harmful to the plants, although it no longer serves such special foods as taralli and oranges.

Second Sunday in June

AMALFI (Campania) A lemon *sagra,* organized by the towns of Amalfi and Massalubrense, is celebrated in each in alternate years. In the historic arsenal, where ships were built for the ancient sea republic of Naples, booths exhibits every type of lemon as well as products based on them such as fogli, moist raisins permeated with the fragrance of lemon from being wrapped in a lemon leaf.

CATTOLICA (Emilia-Romagna) Thousands of fish cooked on the spit and dozens of liters of Romagna wines are the ingredients with which the fishermen of Cattolica celebrate the abundance of the Adriatic. The fish are grilled in typical boat ovens called *foconi,* which are boxes full of sand and burning coals. The fish are brushed with olive oil and herbs, set on skewers placed on vertical spits in the sand, cooked, and distributed free to all.

Third Sunday in June

CHIAMPO (Veneto) Bags of the town's famous cherries are distributed at bargain prices, while polenta and sausages are cooked in great quantities and served with wine. A dance takes place in the piazza at night.

FOGLIANO REDIPUGLIA (Friuli) A festive event offering the mushrooms and wine of the area occurs on the second or third Sunday of the month.

June 21

SPELLO (Umbria) and *GENZANO* (Latium) Astonishingly rich and beautiful pictures made entirely of flower petals become a carpet laid on the main street of a charming medieval town in Umbria and on the long street ascending to the church in Genzano, where the practice began. Similar celebrations are held in *ASSISI* (Umbria) and *BOLSENA* (Latium). It is an old tradition that Italians eat flowers—many menus feature zucchini flowers dipped in batter and fried, although these days it is rare to find once popular fried wisteria—but no such dish is served at the celebration of the Infiorata.

CAMPOBASSO (Molise) For more than two centuries living Mysteries—children dressed as angels, devils, and saints—have hung suspended below the figure of the Madonna in tableaux of religious scenes that pass through the town to celebrate Corpus Christi.

June 22

NOLA (Campania) is famous for an astonishing rite of male power in which teams of men carry and dance seventy-five-foot-tall decorated obelisks through the town. See pages 83–88.

June 23 · Eve of the Feast of San Giovanni Battista (Saint John the Baptist)

SPILAMBERTO (Emilia-Romagna) A contest that awards a prize to the best local balsamic vinegar begins with a professional tasting and ends with a meal in a local restaurant in which each course is made with the famous vinegar. See page 95.

GRELLO (Umbria) The rites of fire traditional on San Giovanni's Eve inspired this village near Gualdo Tadino to create a festival in 1982 incorporating many elements of the ancient celebrations. Teams from the village race through fields with blazing firebrands and the winners light a spectacular pyre of hay in triumph. Local foods made at home and grilled on the piazza are part of the celebration. See page 93.

June 24 · Feast of San Giovanni

FLORENCE (Tuscany) Three famous soccer games are held on June 24, 26, and 27, with four squadrons of twenty-seven men each in medieval dress who play the national sport in much the same way that medieval warriors went to battle. Mayhem and violence are often associated with a local tournament, which is preceded by a colorful costumed procession on the Feast Day of San Giovanni Battista, patron saint of Florence.

ROME (Latium) San Giovanni is celebrated in the San Giovanni Laterano district of Rome by restaurants and trattorie moving tables, chairs, and long counters into the streets and serving snails in a spicy tomato-based sauce. See page 94.

GENOA (Liguria) puts on a spectacular celebration as fifty confraternities go to sea in beautiful boats.

FORMIA (Latium) A gigantic pan fries fish from the Adriatic in epic proportions.

June 24 · or Just After the Summer Solstice

FAVIGNANA (Sicily) Tuna come to spawn in the warm waters off the coast of Trapani and are harvested in a bloody rite known as the mattanza, the killing. The fish are trapped in a system of strong nets anchored at sea, and they are gradually pushed into a series of ever narrower openings, which lead to the death chamber. When the death chamber is full of fish, it is hoisted to the surface and heaved into the center of waiting fishing boats. In a rite as old as the Phoenicians, the tuna are harpooned under the direction of *il rais* (from the Arabic for chief) while the fishermen sing a mournful dirge and hoist the enormous bodies on board ship as the waters turn red with blood.

Last Sunday in June

PISA (Tuscany) the Gioco del Ponte, the Game of the Bridge, is essentially a tug-of-war played by six teams of twenty men dressed in Renaissance costumes who are intent on capturing half of the bridge held by their adversaries. A costumed procession winds along the banks of the Arno River prior to the fierce combat. The event continues a tradition that began in 1568 when the city was divided in two factions, one on each side of the river. The winning team used to celebrate with a big banquet in the streets while the losers retired to the darkness of their neighborhood in defeat.

June 28 and 29 · Feast of San Pietro e Paolo (Saints Peter and Paul)

VIADANA (Lombardy) holds a *sagra* of prosciutto, canteloupe, and Lambrusco wines, a true Italian triumvirate. The sweet orange-fleshed melon, a worthy companion to fine prosciutto, got its name from Cantalupo in the Sabine region, where it was grown in the papal gardens; it then spread to the rest of Italy through the network of papal properties. Inside the seventeenth-century church hangs a painting of the town patron surrounded by melons.

ISERNIA (Molise) The Feast of San Pietro e Paolo was begun by Count Ruggiero di Celano in 1254 and continues today as the town famous for its onions brings them out for a celebration.

PALAZZOLO ACREIDE (Sicily) As bands play, *cudduri*, little wreath-shaped votive breads dedicated to the saint, are taken to church on a cart, blessed, and auctioned off.

July 1–10

FANO (the Marches) A summertime carnival on the Adriatic features gigantic floats and a fish *sagra*. Local specialties include vincisgrassi, a rich lasagne with chicken livers, sweetbreads and brains, besciamella sauce, and black truffles. It gets its name from the Austrian general who commanded troops in the Marches. Also served are tripe marinated in a local white wine and porchetta.

July 2

SIENA (Tuscany) The Palio, Italy's most famous horse race, is run on a track laid down around the Campo in the center of the city. See page 139.

MATERA (Basilicata) As part of the major religious feast of Basilicata, everyone in the crowd watching the procession of the statue of the Madonna of Bruna descends on the ornately decorated cart on which it is transported and destroys it. Legend says that the ritual commemorates a time when the Saracens held much of southern Italy in their sway and stole a statue of the Virgin from Matera on one of their raids, although the crazed destruction sounds like a spectacular survival of the orgies of Bacchus and Dionysius. The Madonna was recaptured, so the story goes, but the city decided to prevent a recurrence of the theft by destroying the cart necessary for its transport. Every year a new large and elaborate cart is drawn through town and every year it is duly broken into tiny pieces. Eating is not connected with this ritual because there is no need for food to be blessed, since everyone gets to take home a small piece of the Madonna.

July 2 · or Thursday before the First Sunday in July

CAMASTRA (Sicily) Breads shaped like arms, feet, legs, hands, and other ex-voto forms are baked for the Festa of San Calogero.

First Sunday in July

ARICCIA (Latium) A *sagra* of porchetta from a town famous for its enormous roasted pigs, fragrant with rosemary, garlic, and salt. Porchetta is the archetypal festival food all over Italy, and if few are actually roasted on the spot, Ariccia proudly boasts special *rosticcerie* and ovens devoted primarily to cooking the huge pigs.

First or Second Weekend in July

BAGNARA CALABRA (Calabria) A festival celebrates the swordfish that spawn in the warm waters of the Mediterranean. At the height of the season, thousands of swordfish once filled the sea and were hunted down by fishermen on boats with a sixty-foot-tall steel mast. A man in a tiny cage at the top of the mast could see entire schools of fish and would shout down to a harpoonist perched on a catwalk ready to thrust a double-pronged long spear into his prey. Swordfish still spawn in these warm waters and are fished out in great numbers. For the *sagra* in their honor, one of the strange high-masted special boats called *ontri* used in capturing the fish is pulled up into the piazza, where involtini, rolls of swordfish, are served with a sauce of olive oil, lemon, and oregano. A wreath of bay leaves is thrown into the sea in memory of drowned fishermen.

Second Sunday in July

CARPINETI (Emilia-Romagna) For a Sagra della Porchetta, in a region famous for its prosciutto and pork products, only young tender pigs are cooked and sold on the piazza. The porchetta has been part of public celebrations of joy since 1249, when, according to Alessandro Tassoni in *La secchia rapita* (in my very loose and nonpoetic paraphrase), at the end of a war prisoners were exchanged and the regiment joyfully tossed a cooked pig from the window, decreeing that the victory would be commemorated in just such a way every year.

July 13–15

PALERMO (Sicily) The Feast of Santa Rosalia, patron saint of the city, lasts for three days and includes a procession to the sea, fireworks, dance and music concerts, and such special foods as tiny local snails and ice-cream–like puddings. See page 114.

July 19

VENICE (Veneto) A feast celebrating the end of the plague in 1576 culminates in a spectacular display of fireworks on the Grand Canal, where hundreds of Venetians enjoy nocturnal picnics and dinners on gondolas and all manner of other boats while waiting for the main event. See page 124.

July 20

PESCHICI (Apulia) For the festival of Sant'Elia, proprietors of the olive-oil presses not only make and sell their oils, but also produce special breads that are sold to finance the events of the day.

Third Sunday in July

LIVORNO (Tuscany) celebrates the fish soup called *cacciucco* which is full of octopus, squid, mullet, and mussels and is typical of the Tuscan coast.

July 19–26

ROME (Latium) The people of Trastevere, the neighborhood on the "left bank" of Rome, celebrate the festival of Noiantri (translation: "our very own") for seven days, eating mountains of pasta and meters of grilled lamb and chicken. They sit outside in the piazza, under strings of lights, drinking quantities of wine and dancing and singing. The festival honors the Virgin of Carmine, "their" Madonna, who is worshiped in the church of Sant'Agata alla Lungaretta, but it is difficult to detect many religious nuances as people eat and drink with abandon.

July 25

ALTOPASCIO (Lucca, Tuscany) The cauldron of Altopascio was once full of a thick minestrone that was given free to pilgrims stopping on their way to or from Rome, especially during the Holy Year. The friars cooked a pot of soup twice a week at the abbey; the custom continues, but the cauldron is now filled with pasta and distributed in commemoration of the earlier event. A crossbow contest and many dance and theatrical events add to the festivities.

July 26

IELSI (Campobasso, Molise) For a grain festival the main street is the scene of a procession of floats elaborately decorated with sheaves of wheat braided and woven to represent various themes from history and religion. A simple pizzalike bread is the traditional food of the day. Bands, dancers in local costume, and a market complete the celebration.

Last Sunday in July

TEGLIA (Lombardy) A *sagra* celebrates pizzoccheri, the famous buckwheat tagliatelle of the mountainous Valtellina region.

SISSA (Emilia-Romagna) Italians are crazy about watermelon. Whoever eats the most watermelon in this tiny town's contest wins the Italian championship. All summer long chunks and slices of watermelon are piled in great pyramids under little showers of cooling water in city squares and along country roads.

PASSIGNANO SUL TRASIMENO (Umbria) Fish are fried in an enormous frying pan and offered to all visitors at this small town on Umbria's largest lake.

MOLA (Apulia) Many-tentacled octopus is cooked in many ways and served.

Sometime Toward the End of July

MONTE PORZIO CATONE (Latium) celebrates apricots, which have been grown in Italy since 50 B.C., although it took the Saracen invasion to spread and make them popular.

 AUGUST

Sometime in August

NOTO (Sicily) A *sagra* of gelato comes along just when the air seems on fire in Sicily, although cassata siciliana, cannoli, and other traditional desserts are served too.

First Two Weeks in August

MONTEFIASCONE (Latium) A *sagra* celebrates Est! Est! Est!, the famous white wine of the region. The story goes that when a German cardinal named Johann Fugger was traveling to Rome for the coronation of Emperor Henry V in 1110, he sent his steward ahead to scout for inns that had good wine and told him to mark the legend *Est* (It Is) on the door. The cardinal followed, and when he got to Montefiascone, he found his scout in a drunken stupor at a tavern on whose door he had written *Est! Est! Est!* The story may be more enchanting than the wine, which is a bit sweet. At the same time *sbroscia,* a fish soup made with bread and vegetables, is served.

First Sunday in August

PIEVEPELAGO (Emilia-Romagna) A *sagra* celebrates blackberries, blueberries, and mushrooms that grow wild in the forests of the lower Apennines.

CASTEL GANDOLFO (Latium) Peaches in baskets, boxes, and counters fill up the piazza in the little town where the pope has his summer residence. Girls in local costume go to the papal villa and present him with a box of the very ripest and juiciest fruit, but everyone else lines up in the piazza to taste the delicious peaches.

CAPRACOTTA (the Marches) An ancient *sagra* of hospitality offers everyone tastes of pezzata, a traditional shepherds' dish of lamb and kid cut in pieces and cooked over a hot fire. Pezzata is one of the specialties of pastoral life in southern Italy and is served on this day in the green fields of Prato Gentile accompanied by singing and dancing.

ASCOLI PICENO (the Marches) holds a *quintana,* a competition whose name comes from the street that was dedicated to games in Roman encampments. Six districts of the city participate in processions in medieval dress and in jousts on horseback much like the one held in Arezzo in early September.

Second Sunday in August

PORTO SAN GIORGIO (the Marches) A gigantic pan, fifteen feet in diameter with a twenty-four-foot-long handle, is used to cook more than five hundred pounds of the famous little calamari of the area.

SALTARA (the Marches) A festival in honor of the berlingozzo, a traditional Alkermes-flavored cookie, was once held in mid-May, and the biscotti were tossed right into the crowd from passing floats. Now behavior is more decorous and the biscotti are available at tables in the piazza.

Pizza seller, engraving from Lo Spassatiempo *by Borricelli*

SAN VITO LO CAPO (Sicily) Couscous, an Arab dish that has become the gastronomical centerpiece of Trapani's cuisine, is cooked in fish broth and served with other typical dishes in a weeklong celebration of food and wine in this city.

August 12–16

FELITTO (Campania) For the Sagra del Fusillo, town cooks first take a kilogram of durum flour, add six fresh eggs from free-range chickens, a pinch of salt and a few drops of warm water, and make a dough that they wrap around a special corkscrew-shaped iron rod and *ecco!* fusilli, a splendid pasta to be tossed with Neapolitan sauces.

August 14

CORTONA (Tuscany) Tuscan beef is cooked on the largest grill in Italy in a Texas-scale festival.

SASSARI (Sardinia) Enormous "candles," like the Ceri of Gubbio, weighing more than eight hundred pounds, are "danced" by groups from eight trade guilds and offered to the Madonna in memory of her ending a terrible plague upon the city in 1652.

PIAZZA ARMERINA (Sicily) The Palio degli Normanni is a beautiful historical procession re-creating the historic arrival in the city of Count Ruggero and his Norman troops. A knightly joust is also held in this town, which boasts a late-Roman villa with spectacular mosaics that include scenes of hunting and bathing and views of the first bikini. Traditional almond-paste cookies are offered to guests.

August 15

LAVAGNA (Liguria) The Torta dei Fieschi, a cake that stands nineteen feet high, is the centerpiece of a celebration, and is served to everyone in the piazza after they take part in a ritual that has romance as its inspiration. See page 153.

GRAZIE DI CURTATONE (Lombardy) A traditional agricultural fair that has gone on since the sixteenth-century is held alongside a much newer competition of itinerant *madonnari*, artists who, using only pastels, create phenomenal three-dimensional pictures with religious themes on the streets of the town. People eat panini with the cotechino sausage of the town.

VILLA SANTO STEFANO (Abruzzo) At the Feast of San Rocco the local ceci bean soup called *la panarda* is cooked in twenty enormous copper caldrons. The soup is flavored with olive oil, salt, pepper, and rosemary. A wheel of homemade country-style bread, called *la pagnotta di San Rocco*, was once served as part of the celebration, but it seems to have disappeared.

ARNAD (Val d'Aosta) A *festa* celebrates lardo, snowy-white cured pork fat that is streaked with meat.

CAMPOFILONE (the Marches) A long-standing *sagra* of pasta celebrates capellini, a type of pasta cut as fine as a strand of hair.

August 16

FOGLIANISE (Campania) For the traditional yearly *sagra* of grain in a tiny town near Benevento, villagers make elaborate floats out of grain and straw. The floats may contain a life-sized Moses presenting the Ten Commandments, the entire Parthenon, or other famous churches and monuments, but whatever they represent, they are always intricately woven.

PALMI (Calabria) An extraordinary procession of penitents walking on bare feet, wearing capes of thorns, and flagellating themselves. In the evening the thorns are burned in a blazing bonfire.

SIENA (Tuscany) Italy's most famous festival features a fiercely competitive horse race in the medieval piazza. See page 139.

Third Sunday in August

AMATRICE (Latium) A feast is held in which thousands of plates of pasta all'amatriciana, spaghetti made with pork (guanciale), tomatoes, and bits of hot red pepper are served sprinkled with Parmesan cheese. Folkloristic groups and musical bands add color. See recipe on page 77.

LA THUILE (Val d'Aosta) The Fête des Bergers re-creates a fifteenth-century tradition of a "battle" between cows from the Val d'Aosta and those from Savoy to determine which is the strongest. Everyone gets samples of the local cheeses.

August 24, 25, and 26 · Feast of Sant'Oranzo

LECCE (Apulia) On the Feast Day of Sant'Oranzo, the patron saint of Lecce, a baroque town that has been called the Florence of the south, it is traditional to eat roosters that have just begun to crow. The fowl is baked in layers with eggplant, tomato sauce, basil, and pecorino cheese.

Fourth Sunday in August

CORTEMILIA (Piedmont) A *sagra* celebrates the famous *tonda e gentile* hazelnuts of Piedmont that appear in such famous desserts as torta di nocciole (hazelnut cake) and giandujotti combined with chocolate.

SAN DANIELE DEL FRIULI (Friuli) The prosciutto of San Daniele is among the most famous in Italy for its fine taste and silky texture. It is celebrated at the end of August with music, games, and a parade of citizens dressed up to look like the local prosciutto.

End of August

POLSI (Calabria) Hundreds of lambs are slaughtered in honor of the Madonna of Polsi, whose sanctuary is visited by an uninterrupted procession of visitors from both Ionian and Tyrrhenian coasts.

 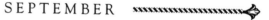

SEPTEMBER

Sometime in September

ANGRI (Campania) It took until the nineteenth century for the tomato to conquer most of Italy, and now the plum-shaped San Marzano and other varieties grown nearby are the primary ingredient of Neapolitan pizza and pasta. For this celebration tomatoes are cooked in sauces that will be served on three types of pasta. The many types of Italian tomatoes include one called *francescino,* which is long and has a little bump at one end, like a pretty French girl with a snub nose. It is easy to see that Italy is a male-oriented society in which women are referred to in gastronomical terms and things gastronomical are given women's names.

September 3

VITERBO (Latium) holds a spectacular nighttime festival in honor of Santa Rosa, the town's patron saint, at which men hoist huge illuminated towers and carry them on their shoulders in a test of strength like the Ceri of Gubbio and the Gigli of Nola.

First Sunday in September

AREZZO (Tuscany) After parades and blessings, and after crowds of people have poured into the city's beautiful Piazza Grande, horsemen in Renaissance dress compete in the Joust of the Saracen. In this competition they ride full tilt at a larger-than-life-sized figure of a Saracen in the medieval square. In its left hand it holds a target of steel and in the right, a whip with lead balls covered in leather. The figure is set on a swivel base, so as each rider hits the target, he must avoid blows from the whip as the figure pivots around. Country food served at the festival includes sausages grilled on an open fire, finocchietta salame, and fresh pecorino cheese on heavy crunchy breads.

VENICE (Veneto) The most sumptuous regatta of the year celebrates the return of Venetians from their summers in the countryside. It begins with a cortege of gondolas and boats from earlier centuries bearing passengers in historical costumes and it ends with a glorious race.

PIENZA (Tuscany) A fair honoring the pecorino cheese made in the hills of southern Tuscany fills the main street of a lovely Renaissance town. See page 156.

CARMAGNOLA (Piedmont) Thick meaty sweet peppers, which are famous all over Italy, are the focus of a local *sagra*.

LESIGNANO DE BAGNI (Emilia-Romagna) There is more to celebrating rosemary than eating it, since a contest of various dishes fragrant with the herb places it in its cultural context by cooking it in the traditional recipes of the Parma countryside.

September 7

FLORENCE (Tuscany) The festival of the Rificolone began as a celebration of Grand Duke Cosimo de' Medici's triumph over Siena, when that city, the last republican outpost in Tuscany, finally capitulated to Florentine rule. People streamed into the Piazza Santissima Annunziata from the surrounding hills and villages, carrying homemade lanterns to guide them from the Renaissance piazza to the banks of the Arno. At night the lanterns were set to float on the river, shimmering magically, lighting up the darkness. During the daytime people brought food from their farms, wheels of pecorino cheese, rounds of bread, and heaps of juicy watermelons that they ate with brigidini, anise-flavored wafer cookies, and berlingozzi, sweet low cakes made with fennel seeds.

First Two Weeks in September

ASTI (Piedmont) The Festa del Vino Douja d'Or, a new event named for a rustic wine container once used in the countryside, serves a great variety of foods and wines from the region.

Second Sunday in September

MAROSTICA (Veneto) is notable for a famous living chess game that is played in the piazza of the castle. The piazza resembles a giant chessboard and the game is played with people dressed as traditional chess pieces. The festival takes place in even-numbered years.

SANSEPOLCRO (Tuscany) and *GUBBIO* (Umbria) A crossbow tournament alternates between the two cities each year. A procession in Renaissance dress is inspired by the paintings of Piero della Francesca, whose Resurrection hangs in the Sansepolcro museum.

QUARTU SANT'ELENA (Sardinia) A festival in honor of the mother of Emperor Constantine includes a costumed procession in which girls in traditional costumes ride on floats filled with zibbibo grapes. Counters sell pabassinas, spicy raisin and nut cookies, and such orange- and lemon-flavored Sardinian sweets as pirichittus. See page 189.

Second and Third Sundays in September

BUDOIA (Friuli) A fair featuring more than four hundred types of mushrooms offers mushroom walks through the hillsides, and sets up kiosks for tasting mushrooms and polenta. If a proposed law passes to protect forests from being denuded, people will need to have a mushroom "hunting license" that will limit them to three kilograms a person. So this fair is a particularly good opportunity to see and taste these specialties.

BAROLO (Piedmont) To celebrate the wines made in the Langhe region of Piedmont, this village offers samples of Barolo, Barbaresco, Barbera, and Nebbiolo wines.

SOAVE (Veneto) celebrates Soave wine and its grapes.

POLIGNANO A MARE (Apulia) As part of the observance of the Festa del Cristo, Christ Crucified, there are tables of lamb involtini, lamb from the spit, and gnemeriide, a rich lamb dish combining lamb giblets, aromatic herbs, tomatoes, and pecorino cheese.

BAGNOLA DI SANTA FIORA (Tuscany) A *sagra* of funghi Porcini in a town on the slopes of Monte Amiata.

September 13 and 14

LUCCA (Tuscany) The Feast of the Holy Cross begins with a candlelight procession from San Frediano, a medieval basilica, to the church of San Martino. The *festa* is in honor of the Holy Face, Il Volto Santo, an enormous crucifix found by a pilgrim in the Holy Land that was said to have been entrusted to a ship without helmsmen. The boat landed not far from Lucca, so the story goes, where the crucifix was collected by the people of Lucca who brought it to the city in 782. A fair is held the following day.

Third Sunday in September

ASTI (Piedmont) One of Italy's oldest palios is held with eight hundred people in sumptuous Renaissance costumes and more than one hundred horses. They parade from the cathedral to the playing field, where jockeys ride bareback in a breakneck race.

CEVA (Piedmont) holds a great mushroom fair and festival.

GREVE IN CHIANTI (Tuscany) A fair and exposition of Chianti wines offers tastes of those wines and of typical local delicacies such as schiacciata all'uva, a briochelike sweet bread layered with wine grapes. It is very similar to the peppery panepazzo (crazy bread) once made in Chianti during the *vendemmia*. A dance and concert in the piazza of Castello di Montefiorale, a village near Greve, end at midnight with free samples of pappardelle sulla lepre, wide lasagne-like noodles with a rabbit or hare sauce. See page 183.

FOLIGNO (Umbria) An evening of festivities and costumed processions precedes the Quintana, an event for which ten costumed riders representing the districts of the city gallop toward the figure of a huge Roman warrior. From the figure's left hand rises the banner of the city, and the right hand holds out a ring into which the rider must thrust his lance without touching the warrior itself. The Quintana was at its most splendid in the eighteenth century, when the celebration was part of the Carnival season and took place at night with flaming torches lighting the course. People go to the *taverne* and *osterie* of the districts in the days before the Quintana and eat such specialties as schiacciata con cipolla e salvia; the vegetable soup called *acquacotta*; Umbrian bruschetta; zuppa di cicerchie, a soup made of a sort of vetch; and a frittata settembrina made with asparagus, artichoke, wild fennel, and herbs.

PEDACE (Calabria) For the religious Festa dell'Addolorata, a special type of cuccia made with goat or pork is served.

September 19

NAPLES (Campania) At the famous Feast of San Gennaro swarms of the faithful gather in tense crowds to wait for the annual miracle in which the saint's blood liquefies. In Naples the event is dizzying and claustrophic, but a smaller, less dramatic feast in the saint's honor takes place in

Praiano, on the Amalfi Drive, just down the coast from Naples, where people eat maccheroni with eggplant and peppers and coniglio in umido, braised rabbit.

Fourth Weekend in September

CAPALBIO (Tuscany) A *sagra* in honor of wild boar includes traditional specialities such as acquacotta, a vegetable soup, and polenta dei carbonei. See pages 161–166.

MORTARA (Lombardy) A celebration of goose as it tastes when made into plump salame d'oca. See page 167.

Last Sunday in September · Festa of San Michele (Saint Michael)

CARBONARA (Apulia) fills up with dense crowds of people who have come to celebrate the saint with fires and with mutton chops. The mutton is raised with special care in the village, grilled over a fire made of branches of thyme and almond and hazelnut shells, served with celery and olives, and washed down with quantities of wine.

IMPRUNETA (Tuscany) The Festa dell'Uva, one of the oldest in Tuscany, features floats with the theme of grapes. Food served includes a beef stew called *il peposo,* made with garlic, tomatoes, and lots of pepper and cooked very slowly over six or seven hours. It used to be eaten at the end of the wheat harvest for the day of thanksgiving when the fields had been threshed.

 OCTOBER

October 1 and First Week in October

ALBA (Piedmont) The Tournament of the Hundred Towers takes place in September and is followed two weeks later by the Palio of Donkeys which coincides with the arrival of white truffles. In early October a truffle fair perfumes the city and honors its traditional dishes with shavings of musky white truffle. See page 209.

Sometime in October

CHALLAND-SAINT-ANSELME (Val d'Aosta) A traditional chestnut roast is accompanied by mulled wine.

FIE ALLO SCILAR (Bolzano, Alto Adige) In this area there is a tradition called *Torggellan* in which people walk from town to town to visit houses and *trattorie* in the countryside to taste the new wine of the year and eat speck, sausages, walnuts, and roasted chestnuts.

BERGAMO (Lombardy) celebrates its famous polenta e osei, polenta and little game birds. Restaurants and inns serve this savory dish while bakeries create a sweet polenta cake topped with tiny birds made of chocolate.

MARINO (Latium) Wine flows freely from a fountain in the central piazza and thousands of bottles of wine produced in the nearby countryside are celebrated in one of Italy's most famous wine festivals. Slices of porchetta and clusters of grapes are also available. In nearby Frascati a cookie is baked in the shape of a woman with three breasts; legend has it that the middle one is for wine.

CAROSINO (Taranto, Apulia) Wine—red, white, and rosé—flows freely from a fountain in the Piazza Vittorio Emanuele.

October 3

ASSISI (Umbria) A solemn religious celebration of San Francesco (Saint Francis) draws thousands of pilgrims but serves no special food.

First Sunday in October

CASALE DI PARI (Tuscany) A *sagra* of the rich umbrella-shaped wild mushrooms called *funghi porcini*, serves them roasted, stewed, and with polenta. Other local specialties are available.

SAN BENEDETTO PO (Lombardy) A great gastronomic event that celebrates the local wild ducks (now raised in captivity) finds restaurants set up around the piazza serving maccheroni al nedar, pasta with a duck sauce, and anatra in umido, the same duck served braised. Artisans and farmers sell their wares in a country fair atmosphere. There is even a goose race (since ducks can't run) and a pole to climb that is slippery with duck fat. The event continues into the evening when there is dancing in the square. Don't miss the city's museum with its splendid collection of the tools of daily life.

VILLASTRADA (Lombardy) What was once a day celebrating zucca, the enormous pumpkin of Mantua, has now become an entire week devoted to its virtues. No one is quite sure whether the zucca referred to in an eleventh-century medical handbook is the pumpkin we know today, but it is certain that zucca was eaten widely in medieval and Renaissance times. Local specialties include riso al zucca, a pumpkin-flavored dish in which the pumpkin virtually disappears into the creamy rice.

Second Week in October

CAMIGLIATELLO SILANO (Calabria) At an exhibit of mushrooms, meals are served that are based on fresh mushrooms from the mountainous Sila area of Calabria.

MORRA (Umbria) A celebration in a tiny Umbrian village that begins by beating chestnut trees so that the prickly-shelled nuts fall; once collected they are turned into dozens of chestnut sweets: tortes, castagnaccio, crescentine, chestnut pralines, and chestnut "kisses."

Second Sunday in October

MERANO (Bolzano) A grape *sagra* in the countryside where beer meets wine has a meticulously organized Tyrolean parade, band music, and musical events in the handsome Kurhaus and Kunsthalle. See page 195.

ROANA (Veneto) The Sagra of Santa Giustina is celebrated with races, games, and musetto, a kind of local cotechino, along with polenta and tosella, a cheese cooked in melted butter.

VILLA SANTA MARIA (Abruzzo) Three days of spirited cooking in a small mountain village known as the home of chefs. See page 170.

Third Sunday in October

MARRADI (Tuscany) Polenta is made from chestnut flour according to a very old recipe.

TEOLO (Veneto) A chestnut festival offers roasted chestnuts and a spectacular variety of side dishes.

TREVI (Umbria) has a *sagra* of local celery and sausage, a perfect marriage since the crunchy celery cuts the fattiness of the sausage. Stalks of celery are dipped in a mixture of extra-virgin olive oil, salt, and pepper that is called *cazzimperio* in Umbria and *pinzimonio* in Tuscany.

October 25 · Feast of San Crispino (Saint Crispin)

ACQUAVIVA DELLE FONTE (Apulia) In Apulia San Crispino's Day has become the Sagra del Calzone in recognition of the food of the feast. This particular calzone is filled with sautéed red onions, aged ricotta cheese, tomatoes, grated pecorino cheese, and black olives, and is cooked in a woodburning oven. The word *calzone* may have existed in medieval Latin as early as 1170, according to a reference in Padua, but Luigi Sada, a scholar of Pugliese gastronomy, finds Apulia to be the center from which calzone radiated across Italy after 1400. Certainly it turns up at almost every holiday in Apulia from Carnival, Lent, and San Giuseppe, through Easter, All Souls' Day, and Christmas, although the filling depends on seasonal ingredients and the form on local tradition.

Fourth Sunday in October

MONTALCINO (Tuscany) A thrush *sagra* is celebrated in the center of the region where the tiny birds stop to eat juniper berries. The event was just one part of the city's festivities at the end of the fourteenth century, and the men in the event, such as those in the costumed procession, still wear the insignia of medieval arts, trades, and arms, recalling the return of noblemen from the hunt. Today grills cook the game birds, which are served with bread and the famous local red wines. After an afternoon archery contest, homemade local spaghetti called *pinci* or *pici* are served with a game sauce.

NUS OR LA THUILE (Val d'Aosta) To celebrate the return of the milk cows from their summer pasturage each year, towns in this Alpine valley host a contest in which the cows vie to see which is the strongest. Earlier competitions have already winnowed the field, so the one that wins now becomes the queen and is crowned with flowers, wears a garland of ribbons, and marches at the head of a parade as bands play music. Traditional foods include Fontina cheese, made from the cow's milk, served with polenta; grilled sausages; and a veal stew called *spezzatino*.

ARITZO (Sardinia) and *PERLOZ* (Val d'Aosta) Chestnut festivals are held at these antipodes of Italy. The Sardinian *sagra* offers hazelnuts, along with singing and dancing, and young boys in traditional costume dash around with cowbells tied around their waists.

End of October

RONCEGNO (Trentino) A festival of chestnuts celebrates the same products that once graced the tables of the rulers of the Austro-Hungarian Empire.

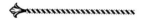

November 1 · All Saints' Day

PALERMO (Sicily) Legend has it that the dead leave their tombs and raid all the best pastry shops in town to bring children delicious gifts. A fair in the Vucciria district features all sorts of desserts made with almond paste. Traditional regional dishes are served all over Italy on this day— from a ceci-based soup in Piedmont to a calzone filled with anchovies, almonds, pine nuts, and raisins in Apulia. The pope lays chrysanthemums, the Italian flowers of the dead, on graves in Rome's largest cemetery. See pages 221–223.

November 2 · All Souls' Day

PERUGIA (Umbria) A secular Fair of the Dead is held at the Pian di Massiano, where hundreds of stalls sell local crafts and sweets, including those known as *stinchetti,* tibia-shaped cookies made especially for I Morti.

ANDRATE (Piedmont) and *PONTREMOLI* (Tuscany) Chestnut festivals celebrate both marroni and castagne, different varieties of the nut. Marroni are richer, more flavorful, and generally become marrons glâcés preserved in a sugar syrup or are baked into Monte Bianco, a rich cake shaped like the mountain for which it is named. In Tuscany chestnuts have different names depending on how they are cooked: *bruciate* (roasted); *ballote* (boiled); they also become castagnaccio, a flat country cake made of chestnut flour and sprinkled with pine nuts, and necci, hot chestnut crepes filled with fresh ricotta or pecorino cheese.

November 7

SANT'AMBROGIO DI VALPOLICELLA (Veneto) A *festa* centers around a huge soup of fava beans, a food closely connected to the Day of the Dead and immortal spirits. The soup is offered with roasted chestnuts and wine just before San Martino's Day.

November 11 · San Martino's Day (Saint Martin)

SIGILLO (Umbria) Chestnuts and the new wine of the year are ritual foods for San Martino's Day. During Roman times chestnuts were called "Jupiter's acorns" and were shepherds' fare. They were as likely to be ground into flour to make bread as roasted in a fire, the way they are here.

PETTENASCO (Piedmont) Loaves of bread are blessed and offered in an ancient ritual to the faithful who bring their own harvest produce to the church. The event ends with tasting new wines, singing, and dancing.

NERETO (Abruzzo) San Martino is honored in a gastronomic Sagra del Pitone in which turkey is cooked in the style of a porchetta, its cavity filled with herbs from the hillside. San Martino's Day is a thanksgiving that celebrates the end of the agricultural year with chestnuts, turkey, and goose.

PALERMO (Sicily) Sweets prevail in Sicily. Biscotti of San Martino, the cookies of the day, come filled with creamy ricotta, jam, or fruit gelatin. Sfinci di San Martino, plump fried bignè, are dipped in honey.

Third Weekend in November

TERRA DEL SOLE (Emilia-Romagna) An ancient celebration is observed in honor of the end of the agricultural year. The fruits of the earth are blessed in the morning, an enormous fire is lit in the afternoon, and sweets and traditional foods are eaten throughout the day.

SAN GIORGIO VALPOLICELLA (Veneto) A *sagra* recalls an ancient pagan festival by cooking an enormous soup of fava beans and distributing it with roast chestnuts and wine.

November 21

VENICE (Veneto) Devoted Venetians make their way across a temporary pontoon bridge to the church of Santa Maria della Salute, built by the baroque architect Baldassare Longhena in gratitude to the Madonna for the end of the plague in 1630. A traditional dish of that time, now rarely found, is called *la castradina,* smoked salted mutton, which is boiled and eaten with mountains of Savoy cabbage.

Last Sunday in November

GORGONZOLA (Lombardy) Polenta is cooked in the piazza in the traditional unlined copper cauldron named *il paiolo,* and it is served with the famous cheese of the city from which it takes its name.

PRESICCE (Apulia) has a feast of *triglie,* red mullet, in honor of Sant'Andrea.

PESCARA (Abruzzo) At a regatta for Sant'Andrea the rich resources of the sea are drawn upon by serving fish cooked in various ways and selling them on a long, brightly decorated pier.

 DECEMBER

December 5 and 6

MONTELEONE DI SPOLETO (Umbria) Farro di San Nicola, a soup based on the ancient grain called *farro,* is distributed by the parish priest in homage to the saint, a practice that recalls an ancient ritual of giving soup to the poor. While the priest is preparing the soup, elementary school teachers give out chestnuts and wine to everyone.

POLLUTRI (Chieti, Abruzzo) Fava beans are cooked in twelve great copper cauldrons in front of the church of San Nicola. At the first pealing of the bells, a fire is lit under the pots; at the second, handfuls of salt are thrown in, and at the third, the beans are seasoned with olive oil and distributed in memory of San Nicola, who once brought six fishing boats loaded with just such beans in time to save the community from starvation.

CASTELVETERE IN VALFORTORE (Benevento, Campania) Chests of bread are blessed and distributed to honor the Feast Day of San Nicola.

TARVISIO AND TRIESTE (Friuli) The Cortege of San Nicola, bringer of gifts, proceeds down the main street of the village accompanied by masked demons known as *krampus,* who wear huge masks of the devil. They carry sticks and chase the children in a scary game. Before the game begins, a figure dressed as San Nicola hands out a lightly sweetened bread made in the shape of a devil.

December 7

MILAN (Lombardy) The Feast Day of Sant'Ambrogio (Saint Ambrose), the city's patron saint, is honored by the fair of O bei, O bei, which is held in front of the handsome medieval basilica of Sant'Ambrogio. Toys and sweets, antiques and books, and bargains of many types can be found at the fair. The *sagra* is perfumed with the aroma of tortelli frying and scotti, chestnuts roasting.

Second Weekend of December

TREVISO (Veneto) A market under the loggia of a fourteenth-century palazzo celebrates radicchio rosso, the famous crisp, long-leaf, red-tinged chicory of the city. Radicchio is used to make gastronomic specialties of the city that range from elegant stuffed guinea fowl to humbler radicchio and bean soup.

CASTELFRANCO VENETO (Treviso, Veneto) Here's another fair dedicated to a different variety of radicchio with fat crimson heads of a slightly bitterer variety.

CARRÙ (Cuneo, Piedmont) The Feast of the Fat Bulls, *bue grossi,* honors the great steer that are the progenitors of today's *razza piemontese,* a lean kind of beef that is used to make bollito misto, mixed boiled meats, and brasato al Barolo, beef braised in Barolo wine.

December 13 · Santa Lucia (Saint Lucy)

LENNA (Bergamo, Lombardy) Counters and stalls full of toys, food, and games are set out for the celebration of Santa Lucia. The fair was once much bigger and full of every kind of sweet, including those known as *baci di dama,* sugary treats that legend says so attracted the donkey on which Santa Lucia rode that he stopped at every house where the sweets had been placed outside, and left presents for the children in exchange.

SYRACUSE (Sicily) A torchlight procession honors Santa Lucia, who is remembered each year with cuccia, a dish made with wheat berries, to recall her miracle of bringing grain to starving Sicily. See page 240.

December 24

LERICI and *TELLARO* (Liguria) Leaving the illuminated city of Lerici, a procession of torchlit boats sails in the calm Tyrrhenian Sea, where men in black rubber suits dive repeatedly and finally surface holding a statue of the Christ Child.

Last Sunday in December

POSITANO (Amalfi, Campania) Neither ancient nor authentic, although certainly picturesque, is the *zeppolata sulla spiaggia,* a feast where fritters are served on the beach with hot sausages.

SELECTED BIBLIOGRAPHY

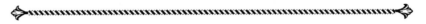

GENERAL

Alberini, Massimo. "Dall'antico pan di Natale al moderno panettone farcito," *L'Accademia* (6: 99–101).

———. *Liguria a Tavola: itinerario gastronomico da Nizza a Lerico.* Milan: Longanesi and Co., 1965.

———. *Piemontesi a Tavola: Itinerario gastronomico da Novara alle Alpi.* Milan: Longanesi and Co., 1967.

———. *Storia del pranzo all'italiana.* Milan: Rizzoli, 1966.

———. "La zuppiera a Natale," *La Cucina Italiana,* December 1986, pp. 110–112.

Alberini, Massimo, and Giorgio Mistretta. *Guida all'Italia Gastronomica.* Milan: Touring Club Italiano, 1984.

Angiuli, Emanuela. "Suor Clarisse e fornai sulla Murgia," *La Gola,* Vol. 2, December 1982–January 1983 (3:5).

Annoscia, Enrico. "La cucina sacrale in Puglia," *La Gola,* Vol. 6, December 1987 (32–34).

Artusi, Luciano, and Silvano Gabbrielli. *Gioco, giostra, palio in Toscana.* Florence: Edizione S.P. 44, 1978.

Artusi, Pellegrino. *La scienza in cucina e l'arte di mangiar bene.* Introduzione e note di Piero Camporesi. Turin: Giulio Einaudi Editore, 1985.

Ashby, Thomas. *Some Italian Scenes and Festivals.* London: 1929.

Avella, Leonardo. *La festa dei Gigli.* Naples: Ler, 1979.

Bagnoli, R., F. Fava, and M. Garzonio. *Tradizioni e feste popolari milanesi di ieri e di oggi.* Milan: Libreria Meraviglia Editrice, 1984.

Barolini, Helen. *Festa: Recipes and Recollections of Italian Holidays.* San Diego, New York, London: Harcourt Brace Jovanovich, 1988.

Begg, Ean. *The Black Madonna.* London, Boston, Henley, England: Arkana, 1985.

Berger, Pamela. *The Goddess Obscured: Transformation of the Grain Protectress from Goddess to Saint.* Boston: Beacon Press, 1985.

Birnbaum, Lucia Chiavola. "Folklore and Italian Women," *Insieme,* Fall, 1986, pp. 23–26.

———. *Liberazione della Donna, Feminism in Italy.* Middletown, Conn.: Wesleyan University Press, 1986.

Braudel, Fernand. *The Structures of Everyday Life: Civilization and Capitalism. 15th to 18th century.* Vol. 1. Translated by Sian Reynolds. New York: Harper and Row, 1978.

Brugnoli, Pierpaolo. *Alcune considerazioni sulla tradizione popolare de "El bacanal del gnoco."* Verona: 1988.

Burke, Peter. *Popular Culture in Early Modern Europe.* New York: New York University Press, 1978.

Buttitta, Antonio. *I colori del sole: arte popolari in Sicilia.* Palermo: S. F. Flaccovio Editore, 1985.

———. *Pasqua in Sicilia.* Palermo: Grafindustria, 1978.

———, Rita Cedrini, Salvatore d'Onofrio, Dino Barrac, Nino Cangemi, et al.: "Pasqua, riti e feste in Sicilia," *Giornale di Sicilia,* March 23, 1989, pp. 27–38.

Bynum, Caroline Walker. *Holy Feast and Holy Fast.* Berkeley and Los Angeles: University of California Press, 1987.

Callen, Anna Theresa. "The Flavors of Abruzzi," *Gourmet,* Vol. 56, October 1984 (10:78–88).

Campbell, Joseph. *The Masks of God: Occidental Mythology.* New York: Penguin Books, 1985.

———. *The Masks of God: Primitive Mythology.* New York: Penguin Books, 1969.

Camporesi, Piero. *Alimentazione folclore società.* Parma: Pratiche Editrice, 1980.

———. *Bread of Dreams: Food and Fantasy in Early Modern Europe.* Translated by David Gentilcore. Cambridge, England: Polity Press, 1989.

Capuozzo, Toni, and Michele Neri. *Le guide di panorama: feste e sagre dei paesi italiani.* Milan: Arnoldo Mondadori Editore, 1985.

Cardini, Franco. *I giorni del sacro: il libro delle feste.* Novara: Edipem, 1983.

Carnacina, Luigi, and Vincenzo Buonassisi. *Il libro della polenta.* Florence: Giunti-Martello, 1974.

Casagrande, Giovanna. *Gola e preghiera nella clausura dell'ultimo '500.* Foligno: Edizioni dell'Arquata, 1988.

Cattabiani, Alfredo. *Calendario: le feste, i miti, le leggende e i riti dell'anno.* Milan: Rusconi, 1988.

Cavalcanti, Ottavio. "Dolci e fuochi di Natale," *La Gola,* Vol. 2 (December 1982: 6–7).

———. "Le feste del grano nel sud," *La Gola,* Vol. 2 (December 1982:3).

Charles, Teresa. *La fiera di Sant'Orso.* Ivrea: Privli and Verlucca, 1988.

Chiocchio, Nino. *I serpari a Cocullo.* Rome: Associazione Abruzzese di Roma, n.d.

Cioffari, P. Gerardo. *Documenti per la storia della festa di S. Nicola.* Bari: Centro Studi Nicolani, n.d.

Clemente, Pietro. *Il linguaggio il corpo la festa.* Milan: Franco Angeli, 1983.

Cocchiara, Giuseppe. *Il Paese di Cuccagna, e altri studi di folklore.* Turin: Boringhieri, 1980.

Colangeli, Mario. *Le feste dell'anno. Almanacco delle feste popolari italiane.* Milan: SugarCo, 1977.

Colangeli, Mario, and Anna Fraschetti. *Alla scoperta delle feste e sagre popolari nel Lazio.* Rome: Editrice I Dioscuri, 1981.

Couffignal, Huguette. *La cucina povera.* Milan: Rizzoli Biblioteca Universal, 1982.

Cunsolo, Felice. *Guida gastronomica d'Italia*. Novara: Istituto Geografico de Agostini, 1975.

Cusatelli, Giorgio. *Ucci, Ucci, piccolo manuale di gastronomia fiabesca*. Milan: Emme Edizioni, 1983.

Cusumano, Antonio. *Pane e dolci della Valle del Belice. Piccolo biblioteca delle tradizione popolari siciliane*. No. 6. Ghibellina: Nando Russo Editore, 1982.

Davidson, Alan. *Il mare in pentola*. Milan: Arnoldo Mondadori, 1972.

De Bellis, Augusto. *Il cacio pecorino, tra storia e tradizione*. Montepulciano: Editore del Grifo, 1982.

De Gubernatis, A. *Usi Natalizi in Italia*. Milan: Arnaldo Forni Editore, 1986.

Del Conte, Anna. *Gastronomy of Italy*. New York: Prentice-Hall Press, 1987.

Delitala, Enrica. "Pane e carne in un'isola del mediterraneo. Buoni da mangiare, buoni da donare," *Brads*, Vol. 10, 1981 (10:38–41).

Del Ninno, Maurizio. *Un rito e i suoi segni: la corsa dei ceri*. Urbino: Argalia, 1976.

De Martino, Ernesto. *Sud e Magia*. Milan: Feltrinelli, 1982.

de Paolis, Carlo. "La Festa di San Giovanni a Civitavecchia," *L'Accademia*. May 1987.

De Simone, Roberto, and Annabella Rossi. *Carnevale si chiamava Vincenzo, rituali di carnevale in Campania*. Rome: De Luca Editore, 1977.

Detienne, Marcel. *Dionysos at Large*. Translated by Arthur Goldhammer. Cambridge: Harvard University Press, 1989.

De Vittoriis-Medori, Angelo. "La Tavola di Natale in Abruzzo," *L'Accademia*, No. 6, June 1985 (5–7).

———. "L'uovo e l'agnello sulla tavola di Pasqua," *L'Accademia*, No. 2, 1986 (8–12).

Di Corato, Riccardo. *Le delizie del divin porcello*. Milan: Idealibri, 1984.

Di Lampedusa, Giuseppe. *The Leopard*. Translated by Archibald Colquhoun. London: William Collins Sons, 1961.

Di Lello, Antonio. *Storia di Villa S. Maria*. Lanciano: Casa Editrice Itinerari, 1978.

Di Natale, Maria Concetta. *Conoscere Palermo*. Palermo: Edizioni Guida, 1986.

Di Nola, Alfonso M. *Gli aspetti magico-religiosi di una cultura subalterna italiana*. Turin: Boringhieri, 1976.

Di Stasi, Lawrence. *Mal Occhio. The Underside of Vision*. Berkeley: North Point Press, 1981.

Di Verdura, Fulco. *The Happy Summer Days: A Sicilian Childhood*. London: Weidenfeld and Nicholson, 1976.

Drower, E. S. "The Ritual Meal," *Folk-lore*, Vol. 45, 1937, pp. 226–244.

Dryansky, G. Y. "A Special, Ancient, and Enduring Madness," *European Travel and Life*, July-August 1986, pp. 84–89, 124–125.

Dundes, Alan, and Alessandro Falassi. *La Terra in Piazza. An Interpretation of the Palio of Siena*. Berkeley and Los Angeles: University of California Press, 1975.

Eliade, Mircea. *A History of Religious Ideas. From the Stone Age to the Eleusinian Mysteries*. Vol. 1. Translated by Willard R. Trask. Chicago: University of Chicago Press, 1978.

———. *Patterns in Comparative Religion*. Translated by Rosemary Smeed. New York: Meridian, 1974.

———. *The Sacred and the Profane. The Nature of Illusion*. Translated by Willard R. Trask. New York: Harper and Row, 1961.

Faccioli, Emilio. "La Cucina." *Enciclopedia Einaudi*, Vol. 5, pp. 981–1030.

———. "Guerra e pace tra Carnevale e Quaresima," *La Gola*, Vol. 4, February 1985 (28: 6–7).

Falassi, Alessandro. *Italian Folklore: An Annotated Bibliography*. New York: Garland Publishing Co., 1985.

———. "I Percorsi del risotto," in *Cucina, cultura, società*. Milan: Shakespeare and Co., 1982.

———, ed. *La Festa*. Milan: Electa, 1988.

———, ed. *Time out of Time, Essays on the Festival*. Albuquerque: University of New Mexico Press, 1987.

———, and Guiliano Catoni. *Palio*. Milan: Electa, 1983.

———, Riccardo di Corato, and P. Stiaccini. *Pan che canti, vin che salti*. Mantua: Editrice I Torchi Chiantigiani, 1979.

Ferrarotti, Franco. *Italy: An Unauthorized Portrait*. Vicenza: Alitalia, 1975.

Finley, M. I., D. Mack Smith, and C.J.H. Duggan. *A History of Sicily*. London: Chatto and Windus, 1986.

Frazer, Sir James G. *The Golden Bough: A Study in Magic and Religion*. Abridged version. New York: The Macmillan Co., 1958.

Gadda, Carlo Emilio. *That Awful Mess on Via Merulana*. Translated by William Weaver. New York: Braziller, 1984.

Gadon, Elinor W. *The Once and Future Goddess*. San Francisco: Harper and Row, 1989.

Galanti, Bianca Maria. "Tradizioni gastronomiche d'Italia: uova e dolci pasquali," *Lares*, 24. (1958), pp. 17–41.

Gallini, C. *Il consumo del sacro: feste lunghe in Sardegna*. Bari: Editore Laterza, 1971.

Gautsch, Walter. *Carnevale: Le origini, la storia, le maschere, le tradizioni del carnevale italiano*. Vimercate: Libreria Meravigli, n.d.

Giancristofaro, Emiliano. *Totemajje: viaggio nella cultura popolare abruzzese*. Lanciano: R. Carabba Editore, 1978.

Gleijeses, Vittorio. *Feste, farina, e forca*. Naples: Società Editrice Napoletana, 1977.

———. *Piccola Storia del Carnevale*. Naples: Marotta, 1971.

Goethe, J. W. *Italian Journey 1786–1788*. Translated by W. H. Auden and Elizabeth Mayer. San Francisco: North Point Press, 1982.

Goria, Giovanni. "Civiltà gastronomiche delle regioni italiane" and "Le mense imbandite," a series of articles in *L'Informatore Alimentare*, 1986–1987.

Grasselli, Silvana. "Antiche usanze natalize nelle case di Cortina," *L'Accademia,* 1987 (1:5–7).

Guagnini, Enrico. "Storie e storielle d'uova," *La Gola,* Vol. 2, April 1983 (6:6).

Harris, Lis. "Annals of Intrigue: The Palio," *The New Yorker,* June 5, 1989, pp. 83–104.

Harrison, Barbara Grizzuti. *Italian Days.* New York: Weidenfeld and Nicholson, 1989.

Hartcup, John and Adeline. *Spello. Life Today in Ancient Umbria.* London, New York: Allison and Busby, 1985.

Haycraft, John. *Italian Labyrinth: Italy in the 1980's.* London: Secker and Warburg, 1985.

Heaton, Eliza. *By-paths of Sicily.* New York: E. P. Dutton, 1920.

Henisch, Bridget Ann. *Fast and Feast: Food in Medieval Society.* University Park: Pennsylvania State University Press, 1976.

Heywood, William. *Palio and Ponte, an Account of the Sports of Central Italy from the Age of Dante to the 20th Century.* London: Methuen and Co., 1904.

Hooker, Katherine. *Byways in Southern Tuscany.* New York: Charles Scribner's Sons, 1918.

Incontri Lotteringhi della Stufa, Maria Luisa. *Desinari e cene dai tempi remoti alla cucina toscana del XV secolo.* Florence: Olimpia, 1965.

———. *Pranzi e conviti. La cucina toscana dal XVI secolo ai giorni d'oggi.* Florence: Olimpia, 1965.

Innocenti, Carlo, and Domenico Zannler, ed. *Tradizioni epifaniche in provincia di Udine.* Provincia di Udine Assessorato al Turismo, n.d.

Isgro, Giovanni. *Feste barocche a Palermo.* Palermo: S. F. Flaccovio Editore, 1986.

Istituto Geografico de Agostini. *Lazio invito a tavola.* Novara: 1977.

James, Edwin Oliver. *Seasonal Feasts and Festivals.* London: Thames and Hudson, 1961.

James, Henry. *Italian Hours.* New York: Grove Press, 1959.

Jandl, Brigitte. *Almanacco Lombardo—alla scoperta delle feste popolari, sagre, e fiere di Lombardia.* Rome: Messaggerie del Libro, 1982.

Jannattoni, Livio. *Il ghiottone romano.* Milan: Bramante Editrice, 1965.

Kertzer, David. "Politics and Ritual: The Communist Festa in Italy," *Anthropology Quarterly,* Vol. 4, 1974 (374–389).

Kubly, Herbert. *An American in Italy.* New York: Simon and Schuster, 1955.

———. *Easter in Sicily.* New York: Simon and Schuster, 1956.

Kummer, Corby. "A Better Omelet," *Atlantic,* Vol. 264 (10:99–101).

Lancelloti, Arturo. *Feste tradizionali.* Vols. 1 and 2. Milan: Società Editrice Libraria, 1950.

Lawrence, D. H. *Etruscan Places.* New York: Penguin Books, 1981.

Lenotti, Tullio. *Bacanal del gnoco.* Verona: Edizioni di "Vita Veronese," 1985.

————. *Il carnevale veronese*. Verona: Vita Veronese, 1948.

Levi, Carlo. *Words Are Stones*. New York: Farrar Straus, 1958.

Limiti, M. *Umbria, folklore. 100 feste religiose popolari tradizionali*. Perugia: Sigla Tre, 1985.

Lloyd, Susan Caperna. "Trapani's Grand Procession," *Attenzione*, Vol. 7, April 1985 (4:42–47).

Manconi, Francesco. *Il lavoro dei Sardi*. Sassari: Edizione Gallizzi, 1983.

Mantovano, Giuseppe. *L'avventura del cibo: origini, misteri, storie e simboli nel nostro mangiare quotidiano*. Rome: Gremese, 1989.

————. *La cucina italiana: origini, storia e segreti*. Rome: Newton Compton, 1985.

Maxwell, Gavin. *The Ten Pains of Death*. New York: E. P. Dutton, 1959.

Mazzarotto, Bianca Tamassia. *Le feste veneziane: i giochi popolari, le cerimonie religiose e di governo*. Florence: Sansoni, 1980.

Medagliani, Eugenio and Fernanda Gosetti. With an essay by Professor Peter Kubelka. *Pastario, or Atlas of Italian Pastas*. Crusinallo: Alessi, 1985.

Menichetti, Piero Luigi. *I ceri di Gubbio dal XII secolo*. Città di Castello: Tipolito-Rubini and Petruzzi, 1982.

Merlino, Italo Vincenzo. *Le panicelle di San Biagio a Taranta Peligna*. Privately printed, 1987.

Messina, Lucio. *I riti della settimana santa e della pasqua a Palermo e nella sua provincia*. Palermo: Foglie Notizie, 1979.

Migliari, Maria Luisa, and Alida Azzola. *Storia della gastronomia*. Novara: Edipem, 1978.

Monaco, Franco. *Manifestazioni italiane*. Roma: Guiditalia, n.d.

————. *What's on in Italian Folklore*. Rome: ACI, 1967.

Monelli, Paolo. *Il ghiottone errante, viaggio gastronomico attraverso l'Italia*. Milan: Garzanti, 1935.

————. "Natale in una famiglia in Bologna d'altri tempi," *L'Accademia*, No. 6, 1986 (4–6).

Morris, James. *The World of Venice*. New York: Pantheon Books, 1960.

Morton, H. V. *A Traveler in Italy*. New York: Dodd Mead and Co., 1964.

————. *A Traveler in Southern Italy*. London: Methuen and Co., 1983.

Musso, Giuseppe Maria. *Ed è subito carnevale*. Ivrea: Princolor, 1982.

Nichols, Peter. *Italia, Italia*. London: Macmillan, 1973.

Nistri, Rossano. "La notte dei prodigi," *La Gola*, Vol. 6, December 1987 (51–52).

————. "La rava, la fava e la befana," *La Gola*, Vol. 5, November-December 1986 (49: 14–15).

Norwich, John Julius. *A History of Venice*. New York: Alfred A. Knopf, 1982.

O'Faolain, Sean. *Autumn in Italy*. New York: Devin-Adair, 1953.

————. *A Summer in Italy*. New York: Devin-Adair, 1950.

Olson, Carl. *The Book of the Goddess*. New York: Crossroads Press, 1988.

Origo, Iris. *The Merchant of Prato*. Boston: David Godine, 1986.

Paola, Donna. "La leggenda del panettone," *La Cucina Italiana,* December 1958, pp. 40–41.

Partner, Peter. *Renaissance Rome, 1500–1559: A Portrait of a Society.* Berkeley: University of California Press, 1976.

Pepper, Curtis Bill. "Italy's Festive Province," *Signature,* 1984, pp. 36–39, 66–72.

Peppoloni, Venenzo. *'Na vorda era cusci (un paese si racconta).* Foligno: Mancinie Valeri, 1981.

Pinna, Gabriella. "Panificazione e pasticceria in Sardegna alla metà dell'ottocento: saggio di repertorio," *Brads,* 1968, Vol. 3 (54–59).

Pitrè, Giuseppe. *La famiglia, la casa, la vita del popolo siciliano.* Palermo: Il Vespro, 1913.

———. *Feste patronali in Sicilia.* Palermo: Clausen, 1900.

———. *Spettacoli e feste popolari siciliane.* Palermo: Lanziel, 1881.

Pontoni, Germano. *Il libro dell'oca: storia, tradizioni e gastronomia.* Udine: Istituto per l'Enciclopedia del Friuli Venezia Giulia, 1987.

Priori, Domenico. "Feasts for S. Antonio," *Lares,* 26.

Projeta, Giuseppe. *Dente cura dente.* Udine: Società Filologica Friulana, 1989.

Righi Parenti, Giovanni. "Quindici ingredienti più acqua e fuoco per fare il pampepato di Siena," *L'Accademia,* No. 1, 1987(51).

Riva, Giorgio. *Le sagre e le feste popolari italiane.* Milan: Editrice Bibliografica, 1978.

Roghi, Bianca, and Maria Luisa Valeri. *Pane, olio e sale, uno sguardo al passato della Valdichiana.* Montepulciano: Editore del Grifo, 1988.

Romer, Elizabeth. *The Tuscan Year. Life and Food in an Italian Valley.* New York: Atheneum, 1985.

Root, Waverley. *The Food of Italy.* New York: Atheneum, 1971.

Rossi, A. *Le feste dei poveri.* Bari: Laterza, 1971.

Santoro, Rodo. *Il carro del festino. Storia dei carri di Santa Rosalia.* Palermo: Enchiridion, 1984.

Sada, Luigi, and Anna Papa. *L'hospitium sanctinicolai di Bari.* Bari: Centro Studi Nicolaiani, 1988.

Sardi, Francesco Saba. "La Tavola di Natale," *La Gola,* Vol. 2, November 1982 (1:4).

Scafoglio, Domenico. *La maschera della cuccagna: spreco, rivolta e sacrificio nel carnevale napoletano nel 1764.* Naples: Collonnese Editore, 1981.

Scardova, Roberto. "Una Maialata," *La Gola,* Vol. 3, February 1984 (16:24).

Schevill, Ferdinand. *Siena: The Story of a Medieval Commune.* New York: Charles Scribner's Sons, 1909.

Sciascia, Leonardo. "Feste religiose in Sicilia." Bari: Leonardo da Vinci Editrice, 1965.

———. *La corda pazza: scrittori e cose della Sicilia.* Turin: Giulio Einaudi Editore, 1982.

Seward, Desmond. *A Traveler's Companion: Naples.* New York: Atheneum, 1986.

Simeti, Mary Taylor. *On Persephone's Island. A Sicilian Journal*. Berkeley: North Point Press, 1987.

———. *Pomp and Sustenance. Twenty-Five Centuries of Sicilian Food*. New York: Alfred A. Knopf, 1989.

Sisci, Rocco. *La caccia al pesce spada nello stretto di Messina*. Messina: Edizioni Dr. Antonino Sfameni, 1984.

Sitwell, Sacheverell. "Festivals of Italy," in *Primitive Scenes and Festivals*. London: Faber and Faber, 1942.

Sozi, Giuliano. *Spello, guida storico-artistica*. Spello: Pro Loco, 1987.

Spicer, Dorothy Gladys. "Festivals of Italy," in *Festivals of Western Europe*. New York: Wilson, 1958.

Teti, Vito. "Carnevale abolito dall'abbondanza," *La Gola*, Vol. 3, February 1984 (16:9).

———. "Carni e maccarruni assai," *La Gola*, Vol. 4, February 1985 (28:9–10).

———. *Il pane, la beffa, e la festa*. Florence: Guaraldi, 1976.

Toor, Frances. *Festivals and Folkways of Europe*. New York: Crown, 1953.

Toschi, Paolo. *Invito al folklore italiano, le regione e le feste*. Rome: Editrice Studium, 1963.

———. *Le origini del teatro italiano: origini rituale della rappresentazione popolare in Italia*. Turin: Paolo Boringhieri, 1976.

Touring Club Italiano. "Il folklore. Tradizioni, vita, e arti popolari," in *Conosci l' Italia*. Vol. 7. *Folklore*. Milan: Touring Club, 1961.

———. *Guida gastronomica d'Italia*. Milan: Touring Club Italiano, 1931.

Uccello, Antonio. *Pani e dolci di Sicilia*. Palermo: Sellerio Editore, 1976.

Valeri, V. "Feste." *Enciclopedia Einaudi*. Vol. VI. Turin: 1977.

Vergani, Orio. "La Tavola di Natale in Abruzzo," *L'Accademia*, No. 6, June 1985 (6–7).

Virdis, Riccardo. "Nenneri per la settimana santa e per San Giovanni in Ogliastra," *Brads*, Vol. 5, 1974 (63–69).

Walker, Barbara. *The Woman's Encyclopedia of Myths and Secrets*. San Francisco: Harper and Row, 1983.

Warner, Marina. *Alone of All Her Sex. The Myth and the Cult of the Virgin Mary*. New York: Vintage Books, 1976.

Whiteridge, Thomas Northcote. "The Dancing Tower Processions of Italy," *Folklore*, Vol. 16, 1905, pp. 243–259.

COOKBOOKS

Antonini, Giuseppina Perusini. *Mangiare e bere friulano*. Milan: Franco Angeli Editore, 1984.

Bergonzini, Renato. *In cucina con l'aceto balsamico*. Bologna: Mundici and Zanetti Editori, 1987.

Bonacina, Gianni. *Vini e cibi dell'Umbria. Guida sistematica alle attività enoga-stronomiche e alimentari della regione.* Genoa: Gianni Bonacina, n.d.

Boni, Ada. *La cucina romana.* Rome: Newton Compton, 1929.

Bozzi, Ottorino Perna. *La Lombardia in cucina. Storia e ricette di piatti tradizionali lombardi.* Florence: Martello-Giunti, 1982.

——. *Vecchia Brianza in cucina.* Florence: Martello-Giunti, 1979.

——. *Vecchia Milano in cucina.* Florence: Martello-Giunti, 1975.

Braccili, Luigi. *Abruzzo in cucina.* Pescara: Constantini Editore, 1988.

Caminiti, M., L. Pasquini, and G. Quondamatteo. *Mangiari di Romagna.* Bologna: Guidianie Rosa Editore, 1964.

Capnist, Giovanni. *La cucina veronese.* Padua: F. Mursia, 1987.

——. *I dolci del Veneto.* Padua: Franco Muzzio Editore, 1983.

Cappacchi, Guglielmo. *La cucina popolare parmigiana.* Parma: Artegrafica Silva Parma, 1985.

Caredda, Gian Paolo. *Gastronomia in Sardegna.* Genoa: Sagep Editrice, 1988.

Cascino, Francesco Paolo. *Cucina di Sicilia.* Palermo: Lorenzo Misuraca Editore, 1980.

Cavalcanti, Ottavio. *Il libro d'oro della cucina e dei vini di Calabria e Basilicata.* Milan: U. Mursia, 1979.

Codacci, Leo. *Civiltà della tavola contadina. 190 ricette e tanti buoni consigli.* Florence: Sansoni, 1981.

Colacchi, Marina, and Pino Simone. *La cucina tradizionale italiana Milano e Lombardia.* Rome: Panda Libri, 1989.

Coppini, Remo. *Umbria a tavola. Anedotti, folclore, tradizioni, usanze e . . . ricette.* Perugia: Edizioni Guerra, 1983.

Coria, Giuseppe. *Profumi di Sicilia. Il libro della cucina siciliana.* Palermo: Vito Cavallotto Editore, 1981.

Correnti, Pino. *Il libro d'oro della cucina e dei vini di Sicilia.* Milan: U. Mursia, 1985.

Corsi, Guglielma. *Un secolo di cucina umbra.* Assisi: S. Maria degli Angeli, 1980.

Da Mosto, Ranieri. *Il Veneto in cucina.* Florence: Martello-Giunti, 1974.

Delegazione di Bolzano. Accademia Italiana della Cucina. *I venti anni 1963–1983.* Calliano: Manfrini F. Arti Grafiche Vallagarina, 1983.

Di Lello, Antonio, and Antonio Stanziani. *La cucina dei grandi cuochi di Villa Santa Maria.* Chieti: Solfanelli, 1984.

Di Napoli Oliver, Fiametta. *La grande cucina siciliana.* Milan: Moizzi Editore, 1976.

Feslikenian, Franca. *Cucina e vini del Lazio.* Milan: U. Mursia, 1973.

Filiputti, Walter, ed. *Cucina del Friuli Venezia Giulia con 10 grandi ristoratori.* Plaino: Istituto per l'enciclopedia del Friuli Venezia Giulia, 1984.

Francesconi, Jeanne Carola. *La cucina napoletana.* Naples: Edizione del Delfino, 1965.

Galluzzi, M. A. Iori, and N. Iori. *La cucina reggiana*. Padua: Franco Muzzio Editore, 1987.

Goria, Giovanni, and Claudia Verro. *In cucina a quattro mani*. Chieri: Daniela Piazza, 1985.

Gosetti, Fernanda. *Il dolcissimo. Torte, pasticcini, e desserts*. Milan: Fabbri, 1984.

Gosetti della Salda, Anna. *Le ricette regionali italiane*. Milan: La Cucina Italiana, 1967.

Gray, Patience. *Honey from a Weed. Fasting and Feasting in Tuscany, Catalonia, the Cyclades, and Apulia*. London: Prospect Books, 1986.

Iannotta, Galluzzi Iori. *La cucina ferrarese*. Padua: Franco Muzzio and Co., 1987.

Laurenti, Mathilde. *La vera cucina romana*. Rome: Colonna Editore, 1986.

Lingua, Paolo. *La cucina dei Genovesi*. Padua: F. Mursia, 1982.

Lorini, Tebaldo. *Mugello in Cucina. Storie, prodotti, tradizioni, ricette*. Borgo S. Lorenzo: 1985.

Lucrezi, Nice Cortelli. *Le ricette della nonna. L'arte del mangiar bene in Abruzzo*. L'Aquila: Japadre Editore, 1974.

Luisa, Maria. *Cucina canavesana*. Ivrea: Edizioni Nuova Europa, 1987.

Maffioli, Giuseppe. *Cucina e vini nelle Tre Venezie*. Milan: U. Mursia, 1972.

———. *La cucina trevigiana*. Padua: F. Mursia, 1981.

———. *La cucina veneziana*. Padua: F. Mursia, 1982.

Mannucci, Umberto. *Bisenzio tradizioni e cucina*. Prato: Edizioni del Palazzo, 1981.

Marinone, Renzo. *Cucina racontata. L'alimentazione tradizionale tra scienza e memoria*. Cavallermaggiore: Edizioni Gribaudo, 1988.

———. *Curiosando in cucina. Tradizioni cuneesi e ricette alla piemontese*. Cavallermaggiore: Edizioni Gribaudo, 1978.

Mencarelli, Rudolfo. *Le ricette eugubine*. Assisi: Santa Maria degli Angeli, 1988.

Menichetti, Piero, and Luciana Menichetti Panfili. *Vecchia cucina eugubina*. Città di Castello: Ikuvium Arte S.A.S., 1984.

Molossi, Baldassare. *La grande cucina di Parma*. Parma: Azzali, 1985.

Novelli, Renato. *Le Marche a Tavola. La tradizione gastronomica regionale*. Ancona: Il Lavoro Editoriale, 1987.

Olivero, Nello. *Storie e curiosità del mangiar napoletano*. Naples: Edizioni Scientifiche Italiane, 1983.

Petroni, Paolo. *Il libro della vera cucina bolognese*. Florence: Bonechi, 1978.

———. *Il libro della vera cucina fiorentina*. Florence: Bonechi, 1974.

Piccinardi, Antonio. *Il libro della vera cucina milanese. 166 ricette dagli antipasti ai dolci*. Florence: Bonechi, 1989.

Pomar, Anna. *La cucina tradizionale siciliana*. Rome: Giuseppe Brancato Editore, 1984.

Porcaro, Giuseppe. *Sapore di Napoli. Storia della pizza napoletana*. Naples: Adriano Gallina Editore, 1985.

Portinari, Laura Gras. *Cucina e vini del Piemonte e della Valle d'Aosta.* Milan: U. Mursia, 1974.

Quondamatteo, Gianni, Luigi Pasquini, and Marcello Caminiti. *Mangiari di Romagna.* Bologna: Guidicini and Rosa Editori, 1979.

Ragusa, Vittorio. *La vera cucina casereccia a Roma e nel Lazio.* Rome: Iedep, 1985.

Raris, Fernando and Tina. *La strada del fungo e del tartufo.* Milan: Fabbri Editori, 1978.

Righi Parenti, Giovanni. *La grande cucina toscana.* Vols. 1 and 2. Milan: SugarCo, 1982.

———. *Mangiare in contrada . . . ovvero piatti per 17 cene.* Siena: Edizioni Periccioli, 1985.

Sada, Luigi. *Puglia. The traditional Italian cooking.* Milan: Edizioni Sipiel, 1989.

Sandri, Amedeo. *La polenta nella cucina veneta.* Padua: Franco Muzzio and Co., 1930.

Sapio Bartelletti, N. *La cucina siciliana nobile e popolare.* Milan: 1985.

Sassu, Antonio. *La vera cucina in Sardegna.* Rome: Anthropos, 1983.

Testa, Itala. *Cucina di Sardegna.* Vols. 1 and 2. Editrice Altair, 1982.

Touring Club Italiano. *"Il folklore. Tradizioni, vita, e arti popolari,"* in *Conosci l'Italia.* Vol. XI. Milan: Touring Club Italiano, 1967.

Trombetta, Silvia. *Dolci tradizionali siciliani.* Catania: Brancato, 1988.

Valerio, Nico. *La tavola degli antichi.* Milan: Arnoldo Mondadori Editore, 1989.

Zaniboni, Maria Riviecero. *Cucina e vini di Napoli e della Campania.* Milan: U. Mursia, 1975.

INDEX

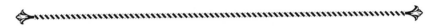

*Note: page numbers in **boldface** refer to recipes*

Taverna dei Capitani
(Gubbio), 45
Tavola Bona, La, 44–46, 47
Teglia, 481
Tellaro, 498
Teolo, 468, 492
Teramo, 17, 470
Termeno, 462
Terni, 434
Terra del Sole, 495
Thesmorphoria, 238
Thrush, 137–38, 493
Timbale, artichoke, **150**
Tinca, minestra di, **380**
Tofeja, 348, **356**
Tomato(es)
in bread salad perfumed with
balsamic vinegar, **103**
celebration of, 486
sauce, Abruzzo, **327**
Tombola, 252
Tonco, 386
Tonnara de Capo Vico, 474
Torciglione, 288, **295**
II, **296**
Torcolo di Santa Costanza, **234**
Tordo, 137–38
Torggellan, 197, 491
Toro, 466
Torre, 386
Torrone, 259
Torta
di farina di grano saraceno,
199
dei Fieschi, 152, **154**
di nocciole, 212, **216**
pasqualina, 421
Tortelli di erbette, **103**
Toschi, Pietro, 12, 236
Tossignano, 463
polenta celebration in,
373–76
Tournament of the Hundred
Towers, 490
Trapani, 13, 409–14, 466, 467
Tredozio, 467

Trentino, calendar of events,
462, 493
Trevi, 492
Treviso, 223, 385, 497
Trieste, 259, 350, 497
Triumphs of gluttony, 12
Truffle(s), 464
fair in Alba, 208–17, 490
hunting for, 211–12
Truffle cookies, chocolate
hazelnut, **217**
Tuna, killing (*mattanza*), 20,
477–78
Turin, 347
Turini, spaghetti con i, **79**
Turkey, 238, 256, 386, 495
roast
herb-scented, from
Nereto, **239**
scented with rosemary and
pancetta, **206**
Turnovers, sweet ricotta-filled,
403
Tuscan grape harvest sweet
bread, **183**
Tuscania, 459
Tuscany, 18, 201, 225, 231,
258, 287, 288, 313,
350, 361, 364, 384,
387, 389, 424
boar festival in Capalbio,
161–66
calendar of events, 463, 468,
474, 477, 481, 484,
486–94
fair of pecorino cheese in
Pienza, 156–60
Festival of the Cauldron in
Altopascio, 128–29
wheat harvest in the Val di
Chiana, 106–13
wine grape festival in Greve
in Chianti, 177–85

Ubaldo, Sant', 43–46, 48
Udine, 304, 384–85

Umbria, 225, 244, 256, 258,
287, 288, 314, 350,
361, 388, 424, 434
calendar of events, 464, 474,
467, 477, 482, 488,
489, 491, 492, 494, 496
carpets of flowers at Spello,
71–81
festival of Saint John the
Baptist and
Midsummer's Eve day in
Grello, 91–103
race of the candles in
Gubbio, 42–59
wine grape crush in Alba
and Todi, 201–7
Uva
sagra dell', 490
in Greve in Chianti,
177–85
in Merano, 195–200
in Quartu Sant'Elena,
186–94
schiacciata all', **183**

Val d'Aosta, calendar of
events, 459–60, 468,
485, 491, 493
Val di Chiana, wheat harvest
in, 106–13
Valentine, Saint, 10
Feast Day of, 475–76
Valguarnera Canopepe, 466
Vallelunga, 428
Valvenosta, 197
Vasari, Giorgio, 10
Vecchia, La (Old Woman),
254, 385–87
Vegetable(s)
frittata, **433**
and garbanzo minestrone
from Piedmont, **226**
hot bath of olive oil,
anchovies, and garlic
for, **205**